W9-CPO-891

The International Business Dictionary and Reference

The International Business Dictionary and Reference

Lewis A. Presner, Ph.D.

John Wiley & Sons, Inc.

New York   Chichester   Brisbane   Toronto   Singapore

In recognition of the importance of preserving what has been written, it is a policy of John Wiley & Sons, Inc., to have books of
enduring value published in the United States printed on acid-free
paper, and we exert our best efforts to that end.

This publication is designed to provide accurate and
authoritative information in regard to the subject
matter covered. It is sold with the understanding that
the publisher is not engaged in rendering legal, accounting,
or other professional service. If legal advice or other
expert assistance is required, the services of a competent
professional person should be sought. *From a Declaration
of Principles jointly adopted by a Committee of the
American Bar Association and a Committee of Publishers.*

Library of Congress Cataloging-in-Publication Data:

Presner, Lewis A., 1945–
    The international business dictionary and reference /
Lewis A. Presner.
        p.   cm.
    Includes bibliographical references.
    ISBN 0-471-54594-5

    1. International economic relations—Encyclopedias.
2. International finance—Encyclopedias.   3. International
relations—Encyclopedias.   4. Export marketing—Encyclopedias.
5. International law—Encyclopedias.   6. Banks and banking,
International—Encyclopedias.   I. Title.
    HF 1359.P74   1991   91-9328
    658'.049'03—dc20

Printed in the United States of America

10 9 8 7 6 5 4 3 2 1

For Edith
who always knew I could do it
and
to whom I owe all

Preface

This is the first work of its kind to be written and published in the English language anywhere in the world. As astounding as this may seem, it is true: before this work existed, there was nothing comparable to it for study, reference, or as a desktop working guide. Thus, I am proud to be its author and to have John Wiley & Sons as its esteemed publisher.

When I approached John Mahaney at John Wiley, initially he was somewhat surprised at my claim about the uniqueness of this work. But he was able to verify my claim. Why is it unique?

I think the reason is that few working scholars are truly *integrative* in their approach to, let alone in their understanding of, the interdisciplinary dynamics of international business. This is so both at the undergraduate business school level and at the postgraduate level. Unfortunately, it is also true at the level of industrial and commercial practice in "the real world" where it counts the most.

The cause of this is, in my judgment, the overweening preoccupation of academics with the jealous guarding of the turf of their specialized fields. This behavior has hobbled generations of students in their international business training; and, as a logical consequence, it has deprived private-sector business people and public-sector government officials of informed and sensitive individuals who, by their actions, create and promote tolerant international relations that lead to profitable international business dealings.

How many opportunities have been lost to our competitors? How much time has been wasted? How many avoidable mistakes have been made, never to be undone? How much money has been unwittingly spent or squandered? No more.

To remedy past errors, to avoid making new ones, and to contribute to success in the real world, I have used a cross-disciplinary approach in writing this work. As my "model," I studied important international business success stories and sought the reasons for their success. The answer was always the same: they all used cross- and interdisciplinary approaches to decision making. So I did, too. Thus, my going-in position was that (1) the work I was writing had to be essentially *integrative* in nature versus *disintegrative*; (2) it had to analyze, master, understand, and communicate the core meanings in all the component vocabularies of the subject, for example, International Marketing,

International Law, International Economics, International Banking and Finance, International Physical Distribution and Logistics, and International Relations/Politics; and (3) it had to tie together the *commonalities* rather than dwell (annoyingly) on the differences. This strategy and the tactics used to implement it took years of diligent work, during which time I learned how to artfully splice together theory and practical experience. I hope I have succeeded.

LEWIS A. PRESNER

Ontario, Canada
August 1991

Acknowledgments

Any work of this scope owes unpayable debts to people in many fields. The following outstanding individuals merit special thanks: Philip Kotler, The S.C. Johnson & Son Distinguished Professor of International Marketing, Northwestern University, for his encouragement over the years; Max Lupul, Professor of Marketing, California State University at Northridge, for his pragmatism, which helped liberate my own thinking; Philip Cateora, Head, Marketing and International Business Division, University of Colorado at Boulder, Vern Terpstra, Professor of International Business, School of Business Administration, University of Michigan, and Michael Czinkota, Professor, Georgetown University, for their contributions to my early "global perspective" through their many fine professional works; Roger Layton, Professor of Marketing, University of New South Wales, and Hans Thorelli, Professor of Marketing, Indiana University, for providing important cross-cultural insights; Kjell Gronhaug, Norwegian School of Economics and Business Administration, and Gerry Wind, The Wharton School, University of Pennsylvania, for the lasting impression each made on me and, in so doing, helping to shape my ideas; Nick Dholakia, University of Rhode Island, for sharing with me his insights on developmental economics; Klaus Tolzien, Nestlé, S.A., Vevey, Switzerland, for helping me understand and master the intricacies of West African business relationships; Daniel Ofori, Ghana Broadcasting Corporation, for cultural education; Peter Umney, Graham & Gillies (West Africa), Lagos, Nigeria, for the autonomy to manage difficult African assignments; Mort Rosenbloom, Associated Press, Lagos, Nigeria, for the opportunity to hone professional skills under fire; Ed Lannert, Unicef (Zambia), for his patience, which guided me through my work in Zambia; Angel Muños Bellver (Rio de Janeiro) and José Luis Molina Vega (Mérida, Mexico), for teaching me survival skills in international business in Latin America; Henry Lum (Price Waterhouse, Washington, D.C.), for opening my mind to Asia; Eugene Decaire, Charles Ewert, and H. Richard Hird, Professors of Computer Science, Law, and Economics, respectively, at Durham College, for research assistance; Midge Day and Gwen Tredwell, Professors of Legal Office Administration, Durham College, for professional support; Dr. Sven Britton, Stockholm, Sweden; and Albert van Danzig, Schreveningen, Holland.

The actual translation of my ideas into the physical reality that is this book would not have been possible without the following people, who have earned my respect: John Mahaney (Wiley—editor); Judy Cardanha, Providence, Rhode Island (copy editor); Maggie Dana, Old Saybrook, Connecticut (Pageworks—design and typesetting); Gloria Fuzia (Wiley—editorial assistant), and Mary Daniello (Wiley—production management).

Finally, I alone am accountable for any errors or shortcomings in this book. The responsibility for any misperceptions, however, remains with the reader.

L.A.P.

Contents

Introduction

The following introduction explains the plan of this book in order that readers may make the best use of it.

ALPHABETICAL SYSTEM OF ARRANGEMENT

The aim of this volume is to present a comprehensive and accurate cross-disciplinary interpretation of the vocabulary of international business. Hundreds of thousands of works (books, journals, abstracts, theses, essays, newspaper and magazine articles, interviews, and radio and television broadcasts on domestic and international frequencies) have been culled in English, in original versions in French and Spanish, and in English translations of works in major world languages, plus regional languages (for example, Punjabi, Kiswahili). The result has been an *alphabetical system of arrangement*, using the English language alphabet (A–Z). Thus, if you are looking for *tariff*, you look under "T"; for World Bank, under "W"; and so on.

APPENDICES

There are seven Appendices in this volume as follows:

- Appendix I: Foreign Exchange Contracts Vocabulary
- Appendix II: Foreign Exchange Risk Vocabulary
- Appendix III: Nonuniform Terms of Trade: Non-Incoterms
- Appendix IV: Uniform Terms of Trade: Incoterms
- Appendix V: International Organizations
- Appendix VI: International Law Vocabulary
- Appendix VII: Selected Information Sources

Each Appendix was developed to include information germane to the subject as a whole, but necessitating special "topical" treatment. This was done to assist the reader: if you know the "topic" area, it is simply easier to access the appropriate "topic" Appendix, rather than search alphabetically in the main body of the book. For example, if an experienced exporter wanted to clarify the exact meaning of *Cost, Insurance and Freight . . . (named port of destination/import)* and knew it was an "Incoterm," then Appendix IV could be accessed directly, and *Cost, Insurance, and Freight . . . (named port of destination/import)* could be clarified.

Appendix V and Appendix VII are subdivided as follows:

Appendix V: International Organizations

A. International Trade Groups (ITGs)
B. International Commercial/Financial Groups (ICFGs)
C. International Political Groups (IPGs)
D. International Organizations of the United Nations System
E. International Commodity Groups (ICGs)

Appendix VII: Selected Information Sources

A. United Nations System
B. Canadian Government
C. United States Government
D. Quasi-Government Organizations
E. International Organizations

GEOGRAPHIC REFERENCE GUIDES OF KEY TERMS

The major problem with any alphabetical arrangement of word listings is that unless the reader knows what to look for, the search can be endless, and possibly fruitless. Thus, there are eight multipurpose geographical Reference Guides of Key Terms. Each one deals with those words and ideas listed in the main entries of the book but separates groups of items on a geographic basis. They are as follows:

1. Global Reference Guide of Key Terms
2. North American Reference Guide of Key Terms
3. Latin American and Caribbean Reference Guide of Key Terms
4. West European Reference Guide of Key Terms
5. East European Reference Guide of Key Terms
6. Middle East Reference Guide of Key Terms
7. African Reference Guide of Key Terms
8. Asian Reference Guide of Key Terms

The intent of these Reference Guides is to assist the reader in making excellent use of this book. Every term is listed in at least one appropriate Reference Guide; and where there is important cross-functionality, terms are listed in more than one guide. For example, the term *bilateral trade agreement* is listed in the North American Reference Guide of Key Terms since it is most commonly referred to, by North American readers, as a trading arrangement between the United States and Canada, or between the United States and Mexico, or between Canada and Mexico. On the other hand, the term *boycott* is listed in the Global Reference Guide of Key Terms since it has, potentially at least, worldwide usage. It is also cross-listed in the Middle East Reference Guide of Key Terms, as is *Arab boycott of Israel*, since the term has special geographical applicability.

The Reference Guides were also designed for their power to logically arrange entries. For example, *tariff* is most logically found in the Global Reference Guide of Key Terms since a tariff has worldwide application, albeit in every geographic region. Consequently, listing *tariff* in the Global Reference Guide of Key Terms is more logical and less redundant than listing it in each of the geographic Reference Guides.

The following "search strategy" is recommended to make best use of the Reference Guides and of the alphabetic system:

1. If you seek a term with the greatest general applicability, look first in the Global Reference Guide of Key Terms, or simply look for it under its alphabetic listing (A–Z).
2. If you have an idea of the geographic applicability of the entry, search the appropriate geographic Reference Guide.

Thus, the geographic Reference Guides were designed to be useful in several specific ways. First of all, they are eminently suited to experienced exporters who are major traders internationally, who know trading geography, and who wish to expand their operations to the global arena.

Secondly, the geographic Reference Guides can functionally assist sophisticated exporters who traditionally trade with one region (for example, West Europe) and who are considering trading with another one (for example, East Europe). In such cases, the geographic Reference Guides can be ideal for "topical research."

Thirdly, for the novice trader or the student, the geographic Reference Guides will be profitable and useful tools to immediately assist one in getting started in a new geographic market.

TOPICAL REFERENCE GUIDES

Two Reference Guides are provided to assist the reader to access information by specific "topic":

9. Foreign Language Reference Guide of Key Terms
10. International Law Reference Guide of Key Terms

The Foreign Language Reference Guide of Key Terms lists every term not yet "naturalized" into the English language. For example, *aduana* and *douane* are words from Spanish and French, respectively, that are still "foreign," and are, thus, listed in the Foreign Language Reference Guide of Key Terms. On the other hand, the term *laissez-faire* has become "naturalized" into standard American English and its variations, and it is, thus, listed in the Global Reference Guide of Key Terms.

The provision of an International Law Reference Guide of Key Terms was based on the acknowledgment that business life in general, and international business life in particular, is becoming more litigious. To afford the reader access to important terms and ideas under this topic, the International Law Reference Guide of Key Terms was compiled. Page references for terms or ideas in this particular Guide refer to Appendix VI: International Law Vocabulary, where every item is listed alphabetically. (There are a few important exceptions.) Thus, international law vocabulary can be accessed directly with Appendix VI or via the International Law Reference Guide of Key Terms if the reader wants the exact page without having to leaf through the pages of Appendix VI.

CROSS-REFERENCING

A main alphabetic entry under "A" is listed as follows:

Arab Bank for Economic Development in Africa (ABEDA), also known as *Banque Arabe pour le Développement Économique en Afrique (BADEA)*

This entry is followed by a thorough explanation of the organization: what it is, what its origins are, and the role it plays in the world. At the end of the main entry, the following cross-references are provided:

See also Organization of African Unity; Arab League; Appendix V (B).

At once, one can see that the cross-reference to the Organization of African Unity places the head word in an appropriate African perspective, while reference to the *Arab League* gives notice of the embeddedness of the organization within an Arab/Islamic context. Both target references have key importance since each is individually listed as a main entry. Further, there is a cross-reference to "Appendix V (B)" where the organization, together with all other organizations in the same functional class, are listed. This deep cross-referencing facilitates further research (1) on the initial main entry itself, (2) on comparative organizations, and, in this example, (3) on the entire subject of international commercial/financial groups.

From these cross-references, the reader now has learned that the main entry is now part of an "African topic"; and perhaps the next time it is accessed, the reader might wish to exercise the option of going directly to the African Reference Guide of Key Terms to find the exact page listing.

As a final observation, it should be noted that every main entry listed in "Appendix V (B): International Commercial/Financial Groups (ICFGs)" is cross-referenced to other informationally relevant main entries in the book, which may have another series of cross-references either to the Appendices or to the Reference Guides or to both. The reader is thus provided with a fabric of informationally rich threads, each layer of which ramifies through other informational layers, the whole being a network of accurate, wide-ranging information, accessible in a number of ways:

1. from individual main entires,
2. from listings in the Appendices, or
3. from secondary entries cross-referenced
   - from main entries,
   - from Appendix listings, or
   - from the Reference Guides.

It is worth noting that because the Appendices are so strong in their referential power, they bind all the special-use vocabularies of this volume together into a single body of knowledge *as a communications tool*. The result is an integrated, high-level international marketing vocabulary of depth and power.

NEW WORDS

Some main entries in the vocabulary listings, in the Appendices, and in the Reference Guides are classified as New Words (NW). New words are always followed by •NW•. For example,

birdyback •NW•

to highlight the new word prominently.

These •NW• entries are different both from words naturalized into standard American English (e.g., oligopoly) and from those listed in the Reference Guide of Key Foreign Terms (e.g., *carnet*). What makes a word, or expression, a *new word*? Reference to those •NW• entries, like *birdyback*, will indicate they are more than faddish "buzz words": •NW• words (1) have a genuine meaning; (2) have practical application, that is, are used in the main course of international business; and (3) have been coined by their users as a way of "making up the language necessary to do the job."

A NOTE ON STYLE

The writing style of this reference, including abbreviations, has been modeled on the *Concise Oxford English Dictionary*. It is an eminently respected lexicon and readers are referred to it.

In this book—unlike in any standard dictionary—the comprehensive treatment of the entries has necessitated an innovative stylistic device to assist the reader to get the full benefit from every entry.

First of all, *examples* supporting the entries are keyed with the word **Example** and indented and printed in smaller type.

Under *clean bill of lading* is found:

Example: A clean bill gives the goods loaded on board the carrier a clean bill of health.

Some of the examples are events drawn from actual happenings. Others are constructed scenarios to illustrate a particular word, phrase, or idea. To take literally every example provided is to see either the world as an incredibly bizarre place or the author as having an incredibly droll sense of humor. It is important to remember this: the example is simply an example, whether actual or constructed.

Secondly, *explanations* are also printed in smaller type, set off with rules above and below them.

Under *economic integration* is found:

It is suggested that harmonization itself acts as an incentive for more integrated economic activity and for economic bloc-building.

They may (1) provide important information to support a meaning, (2) balance a meaning either with opposing facts or contrary viewpoints, or (3) simply provide a contrasting and comparative viewpoint. The same caveat provided for the "examples" pertains to the "explanations." In this case, to take literally every explanation is to conclude that the author is variously sarcastic or cynical, mocking or mendacious. Again, remember this: the explanation is simply an explanation, intended to explain and using the entire repertoire of allowable literary license.

A FINAL NOTE ON THE BIBLIOGRAPHY

In yet another way, this dictionary is like no other: one can actually read it like a regular nonfiction book. This is not accidental. In devising this work, I did what many academics would call a "beastly thing": I took all the research sources and consolidated them into a single bibliography at the end of the book. Had I taken the orthodox academic approach and documented every lexical entry, every supporting example, and every clarifying explanation (including cross-references within every example and explanation), the result on a "rolling" basis would have been a work of under 300 actual dictionary pages sprinkled among over 1,000 pages of footnotes and annotations! Such a rigid academic format would have choked the life out of the content. This I refused to do.

Thus, to make the book fundamentally readable and useful, I defoliated the tree-book of its customary leafage-footnotes, moving the fallen references into one enormous pile-bibliography at the end. Conventional academics will certainly find this approach unorthodox. They may even disapprove. However, I know that all *cognoscenti* will cheer this eclecticism in the interests of the worthwhile goal: readability versus obscurity, and ease-of-use versus heavy slogging. I hope I have achieved this goal.

above-the-line items *See* autonomous transactions.

absolute advantage is the greater normative efficiency that one nation has or may
have over another (or others) in the production of a commodity or service.
   That was the economic basis of international trade, according to Adam
Smith.
   Cf. comparative advantage.
   See also laissez-faire.

accelerated tariff elimination is mutual agreement to increase the pace of tariff
reduction within the framework of international agreements.
   The Canada-U.S. Free Trade Agreement (FTA) of 1989 has as its ultimate
goal the total elimination of all tariffs between the two countries by January
1, 1998. Periodically, detailed lists of requests emanate from either the Canadian or the U.S. government to accelerate tariff elimination under the FTA.
These lists originate in petitions from private industry associations and non-
governmental organizations charged with providing their governments with
ongoing advice on the outcome of implementation of the FTA.

In 1989, over 350 Canadian companies and industry associations and more than 200
U.S. firms petitioned their governments for accelerated tariff elimination under FTA.
Following extensive discussions on those requests, accelerated elimination of duties
was agreed to on over 400 tariff items covering CAD $6 billion in Canada-U.S. trade.

   Further, the FTA itself provides for accelerated elimination of tariffs on
specified goods in the FTA tariff schedules. Decisions on these areas are
subject to consultation between the Canadian and U.S. governments at the
FTA Commission level.
   See also FTA Commission.

acceptance financing is a method of obtaining short-term credit used by exporters.

If the exporter needs working capital and offers the draft for payment in advance of its maturity date, the bank that accepts it is called an accepting bank, and the draft, when accepted, is called a banker's acceptance.

When the draft is accepted by the bank, the exporter is paid a discounted value for the draft (i.e., the face value of the draft less a percentage). This percentage may be the prevailing bank rate, an interbank rate, such as the London interbank offer rate (LIBOR), or a percentage determined by the nature of the risk associated with the time between when the draft was drawn and its ultimate maturity date.

The accepting bank undertakes to pay the face value of the draft at maturity to the party tendering the draft for payment.

See also export financing; accepting bank; documentary credit; London interbank offer rate.

accepted bill of exchange *See* trade acceptance.

accepting bank is the bank that endorses a documentary draft for payment.

When banks endorse a sight draft, they accept it for immediate payment.

More commonly, a bank's endorsement of a term draft acknowledges its agreement to pay the face value of the draft upon maturity or to discount the instrument (i.e., liquidate it at a discount) in favor of the beneficiary (the exporter) before the maturity date.

See also acceptance financing.

accession is the process of agreeing to or becoming a contracting member of a multilateral agreement, such as the General Agreement on Tariffs and Trade (GATT).

See also General Agreement on Tariffs and Trade; multilateral agreements.

accommodating transactions are international transactions, often referred to as "below-the-line items," that are exchanges in official reserve assets of, and of foreign official assets in, a country that are required to balance international cash flows.

A country's accommodating transactions comprise its official reserve account. The balance on this account (whether in surplus or in deficit) is called a country's official settlements balance.

Cf. autonomous transactions.

See also Bank for International Settlements.

acculturation is the process of adapting oneself to a culture of a host country.

across-the-board tariff reductions (ATB tariff reductions), also called *linear reduction of tariffs*, is a process involving an agreement between countries, usually in a given round of General Agreement on Tariffs and Trade (GATT) trade negotiations, to abate by a fixed percentage all tariffs maintained in all countries that are Contracting Parties to the agreement.

This process is sometimes used to obviate the necessarily protracted bargaining involved in negotiations of item-by-item tariff reductions.
Cf. item-by-item tariff reductions.

adjustment (adjustment policies) refers to specific measures used by governments aimed at correcting a balance of payments disequilibrium.
The government actions taken can be changes in

1. *fiscal policy*, that is, government spending and taxes;
2. *monetary policy*, that is, interest rates and the money supply;
3. *exchange controls*, that is, direct controls over foreign exchange;
4. *commercial controls*, that is, tariffs, quotas, and quantitative restrictions, for example, voluntary export restraints (VERs);
5. *nontariff barriers* (NTBs), such as administrative and technical regulations.

   Example: Whenever the International Monetary Fund (IMF) assists a nation with a temporary balance of payments deficit, it requires the government to undertake a program of adjustment.

   Cf. balance of trade.
   See also International Monetary Fund.

administrative law judge (ALJ) is a jurist who presides over tribunals and hearings into civil matters in the United States.

   Example: Notice is hereby given that the U.S. International Trade Commission (USITC) has determined not to review the presiding ALJ's initial determination in the investigation on the basis of a settlement agreement between the parties.

   See also initial determination.

administrative protection order (APO) is a directive that is issued by the U.S. International Trade Commission (USITC) in connection with investigations under Title VII of the Tariff Act of 1930 and that requires the Commission—under Section 1332 of the Omnibus Trade and Competitiveness Act of 1988—to release to the authorized representatives of interested parties in dumping and countervailing duty investigations the business proprietary information (BPI) collected by the USITC in the course of such investigations.
The USITC, using implemented procedures governing the release of BPI under an APO, only provides BPI to authorized applicants who agree to be bound by the terms and conditions of the APO.

The main function of APOs is to protect the BPI of those who are parties to USITC investigations from having their BPI disseminated to unauthorized persons who might be in a position to use the BPI to misuse confidential information commercially. Such dissemination may occur (1) willfully; or (2) by failing to "bracket" BPI, which leads to inadvertent disclosure; or (3) by failing to supervise junior attorneys and inexperienced clerical people in the proper handling of BPI at the law firms; or (4) by failing to destroy documents containing BPI (upon the termination of an USITC investigation), subject to the right to retain the documents during a judicial review of a USITC determination.

USITC sanctions for APO violations serve the interests of preserving the confidence of submitters of BPI in the USITC as a credible and reliable protector of BPI, punishing breachers, and deterring future violations by past offenders and by others in a position to potentially offend. Sanctions include (1) forfeiture of legal practice before the USITC for up to seven years, (2) referral to a U.S. Attorney (for potential criminal prosecution), (3) referral to an appropriate professional organization for discipline by its ethics advisor or ethics committee, (4) disallowing the information presented by any offender on behalf of the party represented, and (5) denial of further access to BPI in a current or any future proceedings before the USITC.

See also U.S. International Trade Commission.

aduana, the Spanish for "customs," is the equivalent of customs *duty*.

ad val. See ad valorem duty.

ad valorem (ad val.) is from the Latin meaning "in proportion to the value."
See also ad valorem duty.

ad valorem duty, also called *ad valorem tariff*, is a tax expressed or calculated as a percentage of the value of goods cleared through the customs authority imposing the charge.
A duty of 10 percent ad valorem means a surcharge of 10 percent of the value payable to customs.
Cf. antidumping duty; compound duty; countervailing duty; end-use tariff; specific duty; optimum tariff; prohibitive tariff.

advance payment See payment in advance.

advising bank is the exporter's bank that notifies ("advises") the exporter that the importer's bank (the issuing bank) has provided a letter of credit on behalf of the importer, to the credit of the exporter (the beneficiary).
Cf. issuing bank.
See also letter of credit.

Advisory Committee on Trade Policy Negotiations See U.S. Advisory Committee on Trade Negotiations.

affiliate See subsidiary.

affirmative action/equal opportunity/pay equity (AA/EO/PE) refers to the shift of political power away from the free interaction of market forces toward managed market economics where government intervention influences, guides and directs the terms for the supply of, and demand for, labor.
AA/EO/PE consists of three components:

1. *Affirmative Action (AA)*: the legal mandate to preferentially favor women and minorities in hiring, this policy began in 1964 in the United States following the passage of the U.S. Civil Rights Act, and it resulted in preferential hiring of blacks to achieve "racial balance."

2. *Equal Opportunity (EO)* (called Employment Equity (EE) in Canada): laws that uphold the right of "equal access" to employment by women and minorities.
3. *Pay Equity (PE)*: the concept of "equal pay for work of equal value," and the adjustment of wages and salaries to reflect this by rectifying past pay differentials.

In recent years, AA/EO/PE has been expanded beyond its original mandate. In many jurisdictions, the AA/EO components have provisions for equal access to jobs by people regardless of their "sexual orientation" (i.e., lesbians and homosexuals), by those who suffer from and are carriers of acquired immune deficiency syndrome (AIDS), and by those who may be mentally or physically handicapped, or others such as Vietnam Era Veterans and aboriginal peoples.

The basis for AA/EO/PE labor-market management derives from what has been called "structural and historical discrimination" primarily against women and non-white-skinned people. AA/EO/PE seeks to redress these "historical inequities" by grouping the victims of employment discrimination into classes called "protected minorities," and then differentially discriminating in their favor. This strategy is called "preferential treatment" by its supporters and "reverse discrimination" by its detractors.

Free trade ideologues and supply-side economists make a strong argument against AA/EO/PE because of its artificial market-distorting effects. They argue that wherever AA/EO/PE operates by favoring employment opportunity on the basis of anything other than merit, the result is not simply mediocrity (*See* Hird's Law), but a real deterioration of the competitive comparative advantage of the employer company, industry, or nation.

The suggestion here is that, in the same way that nontariff barriers (NTBs) retard trade creation, so too AA/EO/PE deprives the market of the most rational allocation of labor resources. It is argued that this is especially true where the AA component sets "hiring quotas" for the protected minorities. Thus, when the market is forced to adjust itself to these quotas, AA/EO/PE acts as a *value subtracter* in making the cost of the end-product less valuable than the sum of its production inputs.

Example: Under U.S. and Canadian AA/EO laws, an automotive aftermarket manufacturer had to preferentially hire so many handicapped and female workers that the outcome produced such costly rework problems, such badly backed-up distribution requirements planning, and such dislocated customer service that the Japanese customer would not accept the order, the cost of which now exceeded the original export quotation. The Japanese cancelled the order and redirected it to Singaporean and Taiwanese foreign trade zones (FTZs) where current U.S. and Canadian AA/EO/PE laws had no jurisdiction.

Thus, free traders argue, it is illusory to expect any industry or nation to be able to accelerate trade creation and wealth production simply by implementing "liberalization" and "deregulation." Much more is required, they say, including a "friendly business environment." To this end, there is considerable evidence to suggest that wherever international businesses find their market freedom delimited by AA/EO/PE policies, they are likely to seek ways to evade compliance with such unfriendly government regulations, including fleeing the jurisdiction in a search for more "friendly business environments."

The success of FTZs worldwide and of the Caribbean Basin Initiative (CBI) regionally can be viewed as such freedom-seeking international-marketing attempts to operate clear of heavy-handed AA/EO/PE controls wielded by government bureaucrats who, claiming to act in the interests of the market, may be more accountable to the major stake-holders in the AA/EO/PE industry: government and parastate agencies, and nongovernment organizations (NGOs), the third-party beneficiaries of public funding.

The foregoing is not advanced to suggest that a reversal of AA/EO/PE is desirable. It is simply meant to illustrate the enormous opportunity costs involved (i.e., the wealth that might have been generated but that would be foregone) when, in a competitive international business environment, well-intentioned individuals flee the market seeking the support of the state to redress wrongs claimed to have been due to "market failure." Ironically, "Hird's Law" seems the inevitable result since it is the intervention of government that deforms the market and that results in the kind of "market failure" that was claimed to have been the original cause of the problem.

See also foreign trade zone; Caribbean Basin Initiative; "Did SMIOHO or did SMIOAQ?"; Hird's Law.

affirmative dumping determination is a final decision that a country has engaged in the marketing of products below fair market value and is thus subject to antidumping duty orders or other measures under U.S. or Canadian law.
See also dumping.

affreightment *See* contract of affreightment.

African Development Bank (AfDB), one of the multilateral development banks (MDBs), is an international financial organization that is an executing agency for projects of the United Nations Development Program (UNDP).

The AfDB is headquartered in Abidjan, with regional offices in Yaoundé, Harare, Rabat, Addis Ababa, Conakry, and London. AfDB members comprise 50 regional African nations and 25 nonregional ones. The AfDB Group consists of the AfDB proper, the African Development Fund (AfDF), and the Nigerian Trust Fund (NTF).

The AfDB stimulates regional economic growth by granting loans and providing technical assistance to projects and programs of its member countries.

Main sectors for concessional financing are social infrastructure, public utilities, agriculture, transport, and development banking.

See also multilateral development banks; technical assistance; concessional financing; near-commercial lending terms; Appendix V (B); United Nations Development Program.

African Groundnut Council (AGC), also known as *Conseil Africain de l'Arachide (CAA)*, is an international commodity group (ICG), formed in 1964, to (1) promote consumption of the product, (2) organize and exchange information on efficient production and marketing among producers, and (3) influence customers in an attempt to attain consistently predictable and profitable prices for producers of the commodity.

The AGC has its headquarters in Lagos, Nigeria, and comprises the following producer-member nations: Gambia, Mali, Niger, Nigeria, Sénégal, Sudan, and Burkina Faso.

Cf. international cartel.

See also Appendix V (E).

African Timber Organization (ATO), also known as *Organisation Africaine du Bois (OAB)*, is an international commodity group (ICG) formed in 1975 to coordinate ways and means among producer-member nations of influencing the prices of wood in the global market.

The ATO has its headquarters in Libreville, Gabon, and comprises the following producer-member nations: Cameroon, Central African Republic, Congo, Equatorial Guinea, Gabon, Ghana, Côte d'Ivoire, Liberia, Malagasy Republic, Tanzania, and Zaire.

Cf. international cartel.

See also Appendix V (E).

AG (A.G.), the abbreviation of the German *Aktien-Gesellschaft*, is the designation for a joint-stock company in the Federal Republic of Germany (FRG).

The equivalent term in Canada and the United States is a limited company (Ltd.) or an incorporated company (Inc.), whose incorporation limits its liability.

Agreement Corporation *See* Edge Corporation.

Agreement on Antidumping Practices, known as the *Antidumping Code*, is an international agreement resulting from the Tokyo Round of Multilateral Trade Negotiations.

The agreement came into force in January 1980, replacing the previous code negotiated during the Kennedy Round of General Agreement on Tariffs and Trade (GATT) negotiations.

The essence of the agreement is the establishment of conditions under which antidumping duties may be legally imposed by a country as its defense against what it determines are dumped imports.

By the agreement, *dumped goods* can be defined as "imports that are sold at prices below those charged in the domestic, national market of the producer-country."

The agreement sets out the process by which claims of dumping can be investigated and antidumping actions taken.

The process rests on international concensus for the semiannual reporting of dumping claims to GATT and on the establishment (by the GATT Council) of dispute-settlement panels to arbitrate between disputing parties. What is crucial is that the determinations of these GATT settlement panels are neither binding on any party to the dispute nor enforceable by GATT.

On judgment, the Canada-U.S. Free Trade Agreement of 1989 (FTA), compared to the GATT Agreement on Antidumping Practices, has a more expeditious process for both establishing dispute-settlement panels and for ensuring compliance by the parties with the binding decisions of the panels established to hear disputes arising from the FTA.

Cf. Canada-U.S. Free Trade Agreement of 1989.
See also Tokyo Round.

Agreement on Customs Valuation, known as the *Customs Valuation Code*, is an international agreement resulting from the Tokyo Round of Multilateral Trade Negotiations.

The Agreement replaced many different hitherto existing arbitrary systems of customs valuation with a set of transparent rules to afford Contracting Parties a fair, neutral, and uniform process of valuing goods for the purpose of levying customs duties.

The objective of this Agreement was to proliferate a single harmonized system of customs valuation globally, thus further establishing rational rules in the interests of liberalizing trade practices and procedures worldwide.

See also Tokyo Round; Harmonized Commodity Description and Coding System.

Agreement on Government Procurement, known as the *Government Procurement Code*, is an international agreement resulting from the Tokyo Round of Multilateral Trade Negotiations.

The Agreement, signed by 12 countries as of the end of 1988, was specifically designed to establish a uniform set of worldwide practices applicable to government procurement. The aim was to liberalize the procurement process, affording all bidders a fair chance to tender for government contracts, without discrimination.

Recent work by the General Agreement on Tariffs and Trade (GATT) Committee on Government Procurement has sought to broaden the Agreement to encompass local government authorities and quasi-government bodies that request tenders. This work accelerated after the Protocol of Amendments (to the Agreement) took effect on February 14, 1988. This Protocol lowered the threshold for all government contracts that could be bid for by foreign suppliers, from SDR 150,000 to SDR 130,000. Further, the Committee has sought to include government service contracts in a broadened definition of government procurement; and it is especially this latter sector that is being vigorously addressed during the current Uruguay Round of GATT talks.

See also Tokyo Round.

Agreement on Import Licensing, known as the *Licensing Code*, is an international agreement resulting from the Tokyo Round of Multilateral Trade Negotiations.

This Agreement, signed by 27 countries as of the end of 1988, was intended to ensure that international licensing procedures per se do not act as trade barriers and that transparent licensing procedures are used (i.e., the administration of licensing be effected in a straightforward and nondiscriminatory way).

See also Tokyo Round.

Agreement on the Interpretation and Application of Articles VI, XVI, and XXIII of the General Agreement on Tariffs and Trade (GATT)
See Subsidies (and Countervailing Measures) Code.

Agreement on Technical Barriers to Trade *See* Standards Code.

Agreement on Trade in Civil Aircraft is an international agreement resulting from the Tokyo Round of Multilateral Trade Negotiations.

This Agreement became effective on January 1, 1988, and by the end of 1988, it had the signatures of 22 countries. It was the only agreement covering manufactured goods that was negotiated during the Tokyo Round.

The essence of this Agreement, signed by all the world's manufacturers of civil aircraft (except the Soviet Union), was (1) the elimination of all duties on aircraft and aircraft parts, (2) the liberalizing of government procurement procedures for civil aircraft, and (3) the agreement on guidelines for the production of aircraft.

See also Tokyo Round; standards; nontariff barriers.

aid *See* official development assistance.

air waybill *See* bill of lading.

allocations under lines of credit, established by Canada's Export Development Corporation (EDC), are lines of credit with private banks and public agencies in foreign countries to facilitate medium- and long-term export financing to foreign buyers of Canadian capital goods and services.

These umbrella-like agreements provide financial encouragement for foreign buyers where local governments or local markets cannot provide the required financing.

See also Export Development Corporation.

all-risk clause is an insurance provision covering all damage to or loss of goods, except that of inherent vice (i.e., self-caused).

"Always Say Yes" •NW• refers to the strategic Western management application of the "Yes, Yes" paradigm involving the Japanese strategy of *nemawashi* that management believes can be successfully imported and applied to a Western hierarchy.

This approach presumes Western business problems are more amenable to solution when group-based tactics are used instead of more conventional individual-oriented decision-making methods.

Such problems are termed "nem-problems" (after *nemawashi*).

Tests of "Always Say Yes" in the business workplace reveal many interesting results. For instance, subjecting nem-problems to group-based tactics tends to make compliance difficult whenever a Western manager who must implement a decision is perceived by his or her subordinates as having an inferior level of education or experience. The situation is compounded when assertive subordinates refuse to restrain their ego drives and demand democratic participation. In such cases, a manager is forced to achieve his or her will brusquely, without demonstrating Japanese-type concern or respect ("saving face") for the group members. From the "Always Say Yes" perspective, the result is a perception of "management tyranny" and of top-down decision making, exactly the opposite of management's intent: in other words, a conventional "nem-hostile" American-style decision-making process.

Analysis of the cultural borrowing component of "Always Say Yes" suggests a finding that may be generalized to decision making worldwide: whenever difficulties arise in solving nem-problems, the cause may be related to some measure of ethnocentrism on the part of the cultural borrowers. Thus, in cases where "nem-friendly" solutions using "Always Say Yes" tactics seem to elude Western managers, the reason may lie in the fact that managers inexperienced in the area of cultural anthropology have trouble applying cross-cultural management ideas successfully.

This raises a cultural caveat for all Western managers who seek to implement "Always Say Yes" and other cross-cultural decision-making strategies. First of all, they are cautioned not to be too easily impressed by what they may want to believe are sophisticated decision-making concepts in general and by Japanese tactics in particular. Second, they should approach the question of cultural borrowing with extreme care, recalling the words of the English philosopher Thomas More, who was beheaded by King Henry VIII: "Never be too trusting."

Western managers thus should restrain themselves from ingenuously agreeing that nem-problems are more easily solved via group-based approaches instead of more conventional American-style individual-oriented decision making.

Lack of attention to the soft side of international business is a predictable reason for management difficulty in this field, especially in cases where managers often seek a "quick fix" to genuinely complex international business issues.

Cf. "Yes, Yes."

See also nemawashi; cultural borrowing; ethnocentrism; soft side of international marketing.

Amazonian Cooperation Treaty (ACT), also called the *Amazon Pact*, is an agreement among all the countries of the Amazon Basin to cooperate in the economic development of their respective Amazon regions, including the proper use and preservation of the natural environment.

The treaty was signed in 1978 by the following countries: Bolivia, Brazil, Colombia, Ecuador, Guyana, Perú, Suriname, and Venezuela. The headquarters are in Brasilia, Brazil.

See also Appendix V (B).

American selling price (ASP) is a now-defunct method of calculating import duties on goods imported into the United States.

The duty was calculated (for certain categories of goods) by multiplying the tariff rate by the price of the U.S. domestic good with which the import competed. This was in contrast to the standard international practice of multiplying the tariff rate by the price of the imported good itself.

The United States agreed in the Tokyo Round to phase out the ASP method of calculation in 1981.

See also valuation.

Andean Common Market (ANCOM), also known as *El Pacto Andino, El Grupo Andino* (Andean Group), The Cartagena Agreement, and the Andean Development

Corporation, is a free trade area, established in 1969, comprising Bolivia, Chile, Colombia, Ecuador, Perú, and Venezuela.

ANCOM is a subgroup of a larger regional economic organization, the Latin American Integration Association (LAIA).

See also common market.

anglophone, from *Anglo* meaning "English" and *phone* (in Greek) meaning "voice," is a national of a country (not necessarily England) whose mother tongue or predominant language choice is the English language.

Cf. francophone.

anonymizing •NW• from the Greek *anonumos,* meaning "nameless," is the process whereby something is deprived of its unique identity.

See also dirty money.

antidumping code (anti-dumping code) is a code of conduct negotiated under the General Agreement on Tariffs and Trade (GATT) during the Kennedy Round and Tokyo Round of multilateral trade negotiations (MTN).

The talks established standards, both substantive and procedural, for national antidumping activities.

See also Kennedy Round; Tokyo Round.

antidumping duty (anti-dumping duty) is a tax imposed by an importing country on imports that are priced below the normal market price of the goods in the exporter's domestic market and that cause injury (i.e., loss of sales and/or market share) to domestic industry.

Sometimes it is called a punitive tariff. It should not be confused with a countervailing duty.

Cf. countervailing duty.

See also dumping; duty; less than fair value.

appreciation is the decrease in the domestic currency price of a foreign currency.

Appreciation of domestic currency occurs due to the relative higher valuation of a domestic currency in terms of a foreign currency, and consequently, the lower price of a foreign currency.

Cf. depreciation.

Arab Bank for Economic Development in Africa (ABEDA), also known as *Banque Arabe pour le Développement Économique en Afrique (BADEA),* is a regional economic development bank established at the Summit Conference of the Arab League in Algiers in 1973.

In 1975, the ABEDA commenced operations. The mandate of the organization is to provide financing and technical assistance for development projects in subscriber countries (who may all be members of the Organization of African Unity (OAU) except African countries who are Arab League members).

The ABEDA has close relations with the African Development Bank (AfDB), an executing agency of the United Nations Development Program (UNDP), with subregional banks in Central and West Africa and with specialized Arab development agencies and funds.

See also Organization of African Countries; Arab League; Appendix V (B).

Arab Boycott of Israel is an embargo agreed to in 1948 by Arab countries to (1) ban all direct trade between themselves and Israel, (2) blacklist all non-Israeli companies adjudged to have invested in Israel, and (3) place conditions in contracts with foreign companies whereby they agree not to deal with any blacklisted company in the procurement of goods and/or services for project work in any Arab country.

Amendments to the U.S. Export Administration Act (plus strict administrative regulations) forbid compliance by U.S. companies with the Arab Boycott.

For example, a U.S. firm exporting from Greece to Syria risks being fined by U.S. authorities if it issues negative certificates of origin that specifically certify that the goods in question did not come either directly or indirectly from Israel.

Cf. embargo; blacklist.

See also certificate of origin.

Arab Common Market (ACM) is a customs union formed in 1965 between Egypt, Iraq, Sudan, Syria, the United Arab Emirates, and Yemen under the auspices of the Council of Arab Economic Unity.

See also customs union; Appendix V (A).

Arab Cooperation Council (ACC) is a Middle Eastern regional group, formed in February 1989, that comprises Egypt, Iraq, Jordan, and Yemen.

Originally perceived of as a new force for moderation in the Middle East, the ACC has not, since February 24, 1990, onwards, enjoyed this reputation. On that date in Amman, Jordan, on the first anniversary of the ACC, President Saddam Hussein of Iraq broadcast an alarmingly anti-American speech, one that later proved to be the forerunner of Iraq's aggressive, expansionist behavior to exert mastery over the Persian Gulf.

Cf. Gulf Cooperation Council.

See also Gulf Crisis.

Arab Fund for Economic and Social Development (AFESD) is an international financial organization established in 1968 (and operational in 1972) that aims to stimulate development via economic and social programs exclusively in Arab states.

The Fund comprises 21 members including the Palestine Liberation Organization (PLO), which has been given *de jure* recognition. It has its headquarters in Kuwait City, Kuwait.

See also Appendix V (B).

Arab League, also known as *The League of Arab States,* is an agreement, established in 1945 (after the end of World War II and prior to the *de jure* establishment of Israel), among Arab states for (1) mutual support; (2) cooperation in social, economic, and cultural programs; and (3) coordination in mutual defense.

Its headquarters are in Cairo, Egypt. The League is committed to both broadly international as well as infra-Arab "causes." For example, in 1957, the Arab Economic Council of the Arab League founded the Council of Arab Economic Unity. First operational in 1965, it was an essentially political body that focused on regional economic development within Arab countries.

At the Arab League Summit Conference held in Algiers in 1973, the Arab Bank for Economic Development in Africa was established to finance development projects.

At the Arab League meeting in 1976 in Rabat, Morocco, the framework for the establishment of the Arab Monetary Fund was agreed upon.

Arab League members consist of: Algeria, Bahrain, Djibouti, Egypt, Iraq, Jordan, Kuwait, Lebanon, Libya, Mauritania, Morocco, Oman, Palestine Liberation Organization (PLO), Qatar, Saudi Arabia, Somalia, Sudan, Syria, Tunisia, and Yemen (formerly Yemen (Aden) and Yemen (San'a)).

Cf. Organization of the Islamic Conference.

See also Arab Bank for Economic Development in Africa; Arab Monetary Fund.

Arab Mahgreb Union (AMU) *See* Mahgreb Common Market.

Arab Monetary Fund (AMF) is an international financial organization established to assist member countries cope with their balance of payments problems, as well as to promote Arab economic development and Arab monetary cooperation.

The AMF was established in Rabat, Morocco, at an Arab League meeting in 1976. It has its headquarters in Abu Dhabi, United Arab Emirates (UAE). The AMF's membership comprises all Arab countries including the Palestine Liberation Organization (which has been given *de jure* recognition).

The accounting unit of the AMF is the Arab dinar (AD), which is equivalent to one Special Drawing Right (1 SDR) of the International Monetary Fund (IMF).

The AMF maintains strong working relations with the IMF and with all international organizations in the fields of commerce, finance, and development, including the World Bank Group and the Bank for International Settlements (BIS).

See also Appendix V (B).

Arab Union (now defunct) was a political agreement, established in 1958 by Jordan and Iraq, as a mutual defense pact to counter the United Arab Republic.

Cf. United Arab Republic.

arbitrage *See* Appendix II.

arbitration *See* Appendix VI.

arbitration clause *See* Appendix VI.

Area Control List *See* Export and Import Permits Act.

arm's length (arm's-length transaction/agreement) is
1. a contract between two or more parties to which they would have agreed had the parties been unrelated or unaffiliated;
2. a contract between two or more parties related by their common interest in the outcome of some enterprise, whereby the activities between the parties are carried out through some third party that has no related interest in the outcome of the matter.

The extraterritorial application of U.S. antitrust laws prohibits U.S. firms overseas from acting in ways that might be interpreted as restraining trade. To achieve market penetration and market dominance in foreign markets, U.S. firms sometimes transact business at arm's length so as to avoid the perception of collusive practices. This involves the establishment of "shell companies" and other offshore phantom entities with which U.S. companies do business at a distance to avoid U.S. antitrust laws.

Arrangement Regarding Bovine Meat is an international agreement resulting from the Tokyo Round of Multilateral Trade Negotiations.

It has been signed by 27 countries plus the European Economic Community (EEC) as a single unit, which account for almost 85 percent of total world exports of beef. The Agreement is overseen by the International Meat Council (IMC).

The objectives of the Agreement are (1) to promote the liberalization of world trade in beef, (2) to discourage the use of voluntary restraint agreements (VRAs) by countries, and (3) to monitor the use of unnecessarily restrictive trade measures by producer-exporter countries.

See also Tokyo Round.

Asian and Pacific Coconut Community (APCC) is an international commodity group (ICG) formed in 1969 to share information on increasing the efficiency of production, processing, and research of the raw commodity (and its by-products) among producer-member countries.

In the long run, the APCC aims to increase its control over down-stream pricing of the commodity and its by-products.

The APCC has its headquarters in Jakarta, Indonesia, and comprises the following producer-members: India, Indonesia, Malaysia, Papua New Guinea (PNG), the Philippines, Solomon Islands, Sri Lanka, Thailand, Vanuatu, and Western Samoa.

Cf. international cartel.

See also Appendix V (E); down-stream pricing.

Asian and Pacific Council (APC) is a consultative group that brings together seven regional members to discuss economic, social, and cultural matters.

It was established in 1966 in Tokyo and comprises Australia, Japan, New

Zealand, the Philippines, Republic of Korea (South Korea), Republic of China (Taiwan), and Thailand.
 Cf. Nordic Council.
 See also Appendix V (B).

Asian Development Bank (AsDB, ADB), one of the multilateral development banks (MDBs), is an international financial organization that is an executing agency for projects of the United Nations Development Program (UNDP).
 The AsDB is headquartered in Manila, the Philippines, and comprises 31 regional and 14 nonregional members.
 The AsDB stimulates regional economic growth by granting loans and providing technical assistance to projects and programs of its member countries.
 Main sectors for concessional financing and near-commercial lending terms are agriculture and agro-industry, transport and communications, energy, industry and nonfuel minerals, urban development, sanitation and water supply, education, and health.
 See also multilateral development banks; United Nations Development Program; Appendix V (B).

Asian Productivity Organization (APO) is an international organization dedicated to increasing the productivity of industry (1) in each of its member countries in particular and (2) in the Asian economic region in general.
 Established in 1971 with headquarters in Tokyo, the organization has helped to found productivity councils in each of its 14 member countries. These bodies act as centers of influence to get and disseminate information to national industries on ways and means of increasing industrial productivity in the nation.
 Together with Japanese technical assistance in the form of know-how, patents, processes, on-the-job training (OJT), seminars, and courses, concepts such as quality circles and kan ban systems have been taught and implemented in the APO's Asian-member countries.

These countries (the "periphery") have become to Japan (the "core") what countries in East Europe are to the Soviet Union or what those in Latin America are to the United States.

 See also Appendix V (B); yen diplomacy.

Asia-Pacific Economic Cooperation Group (APEC) *See* Pacific Economic Cooperation Group.

associated financing •NW• is a managed-financing classification of the Development Assistance Committee (DAC) of the Organization for Economic Cooperation and Development (OECD).
 It comprises export credits extended (1) on market terms of interest; (2)

on mixed credit terms; and (3) on concessional financing, mainly in the form of official development assistance (ODA).

  Cf. OECD Concensus.

  See also concessional financing.

Association of Iron Ore Exporting Countries (AIOEC) (also known as *Association des Pays Exportateurs de Minerai de Fer (APEMF)*) is an international commodity group (ICG) formed in 1975, to establish a mechanism for collaboration among exporter-members in the fields of exploration for and the processing and marketing of the commodity and to secure higher and more profitable world prices.

  The AIOEC's headquarters are in Geneva, Switzerland, and membership comprises the following countries: Algeria, Australia, India, Liberia, Mauritania, Perú, Sierra Leone, Sweden, and Venezuela.

  Cf. international cartel.

  See also Appendix V (E).

Association of Natural Rubber Producing Countries (ANRPC) is an international commodity group (ICG), formed in 1970 as a mechanism for collaboration among producer-member countries, aimed at stabilizing prices and securing fair and profitable returns for exporters.

  The ANRPC has a close relationship with the United Nations Conference on Trade and Development (UNCTAD). Under UNCTAD, an international commodity agreement (ICA) was negotiated and signed as the International Rubber Agreement (IRA).

  The IRA provides a mechanism whereby members of the ANRPC are bound to maintain on-hand buffer stocks of the commodity and to make them available in the world market, if the world price rises above a pre-agreed trigger price.

  On the other hand, if world supply exceeds demand and the world price falls below a pre-agreed price floor (i.e., a minimum price), ANRPC members will buy up the world surplus and hold it in inventory to reduce supply and force up the world price to within a boundary range.

  The ANRPC has its headquarters in Kuala Lumpur, Malaysia, and its membership comprises the following countries: India, Indonesia, Malaysia, Papua New Guinea (PNG), Singapore, Sri Lanka, and Thailand.

  Cf. international cartel; international commodity agreement.

  See also Appendix V (E).

Association of Southeast Asian Nations (ASEAN) is a free trade area, established in 1967, comprising Singapore, Indonesia, Thailand, Brunei, Malaysia, and the Philippines.

  See also Appendix V (A).

ASYCUDA, the abbreviation for **A**utomated **S**ystem for **Cu**stoms **Da**ta, is the automated (electronic) customs system of Africa. ASYCUDA was developed under the auspices of the United Nations Conference on Trade and Development (UNCTAD).

ASYCUDA comprises computer software that handles customs declarations, accounting procedures, cargo movement, warehousing, and import/export licenses. The aim is to assist African governments in international trade relations (1) by producing accurate statistical data and (2) by generating information such as duties payable on imports and the reconciliation of amounts due versus amounts paid. The statistical data are designed to assist governments monitor their foreign trade, minimize dishonest customs declarations, and maintain surveillance and control of the trade in "controlled goods" (e.g., weapons, munitions) and in contraband goods (e.g., drugs).

The history of ASYCUDA began in 1981 when members of the Economic Community of West African States (ECOWAS) approached UNCTAD and the government of France. It took until 1985 for ASYCUDA to be fully written and debugged, and then implemented. Unfortunately, the original system was noninteractive. It was only in 1991, with the launch of a new version, that electronic data transfer was possible between members of the ASYCUDA network and between ASYCUDA and nonnetwork members (with full intra- and intersystem compatibility). ASYCUDA has now been installed in 27 countries with 50 others interested, including ASEAN, the Association of Southeast Asian Nations.

See also United Nations Conference on Trade and Development; Economic Community of West African States.

Australian dollar area *See* currency area.

Australia-New Zealand-U.S. Security Treaty (ANZUS Pact) is a mutual defense treaty, established in 1951, whereby the United States assumed the leadership (from the United Kingdom) to underwrite the military defense of Australia and New Zealand in a "containment" of (what was perceived to have been) Communist political expansion during the 30-year (1950–1980) so-called Cold War period.

The ANZUS Pact is a paper treaty only, following (1) the refusal of New Zealand to permit U.S. nuclear submarines to berth in its harbors and (2) the U.S. response whereby it withdrew its commitments under the treaty to New Zealand in the late 1980s.

See also Appendix V (C).

autarky is self-imposed isolation, characterized by the absence of trade and diplomatic relations with governments and international organizations/associations.
Cf. economic nationalism; open economy.

Automotive Products Trade Agreement, also known as *The Auto Pact*, is a Canada-U.S. sectoral trade agreement entered into in 1965, aimed at providing both nations with duty-free entry of new cars and original automotive equipment parts.
The outcome of The Auto Pact has been the growth and economic rationalization of the North American automotive industry.
Cf. Canada-U.S. Free Trade Agreement of 1989.
See also sectoral trade agreement.

autonomous transactions, sometimes referred to as "above-the-line items," are international transactions that occur for profit and are thus included in the current account and capital account of a country.

These cash flows exclude unilateral transfers, and they are independent of balance of payments considerations.

Cf. accommodating transactions.

b

B-13 is the Canadian Export Declaration form.

    See also export declaration.

back translation (back-translation) is the rendering of intellectual property (e.g., labels, promotional materials, instruction manuals) in a reverse direction from the original rendition.

    In the first translation, the process moves from a source language to a target language (e.g., from English, the source, to Spanish, the target). Back translation reverses the process: the original rendition of the Spanish (target) is retranslated (i.e., translated back) to English (source) by a person other than the one who did the first "forward" translation.

    Cf. translation.

bagged cargo is a colloquial term for a commodity classification used in international physical distribution and logistics (PD/L) that refers to goods that are placed in individual shipping sacks made of canvas, jute, or synthetic material.

    These are, in turn, reloaded into shipping containers, lighters, and the cargo holds of transportation carriers.

    Cf. base produce; commodity.

Baghdad Pact *See* Central Treaty Organization.

baksheesh (bakshish) *See* bribery.

balance of concessions *See* reciprocity.

balance of payments (BOP) is a summary statement of a country's credit and debit transactions with other countries and international organizations/associations during a particular time period, usually 12 months.

The transactions that comprise the BOP are divided into two groups: the current account and the capital account.

Cf. surplus (in the balance of payments); balance of trade.

See also capital account; current account; deficit (in the balance of payments).

balance of trade (BOT), a key component of the balance of payments (BOP), is the difference that results when a nation's receipts from merchandise exports are compared with its expenditures on merchandise imports.

If the receipts from merchandise exports are greater than the nation's expenditures on merchandise imports, the difference is a surplus.

If the expenditures on merchandise imports are greater than the nation's receipts from merchandise exports, the difference is a deficit.

Cf. balance of payments.

banana republic, a derogatory variation of *branch plant economy*,

1. originally referred to Central American republics (e.g., Honduras, Nicaragua) whose political economies were entirely dependent upon exports of bananas to the United States;
2. denotes "one-crop economies": developing countries limited to and dependent on the production and export of one commodity (or a limited number of them) for their economic development. Examples of these are Zambia (copper), Zaire (base metals), Jamaica (sugar, bauxite), Perú (minerals, anchovies); and
3. connotes a political economy that, as a consequence of its dependent development, comprises people of lesser value and of lower moral behavior.

bank, from the Latin *banca* meaning "bench," is an institution, whether privately- or state-owned, that acts as an information storage-and-retrieval system, involving signals in the form of documentation (e.g., drafts, letters of credit, deposit slips, promissory notes) to manage money in certain explicit ways.

Every country has a national bank that issues the country's currency. This institution is called a "central" bank, and its responsibilities may involve developing a government's monetary policy, but certainly involve implementing it.

See also central bank; monetarism.

Bank of Central African States (BCAS), officially, *Banque des États de l'Afrique Centrale (BEAC)*, established in 1955, is a regional international financial institution that acts as the exclusive issuer of bank notes and coins (CFA franc) circulated in the subscriber-member countries.

The Bank services members of the Central African Economic Community (CAEF), officially, *Communauté Économique des États de l'Afrique Centrale (CEEAC)*, a regional trade group, formed in 1983, of countries that were all former French colonies.

The BCAS has its headquarters in Yaoundé, Cameroon. Its membership comprises Cameroon, Central African Republic, Chad, Congo, and Gabon.

Cf. Central Bank of West African States; West African Monetary Union.

See also Appendix V (B); *CFA franc.*

Bank Documentary Credit Insurance (BDCI) is an insurance program of the Export Development Corporation (EDC) that provides "cover" for banks that are involved in export credit financing.

Here is how the BDCI works:

1. A Canadian exporter wants its Canadian bank to back up a documentary credit issued by the bank of its foreign customer. The credit is commonly an irrevocable letter of credit.
2. The Canadian bank takes out a BDCI policy with the Export Development Corporation (EDC).
3. The exporter's documentary credit is now "covered" against any potential losses, and it can be presented to the bank and used against which to draw term drafts to capitalize the exporter.

See also Export Development Corporation; export financing; documentary credits.

banker's acceptance (bank acceptance) is the assent by a bank to honor for payment a draft presented to it for payment at some future date.

See also acceptance financing; term documentary draft.

Bank for International Settlements (BIS) is an international organization that was established in 1930 as a neutral intermediary to promote cooperation among the world's central banks by assisting organizations such as the International Monetary Fund (IMF) to effect international balance of payments settlements.

The BIS' headquarters are in Basel, Switzerland. The Bank for International Settlements is the designated forum for the settlement of disputes among G-10 members.

See also International Monetary Fund.

barter, a type of countertrade transaction, is an agreement between exporter and importer covering the exchange of specific goods-for-goods under one contract.

The exchange does not necessarily occur simultaneously, and it does not preclude the involvement of third parties.

A variation of "pure" barter (i.e., 100 percent goods-for-goods exchange) involves an agreement that specifies the goods exchanged and the balance involving payment in currency.

See also countertrade.

Cf. buy-back; compensation trade; cooperation contracts; counterpurchase; offset deals; switch deals.

Basel (Basle) Accord is an international, multilateral agreement signed by the Group of 10 (G-10) in Basel, Switzerland, that clearly stated its purpose: by 1992, all international commercial banks from the G-10 (plus Luxembourg) must achieve a ratio of capital/risk-weighted assets of eight percent.

To assist G-10 members to achieve this goal, the Accord comprises three parts:

1. a definition of the capital of commercial banks;

2. the application of risk weights to different categories of commercial bank assets;
3. the treatment of off-balance sheet activities.

Point 1 is the most important and germane:

The Definition of Capital

Commercial bank capital consists of two types:

- Tier-One Capital (T1C)—the common stock and retained earnings of a commercial bank (by 1992, T1C must amount to 4 percent of the bank's risk-weighted assets);
- Tier-Two Capital (T2C)—the additional 4 percent of the required capital-to-asset ratio.

The greater the diversity of capital items that are allowed into T2C the easier it will be for banks to meet the standards of the Accord.

Underlying the theory of the Accord is that the amount of capital a commercial bank is required to hold should be directly related to the credit risks of its asset portfolio.
Since U.S. and Canadian companies capitalize companies mainly via debt instruments, while the Japanese do so mainly via equity, there is something fundamentally divergent about the way each perceives risks and, consequently, about their particular perceptions of how to generate capital for what some perceive as extremely risky Third World investments, but what others see as essential capital investments in long-run political stability that will ensure the openness of capital markets worldwide.

See also Bank for International Settlements; Group of 10.

base produce is a commodity classification used in international physical distribution and logistics (PD/L) that comprises unprocessed agricultural goods in bulk form.
Examples of base produce are wool, fresh fruit, tea, coffee, jute, and tobacco.
Cf. bulk cargo; commodity.

basic balance is the net balance on all of a nation's long-term capital and current account transactions.

beggar-thy-neighbor policy is a set of actions characterized by the raising of tariffs and nontariff barriers (NTBs) aimed at reducing imports and, thus, increasing domestic output.
The outcome of this avowedly protectionist policy is usually retaliation by the trading partners of the protectionist nation. This results in continuing rounds of tariff hikes by all the trading nations, reduces total exports, and worsens international economic relations.
The Smoot-Hawley Tariff Act of 1930 is frequently cited as one of the most notable examples of this protectionist policy.
It has been argued that it was this act that greatly exacerbated The Great Depression (1929–1935), actively worsening the international economic situation and, thus, facilitating the rise to power of totalitarian regimes during the period.
See also nontariff barriers; protectionist policy; Smoot-Hawley Tariff Act of 1930.

belly cargo is goods stowed in the lower hold of a transport carrier, usually an aircraft or a ship.
Cf. deck cargo.

beneficiary is the party in whose financial favor a documentary credit is issued. In international trade, the beneficiary would be the exporter.
See also documentary credit.

Belgium-Netherlands-Luxembourg Customs Union *See* Benelux.

below-the-line items *See* accommodating transactions.

benefit allowance refers to specific incentives offered to executives to encourage them to accept overseas postings.

1. *Cost-of-Living Allowance:* the financial adjustment paid to executives as a result of facing increased costs of living in a foreign city.

   Example: If an executive were moving from Detroit to Tokyo and the intercity cost of living in Tokyo was 50 percent higher than in Detroit, the executive would receive an allowance equal to 50 percent of spendable income.

   Cost-of-living allowances are usually company-specific computations using standard price indices from the Canadian Department of National Revenue and the U.S. Department of Commerce.
2. *Education Allowance:* the financial adjustment paid to executives to cover expenses incurred in educating their children overseas to standards comparable to those in the expatriates' home countries.
3. *Housing Allowance:* the financial adjustment paid to executives to cover costs for housing overseas in excess of some basic deductible or fixed percentage of income, to enable executives to afford housing comparable to what they would be able to afford in their home countries.
4. *Relocation Allowance:* the direct payment to executives to cover the costs of moving personal and household goods to and from an overseas posting and the costs of travel to and from the foreign post by the executive, spouse, and children.
5. *Vacation Allowance:* either the salary adjustment made or reimbursement for costs incurred in specific periodic travel to the expatriates' home countries for vacations.

   See also benefits for international service.

benefit differential refers to specific incentives offered to executives to encourage them to accept overseas postings.

1. *Hardship Differential:* a percentage of base pay included in the total salary paid to the executive to compensate for actual or perceived hardship in the location due to unhealthy or difficult living conditions.
2. *Danger Differential:* a percentage of base pay included in the total salary paid to the executive to compensate for political risks in the foreign country. (Executive pay in politically unstable countries has been termed "danger pay.")

benefit gratuity, also called *foreign service premium* and *end-of-contract gratuity*, is a specific financial incentive offered to executives to encourage them to accept (and complete) overseas postings.

It consists of a percentage of base salary paid to the executive in one lump sum upon the completion of the assignment (if the executive is a national expatriate) or upon the completion of the contract (if the executive is a foreign expatriate).

See also benefits for international service.

benefits for international service is a term referring to the "total package" of salary and nonsalary incentives offered to executives (national expatriates and sometimes foreign expatriates) to work outside of their countries.

See also benefit allowance; benefit differential; benefit gratuity.

Benelux, the acronym for **Belgium-Netherlands-Lux**embourg Customs Union, is a customs union established in 1947 and comprising Belgium, Luxembourg, and the Netherlands.

The Benelux is now incorporated into the European Economic Community (EEC).

See also common market; Appendix V (A).

Berne Convention (for the Protection of Literary and Artistic Works of 1886) is an international agreement, originally signed in 1886 and currently signed by 80 countries, that is the oldest international treaty in the field of copyright.

The Convention established an international system of national treatment in the protection of the intellectual property of authors, being creators of literary and artistic works (e.g., novels, music, works of fine art, and motion pictures). A country that is a party to the Convention must grant the same protection to the works of authors from any other country that is also a party to the Convention as it grants to its own nationals.

Under the Convention, the minimum standards include rights for the authors to permit or prohibit copying or reproduction of their works in any manner or any form. Authors' rights under the Convention are limited to a minimum term of the author's life plus 50 years (after the author's death).

The Convention is administered by the World Intellectual Property Organization (WIPO).

Cf. Paris Convention.

See also World Intellectual Property Organization.

Berne Union is a worldwide association of export credit insurers such as the Canadian Export Development Corporation (EDC) and the Export-Import Bank of the United States (Eximbank).

The association meets annually to establish the equivalent of price floors in export credit insurance. It does this in order to establish the upper limits of insurability without creating unduly competitive conditions among the world's industrial countries.

Besides Western developed-country members, the association also includes export credit agencies from a number of developing countries, such as Mexico, that have significant external debt problems and, consequently, problems in generating export credits.

See also Export Credit Enhanced Leverage.

Bid Security Guarantees (BSGs) is a program of the Export Development Corporation (EDC) whereby the EDC covers a bank (which has financed a bid by a Canadian exporter) and provides the foreign buyer with bid security on behalf of the Canadian exporter.

See also Export Development Corporation; export financing.

bilateral trade refers to transactions between any two nations.

Cf. multilateral trade; trilateral trade.

bilateral trade agreement is a formal exchange accord between two nations.

Cf. multilateral trade agreement; trilateral trade agreement.

bill of exchange is any financial instrument that orders payment of a specified amount either to a specified beneficiary or to the bearer at sight or after a specified number of days after presentation.

Cf. trade acceptance.

See also documentary draft; sight documentary draft; term documentary draft.

bill of lading (b/l) is a document used by exporters, importers, and functional intermediaries to establish (1) a contract of carriage, (2) a receipt for the goods carried, and (3) the transfer of legal title to the goods carried.

There are two types of bills of lading: a straight bill of lading and an order bill of lading.

1. *Straight Bill of Lading:* formally referred to as a *uniform straight bill of lading*, it is the most common b/l documentation. It is non-negotiable: the goods to which the straight b/l is title are consigned directly to the customer or the party named (such as the consignee's agent).
2. *Order Bill of Lading:* formally referred to as a *uniform order bill of lading*, it is a negotiable title document. The goods are consigned to order of the party named on the document, but title can be transferred to anyone else by the carrier or by any other holder of the document.

When carriage is via ocean vessel, a bill of lading is commonly called a marine bill of lading, or ocean bill of lading. When carriage is via inland means (i.e., waterways, motorways, railways, or airways), it is referred to as an inland bill of lading. When the carriage is via air, it is called an air waybill.

Further, all types of bills of lading can be either "clean" or "foul."

See also clean bill of lading; foul bill of lading.

binational dispute-settlement mechanism (of the FTA) is the formal arrangement under the Canada-U.S. Free Trade Agreement of 1989 (FTA) whereby disagreements between Canadian and U.S. parties over the FTA are settled peacefully.

Chapter 18 of the FTA provides for the establishment of binational panels to settle disputes that arise over the interpretation and/or application of the FTA per se.

Chapter 19 of the FTA provides for binding binational dispute settlement in matters dealing with antidumping and countervailing duty cases.

Settlement of FTA disputes consists of three important phases:

1. consultations between the disputing parties under Article 1804 (1) (2) (3);
2. failing resolution of the dispute after the first phase, the convening of the FTA Commission under Article 1805 (1) (2);
3. failing resolution after the second phase, the referral of a dispute to binding arbitration, under Articles 1806 and 1807.

Cf. Court of International Trade.

See also Binational Secretariat; binational (binding) dispute-settlement panel.

binational (binding) dispute-settlement panel is composed of five members, at least two of whom are Canadians and two of whom are Americans, selected from a roster of people, half being Canadians chosen by the Canadian Minister of International Trade and half being Americans chosen by the U.S. Trade Representative (USTR), under Article 1807 (1) of the Canada-U.S. Free Trade Agreement of 1989 (FTA).

Together the panel chooses a person as chair under Article 1807 (3). The purpose of this panel is to expedite the settlement of cases under the FTA involving antidumping and countervailing duty disputes.

Under Chapter 19, Canada and the United States retain the sovereign right to apply their antidumping and countervailing duty laws on imported goods. If a trading party disputes an affirmative dumping declaration, it may request the establishment of a panel to hear the case. The process of panel review replaces hitherto existing judicial review in each country, and the decision of the panel (like the decision of a judicial review) is binding on all parties.

In cases where a panel may have exceeded its legal jurisdiction, or behaved with gross misconduct or conflict of interest, the decision of a binding panel can be taken to an extraordinary challenge committee that, acting like a binational supreme court, may (1) request the panel's decision be altered, (2) overturn the panel's decision, or (3) demand a new panel be established to settle the dispute.

Cf. binational dispute-settlement mechanism.

See also United States Trade Representative.

Binational Secretariat (FTA Binational Secretariat) is a permanent institution established under the Canada-U.S. Free Trade Agreement of 1989 (FTA), having offices in Washington, D.C., managed by an American Secretary, and in Ottawa, managed by a Canadian Secretary.

The function of the Secretariat is to serve as a registry office for panel review procedures involving the binational dispute-settlement mechanisms established under Chapters 18 and 19 of the FTA. Thus, all requests for panel review will be filed with the appropriate office of the Secretariat.

binding agreement is an instrument of formal accord between two or more nations that requires that each country comply with the terms and conditions of it.

binding arbitration is a process in dispute settlement between contracting parties whereby, at the outset, the parties agree to abide by the results of the dispute-settlement procedures.
See also Appendix VI (arbitration).

binding a tariff means agreeing to maintain a particular tariff level against increase or change.

birdyback •NW• is the shipping of containerized cargo via air transport.
See also container.

black money •NW• is wealth generated from criminal activities such as *narco-trafico* (i.e., drug trafficking).
See also dirty money.

blacklist (a verb) means to produce a schedule of the names of people or companies that are deemed to have earned punishment as a consequence of some action.

> **Example:** If Saudi Arabia were to blacklist IBM because of some presumed violation by it of the Arab Boycott, the result might be considerable lost sales to the company but also major problems for the Kingdom because of in-process project work and in-place service contracts.

Cf. Arab Boycott of Israel.

blacklist (a noun) is a schedule of the names of people or companies that are deemed to have earned punishment as a consequence of some action.

> **Example:** New York-based Levi Strauss, Dallas-based Neiman-Marcus, and Toronto-based Dylex Diversified are only three of many U.S. and Canadian companies on the Arab Boycott blacklist.

Cf. blacklist (a verb).

blanket certificate of origin is a government document (to be duly completed by the exporter) that covers continuous shipments of goods from the same exporter to the same importer, and all of which fall under the same customs classification, obviating the need for separate documents for each identical shipment.
Cf. certificate of origin.

blocked account is an account that cannot be freely transferred; it is often referred to as a "frozen" account.
National governments block or freeze bank accounts of foreign governments (or of companies over which they have jurisdiction) in an effort to force compliance with political objectives.

> **Example:** On November 11, 1965, upon the announcement of the Unilateral Declaration of Independence (UDI) by Southern Rhodesia, a British colony,

the British government blocked the Southern Rhodesian bank accounts in the United Kingdom and asked the Canadian and U.S. governments to do the same to Rhodesian accounts within their jurisdictions.

blocked currency is a currency that can neither be transferred into another currency nor into another jurisdiction.

> **Example:** On January 1, 1959, upon the assumption of power by the Cuban government, the U.S. government blocked the conversion of Cuban pesos into U.S. dollars in the United States and the transfer of U.S. dollars in Cuban bank accounts in the United States to any bank account in Cuba.

> Cf. Appendix VI (blocking laws).

bonded goods, sometimes referred to as *goods under bond*, are commodities in bonded storage.

> **Example:** Liquor that is "bottled in bond" has been bottled in a warehouse, and it is only subject to tax when the goods leave the facility.

bonded storage (bonded warehousing) is the process of placing goods in a facility for short- or long-term periods and of not having to pay taxes on them until such time as they leave the facility.

> **Example:** Distilleries put their inventories in bonded warehouses to age, and they do not pay taxes on the liquor until it is bottled and shipped out.

booking number is an Arabic number assigned to a contract of affreightment, used as an identifying reference on a bill of lading.
See also contract of affreightment.

border tax adjustments (border-tax adjustments) refer to the remission of duties or taxes on exported goods to ensure that national tax systems do not act to unfairly impede exports.

bounty, which originated in the United States, is payment by a national government to producers and exporters of goods to strengthen their competitive position in the world market.
Also referred to as a grant or more commonly as a subsidy, this payment is characteristic of policies labelled "protectionist."
Cf. subsidy.
See also protectionism.

boycott is a voluntary refusal to engage in commercial dealings with a nation, corporation, or person.

> **Example:** Very few members of the OECD have agreed to comply with the Arab Boycott of Israel.

> **Example:** Muslim-American leaders in New York City called on the faithful to boycott XYZ because of its avowed determination to sell to Israel through Japan-based intermediaries.

See also embargo; Arab Boycott of Israel.

branch (plant/office/bank) *See* subsidiary.

branch plant economy (branch-plant economy) is a political economy (e.g., Canada) in which direct foreign investment is so widespread and concentrated in key industrial sectors that the direction and pace of its national macroeconomic activities are dependent upon decisions made in another jurisdiction (e.g., the United States).
See also dependent development.

break bulk (break-bulk), often called "deconsolidation," is the process of breaking down large shipments into multiple (smaller) shipments, each destined for a particular consignee.
Cf. make bulk.

break bulk (distribution) center is the place where the process of break bulk occurs.
See also break bulk.

Bretton Woods System is the international monetary system (or gold exchange standard) established after World War II, based on a financial conference held in Bretton Woods, New Hampshire, in July 1944.
The aims of Bretton Woods were to liberalize trade globally by

1. making all national currencies freely convertible,
2. stabilizing exchange rates between national currencies,
3. assisting nations to develop economically, and
4. helping those with short-term balance-of-payments difficulties.

Under Bretton Woods, the International Monetary Fund (IMF) was established.
Bretton Woods collapsed in 1971 (with the signing of the Smithsonian Agreement) after the United States

1. suspended the convertibility of the U.S. dollar into gold,
2. had the dollar devalued (by agreeing to increase the official price of gold from U.S. $35 per ounce to U.S. $38 per ounce), and
3. permitted the U.S. dollar to freely float against other world currencies, thus creating a "dollar standard."

The excess liquidity (i.e., the dollar glut) was created by the United States continuously using its currency to settle its persistent and large balance-of-payments deficits. This created a confidence deficit in the U.S. dollar due to the fact that global supply of U.S. dollars exceeded demand for them, aside from the supply (always necessary) to settle temporary balance-of-payments problems and to provide needed liquidity to sustain global trade.

Cf. seigniorage.
See also international monetary system; Smithsonian Agreement; International Monetary Fund.

bribery refers to payments of money, goods, or services made to public officials or to private business people who are in a position to grant, or to influence the process of granting, some right to which the payor otherwise has no legitimate claim.

When called "bribery" explicitly in law, this behavior constitutes a criminal offense usually under both common law and code law systems in payor and payee countries. (While domestic and foreign bribery are illegal in the United States, in Canada, there are no laws against foreign bribery.)

The practice of making payments of money, goods, or services to private business people in foreign countries has been called "payoffs." While it may be illegal under the U.S. Foreign Corrupt Practices Act of 1977, some types of payoffs may not be illegal under local laws.

The following are classifications of bribery and payoffs:

1. *Facilitating Payments:* small money payments made directly to people to expedite action (in highly bureaucratized countries) and to secure favors.

   These payments are known by a variety of colloquial names around the world:

   - grease, lubrication, emollient, payola, tip, kickbacks, commissions
   - *schmir* (from the Yiddish meaning "smear," "grease")
   - *pourboire* (from the French for "for" + "drink," meaning "tip")
   - *baccone* (from the Italian meaning "little bite")
   - *bustarella* (from the Italian meaning "small envelope")
   - *baksheesh, bakshish* (from the Arabic meaning "gratuity," and the Persian *baksis* meaning "tip")
   - *mordida* (from the Spanish meaning "small bite" or "nip") colloquial in Latin American countries
   - *dash* (from the Bambara (Guinea) *dashee* meaning "favor") colloquial across West Africa
   - *kuroi kiri* (from the Japanese meaning "black mist")

   Where practiced, the making of these payments is considered customary behavior, is not classed as bribery, and is usually not illegal, although potentially embarrassing if publicly disclosed.

2. *Cash Disbursements:* sizeable to large amounts of money surreptitiously paid in advance to beneficiaries via (third party) offshore bank accounts for the purpose of obtaining some favor (e.g., sales contract, tax or tariff ruling).

   Where the disbursements occur after the favor has been granted, they are called "cash kickbacks" when they represent some percentage of the value of the object of the favor (e.g., the contract awarded, the taxes saved).

3. *Political Contributions:* payments made to political parties and candidates before an election to gain favors from the winning party or candidate after the election. When illegal, they constitute extortion and are a criminal offense.

   When the payments occur after the election, they are called "political kickbacks," as they represent a percentage of the value of the object of the favor.

4. *Agents' Commissions:* prepayment of intermediaries whose primary activity (on behalf of the foreign client in the host country) is the illicit influencing and bribing of local public officials aimed at securing contracts for the foreign trader.

   See also U.S. Foreign Corrupt Practices Act of 1977.

broker is a term formerly used interchangeably with *freight broker* and *customs broker.*

This practice caused considerable confusion, since the term *freight broker* itself is a nonstandard variant of "freight forwarder + customs broker."

   See also foreign-freight forwarder.

brokerage fee is the compensation paid by the shipper to the freight broker in return for discharging specific contractual responsibilities.
   See also freight broker; physical distribution.

brown goods is a term used in England to refer to furniture; in the United States and Canada the equivalent term is "consumer durables" or simply "durables."
   Cf. soft goods.

Budapest Treaty on the International Recognition of the Deposit of Microorganisms for the Purposes of Patent Procedure, known as the *Budapest Treaty*, is a multilateral treaty signed by states to afford them substantial protection of intellectual property.
   The treaty is administered by the World Intellectual Property Organization (WIPO).
   See also World Intellectual Property Association.

buffer stock refers to

1. an amount of a commodity purchased to be added to existing stocks when the commodity price falls below an agreed minimum floor price;
2. an amount of a commodity sold out of existing stocks when the commodity price rises above the agreed price.

   See also international commodity agreements.

bulk cargo is a commodity classification used in international physical distribution and logistics (PD/L) that comprises goods in a raw, loose, or otherwise unpackaged form.
   Examples are gain, malt, and cattle feed. Such goods are usually handled in bulk cargo ports by specialized materials handling equipment (e.g., conveyor belts, mechanical shovels/scoops).
   Cf. commodity.

bulk shipping is the ocean carriage of goods in gross form.
   See bulk cargo.

Bureau of Export Administration (BXA) is an operating unit of the U.S. Department of Commerce that was established in 1987 to clearly separate the function of export control from that of export promotion.

Headed by an Under Secretary for Export Administration, the Bureau has two operating subunits:

1. *Export Administration* deals with export licensing, policy analysis, and foreign-availability determinations (i.e., findings as to whether U.S. products can be exported to non-U.S. customers without an export permit/ license).
2. *Export Enforcement* administers compliance with U.S. export-control laws by investigating alleged breaches. The office also ensures compliance with the anti-boycott provisions of the Export Administration Act.

Cf. Export and Import Permits Act.
See also Arab Boycott of Israel; export permit.

business proprietary information (BPI) is intellectual property in the form of documents used by parties (i.e., companies) and by firms that represent them (i.e., attorneys).

BPI is used in civil proceedings such as dumping and antidumping investigations undertaken by the U.S. International Trade Commission.

See also U.S. International Trade Commission; administrative protection order.

bustarella *See* bribery.

buy-back, a type of countertrade transaction, is an agreement between exporter and importer covering the export of specific capital goods under one contract, and the agreement by the importer to pay for them with the resultant output produced by the capital goods that the exporter agrees to buy back or assign under a separate contract.

> **Example:** The Cantree paper mill exported to Latvia will be paid for in deliveries to Cantree's Dutch customers over five years.

Cf. barter; compensation trade; cooperation contracts; counterpurchase; offset deals; switch deals.
See also countertrade.

Buyer Credit Protocol (BCP) is an export financing facility of the Export Development Corporation (EDC) set up to encourage foreign purchase of Canadian goods and services on credit (i.e., deferred-payment terms).

Under the BCP, an agreement is signed between the EDC and a foreign financial institution. It involves the foreign financial institution providing a guarantee for EDC export loans to foreign buyers of Canadian goods and services in that country. Thus, should the foreign buyer default on the EDC loan, the foreign financial institution guarantees to make good on it.

The outcome is the pre-arranging and facilitation of procedures by which foreign institutions can provide guarantees for individual international trade transactions.

Cf. Supplier Credit Protocol.

See also Export Development Corporation; export financing.

buyer credits *See* loans (to foreign importers).

buy national refers to (1) discriminatory government procurement policies that provide preferential margins for national versus foreign suppliers; (2) discriminatory slogans favoring national versus foreign products and suppliers, based on perceived or real threats from imported goods.

> **Example:** Buy America. Buy the cars your neighbors build!
>
> Good food from Ontario . . . there's no place like home.

C

cabotage (cabotage rights), from the French *caboter* meaning "to coast," refers to the right by air carriers in different countries to carry as many passengers and as much freight as possible between as many different centers as can be supported by market demand.

See also open skies agreement.

Cairns Group is a body of 13 countries (which rely on agricultural exports for considerable export earnings) that first met in August 1986 to form an agricultural lobby group to exert influence on the (current) Uruguay Round of multilateral trade negotiations (MTN).

The eponym is drawn from the town of Cairns, in Queensland, Australia, where its inaugural meeting was held.

The efforts exerted by the Group were aimed at having the General Agreement on Tariffs and Trade (GATT) steer a course midway between the polar positions (on agriculture) of the EEC, perceived to be protectionist, and of the United States, perceived to be nonprotectionist and multilaterally oriented.

The original 14 members of the Cairns Group are Argentina, Australia, Brazil, Canada, Chile, Colombia, Fiji (which left after a coup d'état in 1987, but later returned), Hungary, Indonesia, Malaysia, New Zealand, the Philippines, Thailand, and Uruguay.

Canada Account, also referred to as the *Government Account*, is a financial facility provided under Section 31 and an insurance facility provided under Section 27 of the Canadian Export Development Act.

This legislation permits the extension of export credits and export insurance (in the name of the Government of Canada by the EDC) to countries commercially rejected by the Canadian Export Development Corporation (EDC).

The EDC may go "off cover" with a country for a variety of reasons: (1) it may be judged to be commercially uncreditworthy; (2) the EDC may already have a large "exposure" in the country in question; (3) there may be political considerations that mitigate against commercial lending but that make the extension of credit in the national interest, and, thereby, legitimate the use of the Canada Account facility.

The Canada Account is used whenever the EDC extends export credits and insurance on a concessional basis, since the extension of concessional financing is a government undertaking according to the Organization for Economic Cooperation and Development (OECD) Concensus.

> **Example:** The Canadian Wheat Board (CWB) is the exclusive marketer of Canadian wheat outside Canada. To ensure the continued availability of competitive export financing for the CWB, the Canadian government has established the Credit Grain Sales Program (CGSP).
>
> For grain not marketed directly by the CWB, export credits can be arranged through the EDC. The regular commercial credit facilities and the EDC's Canada Account financing and insurance facilities are available on credits of from 3 to 10 years and at interest rates in accordance with the OECD Concensus.
>
> Comparable U.S. government programs are:
>
> 1. GSM-102 Program under the U.S. Commodity Credit Corporation (CCC), whereby guarantees are provided on credits on terms of up to 3 years;
> 2. U.S. Intermediate Agricultural Credit Program, which provides credit for over 3 and up to 10 years;
> 3. U.S. CCC's GSM-5 Blended Credit Program, whereby amounts of interest-free GSM-5 credits are "blended" with guaranteed credits under the GSM-102 Program, thereby affording a total overall lower interest rate for U.S. exporters (this program was introduced to counter the EEC's Common Agricultural Policy (CAP) and its ensuing market distortions resulting from the variable levy).

Cf. Common Agricultural Policy; variable levy.

See also Commodity Credit Corporation; Export Development Corporation; OECD Concensus.

Canada Export Awards, initiated in 1983 and sponsored by the Canadian government's Department of External Affairs and International Trade Canada (EAITC), the functional unit responsible for Canadian international trade policy formation, is a program aimed at promoting international trade-related activities and informing Canadian exporters of the range of government programs and services available to them in support of export marketing.

Winners receive a plaque bearing the Canada Export Award logo and a brief citation of the firm's export accomplishments. The firm also has the right to use the logo in its advertising and promotional materials for three years from the date of receiving the award.

See also export support programs.

Canada-U.S. Free Trade Agreement of 1989 (FTA) is a bilateral commercial treaty that came into force on January 1, 1989.

It is a highly complex arrangement that aims:

1. to integrate the Canadian and U.S. economies with the reduction and ultimate elimination of all trade barriers;
2. to accelerate the unimpeded bidirectional flow of direct investment; and
3. to remove barriers to labor mobility for specified trades and professions between Canada and the United States.

Specifically, the FTA provides for:

1. the elimination of all Canada-U.S. tariffs by January 1, 1998;
2. the use of safeguards and quantitative restrictions where appropriate, in accordance with the GATT provisions;
3. the establishment of a binational dispute-settlement mechanism and a binational dispute-settlement panel to reach binding decisions regarding antidumping and countervailing duty decisions, as well as in other trade matters;
4. the liberalization of sectoral trade in agriculture, energy, and distilled spirits;
5. the mutual extension of national treatment in trade in services (including personal services) and direct investment;
6. the expansion of binational access to government procurement.

See also safeguards; quantitative restrictions; binational dispute-settlement mechanism; binational dispute-settlement panel; national treatment; services; government procurement.

Canadian Commercial Corporation (CCC) is a wholly owned Canadian Crown Corporation, established in 1946, that, in principle, contracts with foreign states, foreign-state companies, and international organizations on behalf of Canadian suppliers as a procurement agency of Canadian export goods and services.

In practice, the CCC is mainly involved as Canada's export packager in the procurement of defense goods under the Canada-U.S. Defense Production Sharing Agreement (DPSA).

Aside from its procurement role, the CCC acts as guarantor for the performance of, and payment to, the Canadian supplier.

As a Crown Corporation, the CCC is accountable to the Canadian legislative branch of government (i.e., the Canadian Parliament) through two executive branch Cabinet Officers: the Secretary of State for External Affairs and the Minister of International Trade, each person being responsible for a distinct, although interdependent, area of the Department of External Affairs and International Trade Canada (EAITC).

Example: On May 3, 1989, the Canadian International Trade Minister announced that REMTEC, of Chambly, Québec, had been awarded a contract through the Canadian Commercial Corporation for the supply of 841 refueling stainless-steel tanker trailers for delivery to the U.S. Army for use in the United States and at overseas locations. Production of the specialized vehicles will extend into 1993, and the U.S. $52-million contract will provide 350 jobs, establishing the company as a major North American supplier of this type of vehicle.

See also Department of External Affairs.

Canadian Export Association (CEA), founded in 1943, is a private, nongovernment organization (NGO), based in Ottawa, whose function is to promote information exchange and to sponsor activities (e.g., seminars, FTA conferences) in support of Canadian exports.

Canadian Import Tribunal (CIT) (defunct) *See* Canadian International Trade Tribunal.

Canadian International Development Agency (CIDA) is the official Canadian government body through which official development assistance (ODA), in the form of grants and loans, is allocated and disbursed.

Before 1960, CIDA's functions were carried out by the External Aid Office (EAO) of the Department of Trade and Commerce (DTC). In 1960, the aid functions of DTC were transferred to the Department of External Affairs (DEA). In 1968, the EAO became CIDA.

CIDA, like its American counterpart, the U.S. International Development Cooperation Agency (USIDCA), is departmentalized. Its major units are (1) a Planning and Economics Branch, (2) a Voluntary Agencies Branch, and (3) an Operations Branch. In 1982, the Operations Branch was restructured to create units for four geographic areas: the Caribbean, Latin America, Africa, and Asia and the Pacific.

CIDA formed the Industrial Cooperation Program (ICP) in 1978 and the Business Cooperation Branch (BCB) in 1984, both of which function to initiate and channel offshore-development projects to Canadian industry either on a commercial or a concessional financial basis.

1. *Structure of CIDA's ODA-Granting Structure*

In 1986 and 1987, the allocations of ODA were as follows:

- 87% is allocated by CIDA, including through the IDRC and other Departments in External Affairs;
- 10% is allocated via the Canadian Department of Finance;
- 3% is allocated via provincial government contributions to NGOs.

2. *Segmentation of CIDA's ODA*

The ODA itself is segmented as follows:

Bilateral aid	30.0%
Multilateral aid	7.2
Bilateral food aid	8.4
Multilateral food	6.6
Other tech. cooperation	6.2
Voluntary contributions	9.9
Humanitarian	2.1
Development banks	23.4
Industrial cooperation	1.3
Administration	4.9
TOTAL	100.0%

3. *Geographic Division of CIDA's ODA*

CIDA's ODA is divided into a variety of geographic initiatives for bilateral delivery purposes:

Anglophone Africa	19.0%
Francophone Africa	23.0
America/Caribbean	16.0
Asia	40.0
General miscellaneous	2.0
TOTAL	100.0%

CIDA's 2 percent General miscellaneous goes, in the main, as follows:

General Miscellaneous 2 Percent

NGO assistance	2.0%
Tech cooperation	15.0
International Financial Institutions	63.0 – U.N. funds
Multilateral food aid	3.0
Miscellaneous	17.0 – Canadian Crown Corps.
TOTAL	100.0%

Of the remaining "Miscellaneous 17%" (of the General Miscellaneous ODA), almost 100 percent is channeled to NGOs or through Canadian Crown Corporation participation in bi- and multilateral-aid development in Asia and the Middle East.

General United Nations funds are passed directly to agencies in the United Nations system. These funds are segregated by headings such as (1) international humanitarian assistance, (2) World Food Program, and (3) assistance disbursements to International Financial Institutions (e.g., IDA, IFC, IBRD, AfDB, Andean Development Corporation).

From the 2 percent allocated to CIDA support of NGOs, CIDA assists a range of Canadian NGOs as follows:

- nonsectarian universities
- sectarian universities
- "councils" and "missions" (e.g., CARE, Aga Khan Foundation of Canada, Canadian UNICEF Committee, Salvation Army, OXFAM-Canada)

From this 2 percent comes CIDA funding for International NGOs, for example:

- Foundation for International Training
- Institute for African Economic and Social Development
- International Committee of the Red Cross (ICRC)
- International Planned Parenthood Federation (IPPF)
- Pan-African Institute for Development
- World Council of Indigenous Peoples

The whole CIDA structure is aimed at providing funding to enable Canadian firms to penetrate LDC markets, initially via feasibility studies, secondly with joint ventures and transfer of technical assistance, and finally via long-term export and direct-investment agreements.

Cf. U.S. International Development Cooperation Agency.

See also concessional financing; Appendix V (E.)

Canadian International Trade Tribunal (CITT) is a Canadian government agency, empowered under the Special Import Measures Act, responsible for (1) reporting its findings in cases on dumping, antidumping, and countervailing duties; and (2) providing the government with advice relating to its findings in particular and relevant to import policy in general.

In the United States, the equivalent Federal government agency is the U.S. International Trade Commission (USITC).

Cf. U.S. International Trade Commission.

See also Special Import Measures Act.

capital account is the specific part of a nation's financial statement that includes a record of cash flows related to international bank transactions and direct investment and to changes in foreign exchange reserves.

The current account is used in the calculation of a nation's balance of payments.

Cf. current account.

See also balance of payments.

capital inflow refers either to an increase in a nation's foreign assets held in the nation or to a reduction in the nation's assets held outside the nation.

Cf. capital outflow.

capitalism is a political-economic set of ideas centered around the concept that, in a society, the ownership of the wealth (capital) be in the hands of private individuals and/or private enterprises and be used primarily for profit generation (i.e., capital accumulation) *vis-à-vis* utility.

A political-economy that is mainly capitalistic but that includes a sizeable segment of public ownership (i.e., capital in the hands of the state) is called a "mixed economy."

Sometimes a capitalist economy is equated with an "open economy." This is not necessarily and always the case. Some capitalist economies (e.g., the United States) are more open than other mixed economies (e.g., Japan); but, comparing the mixed economies of Japan and the United Kingdom, the latter is more open than the former: it is easier for direct investment to flow into the British domestic market, which is less distorted by state protectionist interference, than into Japan, which is more distorted by state protectionist interference.

Cf. socialism; command economy; nonmarket economy.

See also mixed economy.

Capital Movements Code *See* Code of Liberalization of Capital Movements.

capital outflow refers either to a decrease in a nation's foreign assets held in the nation or to an increase in the nation's assets held outside the nation.
Cf. capital inflow.

CAPRI Project is a major intergovernmental program involving International Cooperation in the Classification of Search Files according to the International Patent Classification (IPC), which completed its work in 1988.
The CAPRI Project was begun in 1975, under the auspices of the World Intellectual Property Organization (WIPO), in cooperation with the following international *bureaux*: International Patent Documentation Center (IPDOC) in Austria, the West German Patent Office, the European Patent Office (EPO) in Paris, the Japanese Patent Office, and the Soviet Union Patent Office.

The Soviet Union Patent Office is known officially as the State Committee for Inventions and Discoveries of the Soviet Union.

The aims of the Project were (1) the collection of patent documents, (2) the reclassifying of them according to the IPC international standard in machine-readable forms, and (3) the storing of the data as a computer data base (dbase).
The CAPRI data base (CDB) was created from a total of 16 million documents from the following countries: Austria, France, the former Federal Republic of Germany (FRG), Japan, Switzerland, Soviet Union, the United Kingdom, and the United States. It contains inventories of all 614 IPC subclasses, each one containing between 5,000 and 100,000 references, depending on the scope of the subclass and the nature of the technology involved in the subclass entries.
See also World Intellectual Property Organization; intellectual property.

cargo, used interchangeably with *freight*, is goods in some stage of physical movement, usually between seller and buyer, traditionally aboard some mode of water transport, usually an ocean liner.

> **Example:** The railway freight went to the loading dock by truck, was hoisted aboard the ship, and was placed in the cargo hold.

Cf. freight.

cargo consolidation is a variation of *consolidation*.
See also make bulk.

Caribbean Basin Economic Recovery Act (CBERA) refers to U.S. legislation (Title II of Public Law No. 98-67, implemented by Presidential Proclamation 5133 of November 30, 1983) that affords nonreciprocal tariff preferences (i.e., duty-free entry) to developing countries in the Caribbean Basin, allegedly aimed at their economic development.
The CBERA, scheduled to remain in effect until September 30, 1995, was

the legal basis under which U.S. President Ronald Reagan implemented the Caribbean Basin Initiative (CBI).

See also Caribbean Basin Initiative.

Caribbean Basin Initiative (CBI) is a political program (based on the Puerto Rican Model) comprising economic arrangements between the United States and Caribbean countries, announced in February 1982 by U.S. President Reagan at a meeting of the Organization of American States (OAS).

Subsequently, the U.S. Congress enacted the Caribbean Basin Economic Recovery Act of 1983, which was signed into law in August 1983 and which came into force on January 1, 1984.

The CBI originally designated 20 regional countries as beneficiaries of the program: Antigua and Barbuda, Barbados, Belize, the British Virgin Islands, Costa Rica, Dominica, Dominican Republic, El Salvador, Grenada, Guatemala, Haïti, Honduras, Jamaica, Montserrat, Netherlands Antilles, Panamá, St. Kitts-Nevis, St. Lucia, St. Vincent and the Grenadines, and Trinidad and Tobago. In 1985, Bahamas was added, as was Aruba in 1986.

The CBI created several incentives for (predominantly) U.S. companies to locate manufacturing plants in the designated beneficiaries:

1. There are 12 years of duty-free access for U.S. imports from those countries.
2. Operational expenses for U.S. companies located in the designated Caribbean countries are deductible from U.S. taxable income under a Tax Information Exchange Agreement (TIEA) signed with the United States.
3. Designated beneficiaries taking advantage of the CBI qualify for enhanced levels of U.S. "foreign aid," comprising ODA, BOP support, and price stabilization assistance.
4. Under U.S. tax law (Section 936 of the IRS Tax Code) designated Caribbean countries with TIEAs are eligible for funding from U.S. firms that wish to establish plants in designated countries of the Caribbean.

The CBI is a political initiative in the form of U.S. international trade policy, designed to expand the reach of U.S. global marketing to Western hemispheric offshore centers within the geopolitical and military orbit of the United States, where low-cost labor, inexpensively available raw materials, and lucrative tax incentives for U.S. corporations encourage the formation of dedicated foreign trade zones whose nontraditional exports are marketable at competitive prices globally.

Cf. Puerto Rican Model; yen diplomacy; Japan Sea Basin.

See also foreign trade zone; Foreign Sales Corporation; official development assistance; Caribbean Basin Economic Recovery Act.

Caribbean-Canadian Economic Trade Development Assistance Program (CARIBCAN) is a multilateral, Canadian, ODA program launched in 1986, granting preferential, one-way, duty-free entry of goods to Canada from designated Caribbean countries.

CARIBCAN designated the countries of the so-called Commonwealth Caribbean, countries that were former colonies of Britain, for duty-free access.

Of all the potential beneficiaries, Jamaica is the most economically important to Canada because of its mineral exports (bauxite).

Cf. Caribbean Basin Initiative.

Caribbean Common Market (CARICOM), also known as the *Caribbean Community*, is a regional common market, established in 1973 as the successor to the Caribbean Free Trade Association (CARIFTA); CARICOM consists of the same members as CARIFTA.

See also Caribbean Free Trade Association.

Caribbean Development Bank (CDB), one of the multilateral development banks (MDBs), is an international financial organization that is an executing agency for projects of the United Nations Development Program (UNDP).

The CDB is headquartered in Bridgetown, Barbados, and is comprised of 17 regional members and 4 nonregional members. It stimulates regional economic growth by granting loans and providing technical assistance to projects and programs of its member countries.

Main sectors for concessional financing are agriculture and the agro-industry, transport and communications, energy, industry and nonfuel minerals, urban development, sanitation and water supply, education, and health.

See also multilateral development banks; technical assistance; concessional financing; United Nations Development Program.

Caribbean Development and Cooperation Committee (CDCC) is a permanent subsidiary body of the United Nations Economic Commission for Latin America and the Caribbean (UN/ECLAC), comprising 16 UN/ECLAC members: Antigua and Barbuda, Bahamas, Barbados, Belize, Cuba, Dominica, Dominican Republic, Grenada, Guyana, Haïti, Jamaica, St. Kitts-Nevis, Saint Lucia, Saint Vincent and the Grenadines, Suriname, and Trinidad and Tobago.

There are also five associate members: Aruba, the British Virgin Islands, Montserrat, Netherlands Antilles, and the U.S. Virgin Islands.

The CDCC was established in Trinidad in 1975. The work of the body consists of promotion of cooperation for economic and social development among CDCC members, and between them and other developing countries, in the areas of transportation and communications, agriculture, natural resources and energy, science and technology, and trade.

See also United Nations Economic Commission for Latin America and the Caribbean.

Caribbean Free Trade Association (CARIFTA) is a free trade area, established in 1968, comprising 12 members: Antigua, Barbados, Belize, Dominica, Grenada, Guyana, Jamaica, Montserrat, St. Kitts-Nevis, St. Lucia, St. Vincent and the Grenadines, and Trinidad and Tobago.

In 1973, CARIFTA dissolved as its membership formed a new association that reflected the evolving state of the regional economy.

See also Caribbean Common Market.

Caribbean Group for Cooperation in Economic Development (CGCED) is the regional planning group of the Caribbean Common Market (CARICOM).

carnet •**NW**•, from the French meaning "note book," is a document originated by the International Chamber of Commerce, Paris, France, and now issued by national Chambers of Commerce, which permits goods (1) to be imported into a foreign country *on a temporary basis only*, (2) to then be re-exported from it, thus avoiding normal import duties, and (3) to be ultimately re-imported into the originating country.

Goods used in this manner are referred to as being "covered under *carnet*."

There are two types of *carnets*: (1) the *Admission Temporaire (ATA)* (Temporary Admission) *carnet* and (2) the *Transit International Routier (TIR)* (International Highway Transit) *carnet*. The *ATA carnet* is the most frequently used one; but when there are no direct shipments between shipper and consignee (and the goods must pass in transit via third countries), the *TIR carnet* is used.

Carnets are issued to international marketers who may import such goods as samples, tools, and equipment to be used exclusively for display or demonstration to foreign customers. *Carnets* also cover trade fair exhibit booths and fixtures that visit foreign sites temporarily and then are "bicycled" to others.

The *carnet* applicant must post a security deposit with the Chamber of Commerce that issues the document. (In Canada, the Canadian Chamber of Commerce requirement is 40 percent of the value of the merchandise covered by the *carnet*).

If the goods are not returned to the country within one year from the date of issue of the *carnet*, the *carnet* bearer (1) forfeits the security deposit and (2) is obliged to pay duties on the goods to the customs authorities in the country of sale. Otherwise, the security deposit is refunded when the goods are returned to the originating country and proof of return is established with the local Chamber of Commerce.

The *carnet* system is in use in 30 countries, including Canada, the United States, and Japan, and in 5 of the 12 member states of the EEC (France, Germany, Italy, Portugal, and Spain). All *carnet*-user countries are signatories of the Customs Convention on the *ATA Carnet* for the Temporary Admission of Goods.

See also International Chamber of Commerce.

carriage trade is an archaic term for the patronage of wealthy cliques (e.g., royalty, landed gentry) accorded special privileges on the basis of their social rank. (It derives from the English expression for persons wealthy enough to own a private horse-drawn carriage.)

cartel, domestically, is a group (either of private companies, state enterprises, or any combination of them) that comes together to control the price of a commodity or service by controlling the supply to the local market.

See also international cartel; international commodity agreement.

cash against documents (CAD) is a term of sale agreed to between exporter and importer in which documents transferring title are given to the importer (or its agent) upon payment of the account.

Cf. Appendix III.

See also terms of sale.

cash in advance (CIA) is a term of sale agreed to between exporter and importer in which the importer pays the exporter in advance for a shipment of goods.

Cf. Appendix III.

See also terms of sale.

cash with order (CWO) is a term of sale agreed to between exporter and importer in which the account is settled at the time of the order (i.e., the importer pays the exporter in cash when the order is placed).

Cf. Appendix III.

See also terms of sale.

C.B.D. (CBD), the abbreviation of **c**ash **b**efore **d**elivery, is a term of sale, uncommon in Canada and the United States but used in the United Kingdom, equivalent to the North American term of sale *payment in advance*.

Cf. Appendix III.

Central American Bank for Economic Integration (CABEI), also known as *Banco Centro-Americano de Integración Económica (BCIE)*, is an autonomous body intended to act as the central financial institution of the Central American Common Market (CACM).

The countries that signed the General Treaty of Central American Economic Integration (which founded the CACM) established the CABEI in Managua, Nicaragua, in 1960. These were Costa Rica, El Salvador, Guatemala, Honduras, and Nicaragua.

See also Central American Common Market; Appendix V (B).

Central American Common Market (CACM), officially, *Mercado Común Centroamericano (MCC)*, is a customs union, established in Managua in 1960 by the Treaty of Central American Economic Integration.

It comprises Costa Rica, El Salvador, Guatemala, Honduras, and Nicaragua. The Treaty also established a regional bank to support the common market.

See also Central American Bank for Economic Integration; Appendix V (A).

central bank is the principal institution that controls a nation's monetary holdings.

Depending on the political economy of the nation, the central bank may have relative degrees of autonomy in areas of (1) varying the nation's money supply and (2) requiring and issuing exchange permits.

It is important not to confuse the names of banks. For example, *Banco de Costa Rica* and *Banco Nacional de Costa Rica* are names of private banking institutions. *El Banco Central de Costa Rica* is the name of the central bank of that nation.

In Canada, the central bank is The Bank of Canada. In the United States, it is called The Federal Reserve System.

See also exchange controls; central bank swaps; Appendix II.

Central Bank of West African States (CBWAS), officially, *Banque Centrale des États de l'Afrique de l'Ouest (BCEAO)*, is a regional, international, financial institution, headquartered in Dakar, Sénégal, that acts as the exclusive issuer of notes and coins (*CFA franc*) for the members of the West African Monetary Union (WAMU).

The CBWAS was established in 1955, commenced operations in 1962, and comprises the following member countries: Benin, Côte de'Ivoire, Niger, Sénégal, Togo, and Burkina Faso.

See also West African Monetary Union; *CFA franc*; Appendix V (B).

central bank swaps *See* Appendix II.

Central Treaty Organization (CENTO) was a mutual defense military treaty established in 1959 as the successor to the Baghdad Pact, itself formed in 1955 by Iraq, Iran, Pakistan, Turkey, and Britain.

Following the 1958 coup d'état, CENTO's headquarters were moved from Baghdad, Iraq, to Ankara, Turkey. In 1979, following the Iranian Revolution, Iran withdrew from CENTO, and CENTO exists today only on paper.

Certificate of Health (Fumigation/Inspection) is a document required to be filled out by the exporter of goods, under the appropriate national regulatory authority, to ensure the country of the importer that the goods exported meet established standards of safety, or purity, or cleanliness.

Where trade is bilateral (e.g., between Canada and the United States), the standards may be (1) agreed upon bilaterally, (2) entrenched within existing trade laws, and (3) carried out between the appropriate cooperating departments of agriculture and health (e.g., U.S. Department of Agriculture and the U.S. Customs Service, Agriculture Canada, Health & Welfare Canada, and Customs & Excise Canada).

Standards may be incorporated into bi- and multilateral trade agreements by adopting measures established by such international organizations as the World Health Organization (WHO), the International Chamber of Commerce (ICC), and the Food Agricultural Organization (FAO).

certificate of origin is a form issued by a government that, when duly completed by exporters, becomes a certified document as to the origin of goods for the purpose of establishing the basis upon which to levy the appropriate customs duties.

Certificates of origin can be either shipment-specific (i.e., pertaining to a specific shipment of goods only) or "blanket" (i.e., covering many shipments of identical goods with the same origin).

The basis of the Canada-U.S. Free Trade Agreement of 1989 (FTA) are the "Rules of Origin for Goods," which are contained in the Treaty (Part II, Chapter 3, Article 301-304 and Annex 301.2 (Interpretation) and Rules (Section I-XXI)).

Canadian and American traders must submit duly completed certificates of origin to their international counterparts, the U.S. Customs Service (of the U.S. Internal Revenue Service) and the Customs and Excise Department (of the Canadian Department of National Revenue), respectively, to claim full or partial exemption from customs duties.

Cf. Arab Boycott of Israel (negative certificates of origin).

See also blanket certificate of origin; Canada-U.S. Free Trade Agreement of 1989; rules of origin.

CFA franc (*Communauté francais africain franc*), the franc of the French African community, is the common currency of former colonial French West Africa, originally inspired to ensure the dependence upon France of its African territories by tying the exchangeability of the *CFA franc* to the French franc.

Cf. *CFP franc.*

See also currency area.

CFP franc (*Communauté francais pacifique franc*), the franc of the French Pacific Community, is the common currency of present and former French colonies and French territories in the Pacific Ocean, originally inspired to ensure the dependence upon France of its Pacific region communities by tying the exchangeability of the *CFP franc* to the French franc.

Cf. *CFA franc.*

Chamber of Commerce is a national trade-promoting organization that acts as the focus for distribution of information relevant to the support documentation necessary to sustain international trade.

The individual national Chambers of Commerce, which focus on national and international issues, are different from local Chambers of Commerce, which focus on local issues.

See also International Chamber of Commerce; Appendix IV; *carnet.*

channel manager is a global marketer who specializes in ways and means to keep price escalation as low as possible (in a competitive market situation).

See also price escalation.

charter means to rent an entire vessel or part of its freight space for a particular trip or a stipulated time period.

Thus, a charter party is someone who does the renting, and a charter vessel is the ship that is rented.

CKD (C.K.D.), the abbreviation of completely knocked down, is

1. a precise term used in international physical distribution/logistics (PD/L) to denote commodities to be handled and shipped in disassembled form (e.g., auto parts);
2. a marking used in export packaging on the side of shipping containers to denote that the contents are in disassembled form;
3. a precise term used in international freight forwarding to designate commodities in disassembled form. Goods in such form are imported to take

advantage of low tariff classification, compared to assembled-form imports. The latter are assumed to have intrinsically higher value-added, and, presumably, thereby cause injury to domestic manufacturers. Thus stated, we have an argument for the legitimate use of the tariff to protect manufacturers of assembled-form goods.

See also tariff; effective rate of protection; protectionism.

clean bill of lading (clean b/l) is the document of receipt issued by carriers when goods to be carried by them have been received "in good order" (i.e., without damage to external packaging or internal contents).

Unless a carrier marks on the document (by writing, typing, or stamp) that the goods are not "in good order" in some specified way, it is inferred that the bill of lading is "clean."

It is also referred to as a *clean bill* or a *clean on-board bill of lading*.

Example: A clean bill gives the goods loaded on board the carrier a clean bill of health.

Cf. foul bill of lading.

clean collection is a means of export financing by which the exporter presents to a bank only financial documents (e.g., a draft) to execute payment for goods already shipped.

Documents supporting the shipment (e.g., a bill of lading) have already been sent to the importer.

Cf. documentary collection.

See also export financing; bill of lading; draft; collections.

clear customs is a colloquial term for the process (1) of preparing the appropriate documents (e.g., Certificate of Origin, B-13) for presentation to those authorized to examine and appraise the value of the goods for purposes of imposing either an import duty or an export levy, and (2) of subsequently securing the authorized customs clearance document or stamp attesting to the fact either that whatever duty is payable on the goods has been paid or that the appropriate party has accepted the obligation to pay whatever duty is due on the goods at some future date.

Customs payments or payment "undertakings" secure the customs clearance for the goods to move to the next channel member.

See also customs; customs broker; duty.

closed economy is a political economy not engaging in international trade.

Cf. autarky; open economy.

CMEA *See* Council for Mutual Economic Assistance.

Cocoa Producers' Alliance (COPAL) is an international commodity group (ICG) formed in 1962 (1) to exchange information among producer-member countries, (2) to promote consumption of the commodity, and (3) to ensure the availability of adequate world supplies to ensure remunerative prices and profits to producer-members.

COPAL's headquarters are in Lagos, Nigeria, and it consists of the following member countries: Brazil, Cameroon, Ecuador, Gabon, Ghana, Côte d'Ivoire, Mexico, Nigeria, Sao Tomé and Principe, Togo, and Trinidad and Tobago.

See also Appendix V (E).

COCOM, the abbreviation for **Co**ordinating **Com**mittee for Multilateral Export Controls, is a Paris-based international body of Western, "open economy" countries that coordinates and monitors the export of goods to Warsaw Pact nations to prevent high technology, with potential military applications, from being available to communist nations.

The members of COCOM are Belgium, Canada, Denmark, Germany, France, Greece, Italy, Japan, the Netherlands, Norway, Portugal, Turkey, the United Kingdom, and the United States.

See also open economy; North Atlantic Treaty Organization; Warsaw Pact.

COD (C.O.D), the abbreviation of **c**ash **o**n **d**elivery, is a domestic term of sale that stipulates that the buyer of the goods is responsible for their payment in cash upon their delivery to a specified point.

See also Appendix III.

code law system is a nation's legal system that has its historical basis in specific codes of conduct produced by some paramount authority (either religious or secular) to which the judiciary refers when producing a legal ruling.

In a code law system, three separate codes are usually used as legal reference points: a civil code, a commercial code, and a criminal code.

> **Example:** In 1987, Pakistan decided to proclaim itself an Islamic Republic and adopt the Islamic code law system, based on the Shari'ah. For the previous 40 years (i.e., since its partition from India in 1947), Pakistan had adopted the British common law system.

Cf. common law system.

See also Islamic Law (Shari'ah); international law.

code of conduct is a standard of behavior by multinational enterprises, international associations, international institutions, or nation states deemed acceptable by the international community.

See also Valdez Principles.

Code of Conduct for Liner Conferences is a standard of behavior, established in 1974 under the auspices of the United Nations Conference on Trade and Development, that guaranteed developing countries a share within a conference of the carriage of goods in their seaborne trade with other countries, especially developing ones. The Code came into force in 1983 after the (former) Federal Republic of Germany and the Netherlands ratified it. Since 1983, France, the United Kingdom, Denmark, and Belgium have followed.

See also conference; United Nations Conference on Trade and Development.

Code of Liberalization of Capital Movements, also called the *Capital Movements Code*, is an international standard of conduct agreed to by the members of the Organization of Economic Cooperation and Development (OECD).

The Code commits its signatories to promote the unhindered movement of capital among them. It binds each country to refrain from enacting restrictive measures against direct investment.

However, "sectoral reservations" are permitted: they grant countries the right to afford limited protection to those domestic industry sectors determined to be especially vulnerable to foreign economic takeover.

> **Example:** At a Paris meeting of the OECD, Canada expanded its commitment to the Code. Canada's blanket reservation on direct investment was replaced by specific sectoral reservations in the following industries deemed to require special protection: telecommunications, culture, financial services, air and marine transportation, fishing, and energy.

Cf. protectionism; Investment Canada.
See also direct investment; code of conduct.

co-determination (codetermination) •NW• *See mitbestimmung*.

COFACE, the abbreviation for **C**ompagnie **F**rancaise d'**A**ssurance pour le **C**ommerce **E**xterieure, is the export credit granting agency of the government of France, equivalent to its Canadian counterpart the Export Development Corporation (EDC).
See also Export Development Corporation (EDC).

COFC, the abbreviation for **c**ontainer-**o**n-**f**lat**c**ar, is the loading of containers onto railroad flatcars and the shipping of them via rail.
See also container.

collections is a means of export financing whereby both the exporter and the importer agree to use the services of the exporter's bank to effect receipt of payment from the importer.
Cf. clean collection; documentary collection.

Colombo Plan, officially, *The Colombo Plan for Cooperative Economic and Social Development in Asia and the Pacific*, is one of the world's longest-existing North-South development associations, founded in 1950 at the Commonwealth Foreign Ministers' Meeting in Colombo, Sri Lanka, by 7 countries.

Today, there are 26 members, 23 from within the region plus 3 nonregional members (Canada, the United Kingdom, and the United States).

Operationally established in 1951, with headquarters in Colombo, the Plan promotes economic development by providing financing and technical assistance for development projects to member countries within the region.

The Plan maintains liaison with all international organizations, including the United Nations Development Program (UNDP), its executing agencies, the multilateral development banks (MDBs), and all other international bodies involved in international development.
See also Appendix V (B); Appendix V (D).

combination export manager (CEM) is a domestic-based intermediary who acts as an export sales agent for more than one noncompeting domestic exporter.

The CEM sells under its name to foreign-based enterprises and derives its revenue from sales commissions.

See also indirect exporting.

COMECON *See* Council for Mutual Economic Assistance.

command economy, also called *nonmarket economy*, is a political-economy driven by central planning *vis-à-vis* the forces of market supply and demand.

Such political-economies are characterized by (1) a central planning authority, (2) a Five-Year Plan, (3) centrally controlled production targets and allocation schedules for capital and raw materials, and (4) tight control over international trade, including access to money markets and availability of transferrable currencies.

Countries that have such political-economies are members of the Council for Mutual Economic Assistance (CMEA), commonly called communist countries.

Cf. market economy; mixed economy; capitalism.

See also Council for Mutual Economic Assistance; communism; nonmarket economy.

commercial controls are restrictions imposed by nations on international trade.

When in the form of tariffs and other measures (approved of under the General Agreement on Tariffs and Trade (GATT)), they are known as *official commercial controls*.

However, when these restrictions are in the form of import quotas, exchange controls, and other measures (proscribed under GATT), they are classified as *nontariff barriers*.

Cf. exchange controls; import controls.

See also General Agreement on Tariffs and Trade; nontariff barriers; adjustment.

commercial policies are the regulations that govern a nation's international trade.

When publicly approved by the legitimate political authority in a nation, they are referred to as official commercial policies. When accepted by a nation's government but not publicly approved by it, they are cynically referred to as "unofficial commercial policies."

> **Example:** For many years, unofficial commercial policy of the Soviet Union was to conduct a profitable trade in diamonds with the State of Israel via intermediaries but not to recognize Israel in an official diplomatic way.

commercial presence is representation in a market by a firm seeking to do business there.

See also right of establishment.

commercial risks refer to uncontrollable trading hazards that jeopardize exporters being paid.

The most common commercial risks are (1) insolvency (of the foreign buyer); (2) default (of the foreign buyer); (3) repudiation (by the foreign buyer); and (4) delays in, or interruption of, transit outside the exporter's control, resulting in surcharges.

Cf. political risks.

commodity, also referred to as a *good*, is any useful thing exchanged in trade, notably a physical thing rather than a service.

A good is classified in international physical distribution and logistics (PD/L) by the degree of processing undergone and the form in which it is transported (e.g., bulk cargo, base produce, bagged cargo, dirty cargo).

In international marketing, goods are classified according to the following exchange utility categories:

1. *Financial Goods:* U.S. Treasury Bonds, bankers' acceptances, and currencies (e.g., U.S.D., DEM, JPY, and GBP).
2. *Grains, Fats and Oils:*
   - *grains:* corn, wheat, soybeans, soybean meal, barley, flax seed, oats, canola, rye, and rice;
   - *fats and oils:* cottonseed oil, coconut oil, peanut oil, corn oil, and soybean oil.
3. *Livestock and Meat:* beef, feeder cattle, hogs, and pork bellies.
4. *Foods:* cocoa, cocoa butter, coffee, orange juice, sugar, butter, broiler chickens, eggs, and flour.
5. *Precious Metals:* gold, platinum, silver, and paladium.
6. *Industrial Metals:* aluminum, antimony, copper, lead, nickel, mercury, pig iron, steel scrap, tin, and zinc.
7. *Crude and Refined Petroleum:*
   - *crude:* Saudi Arabian light, North Sea Brent, West Texas Intermediate, and Alaska North Slope.
   - *refined:* fuel oil, leaded and unleaded gasoline.
8. *Mineral Ores:*
   - ferrous ores (e.g., iron ore),
   - non-ferrous ores (e.g., bauxite, potash).
9. *Woods and Fibers:* lumber (of different species and dimensions), cotton, wool, and print cloth.
10. *Miscellaneous Goods:* rubber, cement, and coal.

See also bulk cargo; base produce; bagged cargo; dirty cargo.

commodity agreement *See* international commodity agreement.

Commodity Credit Corporation (CCC) is an operating unit of the U.S. Department of Agriculture under the management of an Under Secretary for International Affairs and Commodity Programs.

The CCC, originally established in 1933, provides, through legislation, (1) supports and protection for U.S. farmers and (2) export credits for their foreign customers. For example, the CCC provides concessional export credits for grains and oilseeds and establishes the support price to U.S. farmers at which it will buy these crops.

Through the Export Enhancement Program (EEP) under the authority of the 1985 U.S. Farm Bill, the CCC provides U.S. farmers with export subsidies for grains and oilseeds. Designed to compete with the export subsidy programs of the EEC under its Common Agricultural Policy (CAP), the EEP lowered traditionally high domestic U.S. support prices and used on-hand surplus agricultural inventories to subsidize exports.

Cf. Canada Account (Comparable U.S. Government Programs); Common Agricultural Policy.

See also nonmarket economy.

commodity price agreement See international commodity agreement.

commodity terms of trade, also referred to as the *net barter terms of trade*, is the ratio of the price index of a nation's exports to the price index of its imports (times 100).

Cf. terms of trade.

Common Agricultural Policy (CAP) is the agricultural policy of the European Economic Community (EEC).

A CAP can refer to an agricultural policy of any common market entity that seeks to harmonize the agricultural policies of each of the common market members, according to the "model" set out by the EEC.

The CAP seeks:

1. to unify the agricultural policies of the 12 EEC members into one harmonized policy;
2. to stabilize farm prices while ensuring stable markets for agricultural products (i.e., supply management);
3. to promote regional agricultural development;
4. to ensure rising living standards for the farm population.

Under the CAP, three prices are used as the main vehicles for agricultural support within the EEC:

1. *Target Price:* the upper end-limit of the price range within which producer prices are permitted to fluctuate.
2. *Threshold Price:* the lowest internal price at which agricultural goods may be imported. (The variable levy is imposed on low import prices to raise them to the threshold price.)

Similarly, an export subsidy, called a variable subsidy, is an amount refunded to agricultural producers to lower export prices to lower world levels.

---

3. *Intervention Price:* the lowest price at which public bodies within the EEC may purchase agricultural goods.

Financing of the CAP is done through the European Agricultural Guidance and Guarantee Fund (EAGGF). This body is responsible for coordinating EEC budget expenditures behind agricultural support of the CAP.

In 1969, a transfer payment instrument called a monetary compensatory amount (MCA) was initiated. Expressed in European Currency Units (ECUs), MCAs are transferred by the EAGGF in the form of export subsidies and import levies for EEC countries with appreciating currencies and of import subsidies and export levies for depreciating currencies.

This is done in an attempt to minimize agriculture price discrepancies in the EEC resulting from exchange rate changes.

The principal mechanics of the CAP are carried out by use of the variable levy and the export subsidy (i.e., the variable subsidy).

Cf. Canada Account (Comparable U.S. government programs).

See also variable levy; export subsidy; Uruguay Round.

common external tariff (CXT) is a concise term referring to the harmonized tariff of a common market.

The principle of a free internal trading area with a common external set of tariffs applied to imports from outside, is the cornerstone of any common market.

Cf. free trade area.

See also common market.

Common Fund for Commodities (CFC) is a source of finance for International Commodity Organizations (ICOs) established (under international commodity agreements (ICAs) that contain buffer stock provisions) by the United Nations Conference on Trade and Development (UNCTAD).

Presently, there are only two ICAs whose buffer stocks are recognized as qualifying for CFC assistance: the International Cocoa Agreement (ICCA) and the International Rubber Agreement (IRA).

The funds for the CFC's First Account will come from capital subscriptions by its 104 member countries (as of July 1989), which will be lent to ICOs on the basis of the loans being guaranteed by stock warrants on the commodities of the ICO.

The Fund's Second Account will help finance commodity measures (other than stocking) such as research, quality and productivity improvement, and market development for producer countries.

Development of the CFC began in Nairobi in 1976 under the aegis of the United Nations Conference on Trade and Development (UNCTAD) and culminated in July 1989 at UNCTAD headquarters in Geneva, Switzerland, where the CFC Agreement was ratified.

See also Appendix V (E); United Nations Conference on Trade and Development.

common law system refers to a nation's legal system that has its historical basis in common practices and legal precedents set by courts through interpretation of rulings and statutes.

England established the common law system that is the basis of the legal systems in almost all of its former colonies, including the United States and Canada.

Common law systems do not preclude the existence of civil codes or criminal codes. Much legal precedent is established by specific judicial reference to the statutes.

The key to a common law system is the process of referring to common practices plus legal precedents and statutes in the interpretation and application of law.

Cf. code law system.

See also international law.

common market is an agreement among sovereign states to form a trading bloc in which (1) all barriers to trade between the members will eventually be removed, (2) trade policies among the members will be harmonized toward the rest of the world, and (3) the movement among members of labor and capital will be unhindered.

Cf. economic union; monetary union; political union; free trade area.

See also European Economic Community; customs union.

Commonwealth is an international organization comprising independent countries that were former colonies of Britain within the British Empire and that accept the sovereign of England (currently Queen Elizabeth II) as the symbolic head of the association.

The Commonwealth is adjudged by some to be nothing more than dismembered remnants of the defunct British Empire. Others see it (and the regular meetings of Commonwealth heads of state and of their deputies) as a means of (1) fostering linkages, (2) coordinating economic development assistance on common problems, and (3) collaborating in the development of strategies on common problems, notably peaceful, nonviolent change.

For global marketers, there are two important events involving the Commonwealth:

1. *1932:* The Ottawa Imperial Conference established a preferential system of tariffs (also known as the Commonwealth Preference System). Under this system, Britain conceded more favorable tariff rates to its bilateral Commonwealth trade partners than to non-Commonwealth traders.
2. *1973:* The United Kingdom withdrew from the European Free Trade Association (EFTA) and joined the European Economic Community (EEC). While maintaining strong ties with the Commonwealth, the United Kingdom had to abandon the Commonwealth Preference System in favor of the common external tariff (CXT) of the EEC.

The Commonwealth maintains strong relations between its own development agency, the Commonwealth Development Corporation (CDC), and all international organizations involved in extending official development assistance (ODA), including major organizations within the United Nations system: the Regional Economic Commissions, the multilateral development banks (MDBs), and the United Nations Development Program (UNDP).

See also Appendix V (B); Appendix V (C).

Communauté Économique de l'Afrique de l'Ouest (CEAO) See West African Economic Community.

Communauté Économique des États de l'Afrique Centrale (CEEAC) See Bank of Central African States.

communism *See* socialism.

comparative advantage is the central concept of international economics and trade that states that those who produce certain goods and services relatively more efficiently should specialize in their production and export, while producing and importing those goods and services in which they have a comparative cost disadvantage.

First introduced by David Ricardo, the concept of comparative advantage substantially modified Adam Smith's theory of absolute advantage.

To promote economics as a science equivalent to the physical sciences, Ricardo's concept has been dubbed the "Law of Comparative Advantage."

Cf. absolute advantage.

compensation refers to the concept that a new and/or equivalent concession may be the required outcome of the withdrawal of a previously negotiated or bound concession.

(This is especially prevalent in bilateral trade negotiations.)

Example: In light of the unilateral reduction in its sugar quota, the Jamaican government demanded talks with the U.S. Administration to discuss the various forms of trade compensation that might be granted.

compensation trade is a type of countertrade transaction that relies upon an agreement between exporter and importer to cover reciprocal purchases of specific goods.

The exchange, under one contract, does not necessarily occur simultaneously. Both deliveries are invoiced in agreed currency with payments going either directly to the supplier or to a clearing account.

A variation of compensation trade occurs where one of the parties to the contract purchases only a fraction of, or, in some cases, an excess of the value of, its delivery, and then transfers the purchase commitment for the balance to third parties.

Cf. barter; buy-back; cooperation contracts; counterpurchase; offset deals; switch deals.

See also countertrade.

competition, in the economic sense, is the behavioral rivalry between buyers and sellers to satisfy their wants and needs at an acceptable price to each.

In both micro- and macroeconomics, the basic laws of supply and demand are used to explain the market forces (i.e., the interplay of sellers and buyers).

In economic theory, moreover, competition has been reduced to certain archetypal forms: perfect competition, imperfect competition (comprising oligopolistic competition and monopoly behavior), and monopolistic competition, often referred to as "competition among many diversified sellers."

Based on these concepts, economic theory is replete with competitive models; and some of those even try to explain competition between the developed countries and the less developed countries (LDCs).

However, most theories about modern types of competitive behavior (in our incredibly complex global world) at the macroeconomic level are less well developed than their counterparts in so-called post-industrial societies like the United States, Canada, and the European Economic Community (EEC). Witness the shortfall between the economic theory and the practice of creating free trade areas, common markets, and customs unions.

Ironically, as individual nations advance toward more sophisticated forms of economic integration, the theories underpinning the success or failure of the efforts still revolve around fairly elementary concepts such as:
- price elasticity of demand,
- misallocations (and misuse) of the factors of production,
- suboptimal production systems, and
- a good understanding, but poor practice, of monetary and fiscal-policy principles.

Cf. sustainable development.
See also dependent development.

compound duty, also known as a *mixed tariff*, is a duty, tax, or tariff expressed or calculated as a combination of an ad valorem and a specific duty.

Cf. ad valorem duty; antidumping duty; countervailing duty; specific duty; end-use tariff; optimum tariff; prohibitive tariff.
See also duty.

Comprehensive Export Schedule (CES) is a list, issued by the U.S. Bureau of Commerce in Washington, D.C., that specifies those goods, the sale of which to buyers outside the territorial jurisdiction of the United States requires an export permit.

Cf. Export and Import Permits Act.
See also export permit.

concensus rates *See* OECD Concensus.

concessional financing refers to credit or "soft loans" extended by industrially developed countries to less developed countries (LDCs) on terms less severe than those offered by competitive money markets.

In Canada, the Canadian International Development Agency (CIDA) provides these kinds of funds, and in the United States, the International Development Cooperation Agency (USIDCA) is the lender.

Typically, the credits or loans adhere to the Organization for Economic Cooperation and Development (OECD) associated financing guidelines: They are characterized by (1) lengthy repayment schedules (e.g., of up to 50 years), (2) extended grace periods, (3) forgiveness of principal and interest payments during the grace periods, and (4) interest rates below the world's competitive money-market rates.

Canada's official position is that it does not use concessional financing to solicit business for Canadian exporters. However, via the Canadian Commercial Corporation (CCC), the Canadian International Development Agency (CIDA), and the Export Development Corporation (EDC), it does use concessional loans to match the lending terms offered by other competitive countries, such as the United States, Germany, and Japan.

> **Example:** Concessional loans are often used to support loans to Third World countries, especially for large turnkey projects. They have also been used to undercut competition in developed markets. The EDC (in apparent violation of the OECD Concensus) at one time supported a large concessional loan to the New York Transit Authority to purchase subway cars from Bombardier Inc., based in Montréal.
>
> Cf. mixed credits; near-concessional lending terms; technology transfer.
> *See also* associated financing; OECD Concensus.

conditionality *See* International Monetary Fund (4. Conditionality).

conference, sometimes called a *shipping conference*, is the coming together of international ocean shipping companies or shipping lines that operate regular services (liner shipping) for the purpose of establishing a framework for agreement on matters such as the setting of freight rates, the pooling of revenue, and the allocation of the number and frequency of individual company sailings.

A conference is essentially an international cartel in services. Its origins go back to 1875 when the conference system was introduced in the England-India (i.e., London-Calcutta) ocean shipping trade.

The original intent was to consolidate the resources of British shipping companies to avoid uneconomic competition between them.

> **Example:** There are four conferences operating in the ocean-cargo shipping trade between Africa and Europe: (1) Continental-West Africa Conference (COWAC), consisting of COWAC North and COWAC South; (2) United Kingdom-West Africa Line (UKWAL); (3) Mediterranean Europe-West Africa Line (MEWAL); (4) Central-West Africa Line (CEWAL).
>
> COWAC North comprises 28 shipping lines and has 35–40 percent of that route's total liner trade. COWAC South's share is 60–70 percent of its route. UKWAL comprises 11 shipping lines and has 55–60 percent of the total liner trade of that route. MEWAL has 21 companies, and its route's trade is 85 percent; and CEWAL has 8 shipping lines, and it does 75 percent of that route's business.

conference line is a shipping company that is a member of a conference.
   Cf. nonconference lines.

conference pricing refers to the agreed prices charged by individual members of a particular conference.
   See also conference.

Conference on Security and Cooperation in Europe (CSCE) is an international organization that grew out of the Helsinki Final Act of 1975.

The CSCE originally started as a specialized series of ongoing meetings (between NATO members and Warsaw Pact members) initially involving military security and human rights, and later involving discussions of information exchange, science, technology, education and culture, trade and industrial cooperation, and environmental protection.

Of most recent importance was the CSCE meeting in Paris in November 1990 to oversee the "burial of the Cold War."

Cf. North Atlantic Treaty Organization.

See also Warsaw Pact; Paris Charter for a New Europe.

confirmed letter of credit is a documentary credit that is underwritten (i.e., "confirmed") by the exporter's bank such that in the event of nonpayment by the issuing bank, the exporter is assured payment by its bank that has recourse either to the importer, the importer's bank, or both.

Among international bankers, the term used *de rigeur* is "confirmed and irrevocable letter of credit." Among international marketers, the irrevocability of the letter of credit is subsumed because of the confirmatory status of it.

Cf. letter of credit (3. irrevocable letter of credit).

See also documentary credit.

confiscation is seizure of foreign assets by a government without compensation to the owners.

Cf. expropriation; nationalization.

consignee, from the Latin *con* meaning "with" and *signare* meaning "to sign," refers to the receiver of an export shipment.

It is commonly used to mean the "customer" or the "buyer" (who "signs for" receipt of the goods).

Cf. consignor.

See also foreign freight forwarder.

consignment is a means of financing exports, such that the exporter is not paid until the goods are sold by the importer.

The process is as follows: the exporter ships goods to the importer; when the importer resells the goods to a third party, title to the goods is transferred, the importer is paid, and payment is made to the exporter, frequently via the importer's bank, which acts as a trustee for the consigned goods.

See also export financing; trust receipt.

consignor, from the Latin *con* meaning "with" and *signare* meaning "to sign," refers to the shipper of export goods.

It is commonly used to mean the seller, meaning the owner who has legal right to ship and sell (by "signing over" title).

Cf. consignee.

See also foreign freight forwarder.

consolidation *See* make bulk.

Consortium Insurance (CI) is an insurance program of the Export Development Corporation (EDC) that protects Canadian members of an export consortium against the call of a performance instrument (e.g., a performance bond) where the other member(s) of the group is/are unable to pay their respective shares.
See also documentary credit; Export Development Corporation.

consular declaration is a formal, written statement made by the diplomatic trade representative in the country of export as to a description of goods, their origin, value, mode of shipment, and destination in the country of intended import.

In the judgment of many international marketers, the surveillance function allegedly carried out by diplomatic officials in the country of export is disingenuous, given the frequently picayune behavior of customs officials in the intended country of import. To them, the consular declaration is a nontariff barrier.

---

consular invoice is a document that contains details of a consular declaration.
See also consular declaration.

consumption effect of a tariff is the reduction in domestic consumption of a good as a result of its increase in price due to a tariff.
Cf. production effect of a tariff; trade effect of a tariff.

container is a rectangular metal box of standardized dimensions, used for shipping goods.
In 1964, the International Standardization Organization (ISO) recommended (via its Technical Committee on Freight Containers) Standard 668 on "Dimensions and Rating of Series I Freight Containers": for international use, containers be of 10-foot, 20-foot, 30-foot, and 40-foot lengths, and 8 feet in width and height.
Since ISO Standard 668, only two changes have been made: the introduction of 8-foot-6-inch-high containers and the increase from 20 tonnes (metric tons) to 24 tonnes in the maximum gross weight permitted per container.
Rapid international adoption of Standard 668 has meant that over 90 percent of all containers used internationally are 20-foot- and 40-foot-long units, with a height of 8 feet 6 inches. Among these, the 20-foot containers is considered the standard, and freight loading capacities are referred to in terms of TEUs, or 20-foot equivalent units.

Non-ISO containers called "high-cubes" and "super-high cubes" made their appearance in the United States after road transport deregulation in the early 1980s. At one time these maverick configured boxes threatened to turn the ISO standard container into a nonstandard item due to their uncontrolled proliferation and the high costs associated with installing capital equipment to deal with them.
For example, high cubes were containers having heights of 9 feet and 9 feet 6 inches, and a length of 40 feet. Super-high cubes were containers with high-cube heights and with lengths over 40 feet—some of them 45 feet, 48 feet, and 53 feet long!!
In the continuing effort to harmonize containerization, the ISO has allied itself

with (1) the U.N. Conference on Trade and Development's (UNCTAD's) Committee on Shipping, (2) the U.N. Economic Commission for Europe (UN/ECE) Inland Transport Committee, and (3) the UN/ECE's Working Party of Container Transport. These groups have formidable authority among the world's most important ocean- and air-shipping lines, transportation functional intermediaries, and public regulatory agencies, and they promise those who threaten the disruption of standardized containerization an impossibly uneconomic struggle.

---

containerization refers to the usage of containers for international trade.

This process has been standardized worldwide in the following types of intermodal transport:

1. **COFC** (abbreviation for **container-on-flatcar**): the loading of containers onto railroad flatcars and the shipping of them via rail;
2. **birdyback •NW•**: the shipping of containerized cargo via air transport;
3. **fishyback •NW•**: the shipping of containerized cargo via ocean liners;
4. **TOFC** (abbreviation for **trailer-on-flatcar**): the loading of trailers (on which containers have already been loaded) onto railroad flatcars, and shipping them via rail.

container ship (container shipping) is an ocean-going vessel designed and constructed exclusively for the business of transporting containers.

With this transport mode, the capacity of a container ship is expressed in 20-foot equivalent units, or TEUs, (i.e., the number of 20-foot containers it can carry).

See also container.

contingency protection is a Canadian term that refers collectively to antidumping and countervailing duties and measures as used by the U.S. government and that the United States itself has called unfair trade practices when these retaliatory measures are used by third countries.

See also antidumping duty; countervailing duty.

contraband, from the Italian *contra* meaning "against" and *bando* meaning "decree," is goods prohibited from trade, especially in wartime, and thus, if imported, smuggled.

Cf. black market goods.

contract manufacturing is a formal agreement between corporations for the purpose of cooperating in manufacturing, whereby each of the signatories undertakes to dedicate a percentage of its resources to the production of a specified item or component, to be shipped to a designated place for its subsequent processing or assembly by another of the parties to the agreement.

> **Example:** The so-called joint venture between Chrysler U.S.A. and Mitsubishi Japan is, in fact, a long-term contract manufacturing agreement. Among other things, it involves Mitsubishi casting and machining automotive engines and shipping them to U.S. West Coast ports for assembly onto car platforms designed and fabricated by Chrysler.

Cf. joint venture; production sharing.

contract of affreightment is an agreement by a water transport carrier to provide cargo space on a vessel at a specified price and at a specified time to accommodate a shipper who then becomes liable for payment of the carrier even if the carrier cannot fulfill its responsibility to ship the goods.

See also booking number.

convertible currency, a variation of *reserve currency*, is the money of a nation or group of nations that can be easily exchanged for the money of other nations (i.e., money that enjoys international confidence and, consequently, a high level of transactionability).

> **Example:** When requesting payment for its publications, *Ediciones Cubanas* requires remittances in a convertible currency and gives preferential subscription rates for payments made in any of the currencies in the IMF basket and especially for U.S. dollars.

See also reserve currency country; International Monetary Fund.

cooperation (cooperation contract) is a type of countertrade transaction, sometimes referred to as a *cooperation agreement* that takes the form of a long-term contract for economic cooperation between two countries, usually under one master contract involving continuous purchases of related goods and services.

The cooperation contract has two forms:

1.   a series of buy-back subcontracts enabling the importer to pay the exporter with products derived from the goods originally exported, and
2.   the sale of technical know-how, patents, and processes by an exporter to a joint venture that repays the exporter from the sales proceeds of the enterprise.

> **Example:** Germany entered into a major cooperation contract with the Soviet Union when it agreed to supply steel tubing for the Siberian Gas Pipeline. The tubing, supplied over a period of 10 years, will be paid for by continuous through-put of Siberian natural gas directly to German industries that will, in turn, pay the steel companies that supplied the original product.

Cf. barter; buy-back; compensation trade; counterpurchase; offset deals; switch deals.

See also countertrade.

Coordinating Committee for Multilateral Export Controls *See* COCOM.

co-production (coproduction) is a component of a type of countertrade transaction called direct offsets, in which an exporter receives payment contingent upon permitting the importer to locally ("offshore") produce a part of the total export contract.

The subcontract is usually a straight commercial arrangement that may include licensed production.

Cf. production sharing.

See also offset deals (direct offsets).

correspondent (correspondent relationship) is a reciprocal agreement between two banks doing business internationally to provide service to each other's customers.

> **Example:** In the Caribbean, the Bank of Nova Scotia has a correspondent relationship with the Royal Bank of Canada, each to offer the other's customers use of its services in markets where the other has no local offices. In Canada, such an arrangement might be a restrictive trade practice and a violation of the Competition Act.

cost of living allowance *See* benefit allowance.

Council of Arab Economic Unity (CAEU) is an international Arab organization established in 1957 by the Arab Economic Council of the Arab League.

The Council's aims are regional in focus. They concentrate on economic cooperation and integration of the political economies of Arab countries.

The CAEU's membership consists of Iraq, Jordan, Kuwait, Libya, Mauritania, Somalia, Sudan, Syria, United Arab Emirates (U.A.E.), Yemen, comprising former Yemen (Aden) and former Yemen (San'a), and the Palestine Liberation Organization (PLO), which has been given *de jure* recognition.

See also Arab League; Appendix V (B); Arab Common Market.

Council of Canadian Trading Houses (CCTH) is a national association organized under the auspices of the Canadian Export Association (CEA).

The CCTH is responsible for the following activities:

1. establishing the accreditation criteria for Canadian trading houses;
2. administering the accreditation process for appropriate and legal use of the title *trading house* in Canada;
3. promoting information on the use of trading houses in Canada;
4. providing Canadian exporters with information on, and to refer them to, the appropriate accredited trading house.

See also trading house.

Council of Europe is an international organization with a regional European focus that provides the framework for the increased unity and solidarity among its members to assist in the process of their economic development.

The desire for political unity among Western European nations arose initially as a need for a counterforce against the perceived threat from the Soviet Union and the Warsaw Treaty Organization and, secondarily, as a counterweight against the perceived economic ambitions of the United States.

This desire first expressed itself as The Congress of Europe in The Hague in 1948. The Congress produced an initiative by Belgium, France, Luxembourg, the Netherlands, and the United Kingdom, all signers of the Brussels Treaty Organization (BTO) in 1948. In 1949, the five BTO countries plus Denmark, Ireland, Italy, Norway, and Sweden signed the Statute of the Council in London, which created the Council of Europe.

These 10 original members have been joined by 11 other European nations. This gives the Council of Europe a membership of all Western European countries except for Switzerland, Andorra, Monaco, San Marino, and The Vatican.

The Council of Europe focuses its work in certain specific fields: (1) human rights, (2) social and economic matters, (3) education and cultural affairs, (4) youth, (5) public health, (6) environment and regional planning, (7) regional and municipal government, and (8) crime prevention. It is also active in the areas of human rights, labor, intellectual property, communications, and transportation.

The Council, through its Parliamentary Assembly (referred to as the Consultative Assembly) and its Committee of Ministers, maintains close relations with the European Parliament of the EEC, with other EEC bodies, and with other regional and international organizations.

See also Appendix V (B).

Council for Mutual Economic Assistance (CMEA), also known as *COMECON*, was a free-trade-like group, politically dominated by the Soviet Union, that was established in 1949 to encourage economic integration of the countries of the Eastern European Bloc and, consequently, dependence on the Soviet Union.

On February 25, 1991, after two years of upheaval in East Europe, the CMEA formally dissolved.

Originally comprised of only European communist countries, the CMEA (until its formal dissolution) consisted of "fraternal members" globally. Its membership comprised: Cuba, Czechoslovakia, Finland (associate member), the former German Democratic Republic, Hungary, Mongolia, Poland, Romania, the Soviet Union, and Vietnam.

Cf. open economy.

See also closed economy; Warsaw Pact.

counterpurchase, a type of countertrade transaction, is an agreement between exporter and importer that covers two linked contracts and two linked transactions, as follows:

- *Contract A:* this formalizes the sale of goods at a negotiated and agreed price; the importer pays the exporter in an agreed-upon currency, contingent upon acceptance and execution of Contract B.
- *Contract B:* this is the counterpurchase agreement, which obligates the exporter to purchase goods from the importer valued at a percentage of Contract A, over a specified period of time.

   Example: When the New York-based company concluded a deal to export Tennessee bourbon, it little expected to have to sign a contract obligating it to counterpurchase $150,000 worth of clove cigarettes, 50 percent of the value of the liquor contract.

Cf. barter; buy-back; compensation trade; cooperation contracts; offset deals; switch deals.

See also countertrade.

countertrade is

1. international trade where an export sale is contingent upon a reciprocal purchase or undertaking by the exporter; and/or
2. international trade involving payment in anything other than 100 percent currency by the importer.

Cf. production sharing.

See also barter; buy-back; compensation trade; cooperation contracts; counterpurchase; offset deals; switch deals.

countervailing duty, referred to as a *punitive duty* when levied after material injury occurs to domestic producers, is extra charges levied by an importing country on goods exported to it that were produced with help from subsidies.

The aim is to offset the subsidy so that the less expensive imports do not further materially damage domestic producers who supply the local market with nonsubsidized goods. The effect of the countervailing duty is to increase the price of the cheaper imported goods by the differential between their value and that of the more expensive domestic goods.

Cf. antidumping duty; ad valorem duty; compound duty; specific duty; optimum tariff; prohibitive tariff.

See also duty; consumption effect of a tariff.

Court of International Trade (CIT) is a special U.S. court established to hear appeals on parajudicial and administrative trade decisions.

Unless unfavorable decisions from the U.S. International Trade Commission or the U.S. International Trade Administration are treaty-bound, (e.g., decisions by the binational dispute-settlement mechanism of the Canada-U.S. Free Trade Agreement (FTA) of 1989), they can be appealed to the CIT by the Canadian government on behalf of companies who have sustained injury or who perceive they will be injured by those decisions.

Cf. binational dispute-settlement mechanism.

See also United States International Trade commission; United States International Trade Administration.

covered interest arbitrage *See* Appendix II.

covered under *carnet* refers to export goods making temporary trips to foreign countries, then being re-exported from them, and ultimately being re-imported to their originating country, under the authority of an ICC *carnet*.

See also carnet.

crédit mixte See mixed credit.

credit protocol is a financial agreement, signed between official credit-granting agencies (in different countries), that permits the buyers in one country to use foreign credit to finance their imports.

Example: The credit protocol signed between Canada and Den Norske

Creditbank allows Norwegian buyers to use Export Development Corporation (EDC) financing when sourcing goods and services in Canada.

See also Export Development Corporation; export financing.

crédit tranche, from the French *crédit* meaning "credit" and *tranche* meaning "slice," is the amount that a member of the International Monetary Fund (IMF) can borrow from the Fund, beyond its gold *tranche*.

See also International Monetary Fund.

credit transactions, in international economics, refers to exchanges that involve receipt of time-phased payments from foreign individuals, companies, and/or governments.

crawling peg system *See* exchange rates.

Crisis in the Gulf *See* Gulf Crisis.

cross subsidization (cross-subsidization) is an international marketing strategy whereby a company uses earnings in one foreign market to support its marketing efforts in another foreign market.

Implicit in this process is the suggestion that the earnings used for the cross subsidization effort come from successful marketing work and that they go to support a different (and possibly flagging) product or product line in another market. Sometimes the product being cross subsidized is being offered at predatory prices with market monopolization as the ultimate objective. In this case, the short-run losses incurred are cross subsidized by the successful product.

cross trader (cross-trader) refers to a shipping line that provides cargo service between ports in two or more different countries and that is not under the national flag of any of them.

The Code of Conduct for Liner Conferences guarantees developing countries a share of liner service within a conference according to the "40-40-20 Rule": 40 percent for a developing country at one end of the service, 40 percent for a developed country at the other end, and 20 percent for cross traders (i.e., shipping lines of other countries that are nonconference members).

Cf. outsider.
See also conference.

Crown Corporation is a legal limited liability company owned at least 51 percent (but more customarily 100 percent) by the Federal Government of Canada. When such an enterprise is owned by a Canadian Provincial government, it is called a *Provincial Crown Corporation*. Regardless of the level of government ownership, these state-owned entities are engaged either in "state trading," "state service," or "state production (manufacturing)" operations.

Cf. state trading nation; command economy.
See also mixed economy.

cultural adiaphora are behaviors in which an out-member in a foreign culture may engage.

> **Example:** It is traditionally expected that expatriate Europeans in Ghana will employ house servants for manual tasks; and, therefore, it is perceived as somewhat amusing—although not *verboten*—to see expatriate European women doing laundry by hand while their European spouses tune up the car.

cultural adoption, a variation of *cultural borrowing*, is the process of people in one society actively using the ideas, things, and behaviors from a culture different from their own, resulting in the modification of the society's behaviors.

> A test of positive adoption in sociological analysis is seeing if behaviors in one society have been modified by the borrowings from another.

cultural borrowing is the long-term adoption of symbols and technology of one society by another.

> **Example:** *"Qu'est ce que vous aller faire ce* weekend?" said Sam Pais, the Cuban-born Miami entrepreneur to Nabih Eid, his Lebanese dinner guest, as they relaxed aboard the yacht El Rais, sipping Mogen David wine and nibbling hors d'oeuvres of cold ptarmigan and Peruvian ceviche, flown into St. Tropez especially for the bankers' meeting.

cultural caveat refers to the care to be used prior to borrowing and adopting foreign behaviors.
> *See also* "Always Say Yes."

cultural change refers to the enduring behavioral modifications evoked in members of a society as a result of (1) exposing its members to differential cultural stimuli (i.e., products of a different culture such as language, music, and technology) and (2) having these stimuli adopted by the exposed members.
> *See also* cultural adoption.

cultural exclusives are behaviors in which out-members of a culture are prohibited from engaging.

> Conversely, *cultural inclusives* denote behaviors in which only in-members of a group may engage.

> **Example:** While Muslims are permitted into churches only if they remove their headgear and into synagogues only if they don headgear, neither Christians nor Jews are permitted to enter mosques even if they consent to the customary Muslim practice of removing their footwear beforehand.

> Cf. cultural inclusives.

cultural imperialism refers to the negative perception that a foreign culture gradually displaces a national culture by either eroding, undermining, assimilating, or extinguishing it and substituting alien things for those displaced.

It is a pejorative label used to defend indigenous culture by labeling as negative the process of change.

> **Examples:** In Canada, nationalists often cite the use of American spellings (e.g., labor v. labour) as evidence of "creeping cultural imperialism."
>
> The Province of Québec passed the language law Bill 101, making French the official language of the workplace, in an attempt to protect the Québecois heritage against what was perceived as anglophone cultural imperialism.
>
> The Latinization of South Florida is perceived by many Americans to be the revenge of Fidel Castro via cultural imperialism.

cultural inclusives are behaviors in which only in-members of a group may engage.

> Conversely, *cultural exclusives* denotes behaviors in which out-members of a culture are prohibited from engaging.

Cf. cultural exclusives.

cultural lag refers to the ethnocentric attitude that is perceived to account for the (predominantly) technological differences between countries and, by inference, the differing levels of economic development.

> In the 1960s and 1970s, the enormous, worldwide "economic development" efforts aimed at Africa, Asia, and Latin America by the North produced only a few genuine "economic miracles," as the *newly industrialized countries* (NICs) are called.
>
> These miracles were less a product of slow, evolutionary social change (the "trickle-up effect") than of (1) massive capital investment into specific industrial sectors (managed by governments), (2) the virtual destruction of traditional land tenure (and traditional agricultural practices), and (3) the massification of urban dwellers, relying on their cheap labor as the most valuable industrial input. In Japan, where this formula was so spectacularly successful, the "demon of industrial growth" has frightened Americans (since Japanese lifetime-employment policies were characteristic of a 20-year fast-growth cycle). It is now rapidly being abandoned in favor of relocating Japanese subsidiaries in low-cost Pacific Rim countries such as Indonesia, Thailand, and Mynamar (formerly Burma).

Cf. Puerto Rican Model.
See also Japan Sea Basin; yen diplomacy; currency area (3. The yen area); ethnocentrism; dependent development.

cultural mosaic •NW• *See* multicultural.

cultural sovereignty is, in theory, the right of a country to dictate, establish, and control all the politico-economic conditions of its domestic life; in practice, it is a term used by nationalists in their perceived protection of a country's intellectual property (e.g., T.V. programs, films, books, magazines).

It suggests the condition whereby government authority should be used to create and protect an internal market for a country's cultural products.

> In a Canadian context, those who see cultural sovereignty as an issue deserving of government protection are economic nationalists who tend to overvalue (rather than undervalue) Canadian things and events based on their economic stake in them. Thus

arises the predictable protectionist fear that Canadian cultural values, perceived to be distinct from American cultural values, will be displaced by the American cultural values, anonymized to death in that most fearful of all homogenizers, the Great American Melting Pot.

> Cf. cultural mosaic.
> *See also* cultural imperialism.

cultural universals are behaviors of any culture that are considered to have equal analogs (or equal prohibitions) in every other culture.

> In the realm of nonverbal communication, only one behavior is considered to be a uniformly understood cultural universal: smiling.

culture is the entire array of symbols, institutions, roles, and behaviors that comprise social structure.
> *See also* social structure.

culture shock (cultural shock) is the initial short-lived behavioral reactions of a person who enters a society that is significantly different from the person's own acculturating society.

currency abbreviation is, in the English language, the written, nonsymbolic, short form in Arabic-letter spelling for the world's major currencies, as adopted by the International Standardization Organization (ISO):

Currency	*ISO Standard Abbreviation*
Australian dollar	ASD
Belgian franc	BEF
British pound sterling	GBP
Canadian dollar	CAD
Danish krone	DKK
Deutsche mark	DEM
Dutch guilder	NLG
French franc	FRF
Greek drachma	GRD
Irish pound	IEP
Italian lira	ITL
Japanese yen	JPY
Luxembourg franc	LUF
Portuguese escudo	PTE
Spanish peseta	ESP
Swiss franc	CHF
U.S. dollar	USD

> *See also* currency area.

currency area is a group of associated countries, called the *periphery*, whose individual currencies are each "pegged" to the currency of one country at the "core."

1. The *sterling area* or *sterling bloc* refers to those LDCs whose individual currencies are pegged to the British pound (GBP) by virtue of their historical ties to Britain as former colonies and their ongoing dependence on Britain regarding the marketing of commodities.

2. The *franc area* or *Franc Zone* or *French Community* refers to 14 independent (mainly African, but also Asian and Pacific) LDCs whose individual currencies are denominated as the *CFA franc*, a currency pegged to the French franc (FRF) and, thus, freely convertible with it in franc-area countries, as well as in other major regional countries (e.g., Nigeria).

3. The *yen area* or *yen bloc* refers to those Pacific Rim newly industrialized countries (NICs) who have close ongoing ties in technology, finance, and trade with Japan. No central bank or common currency has, as yet, been established to tie the Asia-Pacific periphery to the Japanese core.

4. The *U.S. dollar area*, customarily referred to simply as the *dollar area*, refers, strictly speaking, to all political-economies in the Caribbean (except Cuba), where there is complete monetary dependency on the U.S. dollar (USD), only partial convertibility of local currencies, and no convertibility in the United States or in the rest of the world. The U.S. dollar has exchange linkages with some countries in Africa, (e.g., Liberia, Zambia), Asia (e.g., the Philippines), and in Latin America (e.g., Panamá).

5. The *Australian dollar area* comprises eight states of the South Pacific (Solomon Islands, Papua New Guinea (PNG), Kiribati, Vanuatu, Tuvalu, Western Samoa, Fiji, and Tonga). The eight national currencies are linked to the Australian dollar by virtue of Australian economic domination of the region.

See also CFA franc; West African Monetary Union; Central Bank of West African States; Bank of Central African States; yen diplomacy; Pacific Economic Cooperation Group.

currency convertibility refers to the relative ease (or lack of ease) involved in exchanging one nation's money for another's.

It also refers to the measure of the restrictions that limit the exchange of national currencies.

Cf. transactionability.

currency exchange controls *See* exchange controls.

current account is the part of a nation's balance of payments that records all current sales and purchase transactions (including exports and imports), invisible trade (transactions for services), interest and transfer payments (including unilateral transfers), and profits from foreign operations.

Cf. capital account.

See also balance of payments.

customs is a designated area, either at a border point or at some inland port of destination, where goods (either imported into or exported out of a country) can be examined and appraised by duly authorized customs officers.

The examination will determine the goods' origin and destination and their appraisal value, the purpose being to levy an appropriate tax on them. A tax levied on imports is a customs import duty; a tax levied on exports is a customs export levy.

See also duty.

Customs Act is the Canadian legislation under which the customs procedures in Canada have been authorized and implemented.

customs broker is a company whose business is exclusively that of preparing and processing the required documentation for customs authorities, the purpose being to get the goods cleared through customs at rates of duty most favorable to the party who hires the broker.

The company is known under different names, depending on who contracts for its services:

1. *Export Customs Broker:* When the exporter hires the broker, the broker is responsible for ensuring that the goods "clear customs" of the foreign country (i.e., the country of import).
2. *Import Customs Broker:* When the importer hires the broker, the broker is responsible for ensuring that the goods clear the customs of the foreign country (i.e., the country of export).

Cf. broker.
See also foreign freight forwarder; clear customs.

customs classification refers to (1) the category in which a good is placed for the purpose of levying a duty or tariff; and/or (2) the procedure for, or method of, determining the tariff category in a nation's nomenclature system, used for classifying internationally traded goods.

customs clearing agent is another name for a customs broker.
See customs broker. *See also* foreign freight forwarder.

Customs Cooperation Council (CCC) is an international organization formed in 1950 to study questions relating to the development of a globally uniform customs classification system whereby interpretation, documentation, and application of all matters relating to customs affairs would be standardized.

The CCC has its headquarters in Brussels, Belgium, and its membership comprises more than 90 countries.

See also Customs Cooperation Council Nomenclature; customs harmonization.

Customs Cooperation Council Nomenclature (CCCN) is a custom system, designed by the Customs Cooperation Council, for classifying goods for the purpose of customs valuation.

Formerly, it was known as the Brussels Tariff Nomenclature (BTN).

Most members of the Organization for Economic Cooperation and Development (OECD) traditionally classified the goods they imported according to the CCCN. However, as of January 1, 1988, when the Harmonized Commodity Description and

Coding System, known as the Harmonized System (HS), was put into effect, most of them converted to it.

The United States and Canada have adopted the Harmonized System for the purpose of customs valuation under the Canada-U.S. Free Trade Agreement of 1989.

See also Customs Cooperation Council.

customs duty *See* duty.

Customs and Economic Union of Central Africa (CEUCA), also known as *Union Douanière et Économique de l'Afrique Centrale (UDEAC)*, is an international trade group (ITG) that aims to establish a common market entity among its Central African member countries.

The CEUCA was established in 1964 by the Brazzaville (Congo) Treaty and became operational in 1966. Its membership comprises Cameroon, Central African Republic, Chad, Congo, and Gabon.

The CEUCA replaced the *Union Douanière Équatoriale (UDE)*, which was formed in 1959 by the Central African Republic, Chad, Congo, and Gabon (without Cameroon).

The following are this common market's major achievements to date:

1. It brought about total liberalization of trade among members and application of a common external tariff (CXT) to goods imported from nonmembers.
2. The right of establishment (within the CEUCA) has been extended to citizens of all member countries.
3. Direct investment is uniformly monitored and regulated, and a common taxation system is in force.
4. Monetary policy is coordinated by The Bank of Central African States (BCAS), which is the issuing bank of the common market.
5. Development financing has been addressed by the establishment of the Solidarity Fund, supplemented by the Development Bank of Central African States (officially, *Banque de Developpement des États Central de l'Afrique (BDECA)*) established in 1976 in Brazzaville, Congo.

The CEUCA has established relations with the United Nations Economic Commission for Africa (UN/ECA), with international development agencies, and with executing agencies of the United Nations Development Program (UNDP).

See also common market; right of establishment; Appendix V (A), (B), (C).

customs harmonization is the ongoing process to increase the standardization of customs procedures and nomenclatures globally.

The Customs Cooperation Council (CCC), under whose aegis the Customs Cooperation Council Nomenclature (CCCN) operates, has developed the new internationally accepted Harmonized Commodity Description and Coding System, which has, effectively, replaced the CCCN as of January 1, 1988.

Cf. Harmonized Commodity Description and Coding System.

See also Kyoto Convention; customs classification; Customs Cooperation Council; Customs Cooperation Council Nomenclature.

Customs Tariff Act refers to Canadian legislation under which the legal framework was established and implemented for the collection of duties, including regulations governing duty drawbacks and duty remission.

See also duty drawback; duty remission.

customs union, from the German *Zollverein* meaning "customs league," is a concept defined in the General Agreement on Tariffs and Trade (GATT), Part III, Article XXIV, 8(a), "to mean the substitution of a single customs territory for two or more customs territories . . . ," and meaning the unification of different customs tariffs into a single customs tariff.

The term was first used after the joining of the Prussian free-trade area by Bavaria, in 1829, and by Saxony, in 1834, to establish a pan-German *Zollverein*.

Cf. *Zoll*.

See also free trade area; common market; Appendix V (A).

Customs Valuation Code *See* Agreement on Customs Valuation.

DAC (**D**evelopment **A**ssistance **C**ommittee (of the Organization for Economic Development)) *See* Development Assistance Committee; Organization for Economic Cooperation and Development.

D/A sight draft (**d**ocuments (against) **a**cceptance sight draft) is a method of payment for exports whereby the document transferring title to the goods (i.e., the bill of lading) is released against the acceptance by the importer of the obligation to pay.
> Cf. DOA; D/P draft.
> *See also* documentary draft; documentary collection.

Danube Commission is an international organization whose purpose is to regulate navigation, to ensure facilities for shipping, and to coordinate regulations for navigation, customs, and sanitation on the Danube River.
> The Commission was established by the Belgrade Convention signed in Belgrade, Yugoslavia, in 1949. Its members are Austria, Bulgaria, Czechoslovakia, Hungary, Romania, the U.S.S.R., and Yugoslavia.
> *See also* Appendix V (B).

Darwin's Law (of Evolution) is the observation that the result of competition among living species is the survival of the fittest.
> It was named after the English naturalist, Charles Darwin.

dash *See* bribery.

dealer is a foreign-based enterprise that works (usually under contract) for a foreign-based distributor from which it buys goods for resale to consumers and/or industrial users.

If the contract binds the distributor not to sell the same products to another competitive dealer within a specific trading area, then the dealer is said to have an exclusive dealership.

Cf. distributor.

debt buy-backs refers to a debt-reduction technique whereby a debtor country purchases ("buys back") its financial obligations (1) at a discount and (2) for cash.

> **Example:** In 1988, Bolivia purchased 40 percent of its U.S. $335 million debt at an (average) discount of 89 percent. Bolivia was so short of cash that international aid agencies had to "front" the deal.

See also debt-reduction techniques.

debt-equity swaps refers to a debt-reduction technique in which there is the exchange by a debtor country of portions of its external debt for ownership in state-owned enterprises.

This is what occurs: (1) the buyer of the debt (at a discount on the secondary market) makes a loan to the debtor country; (2) the buyer then obtains (in exchange) local currency at its full face value; and (3) the buyer then uses this local currency to purchase local equity in the country.

> **Example:** To give themselves breathing room, many Third World debtor countries have tried to interest their developed-country bank creditors in debt-equity swaps involving state enterprises such as telephone companies and hydroelectric projects. Very few Western banks have been interested.

See also debt-reduction techniques.

debt forgiveness, when related to the foreign debt of countries, refers to actions that write off portions of the principal, the interest, or both, by bankers to whom these amounts are owed by foreign governments.

> **Example:** In recent years, banks have attempted to reduce their Third World loans by selling them at steep discounts through a loosely formed market in New York called a "secondary market." Typically, the debt is sold at discounts yielding 40–60 cents on the dollar and is exchanged with the borrowers for local currency.
>
> For example, a loan for U.S. $10 million owed by a Chilean bank to J.P. Morgan & Co. may be sold to an Argentine bank at, say, a 40-percent discount, and J.P. Morgan would immediately receive U.S. $6 million in Argentine australs.
>
> Some Canadian banks have sold their Third World debts to get them off their balance sheets as nonperforming assets. The Toronto-Dominion Bank and the Canadian Imperial Bank of Commerce, both of Toronto, engage in this practice and consider it a form of debt forgiveness since the discounts reflect the expectation that only a portion of the loans will ever be repaid.

See also nonperforming assets; debt-reduction techniques.

Debt Management and Financial Analysis System (DMFAS) is a computerized system developed by the U.N. Conference on Trade and Development

(UNCTAD) at the request of debtor countries to Paris Club members to assist them in formulating policies in the areas of management and rescheduling of their external debt.

The DMFAS was installed during the 1980s in a number of less developed countries, including Costa Rica, Egypt, El Salvador, Guatemala, Haïti, Honduras, Nicaragua, Pakistan, Trinidad and Tobago, Togo, Uganda, Zambia, and Zimbabwe. Plans are in process to implement the DMFAS in Burundi, Djibouti, Ethiopia, Indonesia, Rwanda, and Sudan.

The DMFAS is implemented in three language versions: English, French, and Spanish. It is provided through UNCTAD's Technical Cooperation Program of the UNCTAD Secretariat in Geneva, financed as technical assistance projects by the United Nations Development Program (UNDP). Country-adopters are offered user training, and they are supported by economists and data processing specialists with the Resources for Development Program at UNCTAD's Secretariat in Geneva.

See also external debt; debt rescheduling; debt-reduction techniques; Paris Club.

debt overhang, a variation of *debt servicing*, refers to the payments of a country's external debt determined by some negotiation process between the debtor country and its creditors, resulting in payments tied to the economic performance of the debtor country rather than the strict contractual terms of the debt.

See also debt servicing.

debt-reduction techniques are methods by which a foreign creditor lessens the perceived harshness of the repayment conditions under which a debtor country will honor its financial obligations, or its collective external debt.

These techniques can be called debt rescheduling, debt-equity swaps, debt buy-backs, exchange of debt claims, and reduced-debt servicing.

Cf. Paris Club.

See also debt rescheduling; debt-equity swaps; debt buy-backs; exchange of debt claims; reduced-debt servicing.

debt rescheduling is a technique used by the Paris Club creditors for reducing the external debt owed to foreign creditors by a debtor country.

Under the heading of *multiyear rescheduling arrangements (MYRAs)*, the Paris Club uses the *Toronto Terms* of "Menu Options" in dealing with creditor countries:

1. *Partial Cancellation (Option A):* cancellation of one-third of the consolidated external-debt obligations, and the rescheduling of the remaining two-thirds
   - at a market rate of interest,
   - over a 14-year period,
   - with an 8-year grace period.
2. *Extended Measures (Option B):* no cancellation of any external-debt obligations, but

- consolidation of all external debt,
- rescheduling it over a 25-year period,
- at a market rate of interest,
- with a 14-year grace period.

3. *Concessional Interest Rates (Option C):* no cancellation of any external debt obligations, but
   - consolidation of all external debt,
   - rescheduling it over a 14-year period,
   - with an 8-year grace period,
   - at a concessional rate of interest.

Within this context, the concessional rate means that whatever the market rate of interest is, it would be reduced either by 50 percent or by 3 1/2 percentage points, whichever is less, over the term of the repayment.

Apart from any of the above Options, the Paris Club offers the provision for the repayment of development aid assistance in the form of loans on a

- rescheduled basis of a 25-year period,
- with a 14-year grace period,
- at concessional rates of interest,
- as well as an "intermediate repayment category" called the *Venice Terms*. Cf. Paris Club.
  See also debt-reduction techniques; Toronto Terms; Venice Terms.

debt servicing, also referred to as *foreign debt servicing*, is the ability to service the external debt, or the capacity of a debtor country to actually repay foreign creditors the principal and interest on funds borrowed from its export earnings of hard currency.
  See also debt rescheduling.

deck cargo refers to goods stowed on the deck of a ship.
  Cf. belly cargo.

deconsolidation *See* break-bulk.

default is the late payment of the interest- and/or principal-owing portion of a country's external debt.
  Cf. nonperforming assets.

deficit (in the balance of payments) is the excess of debits over credits in the current account and capital account (or autonomous transactions), which is equal to the net credit balance in the official reserve account (or accommodating transactions).
  Cf. credit (in the balance of payments).
  See also balance of payments.

deindustrialize (deindustrialization) is the sustained flight of capital from a developed country (where returns are less advantageous) to other industrial, developed countries (where the returns are better).

Example: Since January 1, 1989, when the Canada-U.S. Free Trade Agreement (FTA) went into effect, Canada has undergone considerable deindustrialization. Evidence for this is shown in (1) the highest levels of unemployment; (2) the steadiest ongoing erosion of Canada's merchandise trade balance; and (3) the largest number of permanent plant closings in manufacturing since the Great Depression in the 1929–1935 era.

Opponents of the FTA cite the flight of U.S. capital from Canada's high-cost economy as the underlying cause of the country's woes. Others blame (1) the worldwide recession that began in 1990; (2) the upward pressure on oil prices as a result of the Gulf Crisis; and (3) the competitive onslaught of Japan and Europe as the deeper, "structural causes."

del credere **agent**, from the Italian meaning "of trust," used in the United Kingdom, is a private, facilitating intermediary who is paid a commission for undertaking to act as guarantor that a buyer is solvent and who thus undertakes to honor payments due to the seller should the buyer default.

In Canada, the institution that provides such guarantees (to Canadian exporters) is the Export Development Corporation (EDC). In the United States, it is the Overseas Private Investment Corporation (OPIC).

See also Export Development Corporation; U.S. International Development Cooperation Agency (4. Overseas Private Investment Corporation).

delincuencia organizada, from the Spanish meaning "organized delinquency," is a polite expression for *narco-trafico*, the illegal international narcotics trade that, in the Western Hemisphere, is based in the rival Colombian cities of Medellin and Cali.

Delors Report, officially, "Report on Economic and Monetary Union in the European Community," is a document, presented in April 1989, (1) that was originally prepared by a Committee, itself appointed by the European Council at its Hanover, Germany, summit in June 1988, (2) that was chaired by Jacques Delors, President of the European Commission, and (3) that presented certain necessary and concrete steps to achieve European monetary integration at the June 26–27, 1989, meeting of the European Council held in Madrid.

The Report made the following points:

1. The three essential characteristics of a monetary union are total and irreversible convertibility of currencies; complete freedom of capital movements (in fully integrated capital markets); and irrevocably fixed exchange rates, with no fluctuation between members' currencies.
2. For the European Economic Community (EEC), the first two characteristics have been or will be met when the program for a Single Market of Europe in 1992 is complete. The third is the most essential for a monetary union and has not yet been met in the EEC.
3. The adoption of fixed exchange rates, to speed the acceptance of a single European currency, should be accomplished as soon as possible to accelerate the European monetary union, to demonstrate the irreversibility of the union, to eliminate the costs of currency conversions, and to give the union a new common international currency.

4. The establishment should take the place of a permanent, central monetary institution (called the European System of Central Banks), through which a common monetary policy could be developed to manage daily monetary operations, money supply, credit policy, and interest rates.

The date of July 1, 1990, was specified by the European Council that adopted the Delors Report as the date upon which to commence the first stage of European economic and monetary union, based on the recommendations in the Delors Report: "to bring all EEC members fully into the existing European Monetary System (EMS) of fixed, but adjustable, exchange rate parities." By mid-1990, the United Kingdom should join. (It did on October 8, 1990.)

The second stage would be scheduled to start by mid-1990 and would involve points 3 and 4.

The third stage would mean the fully operational nature of the Single European Market, with a single central bank and a single international currency.

Given the fact that the EMS has, until now, failed to bring about monetary unification and that the European Currency Unit (ECU) has never become more than an accounting unit, it strains even the most positive imagination as to how the "Delorsian dream of 1992" will be fully achieved within the guidelines of his Report.

Cf. economic union; monetary union; political union.

See also European Economic Community; European Monetary System; European Currency Unit.

DEM, the abbreviation for **Deutsche mark**, is the currency of Germany according to the terminology of the International Standardization Organization (ISO).

demand side economics (demand-side economics) *See* Keynesian economics.

demurrage, from the French *demeurer* meaning "to stay," refers to (1) excess time for loading/unloading a vessel that is caused by the shipper; and (2) charges levied by carriers on users of the mode of transport who delay in unloading and returning the vehicles and/or containers used to transport the goods.

It is sometimes called "demurrage and detention."

> **Example:** The terms of sale were FAS (Halifax). As scheduled, the COFC shipment arrived at the port but was unable to unload because of the late arrival of the ship. Even though not the fault of the exporter, demurrage was charged by the railway, which was then charged back to the seller. Whether the Canadian exporter can add this demurrage to the export invoice for the U.S. customer all depends on the sales contract, which may not allow for any additional charges beyond the explicit FAS terms of sale agreed to.

Cf. detention.

denationalization (de-nationalization) *See* privatization.

Department of External Affairs (DEA) is the legal name for the Canadian Federal Government ministry that, until 1982, was responsible for (1) the diplomatic relations between Canada and other countries, (2) the political relationship between Canada and its treaty allies, and (3) the arrangements between Canada and international organizations having global, regional, and area interests.

In 1982, international trade, which had hitherto been under the jurisdiction of the (then) Department of Industry, Trade, and Commerce (ITC), was moved to DEA. DEA was now (additionally) responsible for (1) negotiating and implementing international trade agreements, (2) developing Canadian international trade policy, and (3) implementing it through a worldwide network of trade missions, trade commissioners, and trade programs.

In 1989, in line with DEA's expanded functions, the Department officially adopted the applied title of External Affairs and International Trade Canada (EAITC). The legal name of *Department of External Affairs* remains unchanged.

The Minister of International Trade is the Cabinet Officer in DEA responsible for the development of international trade policy and for the execution of its programs and activities. She/he is the counterpart of the U.S. Trade Representative.

The Cabinet Officer in DEA responsible for Canada's diplomatic activities is the Secretary of State for External Affairs, whose U.S. counterpart is the Secretary of State.

Very much like its U.S. analog, DEA has numerous operating units (e.g., the Free Trade Policy and Operations/Free Trade Policy Bureau, the Working Group on Subsidies and Trade Remedies, the Free Trade Management Bureau, U.S. Relations/U.S. Relations Bureau, and the U.S. Trade, Tourism, and Investment Development Bureau).

See also International Trade Center.

Department of Regional Economic Expansion *See* Industry, Science and Technology Canada.

Department of Regional Industrial Expansion *See* Industry, Science and Technology Canada.

dependent development is the perception by developing countries (1) that their development is contingent upon and controlled by developed countries and (2) that the developed countries seek to maintain their dominance over the less developed countries (LDCs) by willful manipulation of the global economy (e.g., money markets where interest rates are high, and commodity markets where prices for LDC exports are low).

> **Example:** The dependent-development world view is central to the Latin American Economic System (LAES), where resentment against U.S. direct investment has been labeled everything from the traditional epithet "Yanqui imperialism" to the more courteous phrase "the excesses of American free market capitalism."

> Cf. New International Economic Order.
> *See also* Latin American Economic System.

depreciation *See* Appendix II.

destabilization speculation *See* Appendix II.

detention refers to charges levied by carriers on users of the mode of transport who retain possession of the transport equipment beyond the time necessary to unload the goods.

Since the concept of detention incorporates that of demurrage, practice is to include one with the other and to refer to the extra charges incurred as "demurrage and detention."

Cf. demurrage.

devaluation *See* Appendix II.

developed country is (1) a culture-based term that denotes those nations that have attained relatively high standards in such matters as per capita income and life expectancy and low standards in such matters as infant mortality and that distinguishes them from others that have achieved lower comparable standards; and is (2) an ethnocentric label used to denote nations that are more industrialized than others and that, by inference, have ways of life that are to be more highly valued than those of other nations that are less industrialized.

The fact that most developed countries are in the northern hemisphere has given rise to the collective reference to them as "The North."

> **Example:** Canada, with a per capita income of $13,670 per annum, a life expectancy of 76.3 years, a 97.3 percent literacy rate, and an infant mortality rate of less than 12 deaths per 1,000 live births, considers itself one of the most developed nations in the world.

Cf. developing country; sustainable development.
See also less developed country; least developed country; Third World.

developing country is (1) a culture-based term that denotes those nations that have attained relatively low standards in such matters as per capita income and life expectancy and high ones in such matters as infant mortality and that distinguishes them from others that have achieved "better" comparable standards; and is (2) a derogatory ethnocentric label used to denote nations that are less industrialized than others and that, by inference, have ways of life that are to be less highly valued than those of other nations that are more industrialized.

The fact that most developing countries are in the Southern hemisphere has given rise to the collective reference to them as "The South." They are also known collectively as the "Third World."

> **Example:** Nepal, with a per capita income of $160 per annum, life expectancy of 47.9 years, a 68.3 percent literacy rate, and an infant mortality rate of more than 70 deaths per 1,000 live births, is classified as one of the developing nations in the world.

Cf. developed country; sustainable development.
See also less developed country; least developed country; Third World.

Development Assistance Committee (DAC) is a body comprising 19 members of the Organization for Economic Cooperation and Development (OECD), responsible for coordinating official development assistance (ODA) among its members.

Cf. OPEC Fund for International Development.

See also official development assistance.

Development Center of the Organization of Economic Cooperation and Development (OECD) is an autonomous operating unit of the OECD, established in 1961 by a decision of the OECD Council.

The purpose of the Center is to pool the knowledge and experience in OECD member countries and to make this knowledge and experience available to all countries in the process of economic and social development.

> **Example:** From the viewpoint of non-OECD members in Asia, Africa, and Latin America, the Development Center may be perceived, at worst, as "neocolonialist," and, at best, as a means to extend the dependence of developing countries (the "periphery") on developed countries (the "core"). Thus, the LDCs have argued that the Development Center is nonprogressive in that it impedes any genuine attempts to create a New International Economic Order (NIEO).

Cf. New International Economic Order.

See also International Development Information Network.

"Did SMIOHO or did SMIOAQ?" •NW•, meaning "Did she make it on her own or did she make it on a quota?", is an expression for the doubt about whether a person has been hired based on merit or on an affirmative action (AA) "hiring quota."

Misgivings such as this breed and reinforce resentment both in people denied job opportunities simply because they are not members of "protected minorities" and in those "targeted minority" group members about whom sexual or racial inferiority is presumed (the presumption that leads to the job discrimination that the AA "quota system" is assumed to redress).

> **Example:** These doubts feed a syndrome of declining workplace morale, initiative, and productivity and of increasing absenteeism, job restriction, and production costs. The end effect of all this is the inevitable (and predictable) deterioration in comparative advantage in the dynamic, competitive, international business environment.

See also affirmative action/equal opportunity/pay equity.

direct exporting refers to all the activities involving the sale and transmittal of goods directly from exporter to importer.

Direct exporting does not exist where any intermediary takes title to the goods for reprocessing, repackaging, consolidation/deconsolidation, transshipment, and/or warehousing for the purpose of resale.

> **Example:** The American company claimed it was direct exporting tools to its Canadian subsidiary. The Canadians were, in turn, reselling the imports to

Cuba, something disallowed to U.S. firms under the Trading with the Enemy Act.

The U.S. government tried to obtain an injunction against what it claimed were direct exports using indirect means to purposely evade the law. It claimed the American firm had prior knowledge of the resale to an "enemy" country. The firm resisted the claim, stating that to the best of its knowledge, all its exports were direct exports to Canadian end-users. It denied prior knowledge of any resale to Cuba, and it insisted its subsidiaries were autonomous in terms of those to whom they direct exported.

Cf. indirect exporting.

direct investment, often termed *foreign direct investment* or *international direct investment*, is the capital flow into a country by private individuals and corporations who retain ownership over the use of the invested capital.

In Canada, the term used to denote these capital flows is *foreign investment*.

See also Foreign Investment Review Agency; Investment Canada.

dirigisme, from the French meaning "planning," connotes the heavy hand of government, and especially government bureaucracy, in the organizing and control of a country's macroeconomic domestic policies, as well as in its trade policy.

A country that is highly *dirigiste* is a "planned economy," such as a command socialist political economy, as opposed to a free-market economy (e.g., the United States and Canada).

In domestic economic activities, a government that reduces its *dirigisme* engages in privatization, extricating government from involvement in various sectors (e.g., airlines: Air Canada, British Airways).

In trade policy, it is suggested that the greater the scope and span of *dirigisme* in a political economy, the greater the level of protectionism. Thus, it is somewhat ironic that with the accelerating drive toward full European monetary and economic integration, as the 1992 target date approaches, internal European *dirigisme* continues to decline dramatically while outward-oriented *dirigiste* policies and behaviors fail to decelerate.

The same cannot be said for the traditional Japanese *dirigiste* industrial strategy, which hopefully may be undergoing modification as a result of the U.S.-Japan Structural Impediments Initiative (SII).

See also Common Agricultural Policy; Structural Impediments Initiative.

dirty cargo is a commodity classification used in international physical distribution and logistics (PD/L) that refers to any goods that are in an unclean or unsanitary condition and that are transported either as bulk cargo or as cargo in containers with disposable linings.

Examples of dirty cargo are wet hides, manure, animal bones, and animal skins.

Cf. commodity.

dirty float *See* Appendix II.

dirty floating *See* Appendix II.

dirty money is the financial proceeds of illegal and/or dubious international business transactions.

There are two distinct classes of dirty money: (1) "black money" and (2) "gray money."

1. *Black money* is wealth generated from criminal activities such as *narcotrafico*.
2. *Gray money* is wealth generated as the proceeds of dubious business transactions. These include the "laundering" of black money, the evasion of currency control laws in countries that control foreign exchange, and the generating of tax-free profits in offshore tax havens.

Cf. black market; gray market; *delincuencia organizada.*
See also offshore banking.

DISC *See* Domestic International Sales Corporation.

discounting is the act of reducing the value of a negotiable instrument offered for sale.

See also purchase of drawings under a documentary credit.

discounting of accepted bills of exchange *See* purchase of drawings under a documentary credit.

discounting of drawings under a letter of credit *See* purchase of drawings under a documentary credit.

dispute-settlement system refers to institutional provisions in an international trade agreement consisting of rules and procedures mutually agreed on, whereby differences and disagreements between the contracting parties can be reconciled peacefully.

There are two types of dispute-settlement mechanisms: (1) the binational dispute-settlement mechanism and (2) the GATT dispute-settlement system.

1. *Binational Dispute-Settlement Mechanism:* this is a system for the reconciliation of trade disputes between two parties (that is, two states) that have entered into a trade agreement, formalized in a treaty. The dispute-settlement mechanism is invariably enshrined in the treaty, and both parties are bound by it.
2. *General Agreement on Tariffs and Trade (GATT) Dispute-Settlement System:* this is an arrangement for the reconciliation of trade disputes between two or more Contracting Parties to GATT.

Where Contracting Parties have no formal trade treaty governing their actions or no binational dispute-settlement mechanism, the GATT dispute settlement process is available to them.

Usually, even states that have signed trade treaties bind themselves to behave in ways that are GATT-consistent, thus giving GATT supranational legal authority where international trade is concerned.

See also binational dispute-settlement mechanism (of the FTA); GATT dispute-settlement system.

distributor is a foreign-based enterprise that works under contract for an exporter in the offshore target market. The distributor imports directly from the exporter and, where required, performs the marketing functions of sales, service, promotion, and distribution (e.g., opening new dealerships). Where a distributor has exclusivity of product lines and/or sales territories, it is called an "exclusive" distributor.

Cf. dealer.

DOA (documents on acceptance) is a method of payment for exports whereby the documents transferring title to the goods are released on the acceptance by the importer of the obligation to pay the time draft.

Cf. D/A sight draft; D/P draft.

See also documentary draft; documentary collection.

dock receipt is documentary evidence given for a shipment received at a designated wharf, pier, or quay.

When delivery is complete, the "ticket," as it is sometimes called, is endorsed by an authorized member of the carrier of the goods, then handed over to the operator of the vessel or the operator's agent. The document now serves as a basis for the preparation of the bill of lading by the carrier.

See also bill of lading.

documentary collection is a term referring to the means of export financing in which specific documents are used to effect payment.

The documents consist of a bill of exchange (draft) drawn on the importer accompanied by commercial documents (e.g., bill of lading, insurance certificate, export invoice). When drafts are unaccompanied by commercial documents, the process is called a "clean collection."

If the draft is drawn at sight, the exporter is paid when the importer receives the documents.

If the draft is a term draft, the exporter is paid on the maturity date of the draft, and documents are released to the importer against acceptance of the obligation to pay.

See also D/A sight draft; D/P draft; bill of exchange; collections; draft; export financing.

documentary credit is an instrument issued by a bank at the request of an importer in favor of an exporter.

When a bank opens this credit, it (1) accepts the obligation for payment, (2) assumes all the risks involved with nonperformance of the exporter, and (3) accepts the responsibility to collect payment from the importer on whose behalf it extended the credit.

There are two major types of documentary credits: (1) sight documentary credits and (2) term documentary credits.

1. *Sight Documentary Credits:* this documentary credit calls for a sight draft (also called a sight documentary draft). This means the exporter is entitled to be paid at sight (i.e., to be paid upon presentation to the bank of the financial instrument plus documents).
2. *Term Documentary Credits:* this documentary credit calls for a term draft (also called a term documentary draft). This means that the documentary credit permits payments over time, and the term draft is permitted to be drawn (paid) over the time periods specified in the credit (e.g., 30, 60, 90 days, or longer).

This credit instrument is formally referred to as a *commercial letter of credit*. In international marketing and financial parlance, it is simply called a *letter of credit*.

Cf. letter of credit; confirmed letter of credit; irrevocable letter of credit; documentary draft.
See also export financing.

documentary draft, colloquially called a *bill of exchange*, or simply a *draft*, is a financial instrument against which payment is made by a bank only when accompanied by supporting documents (e.g., bill of lading, export invoice, customs invoice, insurance certificate).

There are two major types of documentary drafts: (1) sight documentary drafts and (2) term documentary drafts.

1. *Sight Documentary Drafts:* these financial instruments require immediate payment when accompanied by the sight documentary credit plus supporting documents and presented to a bank by the exporter.
2. *Term Documentary Drafts:* these financial instruments permit payments to be made (drawn) after presentation, over the time periods specified in the term credit (e.g., 30, 60, 90 days, or longer), when presented to a bank with the term documentary credit plus supporting documents by the exporter.

See also bill of exchange; draft.

dollar, from the Low German *daler* meaning "dollar," is a currency of the following countries: Australia, Bahamas, Barbados, Bermuda, Canada, Hong Kong, Jamaica, New Zealand, Singapore, Taiwan, Trinidad and Tobago, and the United States. First minted in Sankt Joachimsthal, Bavaria, the *daler* was originally called the *Joachimsthaler*.

In each country, the dollar currency is issued exclusively by the nation's central bank. In the United States, Canada, and Germany these are the U.S. Federal Reserve System, the Bank of Canada, and the Bundesbank, respectively.

The dollar is represented in written form by the dollar sign, which is the currency symbol "$."

Example: The "$" has been borrowed by countries such as Mexico to represent their own national currencies. One hundred Mexican pesos is written $100.

dollar glut is any excess supply of U.S. dollars in the hands of foreign monetary authorities outside the United States.

dollar overhang is the large amount of U.S. dollars held by foreigners (mainly foreign financial institutions) as a result of past deficits in the balance of payments by the United States.

 The movement of these massive amounts of U.S. dollars from one monetary center to another (e.g., from London to Tokyo) results in exchange rate fluctuations of considerable magnitude, which in turn affect decisions regarding direct investment.

dollar standard is the system under which the U.S. dollar remained an international reserve currency without any gold backing.

 (The accord that formed the basis of the system was called the Smithsonian Agreement.)

 Cf. Bretton Woods System.

domestic agent middleman *See* manufacturer's export agent.

domestication is the gradual transfer to foreign nationals (by international and global companies) of domestic capital assets (e.g., property, technology, installations) and intellectual property (e.g., patents, processes).

> **Example:** To enhance its energy self-sufficiency policy, the Canadian government slowly purchased the assets of British Petroleum (refining) and Petrofina (distribution) and consolidated them in a new Crown Corporation (parastate agency) called Petro-Canada.
>
> The domestication of the petroleum industry in Canada was aimed at making the country self-sufficient in petroleum, oil, and lubricants, not at reducing, hindering, or obstructing trade in these goods with the United States.

 Cf. confiscation; expropriation; nationalization.

domestic content requirements (DCR) is the demand that goods must contain a certain percentage of national content by way of domestic factors of production, namely, land, labor, and capital.

 DCRs are sometimes cited as a type of nontariff barrier.

> **Example:** To qualify for deferred taxation on profits and for training grants for upgrading labor, the Canadian government insisted that the machine parts produced for export by the Japanese company resident in Vancouver contain no less than 60 percent Canadian content of materials and labor.

 Cf. nontariff barriers.
 See also investment performance requirements.

domestic debt refers to financial obligations owed by the citizens of a country to other citizens of that same country, payable in the currency of that country.

 The costs of servicing this debt are a domestic transfer between national borrowers and national lenders.

 Cf. external debt.

Domestic International Sales Corporation (DISC) is a type of special U.S. corporation as authorized by the U.S. Tax Revenue Act of 1971 and as amended by the Tax Reform Act of 1984.

This legislation was intended to stimulate exports by reducing the effective tax rate on export income. The legislation also permitted exporters to borrow from the U.S. Treasury at reduced rates of interest.

To qualify, the DISC had to derive 95 percent of its gross income from exports, and it was required neither to operate independently of a parent corporation nor to maintain sales facilities outside the United States.

There neither was, nor is, any Canadian legislation equivalent to U.S. DISC-empowering laws.

The DISC, which was extremely popular in the 1970s, has been largely displaced by the U.S. Foreign Sales Corporation (FSC), which provides lucrative export sales and profit incentives to U.S. firms.

See also Foreign Sales Corporation.

domestic value-added is the market price of the final good, *minus* the cost of the imported inputs that went into the production of the good.

Cf. value-added tax.

douane, from the French meaning "customs," is a place (e.g., customs post) or a duty.

Exempt de douane means "duty free." *Soumis à la douane* means "submitted to duty."

Thus, a customs officer in French is *un douanier* (male) or *une douanière* (female).

See also customs.

double-stack container train (DST) is a train that, by virtue of the fact it carries containers in a "stacked configuration" (instead of the more conventional arrangements of trailer-on-flat-car (TOFC) and container-on-flat-car (COFC)) doubles the freight-carrying capacity of rail cars.

> **Example:** In Canada, both the Canadian National Railway (CNR) and the Canadian Pacific Railway (CPR) originally postponed the introduction of DSTs because heavier containers are used in Canada *vis-à-vis* the United States and because Canada has relatively lower traffic volume routes.
>
> However, as of 1989, the CNR had begun a DST service from Vancouver to Toronto, and they are considering a similar service from Halifax to Central Canada.
>
> *See also* piggyback.

down-stream pricing •NW• refers to the process of establishing a market value for goods that are derived from, or produced as by-products of, primary commodities.

International marketers who control down-stream pricing have more control over the price of the original commodity (from which the by-products are derived) than the owners of the original commodity.

Example: Anglo-American soap manufacturers have more control over the world price of coconuts than those countries who are members of the Asian and Pacific Coconut Community (APCC) and who produce the coconuts from which the oil is used to manufacture the soap.

Cf. up-stream pricing •NW•.
See also commodity.

D/P draft (**d**ocuments (against) **p**ayment) refers to a method of payment for exports whereby the documents transferring title to the goods are released only after the importer has paid the value of the draft issued against him or her.
Cf. D/A draft; DOA.
See also documentary draft; documentary collection.

draft is a financial instrument drawn on the importer's bank that requires payment to the bearer.
See also documentary draft; bill of exchange.

draught, from the Old German *dragan* meaning "draw," is the British-Canadian English (BCE) variation of *draft*.

drawback is a colloquial variation of *duty drawback*.

drawee is the party, usually the importer, against whom a draft is drawn and who is responsible for honoring, or paying, the draft.

drawer is the party, usually the exporter, who originates, or draws, the draft that requests payment.

dumping is the act of exporting goods for sale in a country below the normal market price of the goods in the domestic market of the exporter.
See also less than fair value; predatory dumping; persistent dumping; sporadic dumping; antidumping duty.

duty is a tax or tariff imposed by the customs authority of a nation on goods moving either into or out of that nation.
When the charge is levied on a nation's exports, it is an export levy; and when the tax is added to goods imported into a nation, it is an import duty. The term *tariff* is equivalent to *duty*, and when the two are used interchangeably within the same context, they have identical meaning. The use of a tariff gives rise to important and quantifiable economic outcomes, such as the consumption effect of a tariff, the production effect, the revenue effect, and the trade effect.
Cf. nontariff barriers; surcharge.
See also ad valorem duty; antidumping duty; compound duty; countervailing duty; mixed tariff; optimum tariff; prohibitive tariff; punitive tariff; specific duty; end-use tariff; scientific tariff; consumption effect of a tariff; production effect of a tariff; revenue effect of a tariff; trade effect of a tariff.

duty drawback, also referred to colloquially as *drawback*, is a refund to the original importer of an import duty levied on the goods of that importer, when the goods originally imported are further processed and then re-exported.

> **Example:** The Canadian Chainsaw Company imported 500 pistons from Detroit. All these parts were subject to a specific duty of 25 percent. The company could claim a drawback of the duty paid only on the 425 of them that were chromed, assembled into powerheads, and re-exported to the United States. No duty drawback could be claimed on the remaining 75 that were sold in Canada.

> Cf. duty remission.
> *See also* Customs Tariff Act.

duty free port (DFP) *See* foreign trade zone.

duty free shop *See* foreign trade zone.

duty free zone (DFZ) *See* foreign trade zone.

duty remission is a refund of an import duty to an importer by the government that originally levied it contingent upon the importer engaging in export production and, thereby, creating employment and tax revenue.

Thus, a duty remission program is a government-originated incentive plan to stimulate specific industrial growth and exports.

Under this definition, any duty remission program would be an unfair trade practice since it is designed for export targeting under the Omnibus Trade Act of 1988.

> **Example:** The Canadian government introduced a duty remission scheme involving export-oriented growth incentives for the Canadian high-tech industry and countries of the Association of Southeast Asian Nations (ASEAN). All imports into Canada of "scheduled" electronic components from ASEAN would qualify for duty remission provided that finished goods (containing the "scheduled" imports) were exported to ASEAN.

> Cf. duty drawback.
> *See also* Customs Tariff Act.

D.V.1 (Declaration of Particulars Relating to Customs Value) *See* Single Administrative Document.

e

East African Economic Community (EAEC), also known as the *East African Customs Union* and the *East African Community*, was a customs union established in 1967, comprising Kenya, Uganda, and Tanzania. The EAEC dissolved in 1978 after serious political dissension and open hostilities in the region between Tanzania and Uganda.

> Cf. Preferential Trade Area for Eastern and Southern African States.
> *See also* Appendix V (A).

East Asian Economic Grouping (EAEG) refers to a proposal made by Malaysian Prime Minister Mahathir Mohammed in December 1990 to found a new trade association comprising (1) the six members of the Association of Southeast Asian Nations (ASEAN)—Brunei, Indonesia, Malaysia, the Philippines, Singapore, and Thailand; (2) China, Taiwan, Hong Kong, South Korea, Vietnam, and Myanmar (formerly Burma); and (3) Japan, which has not yet assented to membership.

The idea to form EAEG seems to have originated in resentment (by Malaysia and perhaps by other Third World countries) of their perceived victimization by unfair trading practices and by structural discrimination in world trade. Malaysia's chief hard-currency export, palm oil, has been countervailed by the United States and Europe, and blocked by anti-cholesterol awareness movements that successfully lobbied Western governments. Malaysia's lucrative timber-export business, like that in Brazil, has been turned into an environmental issue by holier-than-thou Westerners.

The six ASEAN countries are already members of the Asia-Pacific Economic Cooperation Group (APEC), initiated in 1989 by Australia, which also dominates the Cairns Group. Japan and New Zealand·are also ASEAN members, as are Canada and the United States, the two Pacific-boundary nonregional members.

Even if Japan does opt for membership, the EAEG does not appear to have good prospects for success. The reasons are varied. First of all, the new regional bloc would be dwarfed by both the European Economic Community (EEC) and the United States in terms of purchasing power. Secondly, many of EAEG's members have dubious long-range prospects. For example, Vietnam is an impoverished nonmarket economy. China's potential for political instability, anathema to foreign investment and trade, is infinite. Hong Kong's survival as a cosmopolitan banking and trading center after 1997 (when China takes it over) is in genuine doubt. Finally, in terms of Japan's enormous long range potential, a truly multilateral, worldwide, open trading system under the General Agreement on Tariffs and Trade (GATT) would be to Japan's advantage rather than a range of regional blocs whose long-term survival is far less certain.

See also Asia-Pacific Economic Cooperation Group; Association of Southeast Asian Nations; Cairns Group; regionalization of trade.

Eastern and Southern African Trade and Development Bank is the official name of the bank for the Preferential Trade Area (PTA) of Eastern and Southern African States.

EC 92 is a colloquial variation of *Europe 1992*.

Economic Community of Great Lakes Countries (ECGC), officially, *Communauté Économique des Pays des Grands Lacs (CEPGL)*, is an international organization (with a regional focus) whose purpose is to foster cooperation in economics and political matters among member countries.

Through its Multinational Programming and Operational Center (MULPOC), the organization selects sectors (e.g., transportation) for project development and works closely with international agencies such as the U.N. Economic Commission for Africa (UN/ECA) to implement them.

Established in Rwanda in 1976, the membership comprises Burundi, Rwanda, and Zaire. Headquarters are in Gisenyi, Rwanda.

See also Appendix V (B); U.N. Economic Commission for Africa.

Economic Community of West African States (ECOWAS), also known as the *Economic Community of West Africa* (ECWA), is a free trade area, established in 1975, comprising 16 regional members: Benin (formerly, Dahomey), Burkina Faso (formerly, Upper Volta), Cape Verde, Côte d'Ivoire, Gambia, Guinea, Guinea-Bissau, Ghana, Liberia, Mali, Mauritania, Niger, Nigeria, Sénégal, Togo, and Sierra Leone.

The ECOWAS Treaty, signed in Lagos, Nigeria, was the culmination of work under the auspices of the Organization of African Unity (OAU) to forge a unified, economic, integrated organization among francophone and anglophone West African states. The success of the (French-speaking) West African Economic Community was, together with the Declaration on African Cooperation, Development, and Economic Independence at the OAU meeting in Addis Ababa in 1973, sufficient incentive for African heads of state to found ECOWAS.

The objective of ECOWAS is to establish a common market among its members. To achieve this, ECOWAS is working toward the following goals:

1. the elimination of all customs duties, tariffs, and nontariff barriers within the Community;

2. the establishment of a common external tariff (CXT) and common trade policies with non-Community members;
3. the harmonization of all economic planning in all economic sectors and the coordination (and eventual harmonization) of all industrial, monetary, and financial policies within the Community.

ECOWAS has close links with the West African Economic Community (WAEC), the Entente Council, and other regional international trading groups, such as the Andean Common Market (ANCOM) and the European Economic Community (EEC).

See also harmonization; West African Economic Community; Entente Council; Appendix V (A).

economic integration is the policy and practice of actively working to harmonize the differing national commercial procedures and laws and to progressively reduce (and ultimately eliminate) trade barriers among countries that come together to form larger trading blocs.

It is suggested that harmonization itself acts as an incentive for more integrated economic activity and for economic bloc-building.

See also harmonization; common market.

economic-monetary union *See* EMU.

economic nationalism refers to ethnocentric attitudes, behaviors, and especially political-economic policies that involve an overweening preoccupation with, and over-valuation of, domestic economic issues (e.g., ownership and concentration of capital, commercial policy, and market access by foreigners).

The aim of its proponents, who are usually the society's economic élite, is to wield the levers of protectionism, initially to restrict foreign imports and secondarily to block market access by foreigners, all in the name of "guarding national interests against foreign influences."

In an extreme form, economic nationalism becomes isolation, otherwise called autarky.

Economic nationalism was the bedrock of Canada's National Policy under Sir John A. Macdonald (in the late nineteenth century): high tariff walls were erected to keep out direct U.S. exports and to "protect" Canadian infant industries; but the same high tariffs were calculated to act as an incentive to attract U.S. subsidiaries to found permanent factories in Canada.

Cf. autarky.
See also infant industry.

economic union is an agreement among sovereign states to form a trading bloc in which

1. all barriers to trade among the members will eventually be removed;
2. trade policies among the members will be harmonized toward the rest of the world;

3. the movement among members of labor and capital will be free (i.e., without impediment); and
4. the monetary, fiscal, and tax policies of members will be brought into alignment and unified.
Cf. common market; political union; free trade area; customs union.
See also harmonize.

Edge Corporation, also called an *Agreement Corporation*, is a U.S. bank branch or a subsidiary of a U.S. corporation established for the sole purpose of engaging in international banking activities.

The U.S. banking authorities, as of 1981, authorized U.S. banks to establish Edge Corporations as a competitive tool against non-U.S. international banking centers (IBCs). Specifically, the Edge Corporation is exempt from domestic U.S. banking and competition legislation regarding pricing and restrictive trade practice behavior.

See also international financial centers.

education allowance *See* benefit allowance.

EEC (EC) is the abbreviation for European Economic Community.

EEC-EFTA linkage refers to the 1972 accord between the (then 10, now 12) members of the European Economic Community (EEC) and the 6 members of the European Free Trade Association (EFTA).

This agreement effectively formed one, single, European, free trade area. International agreements were signed between the EEC and each of the members of EFTA providing for reducing tariffs and nontariff measures on manufactured goods. The agreements also provided for some reciprocal concessions on agricultural commodities.

See also European Economic Space; reciprocity.

effective access *See* reciprocity.

effective exchange rate *See* Appendix II.

effective market access *See* effective access.

effective rate of protection is the actual percentage by which domestic prices of goods are protected by tariffs to increase their costs to consumers, so as to dissuade them from purchasing cheaper, imported goods.

It is argued that the effective rate of protection also protects domestic manufacturers who supply imported inputs to the main manufacturer (and whose imports are subject to the tariff). There is derived protection as well for the domestic jobs saved because of the tariff.

While these arguments in favor of the protective tariff are rational, they are not in consonance with the practice of free trade. Furthermore, the jobs saved and the industries protected are inefficient tariff effects, achieved at the expense of efficient, low-cost production.

The "classical formula" for the effective rate of protection (*g*) is:

$$g = \frac{V_1 - V}{V}$$

where V_1 is the value *after* the tariff is applied and V is the value added *before* the tariff is applied.

The formula is derived from the typical calculations that follow to illustrate the effective rate of protection:

Step 1: Foreign Production for Domestic Consumption

	Export selling price/unit for good "X"	$200.00
minus	Production cost/unit for good "X"	–120.00
equals	Value-added in world prices for good "X"	$ 80.00

Step 2: Addition of Tariff of 10 Percent

	Export selling price/unit for good "X"	$200.00
plus	10-percent tariff imposed on import good "X"	+ 20.00
equals	Increased price to domestic buyers of good "X"	$220.00

Step 3: Calculation of Effective Rate of Protection

	New domestic price after tariff "protection"	$220.00
minus	Production cost/unit for good "X"	–120.00
equals	New value-added (in domestic prices)	$100.00
minus	Value-added in world prices	– 80.00
equals	Difference in value-added due to tariff cost	$ 20.00
divided by	Value-added in world prices	$\dfrac{20.00}{80.00} = 25\%$
equals	Effective Rate of Protection	
compared to	Nominal Rate of Protection	$\dfrac{20.00}{200.00} = 10\%$

Cf. nominal rate of protection.

See also production effect of a tariff; consumption effect of a tariff; protectionism; infant industry argument; Generalized System of Preferences.

efficiency of foreign exchange markets *See* Appendix II.

EFTA is the abbreviation for European Free Trade Association.

embargo, often referred to as *trade sanctions,* or simply as *sanctions,* is (1) a government ban on exports or imports, usually issued during (but not restricted to) wartime, with respect to specific products, specific modes of transport, and/or specific countries; or (2) any law that forbids trade in specific goods and/or via specific modes of transport and/or with specific countries.

Example: The United Nations arms embargo against South Africa requires all signatory nations to ban not only direct sales but also to prohibit any shipments using vessels registered in their countries or any transshipments via their ports.

Embargoes are (often barely) involuntary, in that failure to comply with them may result in outcomes legitimated by the authority that invoked them.

Example: The Arab embargo against all trade with Israel (known as the Arab Boycott) permits any Arab country to legally seize the assets of a resident foreign company upon discovery that the company has traded with Israel.

Example: The United Nations failed to adopt overall trade sanctions against South Africa, but it did succeed in having a Resolution on an arms embargo passed by a two-thirds majority of the General Assembly, to which Canada was a signatory.

Cf. boycott.
See also Appendix VI (sanction); Arab Boycott of Israel.

EMU (**e**conomic-**m**onetary **u**nion) refers to the (anticipated) successful integrated outcome of Europe's attempts to integrate itself economically, monetarily, and commercially by 1992.
See also Europe 1992.

end-of-contract gratuity *See* benefit gratuity.

end-use certificate is an official Canadian government "control document" that is issued to importers and designates the specific end-use of the goods being imported.

Example: End-use certificates, issued by the Canadian Grain Commission under the provisions of the Canada Grain Act, stipulate that a shipment of oats must be used at the processing facility to which it is sent and that it must be denatured so that it does not enter the human end-use grain-marketing system.

end-use tariff is the duty rate used to classify an item dependent upon the use to which the imported good is put.

Example: Books imported into Canada for use in schools, colleges, and universities have always been subject to a lower end-use tariff than books imported for straight commercial resale.

Cf. ad valorem duty; antidumping duty; compound duty; countervailing duty; specific duty; optimum tariff; prohibitive tariff.
See also duty.

Entente Council, also known as *Conseil de l'Entente,* is an international association whose purpose is to promote the enhancement of peaceful, harmonized relations in mutually important matters of economic and political interest to member countries via the Council's Solidarity Fund and its Mutual Aid and Loan Guarantee Fund, two vehicles for mobilizing financing to promote economic growth in the region.

Established in 1959 in Abidjan, Côte d'Ivoire, the group comprises Benin, Burkina Faso, Côte d'Ivoire, Niger, and Togo.

See also Appendix V (B).

Enterprise for the Americas Initiative (EAI) refers to the announcement by the U.S. government in June 1990 that the Executive branch of the federal government would, through legislation-empowering negotiation, seek the creation of a Western hemisphere-wide free trade area (a "megamarket" FTA) comprising North America and South America.

The Administration's initiative involves plans to negotiate agreements that cover trade and investment with countries on the Latin America mainland and in the Caribbean. (Such negotiations have begun with Mexico.) The short-term aim of the United States is to forge a free trade agreement (FTA) with Mexico by 1994 to provide reciprocal access to each other's markets, akin to the market access successfully negotiated between the United States and Canada under the Canada-U.S. Free Trade Agreement of 1989.

Cf. Caribbean Basin Initiative; Puerto Rican Model; Canada-U.S. Free Trade Agreement of 1989; North American Free Trade Agreement.

See also free trade area; customs union.

entrepôt trade, from the French meaning "warehouse," is the business of re-exporting (i.e., importing goods for the purpose of processing or reprocessing them and/or repackaging them, exclusively for export).

These activities frequently involve consolidation, deconsolidation, and transshipment.

EPRG [framework] (**e**thnocentrism, **p**olycentrism, **r**egiocentrism, **g**lobalism) is a conceptual outline of the stages of international involvement through which a company moves in the progression from commerce exclusively within the company's home country to trade with the world.

These states are depicted as follows:

1. *Ethnocentrism:* commerce exclusively within one's home country.
2. *Polycentrism:* commercial orientation to the needs of individual markets within the host country or within a region, excluding regional commonalities.
3. *Regiocentrism:* commercial orientation to the needs of regional markets, recognizing and accepting regional commonalities.
4. *Globalism:* commercial orientation on a world basis, ignoring regional commonalities, sourcing the least expensive production factors worldwide, and marketing a standardized product.

equitable treatment is a type of friendship, commerce, and navigation (FCN) treaty whereby laws and regulations that govern marketing of domestic goods in each signatory country are applied in a reasonable way in accordance with international law and the Principles of International Trade under the General Agreement on Tariffs and Trade (GATT) to all goods otherwise denoted as "foreign" or "imported."

See also Appendix VI (friendship, commerce, and navigation (FCN) treaty).

equivalence of advantages *See* reciprocity.

equivalent access *See* reciprocity.

equivalent treatment *See* reciprocity.

escape clause is a section in a commercial agreement (provided for in Article XIX of the General Agreement on Tariffs and Trade) permitting a signatory nation to "suspend tariffs" (or other concessions) when imports threaten to (or actually) cause serious material injury to domestic producers of goods competitive to those imported.

In the United States, the "suspending of tariffs" begins when the U.S. International Trade Commission (USITC) responds to an industry petition that it is being injured by imports. The USITC investigates and recommends tariff suspension to the president, who responds by executing the tariff suspension.

This may be done, for example, under the authority granted the U.S. president by the Omnibus Trade Act of 1988.

In Canada, tariff suspension is carried out by an Order in Council (from the government), which is a response to Sectoral Advisory Committee recommendations on behalf of petitions by an industry claiming injury due to competitive imports.

In both countries, committees of the legislative branches of government (i.e., House and Senate Committees in the United States and in Canada) may investigate the decision of the executive branch prior to legislative approval, which must ultimately be sought (and granted) for the tariff suspension.

See also safeguards; Trade Reform Act of 1974; General Agreement on Tariffs and Trade; tariff suspension.

establishment *See* right of establishment.

ethnocentrism (ethnocentric), from the Greek *ethnos* meaning "nation" and *kentrikos* meaning "center," refers to (1) the over-valuing of one's own culture, placing it at the center of one's world view and using it as the yardstick with which to measure others; (2) the preoccupation with domestic commerce to the exclusion of interest and involvement in trading outside of one's home country.

See also EPRG [framework].

ethnographic, from the Greek *ethnos* meaning "nation" and *graphos* meaning "writing," refers to a description of different groups of people who have varying national allegiances.
    See also ethnostructure •NW•.

ethnostructure •NW•, condensation of *ethnographic* and *structure*, refers to a description of the number, variety, residence, mobility, and other germane facts about the relations among people who live in a country but who have differing national allegiances.
    See also multiculturalism.

EUR 1 Form is a document that must be filled out by African, Caribbean, and Pacific (ACP) countries that are members of the Lomé Convention for all their exports to the European Economic Community (EEC) in order to qualify for preferential duties.
    See also Lomé Convention.

Eurobond *See* Appendix I.

Eurocommercial paper *See* Appendix I.

Eurocurrency *See* Appendix I.

Eurocurrency deposit *See* Appendix I.

Eurodollar deposits *See* Appendix I.

Eurodollars *See* Appendix I.

Eurolira *See* Appendix I.

Euromarkets began as (1) locations in Western Europe in general (e.g., Zurich) and in the European Economic Community (EEC) in particular (e.g., London, Frankfurt) where currencies are bought and sold both on a spot and on a forward basis; and expanded to be (2) locations in international financial centers anywhere in the world where Eurocurrencies are traded.
    See also Appendix I; Appendix II.

Euromarks *See* Appendix I.

Euronotes *See* Appendix I.

Europe 1992, or, in the colloquial form, "Europe '92," refers to

    1. the concept that the achievement of a single, integrated, economic union of European states, represented by the European Economic Community (EEC), would be completed by the year 1992;

As European economic integration has moved from the Treaty of Rome (1957) to the EEC White Paper on "Completing the Internal Market" (1985), explicit mention was made in the latter document of achieving by 1992 an area without internal frontiers in which the free movement of goods, services, persons, and capital is ensured. The Single European Act (1987) reaffirmed the date, as did the Delors Report (June 1989).

2. an idea promoted in the United States and Canada that, come 1992, an economic fortress Europe will have been erected that will be virtually impregnable behind unassailably high, common exclusionary tariff walls unless and until the North American private sector takes the initiative to forge international corporate alliances with European enterprise.

See also Delors Report; Single European Act; global alliancing •NW•.

European Bank for Reconstruction and Development (EBRD), also known by its official French name, *La Banque européenne de Reconstruction et Développement (BERD),* and colloquially as *The European Bank,* is a permanent financial institution of the European Economic Community (EEC) established in Paris in mid-January 1990 originally by the 12 members of the EEC, 8 East European states, and 14 other developed countries.

On April 5, 1991, the EBRD (now operating from headquarters in London) opened its doors. Its inaugural ceremony was held at the London-based headquarters of the International Maritime Organization (IMO) and was attended by 30 nations.

The original goal of the EBRD was to generate development credits (i.e., concessional financing) for productive investment by the private sector in the emerging democracies in East Europe. Subsequently, the EBRD was structured from a combination of development and commercial banks. With initial capital of $12 billion, it plans to channel 60 percent of its financing to the private sector. It is the first international financial agency to have the Soviet Union as a charter member.

The EBRD's shareholding structure is as follows:

- 51 percent is held by the EEC (which includes the European Commission and the European Investment Bank);
- 14.2 percent is held by other non-European countries (Australia, Canada, Egypt, Japan, South Korea, Mexico, Morocco, and New Zealand);
- 11.4 percent is held by other European members (Austria, Cyprus, Finland, Iceland, Israel, Liechtenstein, Malta, Norway, Sweden, Switzerland, and Turkey);
- 10 percent is held by the United States;
- 8 percent is held by the Soviet Union;
- 5.4 percent is held by "borrowing members" (Bulgaria, Czechoslovakia, Hungary, Poland, Romania, and Yugoslavia).

The rapid, ongoing process of transforming East Europe from a nonmarket, command economy to a "mixed economy" (and ultimately, perhaps, to a purely "private economy") is a process perceived by the EBRD as having long-range potential. As a target market, East Europe is significant in size but lacks the capital production base and the distribution infrastructure for the rapid diffusion of Western marketing processes. Depending on the pace of political liberalization and ensuing privatization in East Europe as well as the political risks assessed as part of the process, the EBRD expects to lend East Europe no more than $200 million to $300 million in 1991, raising the amount to at least $1 billion by 1996. It is worth noting that upon the insistence of the United States, the Soviet Union is limited (for three years) to borrowing only the amount it contributes.

Thus the EBRD is a formal institution designed to accelerate economic industrial development in East Europe. The goal is to transform the region into an open, market economy. The next step would be to merge a unified East Europe with the European Economic Space (the union of the EEC and EFTA) to create a Pan-European economic-monetary union (EMU), incorporating the whole European continent in one "Grand European Unification." This has been the political aim of European statesmen from emperors like Charlemagne and Napoleon to tyrants like Hitler, and modern state-crafters like Jacques Delors.

Cf. European Free Trade Association; European Economic Space.
See also European Economic Community; European Investment Bank.

European Community (EC) is the "Euroterm" for the *European Economic Community (EEC)*.

European Community of Research and Technology (ECRT) are framework programs derived from the Single European Act (of 1987) whereby European Economic Community (EEC) member countries would concentrate on research and technology (R&T) cooperatively to generate the maximum beneficial outcomes to Europe in competition with the United States and Japan.

The 1987–1991 R&T Framework Program comprised the following eight fields of activity, listed with the EEC's financial allocations to each in European Currency Units (ECU).

Activity	*Million ECU*
1. Quality of Life	375
2. Information and Communications	2,275
3. Modernization of Industrial Sectors	845
4. Biological Programs	280
5. Energy	1,173
6. Science and Technology for Development	80
7. Marine Resources	80
8. European Scientific and Technical Cooperation	288
TOTAL (of all research and technology)	5,396

The above-mentioned R&T developmental activities take place in three ways:

1. *In-House Research:* this work is carried out at one of four Joint (European) Research Centers in Belgium, Germany, Italy, and the Netherlands;

2. *Shared-Cost or Contract Research:* work is carried out at European universities and research centers and in EEC-based companies, all of which are supported by EEC financial aid;

3. *Concerted-Action Projects:* these are priority, high-cost research efforts, conducted by national-level Euro-institutions, with close coordination paid by EEC funding.

The critical idea here is that the EEC has made a serious, long-term commitment to major R&T development via the framework programs. The ultimate aim of this enormous, regional concentration of brain power and financial resources is to transform the EEC into the world leader in scientific research and technology *vis-à-vis* the United States and Japan.

See also Single European Act.

European Currency Unit (ECU, Ecu) is the unit of account of the European Economic Community (EEC) as defined by the European Monetary System (EMS), based on weighted averages of the currencies of all EEC members, plus the U.S. dollar.

Example: For example, the following are the ECU's values in national currency as of December 31, 1990. The currency abbreviations used are those adopted by the International Standardization Organization (ISO):

1.	DEM	2.04
2.	GBP	0.71
3.	FRF	6.95
4.	ITL	1540.26
5.	NLG	2.30
6.	ESP	130.60
7.	BEF	42.18
8.	LUF	42.18
9.	DKK	7.88
10.	GRD	214.06
11.	IEP	0.77
12.	PTE	182.82
13.	USD	1.36

For EEC companies, using the ECU as the monetary unit of settlement has distinct advantages over any single currency. Since the ECU is the weighted average of all EEC currencies, each EEC currency is less likely to deviate against the ECU than against any individual EEC currency. The ECU is thus the EEC "currency of choice" when European importers and exporters cooperate to share the risk of exchange rate fluctuations during the course of a transaction.

See also European Monetary System; European Investment Bank; European Economic Community; European Exchange Rate Mechanism; International Standardization Organization.

European Economic Community (EEC) refers to the agreement (formalized by the Treaty of Rome in 1957) that joined Belgium, the (then) Federal Republic of Germany, France, Italy, Luxembourg, and the Netherlands into a common market in 1958 (known as the "Inner Six"); expanded to 9 with the joining of Denmark, Ireland, and the United Kingdom in 1973; to 10 with Greece in 1981; and to the current 12 with Spain and Portugal joining in 1986.

The EEC is the term normally used by North Americans. Europeans call it alternatively the European Community (EC), the Common Market, or simply The Community. With the approach of *Europe 1992*, the "Euroterm" European Community is expected to grow in popularity and increased use, eventually gaining supremacy over European Economic Community.

Cf. European Free Trade Association; Outer Seven; economic union; monetary union; political union; preferential trade area; free trade area.
See also common market; Delors Report; Single European Act.

European Economic Space (EES), also called *European Economic Area (EEA)*, is the concept that originated with the Luxembourg Declaration of 1984 that envisioned intensified cooperation between the European Economic Community (EEC) and the European Free Trade Association (EFTA), the creation of the EES, but that left it politically undefined.

In January 1989, European Economic Community (EEC) Commission president Jacques Delors called for a "more structured relationship between the EEC and EFTA." In March 1989, the Oslo Declaration promoted the "ways and means of a more structured partnership," and in December 1989, ministers from the EEC and EFTA countries agreed to begin formal negotiations to accelerate economic integration of the two communities. Negotiations began in June 1990. An anticipated completion date is the end of 1992, when it is expected that the terms of entry for EFTA countries into the EEC will be formally announced.

At some hitherto unspecified future date, a politically unified Europe with supranational institutions is likely, given the plans for "Europe 1992" and the EES. Whether this entity (called "Fortress Europe") will be preceded or followed by a "Fortress America" is purely speculative; but this discussion betrays fears of retreat into protectionism and an end to today's open and multilateral world trading system.

There is genuine uncertainty (and fear) that the outcomes of the current Uruguay Round of Multilateral Trade Negotiations (MTN) and, indeed, the entire General Agreement on Tariffs and Trade (GATT) framework will not continue to be perceived as worthwhile liberalizing mechanisms for an open, world trading system.

If this spirit wins out, regionalism will overtake globalism and, given the ultimate scarcity of all factors of production and resources, sustainable development will fail. The world economy may not be resilient enough to withstand a domino catastrophe (sometimes called the "cascade effect") of a retreat of the Trilateral Commission into regional fortresses.

Cf. European Bank for Reconstruction and Development.
See also European Economic Community; European Free Trade Association; EEC-EFTA linkage; Europe 1992; Delors Report; Single European Act.

European Exchange Rate Mechanism (ERM) is a system of fixed (though adjustable) exchange rates, which underpins the European Monetary System (EMS).

The countries participating in the ERM are Belgium, Luxembourg, Denmark, France, Germany, Ireland, Italy, the Netherlands, Spain, and the United Kingdom (which finally joined on October 8, 1990), being 10 of the 12 EEC members. Each ERM member has a central exchange rate (for its national currency) relative to the European Currency Unit (ECU). Except for the Spanish peseta, when the national currency of an ERM country fluctuates by plus or minus 2.5 percent (relative to its central rate), the country's central bank is obliged to intervene (with unlimited liability) to attempt to stabilize the currency. The pound sterling (£) has been allowed to fluctuate by up to 6 percent on either side of its bilateral "central parity rate" against other ERM currencies. This rate is £0.696 per ECU.

Each ERM currency has its own "threshold of divergence." The threshold referred to is 75 percent of the "maximum divergence spread" (being three-fourths of the limits of the currency's fluctuation); and each currency's threshold is set on the basis of a "divergence indicator." This indicator plots the relative divergence of every ERM country relative to the divergence of every other ERM currency and measured against the weighted average movement of the currencies in the ECU basket.

When monetary authorities of ERM countries agree that there are "fundamental divergences" in economic performance of the ERM members, they may recommend (to their governments and to the European Commission) that there be a "realignment" of some (or all) of the relationships of the central rates of exchange of ERM member currencies.

See also European Currency Unit; European Investment Bank; European Monetary Cooperation Fund; European Economic Community.

European Free Trade Association (EFTA) is an agreement, established by the Treaty of Stockholm in 1959 and formalized in 1960, that joined Austria, Denmark, Norway, Portugal, Sweden, Switzerland, and the United Kingdom into a free trade area. (Finland was an associate member.)

With the exit from EFTA of Denmark, Portugal, and the United Kingdom to join the EEC and with the joining of Iceland to EFTA, EFTA's membership is now six, including the associate member Finland.

Cf. common market; European Economic Community.
See also free trade area; European Economic Space.

European Investment Bank (EIB) is an institution established in 1958 under the Treaty of Rome that founded the European Economic Community (EEC).

The EIB is the financial institution for long-term lending in the EEC. Its mission is to finance industry, energy, and infrastructure projects in EEC member countries and to finance development projects in less developed countries in which EEC member countries themselves (or the EEC itself) has politico-commercial interests on a long-term basis.

The EIB transacts its affairs in all the currencies of the EEC member countries and in other transferable currencies (e.g., the Japanese yen and the

U.S. dollar). The EIB currency of account is the European Currency Unit (ECU).

Cf. European Monetary Cooperation Fund.

See also European Currency Unit; European Monetary Cooperation Fund; European Monetary System; European Economic Community; Lomé Convention (Lomé IV).

European Monetary Cooperation Fund (EMCF), an institution of the European Monetary System (EMS), was established to provide short- and medium-term balance of payments (BOP) assistance to members of the European Economic Community (EEC).

Cf. European Investment Bank.

See also European Monetary System; European Exchange Rate Mechanism; European Currency Unit; European Economic Community.

European Monetary System (EMS) is the organization formed in 1979 by the members of the European Economic Community (EEC) in line with the policy of harmonization of all rules and regulations aimed at the reduction (and eventual elimination) of all barriers to trade in goods and services in the EEC.

The EMS is based on the creation of the European Currency Unit (ECU) and the European Exchange Rate Mechanism (ERM) and on the formation of the European Monetary Fund (EMF), the European Investment Bank (EIB), and the European Monetary Cooperation Fund (EMCF).

The following were the development phases of the EMS:

1. *March 1979–March 1983:* the system was started up, and countries were oriented toward working within it;
2. *March 1983–1987:* the system aimed at internal monetary stability; the German mark (DEM) emerged as the "anchor currency" of the EMS.
3. *September 1987:* based on the Basel/Nyborg Agreement, EEC banks began using the short-term EMS financing facility for intervention.
4. *May 1986:* after the Single European Act was adopted, the EEC Commission proposed a timetable for liberalization of capital movements.
5. *June 1988:* the EEC Council of Ministers directed most EEC countries to liberalize their capital movements completely by July 1, 1990; Greece, Ireland, Portugal, and Spain were permitted deferment of liberalization.
6. *April 1989:* the Delors Report set out a strategy for complete economic-monetary union (EMU), especially establishing the European System of Central Banks (ESCB) and the adoption of a single currency.
7. *December 1989:* the EEC Commission issued the "Second Banking Directive" that allowed centralized governance of the authority over credit/financial institutions in the EEC.

By July 1990, most EEC members had liberalized all capital movements.

See also Delors Report; Single European Act; economic-monetary union; European Currency Unit; European Exchange Rate Mechanism; European Investment Bank; European Monetary Cooperation Fund; European Economic Community.

European Organization for Testing and Certification (EOTC) is a technical body of the European Economic Community (EEC) intended to be the technical support arm for the unified European community.

The EOTC was formed in Brussels in April 1990. Its activity consists of supervising product testing and certification in the EEC and in the European Free Trade Association (EFTA). The EOTC comprises 45 technical experts from industry, labor, and consumer groups, the EEC, and the EFTA. These people oversee the work of the EEC's private testing organizations: (1) the European Committee for Standardization (CEN); (2) the European Committee for Electrotechnical Standardization (CENELEC); (3) the European Telecommunications Standards Institute (ETSI); and (4) the European Quality System (EQS).

The EEC is determined to improve the process for developing "European Standards." On October 8, 1990, it issued its now famous "Green Paper on Standards." This is a contentious document, and it recommends a number of things to the European Commission that will prove to be impediments to smooth international cooperation.

The Green Paper

1. urges the formation of closer ties with East Europe;
2. discourages informal participation by non-European countries in the work of European standards bodies;
3. recommends EEC standards be promoted outside of the EEC and EFTA;
4. suggests extending technical assistance to non-European regional trade associations (e.g., ASEAN, ANCOM) and to countries in Africa, Asia, and Latin America to enable them to adopt European standards; and
5. suggests that only work not related to EEC product standardization be referred to international standards bodies (i.e., the International Standards Organization).

One can only deduce that the EEC's drive for paramountcy in this field means that the United States and Japan (as well as every other non-European member of the Organization of Economic Cooperation and Development) should be expected to subordinate their interests to European interests and, thus, should adopt European product standards and European certification. This approach does not bode well for peaceful international cooperation between the partners of the Trilateral Commission.

See also regionalization.

European snake, also called *the snake* and *the snake in the tunnel*, is the mechanism whereby the European Inner Six agreed (in March 1972) to permit their national currencies to float conjointly against the U.S. dollar within a "band of fluctuation" of 2.25 percent.

The name *snake* derives from the periodic rising and falling (similar to a serpentine slithering) of the values of European currencies within the band of fluctuation.

This system lasted until March 1973 when (1) the United States, Canada, Japan, the United Kingdom, Italy, and Switzerland decided to let their currencies float independently; and (2) Germany, France, Belgium, Luxembourg, the Netherlands, Denmark, Norway, and Austria agreed to let their currencies float jointly within the 2.25 percent band of fluctuation between the strongest and the weakest currency *vis-à-vis* the U.S. dollar. This was the beginning of the contemporary managed floating exchange rate system.

See also managed floating exchange rate system.

European System of Central Banks (ESCB) *See* Delors Report.

Europe without frontiers is a variation of *Europe 1992*.

Eurosterling (Europounds) *See* Appendix I.

Euroterm is a word or phrase created by European economists and traders in the
European Economic Community (EEC) and by overseas "Europhiles" who
support European economic-monetary union (EMU). The excessive word or
phrase production by institutional European "word factories" (e.g., the European Investment Bank) has been called, derisively, "Eurobabble."

> **Example:** Americans try to get different national laws "into sync" or "to
> mesh." Europeans, in contrast, try to "harmonize" them. Americans, for their
> part, enjoy listening to members of barbershop quartets "harmonize."

Eurotypes are consumer profiles that transcend national boundaries and that are
intended to comprise a socio-cultural map of European consumers after (what
is hoped will be) the successful economic-monetary union of Europe in 1992.

According to Eurotypologists (at the Sorbonne in Paris), each of the 320
million people in West Europe fits one of 16 Eurotypes (e.g., Euro-Pioneer,
Euro-Romantic, Euro-Moralist, Euro-Dandy, Euro-Vigilante).

The French data base, upon which the Eurotype classification system has
been devised, is fee-for-service oriented: private companies pay connection
fees and user fees to access the data.

American psychologists and psycho-sociologists were the original developers of the
Eurotype concept; in the United States, it is called psychographics, a market research
composite of consumer lifestyle (developed in the 1960s and 1970s) based on consumers' attitudes, interests, opinions, and behaviors.

Psychographics enjoyed a heyday in the 1970s in the United States and Canada.
Eventually it was recognized that used alone—as a measure either of consumer-brand
loyalty or of purchase intent—psychographics can lead to highly misleading outcomes.
The reason is that a psychographic data base (let alone an entire classification system
based on it), while frequently insightful, is too persuasively simple a basis upon which
to make serious marketing decisions regarding the positioning of new brands or the
re-positioning of existing ones.

Euroyen *See* Appendix I.

exceptions are special circumstances or unforeseen events that, in multilateral or
bilateral trade agreements, may occur to alter the relationship between the
trading partners or, more commonly, the trading environment itself.

For example, political instability or an outbreak of guerilla insurgency in
a country or region may necessitate the rapid adoption of export/import
controls for security purposes, together with the documentation and attendant delays involved.

Articles XX and XXI of the General Agreement on Tariffs and Trade provide for the basic exceptions that are accepted internationally.
See also General Agreement on Tariffs and Trade.

exchange controls are financial and administrative (nontariff) measures imposed by a government to restrict the outflow of convertible currencies from a country, while sometimes encouraging the inflow of them.

> **Example:** The use of multiple exchange rates in certain Latin American countries is a means to encourage the inflow of dollars while discouraging their outflow.

exchange of debt claims is a technique of external debt reduction whereby holders of debt instruments agree to exchange them (at a discount) for other debt instruments.

> **Example:** The Royal Bank of Canada, holder of tens of millions of dollars in Mexican government bonds, might agree to exchange those bonds (at a discount of 50 percent) for Mexican Railway bonds, deemed more secure by virtue of the fact that they are supported (1) by World Bank financing for expansion of the Mexican railway system and (2) by Canadian export credits (via the Export Development Corporation) for a contract to supply rolling stock to the railway over a 10-year period.

See also debt-reduction techniques.

exchange rate *See* Appendix II.

excise tax is a government levy imposed on the manufacture and sale of certain classes of products, whether produced or imported for domestic consumption.

Excise taxes in Canada originated with the desire of government to curb consumption of certain goods (e.g., liquor, tobacco) by increasing their price to the point where demand for them would become highly elastic.

In contemporary times, excise taxes are part of government fiscal policy and are used to generate revenue from imported goods whose demand is relatively price inelastic (e.g., liquor, luxury cars).

exit bond is a bond issued by a debtor country (e.g., Mexico) to a creditor bank (e.g., The First Bank of Boston), the purpose of which is to permit the creditor to be exempted from future requests for new funds by the debtor country.
See also debt-reduction techniques.

expatriate, abbreviated *expat.*, is a term used to denote any person working and/or living outside of their own country.

A "national expatriate" refers to a person who works overseas for a company from their own country.

Example: It is customary for U.S. firms to compensate American expatriates working for them by at least equalizing the expatriates' total benefit packages with those of American nationals working for the home office in the United States.

A "foreign expatriate" is a person who is a foreign national working in an overseas country that is not his own, and for a foreign company. An alternative term, "third-country national," has enjoyed wide usage to convey the same meaning.

Example: Jorge Rigoberto de Valladolid, a Spanish national with excellent European Community contacts, was recruited by an executive search firm in Manhattan to work in Paris for a U.S. branch office.

Cf. local national.
See also benefits for international service.

expert systems is the most important category of artificial intelligence because from the viewpoint of existing practical application, it has the most advanced current levels of comprehensive knowledge ("expertise") and a means to use it to (1) answer questions, (2) solve problems, and (3) explain the solutions and the way they were reached.

Expert systems comprise two main elements: (1) a knowledge base (i.e., a "data base") and (2) a so-called "inference engine." It is on the basis of the knowledge embodied in the data base and by means of the inference engine that processes that knowledge, that expert systems can be used in highly specialized problem-solving.

Expert systems are well-known tools in medical diagnosis. Less well known is their use in industry, for example, in determining the causes of machine-tool failure. Only recently have expert systems been applied to international business problems.

Example: In international marketing, a computer program called *Company Readiness to Export (CORE)*™ is a state-of-the-art expert system. It was developed by Dr. S. Tamer Cavusgil, Professor of Marketing and International Business, Michigan State University. CORE was developed as a tool to be used by American managers to assist them in assessing a firm's readiness to export. The CORE program generates company ratings along two key dimensions: organization preparedness (i.e., management readiness) and product readiness. Depending on CORE's assessment, the program recommends different and appropriate courses of action. For instance, CORE may recommend that management either (1) refrain from exporting entirely or (2) avoid exporting until preparedness is increased in particular directions proposed by CORE (e.g., financial strength, management training, knowledge of foreign markets).

Thus CORE can be used in a number of ways: (1) as an evaluation tool to assist companies to assess their readiness to export; (2) as a training tool by international business consultants to help prepare their clients for successful exporting; or (3) as an educational tool in business colleges and in export seminars and workshops to help students, novice exporters, and experienced traders learn more about the "initial conditions" that influence the chances for success in export marketing.

In finance, a number of expert systems have been found suitable in areas such as banking, insurance, and portfolio management. In investment planning, one expert system called *Innovator*™ was developed by Professors Sudha Ram of the University of Arizona and Sundaresan Ram of the University of California at Los Angeles. *Innovator* was designed to help financial services organizations (FSOs) plan a financial portfolio. *Innovator* screens financial products and product lines according to their attributes. The evaluation process incorporates "performance factors" (e.g., return on investment) and specific "brand factors" (e.g., company earnings, quality of service), as well as performance considerations. International business people may naturally be interested in "revenue-generators" like CORE. Systems like *Innovator* may be equally useful, but as "risk assessors": they help plan investment portfolios (built from export-generated revenue) that contain (1) foreign equity (i.e., common stock) and (2) foreign debt holdings such as bonds, promissory notes, and accepted bills of exchange.

export, as a verb, means to actively send a good or service out of one sovereign domain to another for purposes of sale (or from areas not designated as sovereign to those so designated); as a noun, it means a good or service actively sent from one sovereign domain to another for purposes of sale (or from areas not designated as sovereign to those so designated).

> **Example:** The parts were made in the parent company's foundry in Singapore's duty free zone (DFZ), transferred to another sister-company plant in Hong Kong's DFZ for machining, then shipped to a company warehouse in Taiwan's DFZ for final assembly and ultimate export to another sister company in Japan. Duties were only paid on the final exports since the company had complied with all the rules of using DFZs.

Cf. import.

Export and Import Bank of Japan (EIBJ) is the official government credit granting agency of Japan.

The EIBJ provides financing facilities such as loans and export credits to buyers of Japanese goods, and it offers joint financing for private and multilateral development banks (MDBs) to support development projects.

Cf. Export Development Corporation; Export Credit Guarantees Department; Export-Import Bank of the United States.

See also export financing.

Export and Import Permits Act refers to Canadian legislation that provides the basis for state authority exercised in the areas of control of exports from and imports into Canada.

1. *Exports:* Exporters in Canada, whether native, naturalized, or foreign, must obtain an export permit prior to contracting to supply any product in any quantity to any foreign buyer, only when subject to the following:
   - *Export Control List (ECL):* a schedule of 150 goods (and of quantities of goods) subject to export control via an export permit.

The ECL contains primarily "strategic materials" and goods for military and nuclear application. In addition, endangered species of flora and fauna are listed.

Canada coordinates and updates the ECL with COCOM, the Coordinating Committee for Multilateral Strategic Export Controls.

- *Area Control List (ACL):* a schedule of specific countries, geographic areas, and trading groups and blocs for which an export permit is required for any goods, not simply those listed in the Export Control List.

Example: Canada has "listed" South Africa and Libya on the ACL, which means that all goods exported to them require permits, in addition to whatever permits may be required to export goods to them that may already be on the ECL, such as guns and ammunition.

2. *Imports:* Importers in Canada, whether native, naturalized, or foreign, must obtain an import permit prior to contracting to bring into Canada any product in any quantity from any foreign supplier, only when subject to the following:
   - *Import Control List:* a schedule of goods (and of quantities of goods) subject to import control via import permit.

Cf. Bureau of Export Administration.
See also export permits; import permits; COCOM.

export broker *See* export jobber.

export buyer is an intermediary, domestically based, who buys surplus production, distressed goods, and discontinued lines (all at reduced prices) for resale to foreign buyers.
See also indirect exporting.

export commission house is an intermediary, domestically based, who acts as a purchasing agent for a foreign importer.
See also indirect exporting.

Export Control List *See* Export and Import Permits Act.

export controls refer to a type of international commodity agreement.
(It is also a (corrupted) variation of *exchange controls*.)
See also international commodity agreement; exchange controls.

export counseling is guidance provided to Canadian exporters by officials of the Department of External Affairs and International Trade Canada (EAITC), most commonly through its International Trade Centers (ITCs) located in the 11 regional offices of the Department of Industry, Science and Technology Canada (ISTC).
See also International Trade Centers.

export credit refers to (1) financing made available to domestic suppliers to generate goods and services for export, and (2) deferred payment terms, loans, or other financial facilities provided to foreign buyers/importers of goods and services.

See also buyer credits; supplier credits.

Export Credit Enhanced Leverage (Excel) is a special export financing program agreed to in October 1989 by the World Bank and official state agencies that extend export financing (e.g., the Canadian Export Development Corporation (EDC) and the Export-Import Bank of the United States (Eximbank)).

As a consequence of the international debt crisis of the 1980s, new money for export credits dried up, and a new export credit facility was needed to assist exporters in the OECD industrialized nations to market their products to Third World countries. Excel was devised to fill the need.

Under the program, national credit insurers (such as Canada's EDC), will provide loans or credit guarantees in parallel with World Bank financing. The funds are channeled to the multilateral development banks (MDBs) (which are the executing agencies of the United Nations Development Program (UNDP)). These banks will then assume the risk on individual private buyers themselves.

The Excel program was organized by the World Bank and the Berne Union, the international association of export credit insurers.

See also Berne Union.

Export Credit Guarantees Department (ECGD) is the official U.K. government agency that offers support for bank financing of exports in the form of guarantees, foreign investment insurance, and interest rate subsidies aimed at reducing the rate from the U.K. market level to a level at which U.K. firms can compete internationally.

Cf. Export Development Corporation; Export-Import Bank of the United States; Export and Import Bank of Japan.

See also export finance.

export declaration, referred to as the *B-13*, is a document required by the Canadian Department of National Revenue, Customs, and Excise and by the U.S. Department of the Treasury-U.S. Customs Service to be duly filled out by exporters (1) for export control and (2) for statistics-gathering purposes.

Cf. Single Administrative Document.

Export Development Corporation (EDC) is a Canadian Crown Corporation that is the official credit-granting agency of the Government of Canada and provides a range of services to Canadian exporters and foreign importers.

The EDC's terms for lending are in line with the Organization for Economic Cooperation and Development (OECD) Concensus arrangements, including its use of the Canada Account, when lending is on a concessional basis. The EDC is more lenient in terms of domestic content requirements (of its national exports) than any of its competitors. For example, the Export-Import Bank of the United States (Eximbank) requires 100 percent U.S. content, but the EDC requires 60 percent domestic content and an overall average of 75 percent.

The following are the (1) financial services, (2) guarantees, (3) credit insurance services, and (4) other insurance services offered by the EDC (each can be found in the alphabetical listings):

1. *Financial Services*
   - Loans to foreign importers
   - Allocations under lines of credit
   - Forfeiting
   - Loan support for services
   - Buyer credit protocol
   - Supplier credit protocol
   - Specialized credit

2. *Guarantees*
   - Specific Transaction Guarantees
   - Performance Security Guarantees
   - Bid Security Guarantees
   - Loan Guarantees

3. *Credit Insurance Services*
   - Global Shipments Comprehensive Insurance
   - Global Contracts Comprehensive Insurance
   - Global Services Comprehensive Insurance
   - Specific Transaction Insurance
   - Bank Documentary Credit Insurance

4. *Other Insurance Services*
   - Loan Pre-Disbursement Insurance
   - Foreign Investment Insurance
   - Performance Security Insurance
   - Consortium Insurance
   - Surety Bond Insurance
   - Short Term Bulk Agriculture Credits Insurance
   - Medium Term Bulk Agriculture Credits Insurance and Guarantee Program

Cf. Export Credit Guarantees Department; Export and Import Bank of Japan; Export-Import Bank of the United States.
See also Canada Account; OECD Concensus; export finance; Export Credit Enhanced Leverage.

export duty is an awkward variation of *export levy*.
See duty.

export education refers to seminars and workshops that are organized by a Canadian International Trade Center (ITC) on behalf of potential (or actual) Canadian exporters to teach the exporters a range of ideas, from the fundamentals of export marketing to correct techniques of export pricing and available Canadian export-support programs.

See also International Trade Centers.

export financing is a means by which exporters can capitalize the sale of their goods or services to a foreign importer.

Depending upon (1) the relationship between the trading principals, (2) the amount of the required funds, (3) the commercial and political risks surrounding the transaction, and (4) the state of the various micro- and macro-economies relative to the goods and/or services being traded, exports can be financed from a variety of money market sources. The following is a comprehensive list of ways and means of financing exports (each can be found in the alphabetical listings):

* acceptance financing
* collections
* consignment
* documentary credit
* factoring foreign accounts receivable
* foreign accounts receivable financing
* foreign accounts receivable purchases
* open account
* payment in advance
* purchase of drawings under a documentary credit
* trade acceptance purchases

Export-Import Bank of the United States (Eximbank) is the official U.S. agency that assists in the financing of U.S. exporters and in insuring their foreign accounts receivable.

Eximbank programs consist of the following:

1. direct loans to foreign buyers,
2. loan guarantees,
3. export insurance, and
4. discounting of foreign receivables.

Like its counterpart in Canada, the Export Development Corporation, Eximbank does not compete with private sector financial institutions. Rather, it works with them to underwrite, co-finance, and insure export transactions in order to make export financing easier, more accessible, and less risky for both the exporter and the exporter's financier.

The Bank also assists U.S. exporters and their private U.S. banks by providing "cover" for some commercial risks. These insurance programs are administered by the Foreign Credit Insurance Association (FCIA).

Cf. Export Development Corporation; Export and Import Bank of Japan; Export Credit Guarantees Department.

See also export financing; Foreign Credit Insurance Association.

export instability *See* Appendix II.

export insurance is a policy taken out (usually by the exporter) to provide coverage (sometimes called "cover") against the risk of nonpayment by the foreign buyer or a financial institution (such as a bank) that has extended credit to the foreign buyer or that has undertaken the payment obligation of the foreign buyer (e.g., via documentary credit).

The risks covered by export insurance fall into two classes: commercial risks and political risks.

See also Export Development Corporation; commercial risks; political risks.

export jobber is an intermediary, domestically based, who buys goods domestically (i.e., takes title) and resells them to foreign buyers, without ever taking physical possession of them. Export jobbers are mainly concerned with arranging transactions in bulk commodities.

See also indirect exporting.

export levy is a tax added to exports from a country.

Cf. import duty.

See also duty.

export license *See* export permit.

export management company (EMC) is an intermediary, domestically based, that specializes in acting for inexperienced domestic exporters.

The EMC can act as a commission sales representative, buying from the local exporter and reselling to foreign buyers. Where an EMC has foreign operations over which it has control or which it owns, it can act as a distributor for a domestic firm, buying locally and exporting to its foreign affiliates.

Cf. combination export manager.

See also indirect exporting.

export merchant is a domestically based company that buys on its own account (i.e., takes title) and sells directly to foreign companies.

Any company that operates in the global market as an international merchant wholesaler is referred to as an export merchant.

See also direct exporting.

export-oriented industrialization refers to the policy and practice of some developing countries to increase their nation's economic output by increasing the output of manufactured goods for export.

Sufficiently large and growing markets for manufactured goods is but one precondition for implementation of this policy. A relatively large and trainable labor pool is another. Capitalization of enterprise is usually (but not always) in private entrepreneurial hands. Laws and regulations that encourage a stable commercial climate are a *sine qua non*, since they usually include deferred taxation and individual rather than collective bargaining.

> **Example:** South Korea, Hong Kong, Taiwan, and Singapore are usually cited as the Pacific Rim's newly industrialized/industrializing countries (NICs) that owe their rapid growth to the policy of export-oriented industrialization.

:ompanies engaged in the preparation of
techniques such as palletization, shrink

xport license, is an official government
prior to engaging in exporting.
ions (e.g., the sale of high-tech computer
tomer), institutions that customarily ex-
nce, and guarantees are not permitted to
required permit.
cific quantities of specific goods permit-
ations.
ainable from the Department of External
_____ ~u..ada (EAITC) in Ottawa. In the United
States, the Bureau of Export Administration (BXA) in Washington, D.C.,
issues them.

Cf. import permit; commercial controls.

See also Export and Import Permits Act; Comprehensive Export Schedule; Bureau of Export Administration.

export pessimism is the term used to describe the expectation that the exports of
both commodities and manufactured goods from less developed countries
cannot grow rapidly, generate export earnings, and form the basis for next-
stage industrialization because of increasing protectionist and technological
practices by developed countries.

> **Example:** Agricultural economists are pessimistic about the rate of export
> growth of specific high-potential agricultural products from West Asia (e.g.,
> sisal, jute) to Europe because of the latter's high rate of innovation in the
> development and adoption of import substitution products.

A traditional complaint that West African groundnut marketing boards have against
the European Economic Community (EEC) is that there is a lower common external
tariff (CXT) levied on the commodity when it is destined for animal feed than when
it is imported as an input for human-food processing.

The result is (1) groundnut importation into EEC member countries to fatten
cattle (at low feed-stock prices) and (2) exportation of high-priced meat to West Africa
for human consumption.

The complaint is that the CXT is neo-protectionist: it acts as an incentive to keep
low-cost feed stock flowing into the EEC (by classifying high-quality groundnut protein
as a low-value input), thus depriving West African producers of the higher prices they
need to afford the European meat output that their misclassified low-cost agricultural
inputs helped to produce.

---

export processing zone (EPZ) *See* foreign trade zone.

export quotas are voluntary restrictions/ceilings, adopted by the government of a
country, on the volume and/or value of goods exported to a specific country
or group of countries.

Six other terms have this equivalent meaning:

1. export restraints,
2. voluntary export restraints (VERs),
3. export restraint arrangements (ERAs),
4. export restraint agreements (ERAs),
5. quantitative restrictions (QRs), and
6. quantitative export restraints (QERs).

A number of other terms have the same core meaning as *export quotas*, but they augment that core with a vocabulary befitting the situation that the term attempts to encompass: orderly marketing arrangements (OMAs), voluntary restraint arrangements (VRAs), and international commodity agreements (ICAs).

Cf. import quotas.

export restraint agreements (ERAs) *See* voluntary restraint agreements (VRAs).

export restraint arrangements (ERAs) *See* voluntary restraint agreements (VRAs).

export restraints *See* export quotas.

export subsidy (export subsidies) refers to government benefits (e.g., direct payments, support prices, tax incentives, training allowances) made available to domestic producers of goods contingent upon their exporting those goods for which the benefits received apply.

In the European Economic Community (EEC), export subsidies, called "variable subsidies," have been formally institutionalized as part of the Common Agricultural Policy (CAP) of the EEC. Their existence forms the basis for the long-running grievance by the United States against EEC agricultural policy activities, especially regarded as protectionist.

Under the General Agreement on Tariffs and Trade (GATT), developed countries are forbidden from using subsidies to support the export of the majority of manufactured goods.

On the other hand, GATT permits less developed countries to subsidize their export manufactures provided that significant material damage does not result to the economies of highly developed countries as a consequence of the export subsidization.

Example: To encourage expansion of Pacific Rim economies—and political democratization as an expected social outcome—Canada has acknowledged higher levels of unemployment in its domestic furniture industry as a result of Asian government export subsidization of the entire low-end, outdoor, summer-furniture market. Asian products now account for over 24 percent of the market, which, by global marketing measurements, is judged to be relatively equitable given the more than reciprocal domination of the Pacific Rim markets by Canadian maple syrup!

If a country determines that a national trading partner is unfairly using export subsidies, the injured country may use the appropriate countervailing duties (and other GATT-approved processes) for obtaining appropriate remedies. In the case of the United States, special, powerful legislation has been passed for the U.S. Trade Representative, in league with the U.S. International Trade Commission (USITC), to take strong action where it is determined that an "unfair trader," using exports subsidies, is causing injury to U.S. commercial interests.

See also General Agreement on Tariffs and Trade; Tokyo Round; Canada-U.S. Free Trade Agreement of 1989; Omnibus Trade Act of 1988; Super 301; U.S. Trade Representative; U.S. International Trade Commission.

export support programs are financial and logistical arrangements developed by a country's department of foreign trade and delivered to domestic exporters via the department's field offices, usually located in the country's important cities.

In Canada, they are financial and logistical arrangements developed by the Department of External Affairs and International Trade Canada (EAITC) and delivered to Canadian exporters via EAITC's International Trade Centers (ITCs) located in the 11 regional offices of the Department of Industry, Science and Technology Canada (ISTC).

Some of the most important programs are the following:

1. *Program for Export Market Development (PEMD):* a comprehensive program of export assistance provided by EAITC, enabling Canadian exporters to
   - make market identification trips,
   - invite potential foreign buyers to Canada,
   - participate in foreign trade fairs,
   - join together in consortia to pool and strengthen their efforts to bid on foreign projects,
   - compete for work on foreign capital projects, and
   - establish a permanent commercial presence in a foreign market.

   PEMD consists not only of technical assistance and logistical support, but also of financial assistance on the basis of the cost-sharing of listed expenses with the exporter and on repaying the support, contingent upon export sales being made.

   Two special PEMD programs, PEMD Food and PEMD Fish, are EAITC's attempts to assist in the development of Canadian exports of agricultural products and of Atlantic groundfish and herring products (and by-products), respectively.

2. *New Exporters to Border States (NEBS):* a program of visits to and intensive consultation with potential U.S. customers in U.S. states bordering Canada, under the auspices of, and supported by, the EAITC and collateral supporting agencies in finance, insurance, transportation, and logistics— it is a "crash course" for small- and medium-sized Canadian firms in the essentials of exporting to the United States.

3. *New Exports to the United States South (NEXUS):* a program of intensive export-market identification, visits to and consultation with potential U.S. export customers in the Sun Belt.

4. *New Exporters Overseas (NEXOS):* a program similar to NEXUS, but directed at potential export markets in Europe, Asia, Latin America, and Africa.

5. *Canada Export Awards:* a program aimed at promoting international trade-related activities and at informing Canadian exporters of the range of government programs and services available to them in support of export marketing.

Cf. Three Pillar Strategy; U.S. International Trade Administration.
See also International Trade Centers.

export targeting is any government program of coordinated actions bestowed on a private company, or on a private industrial sector, the intention of which is to aid it to increase its export competitiveness in its field.

The label can be used by the U.S. government under the authority of the U.S. Omnibus Trade Act of 1988, Subtitle C, Part 1, Section 301 (E).

Countries determined to have engaged in this practice can be dealt with by the U.S. Trade Representative (USTR) under the Act accordingly.

> **Example:** Canadian critics of the Canada-U.S. Free Trade Agreement of 1989 (FTA) see it as doomed to failure since, under Super 301, many long-time Canadian government programs, such as unemployment insurance, industrial training allowances and programs, and government-subsidized loans to industries, can be deemed export targeting by the USTR and subject to retaliatory action under Super 301.

See also Omnibus Trade Act of 1988; Super 301; regional development programs.

export tariff is a tax or duty on goods exported from a country.
Cf. import tariff.
See also duty.

export trade information is data that comprises (1) sources of Canadian suppliers of goods and services, (2) target names of potential customers for Canadian goods and services, and (3) Canadian functional and facilitating intermediaries who can assist in moving goods and services between the Canadian export source and the foreign export target.

Data bases for this information exist in Canada through the network of International Trade Centers (ITCs) maintained in the 11 regional offices of Industry, Science and Technology Canada (ISTC). Canadian exporters may have access to them as follows:

1. *Bureau of Sourcing Suppliers (BOSS):* a computerized data base maintained by the Department of Industry, Science and Technology Canada (ISTC) for use by domestic Canadian traders and by Canadian exporters seeking domestic sources of export goods.

2. *Trade Promotion Events (TPE):* a computerized data base maintained by each ITC and that comprises domestic and foreign trade fairs and trade missions.

3. *World Information Network (WIN):* a computerized data base comprising data on country and sectoral exports by classification and value, designed to update Canadian Trade Commissioners (the equivalent of U.S. Consuls) on export opportunities worldwide and within their sphere of jurisdiction.
4. *International Trade Data Bank (ITDB):* a computerized data base (originating with the U.N. Conference on Trade and Development (UNCTAD) computer tapes) that provides data on commodity flows for the Organization for Economic Cooperation and Development (OECD), trading blocs such as the European Economic Community (EEC), Organization of Petroleum Exporting Countries (OPEC), and less developed countries (LDCs) by country and/or by product classification.

Using the ITDB, a Canadian exporter seeking data on fertilizer inputs by the Association of Southeast Asian Nations (ASEAN) will get the volume of specific fertilizers imported by each ASEAN member and the source of each ASEAN import (i.e., the Canadian exporter's potential export competitors).

Cf. Trade Opportunities Program.
See also International Trade Centers.

export trading company (ETC) is an American company formed and operated for the principal purpose of exporting American goods/services.

Pursuant to the U.S. Export Trading Company Act of 1982, ETCs that are registered as such with the U.S. government (i.e., with the Department of the Treasury's Internal Revenue Service and U.S. Customs Service and the U.S. Department of Justice) are exempt from important provisions of antitrust legislation that would apply were the company to be operating within the legal (territorial) jurisdiction of the U.S. government.

Example: Predatory pricing is an illegal trade practice in the United States. However, given the ruthlessness of European Economic Community (EEC) pharmaceutical manufacturers to penetrate traditional U.S.-dominated Latin American markets, U.S. drug companies have formed ETCs. In one Latin American case, the ETC flooded the local market (under siege from European competitors) with "at cost" or "below cost" products made in non-union U.S.-based free trade areas. The campaign took 10 months. It ended not only with the elimination of EEC products from the market, but also with the collapse of all resident U.S. competitors.

The ETC "price predator" absorbed all significant competition and created a vertically integrated marketing system with the state as the new joint venturer!

The American export trading company is different both in historical origin and in operation from the more widely known international enterprise called simply a trading company.
Cf. trading company.

expropriation is seizure of foreign assets by a government with compensation paid to the owners.
Cf. confiscation; nationalization.

External Affairs and International Trade Canada (EAITC) is the new "applied title" used by the Department of External Affairs (DEA) to project the perception that, in addition to its traditional role as foreign policy maker for Canada, the EAITC functions as the center for the development of international trade policy and its implementation worldwide.

Cf. Industry, Science and Technology Canada.

See also Department of External Affairs.

external debt, from the Spanish *(la) deuda externa* and the French *(la) dette extérieure*, is (1) international financial obligations variously called foreign debt, foreign debt load, international debt, and international debt load; and (2) the large amount of long-term financial obligations (usually denominated in U.S. dollars) owed by the governments (usually of developing countries) to international financial institutions (e.g., the World Bank Group), to governments, and to private banks (in developing countries).

See also debt servicing; Paris Club; International Monetary Fund.

extraterritoriality (extra-territoriality) *See* Appendix VI.

facilitating intermediary is someone in an international marketing channel who, without ever taking physical possession of the goods, provides services that assist the movement of the goods in the direction of the customer.

The following are examples of facilitating intermediaries:

- financial institutions, which issue documentary credits;
- freight forwarders, which purchase cargo capacity, lease trucks, and route shipments;
- insurance companies, which provide "cover" against commercial and political risks;
- customs brokers, who prepare necessary documentation and clear the goods through foreign customs.

factor is (1) a financial institution that purchases the foreign accounts receivable of an exporter without recourse; (2) a foreign-based intermediary that performs all the regular brokerage functions, including the provision of export financing of the transaction.

To cover the cost of extending credit (e.g., opportunity costs and the commercial risks/political risks of nonrepayment), a factor charges fees additional to brokerage fees for the service provided.

Cf. managing agent.

See also factoring (foreign accounts receivable); without-recourse financing.

factoring (foreign accounts receivable) is a means of export financing whereby a financial institution (called a *factor*) purchases the foreign trade debts owed by importers to an exporter.

The factor charges the exporter a fee to underwrite the real losses that will be incurred should the importer fail to pay. Further, if the exporter has provided the importer with credit terms (i.e., time to pay), the factor will purchase the debt at a discount because of the increased commercial risk of nonpayment associated with the extended payment terms.

Cf. *del credere* agent.

See also export finance.

fair trade *See* unfair trade.

fast-track (fast-track procedure) is a political tactic comprising ways and means to accelerate some legal, administrative, or executive action (such as the passage of legislation) by giving it priority attention.

There are fast-track procedures in the U.S. Trade Act of 1974 and in the U.S. Omnibus Trade Act of 1988. Under the latter, the Congress—via the House Committee on Ways and Means and the Senate Committee on Finance—have 60 legislative days from the date of written notice that trade negotiations have begun (say, between the United States and Mexico) to withdraw authority for the U.S. administration to negotiate a trade treaty. As long as neither committee disapproves the negotiations, the president can proceed to negotiate the treaty and present it to Congress for a vote.

Once the president has presented the trade package to Congress, the fast-track procedure gives Congress 90 legislative days either to accept or to reject (but not to amend) the treaty. If the president requires an extension of the fast-track time frame, he can request it, but he must do so at least 90 days before the trade package would otherwise be presented to Congress, and Congress must approve the extension before the 90-day period elapses. In addition, extensions of "fast-track authority" can only be for a maximum of two years.

The fast-track procedures are aimed at assuring foreign governments that the legislative branch of the U.S. government will act expeditiously on an agreement negotiated with the executive branch of government.

The fast-track procedure under which the current North American Free Trade Agreement (NAFTA) is being negotiated trilaterally among the United States, Mexico, and Canada, initiated on September 25, 1990, will require approval by both Congressional committees no later than May 31, 1991. President Bush requested a renewal of fast-track authority on March 1, 1991. If Congress approves the fast-track, the NAFTA may be finalized in 1992, permitting early implementation on January 1, 1993. This timetable assumes, of course, no delay in negotiations requiring the U.S. president to ask Congress for a fast-track extension.

See also Canada-U.S. Free Trade Agreement of 1989; North American Free Trade Agreement.

Federal Maritime Commission (FMC) is a U.S. body that regulates waterborne foreign and domestic offshore commerce to ensure that U.S. international trade is open to all nations on fair terms and that fair rates and conditions exist to permit the commercial market for services to operate without discrimination.

The FMC's regulatory authority derives from the Shipping Act of 1916, the Merchant Marine Act of 1920, the Intercoastal Shipping Act of 1933, the Merchant Marine Act of 1936, and the Shipping Act of 1984.

Cf. nonvessel operating common carrier.

fiscal economics *See* Keynesian economics.

fiscalism *See* Keynesian economics.

fiscal policy refers to government's authority to tax and to redistribute wealth by way of government spending programs.
See also Keynesian economics.

fishyback •NW• is the shipping of containerized cargo via ocean liners.
See also container.

Five Tigers, also called the *Five Dragons*, refer to Hong Kong, Taiwan, Singapore, South Korea, and Thailand.
Thailand was joined to the other four (the Four Tigers) in 1989 by the International Monetary Fund, based on its macroeconomic performance that includes (1) Thailand's real economic growth, which has averaged 9 percent per year over 1987, 1988, and 1989; (2) its per capita GNP, which now exceeds U.S. $1,000; and (3) its (low) inflation, which has been less than 4 percent annually throughout the 1980s.
Cf. Four Tigers.
See also newly industrialized countries.

flag of convenience is a foreign flag under which a ship is registered.

Owners register ocean vessels with the national registry of countries whose maritime regulations regarding such items as safety, experience and fitness of the crew, and navigation standards are relatively lenient and, thus, require fewer expenditures by the owners and operators of the ship.

Food and Agricultural Organization (of the United Nations) **(FAO)** is a specialized agency of the United Nations with headquarters in Rome, Italy.
The FAO is the global coordinator for the following fields:

1. agricultural development;
2. global exchange of new/improved plant species;
3. dissemination of advanced agricultural techniques;
4. combating of animal/plant diseases and improvement of animal husbandry;
5. development and utilization of marine resources;
6. soil erosion control;
7. land reclamation/settlement;
8. geophysical and seismic studies/surveys;
9. mapping (including aerial photography);
10. pilot rural development/demonstration projects.

The FAO is of interest to global marketers because of the possibilities of long-term commercial relationships with this organization based on its ongoing international commitments and its annual procurement of megaquantities of capital goods and services.
See also international organizations.

foreign, from the Latin *foris* meaning "outside," refers to something unfamiliar and, according to E.R. (Ted) Turner, founder of Turner Broadcasting System (TBS), the word "creates a perception of misunderstanding."

> **Example:** There is no such thing as "foreign news" at the Cable News Network (CNN), the main news broadcast unit of TBS. Ted Turner allegedly has warned his staff that any CNN employee who uses the word *foreign* must pay a fine to the United Nations Children's Fund (UNICEF).

Cf. international.
See also ethnocentrism; global marketing.

foreign accounts receivable financing is a means of export financing whereby (1) the exporter uses its lines of credit with a bank to borrow money for terms of 30, 60, 90, or 180 days; or (2) the exporter can sell its foreign accounts receivable to the bank, which may purchase them at a variable discount, depending on the degree of foreign commercial and political risk to payment involved.
See also export financing.

foreign accounts receivable purchases is a means of export financing whereby the exporter sells its foreign invoice acceptances to a financial institution at a variable discount, depending on the degree of foreign commercial and political risk to payment involved.
See also export financing.

Foreign Assistance Act of 1961 is U.S. legislation that grants authority to the executive branch of government for the operation of the Trade and Development Program (TDP) within the framework of the U.S. International Development Cooperation Agency (USIDCA).
See also U.S. International Development Cooperation Agency (3. Trade and Development Program).

foreign branch office, in the age of the multinational corporation (i.e., the 1960s and 1970s), was a foreign-based organization, managed and staffed by national expatriates of the employer's home office; in the age of globalism, it is a nondomestic facility of a corporation, staffed by company employees, regardless of their nationality.
Cf. home office.
See also expatriate.

Foreign Corrupt Practices Act of 1977 is U.S. legislation that prohibits the making of any non-arm's-length payments of cash or goods to any official of a foreign government with whose country a U.S. company does business.
Cf. arm's length.
See also bribery.

Foreign Credit Insurance Association (FCIA), organized by the Export-Import Bank of the United States (Eximbank) in 1961, is an organization that links U.S. insurance companies together to provide U.S. exporters with insurance "cover" exclusively against the commercial risks (mainly default) associated with collecting foreign accounts receivable.

The only American quasi-government body that provides U.S. exporters with "cover" against political risks either to their foreign accounts receivable or their direct foreign investments is the Overseas Private Investment Corporation (OPIC).

Cf. Export Development Corporation.

See also commercial risks; political risks.

foreign debt See external debt.

foreign debt overhang See debt servicing.

foreign exchange (FOREX) refers to the currency of a foreign country.

See also Appendix I.

foreign exchange broker (FOREX broker) is a specialist who facilitates the trading of foreign exchange by matching buyers and sellers, especially in markets where the supply of hard currency is scarce.

foreign exchange controls See exchange controls.

foreign exchange reserve is a variation of reserve currency.

See reserve currency country.

foreign expatriate See expatriate.

foreign external debt See external debt.

Foreign Extraterritorial Measures Act (of 1984) **(FEMA)** is Canadian legislation under which the Canadian government can prohibit any person or company operating in Canada from complying with any U.S. law that prevents trade between Canada and any other country.

Since 1963, the Canadian government has resisted attempts by the U.S. government to interfere with its trade with Cuba and with the right of any U.S. subsidiary to do business with Cuba while legally resident in Canada. In 1984, the passing of the FEMA by the Canadian parliament was the culmination of Canada's formal resistance to U.S. extraterritoriality.

> **Example:** In October 1990, a U.S. bill was passed by Congress containing a measure called the "Mack Amendment" that, had it been passed into law, would have prevented the issuance of any U.S. licenses for trade with Cuba and would have made it unlawful for any U.S. overseas subsidiary to trade with Cuba. In Canada, the U.S. law was immediately blocked by executive order of the Attorney General of Canada, issued under the authority of FEMA. Subsequently, the bill containing the "Mack Amendment" was vetoed by the U.S. president and did not become law. However, in early 1991, the identical provision ("Mack II") was introduced into the U.S. Senate. This measure forms part of the U.S. Export Administration Act Amendments of 1991, which has yet to come before the U.S. president. Unquestionably, the Canadian

government would issue an order blocking application of U.S. extraterritoriality in Canada should the U.S. president sign the bill into law.

See also extraterritoriality.

foreign freight forwarder (FFF), sometimes referred to as an *international freight forwarder*, is a "full-service" domestic-based company that, contracted by a national exporter, is paid fees for carrying out the following:

1. contracting for the services of carriers (on behalf of client shippers);
2. arranging the export packaging of the cargo;
3. coordination of the movement of the goods, now called "the cargo," to the carrier;
4. preparation and processing of required logistical documentation, which may include the bill of lading, packing slips and cargo manifests, delivery orders, and dock receipts;
5. preparation and processing of required customs documentation, which may include consular invoices, export declarations, and certificates of origin;
6. payment of the freight charges for the shipment;
7. offering shipping insurance, materials handling services, warehousing, consolidation (i.e., containerization, "make bulk," and deconsolidation (i.e., "break bulk")), and transshipment.

In the premultimodal logistical world, few companies were integrated to provide all the above services. The result was that physical distribution and logistical and customs arrangements were carried out by combinations of the following companies:

1. freight forwarders (domestic) or freight brokers (domestic);
2. foreign (or international) freight forwarders;
3. customs brokers;
4. customs clearing agents; and
5. export packagers.

Except for small or "odd-lot" shipments (the size or nature of which may best be handled by separate forwarding and customs broking companies), global freight forwarding and customs broking are integrated functions.

Where "non-full-service" domestic freight forwarders are called upon by the shipper to provide customs broking services (usually in smaller centers), a special brokerage fee is payable since the freight forwarder is acting as a customs broker (and, presumably, is licensed to do so).

foreign investment *See* direct investment.

Foreign Investment Insurance (FII) is an insurance program of the Export Development Corporation (EDC) that protects Canadians who invest in foreign countries.

FII service provides "cover" for the following three categories of political risks: (1) inconvertibility; (2) expropriation; and (3) war, revolution, and in-

surrection. The Canadian investor can apply for an insurance contract covering all or any combination of these risks for periods of up to 15 years.
Cf. Overseas Private Investment Corporation.
See also Export Development Corporation.

foreign investment law is legislation in socialist command economies, which governs:

1. the introduction of direct investment into these political-economies;
2. the type, size, number, and nature of the legal economic enterprises in which direct investment can be involved;
3. the sectors of economic activity in which the business firms can operate; and
4. the rules governing the rights to use intellectual property, transfer technology, and remit profits to the parent company.

> **Example:** The Polish Foreign Investment Law, officially entitled "The Law on Economic Activity with the Participation of Foreign Bodies," was passed on December 23, 1988, and came into force on January 1, 1989. Unlike the foreign investment laws in other socialist countries, the Polish Law permits the incorporation and operation of foreign corporations independent of a joint venture partner.
>
> Chapter 1, Article 1.2, of the Polish Law clearly states that economic activity defined as production, construction, trade, and services conducted for profit may be conducted either in the form of a limited-liability company or joint-stock company, meaning companies established jointly by Polish bodies and foreign bodies or exclusively by foreign bodies. The contribution of foreign parties may not be less than 20 percent of the registered capital.

See also nonmarket economy.

Foreign Investment Review Agency (FIRA) was an agency, founded in 1974 by the government of Canada, with the aim of:

1. screening all major direct investment in Canada to ensure that it was desirable from the viewpoint of Canadian economic nationalists (i.e., economic protectionists);
2. monitoring the movement of foreign capital once in Canada to ensure that certain politically designated sectors of the economy (e.g., "cultural industries," publishing) were not encroached upon by non-Canadian capitalists (i.e., the British, pre-World War II, then Americans, post-1945);
3. ensuring that all direct investment in Canada went into enterprise that was of "direct benefit to Canadians" (i.e., generated employment).

In 1985, FIRA was replaced by a new government agency called Investment Canada.
See also Investment Canada.

foreign invoice acceptance is the process of the importer acknowledging receipt of, and agreeing to pay, the export invoice.
Frequently, an importer will accept the obligation to pay an export invoice on terms that deprive the exporter of the capital required to expedite

the order. In such cases, if the importer endorses the invoice as "accepted," this signed document can be presented to a bank for possible sale.

See also foreign accounts receivable purchases; export financing.

foreign sales agent (FSA) is a commission salesperson, resident in a foreign country, who represents a domestic corporation locally.

> **Example:** To effectively "detail" the thousands of retail outlets on the island of Honshu, the U.S. pharmaceutical manufacturer hired teams of foreign sales agents to blitz designated territories. The teams took orders and did in-store merchandising work exclusively on behalf of the firm.

Cf. direct exporting.

Foreign Sales Corporation (FSC) is an export incentive vehicle for U.S. business, whereby a U.S. company, set up under the U.S. Deficit Reduction Act of 1984, can take legal advantage of the U.S. Tax Reform Act of 1984.

Using this strategy, a company elects to be taxed as a U.S. corporation formed in one of more than 30 U.S. Department of the Treasury–approved countries or territories that have a satisfactory Tax Information Exchange Agreement (TIEA) with the United States.

Some of the places that do have satisfactory TIEAs with the United States (and, consequently, have FSCs incorporated within their jurisdictions) are the U.S. Virgin Islands, Guam, and American Samoa.

The competitive advantage of an FSC is that a portion of the combined net income of it and its affiliated U.S. supplier is exempt from tax, contingent upon the percentage of the FSC's net income that was generated by the export of U.S. products.

Thus, the U.S. company is permitted an immediate and permanent benefit through income exclusion of export earnings.

To qualify to receive tax benefits, the FSC must have a maximum of 25 shareholders (with no outstanding preferred stock), maintain an office in an eligible jurisdiction in which it is organized, have at least one nonresident on its Board of Directors, and must not be a member of any Domestic International Sales Corporation (DISC) group.

The FSC is usually a U.S. subsidiary. The parent company uses the FSC as a conduit to which a portion of its foreign-earned profit may be passed in the form of a sales commission. The U.S. parent company reports 77 percent of the net foreign profit from its operations, and the FSC receives a commission of 23 percent, of which 8 percent is taxable and the remaining 15 percent is tax free. The FSC itself must pay quarterly taxes on the 8 percent earned.

At year end, the FSC pays an "after-tax dividend" that is eligible for a 100-percent "dividend-received deduction" by U.S. FSC shareholders.

Under the Canada-U.S. Free Trade Agreement (FTA), the benefits to U.S. companies to have FSCs can be enormous. Given the reducing tariffs on imports of U.S. goods, and the consequent increasing Canadian market potential for them, and the fact that all major U.S. companies operate through U.S. subsidiaries in Canada (which are wholly U.S. owned), U.S. business could legitimately reduce its high capital investment in (marginal) Canadian operations while still benefiting from increasing exports to Canada.

For example, an Ohio manufacturer could incorporate as an FSC in the U.S. Virgin Islands and elect to be taxed there as a U.S. corporation. The firm, working out of, say, Cincinnati, would export indirectly to a Canadian border-state company (an affiliate of its own company) in, say, New York or Vermont, which, in turn, would resell to its wholly U.S.-owned subsidiary in Canada. All that is needed is an annual statement (plus a master bill of materials sold) from the affiliate and the subsidiary in Canada; and the U.S. parent, having incorporated as an FSC in the U.S. Virgin Islands, can take advantage of the U.S. legislation governing exclusion of export income through its FSC and its affiliate.

For tax-reduction purposes, FSCs have generally replaced the U.S. Domestic International Sales Corporation (DISC).

Cf. Domestic International Sales Corporation.
See also Caribbean Basin Initiative.

foreign service premium *See* benefit gratuity.

foreign subsidiary (foreign-owned subsidiary) is a company that is owned by another company (the "parent company") and is located in a country other than the "home country" of the parent company.

foreign tax credit is the accounting credit permitted to Canadian or U.S. taxpayers against tax payable in their home country for tax paid to the foreign government.

Canadian and American citizens can claim this credit when they file their personal income tax each fiscal year.

foreign trade organization (FTO) is an official agency of a government of a nonmarket political-economy (e.g., Technomashimport in the Soviet Union) authorized to purchase from and sell to private companies in market-driven political-economies.

foreign trade zone (FTZ) is the standard American reference to a specifically designated area of a country that receives goods for further processing, assembly, warehousing, consolidation, transshipment, or any legitimate form of value-added activity; the goods are subsequently re-exported.

A foreign trade zone is also known as a:

1. free economic zone (FEZ),
2. free port,
3. free trade zone (FTZ),
4. export processing zone (EPZ),
5. duty free port (DFP),
6. duty free zone (DFZ),
7. *zona franca (ZF),* and
8. special economic zone (SEZ).

Activities in the FTZ are free from any duty/tariff as long as no goods are imported into the country in which the FTZ is an enclave.

Consumer exposure to FTZs comes in the form of the duty free shops at international airports where only passengers with either transit tickets or direct-exit tickets are permitted to purchase duty free goods (i.e., goods upon which import duties would normally be paid were they bought inside the country).

Industry exposure to FTZs comes by way of competitive pressure to drive down variable costs (especially labor costs) and the scanning of the global market for the location of appropriate FTZ facilities.

FOREX is the abbreviation of **for**eign **ex**change, as in:

- FOREX market (foreign exchange market),
- FOREX broker (foreign exchange broker), and
- FOREX trading (foreign exchange trading).

forfaiting is (1) a means of export financing whereby a financial institution purchases any type of deferred debt (for which it pays immediate cash) and endorses the instruments bought without recourse—because there is "no recourse" for payment to anyone except the issuer of the instrument, deferred debt is usually bought at a variable discount based on an assessment of the degree of foreign commercial and political risk to payment involved; and (2) a specific program of deferred-debt purchase by the Export Development Corporation (EDC) to facilitate medium- and long-term financing to foreign buyers of Canadian capital goods and services—under certain conditions, the EDC will purchase promissory notes issued to Canadian exporters by foreign buyers in payment for goods/services on medium-term credit. Foremost of these is that the note be guaranteed by a financial institution (in the buyer's country) by the EDC.

See also without-recourse financing; Export Development Corporation; export financing.

forfeiture is a type of debt repayment in which the importer (who borrows to finance the transaction) repays the factor in installments over an extended period of time.

See also factor.

foul bill of lading, also colloquially known as a *foul bill*, an *unclean bill of lading*, and an *unclean bill*, refers to a bill of lading, issued by the carrier, that bears the notation (usually by writing) that the goods have been received in a damaged condition.

Cf. bill of lading.

Fourth World is an ethnocentric reference to those countries called *least developed countries (LLDCs)*.

Cf. Third World.

See also ethnocentrism.

Four Tigers, also called the *Four Dragons*, is a term for the important newly industrialized countries (NICs) of Hong Kong, Taiwan, Singapore, and South Korea.

Cf. Five Tigers.

See also newly industrialized countries.

framework agreement is a formal understanding that paints the "broad strokes" of agreed trade objectives and the arrangements to be put in place to reach them.

Cf. functional trade agreement.

franc, of unknown origin, possibly derived from *Francorum Rex*, Latin for "King of the Franks," when early (fourteenth century) gold coinage was issued under the authority of the Frankish King, is the currency of France, Belgium, Luxembourg, and Switzerland, issued by the central banks of each country.

The franc was previously represented by "F," "Fr.," and "f." It has been standardized as "F" by the International Organization for Standardization (ISO): 10 CHF = 10 Swiss francs; 10 BEF = 10 Belgian francs; 10 FRF = 10 French francs; 10 LUF = 10 Luxembourg francs.

Cf. *lingua franca*; *CFA franc*; *CFP franc*.

franc area (franc zone) *See* currency area.

franchising is a form of licensing whereby a company (the licensor or franchisor) makes available to a foreign company (the licensee or franchisee), on an exclusive basis, the right to distribute its product and/or service for a fee (a royalty).

Cf. licensing.

franchising agreement is the documentary formalization of a legal franchising process between a franchisor and a franchisee.

See also franchising.

francophone, from *Franco* meaning "French" and *phone* meaning "voice," refers to a national of a country (not necessarily France) whose mother tongue, or predominant language choice, is the French language.

Cf. anglophone.

free economic zone (FEZ) *See* foreign trade zone.

freely convertible currency *See* convertible currency.

free of capture and seizure (FC&S) *See* Appendix III.

Cf. political risks.

free of particular average (FPA) *See* Appendix III.

free of particular average American conditions (FPAAC) *See* Appendix III.

free of particular average English conditions (FPAEC) *See* Appendix III.

freely floating exchange rate system is the system of elastic rates of exchange between different currencies that is determined by the market forces of supply and demand without any government intervention in the foreign exchange market.

See also Appendix II.

free port is an ocean port through which goods may be transshipped without incurring duties.

    See also foreign trade zone.

free trade is (1) an economic concept used to denote trade among nations unimpeded by government restrictions, ideally subject to the laws of supply and demand of the market; (2) a comparative concept used to denote the relative difference in circumstances between trade impeded by government restrictions and the achievement of other circumstances in which international trade would ideally be unhampered by government-imposed restrictions; and (3) a legal concept, rooted in Article XXIV of the General Agreement on Tariffs and Trade (GATT), that allows preferential access to markets when all international trade is flowing "barrier-free."

    See also General Agreement on Tariffs and Trade; Canada-U.S. Free Trade Agreement of 1989.

Free Trade Agreement of 1989 (FTA) *See* Canada-U.S. Free Trade Agreement of 1989.

free trade area (FTA) is (1) a concept defined in the General Agreement on Tariffs and Trade (GATT), Part III, Article XXIV, 8 (a), "to mean a group of two or more customs territories in which the duties and other restrictive regulations of commerce . . . are eliminated in products originating in such territories"; and (2) an agreement among nations to remove all barriers (i.e., tariff and nontariff barriers) to trade among group members, while retaining the barriers of each individual member on trade with nongroup members.

In practice, members of free trade areas maintain actual control over commercial policy for, and trade negotiations with, third countries. This "area of active sovereignty" frequently complicates (and strains) policy discussions (and the climate of amity) when, for example, each of the members of the European Free Trade Association (EFTA) insisted on negotiating separate reciprocal trade treaties with each of the 12 members of the EEC.

    Cf. common market.

    See also European Free Trade Association; European Economic Community.

free trade zone (FTZ) *See* foreign trade zone.

freight is the collective noun for goods either designated for or in the actual process of physical movement, usually from a seller to a buyer, by road, rail, and air carriers.

    Example: The ship's container cargo was unloaded at Halifax, converted into COFC (container-on-flat-car) freight at dockside, and moved by railway to Montréal.

    Cf. cargo; goods.

freight broker (domestic) *See* freight forwarder (domestic).
Cf. broker.

freight forwarder (domestic) is a company whose business was exclusively that of contracting with carriers on behalf of shippers of goods for export and arranging for the goods to arrive at the appropriate inland or ocean port, train terminal, or airport for shipping by the carrier to the consignee.

This function has now been taken over by a more fully integrated intermediary.

See also foreign freight forwarder.

freight villa •NW• is a second house in Japan exclusively for storing personal household goods.

Because of the high price of land in Japan in general and in Tokyo in particular, the cost of storing (seasonal) household items, such as New Year's decorations, is only affordable outside the city where the lower land prices make storage less expensive. The out-of-town storage facilities may consist of a genuine warehouse or they may simply be a room in a private house.

Cf. trunk rooming •NW•.

French Community *See* currency area.

friendship, commerce, and navigation (FCN) treaty *See* Appendix VI.

FSC *See* foreign sales corporation.

FTA Commission is a top-level institution of the Canada-U.S. Free Trade Agreement of 1989 (FTA), established under the authority of Chapter 18 of the Treaty.

The Commission is co-chaired by the U.S. Trade Representative (USTR) and the Canadian Minister of International Trade, and it comprises executive branch members of both governments.

The Commission's key responsibilities are to supervise the implementation and smooth running of the FTA (at the executive levels of both governments) and to participate in the binational dispute-settlement mechanism under Article 1805 (1) (2) of the FTA.

See also binational dispute-settlement mechanism.

FTA Select (Auto) Panel is a group of specialists, appointed by the U.S. Trade Representative (USTR) and the Canadian Minister of International Trade, who comprise a committee (under Article 1004 of the Canada-U.S. Free Trade Agreement of 1989) charged with the task of assessing the state of the North American automotive industry and of proposing public policy measures and private initiatives to improve its competitiveness in domestic and foreign markets.

The formation of this panel is in line with the ongoing consolidation and integration of the North American automotive industry, some of the aims being to reduce the North American production "oversupply," to "rationalize" production costs, and to identify new export market opportunities *vis-à-vis* Japanese and European Economic Community (EEC) competitors.

functional intermediary is someone in an international marketing channel who provides services that in some way physically affect the physical goods and, thereby, assist in their movement in the direction of the customer.

> **Example:** Export packers (who consolidate cargo with protective packaging) and cargo carriers (who actually move the goods along various points between seller and buyer) are examples of functional intermediaries.

functional trade agreement is a trade accord limited in scope to special measures used to "manage trade" between the trading partners.

> **Example:** The formal agreement between Canada and Japan, whereby Japan "voluntarily" agreed to limit its exports of automobiles to Canada, is a functional trade agreement.
>
> When Canada and the European Economic Community (EEC) meet for trade talks, they often seek to work out functional trade agreements to formalize the rules for the reciprocal use of countervailing duties.

> Cf. framework agreement.

fundamental disequilibrium is a macroeconomic situation of a country that is characterized by it having serious, large, and persistent current account imbalances (either a surplus or a deficit), which could lead to unsustainable capital flows.

> The enormous, ongoing, current account surplus of the Japanese has been interpreted by many economists as a fundamentally disequilibrating situation; and the Japanese approach that gave rise to it has been termed "confrontational trade" in comparison to the conventional view of trade as being essentially "equitable" and "reciprocal."
>
> It is suggested that this view explains the growth of protectionist "regionalism" and the increasingly favorable political climate for the introduction and ultimately successful acceptance of the U.S. Omnibus Trade Act of 1988 and, beyond that, the bilateral Canada-U.S. Free Trade Agreement of 1989 and perhaps even a North American Free Trade Agreement (NAFTA).

See also balance of payments; regionalization of trade •NW•.

g

GATT is the abbreviation for **G**eneral **A**greement on **T**ariffs and **T**rade.

GATT Agreements *See* Tokyo Round [for a complete list].

GATT Customs Valuation Code is the multilaterally agreed formula used to appraise imported goods for the purpose of determining the amount of duty payable by the importer in the importing country.

For customs purposes, the Code stipulates that Contracting Parties to GATT and signatories to the Code must use the price actually paid for the goods (termed the "transaction value") rather than their "market price," as the basis for valuing the goods.

See also valuation.

GATT dispute-settlement system is a formal arrangement of rules, procedures, and actions to be followed by the Contracting Parties to GATT for the reconciliation of their differences in matters involving trade with each other.

The first step is a complaint to GATT and the request by the complaining party for GATT to establish a dispute-settlement panel.

Next, the "complainor" presents its evidence to the panel, and the "complainee" responds to the charges.

Following the trying of the merits of the case, the panel renders its judgment. There are mechanisms for appeal of a judgment on various legal grounds; but when the judgment is accepted by the GATT Council (representing all the Contracting Parties to GATT), the "offending party" must comply with the judgment, and it has a reasonable time to do so.

If the "offending party" fails to implement the judgment of the GATT panel within a reasonable time, the "injured party" has remedies available to it. It may request GATT for authority to "suspend substantially equivalent concessions" (i.e., to retaliate).

It may, on the other hand, accept compensation from the "offending party." Such compensation is usually in the form of concessions (i.e., reduced tariffs).

The GATT Council is legally empowered to authorize either retaliation or compensation only to the value of the damage caused. It cannot initiate any compensatory process for "punitive" purposes, as this action would be a deviation into an area of political jurisdiction, which is not the authorized domain of GATT, but rather of such supranational organizations as the United Nations System and the World Court.

Cf. retaliation.

See also U.S. "Superfund"; Appendix VI (retortion).

Gemeinschaft, from the German for "community," is a term, introduced into sociology by Ferdinand Tönnies, taken to mean a society (either Western or non-Western) that is nonindustrial and "traditional" in its social structure.

> **Example:** Marketers in rural India have found that promotional tools such as radio have more long-term influence on potential consumers there than do either television, cinema, or newspaper, because, compared with Bombay, rural Indian societies still remain overwhelmingly *Gemeinschaft*.

Tönnies' meaning varied considerably from modern understanding and current usage. According to him, *Gemeinschaft* is a type of social structure in which family life (and the traditional authority structures within the kinship group, the village, and the town) is at the center of social action, which, in turn, was governed by folkways, customs, mores, and religion. To him, all society originated as *Gemeinschaft*.

Cf. *Gesellschaft*.

GEMSU is the abbreviation for **G**erman **E**conomic, **M**onetary, and **S**ocial **U**nion, the *Treaty Between the Federal Republic of Germany (FRG) and the (German) Democratic Republic (GDR) Establishing a Monetary, Economic and Social Union*, signed May 1990 and in effect as of July 1, 1990.

The GEMSU Treaty binds the FRG and the (former) GDR within a new legal framework of political union, to advance the following principles by way of legislation and implementation: (1) private ownership (especially privatization of all (former) East German state-controlled/owned industry); (2) fiscal discipline (i.e., adoption of market-driven price setting and abolishment of state subsidies to agriculture and industry); (3) federal fiscal structures (i.e., the acceptance of the *Bundesbank* as the central bank); (4) a social safety net (i.e., a social security system, to cushion the impact on (former) East Germans of re-entry into the free market world); and (5) an environmental program (i.e., measures to enforce adherence by "dirty industries" in former East Germany to modern European standards of environmental protection and repair.

> **Example:** On July 1, 1990, the West German mark (DEM) became the legal currency of East Germany whose Ostmark became convertible to DEMs at the rate of 1:1. The high rate of currency exchange was mandated by West German chancellor Helmut Kohl, over the head of the Bundesbank president, Karl Otto Pöhl. Kohl's aim was to stem the massive emigration from East

Germany and to stabilize the East German economy. Since unification, however, unemployment in former East Germany has leaped to 8.9 percent, and many enterprises have gone bankrupt.

In an effort to raise the estimated 20 billion DEM in 1991 needed to help pay for German reunification, Germany's ruling party, the Christian Democratic Union, backed a proposal to levy a 5 percent surcharge on income taxes.

See also German reunification.

General Agreement on Tariffs and Trade (GATT) is a multilateral treaty (signed by 101 nations as of January 11, 1991) the basic aim of which is (1) to liberalize and promote world trade via multilateral trade negotiations, (2) to place world trade on a secure basis, and thereby (3) to contribute to global economic growth and development.

1. *Background:* The General Agreement was negotiated in 1947. It came into force in January 1948. At the time, the 23 nations that signed the General Agreement were in the process of drawing up a charter for a specialized United Nations organization called the International Trade Organization (ITO). It was assumed that the General Agreement would be managed by the ITO.

   However, when the Charter for the ITO was not passed by the required two-thirds of the U.N. General Assembly, plans for the ITO were abandoned. Thus, the General Agreement became the only international instrument that formed the foundation for international trade that was accepted by most of the world's trading nations.

2. *GATT Principles and Rules:* The General Agreement is the only multilateral, international organization that lays down specific rules for international trade. (In addition, the GATT also functions as the principal international body for negotiations about the reduction of tariff and nontariff barriers.)

   The General Agreement itself is complex, and sometimes so are its Rules (embodied in the Articles of the GATT). However, all of them are based on the following fundamental Principles of International Trade:

   - PRINCIPLE 1: *Trade without Discrimination*—All parties that are signatories of the GATT are bound to grant to each other treatment as favorable as they grant to any other nation in the application of import and export tariffs. This is the famous "most-favored-nation (MFN) clause."
   - PRINCIPLE 2: *Protection through Tariffs*—Tariffs are the only internationally acceptable means for protecting domestic industry: commercial measures (i.e., nontariff barriers) are not an acceptable means for protecting domestic industry.
   - PRINCIPLE 3: *A Stable Basis for Trade*—A stable and predictable basis for international trade is provided by the "binding of the tariff levels" negotiated and agreed among the Contracting Parties to the GATT. (Tariff schedules in which "bound" items are listed for each country form an integral part of the GATT.) Provisions exist for the renegotiation of bound tariffs.

- PRINCIPLE 4: *Consultation, Conciliation, and Peaceful Settlement of Differences*—It is expected that all signatories to the GATT will consult with each other in trade matters and will aim to resolve differences in a peaceful manner, including the use of the GATT for hearings on and arbitration of disputed trade matters.

3. *GATT Headquarters:* The Secretariat of the GATT is located in Geneva, Switzerland.

4. *GATT Institutions:* The supreme GATT institution is the Session of Contracting Parties. It is held annually. Consensus is used for arriving at decisions, although voting is used on difficult issues.

   Thus, when GATT members act collectively (either via concensus or vote), they are called Contracting Parties in all GATT documents and in all other documents that make reference to the status of member nations that act in accordance with their legal obligations under the GATT.

   Between Sessions of the Contracting Parties, the GATT Council of Representatives is authorized to act.

5. *GATT Committee Work:* Apart from the United Nations Conference on Trade and Development (UNCTAD), the Trade Negotiations Committee (TNC) of the Group of Negotiations on Goods (GNG) oversees the work of 14 major GATT Standing Committees (or Groups) before, during, and after each round of multilateral trade negotiations. These are as follows:
   a. Negotiating Group on Nontariff Measures,
   b. Negotiating Group on Natural Resource-Based Products,
   c. Negotiating Group on Textiles and Clothing,
   d. Negotiating Group on Agriculture,
   e. Negotiating Group on Tropical Products,
   f. Negotiating Group on Subsidies,
   g. Negotiating Group on GATT Articles,
   h. Negotiating Group on Multilateral Trade Negotiations (MTN) Agreements and Arrangements,
   i. Negotiating Group on Safeguards,
   j. Negotiating Group on Trade-Related Aspects of Intellectual Property Rights (TRIPS),
   k. Negotiating Group on Trade-Related Investment Measures (TRIMS),
   l. Negotiating Group on Dispute Settlement,
   m. Negotiating Group on the Functioning of the GATT System (FOGS),
   n. Group of Negotiations on Services.

   In addition, Working Parties (i.e., ad hoc committees) are established (1) to investigate urgent, current issues; (2) to deal with requests for accession to the GATT; (3) to verify that agreements concluded by member nations are in conformity with the GATT; and (4) to study any issues on which member countries may later wish to make a joint decision.

   Further, in accordance with Principle 4, Panels of Conciliation are established (on an ad hoc basis) to investigate disputes between member countries.

   See also United Nations Conference on Trade and Development; International Trade Center UNCTAD/GATT; round of trade negotiations; Tokyo Round (for the list of GATT Agreements and Codes); Uruguay Round.

General Agreements to Borrow (GAB) is the name for the arrangements under which the International Monetary Fund (IMF) negotiates with the Group of Ten (G-10) to borrow needed funds to augment Fund reserves in order to extend help to nations with balance-of-payments (BOP) difficulties.
See also International Monetary Fund; Group of Ten.

general average *See* Appendix III.

generalized system of preferences (GSP) refers to an agreement developed in 1968 in New Delhi, India, at the second meeting of the United Nations Conference on Trade and Development (UNCTAD II) and first implemented in 1971, whereby 27 developed countries granted nonreciprocal preferences to developing countries (LDCs) (i.e., the developed countries were asked to reduce their import duties in favor of imports from LDCs on a nonreciprocal basis).
The agreement that established the GSP (1) recognizes the need to encourage the growth of manufactured exports from developing countries, and (2) endorses the principle of nonreciprocal grants of preference (i.e., tariff reductions) by developed countries to developing countries to make manufactured exports more competitive.
In operation since 1976, the GSP has grown to involve 16 separate programs established by 27 "preference-giving" countries, comprising 22 industrialized "market economies" and 5 "nonmarket (command) economies" of East Europe.

The GSP has become important to developing countries since it has, under the concept of "equalizing the international terms of trade," artificially increased the comparative advantage of developing countries by forcing developed countries to permit concessions to them. The outcome has resulted in "acceptable levels of injury" to the domestic industries of developed market economies in the name of "equity." These trade concessions (i.e., the reduction of tariffs) increase the export possibilities for developing countries and their potential for export earnings.
The United States enacted the GSP in the Trade Act of 1974 under Title V and renewed it in the Trade and Tariff Act of 1984. The GSP, as adopted by the United States, applies to goods imported from January 1, 1976, to July 4, 1993.

See also GSP Form A; infant industry argument; United Nations Conference on Trade and Development.

Geneva Convention for the Protection of Producers of Phonograms Against Unauthorized Duplication of Their Phonograms, known as the *Geneva Convention*, is a multilateral treaty signed by states to afford them substantial protection of intellectual property.
The treaty is administered by the World Intellectual Property Organization (WIPO).
See also World Intellectual Property Organization.

geocentrism (geocentric) •NW•, from the Greek *geo* meaning "earth" and *kentrikos* meaning "center," is the process of taking a worldview (being globally-oriented) toward a "global marketplace."

See also EPRG [framework].

geographic hole •NW• is the physical absence of a global corporation from a place in one of the regional areas of the world that is perceived to be important; its absence is detrimental to the globalization of the company's market offerings.

> **Example:** Ford Automotive Group has no subsidiaries in Japan. To fill this major geographic hole, Ford owns 25 percent of Mazda and builds the Mazda-designed Tracer in Mexico. With Nissan, Ford will build a Nissan-designed minivan in Ohio and will market it in the United States.
>
> In Korea, where Ford also has another geographic hole, Ford markets the Festiva designed by Ford and made by Kia in Korea.

See also niche.

German Economic, Monetary, and Social Union *See* GEMSU.

German reunification, also called *German unification*, is the concept of bringing together under a single political-economic system the Federal Republic of Germany (FRG), or West Germany, and the Democratic Republic of Germany (DRG), or East Germany.

The two Germanys were created at the end of World War II as a consequence of the National Socialist (Nazi) Government's military defeat by the Allies. The ensuing two political entities correspond to the German territory occupied by the United States, United Kingdom, and France (in the West) and by the Soviet Union (in the East).

The subject of reunifying the two Germanys became a serious issue (1) when the Berlin Wall, erected by the DRG in 1961, was dismantled officially by them in November 1989 and (2) when continuous political change routed (in succession) the communist governments of the DRG, Poland, Czechoslovakia, Bulgaria, and Romania in October to December of 1989.

Thus, German reunification began on November 9, 1989, when the GDR authorities announced they would permit free, unhindered access to and egress from the GDR, following weeks of massive emigration from the country.

The German Economic, Monetary, and Social Union (GEMSU) treaty that unified Germany monetarily took effect July 1, 1990, when the West German mark (DEM) became the legal currency of East Germany. Official unification occurred on October 3, 1990.

The DRG, with a per capita income of U.S. $9,200 compared to the FRG's U.S. $15,800, was an economy centrally planned and thus highly state-subsidized and one in which most of its output was either devoted to meet the minimal needs of the population or to supply the demand in other "fraternal nations" in the Council for Mutual Economic Assistance (CMEA). It was an economy with multiple price structures and one that was not driven by open, free market competition.

In one of many "unification scenarios," the economic burden falling on the FRG comprised (1) an addition of nearly 2 percent to its population due to DRG emigration; (2) steep rises in FRG welfare payments; (3) enormous diversion of resources to provide new resettlement housing; and (4) ultimately the devaluation of the Deutsche mark (DEM), given the monetary unification of the FRG's DEM with the DRG's nonconvertible currency, the Ostmark.

It is estimated that the black-market exchange rate of Ostmarks for DEMs was at least 6:1, compared with the "official" exchange rate of 1:1 in effect on October 3, 1990.

A DEM devaluation would make the currency more attractive to some investors while, at the same time, driving others from it and, thus, accelerating the loss of confidence. Currency traders will move to other currencies that are perceived to be relatively more stable and under less pressure. The prospects will be for a volatile and unsettling period while Europe as a whole is in transition, moving toward the European Economic Space (EES) as the ideal.

For international marketers, the opportunity of an enormous "cheap labor pool" of East European workers exists, but it is one that causes concern among the European Economic Community (EEC) members who fear that new research and development (R&D), investment, production, and marketing will be done in Eastern Europe *vis-à-vis* the EEC or the European Free Trade Association (EFTA).

Cf. European Economic Community.

See also Council for Mutual Economic Assistance; European Economic Space; GEMSU; production sharing.

Gesellschaft, from the German meaning "urban society," is a term, introduced into sociology by Ferdinand Tönnies, taken to mean a society that was Western and industrial in its social structure.

> **Example:** Marketers in Bombay have found it easier to influence potential consumers there than in rural India. The cosmopolitan nature of the city has eroded traditional kinship and religious ties, and pressures to survive and advance have massified people economically.

Tönnies' meaning varied considerably from modern understanding and current usage. According to him, *Gesellschaft* is a type of social structure in which family life (and the traditional authority structures within the kinship group, the village, and the town) is replaced by city life, which itself if directed by nothing except economic means and to nothing except economic goals.

At the center of social action are fearful masses who are governed by impersonal rules, regulations, and laws of the overarching state.

To Tönnies, all society that transformed itself into *Gesellschaft* decayed and lost the close-knit, enduring values of human life.

Cf. *Gemeinschaft*.

glasnost, from the Russian meaning "openness," is an official Soviet political policy of "information sharing" between the Soviet Union and its citizens on the one hand and its international trading partners on the other.

The reason for increased political openness in the Soviet Union is *perestroika* and the urgent need for increased agricultural productivity and for the reverse of industrial stagnation. These goals can only be achieved within a relatively lenient political atmosphere instead of the traditional authoritarian, intolerant, Stalinist approach.

See also perestroika.

global alliancing •NW•, also called *global strategic alliancing* or *international strategic alliancing*, is a global marketing strategy involving, at its core, the formation of major, long-term, cooperative relationships between companies, aimed at sharing the enormous fixed costs incurred in establishing and profitably running global marketing operations.

The institutional outcome of the process is private international agreements (or contracts) called global alliances.

Since automation (and increasingly, robotization) have driven labor costs out of manufacturing, production and attendant research and development (R&D) have become a "fixed-cost activity"; and because the costs of technology and fixed installations are so high, they require enormously large sales of global dimensions (i.e., a worldwide market base) for their amortization.

Global alliances do not necessarily mean reciprocal equity ownership in the partners' companies: they do mean the sharing of (1) intellectual property (e.g., patents, trademarks, trade processes) and of (2) technology, via leasing and contract manufacturing, to generate global demand and to satisfy it.

The traditional "equity-based mind set" that spawned the "joint venture" tends to reduce difficulties to easy, manageable stereotypes instead of seeking rational, value-free answers, regardless of the nationality of the managers and the source of their technology or of their capital.

Cf. global linkage; global marketing; joint venture; contract manufacturing.

Global Contracts Comprehensive Insurance (GCCI) is an insurance program of the Export Development Corporation (EDC), which protects Canadian exporters engaged in continuous international trade. GCCI provides "cover" (from the time the goods are ordered until payment is received) against nonpayment of a credit from an export sale due to commercial risks and political risks.

See also Export Development Corporation; commercial risks; political risks.

global corporation is a profit-making enterprise, usually a private company, that carries out global marketing.

Cf. multinational corporation.

global linkage is a structure involving worldwide networks of interdependent units of finance, transportation, banking, marketing, and logistics.

global marketing is (1) the activity of a global corporation that seeks to achieve long-run, large-scale production efficiencies by producing standardized products of good value and long-term reliability for all consumers (or industrial users) in all segments of all markets; and (2) the marketing of a standardized product on a worldwide basis, with little allowance for, or acceptance of, regional or local differentiation of the marketing-mix strategies.

Example: Coca-Cola is the quintessential global corporation, which markets an identical ingredient formula and primary package worldwide. Of necessity, the labeling on the bottle, and on the secondary containers, varies (e.g., "disfrute Coca-Cola" [Spanish] v. "Savourez Coca-Cola" [French]). But every country's marketing program contains the same core message, the same core consumer promise, and the same core perception of benefit. (In the Coca-Cola "corporate culture," it is called "One sight, one sound.")

At the physical level of corporate control of the global marketing effort is the commitment to global standardization. Every week from every plant where Coke is bottled globally, a random sampling of the product arrives in Atlanta for quality control testing, aimed at ensuring that the product is identical regardless of where it originates.

Cf. multinational marketing.
See also global corporation.

global monetarism is an extreme monetarist position that holds that in the long term, the Law of One Price will prevail throughout the world.

In other words, as the world trading system becomes increasingly integrated, commodity prices for all internationally traded goods (and interest rates) will become homogeneous globally (i.e., will move toward "one price") when expressed in terms of the same currency.

Global monetarism also holds that in the long run, national income will automatically tend toward full employment, but it subsumes an increasing integration of world trading markets.

Global monetarism has (pejoratively) been termed "voodoo economics" and "Reaganomics," after former U.S. president Ronald Reagan, a staunch adherent of the ideas of Milton Friedman, Nobel Laureate in Economics and founder of the Chicago School of neoclassical economics.

One of the bases of this disparagement was the macroeconomic shambles created in Chile following the 1973 military overthrow of the democratically elected socialist government of Salvador Allende by the junta of General Augusto Pinochet. By "Soviet/CMEA-model" standards, Allende's economic programs were radically middle-of-the-socialist-road, à la Yugoslavia.

In contrast to them, Pinochet's clique rapidly implemented the extreme teachings of the Chicago School, regressing Chile from a "neo-quasi-European economy" to a "hewer of wood and drawer of water."

The consequent proletarianization of the Chilean middle classes and the intelligensia tarnished the credibility of Friedman and global monetarism, even though it was the actual implementation of Friedman's ideas that was faulty.

Nevertheless, since it was all done "in the name of Friedman," it cannot but blemish the man, if in no other way than through "consciousness of a kind": association between those who shared a common economic outlook and those who tried to promote and implement it.

See also monetarism.

global scanning •NW• is the process of systematically carrying out a program of monitoring, reviewing, and analyzing data on a specific subject, sector, or industry from multiple sources to detect significant changes in the regional and global environments (technological, legal, political, military) regarding problems and opportunities for a business entity.

To be successful, global scanning involves the following activities:

1. sending informed observers to international trade shows and conferences to assess their competitors;
2. gathering data on government-funded research programs at home and in other countries; and
3. reviewing newspapers, magazines, periodicals, and government publications published in foreign countries on relevant subjects.

Global Services Comprehensive Insurance (GSeCI) is an insurance program of the Export Development Corporation (EDC) that protects Canadian exporters engaged in continuous international trade. GSeCI provides "cover" (during the period the services are performed until payment is received) against nonpayment of a credit from an export sale due to commercial risks and political risks.

See also Export Development Corporation; commercial risks; political risks.

Global Shipments Comprehensive Insurance (GShCI) is an insurance program of the Export Development Corporation (EDC) that protects Canadian exporters engaged in continuous international trade. GShCI provides "cover" (from the time the goods are shipped until payment is received) against nonpayment of a credit from an export sale due to commercial risks and political risks.

See also Export Development Corporation; commercial risks; political risks.

global strategy refers to the methods (but especially the overall plan) used to achieve global marketing objectives.

See also global marketing.

Global System of Trade Preferences *See* Generalized System of Preferences (GSP).

global village •NW• refers to the modern world (according to Marshall McLuhan) that, due to modern means of mass communications, can be reduced to the size of a preindustrial village for communications purposes.

GmbH is the abbreviation for the German *Gesellschaft mit beschrankter Haftung* meaning "organization with limited liability."

Cf. AG.

See also Gesellschaft.

Going Global, a variation of the Three Pillar Strategy, is a worldwide trade approach of the Canadian government to the year 2000.

gold exchange standard *See* Bretton Woods System.

gold export point is the mint parity plus transportation costs of shipping an amount of gold (equal to one unit of the foreign currency) between two countries.

Cf. gold import point.

gold import point is the mint parity minus transportation costs of shipping an amount of gold (equal to one unit of the foreign currency) between two countries.

Cf. gold export point.

gold pool was an international agreement whereby a reservoir of gold was used by the Group of Ten (G-10) in 1961 from which the market in London, England, was supplied to prevent the official price of gold rising above U.S. $35 per ounce.

In 1968, the pool collapsed, and it was replaced by the two-tier gold market.

See also two-tier gold market.

gold standard is the term that refers to the (now-defunct) international monetary system whereby:

1. gold (the most valuable specie, or precious metal) was the exclusive international reserve;
2. intercountry exchange rates fluctuated only within the gold points (i.e., the gold import and export points); and
3. balance-of-payments adjustment was accounted for by the price-specie flow mechanism.

The gold standard operated from *circa* 1870 to 1914, and it was commonly characterized by currency notes on which were printed the words "backed by gold."

Cf. international monetary system.

See also price-specie flow mechanism.

gold tranche, *tranche* from the French meaning "slice," is the 25 percent of a country's International Monetary Fund (IMF) quota required to be paid into the Fund in gold, which then could be borrowed by the contributor country at will.

See also International Monetary Fund.

good *See* commodity.

good neighborly treatment is a type of friendship, commerce, and navigation (FCN) treaty whereby each signatory country agreed that no country (in accordance with international law) had the unilateral right to intervene in the affairs of any other signatory country.

Developed under the U.S. presidential administration of Franklin D. Roosevelt, the Good Neighbor Policy, as it was then called, referred to the climate of reduced political tension between the United States and its Pan-American allies. This resulted from the "nonintervention in the affairs of others" idea enunciated by the United States at the 1933 Pan-American Conference in Montevideo, Uruguay. In international law, the concept contributed to the peaceful settlement of international disputes both in Latin America and elsewhere.

See also Appendix VI (friendship, commerce, and navigation treaty).

Goods and Services Tax (GST) is the name of the Canadian federal government's comprehensive "consumption tax."
See also value-added tax.

Government Accounts *See* Canada Account.

government procurement is the process of acquisition of goods and services by official government agencies.

This process (especially where capital projects are funded by multilateral development banks) involves the submission of bids by multinational corporations or global companies.

It may comprise bid guarantees, performance guarantees, and the appropriate export insurance to provide "cover" (from the time the bid is submitted until the contract is completed).

See also Agreement on Government Procurement; Export Development Corporation; multilateral development banks.

graduation is a term used to refer to the movement of a country from eligibility on either individual generalized system of preferences (GSP)-eligible products or on the entire schedule of them.

Example: Due to Brazil's remarkable industrial development, it is ultimately expected to graduate from GSP eligibility in all classes of semi-manufactured goods.

See also generalized system of preferences.

grandfather clause is a passage in an international trade agreement that provides that certain existing programs and practices are exempted from a specific obligation.

Example: A provision exists in the General Agreement on Tariffs and Trade (GATT) whereby the original Contracting Parties were permitted to accept the general obligations of the GATT despite the fact that there existed, in various member countries, domestic legislation that was contrary to, or inconsistent with, the GATT.

See also General Agreement on Tariffs and Trade; residual restrictions.

gray market refers to the offshore producers and the domestic importers and resellers of gray market goods.

gray market goods are commodities that are either mimics (close duplications called "knock-offs," "pass-offs") or counterfeits of genuine products.

Mimicry is achieved by closely copying product design (usually) in low-wage offshore centers, using low-cost substitute materials.

Example: Clever Gucci and Rolex knock-offs are made in the NICs. Almost impossible to spot at a distance, they use (at best) 10K gold, imitation leather, and rhinestones instead of 18K gold, real leather, and diamonds. The genuine Oyster Shell Rolex sells in the $5,000-to- $18,000 range. A gray market Rolex—albeit without the Rolex three-pointed-crown trade mark—sells for $99.

Counterfeiting is not only the attempt at duplication of the original, but also the representation (the "passing off") of the duplicate as if it were the original.

Example: To sell a "knock-off Rolex" as a "knock-off Rolex" is not illegal unless patents, copyrights, and industrial designs have been infringed. On the other hand, to market jeans that bear genuine Levi Strauss red labels sewn into nongenuine "Levi Strauss" jeans is to manufacture and market counterfeit products.

See also intellectual property.

gray marketing is the process of promoting, displaying, transporting, and selling gray market goods.
See also gray market; gray market goods; intellectual property.

gray money *See* dirty money.

Gresham's law is the observation that "bad money drives out good." It is named after the English businessman and public servant Sir Thomas Gresham.

gross domestic product (GDP) is the value of a country's goods and services produced by residents within the country during a specified accounting period, usually one year.
Cf. gross national product.

gross national product (GNP) is the value of a country's income earned by residents both within and outside the country during a specified accounting period, usually one year.
Cf. gross domestic product.

groupism •NW• is a Japanese concept that the interests of the group supersede the interests of the individual and that all group members are required to subordinate their wishes to those of the group.
This concept is sustained by *tatemae*, which is used among Japanese colleagues in work situations, in contrast to *honne*, which is not.
See also situational conformity; *yoroshiku tanomu* •NW•; *tatemae*; *honne* •NW•; *nemawashi* •NW•.

Group of Five (G-5) refers to the reserve currency countries who are represented in the International Monetary Fund (IMF) "basket": the United States, Germany, Japan, the United Kingdom, and France.

Group of Four (G-4) refers to the four Latin American countries that together form South America's "Southern Cone": Brazil, Argentina, Uruguay, and Paraguay.

Group of One •NW• (G-1) is an ethnocentric self-reference relative to other political-economies.

Group of Seven (G-7) refers to those members of the Organization for Economic Cooperation and Development (OECD) that represent the core developed nations in the world. They are the United States, Japan, Germany, the United Kingdom, France, Canada, and Italy.
    Cf. Group of Thirteen.
    See also reserve currency country; Organization for Economic Cooperation and Development; policy coordination.

Group of Seventy-Seven (G-77) is a group of countries, comprising both the core and the periphery of developing countries in Africa, Asia, and Latin America, that formed at the conclusion of the U.N. Conference on Trade and Development (UNCTAD I) in 1964 in Geneva, Switzerland.
    The Group's Joint Declaration reflected a concensus among the LDCs regarding their perception of unfair treatment by the International Monetary Fund (IMF), in particular, and by the structure of the world trading system, in general. It demanded major income transfers from developed countries to developing ones and a restructuring of the world trading system.
    See also United Nations Conference on Trade and Development; Group of Twenty-Four.

Group of Ten (G-10) is the Group of Seven plus Sweden, Belgium, and the Netherlands.

Group of Thirteen •NW• (G-13) refers to thirteen countries that, in September 1989, formed a group to rival the perceived dominance of the Organization of Economic Cooperation and Development (OECD) by the Group of Seven (G-7).
    Members of the G-13 are as follows: Algeria, Argentina, Egypt, India, Indonesia, Jamaica, Malaysia, Nigeria, Perú, Sénégal, Venezuela, Yugoslavia, and Zimbabwe.
    Cf. Group of Seven.
    See also Organization for Economic Cooperation and Development.

Group of Twenty-Five (G-25) is an informal group whose trade ministers represent from 25 to 30 countries and whose trade interests are neither as narrow as the Cairns Group nor as broadly based as the complete General Agreement on Tariffs and Trade (GATT) group.
    The G-25 meets on an "occasional basis" to informally air international trade concerns (e.g., intellectual property, agricultural subsidies, nontariff barriers) and to form a concensus that can be used in formal GATT negotiations.

Group of Twenty-Four (G-24), officially, the *Intergovernmental Group of Twenty-Four on International Monetary Affairs*, is a core group of nations representative of African, Asian, and Latin American international monetary interests, that was formed at the Group of Seventy-Seven (G-77) meeting in Lima, Perú, in 1972 and that was subsequently given quasi-formal recognition by the International Monetary Fund, whose meetings (of the Interim Development Committee) are timed to occur after those of the G-24 from whom it accepts recommendations.

See also New International Economic Order.

Group of Two •NW• (G-2), comprised of Boston plus the remainder of the world, is an ethnocentric and self-deprecating reference by those who live in Cambridge, Massachusetts, to their paramount position in the intellectual hierarchy of world affairs.

GSP Form A is a document that is used by developing countries exporting goods to developed countries and that must be filled out and accompany the goods in order to qualify for preferential tariff treatment offered to developing countries under the generalized system of preferences (GSP).

See also generalized system of preferences.

GST is the abbreviation for **Goods and Services Tax.**

guest workers is a polite reference to foreign workers "imported" by a government and made available to industry to perform specific tasks for a limited duration.

> **Example:** Agricultural guest workers from the Caribbean islands come to Canada yearly to pick tobacco during the harvest season. The seasonal migration of "surplus labour" is important: the workers fill jobs that Canadians shun because of the low wage rate, and they reduce the burden on their local governments for direct social assistance while remitting scarce foreign exchange to those same governments that are invariably Third World debtor countries.
>
> There have been severe problems in France because of North African guest workers who migrate to Paris (on yearly work visas) and who then become invisible to the immigration authorities (after their visas expire). The underground guest-worker subculture provides a rich labor pool for some industries, but it provides no guarantee of quality production since the turnover is high, making training an impossible investment.
>
> Prior to the Gulf Crisis, millions of guest workers were employed in Iraq and Kuwait. Especially in Kuwait, they performed virtually all the low-level jobs. They mainly hailed from such populous areas as West Asia (e.g., India and Pakistan), Southeast Asia (e.g., Indonesia and Malaysia), and the Middle East (e.g., Palestine (the "West Bank") and Jordan). As a consequence of the Gulf War, all the workers attempted to flee, thus becoming, together with the flight of the persecuted Iraqi Kurds, the largest refugee problem in modern history.

See also Gulf Crisis.

Gulf Cooperation Council (GCC) is an international organization formally established in 1982 in Abu Dhabi, United Arab Emirates (U.A.E.), originally as a political group to counter perceived threats to the sovereignty of its members due to political instability in the Persian Gulf area.

Members of the Council comprise Bahrain, Kuwait, Oman, Qtar, Saudi Arabia, and the United Arab Emirates. The GCC has its headquarters in Riyadh, Saudi Arabia.

The GCC is evolving from a regional mutual defense pact into a comprehensive regional planning organization whose scope encompasses all economic, financial, social, cultural, and commercial areas. To implement regional development programs, the GCC has established a number of specialized commissions.

The GCC has ties with all other important international Arab organizations, including the Organization of Arab Petroleum Exporting Countries (OAPEC), with which it works to develop strategies for the distribution and pricing of oil.

See also Appendix V (C).

Gulf Crisis (Persian Gulf Crisis) •NW• refers to the worldwide political and economic instability precipitated by Iraq's invasion of Kuwait on August 2, 1990. [Colloquial references include the following used by the Cable News Network (CNN) based in Atlanta, Georgia, to describe the course of the Crisis: *"Crisis in the Gulf," "War in the Gulf," "Toward Peace in the Gulf"* and, finally, *"Peace in the Gulf."*]

Prior to the invasion, the Iraqi government, headed by President *Saddam* (from the Arabic meaning "confronter") Hussein, was a major debtor nation, especially to private Western banks as a direct consequence of its financially ruinous eight-year war (1980–1988) with Iran and of falling oil prices worldwide. In the weeks before the invasion, Hussein had demanded the Kuwaiti government restrict its oil production to the OPEC-allotted quota. Hussein accused Kuwait's overproduction of having contributed to the depression of the world oil price to U.S. $22.10 per barrel (bbl.). Iraq was publicly demanding that the world price rise to U.S. $25.00/bbl. The refusal of Kuwait to accede to Iraq's demands to restrict oil production triggered the invasion.

The following are the key events in the Gulf Crisis:

1. *August 6, 1990:* United Nations (U.N.) Security Council Resolution 666 imposed worldwide trade sanctions on Iraq in an effort to force it out of Kuwait nonviolently. All imports into and exports out of Iraq were embargoed, and the embargo was enforced by a naval and air blockade.
2. *December 3, 1990:* U.N. Security Council Resolution 678 authorized the use of force if Iraq did not withdraw from Kuwait by January 15, 1991.
3. *January 17, 1991:* Coalition Forces, essentially comprising the United States, some NATO allies (the United Kingdom, France, and Canada), and some Arab countries (Egypt, Kuwait, and Saudi Arabia), commenced a massive aerial bombardment of Iraq.
4. *February 23, 1991:* Following Iraq's noncompliance with an ultimatum by U.S. president George Bush to "withdraw from Kuwait by noon Eastern

Time on Saturday, February 23rd," the Coalition invaded Kuwait and Iraq militarily.

5. *February 26, 1991:* "Exactly 100 hours later," according to President Bush, a victory cease-fire was declared by him. The Coalition Forces had entirely destroyed the Iraqi armies, evicted them from Kuwait, killed over 100,000 Iraqi soldiers, and sustained total war theater "killed in action" of 79 soldiers, a number later described by United States Field Commander General ("stormin' Norman") Schwarzkopf as "miraculous."

6. *April 3, 1991:* The United Nations passed a "cease-fire resolution" (U.N. Security Council Resolution 687) dictating to Iraq the terms for a permanent cease-fire. Iraq had to accept them if U.N. trade sanctions were to be lifted. The key conditions were: (1) the United Nations to supervise destruction of all Iraq's chemical and biological weapons and ballistic missile systems; (2) Iraq to accept liability for damage resulting from its invasion and occupation of Kuwait, and a fund to be created, drawing from Iraq's oil revenue, to pay claims of Kuwait and of other citizens and corporations; (3) the United Nations to establish and staff a demilitarized zone (10 miles into Iraq and 5 miles into Kuwait); (4) Iraq to declare that it will neither commit nor support international terrorism, nor permit terrorists to operate from its territory; (5) Iraq to cooperate with the International Committee of the Red Cross to repatriate all combatants and others detained during the war.

7. *April 6, 1991:* Iraq's Supreme Revolutionary Command Council accepted, and its 250-seat Parliament voted in favor of, the U.N. terms for the permanent cease-fire that took effect on April 11, 1991.

During the seven-month period of the Gulf Crisis (from the August 2, 1990, invasion to the February 26, 1991, military victory), the world price of oil gyrated wildly from a low of U.S. $22.10 before the invasion to a high of U.S. $38.00. These fluctuations were a result of speculation fueled by fear (1) that the initial shortfall of 2 million barrels per day from Kuwait could not be made up; and (2) that when Saudi Arabia did resupply to fill the need, the world market would be glutted, driving the price down.

During October 1990, the world price hovered around U.S. $40 per barrel. It subsequently began to decline as Saudi Arabia increased oil production by 4 million barrels per day to offset those shipments formerly made by Iraq (under U.N. blockade) and by Kuwait, whose oil supplies and refining and storage facilities had been pillaged by the Iraqi invaders. In the closing days of the war, Iraq sabotaged Kuwaiti oil fields and set fire to 200 high-pressure oil wells. Fear of world oil shortages briefly loomed again then faded following a Saudi Arabian undertaking to produce sufficient oil to meet prewar demand. This action did not please the Organization of Petroleum Exporting Countries (OPEC).

See also Organization of Petroleum Exporting Countries.

habatsu •NW•, from the Japanese meaning "political cliques," is one's personal core of followers and supporters based on self-interest and personal loyalty.

These cliques may comprise the following:

1. *kanryoha* ("former bureaucrats");
2. *tojinha* ("grassroots politicians"), meaning ruling Liberal Democratic Party (LDP) members currently sitting in the parliament (the "Diet");
3. *amakudari* ("descended from earth"), meaning former LDP politicians "parachuted" into bureaucratic sinecures; and
4. current senior bureaucrats, some of whom may be *gikan* ("technical career officials") or *jimukan* ("administrative career officials"), but all of whom will be either directors-general or directors at the top of their government ministries and agencies.

Cf. *keibatsu* •NW•; *nomenklatura* •NW•.

Hague Agreement Concerning the International Deposit of Industrial Designs, known as the *Hague Act of 1960*, is a multilateral treaty signed by states to afford them substantial protection of intellectual property.

The treaty is administered by the World Intellectual Property Organization (WIPO).

See also World Intellectual Property Organization.

Hamburg Rules, a variation of the *United Nations Convention on the Carriage of Goods by Sea*, refers to a set of guidelines formulated in the late 1960s and continually reviewed by the United Nations Conference on Trade and Development (UNCTAD) Working Group on International Shipping Legislation.

The Hamburg Rules provide for an increase in the level of liability of sea carriers regarding loss and damage. The Rules also comprise other measures, including a rise in monetary limitations of the sea carriers' liability.

The aim of the Rules is the establishment of a more equitable regime regarding the rights and obligations of both shippers and ship owners.

See also United Nations Conference on Trade and Development; Code of Conduct for Liner Conferences.

hard currency is a colloquial expression for (1) the money of a country that is easily convertible into other national currencies and (2) the money of one of the reserve currency countries.

Cf. soft currency.

See also reserve currency country.

hard side (of international marketing), often simply called the *hard side*, refers to those areas of the subject that deal with quantifiable processes and outcomes, such as cost trade-offs, profit maximization, and logistics strategy.

Traditionally, these areas have been overvalued, especially in most analytically oriented MBA programs that have tended (1) to regard international marketing as something entirely quantifiable and, thus, (2) to undervalue any "nonquantification orientation" per se.

Cf. soft side (of international marketing).

harmonize (harmonise) means to bring into a state of mutual agreement those things that were not hitherto in such a state.

Thus, when laws in two countries are harmonized with each other, the effect is that each country recognizes the other's laws as being equivalent to its own and as having the same effect.

Example: It is a stated objective of all inter- and supranational organizations that their goals of "integration" rest on the (sometimes) explicit understanding that laws, regulations, and rules in all integrating countries will, as integration proceeds, inevitably be changed so as to enjoy a better "fit" with those of all others.

The rapid and successful economic integrative model of the European Economic Community (EEC) has established the fact that harmonization, especially in areas as complex as agricultural supply and demand management, is the most workable and expeditious tactic to be used when quite different economic systems (with often very different expectations) must be meshed successfully.

See also Common Agricultural Policy.

Harmonized Commodity Description and Coding System, known as the *Harmonized System (HS)*, is the official arrangement of customs classification procedures adopted by Canada (on January 1, 1988) and by the United States (on January 1, 1989) under the terms of the Canada-U.S. Free Trade Agreement of 1989 (FTA).

Compared with the former (low-tech, manually oriented) Customs Cooperation Council Nomenclature (CCCN), known as the "Brussels Nomenclature," the HS encodes information in a digital system that provides a multifunctional design, permitting data to be available for customs tariff valuation and the compilation of statistical information on (1) international trade, (2) production, and (3) physical distribution and logistics. By 1992, it is expected that most of the members of the Organization of Economic Cooperation and Development (OECD) will have converted from the CCCN to the HS.

Example: Canadian Agriculture Minister Don Mazankowski and his U.S. counterpart, Clayton Yeutter, announced that standards for meat and poultry inspection would be harmonized for a one-year test period. Beginning April 1, 1990, there will be no meat inspections whatsoever at any Canada-U.S. border post. This means that transborder shipments of meat and poultry products will now be treated as domestic shipments of domestic products under the Canada-U.S. Free Trade Act of 1989. Since both Canada and the United States have nearly identical domestic meat and poultry inspection standards at processors' plants, the agreement to eliminate border inspection will facilitate trade between the two countries.

Cf. customs harmonization.
See also rules of origin (ii).

Harmonized System (HS) is a colloquial variation of the *Harmonized Commodity Description and Coding System.*

Harmonized System Committee is a unit of the Customs Cooperation Council (CCC) that accepts recommendations for modification of the Harmonized System (HS).
The U.S. International Trade Commission (USITC) is the "lead agency" for U.S. consideration of proposed changes to the HS. According to the public timetable, the USITC is soliciting submissions from U.S. industry that it, in turn, passes along to the Review Committee of the Harmonized System Committee of the Customs Cooperation Council. The review schedule requires the CCC to make final approved decisions by mid-1993. Those HS changes adopted by the CCC would enter into force on January 1, 1996.
Cf. Customs Cooperation Council.
See also Harmonized System; U.S. International Trade Commission.

Harmonized System of Tariff Classification and Statistical Coding is an incorrect phrasing of the "official" *Harmonized Commodity Description and Coding System.*

high-context culture refers to a society in which meaning is communicated between speakers more by nonverbal communications than by what is said explicitly.
Thus, meaning is implicit in the context of a culture.
Cf. low-context culture.
See also situational conformity •NW•.

Hird's Law, named after the Canadian economist H. Richard Hird, is the observation that the ultimate result of distortions caused by prolonged government intervention in the marketplace is the triumph of mediocrity.

home country is the domestic base of a national company engaged in trade with and investment in foreign countries.

honne •NW•, from the Japanese meaning "true personal intentions," refers to private ideas, including anxieties, animosities, tensions, and resentments, that Japanese keep hidden when involved in behavior with groups.

Release of *honne* is restricted to environments where Japanese have close personal relationships characterized by high levels of mutual trust.

The North American view of the "*tatemae-honne* complex" is that it is one of Japanese hypocrisy. This is ironic since *tatemae* group behavior is considered predictable and stabilizing from the Japanese standpoint but artificial, ambivalent, and two-faced from the North American perspective.

Cf. *tatemae* •NW•.

See also groupism •NW•.

host country is the target country of direct (foreign) investment and in which a business operates outside of its domestic jurisdiction.

host government is a foreign government that heads the state in which a business operates outside of its domestic jurisdiction.

host national is a citizen of the state in which a business operates outside of its domestic jurisdiction.

A host national, sometimes called a "local national," who works overseas for a company from his own country is called a "national expatriate."

See also expatriate.

housing allowance *See* benefit allowance.

HS, the abbreviation for **Harmonized System**, is officially the abbreviation for *Harmonized Commodity Description and Coding System*.

The HS is incorrectly used as an abbreviation for *Harmonized System of Tariff Classification and Statistical Coding*, which itself is a misphrasing of the "official" long form.

See also Harmonized Commodity Description and Coding System.

HTS is the abbreviation of **Harmonized Tariff Schedule** of the United States that, effective January 1, 1989, replaced the former Tariff Schedules of the United States (TSUS).

The HTS is based on the internationally adopted Harmonized Commodity Description and Coding System, known as the Harmonized System (HS).

See also Harmonized Commodity Description and Coding System.

HTSUS is the abbreviation of **Harmonized Tariff System** of the United States, which was used commonly before January 1, 1989.

Cf. HTS.

See also Harmonized Commodity Description and Coding System.

human co-working model organization •NW• is an industrial organization in Japan that rests on the concept of groupism, in contrast to North American and European organizations.

Based on the concepts of situational conformity, *yoroshiku tanomu*, and moral responsibility, the Japanese organization "core members" (i.e., management) work to establish networks of cooperative and friendly relations among all workers and to strengthen the self-esteem of workers, who are not regarded as disposable parts (as they are perceived to be in American and European organizations).

See also machine model organization.

identical reciprocity *See* reciprocity.

identical treatment is a type of friendship, commerce, and navigation (FCN) treaty whereby laws and regulations that govern marketing of domestic goods in each signatory country are applied in exactly the same way to all goods otherwise denoted as "foreign" or "imported."

    See also Appendix VI (friendship, commerce, and navigation treaty).

import, as a verb, means to actively bring a good or service into one sovereign domain from another, or from areas not designated as sovereign to those so designated, in order to be sold; as a noun, it means a good or service actively brought into one sovereign domain from another, or from areas not designated as sovereign to those so designated, in order to be sold.

> **Example:** The parts were made in the parent company's foundry in Singapore's duty free zone (DFZ), transferred to another sister-company plant in Hong Kong's DFZ for machining, then shipped to a company warehouse in Taipei's DFZ for final assembly and ultimate import by another sister company in Japan. Duties were only paid on the final imports since the company had complied with all the rules of using DFZs.

> Cf. export.
> *See also* duty.

Import Allocation Certificate is a document that Japan's Ministry of International Trade and Industry (MITI) requires Japanese importers to fill out and submit to a foreign exchange (FOREX) bank as a prerequisite for the importer to obtain an import permit.

    Where imports are subject to import quotas, the certificate plus the permit issued by the FOREX bank plus the mark sheet must be presented to

Japanese customs authorities by the Japanese importer to clear them through customs.
    See also quantity restrictions; FOREX; mark sheet.

Import Control List *See* Export and Import Permits Act.

import controls *See* commercial controls; export controls.

import duty is a tax on goods imported into a country.
    Cf. export levy.

import policy refers to the course of action set by a domestic government to create a favorable politico-economic environment (1) initially to attract foreign imports and (2) ultimately to attract "serious" (being a large amount of long-term) direct investment.
    Cf. import substitution.

import quotas, colloquially classed as nontariff barriers, are restrictions or ceilings adopted by the government of a country on the volume and/or value of goods imported to a specific country or group of countries.
    Cf. export quotas.
    See also nontariff barriers.

import substitution is a course of action of a domestic government to encourage the replacement of imported goods with domestically manufactured ones.
    The term suggests that any government that adopts an import substitution policy embarks on an industrial policy that may involve certain import policy objectives.

> **Example:** It has been claimed that Canada's National Policy, originally introduced by Sir John A. MacDonald, was a clever import substitution policy. It erected tariff barriers ostensibly to exclude U.S. exports to Canada. However, the result was the import of massive U.S. direct investment that flowed into new Canadian-based, U.S.-owned factories. From them, sufficient goods were produced not only to satisfy domestic demands (thereby replacing U.S. imported goods) but also to create a Canadian industrial export sector that became globally competitive to the U.S. parent.)

    Cf. import policy.
    See also industrial policy.

Import Trade Control Order Notices are written directives issued by Japan's Ministry of International Trade and Industry (MITI) that specify which imported goods are subject to import quotas.
    See also quantity restrictions.

Incoterms (International Commercial Terms) are standard definitions of international terms of sale, established by the International Chamber of Commerce (ICC) in Paris and distributed by affiliated Chambers of Commerce.
    Cf. Appendix III.
    See also International Chamber of Commerce; Appendix IV.

indirect exporting refers to export sales by a domestic-based company to a foreign buyer via a domestically based intermediary.

See also combination export manager; export broker; export buyer; export commission house; export management company; export jobber; manufacturer's export agent; trading house.

industrial espionage is surreptitious surveillance of a company's activities, which may or may not be followed by theft or unauthorized use of its proprietary intellectual property (in the form of patents, processes, and other "trade secrets").

industrialization through import substitution *See* import substitution.

industrial policy is the course of action set by a government to influence the development of domestic industrial sectors in particular and the direction of national industrial growth in general.

A government's industrial policy may comprise such instruments as subsidies (direct and indirect), tax incentives, regional development programs, training programs for workers, and research and development (R&D) assistance.

> **Example:** Canadian industrial policy has come under frequent attack from various U.S. industrial sectors. They have claimed that, under the guise of assisting domestic industry, the Canadian government has really been subsidizing the development of competitive export industries. Such alleged activities are contrary to both the Canada-U.S. Free Trade Agreement and the General Agreement on Tariffs and Trade (GATT).

The U.S. Omnibus Trade Act of 1988 (Section 301) prohibits foreign governments engaging in export targeting. The rationale is that since export targeting uses government leverage to enhance export effectiveness, it is implicitly unfair and thus deserving of action by the U.S. Trade Representative.

Cf. import substitution; deindustrialization.
See also Super 301; export targeting; industrial targeting.

industrial sabotage is the act of willfully destroying or rendering useless a company's capital, especially its physical premises, inventories, and equipment, and including its intellectual property such as computer programs.

> **Example:** On the day before the strike, the workers purposely wrecked the foundry and the machine shops in Libya. Unknown to them, they had secret support from some of the managers who were Libyan nationals and who were working hard to insert computer viruses into some of the company's key software, especially the sales forecasting models.

industrial targeting is an expression used to convey the process of selecting a particular industry (or industrial sector) for special attention by a national government.

> **Example:** The Canadian government has an industrial policy that targets high-tech industries in Silicon Valley North for development with a view to exporting to the United States.

Industry, Science and Technology Canada (ISTC) is the new name for the Canadian federal government department that is responsible for initiating and implementing domestic programs for trade, regional expansion, and development.

Previously, and for a brief time, ISTC was called the Department of Industry, Science and Technology. This name followed a prior name change from the Department of Regional Economic Expansion (DREE), which was changed, in turn, from the Department of Regional Industrial Expansion (DRIE).

The predecessor institution to all these changes was the ministry's original name, the Department of Industry, Trade and Commerce (ITC). Under this legal name, the ministry was responsible both for domestic and international trade policy and implementation. When, in 1982, the government transferred international trade to the Department of External Affairs (DEA), ITC was left without a clear direction, and it took seven years to reorganize an effective role for it under its new ISTC appellation.

Cf. Department of External Affairs.

See also International Trade Centers.

Industry Sector Advisory Committee (ISAC) is one of the advisory groups to the U.S. government, relied upon during bilateral and multilateral trade negotiations.

See also Advisory Committee on Trade Policy Negotiations.

Industry, Trade and Commerce *See* Industry, Science and Technology Canada.

infant industry is a recently established sector of domestic commerce *vis-à-vis* a well-established domestic business sector.

See also infant industry argument.

infant industry argument refers to the contention that "temporary trade protection" (i.e., tariffs and nontariff barriers) are needed in order to establish an industry and to protect it against better-established and more-efficient foreign competitors.

It is arguable whether new industries—even if soundly based and efficiently managed—can compete against global corporations with their enormous economies of scale and with their determination to maintain global market dominance. It is suggested that a domestic government's direct and indirect subsidies to its infant industries are meritorious so long as they are removed when the infant industry enters the stage of healthy, competitive adulthood. When this stage is reached (and who makes this determination) is a moot point.

At the international level, the rationale underpinning the generalized system of preferences (GSP) is the global analog to the domestic infant industry argument.

Cf. generalized system of preferences.

injury is "damage" caused, or perceived to have been caused, to a domestic industry as a direct result of import competition.

The injury caused may be quantified according to the following accepted measures:

1. decline in output,
2. decline in sales,
3. loss of market share,
4. decline in profits,
5. reduced return on investment (ROI),
6. reduced physical capacity, and
7. increased layoffs and unemployment.

There are two broad classes of injury:

1. *Serious Injury:* this is a requirement for the imposition of safeguards by a government that claims the serious injury.
2. *Material Injury:* this is a requirement for retaliation whereby antidumping and countervailing duties are imposed.

Most governments require that documentary evidence to support injury claims be produced in accordance with administratively acceptable "rules of evidence" and "due process" for escape-clause relief. The GATT requires this as well.

In the United States and Canada, government agencies and committees of the bicameral legislatures conduct the investigations, and in the United States, the president produces a document called a "finding," which is the legitimate basis for escape-clause relief. In Canada, a report is submitted to the government (i.e., the Cabinet), which may issue Cabinet Orders that are later brought before the legislature for approval.

See also antidumping duty; countervailing duty; escape clause; retaliation; safeguards.

inland bill of lading *See* bill of lading.

inland carrier is a mode of transportation (e.g., truck, train) that carries goods between the port of import and inland destinations.

> **Example:** East European importers (and communist inland carriers) rely heavily on The Port of Rotterdam because the West European inland transport infrastructure is more sophisticated and cost-efficient than overland transport from ports on the Baltic, the Black, the Aegean, or the Adriatic Seas.

inland waterways are a complex of lakes, rivers, and canals within the domestic jurisdiction of a country, intended for the carriage of goods.

> **Example:** In Eastern Canada in the nineteenth century, the Trent River System comprised an important, extensive network of water transport infrastructure, permitting imports to be moved at least 100 miles inland from the St. Lawrence River and assisting hinterland producers to bring exports to market. Today, faster and more reliable means are available, and the Trent System is used predominantly for pleasure craft.

Inner Six refers collectively (from 1958 to 1973) to the six members of the European Economic Community (EEC) *vis-à-vis* the Outer Seven, collectively the members of the European Free Trade Association (EFTA).

Cf. Outer Seven.

See also European Economic Community; European Free Trade Association.

intellectual property is a collective term used to refer to ideas or works in the following classes:

1. *industrial property*, meaning legal rights in the form of patents, technological inventions, trademarks, industrial designs, and "appellations of origin";
2. *copyright*, meaning legal rights in the form of literary works, musical works, and artistic works and in films, books, and performances of performing artists in live form and in any recorded format, including photographs, or television, or other visual medium.

To qualify for inclusion in either one or both of the above classes, ideas and/or works must (1) be put into an appropriate formal documentary form and (2) have been filed with the appropriate national authority for the purpose of registering the material to obtain the domestic (and possibly international) legal protection for the works of the authors, owners, or inventors.

The key body that promotes and coordinates international efforts to protect intellectual property and under whose aegis a number of international agreements are administered in this regard is the World Intellectual Property Organization (WIPO).

See also Berne Convention; CAPRI Project; Paris Convention; Patent Cooperation Treaty; Treaty on International Registration of Audiovisual Works; World Intellectual Property Organization.

Inter-African Coffee Organization (IACO), also known as *Organisation Inter-Africaine de Café (OICAFE)*, is an international commodity group (ICG) formed in 1960 with the aim of exchanging information among producer-members on ways and means of achieving optimal production and optimal prices.

The IACO has its headquarters in Abidjan, Côte d'Ivoire, and comprises 22 African producer-member countries.

See also Appendix V (E).

Inter-American Development Bank (officially **IDB**, but sometimes unofficially **IaDB**), one of the multilateral development banks (MDBs), is an international financial organization that is an executing agency for projects of the United Nations Development Program (UNDP).

The IDB operates on a regional basis in Latin America and the Caribbean. Established in 1959, the IDB has its headquarters in Washington, D.C. Its membership is comprised of 25 regional members and 18 nonregional members, including Canada.

The IDB extends loans and technical assistance to its member countries over a variety of activities including agriculture, fisheries, transportation and communications, public health, education, housing, science and technology, urban development, mining, industry, and energy.

See also multilateral development banks; United Nations Development Program.

Inter-American Investment Corporation (IIC) is a financial institution that was established in 1986 as an affiliate of the Inter-American Development Bank (IDB).

With a membership of 33 countries, its mandate is to encourage the establishment, expansion, and modernization of private enterprises in Latin America and the Caribbean. It is structurally related to the IDB's new Private Sector Development Program (PSDP).

Cf. Private Sector Development Program.

See also Inter-American Development Bank.

Inter-American Treaty of Reciprocal Assistance (also known as the *Rio Treaty* or the *Rio Pact*). *See* Organization of American States.

interest arbitrage *See* Appendix II.

interest parity *See* Appendix II.

Inter-governmental Council of Copper Exporting Countries (ICCEC), also known as *Conseil Inter-gouvernemental des Pays Exportateurs de Cuivre (CIPEC)*, is an international commodity group (ICG) formed in 1968 to cooperate and collaborate to effect higher world prices for copper and, consequently, higher earnings for copper producer-member countries.

The organization has its headquarters in Neuilly-sur-Seine, France, and comprises the following producer-members: Chile, Indonesia, Perú, Zaire, and Zambia, with Australia, Mauritania, Papua New Guinea (PNG), and Yugoslavia as associate members.

See also Appendix V (E).

Interim Committee, formally, *Interim Committee of the Board of Governors of the International Monetary Fund (IMF) on the International Monetary System*, established in 1974, advises the Board of Governors of the IMF on the operation of the Fund.

The Committee consists of Governors of the Fund and of others of comparable rank who represent blocs of countries in their decision making. The Committee presently has 22 members.

On January 3, 1990, the Committee selected the Canadian Minister of Finance, the Honorable Michael H. Wilson, as its Chairman.

See also International Monetary Fund.

intermodal (intermodal movement, intermodal transportation), from the Latin *inter* meaning "between" and *modalis* meaning "of the measure," implies the transport of goods among the various modes of transport (i.e., trucks, railways, boats, airplanes, and pipelines).

international, from the Latin meaning "among nations," refers to things that involve dealings outside of one's own country that may be (1) between one's own country and other countries and (2) among countries other than one's own.

According to E. R. (Ted) Turner, founder of Turner Broadcasting System (TBS), "international promotes a sense of unity."

It is the policy of TBS that any person or event that is not part of the United States be referred to as "international" rather than "foreign." Indeed, at the Cable News Network (CNN), the main news broadcast unit of TBS, all news that is not domestic (i.e., American) is called "international news." There is no such thing as "foreign news."

Example: Americans see the International Monetary Fund (IMF) as comprising over 100 "foreign" countries outside of the United States. From the viewpoint of France, however, the IMF consists of over 100 "foreign" countries (including the United States) besides itself. Every country implicitly sees other countries, and even groups of other countries, as "foreign." It is only from a global viewpoint that all countries, "foreign" to each other, can be seen in an interdependent, international light.

Cf. foreign.
See also ethnocentrism; global marketing.

International Air Transport Association (IATA), formerly *International Air Traffic Association*, is an international organization of scheduled airline operators, established in 1945, whose members consist of any airline (1) that has regularly scheduled flights and (2) that is certified by a government eligible for membership in the International Civil Aviation Organization (ICAO).

IATA is involved in the following activities:

• promotion of passenger transport services,
• promotion of air cargo services, and
• promotion of cooperation among air transport companies.

IATA also acts as a forum for the discussion (among its membership) of the airline rates to passengers. In this, IATA has sometimes been perceived as behaving in a collusive, or cartel-like, way.

Cf. international cartel.
See also International Civil Aviation Organization.

International Atomic Energy Agency (IAEA) is an autonomous international organization, established in 1956, that functions under the aegis of the United Nations within the United Nations System, as of 1957.

IAEA headquarters are in Vienna, Austria. Broadly speaking, the IAEA has two main tasks:

1. to promote the peaceful uses for atomic energy (including education, research, and the training of workers and scientists) and
2. to implement controls under the 1970 Treaty of the Non-Proliferation of Nuclear Weapons (NPT).

The IAEA also operates the International Nuclear Information System (INIS) for collection and dissemination of information on nuclear energy subjects. The INIS was established in 1970.

The organization maintains close working relationships with all appropriate U.N. and international bodies. For example, in 1964, the IAEA established the International Center for Theoretical Physics in Trieste, Italy, and now operates it jointly with UNESCO.

From the viewpoint of international marketers, the IAEA procures (1) mainly specialized capital equipment and supplies for in-field projects and (2) some specialized services (e.g., for food-irradiation projects and isotope manufacturing). The main supplies go to the IAEA's three laboratories, one at the IAEA headquarters in Vienna, the second at Seibersdorf, Austria, and the third in Monaco. All procurement is done directly from IAEA headquarters in Vienna, Austria.

Cf. United Nations Industrial Development Organization.

See also Appendix V (D).

International Bank for Economic Cooperation (IBEC) is an international financial institution that was the central bank of the Council for Mutual Economic Assistance (CMEA).

Established in Moscow in 1963 (through the Agreement on Multilateral Payments in Transferable Roubles), the IBEC became operational in 1964.

The IBEC functioned in two major ways:

1. it acted as the central bank for multilateral settlement of trade balances among CMEA member countries;
2. it extended short-term credit (i.e., 360 days or less) to expand foreign trade among member countries.

The unit of account of the IBEC was the Transferable Rouble (TR), which has 0.987412 grams of gold, the same gold content as the Soviet rouble.

The TR has no exchange value outside the Soviet bloc. IBEC may again (as it did in the 1970s) make serious attempts to interest Western bankers in using it in countertrade transactions as an exchange instrument.

The IBEC maintained strong links with all bodies in the Soviet bloc, and especially with the International Investment Bank (IIB).

See also countertrade; International Investment Bank; Warsaw Pact; Council for Mutual Economic Assistance; Appendix V (B).

International Bank for Reconstruction and Development (IBRD) is one of the multilateral development banks (MDBs).

See also World Bank Group.

international banking refers to the processes of borrowing and lending money with the broad aims of (1) providing credit to domestic companies to finance export sales and (2) providing credit to foreign buyers (on behalf of their domestic clients) to finance export purchases.

See also international financial centers.

international banking centers (IBCs) are cities where financial institutions (including commercial banks) transact trade-related business, including financing foreign trade, buying and selling currencies, and foreign accounts receivable.

IBCs is used synonymously with *international financial centers* (IFCs), the latter being a more accurate and comprehensive identification of cities in which global financial operations take place. IBCs are not synonymous with *offshore banking centers* (OBCs).

Cf. international financial centers; offshore banking centers.

International Bauxite Association (IBA) is an international commodity group (ICG) formed in 1974 to collaborate among member countries about ways and means to effect higher prices and profits for the processing and marketing of the commodity.

With headquarters in Kingston, Jamaica, the IBA comprises the following membership: Australia, Dominican Republic, Ghana, Guinea, Guyana, Haïti, Indonesia, Jamaica, Sierra Leone, Suriname, and Yugoslavia.

See also Appendix V (E).

international cartel is an organization consisting of suppliers of a good or service (1) who are located in different countries, (2) who agree (among themselves) to restrict the output of the good or service, and (3) whose aim is increasing the market price of the good or service.

See also Appendix V (E).

International Center for Genetic Engineering and Biotechnology (ICGEB) *See* United Nations Industrial Development Organization.

International Center for Science and High Technology (ICSHT) *See* United Nations Industrial Development Organization.

International Center for Theoretical Physics (ICTP) *See* International Atomic Energy Agency.

International Chamber of Commerce (ICC) is an international organization with headquarters in Paris, France, that acts as the forum for establishing a concensus on matters such as trading practices, commercial documentation, and trade dispute procedures.

In 1940, the ICC established the code of Uniform Customs and Practice for Documentary Credits (which is accepted by over 162 nations). This was the first modern "uniform terms of trade" code. Revised in 1952, 1962, and 1974, these rules (now called "international commercial terms," or Incoterms) attempt to standardize documentation relating to documentary credits and to define clearly the responsibilities of all parties in international trade transactions.

Cf. Chamber of Commerce.

See also Appendix IV; international arbitration.

international channel efficiency is a comparative measure (*vis-à-vis* domestic channel efficiency) based on the degree to which an international channel's investment in various inputs (e.g., transportation, warehousing), required to achieve a given international distribution objective, can be optimized in terms of international channel outputs.

Cf. international channel lag coefficient.

international channel lag coefficient, a measure of the efficiency of international channels, is the ratio of external (uncontrollable) marketing costs, which negatively burden international distribution, to domestic (controllable) marketing costs.

The higher the coefficient, the less efficient the channel and, thus, the more costly the international distribution.

See also international channel efficiency.

International Civil Aviation Organization (ICAO) is a specialized agency of the United Nations, established in 1944, whose membership consists of over 130 nations. ICAO's headquarters are in Montreal, Canada.

ICAO carries out the following activities:

1. improves and promotes aviation safety;
2. raises operational standards;
3. encourages safe design (and operation) of airways, airports, and air navigational facilities.

ICAO operates a Civil Aviation Purchasing Service (CAPS) to assist governments in acquiring equipment for operating civil aviation facilities. From a consultancy viewpoint, CAPS is involved in air transport economics, regional planning, telecommunications, and airport master planning and design. Consequently, global suppliers see CAPS as a potentially profitable procurement target.

International Cocoa Organization (ICCO) is an international commodity group (ICG) that was established in 1973 under the International Cocoa Agreement of 1972, which itself was negotiated under the auspices of the U.N. Conference on Trade and Development.

The ICCO, with its headquarters in London, is responsible for the implementation of ongoing International Cocoa Agreements. It ensures that appropriate quantities of the commodity:

1. are made available to the world market on a continuous basis;
2. are held as buffer stocks, to be released if demand exceeds supply and pushes the world price above an agreed upon "trigger price" toward a "price ceiling";
3. are purchased by producer countries if supply exceeds demand and the world price falls below the negotiated "reference price" (i.e., the "floor price").

Membership of the ICCO comprises 18 commodity-exporting countries (accounting for over 75 percent of world exports) and 22 importing countries (accounting for over 70 percent of world imports).

See also international commodity agreement; international cartel; Common Fund for Commodities; Appendix V (E); United Nations Conference on Trade and Development.

International Coffee Organization (ICO) is an international commodity group (ICG) established in 1963 under the International Coffee Agreement of 1962.

The ICO, with its headquarters in London, is responsible for the implementation of ongoing International Coffee Agreements. It ensures that appropriate quantities of the commodity:

1. are made available to the world market on a continuous basis;
2. are held as buffer stocks, to be released if demand exceeds supply and pushes the world price above an agreed upon "trigger price" toward a "price ceiling";
3. are purchased by producer countries if supply exceeds demand and the world price falls below the negotiated "reference price" (i.e., the "floor price").

Membership of the ICO comprises 47 commodity-exporting countries (accounting for over 99 percent of world exports) and 27 importing countries (accounting for over 90 percent of world imports).

The system of export quotas of the ICO broke down in 1989 when producer-members were unable to reach agreement on quota allocations, and certain major producers like Brazil exceeded their export quota. The consequence was the "collapse of the coffee market," meaning that the sustained high producer prices that the ICO had maintained collapsed.

In March 21, 1991, the Brazilian government temporarily stopped granting export permits for coffee. This move may signal the renewal of the existing but moribund ICO or the creation of a new international coffee quota system.

See also international commodity agreement; international cartel; Appendix V (E); United Nations Conference on Trade and Development.

international commodity agreement (ICA) is a formal accord among producers of a commodity to control the export output of the good in order to stabilize prices and export earnings for it.

ICAs are invariably formed by developing countries that are "one-crop economies" (i.e., nations that depend on a single crop, product, or commodity for their export earnings).

Examples of important ICAs are the International Jute Agreement (IJA), the International Rubber Agreement (IRA), and the International Cocoa Agreement (ICCA).

See also international cartel; Appendix V (E); export quota.

international commodity group (ICG) is an organization of producer countries, consumer countries, or privately affiliated international commodity economists who come together to (1) establish an international cartel, (2) pool resources to negotiate supplier prices, or (3) supply producers and consumers (of the commodities), for a non-economic purpose, with accurate statistics on production and consumption trends, production costs, productivity data, and transportation and logistical data.

When an ICG administers an international commodity agreement (ICA), it is recognized as an International Commodity Organization (ICO) by the global community in general and by the United Nations Conference on Trade and Development (UNCTAD) in particular for the purpose of financial support.

See also Appendix V (E); United Nations Conference on Trade and Development; Common Fund for Commodities.

international commodity organization (ICO) is an international commodity group (ICG) raised to the level of acknowledgment by the United Nations Conference on Trade and Development (UNCTAD) so as to qualify for financial assistance under the Common Fund for Commodities (CFC).

Cf. international commodity agreement; international commodity group.

See also Common Fund for Commodities.

International Cotton Advisory Committee (ICAC) is an international commodity group (ICG) established in 1939 in Washington, D.C., to ensure "supply-side" availability of cotton in the world market by the collaboration among producer-members and by studying and acting upon means to promote increased consumption of the commodity.

The ICAC membership comprises 49 cotton-producing countries, mainly in Asia, Africa, and Latin America.

Cf. international commodity agreement; international cartel.

See also Appendix V (E).

International Court of Justice *See* Appendix VI.

International Dairy Arrangement is an international accord resulting from the Tokyo Round of Multilateral Trade Negotiations (MTN). Sixteen members of the General Agreement on Tariffs and Trade (GATT) have signed the Arrangement: Argentina, Australia, Bulgaria, Egypt, the European Economic Community (EEC), Finland, Hungary, Japan, New Zealand, Norway, Poland, Romania, South Africa, Sweden, Switzerland, and Uruguay.

The Arrangement, overseen by the International Dairy Products Council (IDPC), aims to promote the expansion and liberalization of trade in dairy products worldwide. To this end, the Arrangement establishes minimum export prices (known as "floor prices") for dairy products. These include certain cheeses, whole milk powder, skimmed milk powder, buttermilk powder, butter, and anhydrous milk fat.

The sense of the Agreement is to create an "orderly international marketing environment" in which the dairy industry can flourish internationally without inviting internecine hostilities between major producer groups (e.g., the United States and the EEC).

See also Tokyo Round.

international debt (international debt load) *See* external debt.

international debt rating refers to the classification of banks, municipal corporations (i.e., cities), and other major capital borrowers by international debt-
rating services, according to their credit worthiness.

  When a borrower's debt rating is lowered, it is charged higher rates to
borrow from other financial institutions on the wholesale market. Conversely,
when the debt rating is raised, the cost of borrowing from other financial
institutions declines.

  In the case of banks, their debt ratings can be affected by a variety of
factors: (1) the percentage of their serious loans invested in developing countries (LDCs); (2) the record of repayment of loans by LDCs; (3) the perception
of measured risk of nonrepayment of those loans; and (4) the percentage of
a loans portfolio (and the absolute amounts) tied up in "leveraged loans" (i.e.,
junk bonds and the financing of "leveraged buy-outs" (LBOs)).

  See also international debt-rating services.

international debt-rating services are firms that provide measures of the credit
worthiness of financial institutions (e.g., banks) and other important corporations (e.g., cities and utilities) that are large capital borrowers.

  Recognized companies in the field are Dun & Bradstreet International
and Moody's Investment Service. Other companies (e.g., stock brokers) likewise can provide information about credit worthiness. However, since they
do not deal at "arm's length" with many of the large corporations—but rather
are "managers" of their stock issues—stock brokerage houses are not classified as debt-rating services.

  The ratings provided range as follows:

Credit Worthiness	*Rating*
highest—no risk	Triple-A
marginal risk	Double A1 to Double A3
appreciable risk	Single A

The significance of the range of ratings is not necessarily in the rating itself but in any
change in a rating given to a bank or other international borrower. For example, if
a major Canadian or U.S. bank were to have its rating lowered to Double A1 from
Triple-A by one of the rating services, the change might signal some important shift
(1) in a bank's leveraged-loan portfolio or (2) in its LDC development-loan portfolio.
Further, ratings changes can be important indicators forewarning of impending adjustments either in financial markets or in foreign countries having serious balance-
of-payments disequilibria.

International Development Association (IDA), established in 1960, is an affiliate
of the International Bank for Reconstruction and Development (IBRD).

  The function of the IDA is to negotiate concessional terms of development financing with developing countries and to extend loans at subsidized
rates to them.

  See also World Bank Group; concessional financing.

International Development Information Network (IDIN) is a system of cooperation among five regional associations of development research, with the Development Center of the Organization of Economic Cooperation and Development (OECD) acting as coordinator for the collection, analysis, and distribution of information on research and training institutes and for ongoing research projects in the field of economic and social development.

The five regional associations of development research are (1) EADI (Europe); (2) CODESRIA (Africa); (3) ADIPA (Asia); (4) CLACSO (Latin America); and (5) AICARDES (in the Arab World).

The coordination effort of the Development Center of the OECD is as follows:

Region	Countries	Institutes	Projects
Africa	46	497	1,109
Arab World	20	210	689
Asia	15	n.a.	847
Europe	12	8	n.a.
Latin America	25	n.a.	1,739

n.a. = not available.

See also Development Center of the Organization of Economic Cooperation and Development; European Community of Research and Technology.

International Development Research Center (IDRC) is a Canadian nongovernment organization (NGO) created by Federal legislation (and thus accountable to the Federal parliament through the Canadian Minister of State for External Affairs).

The purpose of the IDRC is to stimulate and support scientific and technical research by developing countries for applications within developing countries.

The (hoped-for) outcomes of Canada's support are export orders for Canadian-made capital goods, operating supplies, technical assistance, and management contracts.

International Finance Corporation (IFC), established in 1956, is an affiliate of the International Bank for Reconstruction and Development (IBRD).

The function of the IFC is to provide development financing for private enterprises in developing countries. It co-invests with governments and private companies either in the enterprise's capital stock or by providing loans to the enterprise, or by a combination of these two arrangements.

The IFC also provides financial and technical assistance to private banks in developing countries to assist them in developing the expertise required to become profitable commercial lenders.

Cf. Japan Special Fund.

See also World Bank Group; near-concessional financing.

international financial centers (IFCs) are cities where international financial institutions (mainly commercial banks) transact business arising from international trade, according to established laws and also orthodox customs and practices.

International banking centers (IBCs) is a frequently used "near-synonym" for IFCs. IFCs itself is used incorrectly as a synonym for *offshore banking centers (OBCs)*.

There are three classes of IFCs:

1. *Global IFCs* (London, New York City, and Tokyo)
2. *Secondary IFCs* (Amsterdam, Brussels, Caracas, Chicago, Frankfurt, Milan, Paris, São Paulo, Sydney, Toronto, and Zurich)
3. *Offshore IFCs* (explained in *offshore banking centers*)

This classification reflects the size and importance of IFCs and their proximity to global trading markets.

The U.S. government has passed special legislation to assist U.S. banks to compete in the global banking area.

Cf. international banking centers.

See also Edge Corporation; Appendix V (B).

international freight broker *See* foreign freight forwarder.

international freight forwarder *See* foreign freight forwarder.

International Fund for Agricultural Development (IFAD) is an international organization of the United Nations System, the purpose of which is to mobilize finances and make loans and grants for agricultural and rural development to developing member states of the United Nations.

Proposals for the establishment of the Fund were made at the 1974 World Food Conference. The accord establishing the Fund was adopted by 91 countries in 1976, and the Fund commenced operations in 1977. The Fund's headquarters are in Rome, Italy.

Membership consists of 135 U.N. countries as follows:

Category I: Developed countries that are members of the Organization for Economic Cooperation and Development (OECD) are contributors to the Fund.

Category II: Developing countries that are members of the Organization of Petroleum Exporting Countries (OPEC) are contributors to the Fund.

Category III: Developing countries that are neither OECD nor OPEC members are recipients of the Fund.

The IFAD is not directly involved in the United Nations Development Program: its major project work is in (1) designing the expansion of existing food-production systems, especially in food-deficient countries, (2) the generation of additional income for poor farmers, and (3) the improvement of levels of nutrition and food distribution in rural areas.

Therefore, from a global marketing viewpoint, the IFAD procures a limited amount of capital goods from local project suppliers, but a large number and variety of individual experts, as well as expert consulting firms. It has close and strong working relations with the Food and Agricultural Organization (FAO), also headquartered in Rome.

See also Appendix V (D).

International Investment Bank (IIB) is an international financial institution that became operational in 1971 through the Agreement on Multilateral Payments in Transferable Roubles, originally signed in Moscow in 1963, by the members of the Council for Mutual Economic Assistance (CMEA).

The Agreement also established the International Bank for Economic Cooperation (IBEC). While the functions of the IBEC were (1) the multilateral settlement of CMEA-member trade balances and (2) the extension of short-term credit, the key function of the IIB was the extension of medium- and long-term credit.

Medium-term (i.e., from 2 to 5 years) and long-term (i.e., from 6 to 15 years) credit facilities were normally granted to any country that subscribed to the principles and aims of the IIB: in practice, only CMEA-member countries (who are also members of the IBEC) were granted credit.

IIB credit was extended for development projects in fields such as energy, health, education and transportation infrastructure, industry, and agriculture.

Like the IBEC, the unit of account of the IIB was the Transferable Rouble (TR), whose value reflects the gold content of the Soviet rouble (i.e., 0.987412 gram).

The IIB maintained strong relations with the IBEC and the CMEA. It had neither formal ties nor working relationships with any autonomous international financial organization of the non-Soviet bloc or with any international financial development organization of the United Nations System.

See also International Bank for Economic Cooperation; Council for Mutual Economic Assistance; Appendix V (B).

international investment position, also called the *balance of international indebtedness*, is the accounting of the amounts and distribution of country A's assets in foreign countries on the one hand, balanced by the amounts and distribution of foreign assets in country A on the other.

> **Example:** In terms of the external debt of some less developed countries (LDCs), it is the worsening of their balance of international indebtedness that is particularly troubling: chronically low commodity prices, which generate poor export earnings and lead to higher yearly balance-of-payments shortfalls, result in reduced LDC domestic capital formation and the increasing LDC inability to service the external debt.

International Joint Commission (IJC) is a bilateral Canada-U.S. body, established in 1909 by the Boundary Waters Treaty.

The IJC is involved in the following:

1. investigating complaints of pollution of those Great Lakes over which Canada and the United States have joint use; and

2. arbitrating questions (brought before it) on use of Canada-U.S. boundary waters (both in the Great Lakes and in the Atlantic, Pacific, and Arctic Oceans) for fishing, energy use, navigation, sanitation, and irrigation.

International Jute Agreement (IJA) is an international commodity agreement (ICA) that went into force on January 1, 1991, and that will run for five years (until December 31, 1996), with the possibility of two extensions of two years each.

Convened under the auspices of the United Nations Conference on Trade and Development (UNCTAD), the IJA represents (1) producer countries that account for 99 percent of world jute exports and (2) consumer countries that comprise 63 percent of world jute imports.

The main purpose of the IJA, as implemented by the International Jute Organization, is to promote the use of the product by developed countries *vis-à-vis* synthetic substitutes.

See also international commodity agreement; United Nations Conference on Trade and Development.

International Labor Organization (ILO) is a specialized agency of the United Nations, established in 1919 under the League of Nations and the oldest surviving League agency.

Integrated into the U.N. in 1946 upon the dissolution of the League of Nations, the ILO is involved in the following major activities:

1. setting international labor standards;
2. providing governments with technical cooperation in the planning and implementation of labor-intensive activities in all sectors of public-works activities;
3. providing assistance to governments in the planning of social institutions regarding (1) human resource administration, (2) industrial relations, and (3) assistance to collective bargaining units and employers' associations.

See also Appendix V (D).

international law *See* Appendix VI.

International Lead and Zinc Study Group (ILZSG), an international commodity group (ICG) established in London in 1959 (ostensibly with the mission of conducting studies and considering problem solutions affecting the industry worldwide), is a body comprised of 31 exclusively consumer-member countries, mainly in West and East Europe, that are primarily concerned about (1) the security of supply of the commodities and (2) the ready availability of desired quantities of the commodities at reasonable prices.

The "security of supply" concern deals mainly with non-European sources of supply (e.g., the Copper Belt in Zambia, Shaba Province in Zaire). The past history of violent political problems affecting both areas concerns the ILZSG.

The "ready availability" concern addressed itself to questions of traditional "command economic management" of the former Council for Mutual Economic Assistance

(CMEA) and of the impact of East Europe's commodity needs on world supply in general and on West European needs in particular.

Cf. international commodity agreement; international cartel.
See also Appendix V (E); Council for Mutual Economic Assistance.

International Maritime Bureau (IMB) is the arm of the Paris-based International Chamber of Commerce (ICC) that acts against fraud, piracy, and other criminal activity in international physical distribution and logistics (PD/L).

IMB agents roam the globe under legal orders issued by national courts and under the authority of the IMB multilateral treaty to which Organization of Economic Cooperation and Development (OECD) members have acceded. The agents search for stolen or diverted goods and ships, "phantom ships" (i.e., maverick ships that handle stolen cargo), and for false and stolen documents (e.g., bills of lading, letters of credit, pilots' licenses, and passports).

> **Example:** Mandalay PLC of Indonesia sold a cargo of lumber to Lucky Lotus Trading Company of Hong Kong. Lucky Lotus opened a letter of credit with Mandalay as the beneficiary. A tight market for ships sent Mandalay scurrying for a carrier as the expiration date of the letter of credit approached.
>
> An international gang of fraud artists in Taiwan—affiliated with the Japanese "*yakuza*" (i.e., "the mob")—secured a vessel for Mandalay through a friendly broker. The name of the ship, *East Star*, had been falsified.
>
> The gang registered the ship with the Panamanian consulate in Singapore. The ship's papers were falsified, and the ship's crew were inexperienced Thais and Burmese for whom false passports had been secured via a "friendly travel agent" in Manila. Forged and stolen birth certificates, residence permits, and work visas had been used to get the passports. Thus, with entirely false documents, the *East Star* arrived in Jakarta, Indonesia; the plywood was loaded, and the ship sailed away.
>
> The stolen cargo eventually arrived in Bombay and via another "friendly agent" was sold to a buyer who accepted the goods, perhaps ignorant of the facts. Via the Taiwanese gang, Mandalay PLC was informed that the *East Star* had sunk in the Indian Ocean. Mandalay thus proceeded to file an insurance claim under its original insurance certificate issued by an insurance company established as a "front" by the Taiwanese gang, which had since "gone bankrupt."
>
> Mandalay PLC never was compensated, and only a complaint lodged with the International Maritime Bureau uncovered the fraud.
>
> *[NOTE: All names and locations in the foregoing example are entirely fictitious and bear no intended resemblance to any person, company, or event. Any resemblance is entirely coincidental.]*

See also International Chamber of Commerce; Appendix VI (Interpol).

International Maritime Organization (IMO) is a specialized agency of the United Nations, involved in the following international activities, including the enforcement of the international Rules of Navigation:

1. establishing safe shipping standards;

2. support of maritime research, training, and administration aimed at supporting the development of national merchant marine services;
3. research into shipbuilding and ship repair, port operations, and aids to navigation;
4. providing training and assistance to prevent and combat marine pollution.

Global marketers see the IMO as a potential profitable target from the viewpoint of its worldwide procurement of significant capital equipment and services.

Canada was the first charter member (1948) of the IMO.

Cf. Appendix VI (Rules of Navigation).

See also Appendix V (B).

International Maritime Satellite Organization (INMARSAT) is an international organization, established in 1979 under the auspices of the United Nations, that began operating in 1982.

Using a global system of land-, sea-, and space-based electronic communications and liaising with the International Maritime Association (IMO), INMARSAT provides international maritime communications in emergency situations and in the interests of increasing global efficiency and safety of maritime transportation, physical distribution, and logistical information management.

INMARSAT is owned by 54 national telecommunications authorities. It currently leases transmission capacity on eight satellites, which cover the Atlantic, Pacific, and Indian Oceans. These reached the end of their operational life by the end of 1990, and four new (more powerful) satellites will be launched to extend and increase demand for navigation telecommunications.

INMARSAT has its headquarters in London, England, where the new systems control center will be installed.

See also Appendix V (B).

international marketing refers to the actions of multinational corporations (MNCs) that seek to achieve long-run, large-scale production efficiencies by tailoring standardized products to local consumer (or industrial-user) needs in the individual segments of local, regional, national, and global markets.

Cf. global marketing.

See also multinational corporations.

international marketing channel is the route (including all functional and facilitating intermediaries in it) used by the seller and the buyer in the export process to move goods, services, and supporting information through those intermediaries to the destination.

See also functional intermediary; facilitating intermediary.

International Monetary Fund (IMF) is a specialized agency of the United Nations, established in 1944 after the Bretton Woods Conference. The membership of the IMF currently totals 155 countries.

Commencing its operations in 1947, the IMF was responsible for two broad categories of operations: (1) establishing a set of rules to be followed by all nations in conducting international financing for international trade and (2) providing borrowing facilities for countries with temporary balance-of-payments problems.

The above two categories have expanded significantly since 1947, in the complexity of both their form and content. What follows is a concise outline of those IMF activities of key interest and importance to global marketers.

1. *The IMF's Lending Facilities:*

    i.   *First Credit Tranche* (formerly, *Gold Tranche*)

         To borrow the first 25 percent of its required Fund deposit, the country must demonstrate reasonable efforts to surmount its balance-of-payments problems. (Repayments of the amount(s) borrowed (called "repurchases") are made in 3.25 to 5 years.)

    ii. *Upper Credit Tranches*

         To borrow any part of the remaining 75 percent of its required depository amount, the country must have a substantial program developed (if not initiated) to overcome its balance-of-payments difficulties. (Repurchases are made in 3.25 to 5 years.)

         The First Credit Tranche and the Upper Credit Tranches are referred to as standby lending facilities.

    iii. *Extended Fund Facility (EFF)*

         This is a medium-term lending program, aimed at overcoming structural balance-of-payments maladjustments. The program is normally 3 years in length but can be extended to 4 years where appropriate. In the first year, the IMF lays down explicit policies and achievement targets for borrowing, and it measures the borrowing nation's performance against the criteria. (Repurchases are made in 4.5 to 10 years.)

    iv. *Enlarged Access Policy (EAP)*

         This is a special lending program, established to augment the financing available under standby lending facilities and EFF and EAP arrangements. (Repurchases are made in 3.5 to 7 years.)

    v.   *Compensatory and Contingency Financing Facility (CCFF)*

         This special lending program, which came into effect in August 1988, replaced the hitherto existing Compensatory Financing Facility (CFF). The new CCFF has two components:
         - *Compensatory Element:* this provides financing to a member country that experiences (a) an export shortfall in any commodity (e.g., copper, rice) and (b) an import cereal cost increase. Both (a) and (b) must have been beyond the control of the borrowing member country.
         - *Contingency Element:* this provides the borrowing country with the assurance that, depending on the continuance of a nation's

Fund-supported adjustment programs, the Fund will continue to assist its borrowers to maintain the momentum of adjustment efforts in the face of unexpected and uncontrollable problems that may arise (e.g., hurricanes, cyclones, third-party oil spills, and punitive political and trade actions).

vi. *Buffer Stock Financing Facility (BSFF)*

This lending program was designed to assist a country to finance its contribution to an IMF-approved international buffer stock (as defined in line with "approved" International Commodity Agreements (ICAs)). (Repurchases are made in 3.25 to 5 years.)

vii. *Structural Adjustment Facility (SAF)*

This lending program provides a developing-country borrower with financing on concessional terms. Fund members who apply for the SAF must (a) be low-per-capita-income countries, (b) have protracted balance-of-payments problems, (c) comply with both IMF and World Bank policy directives in the development of (3-year minimum) structural adjustment programs, and (d) be prepared to "fine tune" the economy periodically in terms of adjustments necessary to bring macroeconomic performance into line with Fund benchmarks. (Repurchases are made in 5.5 to 10 years.)

viii. *Enhanced Structural Adjustment Facility (ESAF)*

This special lending facility (established in December 1987) was designed to augment the SAF. The major differences between the ESAF and the SAF consist of means of access to the ESAF and monitoring country performance.

Access to the ESAF is rigorous, involving yearly policy-framework papers and programs that are developed by the Fund and that must be accepted by the potential borrower.

Monitoring of a country's performance is strict. The process includes quarterly targets, mid-year reviews, and semi-annual and annual reviews.

To gain ongoing IMF support, the borrower not only must comply with the Fund's policies and rules, but also must take immediate and effective adjustments actions, upon the Fund's request, to assist the economy to grow and thereby strengthen its balance-of-payments position. (Repurchases are made in 5.5 to 10 years.)

2. *Special Drawing Right(s) (SDR, SDRs):*

The SDR is an international reserve asset of the IMF. It was created by the Fund in 1969 as the unit of account of the Fund and is allocated to Fund member countries to supplement existing reserve assets. (Each member of the IMF has a "quota" expressed in SDRs that is equal to its subscription in the IMF. Quotas determine voting power in the IMF, which is based on 1 vote per SDR 100,000 of a member's quota plus 250 basic votes. It is critical to note that the size of the quota determines each member's access to the IMF's financial resources and its share in SDR allocations.)

i. *SDR Allocations*

The Fund uses its authority to allocate SDRs and to create unconditional liquidity for SDRs.

ii. *Use of SDRs*

Fund members with balance-of-payments difficulties may use SDRs to acquire a specific transferable currency. There are specific rules set down by the Fund for using SDRs in currency-swap arrangements, forward operations, and loans and grant deals.

iii. *Valuation of SDRs*

The value of the SDR is determined on the basis of a basket of five currencies: the U.S. dollar (USD), the pound sterling (GBP), the Japanese yen (JPY), the French franc (FRF), and the Deutsche mark (DEM). Its value in USD is calculated daily: it is the sum of the values in USD, based on market exchange rates of specified amounts of the five currencies in the SDR valuation basket. The specified amounts in terms of agreed weights are:

Currency	*Agreed Weight*
U.S. dollar (USD)	42 percent
Deutsche mark (DEM)	19 percent
Japanese yen (JPY)	15 percent
French franc (FRF)	12 percent
Pound sterling (GBP)	12 percent
SDR currency basket	100 percent

An example of SDR valuation is provided as follows:

Currency	*A* *Currency Amount*	*B* *Exchange Rate on Aug. 6, 1990*	*C* *U.S. Dollar Equivalent*
mark (DEM)	0.5270	1.57620	0.334348
franc (FRF)	1.0200	5.28800	0.192890
yen (JPY)	33.4000	149.82000	0.222934
pound (GBP)	0.0893	1.87220	0.167187
dollar (USD)	0.4520	1.00000	0.452000
SDR 1 = USD			1.369359

Notes:

Column A: These are the currency components of the basket.

Column B: These are exchange rates in terms of currency units per USD, except for the GBP: it is expressed in USD per GBP.

Column C: This is Column A divided by Column B. (It expresses the USD equivalents of the currency amounts in Column A at the exchange rates in Column B.)

It is worth noting that the SDR interest rate is determined weekly, and it is an average of the yields on short-term domestic obligations in money markets of those countries whose currencies comprise the valuation basket.

iv. *Global Nature of the SDR*

Aside from the Fund's member countries, the following 16 international organizations were designated on July 31, 1988, by the Fund to be "prescribed holders" of SDRs:

- African Development Bank (Abidjan, Côte d'Ivoire)*
- African Development Fund (Abidjan, Côte d'Ivoire)
- Andean Reserve Fund (Bogotá, Colombia)
- Arab Monetary Fund (Abu Dhabi, United Arab Emirates)*
- Asian Development Bank (Manila, Philippines)*
- Bank for International Settlements (Basel, Switzerland)*
- Bank of Central African States (Yaoundé, Cameroon)*
- Central Bank of West African States (Dakar, Sénégal)*
- Eastern and Southern African Trade and Development Bank (Bujumbura, Burundi)*
- Eastern Caribbean Central Bank (Basseterre, St. Kitts)*
- International Bank for Reconstruction and Development (Washington, D.C., U.S.A.)*
- International Development Association (Washington, D.C., U.S.A.)*
- International Fund for Agricultural Development (Rome, Italy)*
- Islamic Development Bank (Jeddah, Saudi Arabia)*
- Nordic Investment Bank (Helsinki, Finland)
- Swiss National Bank (Zurich, Switzerland)

*Entries have alphabetical listings.

Some of these international organizations use the SDR as their "unit of account." All of them use the SDR when they carry out international transactions among themselves and between themselves and other international organizations (e.g., the European Investment Bank (EIB)).

Because of the inherent stability of the SDR, the long-term trend is to use the SDR in global business to denominate financial instruments, to settle financial obligations, and as a basis for establishing credit arrangements not only between national entities, but between trading areas (e.g., EEC and EFTA) and between private enterprises.

3. *Surveillance:*

This is the IMF process of monitoring the actual performance of a country against the benchmarks for that performance as laid down in the Fund's policies and rules that surround each lending facility.

4. *Conditionality:*

This is the express contingency in the Fund's lending policies: the IMF will make available lending facilities to a member country (and will only continue to do so) if the member country follows the policies and rules laid down for it and carries out those macroeconomic "adjustment" actions indicated by the Fund.

5. *Adjustment:*

> This refers to the macroeconomic actions that the Fund requires a member country to adopt to correct its balance of payments problems and, thereby, qualify for Fund support via its lending facilities.

> **Example:** One example of an IMF adjustment demand: increase food prices to create incentives for domestic agriculture and conserve scarce foreign exchange by curbing costly food imports. When followed, such adjustment actions frequently result in major domestic upheaval, as attested to by the 1989 urban food riots in Caracas, Venezuela, and in Buenos Aires, Rosario, and Córdoba, Argentina.

international monetary system (IMS) refers to the institutions, rules, and practices that comprised the global arrangements from 1870 to 1973 for effecting international payments and for settling international balance-of-payments indebtedness.
See also gold standard.

international organization(s) (INTORG, INTORGs) denotes institutions (i.e., agencies, associations, councils, organizations) that operate internationally (i.e., on a worldwide or regional scale/level) and represent the interests of

- individual countries *per se*, or of countries as members of trade, commercial/financial, political groups;
- trade, commercial/financial, political groups *per se*; or
- some important worldwide/regional group, which is dedicated to achieving specific short-, medium-, and/or long-term objectives and, thus, having enduring (i.e., relatively permanent) relationships within the global community.
See also Appendix V (A), (B), (C), (D), (E).

international product life cycle *See* product life cycle.

International Rubber Agreement (IRA), officially, the *International Natural Rubber Agreement*, is an international commodity agreement (ICA) that was signed in 1987 under the auspices of the United Nations Conference on Trade and Development (UNCTAD) as the successor to the former agreement, signed in 1979. The Agreement provides, among the producer countries, for price stabilization via mechanisms similar to other ICAs.
Cf. International Cocoa Agreement.
See also international commodity agreement.

International Rubber Organization (IRO) is an international commodity organization (ICO) formed to administer the International Rubber Agreement (IRA).
See also International Rubber Agreement.

International Rubber Study Group (IRSG) is an international commodity group (ICG) that was established in 1944, with headquarters in London, as a consultative forum for the discussion of problems affecting synthetic and natural rubber.

The IRSG is, in fact, a group of 30 countries, most of whom are either natural-rubber-consumer countries or major synthetic-rubber-producer countries. Very few of its members belong to the Association of Natural Rubber Producing Countries (ANRPC), which is the only ICG that represents their interests exclusively.

Thus, the IRSG represents the developed countries (and the newly indus-trialized (industrializing) countries (NICs)) of the North, while the ANRPC represents the developing, non-industrialized countries of the South.

Cf. international commodity agreement; international cartel.

See also Appendix V (E).

International Standardization Organization (ISO) is an international organiza-tion, founded in 1946 and based in Geneva, Switzerland, responsible for the collaboration with world industrial, scientific, technical, and commercial groups and the coordination and development of uniform technical stan-dards in areas dealing with international commerce (e.g., in transportation, materials handling, and logistics).

> **Example:** In 1964, the ISO recommended (via its Technical Committee on Freight Containers) Standard 668 on "Dimensions and Rating of Series I Freight Containers." This was the idea for a freight container of internation-ally uniform dimensions. This standard has been accepted worldwide and has brought rapid cost reductions in intermodal containerization.

See also Standards Code; container.

International Sugar Agreement (ISA) is an international commodity agreement (ICA) that was signed in 1987 as the successor to the former agreement, signed in 1984.

Since the ISA does not contain economic provisions in relation to inter-national trade in sugar, it is thus unlike the International Cocoa Agreement (ICCA) in that it is not an exclusive representation of the interests of produc-ers *vis-à-vis* consumers.

Rather, the ISA is an agreement for the collaborative work of its 43 exporting and 11 importing member countries, relating to the collecting/distribution of (1) production, export, import, and marketing statistics; (2) consumption statistics; (3) statistics on taxation of the commodity and other fiscal measures that impede sugar consumption; (4) information on the de-velopment of artificial sugar substitutes, which compete with sugar; and (5) climatic and other conditions that can either promote or retard the advance of the production and marketing of sugar worldwide.

The ISA was in force until December 31, 1990, and has been extended to (at the latest) December 31, 1992.

It is expected that if future trends follow past events, a new agreement will be negotiated that will run for at least three years (to December 31, 1995) and that might be extended on a year-to-year basis to December 31, 1997.

At the U.N. Sugar Conference in September 1987, convened in Geneva by the Secretary-General, K.K. Dadzie, of the U.N. Conference on Trade and Development (UNCTAD), the need was stressed to "preserve the ISA framework within which an agreement with economic provisions could be prepared at an early date." UNCTAD thus hopes to elevate the current ISA to an OPEC-style cartel of producers whose control over production and physical distribution of the commodity will have a major impact on sugar's low world price.

See also International Sugar Organization.

International Sugar Organization (ISO) is an international commodity group (ICG), with headquarters in London, that acts to administer the International Sugar Agreement (ISA) of 1984 and all succeeding agreements.

The ISO is a genuinely consultative group among the 43 producer countries and 11 consumer countries that are parties to the ISA. It shares information (and forecasts) on production, shipping, and pricing movement worldwide, thus acting as a "neutral clearing house" for information exchange among its membership, which comprises all producer and consumer nations, regardless of political, ideological, or economic orientation.

Cf. international commodity agreement; international cartel.
See also Appendix V (E).

international takeover is the bid by a foreign company to buy control, in the open market, of a domestic corporation.

> **Example:** From March 1989 onwards, a fierce takeover struggle was waged for Connaught Biosciences Inc., the world-famous vaccine producer. The struggle was between *Institut Mérieux S.A.*, a French serum maker, controlled by the French government, and a coalition of the Swiss drug maker Ciba-Geigy Ltd. and its partner Chiron Corporation of California.
>
> In March 1989, *Mérieux* bid for total control of Connaught. However, the $764-million bid was placed in jeopardy by a higher bid by the Swiss-U.S. team. *Mérieux* had difficulty competing since it is owned 50.4 percent by the French government, which had a range of outstanding projects on hand for *Mérieux*, all of which demanded cash. Connaught stock jumped more than $20 in two days of active trading and closed at $51, more than double its value since *Mérieux's* March offer.

International Telecommunications Satellite Organization (INTELSAT) is an international organization, established in 1964, with headquarters in Washington, D.C.

The purpose of INTELSAT is to efficiently operate and profitably manage a global communications satellite system for peaceful, commercial purposes. For example, such purposes include (but are not limited to):

1. the exchange of data between buyers and sellers involving on-line stock exchanges and commodity exchanges;
2. the interconnection of balance-of-trade and balance-of-payments data files in particular country central banks, with surveillance program data files of the regional multilateral development banks, the World Bank, and the International Monetary Fund (IMF);

3. the interconnection between U.N. Conference on Trade and Development (UNCTAD) data banks (containing information on commodity tariff classifications and rates) and particular developing countries (and international commodity country groups).

See also Appendix V (B); United Nations Conference on Trade and Development.

International Telecommunications Union (ITU) is a specialized agency of the United Nations that

1. executes technical cooperation projects (funded by the United Nations Development Program (UNDP) related to telephone, telegraph, data transmission, radio communication, and television services;
2. assists national governments to organize, manage, and operate telecommunications agencies and equipment; and
3. provides technical and supervisory training for personnel involved in telecommunications services.

International Tin Agreement (ITA) *See* International Tin Council.

International Tin Council (ITC) is an international commodity group (ICG) that was responsible for executing the ongoing International Tin Agreement.

The ITC set "floor prices" and "ceiling prices," established commodity reserves (i.e., "buffer stock"), and had authority to regulate tin exports from producer countries.

Under the aegis of the U.N. Conference on Trade and Development, the 3rd International Tin Agreement (between producer and consumer countries) was

1. signed in 1966;
2. renewed in 1971 (as the 4th International Tin Agreement);
3. renegotiated and re-signed in 1976 (as the 5th International Tin Agreement);
4. extended one year (to 1982) beyond its original 1981 expiration date; and
5. extinguished in 1983 before it could be renegotiated because of a collapse in the world tin market.

The ITC remains extant, and although currently inactive, it has never been dissolved. Its membership comprises over 20 producer and consumer countries, plus the European Economic Community (EEC) as a single trading entity.

See also Appendix V (E).

International Trade Administration *See* U.S. International Trade Administration.

International Trade Advisory Committee (System) (ITACS) is a Canadian system of permanent trade advisory functions that was established in 1989 by the Canadian government to provide private-sector input regarding the implementation of the Canada-U.S. Free Trade Agreement of 1989 (FTA).

The system has two components: (1) the International Trade Advisory

Committee (ITAC) and (2) Sectoral Advisory Groups on International Trade (SAGITs).

The ITAC has broad terms of reference on all international-trade policy issues. It comprises a membership of 45 people from all disciplines, including labor, consumer groups, agriculture, academia, and business; and it broadly represents Canada regionally and demographically.

The 13 SAGITS interact with the government to provide sectoral views of international-trade policy development. In matters dealing with multilateral trade negotiations (MTN), the ITAC/SAGITs provide advice to MTN negotiators.

The SAGITs are as follows: (1) Agriculture; (2) Apparel and Fur; (3) Arts and Culture; (4) Communications, Computer Equipment, and Services; (5) Consumer and Household Products; (6) Energy, Chemicals, and Petrochemicals; (7) Financial Services; (8) Fish and Fish Products; (9) Forest Products; (10) General Services; (11) Industrial and Transportation Equipment; (12) Minerals and Metals; and (13) Textiles, Footwear, and Leather.

The Minister of International Trade has the authority to create new SAGITs if needed.

Cf. Sectoral Advisory Groups on International Trade.

International Trade Centers (ITCs) are units located within the regional offices of Industry, Science and Technology Canada (ISTC), a key function of which is to manage, on behalf of the External Affairs and International Trade Canada (EAITC), those units called ITCs.

Headed by a Senior Trade Commissioner (i.e., a trade consul), each ITC is staffed by experienced EAITC trade officials, by Export Development Corporation (EDC) staff, and by individuals from the Canadian International Development Agency (CIDA).

The range of trade services that the ITCs offer to Canadian exporters are the following, each of which can be found in the alphabetical listings: export counseling, export support programs, export education, export trade information, export financing, and export insurance.

Cf. Department of External Affairs.

International Trade Center UNCTAD/GATT (ITC) is an international organization established under the aegis of the General Agreement of Tariffs and Trade (GATT) in 1964 to assist developing countries to promote their exports.

Since 1968, the ITC has been operated jointly by the GATT and the United Nations Conference on Trade and Development (UNCTAD) in Geneva.

The ITC carries out the following activities:

1. providing developing countries with assistance in devising and implementing export-promotion programs;
2. providing information, technical cooperation, and guidance on export activities relating to financing, packaging, logistics, physical distribution, market research, and promotion;
3. providing training assistance for those who are required to plan and implement export marketing activities in developing countries.

See also General Agreement on Tariffs and Trade; United Nations Conference on Trade and Development.

International Trade Commission *See* U.S. International Trade Commission.

International Trade Organization (ITO) is a now-defunct institution, established after World War II, that was supposed to act globally to regulate, stimulate, and expand international trade.
See also General Agreement on Tariffs and Trade.

international transfer of technology *See* technology transfer.

International Vine and Wine Study Group (IVWSG), officially, *Office Internationale de la Vigne et du Vin (OIVV)*, is an international commodity group (ICG) that acts as a consultative and information exchange forum on (1) the growing and harvesting of grapes; (2) their processing into wine; and (3) the technical, scientific, and economic problems of (1) and (2).
The OIVV was established in 1924, and it has its headquarters in Paris, France.
See also Appendix V (E).

International Wheat Council (IWC) is an international commodity group (ICG), established in 1949 and headquartered in London, England, that was originally given the responsibility of executing what were expected to have been a series of International Wheat Agreements or, as they were then known, Wheat Trade Conventions (WTCs).
The first WTC was signed in 1949 by countries that accounted for over 50 percent of global wheat trade: 5 exporting countries and 40 importing countries. The WTC established (1) a "floor price," a "reference price," a "ceiling price," and a "trigger price" and (2) mechanisms for managing world supply and demand to afford producer countries fair profits and consumer countries equitable prices and assured supply.
The most contemporary (1971) WTC was extended until 1983, but it collapsed because the IWC could establish no concensus for acceptable pricing of wheat, given the "war of agricultural subsidies" being waged between the United States and the European Economic Community. Subsequently, the WTC was renegotiated in 1986.
Cf. international commodity agreement.
See also round of trade negotiations; Appendix V (E).

International Wool Study Group (IWSG) is an international commodity group (ICG) that was established in 1949 with the same framework as the International Lead and Zinc Study Group (ILZSG) and the International Rubber Study Group (IRSG): to consult, study, appraise, and recommend and to share information among group members.
The IWSG comprises 42 producer- and consumer-member countries and is headquartered in London, England.
Cf. International Lead and Zinc Study Group; International Rubber Study Group.
See also Appendix V (E).

intervention currency *See* Appendix II.

Investment Canada is a Canadian government agency that was established in 1985 and that replaced the Canadian Foreign Investment Review Agency (FIRA).

The mandate of FIRA, from its founding in 1974 until its replacement, was essentially one of nationalist economic protectionism. The function of Investment Canada, on the other hand, is expansionist and globally oriented: to actively promote direct foreign investment in Canada.

While assuming an "open for business" posture, the agency carefully monitors all foreign investment to ensure that government obligations both under the General Agreement on Tariffs and Trade and to domestic industry (in terms of competition policy) are protected.

Cf. Foreign Investment Review Agency.

investment performance requirements (IPRs), sometimes cited as a type of *nontariff barrier*, are conditions imposed on foreign investors seeking permission to make direct investments in a country.

The Canadian Foreign Investment Review Agency (FIRA), from its founding in 1974 until its replacement in 1985 by Investment Canada, extracted written commitments from foreign investors in terms of IPRs set down by the Canadian government. For example, the requirement to maintain and increase Canadian jobs was a priority IPR.

Secondly, there was the requirement that the physical product (produced in Canada) contain a minimum of 60 percent Canadian content. Depending on the industry, this requirement might be reduced to 50 percent if the goods were for export.

The formation of some regional international organizations, such as the Latin American Economic System (LAES), may not necessarily be congruent with a marketing outlook that is truly global. With a specific mandate to extricate member countries from "dependence," the LAES suggests that direct foreign investment from sources hitherto perceived as "imperialist" may, if welcome at all, be subject to relatively strict IPRs.

See *also* nontariff barriers; Latin American Economic System.

invisible trade, sometimes referred to as *invisible exports, invisible imports*, and *invisibles*, are items implicitly included in a country's balance of payments even though they neither show up nor are recorded as tangible exports and imports.

Such items comprise financial and legal services, physical distribution services (packaging, handling, transportation), and logistical services (insurance, computer processing).

See *also* balance of payments.

invoice acceptance *See* foreign invoice acceptance.

irrevocable letter of credit *See* letter of credit.

irrevocable transferable letter of credit *See* letter of credit.

Islamic Development Bank (ISDB) is an international Arab financial organization, established by the Organization of the Islamic Conference in 1973, with headquarters in Jeddah, Saudi Arabia.

The ISDB acts, in accordance with Islamic Law, as a bank (1) to directly fund development projects in Arab countries, (2) to invest in major infrastructural projects and take a share of the equity capital as a return on the investment, and (3) to extend loans and loan guarantees to the private and public sectors.

See also Islamic Law; Organization of the Islamic Conference; Appendix V (B).

Islamic Law (*Shari'ah**), as perceived by Muslims, is a system of divinely ordained rules, codified as the *Shari'ah*, that guides the entire conduct of Muslim life.

Therefore, the Islamic Law system differs fundamentally from Western, customary law systems. Western systems govern the relationships among people themselves and between people and the State. The Islamic Law system includes the regulation of these relationships, but includes the relationship between people and God (*Allah**) and between people and their own private consciences. Thus, Islamic Law encompasses all possible human relationships; and since it is divinely ordained, it is static and immutable, something that differs markedly from the customary law systems of Western, secular countries.

The *Shari'ah* comprises two broad categories:

1. *'ibadat**: the ritual (religious) practices of Islam (i.e., the religious obligations of people to *Allah*);
2. *mu'amalat**: the rights and duties of people to each other (secular laws).

The *mu'amalat* consist of the following legal codes:

1. *Penal Code:* comprises crimes against the person and specifies penalties;
2. *Law of Transactions Code:* establishes and defines the core rules of economic behavior;
3. *Family Law Code:* establishes and defines the rights and obligations of family members to each other and between men and women as spouses, and the rules that govern marriage and family formation;
4. *Succession Law Code:* establishes the rules for inheritance and the authority people have to bequeath their possessions and to make use of inheritances.

From the global marketing viewpoint, the Law of Transactions Code is most relevant. One can isolate the following salient features:

1. *Legal Capacity to Transact*: is derived from the physical age of puberty; it is established as 15 years of age for men and women.
2. *Legal Incapacity to Transact*: is derived from the concept of *rashid** (a person of wise or prudent judgment). People under 15 years old are presumed not to "be *rashid*." People can lose their *rashid* by virtue of old age or of mental or physical incapacity or illness.

---

*Transliterated from the Arabic.

3. *Four Basic Types of Transactions*: all economic relations derive from these root exchanges:
   - *Bay**: transfer of title to real estate or chattel for a consideration
   - *Ijarah**: transfer of real estate or chattel for "a right to use" (rent, lease, or hire) for a consideration
   - *Hibah**: gratuitous transfer (a gift) of real estate or chattel, without any expectation of any consideration
   - *Ariyah**: gratuitous transfer (a loan) of real estate or chattel for "a right to use" for a consideration.
4. *The Doctrine of Riba**: the prohibition of usury (i.e., the charging of any form of interest on capital or investments). To comply with Islamic Law, financial institutions (e.g., Islamic Development Bank) receive "considerations" for their funding by means of (1) management fees, (2) administration fees, and (3) by taking an equity capital position in projects they have financed.

Cf. common law systems.
See also Islamic Development Bank.

issuing bank, also called the *opening bank*, is the financial institution that opens or extends the documentary credit at the request of an importer in favor of an exporter and that agrees to pay (to honor) drafts drawn "under it" or "against it" by the exporter who is the "beneficiary," or the payee.
Cf. advising bank.
See also documentary credit; trust receipt.

item-by-item tariff reductions refers to a negotiating strategy used by Contracting Parties to the General Agreement on Tariffs and Trade, usually in a given round of multilateral trade negotiations (MTN).

This technique abjures blanket tariff reductions and, rather, focuses discussion on the amount, extent, and timing of specific tariff abatement by restricting negotiations to "serial bargaining" (i.e., first of all, specific product classes are addressed, followed by detailed talks on every specific product within a particular class).

This negotiating process is sometimes used by countries with particularly "sensitive products." These are goods whose local manufacture is so important to the country that any across-the-board tariff reduction would cause serious economic problems (e.g., balance-of-payments deficits, unemployment, flight of direct investment) and, consequently, political difficulties (e.g., a declared moratorium on external debt payments).

> **Example:** All classes of unprocessed and semiprocessed forestry products are so important as an export earner that the Canadian government considers it wisest to take an item-by-item approach in any talks on tariff reductions affecting the industry.

Cf. liberalization; across-the-board tariff reductions.
See also General Agreement on Tariffs and Trade; round of trade negotiations.

---

*Transliterated from the Arabic.

Jamaica Accords (Jamaica Agreement) is an international arrangement concerning the international monetary system, reached in Jamaica in January 1976.

The Accords were consented to by the U.S. Congress and were ratified by the U.S. president in April 1978.

The Accords (1) recognized the "managed float" and (2) abolished the official price of gold (i.e., U.S. $32 per oz.), permitting it to fluctuate freely on the world market.

Cf. gold standard.

See also managed float.

Japan, Inc., is the name given by Americans to their perception of the smooth, harmonious alliance among Japanese private industry, the Japanese Ministry of International Trade and Industry (MITI), and the Japanese Ministry of Finance (MOF) to dominate world markets.

This perception is based on fear and ignorance, and it has little resemblance to reality. It is not necessarily a fact that Japanese industry, MITI, and MOF have a common international marketing strategy. In fact, the opposite is often the case. While MITI favored only a few large and highly productive companies—and scrapped shipbuilding, coal, and textiles—the MOF favored keeping weak firms alive. This divisiveness—in-fighting among bureaucratic administrators—has contributed greatly to Japan's perceived "leadershipless state."

Another example will illustrate the Japan, Inc., myth. For years, MITI had advised industry that the world market for automobiles was becoming saturated and they should switch investment. But all through the 1980s, Japanese car builders continued to accelerate direct investment in assembly plants in North America, encouraged by MOF-supported Japanese banks.

They were, in other words, directly contributing to the worldwide slowdown in demand for cars, which contributed to the "rationalization" of the global auto industry.

It was like a *kamikaze* who, despite being told World War II was over, was determined to complete his "down the ship's funnel" mission.

Since the facts frequently do not jibe with the preconceived notion of Japan, Inc., as a well-oiled machine bent on overwhelming U.S. industry, they are often ignored in the all too common search for scapegoats for U.S. marketing failures.

Japan Sea Basin (economic cooperation zone) refers to the idea, suggested by Japanese academics and officials of the Japanese Ministry of International Trade and Industry (MITI), that the five nations of the Western Pacific (i.e., Japan, the U.S.S.R., South Korea, North Korea, and China) should form a regional economic cooperation zone.

The purpose of the new "development zone" would be (1) to afford Japan access to cheap and plentiful supplies of labor and raw materials; (2) to promote reform and trade liberalization in the area, especially in nonmarket economies in the region; and (3) to lay the economic groundwork for a new dependence upon Japan (having an abundance of capital and technology) by the other four regional partners who are wealthy only in labor and resources.

Cf. Association of Southeast Asian Nations.
See also yen diplomacy; dependent development.

Japan Special Fund (JSF) is a financial facility created by the Japanese government that makes grants to "co-finance" operations of the multilateral development banks (MDBs) for pre-investment and feasibility studies, small projects, and emergency assistance.

Example: When Hurricane Gilbert hit Jamaica in 1988, it took only 48 hours for the Inter-American Development Bank to approve a $5-million grant from the JSF for the rebuilding of the homes of the disaster victims.

See also multilateral development banks; yen diplomacy.

jinmyaku •NW•, from the Japanese *jin* meaning "personal" and *myaku* meaning "vein" (as in veins of ore), are personal networks of friends and associates that penetrate society at various levels.

These relationships are based on personal and company allegiance rather than family ties.

Cf. *keibatsu* •NW•; *habatsu* •NW•; *kone* •NW•; *paipu* •NW•.

joint venture (JV, J.V., j.v.) is a legal form of business organization between companies in different countries, whereby there is cooperation toward the achievement of common goals between entities that were, prior to the JV, separate.

There are three types of JVs: (1) contractual JVs, (2) equity JVs, and (3) hybrid JVs.

1. *Contractual JVs:* under this type of arrangement, the JV is not created as a separate legal corporate entity. It is an enterprise in the form of an unincorporated association, created to carry out clearly defined activities

and to attain specific goals over a specific period of time. There is a clear separation between the companies that agree to cooperate within this type of JV framework: each of them is responsible for its own liabilities.

2. *Equity JVs:* this arrangement is an enterprise comprising at least two partners and having the following characteristics:
   - formation of a legal corporation with limited liability and the joint management of it by the JV partners;
   - pooled equity in the corporation, from which an equity ratio is determined (e.g., 50–50, 49–51, 30–21–49);
   - profits and losses shared between the partners in proportion to their equity in the JV.

3. *Hybrid JVs:* this commercial agreement is, as its name suggests, a cross between contractual JVs and equity JVs: (1) from the equity JV format, the hybrid JV retains the form of a separate legal entity, but one that is not necessarily a limited-liability corporation; and (2) from the contractual JV format, the hybrid type retains the specificity of time-limited activities and objectives.

The JV is, from the global marketing viewpoint, a less desirable business framework than the "subsidiary format" (i.e., total ownership of the foreign-based enterprise). It is "acceptable" (even up to a 50/50 basis), given the following:

1. The joint venture is a form of business arrangement preferred especially by nonmarket, socialist economies and developing countries. These use the JV to attract capital and management skills either driven out of collectivist economies or disinterested in politically risky, debt-ridden less developed countries.

2. Developing countries (many of which have socialist command economies) lack capital, skilled labor, training facilities, and management expertise. They use the joint-venture framework to domesticate direct investment, which might otherwise be perceived as "economic imperialism."

3. The JV, in other words, permits foreign capital to be attracted to a country (which might have been a former colony of a Western, capitalist economy) on political terms more acceptable to local economic nationalists.

4. In nonmarket, socialist economies, the JV likewise is more acceptable to local political elites. Where complete economic liberalization itself is unacceptable since it would threaten their political authority as a result of the new, unfettered competition in a free world market, the JV "buys them time," and it gains the global marketer an *entrée* into the relatively closed economy.

Thus, the joint venture may be perceived as ranking with countertrade as a strategy to delimit global marketing, by raising political barriers to what would otherwise be the unhindered global movement of the factors of production.

Another view of the joint venture is that of the global marketer who may be somewhat antagonistic to the JV's binding legal structure and the necessity of reciprocal equity swapping. As a consequence of this, the JV is viewed as being a narrow nonglobal world view, one that is (at worst) binational and (at best) regiocentric. These marketers argue that JVs are implicitly inflexible, where flexibility is the *sine qua non* in the global environment. They prefer the global marketing strategy called global alliancing.

Cf. countertrade; contract manufacturing.

See also global alliancing •NW•; foreign investment law; closed economy; command economy; domestication; nontariff barriers.

keibatsu •NW•, from the Japanese, are family groupings generated by marriage among Japanese elite members to facilitate the buildup of contacts.
Cf. *habatsu* •NW•; *jinmyaku* •NW•.

Keidanren •NW•, from the Japanese, is the Federation of Economic Organizations, a national "association of associations" comprising leading associations that themselves include all the companies in major *keiretsu* in Japan.
Keidanren membership includes such associations as the following:

- The Automobile Manufacturers' Association
- The Japan Federation of Bar Associations
- The Shipbuilders' Associations
- The Petroleum Association
- The Chemical Industry Association
- The Japan Foreign Trade Council (representing *sogososha*)
- The Wholesale Businesses' Association
- The National Federation of Rice Marketing Cooperative Associations (Japan's largest rice-wholesaler group)
- The Japan Federation of Construction Contractors
- The Iron and Steel Federation
- The Banking Association

The importance of the *Keidanren* lies not only in its function as the focus for all Japanese industry, trade, and commerce discussions of intrasectoral strategies and building of *jinmyaku*, but also in the fact that it serves as the "first head" of Japan's four-headed *zaikai*.
See also zaikai •NW•.

keiretsu, from the Japanese, are corporate conglomerates whose members cooperate with each other for strategic purposes within the international business environment.

There are three major types of *keiretsu* in Japan: (1) bank-centered *keiretsu*, (2) supply-centered *keiretsu*, and (3) distribution *keiretsu*.

1. Bank-centered *keiretsu* are massive industrial combines of 20 to 45 companies centered around a bank. This structure enables the companies that comprise the core of the *keiretsu* to share financial risk and to allocate investment in economically advantageous ways worldwide. There are 7 major bank-centered *keiretsu* in Japan: Sumitomo, Mitsubishi, Mitsui, Dai Ichi, Kangyo, Fuyo, and Sanwa, comprising 182 companies in all.

2. Supply-centered *keiretsu* are groups of companies vertically integrated along a "supplier chain" dominated by a major manufacturer, a "channel captain." Supply-centered *keiretsu* characterize the automotive and electronics industries. They are well known for the pressure tactics used by channel captains to enforce time, cost, and delivery-schedule compliance by suppliers (and to extract price concessions from them) under strategies such as just-in-time (JIT) supply systems. Examples of important supply-centered *keiretsu* are the NEC group (electronics) and the Canon and Nikon group (semiconductor diffusion). Many of the companies in the supply-centered *keiretsu* are linked to the bank-centered *keiretsu*: the NEC group is owned 25 percent by Sumitomo *keiretsu* banks, and NEC is thus the Sumitomo group's principal electronics company; Canon is the $8-billion diversified electronics company in the Fuyo bank-centered *keiretsu*, while Nikon is in the Mitsubishi *keiretsu*. Canon and Nikon together hold more than 60 percent of the world market in the production of semiconductor capital equipment.

3. Distribution *keiretsu* are webs of relationships tying Japanese wholesalers and retailers to a particular manufacturer who acts as a "channel captains."

    The Japanese Fair Trade Commission (JFTC) issued guidelines on January 17, 1991, to enforce Japan's Antimonopoly Law against distribution *keiretsu* manufacturers who have engaged in systematic protectionist trading practices to restrict competition and exclude foreign companies from entering the Japanese market. Some of these protectionist trading practices are as follows:
    *   payment of rebates by manufacturers to retailers as rewards for not carrying products made by competitors;
    *   payment of special rebates to wholesalers for handling the goods of a single manufacturer ("tied selling");
    *   "joint boycotts" in which rival manufacturers collude to keep out their competitors;
    *   cutbacks in manufacturers' shipments to punish retailers (or to punish wholesalers who, in turn, will punish retailers) who reduce prices below a level established by the manufacturers ("resale-price maintenance").

In the United States, the protectionist business practices cited would be clear criminal violations of laws such as the Clayton Act and the Sherman Antitrust Act; in Canada, they would be equally clear violations of The Competition Act. However, in Japan, the power of *keiretsu* in general and the nature of Japanese culture and consumer behavior are such that the JFTC should not expect success in its enforcement of the Antimonopoly Law. First of all, few Japanese retailers will report violations to the JFTC because they will not want to be "punished" by the overarching power of the "channel captain." Secondly, few retailers will want to disrupt customary practices. The paradigm of the all-powerful patriarchal social structure is the dominant theme here. Thus, those foreign traders who accept the recent JFTC action as proof of its responsiveness to the Structural Impediments Initiative (SII) between Japan and the United States, undertaken in 1990, are either ignorant of the soft side of international marketing in Japan or are willfully blinding themselves to the facts of Japanese ongoing protectionism.

Cf. monopoly.

See also protectionist business practices; Structural Impediments Initiative •NW•.

Keizai Doyukai •NW•, from the Japanese, is "The Committee for Economic Development."

See also zaikai •NW•.

kengen •NW•, from the Japanese meaning "authority," refers to the right or legitimacy of a Japanese manager to issue directives within a predefined work domain.

Since Japanese society is a high-context culture, one can never be entirely sure whether compliance by Japanese workers to management orders flows from acknowledgment of a manager's *kengen* or if the compliance is rooted within the idea of *yoroshiku tanomu*, which itself is embedded within the situational-conformity social framework.

Cf. *ken'i* •NW•.

See also situational conformity •NW•; *yoroshiku tanomu* •NW•; high-context culture; *nemawashi* •NW•.

ken'i •NW•, from the Japanese meaning "personal influence," refers to the capacity of a Japanese manager to influence subordinates based on his "personal power," which derives more from the manager's character than from his social rank and status.

Since Japanese society is a high-context culture, one's *ken'i* is more valued than power one earns through achievement. Thus, Japanese managers are felt to have certain "inborn leadership qualities," which are part of character, rather than "leadership abilities," which are learned.

Cf. *kengen* •NW•.

Kennedy Round, officially, the *Kennedy Round of Trade Negotiations under GATT*, named after U.S. president John F. Kennedy, was the sixth complete set (in an ongoing series) of multilateral trade negotiations (MTNs) held under the aegis of the General Agreement on Tariffs and Trade (GATT).

Initiated in 1963, the round comprised all the world's major trading nations. The U.S. government was authorized to participate under the U.S. Trade Expansion Act of 1962. The Kennedy Round itself was completed successfully in 1967.

Under the Kennedy Round, two important events occurred:

1. a major trade-liberalization agreement was entered into, whereby members of the Organization for Cooperation and Development agreed to reduce customs duties by an average of 35 percent on industrial products;
2. an antidumping code was signed that established the protocols to be followed when a country alleging injury as a result of dumping seeks available remedies.

See also round of trade negotiations; liberalization; antidumping code.

Keynesian economics, also termed *liberal economics, demand-side economics, fiscal economics, fiscalism,* or, eponymously, *Keynesianism,* is a body of economic ideas, named after the economist John Maynard Keynes, that focuses on the core idea that government involvement in the economy is the most intelligent, reliable, and expedient way to moderate the effects of extreme fluctuations in the business cycle.

The modus used by government is called "fiscal policy": government's authority to tax and its power to redistribute wealth by way of government expenditures.

For almost half a century, from the Great Depression (1929–circa 1939) onwards, Keynesian economics has dominated the national macroeconomic policies and practices in the highly industrialized economies of the Organization for Economic Cooperation and Development states. Only during the "Nixon Era" (1968–1973) and the "Reagan Era" (1980–1988) was it displaced in favor of the conservative economics of the monetarists.

Cf. monetarism.

Keynesianism *See* Keynesian economics.

kickbacks *See* bribery.

kone •NW•, from the Japanese, refers to "connections" with important people.
Cf. *jinmyaku* •NW•; *paipu* •NW•.

Kyoto Convention is a major international agreement, administered by the Customs Cooperation Council (CCC) in Brussels, whereby the rules governing the harmonization of global customs practices are amended according to certain protocols, which themselves are reviewed and amended by CCC experts according to the Convention.
See also Customs Cooperation Council.

l

laissez-faire, from the French meaning "let it be," is the philosophy (which replaced mercantilism) that espoused minimum government involvement in the regulation of a country's economic activity.

This was the core idea advocated by Adam Smith and the (so-called) "classical economists" of eighteenth-century Europe. From it, the following argument has been adduced by Milton Friedman and the Chicago School of contemporary "neoclassical economists":

1. minimum government interference is equated with maximum personal freedom;
2. maximum personal freedom is most conducive to individuals achieving their maximum economic benefit;
3. the unfettered competition in the marketplace, which resulted from and accompanied maximum personal economic freedom, rewards the most efficient and thereby creates an incentive that ultimately benefits society as a whole.

Cf. socialism; mercantilism.
See also absolute advantage.

Lake Chad Basin Commission (LCBC), also known as *Commission du Bassin du Lac Chad (CBLC)*, is an international organization established in 1964 to coordinate plans for the economic development of the Chad Basin among neighboring countries of the region.

The members of the LCBC are Cameroon, Chad, Niger, and Nigeria. Headquartered in N'jamena, Chad, the LCBC develops plans for common projects with a regional impact. For example, projects such as the establishment of fisheries and the efficient use of common surface- and groundwater resources in agriculture, animal husbandry, and fishery are recommended to the U.N. Economic Commission for Africa for implementation and funding by the African Development Bank.

The LCBC is one of a number of African regional international organizations dedicated to multilateral cooperation in economic development.

See also United Nations Economic Commission for Africa; African Development Bank.

large-scale industrial transfer (LSIT) is a form of technology transfer whereby manufacturing plants are moved from the "core" (e.g., the United States and Japan) to the "periphery" (e.g., Puerto Rico and Thailand) to take advantage of low-cost industrial inputs (especially cheap labor).

Every major Japanese electronics company (e.g., Sony, Matsushita, Sharp, Fujitsu, and Aiwa) has implemented LSIT.

> **Example:** In Southeast Asia, Japanese LSIT investment has triggered an unprecedented boom in regional trade. For example, at Matsushita Television (Malaysia), over 66 percent of the 47 percent of components that are supplied within the region come from other Matsushita plants in Malaysia and Singapore. Another of Matsushita's Malaysian subsidiaries, Matsushita Electronic Components, sells 35 percent of its products to other Matsushita plants: its resistors go to three nearby T.V. factories and three audio-equipment plants in Singapore and Malaysia and to Matsushita's new fax-machine plant in Singapore. With almost half of its manufacturing already in Southeast Asia, the infrastructure is in place for a new regional-based electronics "empire."

See also technology transfer.

LASH (vessel) (lighter aboard ship) is an ocean-going vessel designed to carry barges and is especially useful in shallow ports where deep-water vessels are unable to berth.

> **Example:** Ocean-bound freight from inland ports such as Memphis and St. Louis would be floated down the Mississippi. At New Orleans, the cargo barges would be towed out to LASH vessels anchored in deep water, and the barges themselves would be loaded onto (or otherwise affixed to) the ships. At the destination, the ship would anchor in deep water, and the barges would be towed into port.

Latin American Association of International Trading Companies (LAAITC), officially, *Asociación Latinoamericano de Traficantes (ALAT)*, is a regional industry association first suggested in Caracas in October 1987 and formally launched in Rio de Janeiro in September 1988 with the assistance of the Inter-American Development Bank (IDB), the United Nations Conference on Trade and Development (UNCTAD), and the Latin American Economic System (SELA).

ALAT's membership comprises representatives from ten Latin American and Caribbean countries: Argentina, Brazil, Colombia, Cuba, Ecuador, El Salvador, Panamá, Perú, Uruguay, and Venezuela. The objectives of ALAT are to provide a common forum for uniting ALAT members, aimed at strengthening members' capacity to generate exports from the region, and to strengthen the process of regional economic integration.

The Brazilian Trading Companies Association (ABECE) was chosen (at Caracas) to establish the ALAT, and Rio de Janeiro was selected as the Association's headquarters with the ABECE as its interim Secretariat.

See also Latin American Integration Association.

Latin American Economic System (LAES), officially *Sistema Económico Latino-americano (SELA)*, a regional international organization that was established in Panamá in 1975, with current headquarters in Caracas, Venezuela, represents the cooperative trade and development interests of its 26 Latin American and Caribbean members.

The LAES is a network of permanent institutions that affords its member countries mechanisms for joint cooperation and collaborative planning and execution of programs and projects. The network aims to better utilize the region's resources by establishing specifically Latin American-based global corporations, to transform indigenous resources in line with the individual and joint developmental goals of member countries.

The System has developed Action Committees *(Comités de Acción)* as follows:

Action Committee On	*Located In*
arts and crafts	Panamá
fertilizers	México City
high-protein food stuffs	Caracas
low-income housing	Quito
sea- and freshwater products	Lima
technological information	Rio de Janeiro
tourism	San José

These Committees design and execute major project work that is financed by, and shared among, members.

For example, work by the Action Committee in Mexico was the model for the establishment of Multifert S.A., the Latin American corporation owned by 11 member countries of the LAES, which markets fertilizer globally.

Funding for the organization is from member countries. An agreement signed with the United Nations Development Program (UNDP) provides for technical cooperation to be made available for project work designed and implemented by the Action Committees.

The LAES is a strong supporter of and has good relations with the U.N. Conference on Trade and Development, which it perceives as a strong defender of policies that provide member countries with equitable prices for commodities and natural resources exported for external processing.

In terms of international influence, the LAES provides its members with a forum for discussion of and a platform to address international organizations on a range of macroeconomic subjects such as the external debt of the region's members and allegedly discriminatory trade laws and practices of the United States.

See also United Nations Conference on Trade and Development; United Nations Development Program; generalized system of preferences.

Latin American Free Trade Association (LAFTA) was a free trade area, established in 1960, comprising Mexico and most Latin American nations of the region.

LAFTA became defunct in 1980 when it evolved into a new economic integration organization.

See also Latin American Integration Association.

Latin American Integration Association (LAIA), also called the *Latin American Association for Integration (LAAI)* and, officially, the *Asociación Latinoamericana De Integración (ALADI)*, is the common market established in 1980 as the successor to LAFTA.

The LAIA consists of all 11 countries of LAFTA including the Andean Common Market countries: Argentina, Bolivia, Brazil, Chile, Colombia, Ecuador, México, Paraguay, Perú, Uruguay, and Venezuela.

The long-term aim of the organization is the integration of the Latin American economies. Efforts in this direction are enhanced through bilateral trade agreements such as the 1985 Program for Cooperation signed by Argentina and Brazil. Private industrial groups and trade associations (such as the Latin American Association of International Trading Companies (ALAT) founded in Rio de Janeiro in 1988), as well as business groups, work to further trade liberalization regionally and to promote reciprocal trade (e.g., between Venezuela and Colombia).

See also Appendix V (A).

laundering (of money), also known as *money laundering*, is the process whereby holders of *dirty money*, usually in the form of cash, inject the money into the vast stream of legitimate, worldwide cash deals (by means of investments, transfers, and deposits).

Detection by authorities is thereby evaded simply because of the colossal volume of cash transactions done on a global basis daily and the "speed of light" rapidity with which global transfers can be effected.

See also offshore banking.

Law of Comparative Advantage *See* comparative advantage.

Law of One Price *See* global monetarism.

least developed country (LLDC) is

1. a culture-based term that denotes nations that have attained the lowest measured standards (e.g., per capita income) or the highest "negative performance" (e.g., infant mortality) and that distinguishes them from others that have achieved higher comparable standards;

Some of the standards applied (by the United Nations) are a gross domestic product (GDP) of U.S. $100 per capita or less, a literacy rate of 20 percent or less of that part of the population old enough to read, and a share of manufacturing in the gross domestic product of 10 percent or less.

2. an ethnocentric label used to denote nations that are the least industrialized and that, by negative inference, have ways of life that are less highly valued than those of other nations that are more industrialized.

At a United Nations Conference on the Least Developed Countries in 1981 (reconvened in Paris in September 1990), there were 31 countries classified as LLDCs. As of 1989, there were 41 of them. Most lie in the zone of 10° to 30° north latitude in Africa; a few are in Asia; and only one (Haïti) is in the Western Hemisphere.

The full list of the 41 LLDCs is as follows: Afghanistan, Bangladesh, Benin, Bhutan, Botswana, Burkina Faso, Burundi, Cape Verde, Central African Republic, Chad, Comoros, Djibouti, Equatorial Guinea, Ethiopia, Gambia, Guinea, Guinea-Bissau, Haïti, Kiribati, Lao People's Democratic Republic, Lesotho, Malawi, Maldives, Mali, Mauritania, Mozambique, Mynamar (formerly Burma), Nepal, Niger, Rwanda, Samoa, São Tomé and Principe, Sierra Leone, Somalia, Sudan, Togo, Tuvalu, Uganda, Tanzania, Vanuatu, and Yemen.

LLDCs comprise 12 percent of world population, generate only 1 percent of world GDP, and use only 1 percent of the world's energy.

All LLDCs are included in the larger group of developing countries known as the Third World.

Cf. developed country; less developed country; sustainable development. *See also* developing country; Third World.

less developed country (LDC) is

1. a culture-based term that denotes a nation that has attained intermediate standards, falling between developed nations and least developed nations; the standards relate to measures such as per capita income, life expectancy, and infant mortality;
2. an ethnocentric label used to denote nations that are less industrialized, falling between developed nations and least developed nations, and that, by negative inference, have ways of life that are less highly valued than those of other nations that are more industrialized.

Most LDCs are in the Southern hemisphere. They include the least developed countries and are known comprehensively as the Third World.

Cf. developed country; least developed country; sustainable development. *See also* developing country; Third World.

less than fair value (LTFV) is a determination by the U.S. International Trade Commission (USITC) that foreign goods have been imported into the United States and sold there at a "dumped price."

Based on this determination, the goods may be the object of antidumping actions under the U.S. Tariff Act of 1930, and the alleged "dumpers" may be dealt with under the U.S. Omnibus Trade Act of 1988.

See also dumping; antidumping duty; U.S. International Trade Commission; Tariff Act of 1930; Omnibus Trade Act of 1988.

letter of credit (l/c), formally, a *commercial letter of credit*, is a "letter of instruction" issued by the importer's bank (the issuing bank) to the exporter that establishes a documentary basis for the exporter getting paid (by drafts drawn on the credit), provided the exporter complies with the exact terms of the credit.

A letter of credit can be of several types:

1. *Revocable Letter of Credit:* the credit that the issuing bank can withdraw unilaterally for whatever reason, without any other party to the transaction concurring.
2. *Confirmed Letter of Credit:* a letter of credit that the exporter's bank agrees to "cover" (i.e., it is agreed the exporter's bank (the advising bank) will "make good" on the l/c in the event that the issuing bank has payment problems).
3. *Irrevocable Letter of Credit:* a written undertaking by the issuing bank that, except with the express consent of all the key parties to the transaction (i.e., importer and its importer's bank, exporter and its exporter's bank), the credit will neither be withdrawn nor amended (an irrevocable letter of credit may be unconfirmed or confirmed).
4. *Irrevocable Transferable Letter of Credit:* a written undertaking by the issuing bank (and its acceptance by the exporter) that the exporter, as beneficiary, has the authority to instruct its bank to assign part proceeds of the credit to a third party (an irrevocable transferable letter of credit may be unconfirmed or confirmed).

While the "transferability" of the l/c may appear to be simply a nicety, it is a truly desirable feature should the exporter seek to liquidate its foreign accounts receivables in favor of one of its nonbank creditors, such as a transport company or other export intermediary.

5. *Revolving Letter of Credit:* a documentary credit establishing the mechanism for a "blanket" credit instrument whereby continuous drawings (via documentary drafts) are made over a specific period of time; and each time drawings are made, the credit is automatically renewed under identical conditions (a revolving letter of credit may be unconfirmed or confirmed).
6. *Back-to-Back Letter of Credit:* when a foreign bank issues an irrevocable l/c in favor of an exporter who may be unable to supply the goods directly, the same exporter arranges for the issuance of a second irrevocable l/c in favor of a domestic supplier (from whom goods must be bought for resale to the foreign buyer); in this case, the exporter assigns the proceeds payable under the foreign bank credit as backing (collateral) for the l/c; the invoice of the exporter will later be substituted for that of the supplier under the second l/c.

Cf. export financing.

See also documentary credit; documentary draft; advising bank; issuing bank; confirming bank.

level playing field is (1) the condition in which there are equally balanced strength and position of the "players" in some international negotiation (e.g., the Multilateral Trade Negotiations of the General Agreement on Tariffs and Trade); or (2) the condition in which the comparative advantages of one "player" is offset to afford the other(s) equal treatment in some international relationship.

> **Example:** In the trade negotiations between country X and country Y, it was agreed that to produce a level playing field, and because of the lack of industrial development of country X, a grace period of 20 years was allowed (by country Y) until tariffs on its goods are reduced to zero.

See also Keynesian economics.

liberalization, as used in *trade liberalization*, is a gradual relaxation, reduction, removal, or elimination of "impediments" to world trade.

These impediments comprise tariffs and nontariff barriers, including in the latter such items as customs fees, surety bonds, export quotas, and all forms of administrative regulations such as end-use permits and licenses.

The liberalization process can occur (1) unilaterally, (2) bilaterally (e.g., the Canada-U.S. Free Trade Agreement of 1989), or (3) multilaterally (e.g., the Multinational Trade Negotiations under the aegis of the General Agreement on Tariffs and Trade).

See also General Agreement on Tariffs and Trade; round of trade negotiations.

LIBOR (London interbank offer rate) *See* Appendix II.

licensed production refers to a component of a type of countertrade transaction called direct offsets in which an exporter agrees to permit all or a part of the total export contract to be produced offshore, based on the acceptance by the importer of technology transfer.

> **Example:** To secure the export contract for extruded plastic components, the Canadian manufacturer had to set up a local plant to make all the components. To offset this transfer of technology, the Canadian exporter demanded a contract binding the local government to disallow the establishment of any competitive plastics extruder in the country for a period of five years. The Canadian licensor agreed on its part not to obsolete the local production or displace it with any more technologically advanced products made under license in neighboring countries, during the same five-year period.)

See also offset deals.

licensing is the international market-penetration strategy whereby a company (the licensor) makes available to a foreign company (the licensee) its technology, industrial processes, trade secrets, and intellectual property for a fee (a royalty).

Cf. franchising.

licensing agreement is the contract between an exporter (the licensor) and an importer (the licensee) to make available to an importer some property of the exporter for a fee.

    See also licensing.

lighter is a flat-bottomed, motorized barge used to transport cargo from a shallow-water (inland) port to a deep-water vessel anchored offshore.

    See also LASH (vessel).

lighterage is the use of small boats (e.g., tow boats, motorized barges, tug boats) to transfer cargo usually between a shallow-water, inland port and the deep-water vessel anchored offshore, but sometimes between vessels themselves.

    See also LASH (vessel).

linear reduction of tariffs *See* across-the-board tariff reductions.

liner shipping is cargo-carrying ocean shipping services between ports in different countries on a regular basis.

    See also conference.

lingua franca, from the Italian *lingua* meaning "tongue" and *franca* meaning "Frankish," the "language of commerce," or the most commonly spoken natural language of an area or region.

Lingua franca derives its sixteenth-century A.D. origin from polyglot traders in the Eastern Mediterranean, mainly Diaspora Jews. Their regionally based commerce influenced their use of language. This resulted in the borrowing of words and phrases from Italian, French, Greek, Arabic, and Spanish and the synthesizing of an original Italian "dialect of trade." The Italians called it *lingua franca* because it sounded to them like a "pidgin French."

Every major trading region of the world has its *lingua franca*:

Trading Region	Lingua Franca
East Europe	*French* and *German* with West Europe *Russian* with USSR.
West Europe	*Russian* and *German* with East Europe *English* and *French* among the European Economic Community and with rest of world
North America	*English* among itself and with rest of world, excluding Québec (*French*)
Latin America	*Spanish* among itself *English* with rest of world
East Africa	*Kiswahili* with Kenya, Tanzania, Uganda, Rwanda, Burundi, Eastern Zaire, and Zambia *English* with rest of world

West Africa	*English* and *French* with rest of world *Hausa* with Nigeria, Niger, Benin, Togo, Ghana, Cameroon, and Chad
North Africa and Middle East	*Arabic* among itself *English* with rest of world
Asia	*English* with rest of world *Chinese* with Southeast Asia

Some other subregional *linguas francas* are:

- *Yiddish:* Lower German dialect of Jewish immigrants from East Europe, spoken in large, important urban centers in the Western Hemisphere (e.g., New York, Chicago, Barcelona, Buenos Aires, São Paulo, Bogotá)
- *Caribbean pidgin-English:* centered in Trinidad and Jamaica, spans all anglophone islands in the region
- *Caribbean patois:* "pidgin-French," spans all francophone and non-anglophone islands

In the Dutch Antilles, a *patois* called *papiamento* is spoken in Aruba and Curaçao (the overseas colonies of Holland), in Guyana (formerly British Guiana), in Suriname (formerly the colony of Dutch Guiana), and in French Guiana (an "overseas *département*" (i.e., colony) of France).

- *Australasian pidgin-English:* a dialect of English spoken by islanders in the Pacific Ocean Basin

linkage (linking) is creation of demand in a second or third international market based upon the movement into that market of the product and/or the target customer from the primary market.

> **Example:** Japanese car manufacturers created export demand for their products in Canada first, by exporting whole vehicles. Then, in the 1970s, when persuaded to manufacture cars in the country, the Japanese used the opportunity to exploit this new manufacturing base as a jump-off point for re-exporting whole vehicles to the U.S. market, their ultimate tertiary target. Eventually, they established manufacturing and assembly plants in the United States, completing the network.
>
> The *linkage* between Japanese car building in Canada and the United States was purposely forged, and after January 1, 1989, it fortuitously took advantage of the FTA (between Canada and the United States) to qualify under it for bidirectional duty-free transshipment of parts.

liquid assets refers to Treasury Bills, common stock, negotiable paper (e.g., trade acceptances) and "demand notes," which quickly can be converted into cash (i.e., transferable currency).

liquidity, from the global marketing viewpoint, is the amount of "international reserves" held in transferable currencies that are readily available to countries to settle temporary balance-of-payments disequilibria.

In practical terms, this means that credits are held in transferable currencies (i.e., in some globally acceptable accounting unit, such as the Special Drawing Right (SDR), or any of the currencies in the "basket" of five IMF currencies that comprise the SDR, or in some IMF facility). These credits are made available from international financial institutions (including the IMF, the IBRD, the BIS, and commercial banks that deal internationally) upon which the central bank of a country can draw when it is requested by a creditor. Such a creditor usually is a central bank or government financial agency acting for a creditor country, or it is a commercial bank acting for itself or as the "lead member" of a creditor consortium.

Thus, this kind of liquidity is made available in order to assist countries make scheduled payments (of principal and/or interest) on a financial obligation, when it cannot otherwise meet that obligation by way of its own current assets (i.e., export earnings) or its own reserves (in transferrable currencies or globally acceptable accounting units).

A disequilibrium in a country's balance of payments that is temporary or short-term means that there is a real basis to support a reasonable expectation that, within a predictable time period, the country will be able to meet its international debt obligations.

Example: Due to the willful dumping of bauxite on the world market by the Soviet Union, it was made impossible for bauxite exporters such as Jamaica and Guyana to keep their balance of payments in equilibrium, at least for 12 to 18 months, until the United States and the European Economic Community (1) reduced production of aluminum and (2) increased their strategic stockpiles of the metal.

Example: The monsoons devastated Western Asia, creating havoc in two key areas: the rice crop in Thailand was destroyed, and the Bangladesh jute industry was devastated.

The outcome of the former catastrophe was a serious shortfall in Thailand's export earnings from rice, which it was not able to make up until the next growing season, several months later. To Bangladesh, the consequence was more severe since not only were its immediate export earnings gone, but it still has to make good on jute contract commitments to foreign buyers. It could only fill those contracts by borrowing (expensive hard currencies) to buy expensive synthetic substitutes for the jute it could not supply.

While only temporary, this "double whammy" set back the jute industry at least two years in estimated export earnings, but over seven years in repaying the monies borrowed to fulfill its contract commitments!

See also Appendix V (B); International Monetary Fund.

Loan Guarantees is a program of the Export Development Corporation (EDC) whereby it pledges itself as loan guarantor to banks and financial institutions that provide export financing to foreign buyers of Canadian goods and services.

See also Export Development Corporation; export financing.

Loan Pre-Disbursement Insurance (LPI), an insurance program of the Export Development Corporation (EDC), which protects Canadian exporters, provides "cover" for the export production risk from the effective date of the export financing until disbursement under the terms of the loan agreement.

See also Export Development Corporation.

Loans (to foreign importers) are loans (to foreign borrowers) by the Export Development Corporation (EDC) to facilitate medium- and long-term export financing to foreign buyers of Canadian capital goods and services.

Although they can be arranged for any export transaction, loans by the EDC to foreign buyers are more applicable for transactions of a size in which the repayment terms are five years or more.

Loans to foreign importers are sometimes called "buyer credits" since credit is extended to the foreign buyer.

See also Export Development Corporation.

Loan Support for Services is an export financing program of the Export Development Corporation (EDC) whereby the EDC's financing facilities are made available to support export transactions involving Canadian services that can be expected to lead to subsequent contracts for Canadian goods.

The EDC recognizes the following services that qualify for loan support:

1. engineering and consulting studies;
2. engineering and consulting services;
3. feasibility studies; and
4. engineering/procurement/construction management services for EPCM projects.

Depending on the potential Canadian capital-goods procurement from these recognized studies and services, EDC's financial support for them can cover periods of from 5 to 7 years.

See also Export Development Corporation.

local national is a person who works for a foreign company in a country of which she or he is a national (i.e., a citizen).

> **Example:** The Africanization (i.e., nationalization) of foreign industry in "Black Africa" (i.e., Africa south of the Sahara) in the 1960s, usually within a year or two after independence, required the firms to replace expatriate managers with local nationals.
>
> This was an immensely popular political move, engineered to be perceived as the "redeeming of colonial debts" by independent Africa at the expense of its former "colonial oppressors." Within a short time, however, management contracts were usually signed between the African governments and the former owners of the expropriated companies.
>
> Cf. expatriates.
> *See also* management contracts.

Lomé Convention, from *Franco-Hausa Lomé*, capital city of the West African country Togo, where the First Lomé Convention, was negotiated, is a multilateral, ongoing commercial agreement entered into by the European Economic

Community (EEC), representing its 12 West European members and over 60 African, Caribbean, and Pacific (ACP) countries.

The First Lomé Convention, colloquially referred to as Lomé I, was signed in 1975. It permitted ACP commodities—mainly comprising raw ores and raw agricultural products—to enter the EEC duty free.

The Second Lomé Convention, "Lomé II," signed in 1979, introduced the *Stabex* and *Sysmin* schemes relating to the use of the European Development Fund to assist in the stabilization of export earnings in general (*Stabex*) and of mineral exports in particular (*Sysmin*).

Succeeding Lomé Conventions have attempted to expand and deepen the number of commodity classes from ACP signatory countries eligible for duty free access to the EEC.

EEC-ACP permanent institutions are the Committee of Ambassadors and the Council of Ministers, which meet annually and semi-annually, respectively.

The ongoing Lomé Conventions (together with the Generalized System of Preferences) have been accused of being a "neocolonialist form of economic imperialism." As a global extension of the infant industry argument, they provide developing countries with preferential duty rates for basic commodities exported, thus keeping ACP "periphery" countries dependent on the EEC "core."

Lomé III came into force in 1986 and expired May 31, 1989. Lomé IV was signed in Lomé, Togo, on December 15, 1989. The new Treaty runs for a 10-year period, until December 14, 1999.

The most significant outcome of Lomé IV is the financial commitment from the EEC: ECU 12 billion are to be allocated to debt relief, investment, and risk capital over the 10-year period. ECU 1.2 billion in funding will come from the European Investment Bank (EIB), and ECU 10.8 billion from the European Development Fund (EDF).

See also infant industry argument; Appendix V (B); *Stabex* •NW•; *Sysmin* •NW•.

London interbank offered rate (London interbank offering rate) is a variation of *London interbank offer rate.*
    See also LIBOR.

London interbank offer rate *See* LIBOR.

Long-Term Agreement on (International Trade in) Cotton Textiles (LTA) was the predecessor international commodity agreement (ICA) to the MultiFiber Arrangement (MFA).
    See also MultiFiber Arrangement.

loon (loonie) •NW• colloquially refers to the new brass/copper $1 coin, minted in 1989 by the Bank of Canada, that replaces all $1 paper notes in circulation and is named for the common loon (bird) pictured on the obverse side, a species of water fowl indigenous to the deciduous temperate forests of Eastern Canada.

The loon is not a popular monetary commodity with U.S. merchants, especially with those located in U.S. border cities, such as Detroit, Michigan, and Bellingham, Washington. Canadian visitors are advised that if they carry any of their domestic currency into the United States, they should bring only Canadian paper currency. The reason: the new coin is heavier and bulkier to handle than traditional $1 paper notes and, thus, is discounted more heavily than its paper equivalent. Travellers report that where the bank rate (or discount) is 15 percent on the Canadian paper dollar (as of May 1991), U.S. merchants have been discounting the loon by up to 20 percent.

For the reason cited and because of the traditional consumer resistance to accept social change easily, the Canadian loon has earned the derisive name of the "loonie," alluding to an alleged "lunacy" of its political initiators.

Louvre Accord, a variation of *Paris Pact*, was the agreement reached in Paris, France, in 1987 among the members of the Group of Five (G-5) plus Canada whereby they agreed to cooperate more closely to increase stability (via dirty floating) of the rates of exchange of their currencies.

See also dirty floating; Group of Five.

low-context culture is a society in which meaning is communicated between speakers predominantly by the language used for communication and less by nonverbal components of the culture or of the communications process. Thus, meaning is made explicit by the language, regardless of the surrounding cultural context in which the verbal communication takes place.

> **Example:** When a business meeting is scheduled for 9:00 A.M. in Zurich, one usually arrives by 8:45 A.M. at the latest, that is, at least 15 minutes early, since the Swiss low-context culture dictates that a nine o'clock meeting starts at nine o'clock sharp.
>
> This near-fanatical preoccupation of the Swiss (and of most other north Europeans) with time-keeping, and with legal documentation, is an outstanding example of low-context cultural explicitness.

Cf. high-context culture.

m

machine model organization •NW• is the Japanese view of North American and European industrial organization, seen as based on the rationality of Protestant work-ethic systems and strategies where (1) profit is an end in itself and (2) nothing is sacred in the pursuit of profit.

This type of social structure makes all the factors of production replaceable over time and demands rational discipline to prevent subjective feelings from arising and adversely influencing rational (i.e., strictly economic) decisions.

Cf. human co-working model organization •NW•.

Madrid Agreement Concerning the International Registration of Marks, known as the *Madrid Agreement*, is a multilateral treaty signed by 22 states (the Madrid Union) to afford them substantial protection of intellectual property.

The treaty is administered by the World Intellectual Property Organization (WIPO). WIPO undertakes to issue an "international registration" with the trademark offices of all the members of the Madrid Union (for examination under their national laws) when a company registers its trademark with one of the Union members and pays a one-time fee. Madrid Union members agree to automatically provide a 20-year protection extension for registering companies.

Cf. Patent Cooperation Treaty.

See also World Intellectual Property Association.

Mahgreb Common Market (MCM), the political name for the official *Arab Mahgreb Union (AMU)*, is a multilateral agreement signed in Marakesh, Morocco, in February 1989 by Algeria, Libya, Mauritania, Morocco, and Tunisia (as the successor to the Mahgreb Permanent Consultative Committee) for the economic integration of the Arab countries of the Mahgreb region of North Africa.

The impetus for the agreement was (1) the need for market regulation as a consequence of significantly increased intra-Mahgreb (mainly bilateral) trade and (2) the need for regional monetary integration as a result of ongoing cooperation among Mahgreb countries, and to establish financial parities among Mahgreb member currencies to facilitate intra-Mahgreb financial dealings.

Cf. Mahgreb Permanent Consultative Committee.

Mahgreb Permanent Consultative Committee (MPCC), also known as the *Permanent Consultative Committee of the Mahgreb (PCCM)*, is a regional international organization, formed with headquarters in Tunis in 1964, with the aim of acting as a forum for economic cooperation among member countries.

The long-term goal of the organization is to establish a regional common market (i.e., the Mahgreb Economic Community).

Members of the MPCC are Algeria, Mauritania, Morocco, and Tunisia. Libya, a founding member, withdrew from the organization in 1970 because of "serious political differences" between it and other members.

See also common market; Appendix V (B).

make bulk (make-bulk), sometimes called *consolidation*, is the process of putting together large shipments from multiple (smaller) shipments to take advantage of large-volume discounts from carriers.

Cf. break bulk.

make-bulk (distribution) center is the place where the process of consolidation occurs.

See also make bulk.

managed float *See* dirty float.

managed floating-exchange rate system is the policy of "administering" the short-term fluctuations in exchange rates by the intervention of government (monetary authorities).

See also dirty float; monetarism.

managed trade is any international commercial transactions that are affected by nonmarket "contaminating effects" such as nontrade measures and quantitative restrictions.

Since virtually all world trade is affected by international agreements involving both supply and demand management, both bi- and multilaterally, all international commerce could be said to be managed.

management contracts are formal, contractual agreements between governments that have expropriated foreign capital and the foreigners whose capital has been "nationalized"; the contracts aim to compensate the former owners for assisting the new ones to operate the firm or industry that has been seized.

See also expropriation.

managing agents are foreign-based intermediaries, hired by nondomestic parent companies, under exclusive agreements to conduct business with foreign governments.

> **Example:** To promote sales of its heavy water nuclear reactors to foreign governments, Atomic Energy of Canada Limited (AECL) has used the services of managing agents as exclusive representatives of the government agency. Because of the enormity of the contracts in dollar terms, sales commissions have been paid to them contingent upon the signing of the contract and not upon actual delivery of the project, which might be 5 to 10 years from the date of signing the commercial contract.

manufacturer's export agent (MEA), traditionally referred to as a *domestic agent middleman*, is a domestic-based intermediary that acts as an export sales agent for a number of noncompeting manufacturers who pay commissions for services rendered.

The MEA carries on business under its own name, and it usually has considerable regional/geographic market experience. For example, one MEA might specialize in the Mahgreb Common Market area, another in the Andean Common Market, and yet another in the Caribbean Common Market.

See also indirect exporting.

manufacturer's representatives (manufacturer's reps) are field sales people who sell the products of an exporting manufacturer from a foreign base of operations, usually within the target-market territory itself.

They may be expatriates of the manufacturer's country, but, more commonly, they are local nationals.

Since manufacturer's reps are hired on the basis of their industry expertise (in wholesaling, retailing, and merchandising), they function almost exclusively as "order takers," with little other marketing involvement, except in relevant areas of after-market service.

Manufacturer's reps are always engaged on a commission basis, either to supplement a company's export sales force or to act as that export sales force itself. Depending on their experience, they may sell:

1. particular product lines,
2. specific products (within particular product lines), or
3. a combination of the first two in a specific geographical area called an exclusive territory.

maquiladora **system**, from the old Spanish *maquila* meaning the "portion of maize that a tenant farmer pays to the landlord at harvest time," refers to the offshore production of goods by global corporations in border cities in northern Mexico that offer the marketer all the advantages of free/foreign trade zone (FTZ) plus the geographical proximity to the United States.

In the 1960s, Mexico's Brazero Program provided U.S. agriculture with migrant labor. In 1964, the program was cancelled by the U.S. government because of illegal permanent migration and settlement by Mexicans. Thus, the *maquiladora* system was created by the Mexican government in 1965 to relieve the political pressure on it due to population pressure and endemic unemployment along its northern border with the United States.

The main *maquiladora* areas are as follows:

Mexican Location	*Proximate U.S. Border City*
Tijuana	San Diego, CA
Matamoros	Brownsville, TX
Nuevo Laredo	Laredo, TX
Ciudad Juarez	El Paso, TX
Nogales	Tucson, AZ

It is estimated there are more than 1,400 plants in the system, which employ in excess of 400,000 people at labor rates the equivalent of U.S. $1.00 per hour. International and global marketers (e.g., Fortune 500 companies) have migrated from high-cost centers in Canada and the United States to the *maquiladoras*.

It is perceived by some Canadian supporters of the Canada-U.S. Free Trade Agreement (FTA) that the *maquiladora* system is a direct threat to Canadian exports to the United States. Canadian accession to the FTA was based on perceptions of "enlarged market access" to the United States. It is claimed that this is being eroded by U.S. firms that, instead of expanding production in Canada, are transferring production to Mexican *maquiladoras* due to the comparative advantage of lower wages paid to Mexican labor and the lower standards of occupational health and safety required in Mexico *vis-à-vis* Canada.

See also production sharing; North American Free Trade Agreement.

marine bill of lading *See* bill of lading.

marine insurance is protective coverage taken out by an exporter (using international water transport) to compensate in the event of loss or damage incurred due to causes explicitly specified in the policy.

Cf. export insurance.

See also Appendix IV (Cost, Insurance, and Freight).

marine insurance certificate is a document attesting to the fact that the exporter has protective coverage against specific risks for specific goods transported by specific international water transport to a specific customer.

In documentary collections involving exports of goods transported by sea, the exporter will be paid only if a marine insurance certificate accompanies the other required documents that are presented to the paying bank.

See also documentary collections.

market access is the ease (or difficulty) of admittance to a foreign market by an exporting country, as follows:

1. When tariff and nontariff barriers are reduced (through multilateral or bilateral trade negotiations), it is said that access has been increased or improved or enhanced.

2.   When restrictions to a foreign market are imposed on exporters, it is said that access to that market has been reduced or lessened.

One of the purposes of the General Agreement on Tariffs and Trade (GATT) in general and of every round of trade negotiations (RTN) in particular is to refine the global framework to improve trade liberalization and, thereby, to increase market access.

See also General Agreement on Tariffs and Trade; liberalization.

market disruption refers to serious economic difficulties in a domestic market (e.g., layoffs, shutdowns, unemployment, flight of direct investment) resulting from a sudden surge of imports into that market.

These difficulties may arise because of dumping. On the other hand, they may be the outcome of a trade agreement (e.g., the Canada-U.S. Free Trade Agreement of 1989) whereby one inefficient producer country is perceived to suffer injury simply as a consequence of its prior economic protectionism.

With dumping, countries have legal remedies available to them under the General Agreement on Tariffs and Trade (GATT). With nondumping market disruption, the parties to the trade agreement will (doubtless) have agreed upon specific market-assistance programs and dispute-settlement mechanisms to deal with the market disruption in one (high-cost, inefficient) producer country, allegedly caused by the sudden import of goods from the other (low-cost, efficient) producer country.

See also General Agreement on Tariffs and Trade; support programs; injury; antidumping duty.

market economy, a variation of *open economy*, is a political-economy run according to market principles of freely operating supply and demand.

Cf. command economy; nonmarket economy.

marketing boards are government and nongovernment agencies established in different countries to manage the supply of agricultural products and, thereby, stabilize agricultural prices and farm incomes.

In Canada, marketing boards operate within both Federal (Government of Canada) and Provincial jurisdictions.

> **Example:** In Canada at the Provincial level, the Ontario Milk Marketing Board (OMMB) (under the authority of the Ontario Provincial Government's Ministry of Agriculture and Food (OMAF)) sells "milk quota"; but it is the Federal Canadian Dairy Commission (CDC) that "supports" the producer price of milk with subsidies.

Domestic price subsidization of agricultural products by marketing boards has resulted simultaneously in (1) the protection (and rewarding) of marginal producers and (2) the accumulation of enormous (expensive) surplus inventories of agricultural commodities.

From the global viewpoint, it is almost impossible to separate the "export component" of the farm subsidy from its "domestic component." For this reason, bilateral and multilateral trade agreements involving agricultural commodities are notoriously difficult to negotiate, if for no other reason than that export subsidies are proscribed under the General Agreement on Tariffs and Trade, and, thus, all trading nations deny using them.

The Canada-U.S. Free Trade Agreement of 1989 is a remarkable and successful major trade agreement in which agricultural commodities figure largely. Its success is due in no small part to the meticulous care with which the negotiators detailed the specifics of every Canadian and U.S. farm-support program and the ways in which domestic subsidies would be identified (and protected) so as not to distort or interfere with Canada-U.S. trade in agricultural commodities.

The worst ongoing failure in the agricultural area is that of the European Economic Community (EEC). To date, it has been unable to establish a truly harmonized (and workable) common agricultural policy (CAP) that comprises *inter alia*, a means to alleviate the onerous financial burden of annual agricultural surpluses. This failure at regional agricultural integration, combined with the truculence of important European (i.e., mainly French) electoral sectors, has resulted in a political restiveness that has smoldered and occasionally flared into open antagonism ("dumping wars") between the United States and the EEC.

See also common agricultural policy; export subsidies.

mark sheet is a "report of import" (equivalent to an "import declaration") required to be submitted by a Japanese importer to a Japanese foreign exchange bank to obtain foreign exchange for imports valued at more than ¥1 million, even when the goods are not subject to import quotas.

See also quantity restrictions; Import Allocation Certificate.

massify (massified, massifying) •NW• is the process of reducing the perceived wants and needs of consumers and end users to the lowest common denominator.

The motive is to cheapen the cost of all the inputs into the production and distribution processes (e.g., cheapening direct labor, materials, and indirect labor, such as marketing). The aim is to develop a standardized product for a massified (homogeneous) market that will adopt the good or service quickly.

See also standardize.

Medium Term Bulk Agriculture Credits Insurance and Guarantee Program is a program of the Export Development Corporation (EDC), designed to provide "cover" for Canadian exporters of bulk commodities from Canada on credit terms.

It was designed for sales with terms beyond 365 days and done by documentary credit (usually irrevocable letter of credit) to private buyers or on open account to public (i.e., state) buyers.

The Medium Term Program was designed for competitive situations where medium-term credit was needed to maintain existing Canadian markets and to penetrate new markets with credit terms equal to those of competitors.

Like the Short Term Program, the Medium Term Program provides coverage against nonrepayment due to commercial and political risks. Unlike the Short Term Program, the Medium Term Program offers a bank a "guarantee option" that works as follows:

1. The exporter's bank extends a loan to a foreign buyer or to a state agency.
2. The EDC provides the exporter's bank with a 100 percent guarantee that the foreign borrowing institution will repay the loan.

3. The exporter's bank is now in a position to offer the exporter discounted rates for term drafts drawn against the original documentary credits, or other types of financing, based on the EDC's guarantee.

Cf. Short Term Bulk Agriculture Credits Insurance.
See also Export Development Corporation; export financing; commercial risks; political risks.

melting pot is a cultural term for the demographic structure of the United States, whereby individual subcultures abandon their distinctiveness and adopt "mainstream" (American) cultural values, expressing their sole allegiance to and affiliation with the United States of America.
Cf. multicultural.

Mercado Común Centroamericano (MCC) See Central American Common Market.

mercantilism is a set of ideas, prevalent among the élite in sixteenth-, seventeenth-, and early-eighteenth-century European society, that stated that national strength was measured according to the following argument: to accumulate the maximum amount of specie (but especially silver and gold), a country must maximize exports, restrict imports, and thus create surpluses of precious metals and traded goods at the expense of competitor countries.

This was the age of capitalism—when Europe's superior technology plundered the world and when European seafaring colonizers (English, French, Spanish, Portuguese, Dutch, Danish, and Swedish) each sought self-interested, unilateral pre-eminence.

Later, in the eighteenth and nineteenth centuries, when technology moved from labor intensiveness, the ideas of mercantilism were replaced by those of laissez-faire.

The modern analogue of mercantilist thinking is neomercantilism, that is, trade policy that stresses the accumulation of trade surpluses via the promotion of economic nationalism and tariff protection rather than global economic integration and free market trade.

Cf. laissez-faire; infant industry argument.

mint parity *See* Appendix II.

Middle East Development Bank (MEDB) is an idea for a new multilateral development bank (MDB) that would, like other MDBs, act as an executing agency for projects of the United Nations Development Program (UNDP).

The MEDB should be headquartered in a regional center such as Qatar, the United Arab Emirates (U.A.E.), or Kuwait (when reconstructed) with excellent infrastructure and telecommunications facilities. Its membership should comprise all regional countries, including Israel, and any Palestinian state born as an outcome of regional peace talks. In addition, the MEDB should contain nonregional members, especially the United States and including Germany and Japan, who contributed substantial finances to the Coalition's successful Persian Gulf War effort.

The MEDB would treat the entire region as its focus for economic growth, granting loans and providing technical assistance to projects of its regional members. The main concentrations for financing would be agriculture, energy, transportation, water supply and sanitation, education, and industrial diversification.

The crucial political challenge of the MEDB would be the consolidation of development financing in support of it as the exclusive secular funding agency for regional development. Presently, funding is dispersed among the following agencies:

- OPEC Fund for International Development (OPEC/FID) in Vienna
- Arab Fund for Economic and Social Development (AFESD) in Kuwait
- Arab Monetary Fund (AMF) in Rabat
- Islamic Development Bank (ISDB) in Jeddah

All of them are underpinned by avowed pan-Islamic ideas, and some (e.g., AFESD) are restricted from dealing with non-Islamic entities.

Long-term economic development for the Middle East region can neither be conceived of nor implemented, as long as development financing in the region remains fragmented and sacred rather than consolidated and secular. Solution to this may take time since its key components involve the following: (1) "desanctification" of The Palestinian Problem by all; (2) recognition and acceptance of Israel by Arab states and of peaceful relations (versus war) as the normal state of affairs; (3) legal settlement of a physical state for the Palestinian people; and (4) the normalization of all international relations by all states in the region.

Cf. OPEC Fund for International Development; Arab Fund for Economic and Social Development; Arab Monetary Fund; Islamic Development Bank. *See also* Appendix V (B); multilateral development banks (MDBs).

mitbestimmung •NW•, from the German meaning "co-determination," is the practice, pioneered in the Federal Republic of Germany (West Germany), of having representatives of labor participating in the management of the company by being members of the board of directors.

The tactic was devised after World War II. In the face of a threatening, communist East Europe, the co-optation of labor by its inclusion within the élite managerial structure of the capitalist enterprise undercut communist appeal to West German workers as "downtrodden and oppressed masses."

Strategically, co-determination assisted in the formation of a climate of industrial peace in West Germany, which formed a backdrop for the renaissance of the political-economy of West Germany and the strength of the Deutsche mark (DEM).

mixed credit •NW•, from the French *crédit mixte*, refers to financial terms extended by developed countries to developing countries, (usually) under the OECD Concensus, whereby a part of the credit that is repayable at "commercial rates" (i.e., at competitive rates established in the money markets in international financial centers) is "mixed" or "blended" with the other part (usually the larger), which is repayable at "below commercial rates" on terms called near-concessional or concessional.

Those who extend mixed credits are usually granters of credit for development purposes (e.g., World Bank Group) or agencies of national governments that extend soft loans (as part of their official development assistance (ODA) programs) to countries seeking either direct foreign aid or affordable financing for development project work.

In Canada and the United States, examples of the latter are the Canadian International Development Agency (CIDA) and the U.S. Agency for International Development (USAID), respectively.

Cf. concessional financing.
See also official development assistance; Development Assistance Committee; OECD Concensus; Appendix V (B).

mixed economy is an open political-economy in which wealth is generated and distributed primarily by private, profit-seeking individuals and corporations, but in which the state owns or controls enterprises in key sectors.

Canada is considered to be this type of political-economy where such sectors as petroleum exploration, refining, and retailing were, for 15 years after 1974, strongly influenced by (the price leader) Petro-Canada Crown Corporation, which was finally privatized in 1989.

In contrast, Mexico is less a mixed economy than a state trading nation. In the petroleum industry, Mexico, like Canada (formerly), has a state-owned oil corporation, PEMEX; but unlike Canada, where Petro-Canada was but one member of a competitive (oligopolistic) marketplace, Mexico's domestic petroleum market (and all petroleum trading into and out of it) is controlled by the exclusive monopoly of PEMEX.

Cf. state trading nation; command economy; socialism.
See also open economy; capitalism; privatization.

mixed tariff is a variation of *compound duty*.

monetarism, also known as *supply side economics*, is the school of economic thought known as the "Chicago School," headed by Nobel Laureate Milton Friedman, which holds that the money supply is the chief determinant of macroeconomic activity both within a country and between countries and groups of countries.
The key ideas of monetarism are as follows:

1. Change in the money supply directly affects and determines, over the long run, the levels of industrial and agricultural production, employment, and prices of goods and services.
2. Fiscal policy (i.e., taxes and expenditures) has little significant effect on business-cycle events, such as inflation, deflation, recession, and depression. Therefore, monetary policy (i.e., the use of the money supply and interest rates by a nation's central monetary authority) is the preferred way to control a national economy.
3. Economic stability can best be promoted by government by following a "simple money rule": increase the money supply at a constant annual rate linked to the growth of the GNP.
4. Reduced government economic involvement equates with increased personal economic freedom, which, in turn, equates with increased personal political freedom.

For international marketers, the importance of monetarism cannot be underestimated. First of all, its pre-eminent feature is that of overvaluing monetary tools and devaluing traditional Keynesian ones. Thus, when in power, monetarists have imposed drastic cuts in government spending (for traditional health, education, and welfare). The worldwide consequence has been a decline in human nutrition, an increase in malnutrition, increasing population flight from marginal rural areas to cities, increased population pressure on urban infrastructures, and a parallel upswing in serious infectious diseases.

Secondly, monetarism's preoccupation with human society as being driven exclusively by economic forces and with human beings as being fundamentally economically motivated has promoted a type of "economic Darwinism" where the distribution of wealth and power has become more tightly concentrated in fewer élite hands worldwide.

Third, the establishment of regional economic trading groups, their rapid politicization, and the formation of numerous international commodity groups may be perceived as a predictable reaction among the "have-not" developing countries whose export earnings have dwindled even as their external debts have grown.

All these events may be seen as a global reaction to the negative socio-economic effects inspired and promoted by global monetarism. International marketers should be mindful of these facts and of these perceptions.

Cf. Keynesian economics.
See also global monetarism.

monetary policy *See* monetarism.

monetary union is a formal, multilateral arrangement between states already integrated in an economic union, whereby there exists (1) ultimately one common currency; (2) total and irreversible convertibility of the (interim) currencies of member countries; (3) complete freedom of capital movements (in fully integrated capital markets); and (4) irrevocably fixed exchange rates, with no fluctuation between members' currencies.

Cf. economic-monetary union; economic union; common market.
See also Delors Report.

money laundering *See* laundering (of money).

money market is (1) the network of a nation's financial institutions that facilitates the lending and borrowing of money for domestic commercial purposes, including the financing of trade and assisting the national government to maintain an equilibrium in its balance of payments; and (2) the network of international financial organizations that facilitates the lending and borrowing of money for global commercial purposes, including the financing of trade, the extending of capital to finance growth in developing countries, and the settling of international balance-of-payments accounts.

See also Appendix V (B); export financing.

money supply is the liquid assets held by individuals, banks, and other financial institutions in a country.

In Canada and the United States, the central monetary authorities are the Bank of Canada and the Federal Reserve System, respectively.

All central banks have the exclusive authority to issue their nation's currency (i.e., notes and coins) and, *inter alia*, to use the tools of monetary policy to stabilize the economies of their respective countries.

See also monetarism.

monopoly, from the Greek *monos* meaning "one" and *poleein* meaning "seller," refers to the form of business organization in which there is a single producer or supplier of a commodity or service and for which there are no close substitutes.

As a result of this condition, the monopolist has significant control over the price at which the product or service will be offered in the marketplace.

In Canada and the United States, attempts to establish monopolies are outlawed by the Competition Act and the Sherman Antitrust Act, respectively. In other words, in domestic marketing, it is a criminal offense to engage in certain specific business practices that unduly lessen, restrict, or restrain trade, with the ultimate aim of seeking to entirely eliminate competition and, thus, to control the market.

Examples of such illegal activities are predatory pricing, price fixing, collusion, and bid rigging.

On the other hand, in international trade, there is no single international law or set of harmonized national laws that criminalize monopoly-formation practices. However, the U.S. government applies the principle of extraterritorial jurisdiction of U.S. antitrust laws to U.S. companies and individuals working outside U.S. territory: all are deemed to fall under the jurisdiction of U.S. laws in general and under the jurisdiction of the Sherman Antitrust Act, in this instance, in particular.

In comparison, the Canadian government does not adhere to the principle of extraterritoriality. Rather, it accepts the principle of domestic jurisdiction in international law: all Canadian citizens and Canadian companies fall under the jurisdiction of the laws of their host countries when Canadian citizens and companies visit or reside in them.

In fact, outside of Canada and the United States, there is little noteworthy history of antimonopoly legislation in the world. International cartels, such as the Organization of Petroleum Exporting Countries (OPEC), figure prominently in global trade and geopolitics.

Cf. oligopoly.

See also international cartel; international law; extraterritoriality; Appendix V (E).

moral responsibility •NW• is a cultural term that (1) in Western society is perceived (and accepted) as the obligation of individuals to behave in ways that are in consonance with natural law, meaning "good behavior" within a context of fundamental fairness and equity; and (2) in Japanese society is the perceived central concept of responsibility by one individual to another, and by individuals to a group, based on close, trusting relations that raise "moral expectations" about appropriate behavior between people.

> **Example:** In the United States, if a supplier fails to deliver goods on time due to unforeseen and uncontrollable circumstances (e.g., the weather), the consignee will probably understand, and the appropriate adjustments will be

made by both parties since it is established that the intervening event was not a willful act (to repudiate a contract).

In Japan, if a Japanese consignor promises to deliver goods on time, the concept of moral responsibility binds him to that obligation, and nothing can release him from it. Assuming that inclement, unforeseen weather halted the shipment, the consignor will be expected to feel shame and guilt at his failure to execute his promise. Regardless of the consignee's response, the consignor's remorse, seen by peers and subordinates within the work group, will reinforce the notion that moral responsibility is inescapable and that the responsible individual has earned his grief. In this way, Japanese peers will learn to avoid making similar mistakes that will place them in similarly vulnerable positions.

moratorium, from the Latin *moratorius* meaning "delaying," is a period of time during which a country does not make payments on the interest- and/or principal-owing portions of its external debt.

Cf. nonperforming assets; default.

See also external debt.

mordida See bribery.

most-favored nation (MFN) refers to the *most-favored-nation principle*, *most-favored-nation treatment*, and the *most-favored-nation clause*.

See General Agreement on Tariffs and Trade (Principles of International Trade: Principle 1).

"mother of all battles" •NW• was the phrase used by Iraqi president Saddam Hussein throughout the Persian Gulf War to evoke the memory among his troops of the decisive Battle of Qadisiya in 636 A.D.

In that engagement, the Arabs united under Islam to defeat the Saassanian (Persian) army and to drive it right to the walls of Saassania's ancient capital, Ctesiphan. The result was that the land west of the Tigris River was gained for Islam.

Since Iraq's defeat in the Gulf War, the phrase "mother of all battles" has been rephrased and used sarcastically (e.g., by United States defense secretary Dick Cheney) to depict the rout of the Iraqi army in the war as the "mother of all retreats."

To Westerners, the phrase is a genuinely "new word" with such rich potential for frivolous fun that the "mother of all (something)" will doubtlessly find a continuing place in vocabularies of wordsmiths. One of them has already described this book as the "mother of all business dictionaries"!

See also Gulf Crisis.

multicultural (multiculturalism), called *cultural mosaic*, refers to the ethnostructure of Canada whereby individual subcultures (e.g., Canadians of German, Polish, and Italian origin) express their own ethnicity, while maintaining primary allegiance to Canada but affiliation with the values of their "country of origin."

This Canadian ethnostructure was first described as a "cultural mosaic" by John Porter, the Canadian sociologist, in a work of the same name. Porter's ideas were critical in that they identified Canada as a "national patchwork" rather than a "unified unitary state." This understanding underpinned the Canadian government's Multicultural Policy of the 1970s.

The Trudeau government's incorporation of multiculturalism into the Canadian Constitution affords, on the one hand, "cultural protection" to minority groups. On the other, it ensures that nation building in Canada, as the homogenization of each ethnic segment into a "national culture" (*à la* United States), has not and will not occur.

The consequences of the delayed formation of a unitary Canadian nation state can be of significant value to global marketers who see the nation-state stage of political-economic integration as an historical barrier impeding the process of integrating countries into ever-larger economic units, such as the European Economic Community (EEC) and the European Economic Space (EES).

Cf. melting pot.

MultiFiber Arrangement (MultiFiber Agreement) (MFA), officially, *The MultiFiber Arrangement Regarding Trade in Textiles*, is an international agreement, negotiated under the General Agreement on Tariffs and Trade (GATT) and acceded to by producer and consumer countries, that permits MFA signatories to apply quantitative (i.e., import) restrictions on textiles when necessary to avert market disruption.

Called an orderly marketing arrangement (OMA), the MFA has been one of the more successful multilateral attempts to manage the global trade in apparel and textiles (although it is no "final solution"). The reason is that the MFA provides a framework for:

1. determining market disruption by measuring market activities and comparing them with MFA benchmarks;
2. determining minimum levels of import restraints necessary to offset market disruption; and
3. negotiating bilateral agreements on issues of bilateral importance between producer and consumer countries.

One of the goals of the Uruguay Round of trade talks is to phase out the MFA. Because of the ongoing success of the MFA, this will be difficult to achieve.

Prior to the MFA, a multilateral arrangement called *The Long-Term Agreement on (International Trade in) Cotton Textiles (LTA)* was the only global OMA in operation. The LTA went into effect in 1962 and was successful for 12 years, despite the fact that it applied only to cotton textiles. In 1974, it was superseded by the MFA, which applied not only to cotton textiles, but also to wool, synthetic fibers, silk fibers, mohair, angora, a range of lesser vegetable fibers, and apparel.

See also market disruption; orderly marketing arrangement.

multilateral agreement is a concurrence or consent, acceded to by three or more countries, usually under the auspices of an international organization, the nature of which can be commercial, political, military, or humanitarian.

A treaty is a covenant that binds the states that sign it through the authority of the citizens whose legislatures must assent to it.

In comparison, a multilateral agreement (formally called an *accord* or *convention*) binds the government that signed it, and, by custom, its successors and, by incorporation, the citizens of the state itself, even though the document is rarely presented to the legislature of the country for formal assent by the representatives of the people.

Therefore, in international law, a multilateral agreement is less binding than a treaty. A multilateral agreement binds by custom and tradition, whereas a treaty is binding by the overwhelming force of popular (democratic) concensus.

Example: The Helsinki Accord, officially known as The *Helsinki Final Act*, was a multilateral agreement signed in 1975 by 35 North Atlantic Treaty Organization and Warsaw Treaty Organization countries. It provides for comprehensive peace, security, and cooperation in human rights, science, culture, and education.

Example: The Geneva Convention of 1949 is the latest in a long series of multilateral agreements on the rules of war and the treatment of prisoners of war and of civilians.

Cf. international agreement.

multilateral development banks (MDBs), frequently called *regional development banks (RDBs)*, are five large financial institutions that:

1. operate regionally on behalf of their members,
2. stimulate economic growth and development within the member countries of the region, and
3. implement the programs of the United Nations Development Program (UNDP).

Example: In addition to the existing five MDBs, the establishment of a new Middle East Development Bank would fund programs of the United Nations Development Program (UNDP) directed through the new United Nations Economic Commission for the Middle East (UN/ECME).

See also African Development Bank; Asian Development Bank; Caribbean Development Bank; Inter-American Development Bank; International Bank for Reconstruction and Development; Middle East Development Bank; United Nations Regional Economic Commissions; United Nations Development Program.

Multilateral Investment Guarantee Agency (MIGA), established in 1987 and in effect since June 1988, is an affiliate of the International Bank for Reconstruction and Development (IBRD).

MIGA's main function is to promote private investment in developing countries through the provision of insurance against noncommercial (i.e., political) risks.

To join MIGA and qualify for its insurance "cover," a country must be a member of both the International Monetary Fund (IMF) and the World Bank.
See also political risks; World Bank Group; International Finance Corporation.

multilateral trade is, strictly speaking, trade among more than four nations; informally, it refers to transactions among three or more countries.
Cf. bilateral trade; trilateral trade; quadrilateral trade.

multilateral trade agreement is, strictly speaking, a formal exchange accord among four or more nations.
Cf. bilateral trade agreement; trilateral trade agreement.
See also multilateral trade.

multilateral trade negotiations (MTN) are understood to refer to (1) present or past formal trade talks held, since 1947, at different locations, under the aegis of the General Agreement on Tariffs and Trade (GATT); or (2) formal meetings for the purpose of commercial bargaining among three or more countries, under the auspices of some international organization (e.g., United Nations Conference on Trade and Development (UNCTAD)), apart from the General Agreement on Tariffs and Trade (GATT).
See also round of trade negotiations.

multinational corporations (MNCs) are profit-making enterprises, usually private profit-making corporations, that carry out marketing on a multinational or international basis.
Other names for MNCs include:

- transnational enterprises (TNEs),
- transnational corporations (TNCs), and
- multinational enterprises (MNEs).

Cf. global corporations.
See also multinational marketing.

multinational enterprises (MNEs) *See* multinational corporations (MNCs).

multinational marketing, derived from the private, profit-based multinational corporation (MNC), is:

1. that stage of marketing (suggested to be the international marketing era of the 1960s and 1970s) when profit-seeking corporations (each as a "profit center") divided up different geographic markets worldwide, segmented each one into its most profitable "target," then tailored goods and services to satisfy that target, either ignoring (or mindless of) the proximity of other markets with similar needs;
2. that stage of (international) marketing considered to be a step of "lesser" (capitalistic) development than global marketing.

Cf. global marketing.
See also international marketing.

multiple exchange rates *See* exchange controls.

Murphy's Law, eponym and origin unknown, is the observation that "whatever can possibly go wrong always will."

It provides a means to cope (sometimes, but not invariably, by way of fatalistic acceptance) with difficulties that arise in international and global marketing that are uncontrollable and whose consequences produce a "cascade effect" of outcomes that are likewise uncontrollable and unpredictable.

In some countries (where monsoons, snow storms, or dust storms interrupt an entire infrastructure, from roads to telephone communications), local nationals have learned to adapt to local climates and to accept the vicissitudes of nature. Often when such adaptations are made by foreign expatriates, the misperception is made by foreign-based expatriates (i.e., home-office executives) that the adapting company officer is "going native": this is a derogatory term for imputing attitudes and behaviors of lesser moral value and lesser social worth to the foreign expatriate who acts in what is perceived as a local (i.e., "native") way.

Experience has shown that foreign expatriates who adopt the Murphy's Law point of view are more likely to be misperceived and misjudged by home-country raters, whereas host-country raters are less likely to misperceive or to misjudge the actions of their foreign expatriates.

See also culture shock.

mutuality of benefits *See* reciprocity.

n

national expatriate *See* expatriate.

nationalization is the process involving the seizure of private property (usually foreign-owned real estate and capital assets) by a government and the unilateral transfer of title to the state.

> **Example:** After the assumption of political power in Cuba on January 1, 1959, by the 24th of July Movement *(El Movimiento de 24 de Julio)*, the government nationalized all direct investment (e.g., sugar mills, oil refineries) in the name of the revolution.

> **Example:** The government of British prime minister Margaret Thatcher has been characterized by a major effort at privatization: the de-nationalization (by way of sale of capital equity) of previously nationalized companies (e.g., state-owned British Overseas Airways Corporation (BOAC) to privately-owned British Airways).

Nationalization does not preclude compensation being paid to the foreign owners.
Cf. confiscation; expropriation.

national security clause is a section written into legislation in the process of being passed by a country's legislature or inserted *post factum* to prevent or to overturn any attempted or actual tariff reduction on specific imported goods.

The purpose of this measure is to protect any national industry that produces for national defense and that would be injured by the importation of foreign defense-related goods.

From this viewpoint, a national security clause has been cited as a protectionist tactic to unfairly protect domestic industry that otherwise would have to compete with foreign competition.

Politically conservative supporters of the tactic suggest that national defense procurement should never be placed in a position of potential supply-related vulnerability simply because a foreign supplier can offer the product at a lower price.

> **Example:** The U.S. Omnibus Trade Act of 1988 contains numerous national security clauses. The president is empowered, on the recommendation of the U.S. Trade Representative, to levy retroactive tariffs (punitive tariffs) if, after investigation, it is proven that countries supplying products related to the national defense of the United States have injured domestic American companies that lost government-procurement contracts on the basis of price alone.

See also injury.

national treatment is a type of friendship, commerce, and navigation (FCN) treaty whereby laws and regulations governing the marketing of domestic goods in countries that signed the treaty are extended to goods designated as "foreign" and "imported" (i.e., originating in the other signatory country).

In the evolution of international marketing systems, the more economically integrated the trading partners and the more harmonized their customs systems, the more thorough and comprehensive the national treatment of goods is by the trading partners.

> **Example:** There is a higher level of national treatment of goods by each member of the European Economic Community (EEC) than there is by Canada and the United States under their Free Trade Agreement. The reason is the higher level and greater extent of economic (and political) integration of the European communities compared to Canada and the United States.

Under the General Agreement on Tariffs and Trade (GATT), every Contracting Party is expected to extend to every other Contracting Party national treatment with respect to the laws and regulations that can affect trade.

A positive inference (called *liberalization*) is drawn when trading partners afford each other national treatment.

Cf. reciprocity.

See also General Agreement on Tariffs and Trade; liberalization; Appendix VI (friendship, commerce, and navigation treaty).

near-concessional financing refers to export credits granted by governments that are slightly more "stiff" (i.e., more market-driven) than the terms of repayment for concessional financing.

> For a middle-range country such as the newly industrialized/industrializing countries (NICs) seeking export credits, the near-concessional lending terms would be more market-oriented and commercial than concessional financing, reflecting their political stability, strong growth, and healthy export-earnings record.

Cf. concessional financing; OECD Concensus.

near-concessional lending terms *See* near-concessional financing.

nemawashi •NW•, from the Japanese meaning "taking care of the roots," refers to the Japanese method used to arrive at group consensus, or decision making via consensus.

The process involves discussion with group members to permit formal, anonymous, face-saving objections to be voiced prior to the acceptance by all members of the decision. This process also prepares the members to accept the decision, in a way akin to the preparation of the ground for planting.

Nemawashi is sometimes considered a cynical method of creating the illusion that group participation actually exists in decision making when the group actually is given only a face-saving opportunity to object prior to having to accept the decision.

A contrasting view is that *nemawashi* does permit genuine, democratic dissent; and, indeed, within Japanese group-oriented culture, *nemawashi* is deemed to be an important tactic for exploring alternative decisions, anticipating conflict, and creating real problem-solving harmony among individuals. This viewpoint deems *nemawashi* to be a polite and judicious way of managing: it harnesses the best that assertive individuals have to offer while maintaining a balance with a group, the majority of whose members may be more amenable to accepting authority.

See also "Always Say Yes"; "Yes, Yes."

neomercantilism is from the Greek *neos* meaning "new" and from the Italian *mercante* meaning "merchant."
See mercantilism.

net IMF position (NIP) is the accounting status of a country (e.g., country X) calculated as follows:

NIP = (X's IMF "quota") − (IMF holdings of X's currency)

See also International Monetary Fund (IMF); liquidity.

net liquidity balance (NLB) is a statement of the accounting position of a country described as the net balance of all transactions comprising all current account, all long-term capital, and all short-term non-liquid-asset transactions.
Cf. balance of payments.

New Exporters to Border States (NEBS) *See* export support programs (2).

New Exporters Overseas (NEXOS) *See* export support programs (4).

New Exports to the U.S. South (NEXUS) *See* export support programs (3).

New International Economic Order •NW• (NIEO) is a perception of global economic relations by developing countries (The South) in Asia, Africa, and Latin America, whereby dependence by them upon developed countries (The North) will be replaced by more equitable relations between North and South.

The NIEO began in 1974 at the Sixth Special Session of the United Nations General Assembly. The General Assembly adopted the Charter of Economic Rights and Duties of States.

The NIEO is not a formal political organization. Nevertheless, it represents a consensus among the world's developing countries that dependent development is neither a desirable nor a perpetually acceptable condition for Third World countries.

See also dependent development.

newly industrialized (industrializing) country (NIC) •NW• is a Third World country that (1) has borrowed (and built on) Western industrial ideology and, as a consequence, (2) has increased its industrial production, per capita income, and per capita consumption dramatically vis-à-vis other developing countries that have not.

> **Example:** South Korea, Taiwan, Hong Kong, and Singapore are the Pacific Rim's NICs, called Asia's Four Tigers.

See also export-oriented industrialization; Five Tigers.

newly industrialized (industrializing) economies (NIEs) See newly industrialized countries.

new money •NW• is

1. in private commercial ventures, supplementary financing made available either to the exporter or the importer from private or quasi-official sources based on explicit conditions being met;
2. in international debt financing (for countries with severe balance-of-payments difficulties), additional funds made available to the government of a debtor nation by members of the Paris Club (i.e., the world's private commercial banks).

For example, in the first case, new money may be made available to a Canadian exporter. Assume that a U.S. importer is unable to borrow U.S. dollars from a U.S. bank, which rejects the terms of sale of the particular deal as too risky. (The U.S. bank says the Canadian exporter should be paid in Canadian dollars in any event.) Suppose the Canadian exporter, on behalf of a potential customer, applied to the Export Development Corporation for a Specific Transaction Guarantee (i.e., for "cover" for the U.S. bank extending credit to the U.S. importer, against repayment default by the exporter). Were the arrangement to be accepted, new money would be made available to finance the trade deal.

In the second case, the new money is made available on terms that "spread the exposure risk" equitably among the lending banks by the "bank advisory committee."

Cf. reduced debt servicing.

See also Export Credit Enhanced Leverage.

Nice Agreement Concerning the International Classification of Goods and Services for the Purposes of the Registration of Marks, known as the *Nice Agreement* or the *Geneva Act (1977) of the Nice Agreement*, is a multilateral treaty signed by states to afford them substantial protection of intellectual property.

The treaty is administered by the World Intellectual Property Organization (WIPO).

See also World Intellectual Property Organization.

niche (niche marketing, niche strategy, nichers) •NW•, from the French meaning "nook," is

1. a specific "position" in the world market, identified by a company, and not serviced by any of its competitors. (After analysis, if it is determined to be worth occupying the niche, the process involves developing a niche strategy to do niche marketing);
2. a game played by global companies to specialize in one particular segment of an already well-developed market. The niche strategy here is market penetration and sales-building, but in ways that do not (ostensibly) threaten the pre-eminent market position of "price leaders."

The nichers who introduced Mitsubishi into the "high-ticket end" of the premium automobile market in California with their Mirage and Gallant models could be viewed as "infinite game players": the Japanese niche marketing (short-run) goal was to independently earn relatively cost-efficient sales and profits without being perceived to endanger the predominant market share position of GM, Chrysler, and Ford. The long-term business goal was to diversify Mitsubishi away from its electronic-home-products core business and to set the stage for serious "infinite game playing."

Example: Like other global corporations, the Ford Automotive Group has developed an array of production and commercial alliances to compensate for geographic holes and to fill niches. Ford's acquisition of the British car company Jaguar in 1989 killed two birds with one stone: it helped Ford fill (1) a niche with an established luxury car entry and (2) a geographic hole, the U.S. offshore market.

niche marketing *See* niche.

nichers *See* niche.

niche strategy *See* niche.

Niger Basin Authority (NBA), officially, *Authorité du Bassin du Niger (ABN)*, is an international regional association formed in 1964 to promote cooperation among its members in the peaceful development of the economic resources of the Niger Basin.

With headquarters in Niamy, Niger, the NBA comprises Benin, Burkina Faso, Cameroon, Chad, Guinea, Côte d'Ivoire, Mali, Niger, and Nigeria. It is one of a number of African regional international organizations dedicated to multilateral cooperation in economic development.

Cf. Lake Chad Basin Commission; Organization for the Development of the Sénégal River.

Nihon Keizai Shimbun •NW•, from the Japanese meaning "Japan financial daily," is the exhaustive financial daily newspaper that reports on the *Nikkei* (i.e., the Tokyo Stock Exchange (TSE)).

It is comparable to *The Wall Street Journal* (re: the New York Stock Exchange (NYSE)), *The Financial Times* (re: the London International Stock Exchange (LSE)), or *The Globe and Mail* (re: the Toronto Stock Exchange (TSE)).

Nikkei is the Japanese name of the Tokyo Stock Exchange (TSE); the measure of its performance is the *Nikkei 225*, the "index" (or average) of 225 important stocks listed on the *Nikkei*.

The *Nikkei 225* is analogous to the NYSE Composite Index, which measures the performance of stock on the New York Stock Exchange in New York City or the Dow Jones Industrial Average (of 500 industrial stocks on the NYSE).

In Canada, the analogue is the TSE 300 Composite Index, which measures the performance of the Toronto Stock Exchange in terms of the movement of 300 listed stocks supposed to be representative of the market as a whole.

See also Nihon Keizai Shimbun •NW•.

Nikkeiren •NW•, from the Japanese, is the "Japan Federation of Employers' Associations."

See also zaikai •NW•.

nomenklatura •NW•, from the Russian meaning "élite," are the top administrative echelons of government in the Soviet Union whose members control all important bureaucratic posts.

All *nomenklatura* officials are members of the Communist Party.

Cf. *habatsu* •NW•.

nominal rate of protection is the tariff rate (as accepted at "face value") as applied to cheaper foreign goods to protect domestic producers from injury from them.

For example, a foreign good "X" imported at $200/unit and subject to a nominal tariff rate of 10 percent would generate $20/unit additional costs for domestic buyers.

The actual costs of protection are hidden until costs of production are known, and calculations are done involving these costs.

Cf. effective rate of protection.

nominal tariff is an archaic term for a tax or duty levied on the final price of a good.

See also ad valorem duty.

nonconference line is a shipping line that offers cargo service but is not a member of a conference.

Cf. conference line.

non-Incoterms (non-INCOTERMS) are terms of commercial sale used in international transactions that have attained a good level of acknowledgment and acceptability among those who use them, but whose usage is neither extensive internationally nor sufficiently intensive (even regionally) to merit legitimation by the International Chamber of Commerce (ICC) as a uniform set of definitions.

Cf. Appendix IV.

See also Appendix III.

nonmarket economy (NME), also called a *communist country*, is a country defined in Section 1316 (18) (A) of the U.S. Omnibus Trade Act of 1988 as any political-economy that does not operate on the principles of cost and pricing structures determined by the free market forces of supply and demand, so that the prices of its goods and services do not reflect their fair market value.

Those countries so defined are listed in general note 3 (b) of the Harmonized Tariff Schedule (HTS) of the United States. As of December 31, 1990, the list comprised the following: Afghanistan, Albania, Bulgaria, Cambodia (Kampuchea), Cuba, Estonia, Laos, Latvia, Lithuania, Mongolia, North Korea, Romania, the USSR, and Vietnam. On October 3, 1990, with the reunification of West Germany with East Germany, the latter was removed from the list of NMEs.

The history of the listing of NMEs dates from the 1950s when the most-favored-nation (MFN) status of communist countries was suspended by the U.S. president in accordance with Section 5 of the Trade Agreements Extension Act of 1951. In other words, beginning in the Cold War era, the U.S. government used the granting of MFN status as an incentive for countries to join the free and democratic world order; or it suspended MFN status when countries did not comply with price setting in accordance with supply and demand. Moreover, Section 402 of the Trade Act of 1974 authorized the president (1) to grant MFN status to countries that met the "freedom of emigration" requirement provided for in this Section (and otherwise referred to as the "Jackson-Vanik Amendment") or (2) to waive full compliance with Jackson-Vanik when assurances have been received. Waivers resulting in MFN treatment were extended to Romania (1975), Hungary (1978), and China (1980).

A waiver of the Jackson-Vanik Amendment was made for Czechoslovakia in February 1990. This was done to accelerate the political liberation of the people from the Warsaw Pact and the Council of Mutual Economic Assistance (CMEA). Consequently, Czechoslovakia was accorded MFN status on November 17, 1990. The Soviet Union itself received a Jackson-Vanik waiver on December 12, 1990, making it eligible for U.S. Department of Agriculture (USDA) guarantees of commercial bank loans (called *loan guarantees*) extended to purchase U.S. agricultural products. (Earlier, in March 1990, the Bush Administration had renewed its long-term grain agreement (LTA) with the Soviet Union, which provides for Soviet minimum annual purchases of 10 million metric tons of U.S. oilseed and grain.)

The immediate purpose of the waiver was to make the USSR immediately eligible for export credit guarantees provided by the USDA for the purchase of U.S. agricultural products. This credit facility was deemed necessary given the "internal price adjustments" undertaken in the Soviet Union (under *perestroika*) that resulted in dramatic food shortages in major Soviet cities, food rationing in Leningrad, and the U.S. fear of political overthrow of the Gorbachev government.

In the interim, however, the following events have angered the U.S. people and their elected representatives: (1) the Soviet military "pacification" of Lithuania in January 1991 and the concurrent claim by Soviet Chairman Gorbachev that he was (literally) asleep while this was going on; and (2) the Soviet government's attempted "peace initiatives" in February 1991 during the Gulf Crisis, which were perceived as a "bailout" of the Saddam Hussein government in Iraq both to save Iraq as a Soviet "client state" for resupply of offensive military weapons and to deflect political opposition by 50 million Muslim citizens of the Soviet Union's southern republics.

However, the USSR cannot receive MFN tariff status until the U.S. Congress approves the U.S.–Soviet trade agreement. Indeed, following the Soviet Union's "crackdown" in Lithuania, the U.S. Senate approved a resolution calling on the president to reconsider the waiver and the extension of credits to the Soviet Union. Finally, the president has the authority to withdraw the loan guarantees themselves. However, withdrawal of them or cancellation of the credits seems unlikely since (1) the powerful U.S. grain trade lobby supports "managed" government-assisted trade with the Soviet Union, (2) there remains ferocious competition between the United States and all members of the Cairns Group and the EEC for export markets of grain, and (3) no formal moves by the Congress against the export credits have yet been initiated.

Cf. market economy; open economy; loan guarantees.

See also most-favored nation; *perestroika*; Warsaw Pact; Council for Mutual Economic Assistance; Gulf Crisis.

nonperforming assets refer to loans to Third World countries (i.e., their external debt) on which payments of either interest and/or repayments of principal have been suspended or cancelled (by the debtor country).

Cf. default.

See also external debt.

nonpublic record is an administrative record that is not open for public scrutiny.

See also record.

nonrecourse financing is the process of making available funds to capitalize a trade transaction in which the provider of capital can look to no one for repayment except the issuer of the instrument being tendered.

See also forfeiting.

nontariff barriers (NTBs), also referred to in United Nations forums, especially those of the United Nations Conference on Trade and Development (UNCTAD), as *nontariff measures (NTMs)*, are restrictions on global trade that are "nontariff" or "nonduty" in nature.

The classes of NTBs are as follows:

1. *Quantitative Restrictions:* unilaterally imposed or bi- or multilaterally negotiated restraints on exports and/or imports, including international commodity agreements (ICAs), voluntary export restraints (VERs), and orderly marketing arrangements (OMAs).

2. *Administrative Regulations:* for example, surety deposits, performance bonds, import/export licenses, customs fees, exchange control permits, investment performance requirements, domestic content requirements, government (Federal, regional, municipal, city, local) procurement practices.
3. *Technical Regulations:* for example, packaging regulations, container-marking requirements, bi- and multilingual requirements, safety codes/ standards.

See also Agreement on Technical Barriers to Trade (Standards Code).

nontraded goods and services are items for which there exists supply and demand (i.e., exporters and importers) but that nevertheless are not traded.

The reason for the nontransaction is that the cost of the invisibles to the potential transaction (mainly the cost of transportation) exceeds either (1) the comparative advantage to be derived from the exchange or (2) the price differential of the products or goods themselves.

Cf. invisible trade.

nonvessel operating common carrier (NVOCC) is a physical distribution/logistical (PD/L) domestically based intermediary that is not an international forwarder.

These companies offer to transport commodities via water (usually marine) carriers, even though they do not operate any ships themselves.

Whereas international air freight forwarders (so-called "IATA agents") do no consolidation and issue no bill of lading (and thus assume no responsibility for the shipment but get a commission from the air carrier), the prime function of NVOCCs is to consolidate and offer these container loads to ocean carriers.

NVOCCs issue bills of lading and thus assume responsibility for the shipment relative to the agreed-upon terms of sale. They do not, however, receive a commission from the ocean carrier for the freight they tender.

The regulations that govern and license the activity of NVOCCs (as well as other PD/L intermediaries) have, since 1961, been administered in the United States by the Federal Maritime Commission (FMC) under the authority of the Shipping Act of 1916 (Section 44).

Cf. foreign freight forwarder.

Nordic Council (NC) is a consultative group formed in 1952, comprising Denmark, Finland, Iceland, Norway, and Sweden, to discuss subjects of common regional interest: economic, social, and legal matters.

Cf. Asian and Pacific Council.

See also Appendix V (B).

no-recourse financing *See* nonrecourse financing.

North American Free Trade Agreement (NAFTA), also referred to as the *North American Free Trade Zone (NAFTZ),* will, if successful, be a multilateral accord between the United States, Canada, and Mexico.

NAFTA would comprise both the Canada-U.S. Free Trade Agreement of 1989 (FTA) and a U.S.-Mexico Free Trade Agreement. (The latter treaty is, as of this writing, being negotiated within the guidelines of fast-track procedures established in U.S. legislation to accelerate the negotiation and implementation process.) The United States initially began bilateral discussions with Mexico on September 25, 1990. Both agreed to have Canada participate in the talks.

If successfully negotiated, NAFTA would thus extend the existing Canada-U.S. Free Trade Agreement market of 275 million people to one of almost 360 million people with the inclusion of a U.S.-Mexico Free Trade Agreement. This combined market would be larger than the 320-million-people market of the 12-member European Economic Community (EEC).

NAFTA itself would be dedicated to (1) phased, full elimination of all import tariffs; (2) elimination of all nontariff barriers; (3) establishment of binding, full, mutual protection for intellectual property rights; and (4) expeditious and equitable dispute-settlement mechanisms.

Canada's support for NAFTA seems to be based on a solid platform of self-interested commercial policy. Canada, not unfairly, simply seeks to ensure its continued open access to the enormous U.S. market, which is ten times larger than its own. Canada fears the growing "balkanization of nations" (e.g., East Europe and the Middle East) and the "regionalization of trade." Indeed, in light of the sudden break in Uruguay Round GATT talks on December 7, 1990, and of the movement to form a new regional trade association (the East Asian Economic Group in February 1991), this fear is not entirely imagined. But this does not necessarily mean that it is in the United States' self-interest to create NAFTA.

For example, the United States International Trade Commission (USITC) has reported that the net benefits to the United States as a result of forming NAFTA would be relatively small, first, because the Mexican economy is only 3.6 percent the size of the U.S. economy, and, second, because most U.S.-Mexico trade is already nondutiable, affording both countries benefits without a NAFTA.

Ironically, while the Canadian government has been championing the NAFTA negotiations in which it has now been included, the USITC has reported that while any U.S.-Mexico free trade agreement (FTA) could decrease U.S.-Canada trade slightly, this decrease would become greater if it were conducted within a trilateral NAFTA framework!

Cf. Canada-U.S. Free Trade Agreement of 1989.

See also regionalization; dispute-settlement system; fast-track.

North Atlantic Treaty Organization (NATO) is an international political group (IPG) arising out of the North Atlantic Treaty signed in 1949 in Washington, D.C.; together with the Treaty under which it was established, NATO is a military organization established for the mutual defense of Western, open economies against perceived and actual threats posed by the relatively (and historically) closed economies of the USSR and its "fraternal allies."

NATO's headquarters are in Brussels, Belgium, and its membership consists of the following countries: Belgium, Canada, Denmark, Germany, Greece, Iceland, Italy, Luxembourg, the Netherlands, Norway, Portugal, Turkey, Spain, the United Kingdom (U.K.), and the United States of America (U.S.A.).

Despite the signing of the Paris Charter for a New Europe on November 22, 1990, and of a Treaty on Conventional Forces in Europe two days earlier, it is a moot point whether *glasnost* and *perestroika* and the clear de-Stalinization of East Europe are sufficient incentives for sustained mutual troop reductions in NATO and the (former) Warsaw Pact. Soviet compliance in accepting a unified Germany was not contingent upon (1) the removal of substantially all NATO troops and equipment from a re-unified Germany and (2) the "political neutralization" of Germany per se (i.e., its nonmembership in any military pact). Initial Soviet troop withdrawals have coincided more with civil unrest in the "balkanizing" USSR than with any long-term interest in geopolitical disengagement from Europe.

For its part, the U.S. government requested and got NATO membership for a unified Germany on a limited basis acceptable to the USSR (i.e., with pledges to reduce U.S. troops in Europe).

Ironically, the most important consideration underlying the Soviet Union's agreeing to Germany being a member of NATO seems to have stemmed from the USSR's internal instability and the opportunity cost of keeping its troops armed, fed, clothed, and trained outside of Soviet territory (where they were not needed) *vis-à-vis* returning them home (where they might be needed).

Cf. Warsaw Treaty Organization.

See also German reunification; open economy; closed economy; Appendix V (C).

Northern Corridor is the transport infrastructure located in East Africa and served by the Port of Mombasa, Kenya.

This system comprises the following components:

1. the railway running from the Port of Mombasa, Kenya, to Nairobi, Kenya, and continuing into Uganda to the capital, Kampala, and beyond that to the Uganda-Zaire border;
2. the highway system that connects Mombasa and Nairobi, continuing into Uganda to Kampala, then on to Kigali, capital of Rwanda, and continuing to Bujumbura, capital of Burundi; and
3. the oil pipeline from the Port of Mombasa to Nairobi.

See also Northern Corridor Transit Agreement.

Northern Corridor Transit Agreement (NCTA) is a multilateral treaty signed on February 19, 1985, by Kenya, Uganda, Burundi, Rwanda, and Tanzania, and by Zaire in 1987, pertaining to the transport infrastructure located in East Africa and served by the Port of Mombasa, Kenya.

The Agreement is an undertaking by each of the signatories to carry out the following:

1. to facilitate the free movement of transit traffic on land routes adapted for international traffic;
2. to remove or reduce the "administrative procedures" that restrain the free movement of international traffic; and
3. to allocate to the region's land-locked countries an area within the Indian Ocean Port of Mombasa, Kenya, to facilitate the transshipment of their commodities.

The Agreement was signed under the auspices of the United Nations Conference on Trade and Development (UNCTAD).

North Pacific Cooperation Security Dialog (NPCSD) is the effort launched by the Canadian minister of external affairs (i.e., the counterpart of the United States secretary of state) to establish a "habit of dialog" in the North Pacific region.

The inaugural meeting of NPCSD took place April 6–9, 1991, in Victoria, British Columbia, and was attended by the region's seven countries: Canada, the United States, the Soviet Union, China, Japan, North Korea, and South Korea.

Cynics see the NPCSD as characteristic of Canada's traditional "boy scout" behavior in international affairs: a facile attempt to portray itself as international "peace keeper." Less cynical observers see the NPCSD initiative to be an extension of Canada's Three Pillar Strategy, and especially of the Pacific Trade Strategy component of it.

With no history of imperialism or of modern military ambitions, Canada can be expected to use diplomatic "confidence-building" tools (such as NPCSD) for extending its influence. Especially in the North Pacific, a region where Canada has considerable difficulty in asserting its own sovereignty over vast stretches of its territorial sea, Canada's own security interests are best enhanced by such applications of peaceful diplomacy.

See also Three Pillar Strategy.

Northwest Atlantic Fisheries Organization (NAFO), formerly, *International Commission for Northwest Atlantic Fisheries (ICNAF)*, is an international organization established in 1979 to manage and protect common fishery resources in the Northwest Atlantic Ocean.

NAFO comprises 12 member countries: the European Economic Community (EEC), Canada, Japan, the United States, USSR, Norway, Iceland, and 6 others.

NAFO sets "catch quotas" (called total allowable catches (TACs)) on a yearly basis; but entities such as the European Economic Community (EEC) set their own quotas, and they overfish the Northwest Atlantic Ocean beyond the 200-mile territorial sea limit of the Atlantic countries, in clear violation of the NAFO agreement.

However, since all maritime countries, including Canada, have domestic jurisdiction (in international law) over commercial activities within their "territorial sea" only within a "200-mile exclusive economic zone," all catches beyond that zone occur on the "high seas" and are thus beyond its territorial jurisdiction.

Flatfish (e.g., flounder, place, and cod) flourish in the sea beyond the 200-mile limit, and lack of appropriate conservation depletes all fish stocks within and without the 200-mile zone. Since 1986, with the accession of Spain and Portugal to the EEC, fish stocks in the Grand Banks and the Flemish Cap have been drastically depleted due to overfishing by the EEC, which in that year first set its own catch quotas in direct violation of NAFO's TACs.

The relatively poor status of the Spanish and Portuguese industrial economies *vis-à-vis* northern Europe has been recognized by the EEC Commission, and especially by the United Kingdom, France, and Germany. Massive amounts of development capital have been channeled to Spain and Portugal for long-range industrial development to bring their economies up to northern European standards because, by 1992/93, harmonization of many outstanding Spanish and Portuguese tariffs will be occurring.

In the interim, the Canadian government alleges that the EEC Commission has willfully permitted (and encouraged) Spain and Portugal to continue with their over-fishing and, consequently, to deplete the Northwest Atlantic fishery.

Short-term, the economic outcomes have been (1) the closing of marginal fish packers in the Canadian Atlantic provinces; (2) their consequent move to the New England states in the United States where costs are lower and markets larger; and (3) the shutdown of hundreds of individual, family-owned, and community-supported fishing boats and the emigration from Atlantic Canada of entire communities.

Long-term, the allegedly blatant disregard of the NAFO Agreement by the EEC and the resulting alleged reckless depletion of the Northwest Atlantic fishery may portend an irreparable situation (i.e., terminal depletion of fish stocks) for all nations that depend on fish from the region.

One lesson to be learned is that whenever a customs union, common market, or economic-monetary union (EMU) is being formed, the success of the union depends crucially on the structure and level of development of each of the member countries. The admission of Spain and Portugal to the EEC may have been unwisely premature, done in overweening political haste to produce an integrated economic-monetary union to compete with an obviously strategically serious U.S. rival. The expansion of the EEC to include such East Europe candidates as Poland and Hungary will be a more cautious and drawn-out affair.

There is little to dispute that the labor-intensive, low-tech industrial structures of Spain and Portugal were so obviously undisciplined and ill-suited for immediate integration with the sophisticated industrial economies of northern Europe that an "adjustment period" had to be provided for their "industrial upgrading." But, based on the facts of the ongoing alleged reckless destruction of the Northwest Atlantic fishery by them, one is impelled to comment that the long-term cost impact on the ecosystem of integrating Iberia into the EEC may be much greater than the long-term benefits.

From a global economic (and legal) overview of the NAFO situation, one might adduce the following:

1. Since it will cost the other ten EEC members countless billions of ECU to har-monize the economies of Spain and Portugal with the disciplined pace of rational economic life of northern Europe, the "Iberian acquisition" may have been an extremely costly decision in terms of the opportunity cost.

2. Since it will cost non-EEC members of NAFO (like Canada) equally enormous sums for known negative third-party effects caused by negative "catch-up time" actions, the EEC may be seen to be competitively malicious and, thus, criminal.

3. Any EMU—European or otherwise—that encourages the willful destruction of one of the globe's most precious protein resources and source of economic ben-efit worldwide—albeit in the name of permitting two of its members adequate "catch-up time"—may be *prima facie* evidence of an "international economic crime against the environment" with "international criminal effects against humanity."

4. Such a competitor might (ideally) be treated as one would a criminal who commit-ted an "economic war crime": it should be held accountable in law. Not to do so would be to jeopardize the very basis of rational economic activity in the world and to permit the world to be squandered and plundered without any regard for the consequences. (In this regard, perhaps Iraq will be held accountable (under United Nations Security Council Resolution 687) for its criminal damage to the world environment, by having willfully set Kuwait's entire oil-well inventory on fire.)

5. If global harmony means anything real, it must be underpinned by a simple moral law: since "growth and development" (let alone sustainable development) is not sustainable given economic behavior that impacts negatively long-term on world resources, IT SHOULD BE A CRIME TO KNOWINGLY MISBEHAVE THUSLY.

However, international law is a concensus-building process initiated by political will. Until there exists the willingness (1) to codify laws under which a sovereign state can be held legally accountable for wrongful (ecology-destroying) behavior and (2) to enforce those laws (supranationally rather than bilaterally) little will be accomplished.

See also Appendix VI (Law of the Sea); Valdez Principles; Gulf Crisis.

O

OCT is the English-language abbreviation for overseas countries and territories of the European Economic Community (EEC); in French, they are called *territoires d'outre-mer (TO)* and *collectivités territoriales (CT)*.

These dependencies comprise the following:

1. *Eleven OCTs of the United Kingdom*: Anguilla, Cayman Islands, Falklands, South Sandwich Islands, Montserrat, Pitcairn, St. Helena, British Antarctic Territory, British Indian Ocean Territories, Turks and Caicos Islands, and British Virgin Islands;
2. *Four TOs of France*: New Caledonia, French Polynesia, French Antarctic Territories and Settlements, and Wallis and Fortuna Islands;
3. *Two CTs of France:* Mayotte and St. Pierre et Miquelon;
4. *Two OCTs of the Netherlands:* Netherlands Antilles (Bonaire, Curaçao, Saba, St. Eustatius, and St. Maarten) and Aruba;
5. *One "Autonomous Region" of Denmark:* Greenland.

The OCTs are Europe's last remnants of its former colonial empires. But their importance derives from their relationship to the EEC. For example, while people from the French OTCs have full French citizenship and enjoy all the benefits of EEC membership, in terms of international business, there is an important distinction between the OTs and the CTs. While the French OTs are "legally autonomous" and can negotiate independent arrangements to implement EEC commercial law, the French CTs are directly subject to French national law and, thus, have no such autonomy. A considerable variety of such permutations and combinations characterize the OCT-EEC arrangement. The suggestion is that international business players should make no blanket assumptions (e.g., that the rules of the commercial game in the EEC are identical to those in the OCTs).

Article 132(5) of the Treaty of Rome states: "In relations between (EEC) Member States and the countries and territories, the right of establishment shall be open on equal terms to all natural and legal persons who are members of a Member State or of one of the countries and territories." However, since the Single European Act applies to the EEC's European territory, not to the OCTs, which are not physically part of Europe, the "completion of the internal market" apparently does not apply to the OCTs, giving them a somewhat curious legal status.

Under EEC law, the OCTs are in an "association" with the EEC. Articles 131–135 of the Treaty of Rome cover the ways and means of this association, and Article 136 sets out the procedure for implementing it. Article 131 states that the aim of the association is "to promote the economic and social development of the countries and territories," and to "establish close economic relations between them and the Community as a whole." These political aims are clearly spelled out in the Preamble to the Treaty of Rome.

In short, having a variety of excess, postcolonial, territorial baggage, the EEC has established a considerable number of explicit rules and regulations for managing its arrangements with them. These include official development assistance (ODA) (i.e., "aid") extended via the various Lomé Conventions and via the European Development Fund.

See also Lomé Convention; right of establishment; Single Act.

ODA is the abbreviation for **o**fficial **d**evelopment **a**ssistance.

OECD is the abbreviation for **O**rganization for **E**conomic **C**ooperation and **D**evelopment.

OECD Concensus, also called *OECD Concensus guidelines*, *OECD Concensus rates*, and *concensus rates*, is an agreement established by the Organization for Economic Cooperation and Development (OECD) to "manage" the terms of official export financing by each of the OECD members according to specific delimiting criteria.

The Concensus, in fact, is collusion by OECD members to limit the free-market competition in export financing.

1. *Export Financing Guidelines*

The criteria applied by the OECD apply on (i) maximum time limits on the maturity of export financing, (ii) minimum (cash) down payments, and (iii) minimum interest rates, as follows:

i. *Maximum time limits:* a range of $8^{1}/_{2}$ to 10 years is recommended, unless the export credits are classified as being a component of official development assistance (ODA), in which case longer maturity terms, classified as concessional financing terms, would apply.

ii. *Minimum (cash) down payments:* no less than 15 percent of the value of the export credit is the guideline.

iii. *Minimum interest rates:* the guidelines are
   - 10.7 percent for least developed countries (LLDCs),
   - 11.9 percent for all less developed countries (LDCs) not classed as LLDCs,
   - 13.6 percent for developed industrial countries.

2. *Mixed Credit Guidelines*

The OECD Concensus, in seeking to keep mixed credits from "contaminating" commercial market rates, suggests that mixed-credit transactions (i.e., export financing with a market-rate element and a concessional-financing component) have their concessional component at a minimum of 20 percent of the total mixed-credit package.

See also export financing; associated financing; concessional financing; mixed credits; official development assistance.

OECD Concensus guidelines *See* OECD Concensus.

OECD Concensus rates *See* OECD Concensus.

official development assistance (ODA) refers to funds provided by the governments of developed countries to those of developing countries for the purpose of assisting the economic and social development of developing political economies.

The thing that differentiates ODA from other types of development funding is that ODA comprises a grant (or concessional) component of at least 25 percent of the value of the ODA package.

ODA from the developed countries—excepting OPEC (Organization of Petroleum Exporting Countries) development assistance and aid from the Council for Mutual Economic Assistance (CMEA)—is coordinated by the Development Assistance Committee (DAC) of the Organization for Economic Cooperation and Development (OECD). The 19 member countries of the DAC are as follows: Australia, Austria, Belgium, Canada, Commission of the European Communities, Denmark, Finland, France, Germany, Ireland, Italy, Japan, Netherlands, New Zealand, Norway, Sweden, Switzerland, United Kingdom, and the United States.

OPEC development assistance is coordinated separately by the OPEC Fund for International Development (OPEC/FID).

The internationally agreed target of 0.70 percent of gross national product (GNP) for ODA has never been achieved by Canada. In 1986/87, the level reached 0.50 percent, up from 0.46 percent in 1985/86.

The OECD's DAC was formed in 1961, following an OECD Resolution on the Common Aid Effort. This recommended the strengthening and expansion of ODA, and its coordination, to increase its effectiveness in the global developmental effort.

In the United States, the official government aid agency is the U.S. International Development Cooperation Agency (USIDCA). In Canada, it is the Canadian International Development Agency (CIDA).

The volume of non-OPEC and non-CMEA ODA is massive. As of 1988, its net value was U.S. $47.58 billion, or 0.35 percent of the GNP of the 19 DAC member countries. It represented fully 50 percent of all capital flows to developing countries. Development assistance from OPEC/FID was valued at U.S. $2 billion, and that from the CMEA exceeded U.S. $5 billion in 1988.

Without ODA, there is little question that all the developmental efforts of the United Nations System, including the World Bank, the United Nations Children's Fund (UNICEF), the International Fund for Agricultural Development (IFAD), the United Nations Environment Program (UNEP), and the United Nations Development Program (UNDP), would be in vain.

Cf. tied aid.

official reserve account *See* accommodating transactions.

official settlements balance is a summary statement of the net debit or net credit position in a country's official reserve account.
See also accommodating transactions.

offset deals are a type of countertrade transaction. The agreement between exporter and importer can be of two types: (1) indirect offsets and (2) direct offsets.

1. With indirect offsets, an exporter receives payment in a variety of ways: (i) by receiving part in cash and by undertaking to counterpurchase nonrelated items, or (ii) by receiving part in cash and by agreeing to assist in the export marketing or unrelated goods.

    Example: Spar Aero-Space, a Canadian company, contracted with the Brazilian state agency Intelbras to build fixed-earth receiving stations for Brazil's telecommunications network. Spar agreed to 50-percent payment in U.S. dollars, the remainder to be paid when Spar successfully export-marketed Brazilian manioc and tropical fruit. Spar Trading Company was established to fulfill the offset agreement.

2. With direct offsets, the exporter receives payment by agreeing to activities directly related to the goods or services being imported: (i) co-production, (ii) subcontract production, (iii) overseas investment, and (iv) technology transfer.

    Cf. barter; buy-back; compensation trade; cooperation contracts; counterpurchase; switch deals.
    See also countertrade; co-production; subcontract production; overseas investment; technology transfer.

offshore banking refers to specific types of transactions that do not take place within the domestic jurisdiction of a country.
See also offshore banking centers.

offshore banking centers (OBCs) (1) is a derogatory term for financial institutions outside the domestic jurisdiction of a country, alleged to be used for unorthodox purposes (e.g., laundering of dirty money, evasion of taxes); or (2) are financial institutions that are either cities or countries or enclaves of cities or countries.
These have been established specifically to attract nonresident banking operations denominated in convertible currencies (e.g., USD, CAD, GBP, DEM, or CHF) by reducing or eliminating "restrictions" (e.g., taxes, disclosure re-

quirements, residency requirements) upon their operations, that might otherwise apply in orthodox international banking centers (IBCs).

OBCs can be of two types:

1. *Functional facilities* may serve as offshoots of, or as adjuncts to, established international financial centers (IFCs). Depending on their size and importance, they may be perceived as "down-scale" (and slightly "less kosher") versions of the larger and more sophisticated IFCs.

   Examples of functional entities are: Bahrain, Hong Kong, Luxembourg, Liechtenstein, Panamá, the Philippines, Singapore, and United Arab Emirates (U.A.E.).

2. *Paper operations* serve essentially to generate documents (e.g., certificates of origin, bills of lading), thus establishing an evidentiary bases for nondomestic financial operations. The purpose of these "paper mills" is to afford their users financial benefits (i.e., to evade (which is criminal) or to avoid (which is not) the payment of taxes, fees, customs duties/levies, and income taxes).

   Examples of paper operations are: Anguilla, Bahamas, Cayman Islands, Jersey, Netherlands Antilles, and the Seychelles.

   Cf. international financial centers.

offshore funds are cash and negotiable instruments, usually denominated in one of the reserve currencies, located in a financial institution outside the domestic jurisdiction of the country.

When the United States refers to offshore funds, it means currency in U.S. dollars located abroad. When the Germans refer to offshore funds, they mean currency denominated in Deutsche marks, located abroad. For the Japanese, it is yen; for the Swiss, the Swiss franc; and so forth.

See also offshore banking centers.

oligopoly, from the Greek *oligos* meaning "few" and *poleein* meaning "sellers," is the form of business organization in which there are only a few suppliers or producers of a product, or a commodity, or a service, which has undergone some differentiation.

As a result of this competitive market condition, the members of the oligopoly have less control than does a monopolist over the price at which the commodity or service will be offered in the market.

Where members of the oligopoly collude to gain more control over price and, thus, restrain competition, they are subject to competition laws.

Cf. monopoly.

Omnibus Trade Act of 1988, the colloquial name for Public Law 100-418: an Act to enhance the competitiveness of American industry, and for other purposes (the official long title), or the Omnibus Trade and Competitiveness Act of 1988 (the official short title), is U.S. legislation enacted on August 23, 1988, intended to improve the comparative advantage of U.S. industry in interna-

tional trade by enhancing the authority of the executive branch of government (specifically the U.S. Trade Representative) in order to improve and
strengthen enforcement of U.S. laws in the following key areas:

1. U.S. rights under trade agreements and responses to foreign trade practices,
2. antidumping and countervailing U.S. duty laws,
3. protection of U.S. intellectual property,
4. U.S. export enhancement/U.S. export controls, and
5. U.S. international financial policy.

See also Super 301.

OPEC Fund for International Development (OPEC/FID) is an autonomous international development agency, established by the Organization of Petroleum
Exporting Countries (OPEC) in Paris, France, in 1976. Headquarters have
been in Vienna, Austria, since 1980.

The OPEC/FID extends official development assistance (ODA) from OPEC
member countries to non-oil-producing developing countries, with the aim of
financing balance-of-payments deficits and development projects. The development assistance granted is in the form of loans on concessional terms of
finance.

Cf. Development Assistance Committee.
See also official development assistance.

open account is a method of export financing whereby the settlement of the account
between the exporter and the importer is made on a regular basis every 30
to 120 days through the routine exchange of statements of account and other
pertinent documents.

See also export financing.

open door treatment is a type of friendship, commerce, and navigation (FCN) treaty
whereby signatory countries agree to treat the nationals of any other signatory country in an equal, nondiscriminatory way with regard to trading in a
specified territory.

The practice originated in the Open Door Policy of the United States as
it was presented to England, France, and Germany in 1899. The U.S. initiative
resulted in Open Door Treaties being signed with each of them. The "open
door" referred to is that of equal access demanded by the United States in
trading with China, a country with whom the Europeans sought to maintain
an exclusive, exploitative relationship.

See also Appendix VI (friendship, commerce, and navigation treaty).

open economy *See* market economy.

opening bank, also called an *issuing bank*, is a financial institution that issues a
letter of credit on behalf of a client and that agrees to pay (or "honor") drafts
drawn under it (or "against it") by the exporter, who is the beneficiary (or the
payee).

Cf. advising bank.
See also documentary credit.

opening skies agreement (open skies) refers to ongoing negotiations between the United States and Canada aimed at updating a 1966 bilateral agreement (last revised in 1974) that stipulates the number of cities that U.S. and Canadian air carriers can serve with passenger and cargo services in each other's country.

The goal of the talks is to deregulate the U.S.-Canada transborder air traffic, allowing free market forces of supply and demand to determine the patterns of routes.

Canadian air carriers now serve only 30 percent of the U.S. market while U.S. carriers serve 90 percent of the Canadian market.

A desirable U.S. objective of the talks is to obtain an "anything goes" agreement, with unlimited operating rights everywhere that demand can support service.

The opposing Canadian view—especially from air cargo companies in Canada—is to protect intra-Canadian routes from U.S. carriers as well as to protect existing Canadian rights of service to and from U.S. cities.

It does seem likely that U.S. air carriers would use their own planes and crews to move Canadian cargo through the U.S. freight hubs. For example, Federal Express ships 1.5 million parcels per night out of its Memphis, Tennessee, hub. Such enormous economies of scale might make survival impossible for major Canadian carriers such as Air Canada which currently provide in excess of 95 percent of air cargo services within the country, and which would likely lose most of it if cross-border rights were awarded to U.S. carriers under an open skies agreement. In expectation of such deregulated competition, Air Canada is likely to increase its "same day service" and its "2nd day service," acknowledging that it will lose most its "next day/overnight service" to U.S. carriers.

See also cabotage; free trade.

OPIC *See* U.S. International Development Cooperation Agency (4. Overseas Private Investment Corporation).

optimum tariff is the "best" duty rate for goods. This is calculated as the rate of duty that maximizes the positive economic benefits that accrue from improvement in the terms of trade of a nation *vis-à-vis* the negative economic effects that result from reductions in the volume of trade (due to the imposition of duties).

Cf. prohibitive tariff.
See also duty.

order bill of lading is a variation of *uniform order bill of lading.*
See bill of lading.

orderly marketing arrangements (OMAs), also called *voluntary restraint arrangements,* refers to bi- and multilateral understandings between producer and consumer countries of commodities arrived at to restrict exports/imports of the particular goods to avoid market disruption in the consumer country.

Cf. voluntary restraint arrangement; export quotas.
See also MultiFiber Arrangement; market disruption.

Organisation Commune Africaine et Mauricienne (OCAM), also known as *African and Mauritian Common Organization (AMCO)*, is a free trade area, established in 1965 at Nouakchoutt, Mauritania, which became operational after the signing of the charter in Antananarivo, Madagascar, in 1966.

The objectives of OCAM are to strengthen and promote solidarity among members to further the economic- and social-development work carried out by the Organization for African Unity (OAU).

OCAM has a rather labyrinthine history, which strongly supports the West African (Akan) proverb that "no path in Africa is ever straight":

1. Originally, OCAM began as a political group, the *Union Africaine et Malagache (UAM)* (African and Malagasy Union (AMU)), comprising 11 French-speaking African states plus Madagascar, established in Antananarivo in 1961.
2. In 1964, UAM transformed itself into the economically focused *Union Africaine et Malagache de Coopération Économique (UAMCE)* (African and Malagasy Economic Cooperation Union (AMECU)).
3. In 1964, UAMCE re-assumed some political (as opposed to strictly economic) goals and changed its charter and its name to the *Organisation Commune Africaine et Malagache (OCAM)* (African and Malagasy Common Organization (AMCO)).
4. In 1970, after the admission of Mauritius to the Organization, OCAM's name was changed to *Organisation Commune Africaine, Malagache et Mauricienne (OCAMM)* (African, Malagasy, and Mauritian Common Organization (AMMCO)).
5. In 1974, Madagascar (among others) withdrew from OCAMM, necessitating the name change to its present appellation.

At present, the following countries are members of OCAM: Benin, Burkina Faso, Central African Republic, Côte d'Ivoire, Gabon, Mauritius, Niger, Rwanda, Sénégal, and Togo.

Present headquarters of OCAM are in Bangui, Central African Republic (CAR). Previous headquarters were in Yaoundé, in Cameroon, and in Antananrivo, Madagascar, but they were moved because of the withdrawal of those nations from the organization.

The original formation of OCAM was encouraged by France, and all of the members were former French colonies. It is suggested that, with the formation of the OAU in 1963, OCAM was seen by France (and by other former European colonialists) as a genuine political counterweight to the OAU, which was always regarded with considerable suspicion and fear by them.

See also Lomé Convention; Organization of African Unity; Appendix V (C).

Organization of African Unity (OAU) is an international regional organization that was established in Addis Ababa, Ethiopia, in 1963.

The membership of the OAU consists of all African states except South Africa (and its pseudo-republics known locally as "homelands"). Namibia (formerly known as Southwest Africa), was occupied by South Africa originally by the authority of the Permanent Mandates Commission of the League of Nations and (until the U.N.-supervised elections in 1989) was held illegally in defiance of a judgment of the International Court of Justice (i.e., The World Court) at The Hague.

The OAU's *raison d'être* is to promote African unity via economic and political cooperation and mutual defense. The formation of the OAU was partly a rational attempt to deal with development challenges and partly a mechanism to satisfy a genuine need to vent anger and resentment at former European colonizers for the years of African powerlessness and exploitation.

See also Appendix V (C).

Organization of American States (OAS) is an international political organization, founded in 1948 at the 9th Pan-American Conference in Bogotá, Colombia.

1. *History:* The OAS's origins stem from the signing of the Act of Chapultepec in 1945 in Mexico City. The Act was a wartime defense pact among hemispheric states, and it laid the foundation for the signing in Rio de Janeiro in 1947 of the Inter-American Treaty of Reciprocal Assistance, commonly known as the Rio Treaty or the Rio Pact.

   The Rio Treaty is a true military accord between American states in the Western Hemisphere, and it acted as the model for NATO and SEATO. The key "mutual defense phrase" in the Treaty states, " . . . an armed attack by any state against an American state shall be considered an attack against all." In 1948, one year after the signing of the Rio Treaty, the OAS was founded to implement the Treaty.

   The OAS originally comprised almost all states of the Americas. Two notable exceptions were Canada and Cuba. Canada, a nonmember, had the status as an "official observer" since 1972. Seventeen years later, it applied for membership, in October 1989, and was unanimously accepted as a full member on November 13, 1989, within two weeks of its application. When formal ratification took place on January 1, 1990, Canada became the thirty-third member of the organization.

   Cuba, on the other hand, was an original member but was suspended by a two-thirds majority of the OAS Council after the 1962 Cuban Missile Crisis.

   The OAS had as its Central Office an agency called the Pan-American Union (PAU). The PAU itself was founded in 1910 when the Commercial Bureau of the International Union of American Republics (IUAR), established in 1890, was selected as the Central Office of the IUAR and named the PAU. The OAS abandoned the name "Pan-American Union" in 1970, when it changed its charter and renamed its Central Office the General Secretariat.

For some time, there seems to have been some confusion between the OAS and the Pan-American Union (PAU), perhaps as a result of their intermingled histories.

2. *Purpose and Functions:* The OAS' *raison d'être* is:
   i.   to act as the formal, legal institution for implementing the Pan-American collective security treaty (i.e., the Rio Treaty);

   ii.   to provide mechanisms for the peaceful settlement of disputes; and

   iii.   to coordinate regional development programs of the Inter-American Development Bank, which was established by the OAS.

Under this plan, (almost) all the political economies of the Americas are targeted for regional integration with the United States and under its defensive military canopy. At least one school of international economics suggests that the OAS is a tool of "American capitalist imperialism," which seeks to create a permanent economic dependency by Latin America on the United States.

See also Inter-American Development Bank; Appendix V (C).

Organization of Arab Petroleum Exporting Countries (OAPEC) is a regional international organization, established in 1968 by Saudi Arabia, Kuwait, and Libya, and later joined by Algeria, Bahrain, Egypt, Iraq, Qtar, Syria, Tunisia, and the United Arab Emirates (U.A.E.). OAPEC has its headquarters in Kuwait City, Kuwait.

The organization has a number of multidisciplinary functions:

1.   to ensure the supply of petroleum to customers at negotiated prices;
2.   to create and promote favorable political conditions conducive to capital investment in the petroleum industry in Arab countries; and
3.   to promote increasing Arab participation in specialized fields of the petroleum industry.

To achieve the first function, OAPEC works closely with the Organization of Petroleum Exporting Countries (OPEC) to ensure that the OAPEC bloc's views are appropriately represented.

To achieve the second function, OAPEC maintains strong relations with bodies such as the Arab League, aimed at ensuring political harmony in the region.

To achieve the third function, OAPEC cooperates with a wide variety of international organizations such as the United Nations Industrial Development Organization (UNIDO) and the United Nations International Maritime Organization (IMO).

As a consequence of OAPEC's efforts, the following joint venture enterprises have been established:

- Arab Maritime Petroleum Transport Company
- Arab Shipbuilding and Repair Yard Company
- Arab Petroleum Services Company
- Arab Petroleum Training Institute
- Arab Petroleum Investments Corporation
- Arab Engineering and Consulting Company

See also Organization of Petroleum Exporting Countries; Appendix V (B).

Organization of Central American States (OCAS), officially, *Organización de Estados Centro-americanos (OECA)*, is an international political organization established in 1962 in Panama City, Panamá, by the Foreign Ministers of the five Central American republics: Costa Rica, El Salvador, Guatemala, Honduras, and Nicaragua. (Panamá is not a member.) OCAS has its headquarters in San Salvador, El Salvador.

The objectives of OCAS are to actively promote and strengthen the bonds of economic, political, and social solidarity among the member states, with the ultimate goal of establishing a single political entity in the region.

These objectives have, in fact, been unattainable to date. First of all, regional economic integration is a process firmly not in the hands of the OCAS, but in those of the Central American Common Market (CACM). This fact badly fractures (and frustrates) OCAS' authority to coordinate regional political unity.

Second, only with the signing of the General Peace Treaty between El Salvador and Honduras in 1980 was the long-standing dispute between these two OCAS members settled. That dispute, which erupted in the notorious "football war" of 1969, negatively affected regional political unity by producing 11 years of additional political uncertainty in a region already racked (1) by ongoing turmoil within Nicaragua, El Salvador, and Guatemala and (2) by U.S.-backed insurgent contras infiltrating Nicaragua from Honduras, who were fighting to oust the Nicaraguan Sandinista government.

The Sandinista government was "cleanly" defeated at the polls (by Violeta Chamorro's UNO Party) in March 1990.

See also Central American Common Market; Appendix V (B).

Organization for the Development of the Sénégal River (ODSR), officially, *Organisation pour la Mise en Valeur du Fleuve Sénégal (OMVFS)*, is a regional international organization established in 1972 to increase cooperation among member countries in the economic exploitation of the resources of the Sénégal Basin.

The ODSR comprises Mali, Mauritania, and Sénégal. Its headquarters are in Dakar, Sénégal. It is one of a number of African regional international organizations dedicated to multilateral cooperation in economic development.

Cf. Lake Chad Basin Commission; Niger Basin Authority.

Organization for Economic Cooperation and Development (OECD) was established in 1961 in Paris, France, to act as a global forum to stimulate world trade and economic development.

The OECD's membership consists of the world's developed countries: Australia, Austria, Belgium, Canada, Denmark, Germany, Finland, France, Greece, Iceland, Ireland, Italy, Japan, Luxembourg, the Netherlands, New Zealand, Norway, Portugal, Spain, Sweden, Switzerland, Turkey, the United Kingdom, the United States, and Yugoslavia. The development of an environment conducive to economic growth of the world's developing countries rests with the OECD.

The OECD replaced the Organization for European Economic Cooperation (OEEC), an organization formed in 1948 to guide the rebuilding of Europe after World War II.

See also Development Assistance Committee; Development Center of the Organization for Economic Cooperation and Development; OECD Concensus; Appendix V (B).

Organization of the Islamic Conference (OIC) is an international Arab organization, formed in Jeddah, Saudi Arabia, in 1971. The OIC aims to strengthen and promote "Islamic solidarity" between member countries by coordinating economic and social activities. (For example, the idea of the Islamic Development Bank was conceived at the OIC's 1973 meeting.)

The OIC comprises more than 40 countries: all the members of the Arab League plus Islamic states in Africa and Asia and the Palestine Liberation Organization (PLO), which has been given *de jure* recognition.

Cf. Arab League.

See also Islamic Development Bank.

Organization of Petroleum Exporting Countries (OPEC) is the most important international commodity group (ICG) in the world. OPEC was officially established in Caracas, Venezuela, in 1961. Its headquarters are in Vienna, Austria.

OPEC's importance derives from two facts: (1) its impact on the world price of oil and, subsequently, on the balance of payments of every country; and (2) the model of a successful international cartel, which OPEC has demonstrated to developing countries whose economies are primarily (if not exclusively) commodity based.

---

1. *Impact on the World Price of Oil*

   Following the inability of OPEC producer countries and Western oil companies to agree upon a timetable for increasing the world price of oil (after the Tehran Conferences in 1973), OPEC unilaterally increased the price from U.S. $2.00 per barrel to U.S. $3.40 per barrel in September 1973 and again to U.S. $11.63 per barrel in December 1973.

   Further, in 1973, OPEC placed a total embargo against oil shipments to the United States and the Netherlands. The United States was targeted because of its open and (what was perceived as) "flagrantly arrogant" political and military support of Israel in the 1973 war between it and Arab states. The Netherlands was embargoed because of its strategic geographic position: Rotterdam, the world's largest port, is located in Holland at the mouth of the Rhine River. The Port of Rotterdam includes the European Common Market's largest oil refinery and transshipment complex. It serves not only major down-stream European ports, such as The Port of Antwerp, but also is the key international transshipment facility for North America, South America, Africa, and the Middle East.

   One effect of OPEC's actions in 1973 (and subsequent price increases in 1975, 1977, 1979, 1980, 1981, and, rising to the "all-time high" of U.S. $42.00 per barrel, 1982) was to drive the non-Western, nonindustrialized, non-oil producing developing countries in Africa, Asia, and Latin America into severe balance of payments deficit positions, with every prospect of them becoming increasingly indebted.

   To assist these countries, OPEC created a Special Fund in 1976, which was renamed the OPEC/Fund for International Development (OPEC/FID) in 1980.

Other long-term effects of OPEC's actions were (1) the strategic drive of Western economies to better integrate their political economies and (2) innovations in the field of energy development and utilization, producing more energy-efficient products, thus reducing their dependence on imported oil and, presumably, increasing their political flexibility in their foreign policy activities.

Evidence of the first is shown by the accelerated drive toward economic, monetary, and (ultimately) political integration (and thus interdependence *vis-à-vis* external dependence) within the European Common Market (EEC). The same movement toward economic and political integration is taking place between Canada and the United States within the framework of the Canada-U.S. Free Trade Act of 1989.

Evidence of the second is found in OPEC's price reduction for oil from the "all-time high" of U.S. $42.00 per barrel in 1982 to an "all-time low" of U.S. $16.00 per barrel in 1988.

One can also adduce, from the reduction of supertanker construction by the Japanese, that Western economies use relatively less oil more efficiently than they did prior to 1973, thus driving the Japanese to reach a diminishing return in the building of very large crude carriers (VLCCs).

2. *The Model of a Successful International Cartel*

In an attempt to emulate the apparent success of OPEC, a number and variety of producer countries have formed international commodity groups (ICGs) with the aim (1) of controlling supply and, thus, (2) of influencing the upward movement of price for a particular commodity.

"Success" can be measured on the basis of the price inelasticity of demand for the commodity in question and, consequently, of the relative lack of substitutes for it, resulting, over time, in a relatively elastic supply response and in an increase in the producer price for it.

It is no coincidence that the New International Economic Order (NIEO) initiative occurred in 1974 on the heels of what appeared to be a dramatically successful confrontation between OPEC (representing the developing world) and Europe and the United States (the developed world).

Cf. international cartel.

See also OPEC Fund for International Development; Gulf Crisis; Appendix V (E).

Outer Seven is a term used (from 1958 until 1973) to refer collectively to the seven members of the European Free Trade Association (EFTA) *vis-à-vis* the Inner Six, a term used to refer collectively to the European Economic Community (EEC).

Cf. Inner Six.

See also European Economic Community; European Free Trade Association.

outsider *See* nonconference line.

outward processing arrangements is a variation of *outward processing relief arrangements*, also called *outward processing*.

> *See* production sharing.

overall reciprocity *See* reciprocity.

Overseas Economic Cooperation Fund (OECF) is a Japanese financial institution, created for the purpose of providing new money via co-financing with Japanese private-sector financial institutions.

> **Example:** The OECF and the Asian Development Bank (ADB) finalized arrangements under which the OECF will make available ¥20 billion for co-financing with the ADB. The ADB borrowed ¥20 billion from a consortium of Japanese insurance companies to be repaid over a 25-year term.

> *See also* yen diplomacy; concessional financing; new money.

overseas investment refers to (1) direct investment in a host country by a foreign investor for the purpose of commercial profit; and (2) a component of a type of countertrade transaction called direct offsets in which an exporter agrees to direct capital investment in the overseas country that is the import customer.

> **Example:** From the exporter's viewpoint, the capital investment in a local soft drink bottling plant was a mandatory requirement of the transaction, without which the American syrup would no longer be purchased. From the importer's viewpoint, the direct investment offset enabled it to reduce its dependence on the U.S. importer by having the investment channeled into a local bottling plant joint venture over which it would have considerable political control, in addition to 50 percent equity.

> *See also* offset deals.

Overseas Private Investment Corporation *See* U.S. International Development Cooperation Agency (4. Overseas Private Investment Corporation).

Pacific 2000 Strategy *See* Three Pillar Strategy.

Pacific Economic Cooperation Conference (PECC) *See* Pacific Economic Cooperation Group.

Pacific Economic Cooperation Group (PECG), also called Pacific Economic Cooperation Conference (PECC) and Asia-Pacific Economic Cooperation Group (APEC), is a body representing countries with international trade interests in the geographic area of the Pacific Rim, which first met in Canberra, Australia (November 6 and 7, 1989), with the aim of establishing a subregional organization on the style of the Organization for Economic Cooperation and Development.

The governments represented by the PECC comprise the six countries of the Association of Southeast Asian Nations (Brunei, Indonesia, Malaysia, the Philippines, Singapore, and Thailand), Australia, Canada, Hong Kong, Japan, New Zealand, South Korea, Taiwan, and the United States.

There are two schools of thought regarding the formation of a formal Pacific trading bloc. The first, which is supportive of it, suggests that efficient regional economic integration is best achieved (1) through formal institutions and (2) in a method akin to the measured steps taken by the European Economic Community (EEC) to integrate Europe, from the Treaty of Rome (in 1957) to the (anticipated) "EMU conclusion."

The second and opposing school suggests that the formation of an integrated Europe will likely herald a new era in protectionism characterized by "Fortress Europe," which, having a common monetary, economic, and trade policy, will have every incentive to protect itself from the competitive onslaught of a North American trading area (which suffers large and continuing trade imbalances as a consequence of its loss of global competitiveness).

On judgment, a successful outcome to the current Uruguay Round of multilateral trade negotiations (MTN), in terms of increased and enhanced trade liberalization, will forestall the need for the development of an inward-looking "Fortress Europe" or for a protectionist Pacific trading bloc.

Cf. Organization for Economic Cooperation and Development; protectionism; Japan Sea Basin.

paipu •**NW**• from the Japanese meaning "pipe," refers to the conduit, entrée, or accessibility to bureaucrats by politicians in Japan, or, more generally, the "access" any person has to someone of importance and power.
Cf. *jinmyaku* •NW•; *kone* •NW•.

palletization is the technique, used by export packers, of using wooden or metal platforms (of standardized dimensions) on which to place large numbers of individual boxes or cartons, thus consolidating a load and facilitating its handling and movement while reducing the chances of damage.

Pan-American Union *See* Organization of American States.

paper fish is the reduction in the quota of fish that were not being caught.
The quotas in question are the total allowable catches (TACs) multilaterally agreed to under the Northwest Atlantic Fisheries Organization (NAFO).
See also Northwest Atlantic Fisheries Organization.

paper gold *See* Special Drawing Right (SDR).

parallel exporting (parallel importing, parallel trading) refers to international commerce in goods by traders who are outside of the official channels but whose operations are entirely legal.

> **Example:** Seeking mass distribution, a Japanese manufacturer established an official U.S. distributor in Los Angeles, California, authorized to import electronic home-entertainment units direct from Japan.
> However, an American entrepreneur in San Diego, California, was able to strike a deal with the Mexican-Japanese joint venture operation in Tijuana, Mexico, where the Japanese firm has a *maquiladora* operation. His parallel operation imported from Mexico units identical to those brought in by the authorized U.S. distributor, but at a 40 percent discount. The goods were distributed through discount stereo stores. As an "unauthorized distributor," the San Diego firm could not warranty the units, but it could afford to sell parallel service contracts, which it did.
> When an increasing number of complaints reached Japan about "substandard service," the authorized U.S. distributor was persuaded to purchase the service contracts of his parallel competitor to ensure that service was carried out according to the Japanese manufacturer's specifications. It was, in truth, an investment in the long-term retention of his contract as official U.S. distributor of the products.

parent company is a company that is engaged in trade with and investment in foreign countries and that owns at least one commercial entity located there, called a foreign subsidiary.

Paris Charter for a New Europe is a multilateral treaty signed in Paris, France, on November 22, 1990, by all the members of the Conference on Security and Cooperation in Europe (CSCE), who committed themselves to a new declaration of human rights for Europe and a final end to the solution of problems via military means.

The signing of the Charter occurred two days after Warsaw Pact and NATO members of the CSCE signed treaties ending the Cold War.

Cf. North Atlantic Treaty Organization.

See also Warsaw Pact; Conference on Security and Cooperation in Europe.

Paris Club is an informal forum where debtor countries meet with representatives of creditor governments, the objective being to negotiate possible debt relief on loans from the creditor governments and on export credits insured or guaranteed by Berne Union agencies of creditor governments.

The Paris Club was formed in 1956, and it meets regularly to negotiate multiyear rescheduling agreements (MYRAs) with debtor countries. From 1983 to 1986, there were 16 meetings. In the 1989 to 1990 period, there were 19 meetings.

The members being Western banks, one might expect that the Club acts in coordination with International Monetary Fund (IMF) initiatives to provide extended lending facilities and to promote structural adjustment in the debtor countries.

Cf. Berne Union; International Monetary Fund.

See also debt rescheduling.

Paris Convention (for the Protection of Industrial Property) is an international agreement among 96 countries whereby the signatories agreed to recognize minimum standards for the protection of specific intellectual property (i.e., patents, industrial designs, and trademarks).

The Convention was signed in 1883, and WIPO performs the administrative functions for the signatories under the Convention.

See also World Intellectual Property Organization.

Paris Pact *See* Louvre Accord.

Parkinson's Law is the observation that "work expands to fill the time available"; it is named after the English sociologist C. Northcote Parkinson.

par value is the official (i.e., government-set) rate of exchange between any of the following:

1. two national currencies;
2. a currency and a specific weight of gold; and
3. a currency and a basket of currencies.

Cf. mint parity.

See also Appendix II.

Patent Cooperation Treaty (PCT) is an international agreement among 49 states, signed in 1970, under the auspices of the World Intellectual Property Organization (WIPO), in Geneva, Switzerland. Signatories to the PCT are as follows: 16 countries in Africa, 5 in the Americas, 6 in Asia and the Pacific region, and 22 in Europe.

The PCT affords each of its 49 members a system whereby a single patent application filed in any of the signatory states affords the successful applicant protection in every other signatory state. (Since October 3, 1990, the PCT has had effect in the former German Democratic Republic as a result of its unification with (former) West Germany.)

Each international PCT application undergoes an "international search" by a national patent office that acts as an International Searching Authority (ISA). Should the applicant require an "international preliminary examination report" to determine whether the claim fulfills the main patentability criteria, the national ISAs act as International Preliminary Examining Authorities (IPEAs). Using the PCT, the ISA and IPEA require the patent claimant to pay only national costs to the applicant's national patent office. It is only when applicants seek patent protection in countries outside their own that they have to pay foreign patent office fees, translation costs, and patent attorney fees.

The PCT names certain "international authorities" to act as IPEAs. These are: (1) Australian Patent Office; (2) Austrian Patent Office; (3) European Patent Office; (4) Japanese Patent Office; (5) Royal Patent & Registration Office (Sweden); (6) United Kingdom Patent Office; (7) the USSR State Committee for Inventions and Discoveries; and (8) the United States Patent and Trademark Office.

In 1990, WIPO's International Bureau with headquarters in Geneva, Switzerland, in cooperation with the European Patent Office, started the production of CD-ROMs, each containing the full text and drawings of 500 published international applications, including the supporting bibliographic data in coded, "machine searchable" form.

Example: On October 2, 1989, Canada became the forty-third country that deposited its instrument of ratification to the PCT. Thus, on January 2, 1990, Canada became the PCT's forty-third contracting party, and, as of that date, Canadian nationals became entitled to file international applications (under the PCT).

See also World Intellectual Property Organization.

payee is the party who is the beneficiary of an export transaction involving the honoring of a draft.

The payee may be the exporter or the drawer (i.e., originator) of the draft; it may also be the exporter's bank or another bearer (i.e., holder) of the draft upon its maturity.

Cf. drawer.

payer is the party who is responsible for honoring a draft at the date of its maturity.

This is usually the importer, the party against whom the draft was drawn, but it may be the importer's bank if the importer defaults and its bank issued an irrevocable letter of credit guaranteeing payment.

Cf. drawee.

payment in advance, also known as *advance payment*, is a means of export financing whereby the importer sends full payment to the exporter (either in one full payment or in a series of payments) prior to receipt of the goods.

　　See also export financing.

payoffs *See* bribery.

perestroika, from the Russian meaning "re-structuring," is the purposeful plan to modernize the Soviet economy by a systematic replacement of the command economy with market-driven, decentralized, entrepreneurial initiatives.

　　The aim is to try to generate and distribute more wealth by stimulating local economic initiatives under central political control.

　　This "staged" (i.e., phased-in) democratization of the Soviet political-economy was initiated by, and is under the political direction, of Mikhail Gorbachev, Chairman of the Communist Party of the Soviet Union (CPSU) and (the first) Executive President of the USSR.

　　Cf. market economy.

　　See also glasnost •NW•; command economy.

Performance Security Guarantees (PSGs) is a program of the Export Development Corporation (EDC) whereby the EDC "covers" (i.e., protects) a bank or other financial institution against a "call of security," usually in the form of a documentary credit, issued to a foreign buyer on behalf of a (Canadian) exporter.

　　See also Export Development Corporation; export financing.

Performance Security Insurance (PSI) is an insurance program of the Export Development Corporation (EDC) that provides Canadian exporters with "cover" (i.e., protection) against a wrongful call by a foreign buyer of a documentary credit, usually an irrevocable letter of credit, provided by the importer's bank to the benefit of the exporter.

　　See also documentary credit; Export Development Corporation.

peril-point provisions refers to a stipulation in U.S. legislation that forbids the president from negotiating any reduction in U.S. tariffs that might possibly be a cause of injury to U.S. domestic industry.

　　See also injury.

persistent dumping is the ongoing inclination or tendency of profit-seeking enterprises resident in one country to export goods for sale in another country at below the normal market price of the goods in the domestic market of the exporter.

　　See also dumping; predatory dumping; sporadic dumping; antidumping duty.

Peter Principle is the observation that "in a hierarchy, every employee tends to rise to his or her level of incompetence"; it is named after the Canadian psychologist and Professor of Education Laurence J. Peter.

phasing *See* transitional measures.

physical distribution (PD), also known as *physical distribution/logistics (PD/L)*, refers to all the activities (excluding production) in the effective and efficient movement of goods from the point of supply (i.e., the exporter) to the point of demand (i.e., the importer).

The core PD activities are (1) transportation, (2) inventory management, and (3) order entry and processing.

Plaza Accord is an international agreement, signed in 1985, among members of the Group of Five (G-5), which called for coordinated action to "bring down the (exchange) value of the U.S. dollar."

The eponym derives from the Plaza Hotel in New York City where the agreement was reached.

plc (PLC) •NW• is the abbreviation of private limited company, used in the U.K. instead of *Inc.*, the abbreviation for *incorporated company*, or *Ltd.*, the abbreviation for *limited company*.

Cf. AG.

policy coordination, also called *economic policy coordination* and the *G-7 process*, refers to the coordination of decision making among the Group of Seven (G-7) that yields improved national policies (for each of the G-7 members) in recognition of their international economic interdependence.

Policy coordination consists of the following:

1. *Meetings of the G-7 Officials:* these occur three times a year: once yearly on their own and then twice in conjunction with meetings of the International Monetary Fund Interim Committee of the Board of Governors and the World Bank-IMF Development Committee.
2. *Meetings of the G-7 Treasury Deputies:* these are held frequently and are tied in with regularly scheduled meetings (e.g., the Paris Club, the Organization for Economic Cooperation and Development).

There have been suggestions to strengthen the process of policy coordination among the G-7 members. Serious proposals have included the following:

1. creating a permanent secretariat (in the same way that the original meetings of the General Agreement on Tariffs and Trade (GATT) gave way to the creation of a GATT Secretariat permanently based in Geneva);
2. including central bankers in the meetings in preministerial discussion and/or in the ministerial coordination sessions themselves; and
3. reducing the number of G-7 participants by having the United Kingdom, France, Germany, and Italy represented by one set of negotiators at some stage along the path to European economic-monetary union (EMU).

This last suggestion would certainly increase the efficiency of the coordination process; but it would de facto change the G-7 into a G-4. To complete the rationalization, Canada thus should, at some stage in its coming EMU with the United States, merge its negotiating interests with its stronger partner, and, assuming that the North American Free Trade Agreement (NAFTA) becomes a reality, Mexico should do the same. The G-7 process would thus be transformed into a G-3 process, a new policy-coordination mechanism among the Trilateral Commission members.

See also Group of Seven; Trilateral Commission; economic-monetary union; North American Free Trade Agreement.

political-economy •NW• is the concept that the rules that govern any national system of economic organization are derived from the rules that define the society's political system.

It is logically correct, therefore, always to refer to a nation's political-economy, since there is no autonomous economy that can operate independent of political rules.

political risks are uncontrollable hazards (associated with the use of, or challenge to, legitimate state authority) that jeopardize exporters being paid.
The following are the most common political risks:

1. blockage of funds (by foreign authorities);
2. obstruction of funds transfer (by foreign authorities);
3. cancellation or nonrenewal of import permits (by foreign authorities);
4. cancellation or nonrenewal of export permits (by authorities in the exporter's country);
5. war, insurrection, revolution, martial law, or state of siege (in the importer's country);
6. war between the importer's country and the exporter's country; and
7. war, insurrection, revolution, martial law, or state of siege in third-party countries through which the exported goods may have been diverted for logistical reasons (before the outbreak of the disruptions).

Cf. commercial risks.
See also Overseas Private Investment Corporation; Multilateral Investment Guarantee Agency; Export Development Corporation (4. Other Insurance Services).

political union is an agreement among sovereign states to form a trading bloc in which

1. all barriers to trade between the members will eventually be removed;
2. trade policies among the members will be harmonized toward the rest of the world;
3. the movement among members of labor and capital will be free (i.e., without impediment);
4. the monetary, fiscal, and tax policies of members will be harmonized; and
5. supranational ("bloc-wide") institutions will have authority to manage the implementation of trade policies and activities on a comprehensive basis.

Cf. economic union; common market; free trade area; customs union.

polycentrism (polycentric), from the Greek *polloi* meaning "many" and *kentrikos* meaning "center," is a commercial orientation toward individual markets within a country or toward individual country markets within a region, excluding regional commonalities between the markets.

> *See also* EPRG [framework].

post-industrial society is a political-economy that has moved from "manufacturing-centered" to "information-centered"; and it is a society whose gross domestic product (GDP) is generated predominantly from "service-centered industries."

> In 1987, according to the General Agreement on Tariffs and Trade (GATT), 63 percent of the GDP of developed countries was generated from services, *vis-à-vis* 1970 when the figure was 55 percent. Over the same 17-year period, the percentage for (selected) developing countries rose marginally from 45 percent to 49 percent.

> Cf. developing country.
> *See also* developed country.

pound, from the Latin *libra* meaning "pound," (1) when called the *pound sterling*, is the currency of the United Kingdom, issued by the Bank of England, represented by the "£" symbol and abbreviated (by the ISO) as GBP; and (2) when used for other jurisdictions, is the currency of them (e.g., Scottish pound, Egyptian pound, Israeli pound), by virtue of Britain's historical relationship of either colonial domination of, or significant influence over, the named country.

> *See also* currency area.

pourboire See bribery.

predatory dumping is the tactic of temporarily selling exported goods in another country below the normal market price of the goods in the exporter's market, with the aim of driving local producers (and often foreign competitors) out of the market.

> Having successfully achieved the goal, prices of the goods are raised by the export-predator who seeks to take maximum advantage of its newly acquired monopoly position.

> **Example:** The European manufacturer of pharmaceuticals used its Miami-based operation to dump antibiotics and analgesics into the Caribbean Basin, penetrating the market and, thus, making traditional American exports prohibitively expensive. In consequence, joint ventures were set up throughout the region, giving monopoly control to foreign-controlled companies that could charge higher prices because of their newly protected status—protected by government, that is, which was the minority joint venturer.

> *See also* dumping; persistent dumping; sporadic dumping; antidumping duty.

predatory pricing is the marketing tactic whereby a company offers its goods or services in the market at prices sufficiently low to drive competitors out of business and to deter market entry by new competitors.

In Canada and the United States, this tactic is adjudged to be an illegal restraint of trade under national legislation.

Cf. less than fair value.

See also monopoly.

preferences are trade concessions granted bilaterally or multilaterally.

Historically, they have been extended by developed countries to developing countries.

Cf. reverse preferences.

See also generalized system of preferences.

preferential trade area (PTA) is a relatively loose type of economic integration whereby lower tariffs are established among members of the international agreement, association, or system *vis-à-vis* nonmembers.

Cf. Preferential Trade Area (PTA) for Eastern and Southern African States.

See also Commonwealth.

Preferential Trade Area (PTA) for Eastern and Southern African States is the successor to the East African Economic Community, which dissolved in 1978; it was formed in 1982 and consists of 15 member countries in East and Southern Africa: Burundi, Comoros, Djibouti, Ethiopia, Kenya, Lesotho, Malawi, Mauritius, Rwanda, Somalia, Swaziland, Tanzania, Uganda, Zambia, and Zimbabwe.

There are five other potential regional members: Angola, Botswana, Madagascar, Mozambique, and the Seychelles.

The PTA has its Secretariat in Lusaka, Zambia, and its bank (which began operations in 1966) is in Bujumbura, Burundi. The PTA Bank is officially called the Eastern and Southern African Trade and Development Bank. It is a "subregional development bank," subordinate to, but strongly supported by, the African Development Bank (ADB), an executing agency of the United Nations Development Program (UNDP). The Bank's financial unit of account is the UAPTA (1 UAPTA = 1 SDR). A PTA "clearing house" was established on February 1, 1984.

The goal of the PTA is to increase trade liberalization (and, consequently, to increase trade) among its members, working within the framework of the United Nations System and its regional development agencies, such as the United Nations Economic Commission for Africa (UN/ECA). To this end, the PTA countries are gradually removing all tariffs and nontariff barriers on intra-PTA trade. As of October 1, 1988, the PTA reduced tariffs by 10 percent, and will continue to do so until it reaches zero tariffs. The process will take from 10 to 15 years, and it will be reviewed to accelerate it or slow it down.

See also Appendix V (A).

preferential trade arrangement *See* preferential trade area.

preferential trade scheme *See* preferential trade area.

preferential trade system *See* preferential trade area.

preferential treatment refers to special tariff reductions provided by treaty members of a preferential trade area.
See also Appendix VI (friendship, commerce, and navigation treaty).

pre-industrial society *See Gemeinschaft*.

Presner's Principle is the observation that within any trading relationship, "no marketing functions can be eliminated, but are simply shifted between channel members;" it is named after the Canadian Professor of Marketing Lewis A. Presner.

price discrimination is the practice whereby some sellers of goods and services (unfairly) charge higher prices to some buyers than others, and the price differentials cannot be attributed to such rational factors as quantity discounts or transportation costs.
Competition laws within Canada and the United States make some types of domestic price discrimination illegal. In international trade, price discrimination is (at a minimum) considered a nontariff barrier (NTB) when a national government has procurement policies that favor national companies *vis-à-vis* foreign companies, even when the foreign suppliers' prices are lower than the national competitors'.
Cf. *keiretsu*.
See also Agreement on Government Procurement; nontariff barriers; protectionist trading practices.

price escalation is a blanket expression used by global marketers to describe the significant increase in price that results when costly exporting functions, such as packaging, consolidation, de-consolidation, transshipment, handling, and insurance, are added to a "basic domestic free on board (FOB) price."
Global marketers who specialize in ways and means to keep price escalation as low as possible (in a competitive market situation) are called *channel managers*.

price-specie *See* gold standard.

price-specie flow mechanism, under the gold standard, was a process whereby there was an "automatic adjustment" in a country's balance of payments.
When a country was in a deficit position, the "mechanism" worked as follows:

1. A country in a deficit trade position lost gold and thus experienced a physical reduction in its money supply.
2. This event caused domestic marketers to reduce domestic prices.
3. This, in turn, stimulated the country's exporters, and, because of low domestic prices, there was little incentive to import expensive goods.
4. The process continued until an equilibrium was established, and the deficit was eliminated.

When a country experienced a balance-of-payments surplus, the "automatic adjustment" worked in this way:

1. A country in a surplus trade position gained gold and thus experienced a physical increase in its money supply.
2. This event caused domestic marketers to increase domestic prices.
3. This, in turn, curbed demand for the country's exports, and, because of high domestic prices, there was much incentive to import cheap goods.
4. The process continued until an equilibrium was established, and the surplus was eliminated.

Cf. gold standard.

price suppression, also called *price repression*, is the forced lowering of domestic prices when imported goods (competing with them) are sold at comparatively lower prices than the domestically produced goods.

> **Example:** When American companies petition the United States International Trade Commission (USITC) claiming injury and demanding that countervailing duties be levied on imported goods, the Americans provide evidence of dumping by showing the decline in their sales (with audited sales records). The American companies attribute the decline to price suppression that they claim they were forced to adopt in order to compete with imported goods that, they claim, were sold at "less than fair value" (i.e., at "dumped" prices).

A direct causal relationship is difficult to draw in every case, especially where industry growth may, for indeterminate reasons, have declined. For example, it may simply be that domestic American producers were offering their products at prices higher than the U.S. market would bear, and that they only discovered this when less costly imports forced them into price suppression. Ironically, more of both domestic and imported goods will now be sold given the "law of downward-sloping demand" (i.e., the lower the offered price for a good, the more of it will be demanded). However, some ethnocentric marketers use "nonprice competition" tools (e.g., "buy American" promotion campaigns) to increase their competitive advantage.

Cf. underselling.
See also buy national.

Principle of Professional Development (PPD) is the sociological explanation of the famous Peter Principle, that is, why people in a hierarchy tend to rise to their level of incompetence.

The Principle of Professional Development states that upward mobility in a hierarchy is less influenced by objective evaluation of the merits of office holders than by assessment of their behavior by their superiors, in passively obeying and in actively complying with "top-down" decisions.

Cf. *nemawashi* •NW•; "Always Say Yes" •NW•.
See also Peter Principle.

principles of international trade (PIT) refers to the four fundamental ideas that are the bases for international trade and that are accepted by the world's trading nations that are Contracting Parties to, and signatories of, the General Agreement on Tariffs and Trade (GATT).

See also General Agreement on Tariffs and Trade.

priority foreign country (PFC) is a country, determined by the U.S. Trade Representative (USTR), to have engaged in "unfair trading acts, policies, and practices."

Aside from those unfair acts designated priority practices, other unfair trading activities comprise the following:

1. denying "adequate and effective protection" of U.S. intellectual property rights,
2. denying "fair and equitable market access to U.S. citizens that rely on intellectual property protection," and
3. not entering into trade negotiations with the United States "in good faith."

Countries designated as PFCs can be the object of action under the U.S. Omnibus Trade Act of 1988.

See also priority practices; Super 301.

priority practices are high-level, unfair trading acts, policies, and practices, by virtue of the fact that they are major barriers and trade-distorting practices, the elimination of which is likely to have the most significant potential to increase United States exports either directly or through the establishment of beneficial precedents.

The "priority practice" designation is made by the U.S. government under the authority of the Omnibus Trade Act of 1988, Subtitle C, Part 1, Section 310(a)(1)(A).

See also priority foreign country; Super 301.

Private Sector Development Program (PSDP) is a new market-driven initiative of the Inter-American Development Bank (IDB) aimed at providing Latin American countries with financial incentives to privatize their economies, thus reducing the market distortions caused by undue state involvement in the local economies.

This new program seeks to consolidate resources from the IDB, the Inter-American Investment Corporation (the IDB's affiliate), and the International Monetary Fund in an effort to liberalize trade regionally, with a Western Hemispheric "mega-market," as envisioned by U.S. president George Bush under his Enterprise for the Americas Initiative, as the goal.

Cf. Caribbean Basin Economic Recovery Act; dependent development; North American Free Trade Agreement.

See also Inter-American Development Bank; Inter-American Investment Corporation; Enterprise for the Americas Initiative.

privatization is the process of purposeful denationalization (i.e., sale to the private sector) of state-owned companies.

The Canadian federal government passed legislation to provide Canadians with an opportunity to share directly in the ownership of the crown corporation Petro-Canada. Privatization will begin with an initial offering of Petro-Canada shares to the public on a date yet to be determined. No individual will be allowed to own more than 10 percent of the total value of the company. Foreign ownership will be limited to 25 percent of the shares issued.

Cf. nationalization.
See also Code of Liberalization of Capital Movements.

production effect of a tariff is the increase in domestic production of a good as a result of its increase in price due to a protective tariff.

Cf. consumption effect of a tariff; trade effect of a tariff.

production sharing is the international marketing concept whereby independent companies in different countries agree to cooperate in the manufacture, handling, and assembly of goods. Legal arrangements may comprise subcontracting (between independent private companies), licensing, and joint ventures with state-owned enterprises in nonmarket economies.

American international traders use production sharing to take advantage of special tariff treatment afforded them (1) under certain sections of the Harmonized Tariff Schedule of the United States (HTS) and (2) under the Generalized System of Preferences (GSP). For example, U.S. firms can ship goods to a Mexican *maquiladora* operation, have them finished (at low labor costs and overhead), and have the goods re-enter the United States either duty free under the GSP or at preferential HTS rates.

In the European Economic Community (EEC), production sharing is called *outward processing*, and agreements under it are referred to as *outward processing relief arrangements*.

Outward processing arrangements with Yugoslavia, Hungary, and Poland account for more than 70 percent of Germany's textile and apparel imports. The move of the Soviet Union (however haltingly) toward a market economy will encourage all EEC members to develop outward processing contracts with it. Regarding the economies of East Europe, the EEC will likely increase its production-sharing arrangements there as these economies face increasing competitive pressures from the integrating EEC internal market and from the rapidly disintegrating Council for Mutual Economic Assistance (CMEA).

See also joint venture; licensing.

product life cycle (PLC), a variation of the *product life cycle model* and the *international product life cycle*, is the idea that all capital intensive products originating in industrial countries will, over time, become relatively standardized and can be manufactured more cheaply in other countries with relatively larger supplies of unskilled labor.

The basis of this hypothesis is the analysis of national differentials in production factors between countries and the observation of the "time lag" involved in the "diffusion of innovation" process, that is, how much time elapses between (1) the original commercialization of a product in industrialized country X and (2) its re-introduction as a cheaper product into industrialized country X. Between (1) and (2), the product is introduced into developing country Y (with highly unskilled labor), adopted there, and then produced in differentiated and cheaper forms.

The implication of this idea for global marketers involves understanding the process of industrialization itself: countries (where rapid development via industrial training reduces the variable cost of labor) have an available supply of low-cost labor in the short run, something essential for serious global production. In the longer run, these same countries, while being newly developed global competitors, drive up their domestic-consumer expectations and, thus, represent newly developed export target markets.

See also newly industrialized countries; large scale industrial transfer.

product shifting, also called *production shifting*, is the switch from the production and export of one good to the production and export of another.

Exporters who readily product shift do so because the shift does not involve costly alternations in production.

> **Example:** In the famous 1989–1991 United States-Canada countervailing duty "pork war," United States International Trade Commissioner Eckes observed (in the USITC's final determination) that the imposition of a countervailing duty on Canadian swine but not on pork created an "extraordinary incentive" for Canadian pork producers to shift from the production and export of live swine to the production and export of fresh, chilled, or frozen pork. One might infer that where efficient producers compete with inefficient ones, even the entirely legal use of countervailing duties may be ineffective to protect the former from "injury" caused by genuinely cheaper imported goods.

A strategic export lesson can be learned from this: once markets open to foreign imports (as the United States, via the Strategic Impediments Initiative, is trying to "open Japan"), the more cost efficient American producers and exporters will become and the more flexible they will be to use product shifting to beat the threat, or actual imposition, of Japanese countervailing duties.

Cf. underselling.

pro forma is a Latin term meaning "for form's sake."
See pro forma invoice.

pro forma invoice, sometimes called a *pro forma set* or a *pro bill set*, is a documentary demand for payment sent to a buyer by a seller in advance of the physical shipment of the goods to permit the buyer to complete some required formalities in the transaction.

> **Example:** In international business, a foreign customer who receives a pro forma invoice may be requested to notify the central bank of the specific cost of goods due to the imported and to apply for the required currency-control documents in order to secure the convertible currency to pay for the goods.

Program for Export Market Development (PEMD) *See* export support programs (1).

prohibitive tariff, also called an *exclusionary tariff*, is (1) a tax on goods imported into a country, the volume of which exceeds a "permitted level" of imports; and (2) a duty high enough to lessen, reduce, and ultimately stop all international trade in the imported commodity subject to the duty.

> **Example:** The U.S. Department of Agriculture (USDA) and U.S. sugar cane and sugar beet growers are concerned that the U.S. sugar industry may not survive worldwide liberalization of the sugar trade. However, the USDA has reassured the industry that it would protect sugar through a tariff rate quota. Such a quota would permit imports of sugar to meet the normal needs of the United States, with a prohibitive tariff on imports above that amount.

> **Example:** To protect national industries, the U.S. government may raise tariffs so high on electronic components imported from the Pacific Rim that it will drive Asian exporters to the edge of bankruptcy—and ultimately to the negotiating table, which would be, of course, the purpose of the exercise.

Cf. optimum tariff.
See also duty.

protected markets refers to buyers and sellers who are sheltered from market disruption by the use of voluntary export restraints (VERs) invoked by exporters of goods to these markets.
> *See also* restrained exporters; voluntary export restraint; market disruption.

protection cost of a tariff, also called the *deadweight loss of a tariff*, is the economic loss of productive efficiency and the distortions in consumption resulting from the effects of tariff protection of inefficient industries.
Cf. infant industry argument.

protectionism is a government policy to restrain, restrict, or diminish trade (that is, imports) bi- or multilaterally by the direct use of tariffs or nontariff barriers for the purpose of shielding allegedly inefficient domestic producers from competition.

> **Example:** Given the near-universal availability of modern production technology, the task of the General Agreement on Tariffs and Trade (GATT) to liberalize trade becomes increasingly difficult. As developing countries produce more and more goods at cheaper and cheaper prices, "stealthy protectionism" (e.g., the use of nontariff barriers) comes to be perceived as a genuinely legitimate means for members of the Organization for Economic Cooperation and Development (such as Canada, the United States, and the European Economic Community) to defend their industrial positions.

> **Example:** The U.S. Agricultural Adjustment Act (AAA) of 1933 protects U.S. farmers by virtually banning (by the use of quotas) imports of raw peanuts and prohibits farmers from expanding sales. This protectionist system, erected in the name of "agricultural self-sufficiency," forces American consumers to pay prices at least 50 percent above world levels, and these protectionist practices enrich a few "Depression farmers" who purchased their production licenses during the 1930s.

To end this protectionist system, the president should suspend the import quotas. This would have at least four immediate, positive third-party effects:

1. it would help poor farmers in Third World countries (especially in Africa) earn decent wages;
2. it would help U.S. consumers reduce their artificially high cost of living;
3. it would send a strong signal to Japan regarding U.S. expectations about Japan's internal rice market; and
4. it would restore peanut butter (dropped by the United States Department of Agriculture from the Federal government's school lunch program) to the lunches of American school children.

See also General Agreement on Tariffs and Trade; liberalization.

protectionist business practices *See* protectionist trading practices.

protectionist trading practices (PTPs), also called *protectionist business practices*, *restrictive business practices*, and *restrictive trading practices*, are the actions of countries that aim to restrict trade.
Cf. *keiretsu*.
See also protectionism; Smoot-Hawley Tariff Act of 1930.

PTA is the abbreviation for **preferential trade area**.

PTA Bank *See* Eastern and Southern African Trade and Development Bank.

Puerto Rican Model •NW• refers to the U.S. strategy of modernizing a small, one-crop economy in Latin America and the Caribbean, as illustrated by the Commonwealth of Puerto Rico.
The "model" is comprised of several components: duty free access to the United States, cheap local labor, and tax incentives (e.g., exemptions on sales and profits) for U.S. companies to relocate a manufacturing unit in the country.
This strategy is the basis of the Caribbean Basin Initiative (CBI).
See also Caribbean Basin Initiative; Foreign Sales Corporation.

punitive duty is an alternative term for *countervailing duty*.
See countervailing duty; duty.

punitive tariff *See* antidumping duty; duty.

purchase of drawings under a documentary credit is a means of export financing whereby the exporter sells a draft drawn against a term documentary credit of which it is the ultimate beneficiary.
The exporter "draws a draft" on the issuing bank under a term credit. The exporter's bank will purchase the draft usually at a discount, depending on an assessment of the degree of credit worthiness of the issuing bank, the length of time until the drafts mature, and the degree of commercial and political risk that may jeopardize payment.

This method of financing exports has been called discounting of drawings under a letter of credit, purchasing of trade acceptances, and discounting of accepted bills of exchange.

Alternately, the exporter can use the term draft to establish a line of credit with his bank, against which he can draw, using the term draft as collateral.

See also export financing; purchase of invoice acceptances; foreign accounts-receivable purchases.

purchasing power parity theory (PPP theory) is a method, popular in the school of economic monetarism, that is used by economists to estimate the "equilibrium exchange rate" when a country is in a state of disequilibrium in terms of its balance of payments.

Cf. relative purchasing power parity theory.

See also monetarism.

Q

Quad, the abbreviation for The **Quad**rilateral Trade Ministers, is a group of four politicians, each of whom holds a cabinet office responsible for international trade within his or her own political jurisdiction and represents the international trade interests of an international trade sector.

The Quad comprises the following:

1. *Canadian Minister of International Trade*, who represents Canada and is a conduit for the interests of the Caribbean and Latin America;
2. *U.S. Trade Representative (USTR)*, who represents the United States, its territories, and dependencies;
3. *Japan's Minister of International Trade and Industry (MITI)*, who speaks for Japan and (arguably) for those political-economies well integrated with Japan's in Asia; and
4. *European (Economic) Community's (EEC) Commissioner for External Relations*, who is responsible for the EEC, including those African, Caribbean, and Pacific (ACP) countries involved with the EEC via the Lomé Convention.

Canada earned the voice of legitimate representation of the Caribbean and Latin American countries by having historically distanced itself from networks of alliances with the United States, such as the Rio Treaty, and the OAS, and, thereby, being perceived by the smaller nations of the Western Hemisphere as a traditional political counterweight to the United States. Canada's application to the OAS (in November 1989) was interpreted in this light.

---

quadrilateral trade refers to transactions among four nations.

Cf. bilateral trade; trilateral trade; multilateral trade.

quadrilateral trade agreement is a formal exchange accord among four nations.
Cf. bilateral trade agreement; trilateral trade agreement.
See also multilateral trade agreement.

quantitative export restraints (QERs) *See* voluntary restraint agreements (VRAs).

quantity restrictions (QRs), also known as *export quotas* or *import quotas*, or simply as *quotas*, are limits on the physical amounts of goods that may be exported or imported.
Under the theory of trade liberalization upon which the General Agreement on Tariffs and Trade (GATT) was founded, all QRs are prohibited, except under specific circumstances. For example, Article XIX of the GATT permits QRs to be used to protect against injury that may result from rapidly rising imports; and Articles XII and XVIII provide for the use of QRs by countries in cases where severe balance of payments difficulties warrant.
Cf. import quotas.
See also export quotas; General Agreement on Tariffs and Trade.

quasi-judicial procedures are ways by which departments, agencies, and tribunals involved in regulatory trade functions make law (in a common law system such as Canada or the United States).
For example, were the U.S. Department of Commerce or the U.S. International Trade Commission (USITC) to levy a countervailing duty against a specific Canadian product, the process whereby the ruling was made and implemented would be under the judicial authority granted by general U.S. trade law and applied to a specific case.

> **Example:** On May 2, 1989, the U.S. Department of Commerce imposed a preliminary countervailing duty of U.S. $3^{1}/_{2}$¢ per pound on Canadian pork exports. As early as March 1985, the United States imposed a preliminary countervailing duty on Canadian live hog and pork exports. But one month later, the duty on pork exports was lifted, while the one on live hogs was retained. Encouraged by certain provisions included in the U.S. Omnibus Trade Act of 1988, U.S. hog producers renewed their petition in 1989. Hearings on the matter were held in the U.S. House of Representatives Agriculture Subcommittee in Iowa, as well as in Washington, D.C.

Cf. United States International Trade Commission.

quota *See* quantity restrictions.

r

rate of effective protection *See* effective rate of protection.

reciprocity, also known as *equivalence of advantages*, *balance of concessions*, and *mutuality of benefits*, is the mutual extension of identical or similar trade benefits or concessions between trading countries.

Depending on the viewpoint of different countries that are parties to trade negotiations, reciprocity is perceived as having various interpretations as follows:

1. *Overall Reciprocity:* the General Agreement on Tariffs and Trade perception of the mutual and equivalent provision of concessions by countries.
2. *Sectoral Reciprocity:* the mutual extension of trade benefits on a sector-for-sector basis (e.g., the reciprocal trade in the automotive, clothing, or chemical sectors of two economies).
3. *National Treatment:* (sometimes called *equivalent treatment*) the extension of laws and regulations governing the marketing of domestic goods in countries that signed a trade treaty to goods designated as "foreign" and "imported" (i.e., originating in the other signatory country).
4. *National Treatment with Effective Access or with Effective Market Access:* the extension of national treatment by country A to country B, contingent on country B permitting the entry of country A's goods into it.
5. *Identical Reciprocity:* the extension of restricted, "legalistic national treatment" (i) that permits foreign firms (in country A) to do only those things that are permitted to their counterpart firms (in country B) and (ii) that prevents foreign firms (in country A) from doing anything beyond that which specifically delimits the behavior of their counterpart firms (in country B).
6. *Equivalent Market Access:* (also called *mirror-image reciprocity*, *comparable effective market access*, and *mutual recognition*) the mutual ac-

knowledgment by trading partners (especially in the European Economic Community (EEC) of 1992) that foreign firms may operate in each other's countries based on their acceptance of the fact that their different regulatory systems (which govern the activity of foreign firms in domestic markets) apply the same essential standards in different ways.

From the EEC viewpoint, mutual recognition would be afforded to all EEC members, but not to non-EEC states importing into the community.

In practice, what reciprocity may mean after 1992 when the Single European Market has been achieved is that no trading partner (not hitherto established in the EEC) can expect anything approaching national treatment unless it permits equivalent access to its market by each of the 12 EEC members!

Thus, there would seem adequate incentive for U.S. and Canadian firms to strategically position for exporting into EEC-based subsidiaries or for joint venture manufacturing within the EEC itself, lest they be shut out because of the reciprocal recognition regulations.

Example: A type of reciprocal deal might be perceived to have occurred if Japan were to eliminate its tariffs that protect inefficient local food producers—thus permitting the United States to enter the Japanese market—in exchange for a U.S. undertaking to in no way hinder Japanese development and penetration of the European Economic Community with Japanese supercomputer products.

reduced debt servicing is a debt-reduction technique whereby banks that are unwilling to provide new money to indebted creditor countries are invited to exchange their claims (to repayment of financial obligations) for bonds exempt from future debt-reduction measures.

As of 1989, this technique for reducing the burden of external debt is entirely theoretical: no member of the Paris Club has exercised this option.

Cf. debt servicing.
See also debt-reduction techniques; Paris Club.

reference zone *See* managed float.

regiocentrism (regiocentric), from the Latin *regio* meaning "district" and the Greek *kentrikos* meaning "center," is a commercial orientation toward regions (i.e., groups of individual countries united into "district markets") *vis-à-vis* individual, disunited country markets.
See also EPRG [framework].

Regional Cooperation for Development (RCD) is a regional international organization, established in 1964, to develop and promote technical cooperation and economic advancement (presumably leading toward trade liberalization and increasing integration of the members' political-economic systems).

The organization has its headquarters in Tehran, Iran, and it comprises Iran, Pakistan, and Turkey.

While all RCD members belong to the Organization of the Islamic Conference (which is an integrating influence), there are some remarkable political differences between them. These are significant enough, at least in the short run, to preclude any possibility that their economies will become well integrated without some prior or concurrent changes in their political systems.

For example, the post-revolutionary Shi'a government of the Islamic Republic of Iran re-adopted the Shari'ah after overthrowing the Palavi regime in 1979. The Islamic Republic of Pakistan on its part re-adopted Islamic Law in 1986 but radically broke with Islamic tradition in electing the world's first Islamic woman prime minister in 1988.

The Islamic Republic of Turkey, on the other hand, abandoned the Shari'ah entirely in 1926 (in favor of entirely secular British common law and Swiss Family Law).

Cf. Organization of the Islamic Conference.

regional development banks (RDBs) *See* multilateral development banks (MDBs).

regional development programs refer to arrangements between the Canadian Federal Government and the Canadian provincial governments, that may comprise some (or all) of the following:

1. the remittance of transfer payments, or "equalization payments," from the Federal Government to "have-not" provinces to raise the incomes of the poorer regions of the country;
2. the establishment of provincial or regional "development agencies" through which
    i.   Federal loans and grants can be made to sustain local industries (at concessional rates of interest),
    ii. applicants can secure needed training and skills development,
    iii. trained and skilled workers can find employment,
    iv. entrepreneurs can secure low-cost financing (at concessional rates of interest) for new businesses, and
    v.   foreign (either out-of-country or out-of-province) investors can be attracted to invest in new or existing businesses having some of the costs (such as training workers, securing serviced land, and installing infrastructure elements) subsidized by the "development agency."

Example: According to the Minister of International Trade, no instrument of Federal policy is more important to this process (in Atlantic Canada) than the Atlantic Canada Opportunities Agency (ACOA). ACOA is about helping business people identify new opportunities, improve productivity, exploit new technology, develop new markets, and create new jobs. ACOA has already out-performed all previous regional economic development schemes, and then some.

To October 1989, Agency officials have fielded more than 68,000 inquiries, received 13,000 applications, approved 6,100 projects, committed $600 million and leveraged $1.7 billion in investment from the private sector. ACOA-aided projects have created 15,000 new jobs and saved 18,000 others. Some 800 new enterprises have been opened, half of those by first-time entrepreneurs.

The Minister had the honor of leading a group of representatives from 27 Atlantic Canadian companies on a trade mission to Boston. The companies were participating in the New Exporters to Border States (NEBS) program, which provides practical information along with first-hand exposure to a nearby marketplace in a northern U.S. state. NEBS encourages Canadian firms that are not now exporting to develop markets "just across the border" as a natural extension of their home market.

In a review of the Agency activity, it was decided to place greater focus on small- and medium-sized enterprises, the kind of companies whose representatives came to Boston with the Minister and the kind of companies that must prosper for Atlantic Canada to prosper.

On judgment, it is a moot point whether Canada's regional development programs are not, in fact, programs of partial export targeting. Critics of the Canada-U.S. Free Trade Agreement (FTA) have suggested that the treaty would erode some of the "traditional elements of Canadian culture," namely, those very components of the above-cited provincial Agency that are responsible for giving Canadian Atlantic-region traders a comparative advantage over their U.S. counterparts in New England.

These critics suggest that the consequent erosion of "Canadian culture" will arise from U.S. development and use of aggressive, expansionist political instruments, such as Section 301 of the Omnibus Trade Act of 1988.

See also export targeting; Super 301.

Regional Economic Commissions *See* United Nations Regional Economic Commissions.

regional economic development programs *See* regional development programs.

regionalization of trade •NW• is a process whereby members of regional geographic groups (1) concentrate and liberalize international trade among themselves; (2) move from customs and economic integration to monetary integration and ultimately to single-market political integration; and (3) move away from liberalized trade on an open, worldwide, multilateral basis.

> **Example:** Ministers of the G-24 nations expressed their concern at regionalization of trade (particularly the Single Market in Europe in 1992) and its eventual negative implications on trade and financial relations with the developing countries.

> Cf. Canada-U.S. Free Trade Agreement of 1989; Pacific Economic Cooperation Group.
> *See also* Europe 1992.

regional trading arrangements are multilateral commerce conducted within a formal geographic framework.
> *See also* Appendix V (A).

reinvoicing (re-invoicing) is a quasi-legal device used by international corporations involving a process whereby a "domestic" (i.e., U.S., Canadian, Japanese, or European Economic Community (EEC)) company (1) imports commodities through an offshore company (established specifically for such a purpose) and then (2) dumps the profits made on the transaction in the offshore tax haven, thus boosting its apparent costs to reduce taxes on the mainland (U.S., Canadian, Japanese, or EEC) firm.

The profits made by the offshore firm can then be repatriated, sometimes in the form of "tax-free loans" from the offshore affiliates to the (U.S., Canadian, Japanese, or EEC) parent companies.

Cf. transfer pricing.

relative purchasing power parity theory is a version of the *purchasing power parity theory*, which puts forward the idea that, over time, the changes in the rate of exchange between currencies of countries (say Canada and the United States) should be proportional to the relative change in price levels between those countries.

Cf. purchasing power parity theory.

See also monetarism.

relocation allowance *See* benefit allowance.

repatriation is the return to one's country of citizenship of nationals and/or assets held in foreign countries.

reprisals *See* retaliation.

reserve currency is a variation of *foreign exchange reserves*.

See reserve currency country.

reserve currency country (RCC) (plural—**reserve currency countries (RCCs)**) is the designation of an important political-economy whose currency is held by other (less important) countries.

The RCCs are, in order of global political-economic importance: the United States, Germany, Japan, the United Kingdom, France, Canada, and Italy.

The currency of each of these countries is called a reserve currency, or a foreign exchange reserve. This refers to the fact that, together with gold, each of these currencies is highly convertible on the world market.

The RCCs are collectively called the Group of Seven (G-7). They represent the core of the Organization for Economic Cooperation and Development (OECD).

See also Organization for Economic Cooperation and Development; Group of Seven.

residual restrictions are quantitative restrictions (QRs) currently in force that were put in place by countries before their accession to the General Agreement on Tariffs and Trade (GATT) and that are, therefore, considered permissible under a grandfather clause in the GATT.

See also grandfather clause; nontariff barriers.

restrained exporters are countries that use voluntary export restraints (VERs) to impede the export of specific goods to specific markets.
See also protected markets; voluntary export restraint.

restrictive business practices *See* protectionist trading practices.

restrictive trading practices *See* protectionist trading practices.

retaliation refers to (1) counterclaims taken by a country in response to what are perceived as offensive actions of its trading partners, including the use of safeguards (in international law, such acts are called retortion); or (2) legal actions, authorized by the General Agreement on Tariffs and Trade (GATT) Council, that an "injured party" may take against an "offending party"; these actions consist of the right to impose new tariffs or to raise the rate of existing tariffs on the imported goods of a country against whom a GATT dispute settlement panel has rendered a judgment that has been accepted by the GATT Council.

Retaliation can either be legitimate, directed against the specific object of the offence, or it can be illegitimate (i.e., retortious), redirected against vulnerable targets for trade actions considered particularly offensive. In the latter case, retaliation is referred to as *reprisals*.

> **Example:** Countervailing duties levied by the United States against Canadian pork exports were perceived not as a legitimate response under the Canada-U.S. Free Trade Act of 1989, but rather as illegitimate and as harassing reprisals for alleged Canadian dumping of steel into the U.S. market.

> *See also* Appendix VI (retortion); injury; safeguards; GATT dispute settlement system.

retortion *See* Appendix VI.

revenue effect of a tariff refers to the income collected by a government that has levied a duty.
See also tariff.

reverse preferences are trade concessions granted by developing countries to developed countries.

> **Example:** Prior to the generalized system of preferences (GSP), the Lomé Convention provided a framework whereby there were reciprocal concessions between European Economic Community (EEC) members and African-, Caribbean-, and Pacific-region developing countries. The developed countries of the EEC extended duty-free access to the EEC for developing-country commodity exports. In exchange, the developing countries permitted preferential access to their markets for EEC-manufactured goods.

> Cf. preferences.
> *See also* generalized system of preferences; reciprocity; Lomé Convention.

revocable letter of credit *See* letter of credit.

revolving letter of credit *See* letter of credit.

right of establishment is a specific form of national treatment whereby foreign direct investors are accorded the same legal, quasi-judicial, and administrative rights to establish and manage enterprises (in a foreign country) as are extended to the country's citizens.

> *See also* national treatment.

***ringi* system** from the Japanese meaning the "piling-up system," is a decision-making process common in Japanese companies.

> Under the *ringi* system, the appearance of full, democratic participation in decision making is maintained as a *ringi-sho* ("circulated document") devised by low-level managers winds its way up the ladder of corporate authority. Authority is asserted by more senior managers who retard or block approval by allowing the *ringi-sho* to "pile up."

Pragmatically speaking, the *ringi* system is a control device used by management. Managers affix their seal only to documents of which they approve. Success in the *ringi* system would seem to depend on the degree to which subordinates can anticipate the needs of their superiors with *ringi-sho* that satisfy them.

As with the *nemawashi* system, a premium on compliance with superiors would appear to be rewarded, and objection to it punished. With the *ringi* system, managers can use a Japanese "carrot-and-stick" (i.e., reward-and-punishment) approach to control particularly entrepreneurial and assertive workers: management can (1) informally disclose (and promote) the identities of the initiators of "good *ringi-sho*" and can (2) subtly disparage the authors of "bad *ringi-sho*."

> Cf. *nemawashi* •NW•.

Rio Treaty, also called the *Rio Pact*, is officially the *Inter-American Treaty of Reciprocal Assistance*.

> *See* Organization of American States.

River Plate Basin System (RPBS), officially, *El Sistema de la Cuenca del Plata (SICDEP)*, is a regional international organization, formed in 1969 under the Treaty of the River Plate Basin, which was signed in Brasilia, Brazil, by Argentina, Bolivia, Brazil, Paraguay, and Uruguay.

> Headquarters of the RPBS are in Buenos Aires, Argentina. The aim of the organization, comparable to like organizations in regional areas of Africa, is to formulate commercial policies, projects, and programs for the coordinated economic development and integration of the natural resources of the River Plate Basin.

> The RPBS has close working relations with other international organizations. For example, the RPBS's Financial Fund (FONPLATA), with offices in Sucre, Bolivia, liaises with the region's development bank, the Inter-American Development Bank (IDB), and with the International Bank for Reconstruction and Development (IBRD), which is the main executing agency for the United Nations Development Program (UNDP).

> Cf. Lake Chad Basin Commission; Niger Basin Authority; Organization for the Development of the Sénégal River.

> *See also* Appendix V (B).

Rome Convention for the Protection of Performers, Producers of Phonograms, and Broadcasting Organizations, known as the *Rome Convention*, is a multilateral treaty signed by states to afford them substantial protection of intellectual property and administered by the World Intellectual Property Organization (WIPO).

    See also World Intellectual Property Organization.

RO-RO (vessel), the abbreviation for **roll-on, roll-off (vessel)**, is an ocean vessel onto which motorized trucks (called "tractors") haul wheeled "trailers" bearing cargo or cargo containers.

    The process involves "rolling on" the trailers at the port of shipment and "rolling (them) off" at the destination.

    See also container.

round of trade negotiations (RTN), also known as *multilateral trade negotiations (MTN)*, refers to meetings (past and present) of signatories to the General Agreement on Tariffs and Trade (GATT) at which there is formal bargaining on commercial subjects, with the ultimate aim of establishing an express concensus (in the form of a Multilateral Agreement) on ways and means to liberalize trade globally (i.e., reduce tariff and nontariff barriers).

    The following is a list of the RTNs completed (or in process) to date:

Inaugural Site of the RTN	*Date of the RTN*
Geneva, Switzerland	1947–1948
Annecy, France	1949
Torquay, England	1950–1951
Geneva, Switzerland	1956
Geneva, Switzerland[1]	1960–1962
Geneva, Switzerland[2]	1963–1967
Tokyo, Japan[3]	1973–1979
Montevideo, Uruguay[4]	1986–1991[5]

[1]referred to as the Dillon Round.

[2]referred to as the Kennedy Round.

[3]referred to as the Tokyo Round.

[4]referred to as the Uruguay Round.

[5]1991 is the year during which it is anticipated the Uruguay Round will be completed, and an Agreement signed by the Contracting Parties to the GATT.

    Cf. multilateral trade negotiations.

    See also General Agreement on Tariffs and Trade.

royalty (royalty payment), under a licensing agreement, is the compensation paid by the licensee to the licensor.

    See also licensing.

rules of origin are (1) regulations put in place either unilaterally, bilaterally, or multilaterally (through negotiation) to determine the source of goods being imported into a country for the purpose of ascertaining what duties (if any) are applicable, and, if applicable, what duty rate will apply; (2) regulations set out in Chapter 3 and in Annex 301.2 of the Canada-U.S. Free Trade Agreement of 1989 that assist in establishing the origin of goods for the purpose of determining what duties are to be levied, based on the Harmonized Commodity Description and Coding System (HS), adopted by Canada on January 1, 1988, and by the United States on January 1, 1989; and (3) international guidelines set out in the Kyoto Customs Convention of 1965 stating that the origination of goods (for export/import purposes) is determined not by local content levels but by the location where "the last substantial process" is performed.

In order to qualify for exemption from duties under the Free Trade Agreement (FTA) of 1989, both Canadian and U.S. exporters must conform to the basic rules of origin under the FTA: the value of materials originating in Canada and/or the United States, plus the direct cost of processing, constitute not less than 50 percent of the value of the goods when exported. Certificates of origin (attesting to this fact) must be submitted to the respective authorities.

The European Commission may be moving toward a redefinition of the rules of origin: goods will be determined to have originated in the place where "the most substantial process" occurs, regardless of when it takes place. The motivation behind this move derives from the proliferation in the European Economic Community (EEC) of what Europeans call Japanese "screwdriver industries." Europeans perceive these as having been established either to avoid dumping duties (especially in consumer electronics) or to circumvent other nontariff barriers established (by the Europeans) to restrain the direct export of Japanese automobiles.

Example: Production of semiconductors involves three main steps: (1) manufacturing the silicon wafer/disc, (2) printing the circuitry on the wafer ("diffusion"), and (3) cutting the wafer into individual chips. Until 1989, the last stage of cutting determined the origin of the product. In 1989, EEC customs authorities directed that the diffusion process by chip makers must be carried out in the EEC. The theory underlying this is that, on the one hand, European chip makers can use high-tech EEC-based diffusion while on the other, they can still use low-cost Third World labor for chip cutting as the last process, while still preserving EEC origin. This would imperil Japanese who manufacture or cut chips in the EEC, but do their diffusion elsewhere. They would be penalized by the new EEC rule of origin.

Cf. Arab Boycott of Israel (negative certificates of origin).
See also certificate of origin; Canada-U.S. Free Trade Agreement of 1989.

S

S.A. (SA), from the Latin plus Greek *societas* meaning "fellowship" and *anonumos* meaning "nameless," is the abbreviation of the French *Société Anonyme*, the Spanish *Sociedad Anónima*, and the Italian *Societa Anonima* and means "limited company" or "corporation."

safeguards are strictly temporary restrictions to trade (in the form of special duties or surcharges or quantitative restrictions (QRs)) levied unilaterally by a government on an emergency basis against imported goods that are adjudged to have caused serious injury to domestic industry.

These measures are legitimate under the General Agreement on Tariffs and Trade (GATT) provided that their imposition is impermanent (i.e., intended to provide short-term relief to national manufacturers) *vis-à-vis* protectionist measures aimed at deliberalizing trade and, thus, implicitly contrary to the GATT's principles of international trade (PIT).

See also injury; retaliation; General Agreement on Tariffs and Trade (2. GATT Principles and Rules); surcharges.

sanction *See* Appendix VI.

Sarl (SARL) is an acronym from the French *societé à responsabilité limitée*, meaning "a company with limited liability."

The meaning of *Sarl* is equivalent to that of the abbreviation *S.A.*

Cf. *S.A.*

Schengen Agreement is an international accord among Belgium, Germany (now incorporating the former German Democratic Republic), France, Luxembourg, and the Netherlands, acceded to on June 19, 1990, whereby individual nationals of the signatory countries will not be subject to "border checks" either when entering or leaving any of the "Schengen countries."

This agreement will come into full force on January 1, 1992. In November 1990, Italy became the sixth full member of the group. A precondition for its membership was the "tightening" of visa requirements for visitors from North Africa. Spain expects to join the Schengen group after its visa controls for North African visitors are tightened. Portugal, too, has applied for membership in the group and, in anticipation of it, established (with Spain) their first control-free border crossing for European Economic Community (EEC) citizens on July 15, 1990.

Originally concluded on June 14, 1985, the agreement is evidence of moves designed to further integrate the European Economic Community in line with the Single European Act of 1987. With full EEC border controls not due to be fully removed until January 1, 1993, the Schengen group has achieved a real "jump start" on the free movement of people over the EEC as a whole.

See also Single European Act.

schmir *See* bribery.

scientific tariff—a name that might fittingly be called the "Leibnitz Tariff" after the independent co-discoverer of the calculus, who is reported to have said that the ideal human situation for problem solving would be for two thinkers, upon approaching some serious mental task, to say to each other, "Let us compute!"—in the realm of international economics, is hypothesized to be the rate of a duty so computed as to result in the equalization of the price of imports and of domestic goods.

Underpinning the computation is the crucial assumption that a tariff is imposed to afford domestic producers relief to "meet the foreign competition"; it assumes that, given temporary protection behind the tariff wall, domestic producers will manage their firms more efficiently to "meet the competition" on the day the tariff is removed.

Historically, there is little evidence that domestic producers use the "protection time" behind the tariff wall for anything except entrenching their market positions. For example, protected by tariffs against inexpensive U.S. beer and by nontariff barriers preventing interprovincial competition, Canadian breweries (prior to the Canada-U.S. Free Trade Agreement (FTA) of 1989) gouged the market with high prices.

In the first six months of the FTA, cheap U.S. beer (imported into the Province of Ontario, for example) so embarrassed Canadian beer producers that they successfully lobbied the Provincial government to slap additional domestic taxes onto the imports to raise their price. (Safeguards were not used by the Canadian Federal government since their use might have been interpreted by the U.S. Trade Representative or the U.S. Department of Commerce as illegal under the FTA.)

See also Free Trade Agreement of 1989; consumption effect of a tariff.

Sectoral Advisory Group(s) on International Trade (SAGIT, plural **SAGITS),** established in 1989 under the aegis of the Canadian Government, are 15 bodies (which represent specific industrial areas) that advise the government on international trade matters in general and on transborder trade relevant to the Canada-U.S. Free Trade Agreement of 1989 in particular.

Cf. International Trade Advisory Committee.

sectoral reciprocity is the process by which governments grant mutual concessions to each other in the trade of goods in specific industrial areas (e.g., the automotive sector and the capital equipment agricultural sector).
See also reciprocity.

sectoral trade agreement is a bi- or multilateral accord limited to commercial exchange relations focused on a particular industry.

> **Example:** The Automotive Products Trade Agreement (the Auto Pact) is a Canada-U.S. (bilateral) sectoral trade agreement.

> **Example:** The Aircraft Agreement (under the General Agreement on Tariffs and Trade) is an example of a multilateral sectoral agreement.

See also Automotive Products Trade Agreement.

seigniorage, from the French *seigneur* meaning "lord" (e.g., the colonial landowner in Québec) refers to the benefits that (theoretically) accrued to the United States—under the Bretton Woods System—(1) as the issuer of the U.S. dollar and (2) when the U.S. dollar was used as an international reserve currency.

The expression arose from the Bretton Woods days (i.e., prior to the collapse of the Bretton Woods System in 1971) when the United States was able to settle its balance of payments deficits with U.S. dollars, since it issued the currency, and thus had the (dubious) incentive to supply excessive world liquidity with large and ongoing balance of payments deficits.

See also Bretton Woods System.

self-reference criteria (SRC) is the ethnocentric framework from which one judges another's culture, by using one's own culture-bound values as the standard against which host-country attitudes and behaviors are measured and judged.
See also ethnocentrism.

senmosha •NW•, from the Japanese meaning "specialized trading company," is an independent trading company, smaller than a *sogoshosha*, that (1) purchases on its own account and (2) limits its commercial activity to marketing goods with a "narrow" product line and a "shallow" product depth.
The *senmosha* specializes in sophisticated industrial products (e.g., medical equipment, electronic components) and in products that are "brand differentiated."
Cf. *sogoshosha* •NW•.

services are economic behaviors that provide what is necessary for the operation, maintenance, and repair of some activity.
Services can be categorized as follows:

1. *construction services* (e.g., site preparation, new construction, maintenance, repair services),
2. *trade services* (e.g., wholesale and retail trade, hospitality services),

3. *transportation, port, and terminal services* (e.g., freight services, passenger transportation services, loading and unloading of transport carriers),
4. *communications services* (e.g., postal and courier services, telecommunications, customs clearing, freight forwarding),
5. *financial services* (e.g., banking, financial leasing, investment services),
6. *insurance services* (e.g., freight insurance, nonfreight insurance),
7. *business and professional services* (e.g., real estate services, advertising, accounting, market research, computer-related services),
8. *educational services* (e.g., training, teaching),
9. *health services* (e.g., hospital and veterinary services),
10. *recreation and cultural services* (e.g., sports facilities, theater and film production and presentations).

Trade in services (provided for in U.S. legislation under the Trade Act of 1974) occurs, for example, when one party exports a service to another (e.g., a turnkey project), extends credit to the other (banking), and protects against nonperformance and default (insurance).

Cf. commodity.

shadow economy refers to the "underground economy" in the Soviet Union, the networks of suppliers and intermediaries (known as *tolkachi*, or "pushers") who provide goods and services to the "underground market" of industrial users and consumers.

This market has been called the "parallel market" since it runs alongside the official, legal, state-controlled market channels.

It is internationally known as the *black market*, and goods sold on it are called *black-market goods*.

> **Example:** Russians have been heard to say that while the shadow economy works all the time, the legitimate economy runs only at night—while the government is sleeping.

shipment consolidation is a variation of consolidation.

See make bulk.

shipper's agent is an international marketing channel facilitating intermediary who purchases "cargo capacity" on transport modes and who then resells this to shippers.

shippers' cooperative is an incorporated company, owned by shippers of goods, run on a not-for-profit basis, which performs the functions of a foreign freight forwarder.

The company's services are available to members and nonmembers alike. However, in accordance with the laws that regulate the behavior of cooperatives, profits (in the form of "patronage dividends") are distributed only to owner-members.

Shipper's Declaration of Canadian Origin is a document required, under Section 10.84 of the U.S. Customs Regulations, to be filled out by the shipper, attesting in documentary form that goods originating in Canada and being exported to the United States are "Canadian articles" according to the Free Trade Agreement (FTA) rules of origin.

See also rules of origin.

shipping association (shippers' association), also called a *transport association* and a *transportation association*, is a group of companies engaged in international trade that come together with the express purpose of "leveraging their resources" to negotiate more favorable shipping rates than those they would receive by individual arrangement.

> **Example:** In the third quarter of 1989, a type of shipping association called the Importers' Transport Council Inc. (ITC) was formed in Canada. The importers involved were Nissan, Saab-Scania, Jaguar, Lada, and Autolion, Canadian distributors for Peugot, BMW, Subaru, and Skocar. ITC was incorporated to negotiate rail and trucking contracts. Recently, ITC signed a Memorandum of Understanding with the Canadian National Railways (CNR) that will lead to a multiyear contract involving significant reductions in freight rates for the importers. As a consequence, CNR will do over 90 percent of the importers' business.
>
> ITC's next project is to land a major Canadian trucking company contract. Data is currently being assembled and analyzed on the origins and destinations of the importers' trucking shipments, as well as their current carriers.

shipping conference *See* conference.

short-life-cycle goods refers to any product in any form likely to become obsolete within four years (as set out in the U.S. Omnibus Trade Act of 1988) from the date of being made available commercially as a consequence of advances in technology.

In the United States, the determination is made by the U.S. International Trade Commission (USITC) and forwarded to the U.S. Trade Representative (USTR) for action where appropriate.

Cf. product life cycle.

Short-Term Bulk Agriculture Credits Insurance is a program of the Export Development Corporation (EDC) aimed at providing "cover" for Canadian exporters of bulk commodities from Canada on credit terms.

It was designed for sales with terms up to 365 days and done by documentary credit (usually irrevocable letter of credit) to private buyers or on open account to public (i.e., state) buyers.

The Short-Term Program provides coverage against nonrepayment due to commercial and political risks.

Cf. Medium-Term Bulk Agriculture Credits Insurance and Guarantee Program.

See also Export Development Corporation; export financing; commercial risks; political risks.

shrink wrapping is the technique, used by export packers, of using strong, flexible plastic film (called shrink film or shrink wrap) to enclose an entire palletized load of boxes or cartons, the aim being to immobilize the goods and, thus, facilitate handling and movement, while reducing the risk of damage.

sight documentary credit *See* documentary credit.

sight documentary draft *See* documentary draft; D/A sight draft.

sight draft *See* documentary draft; sight documentary draft; D/A sight draft.

Single Administrative Document (SAD), officially called the *D.V.1*, the abbreviation for **D**eclaration of Particulars Relating to Customs **V**alue, is a customs document, introduced on January 1, 1989, within the European Economic Community (EEC) to eliminate an estimated 70 different forms in several languages that were previously required by the 12 EEC-member governments at their borders prior to permitting the importation of goods.

    The SAD serves as (1) an export declaration, (2) a transit document, and (3) an import declaration. It is used not only within the EEC but also between the EEC and the European Free Trade Association (EFTA).

The SAD does not eliminate a variety of other "control forms" used at all customs posts worldwide (e.g., health and inspection documents).

    Cf. Schengen Agreement.

Single European Act (SEA), also called the *Single Act*, is a law signed in February 1986. It came into force on July 1, 1987, amending the Treaty of Rome of 1957 and facilitating European economic and monetary integration by permitting decisions to be made by a majority (rather than the formerly required unanimous vote) in the European Council of Ministers on matters relating to the completion of the European internal market.

    The SEA established the end of 1992 as the limiting date for the establishment of an integrated European market for goods, services, and capital.

    See also Delors Report.

situational conformity •NW• is a Japanese concept, derived from the high-context Japanese culture, whereby the domain (i.e., situation, environment) in which events occur requires behavior that is implicitly flexible yet situationally appropriate (i.e., conformist) according to Japanese cultural expectations.

    Cf. low-context culture.

    See also high-context culture; groupism •NW•.

Smithsonian Agreement is the accord reached among the Group of 10 (G-10) nations at the Smithsonian Institution in Washington, D.C., in December 1971, that formally brought the Bretton Woods System to an end.

    See also Bretton Woods System.

Smoot-Hawley Tariff Act of 1930, called *The Smoot-Hawley Act* and, colloquially, *Smoot-Hawley*, is a U.S. law, adjudged in the light of history to have been the most protectionist piece of legislation ever to have been passed by Congress and ratified by the U.S. president.

Raising average U.S. import duties to an historical high of 31 percent in 1932, Smoot-Hawley has earned the invidious reputation of being the single most important event that ushered in (and sustained) The Great Depression of the 1930s by hastening the collapse of global trade.

See also protectionism.

snake *See* European snake.

social democracy *See* mixed economy.

socialism is (1) a political-economic set of ideas centered around the concept that in a society, the ownership of the wealth (i.e, capital) be in the hands of the state and be used primarily as a means of production "for use" (i.e., utility) rather than "for profit"; and (2) a political-economic set of ideas that adheres to the concept that ownership of wealth (i.e., capital) be in the hands of one (i.e., communist) political party (the "vanguard of the proletariat") through which it governs ("in the name of the proletariat"), using the capital as the "common means of production" to generate "social wealth" rather than private profit.

Such a political system is referred to as communism, and its political economy is called a command economy.

Totalitarian command economies claimed to have been particularly successful in accelerating the accumulation of capital in particularly less developed countries (e.g., those in East Europe). There is evidence to support this claim.

There is none, however, to support a contention that a socialist economy produced anything but relative deprivation for and impoverishment of people living under it: the rapid, revolutionary "de-communization" of East Europe (from October 1989 onwards) supports this, as does the mass exodus from East Germany to West Germany (estimated to have been 2,000 to 3,000 people per day) following the opening of the Berlin Wall in November 1989.

Cf. capitalism; market economy.
See also command economy; nonmarket economy.

social structure is (1) the enduring (i.e., long-term), relations among people who play roles in a variety of "social orders" (i.e., social orders being "economic order," "kinship order," "political order," "military order," and "religious order"); and (2) the consequent enduring pattern of impersonal relationships among a society's social institutions that characterizes the "structure of society."

This contemporary, American, rational perspective is the legacy of the iconoclastic sociologist C. Wright Mills.

Cf. ethnostructure; multiculturalism.

Society of Worldwide Interbank Financial Telecommunications (SWIFT) is a global database and communications system for transferring funds between banks in North America, West Europe, and Japan, the Trilateral Commission of the global capitalist system.

soft currency colloquially refers to a country's money that is not easily convertible into other national currencies.
Cf. hard currency.

soft goods refers to, in the United Kingdom, merchandise manufactured from textiles or the textiles themselves.

> In Canada and the United States, the textile business is called, in slang, the "shmatah business," from the Yiddish for "rag," thus, the possible etymology of the "rag trade."
> The only analog in North America for textile goods is "white goods" (specifically, white percale sheets), generally implying "bedding."

See also commodity.

soft loans is a colloquial variation of *concessional financing*.

soft side (of international marketing) •NW• refers to those areas of the subject that deal with nonquantifiable processes and outcomes, such as culture, business customs, and language.

> **Example:** Traditionally, these areas have been undervalued, especially in most analytically oriented Master of Business Administration (MBA) programs, which have tended (1) to regard international marketing as something entirely quantifiable and, thus, (2) to overvalue the quantification-orientation per se.

Cf. hard side (of international marketing).
See also culture; high-context culture; low-context culture.

Software for Market Analysis and Restrictions on Trade (SMART) refers to computer programs, developed jointly by the U.N. Conference on Trade and Development (UNCTAD) and the World Bank, designed to provide developing countries with trade statistics and market information to enable them to effectively participate in rounds of multilateral trade negotiations (MTNs).
The power of the SMART programs will permit users to derive information on international, regional, and subregional trade flows and on tariff and nontariff barriers by commodity by country or by regional trade group.
The SMART system is centered in Geneva, Switzerland, and is funded by the United Nations Development Program (UNDP), which has undertaken the responsibility to disseminate the software and to train potential users in developing countries.
Cf. expert systems.
See also United Nations Conference on Trade and Development.

sogososha (sogo sosha) •NW•, from the Japanese, is a "trading company engaged in direct exporting."
In the United States and Canada, there is no exactly equivalent marketing organization. The closest equivalent entity would be a company operating as

a direct-export trading house (i.e., a company trading directly on its own account or on behalf of other noncompeting companies).

A *sogososha* contrasts with the North American trading house that operates as an indirect exporter.

Cf. indirect exporting.

See also direct exporting.

Southeast Asia Treaty Organization (SEATO) is a mutual defense treaty signed in 1955 under the authority of the Southeast Asia Collective Defense Treaty (SEACDT) of 1954.

The signatories of SEATO are Australia, France, New Zealand, Pakistan, the Philippines, Thailand, the United Kingdom, and the United States.

SEATO was originally established to act as the Asian analog of the North Atlantic Treaty Organization (NATO) in Europe to "contain Communism" and the perceived and actual military threats associated with the Soviet Union, the People's Republic of China (PRC), and their "fraternal allies."

While SEATO dissolved in 1977, the SEACDT under which it was formed remains in force, but it is considered a treaty with the formal force of paper only.

Cf. North Atlantic Treaty Organization; Warsaw Treaty Organization.

Southern African Development Coordination Conference (SADCC) is a regional international organization (with a global institutional infrastructure), established in 1979, with the aim of harmonizing development plans in the region within the framework of lessening the economic dependence of the regional members on South Africa.

Member countries of the SADCC are Angola, Botswana, Lesotho, Malawi, Mozambique, Swaziland, Tanzania, Zambia, and Zimbabwe. Its headquarters are in Gabarone, Botswana.

The SADCC has excellent working relations with international development organizations, with major trading partners, and with major international financial institutions.

See also Appendix V (B).

Southern Cone refers to those countries in South America—Argentina, Chile, Paraguay, and Uruguay—whose combined territory (from 20 to 50 degrees South latitude) is seen as forming the shape of an (ice-cream-type) upright cone.

See also Southern Cone Common Market.

Southern Cone Common Market (SCCM) is a customs union, established in Asunción, Paraguay, on March 26, 1991, that comprises the countries of the South American Southern Cone: Argentina, Chile, Paraguay, and Uruguay.

The idea of the SCCM is to create an integrated regional market of over 200 million people, based on foreign direct investment and driven by export-oriented industrial growth. The plan calls for the harmonization of all internal tariffs of the members and the creation of a common external tariff by December 31, 1994.

The greatest obstacles to be overcome by the four-nation grouping will be the disparate size of their economies, their uneven rates of growth, and their different rates of inflation. Under these circumstances, economic growth for the SCCM demands a high level of political and monetary cooperation among the partners to forge a single monetary policy.

Given the history of the European drive toward economic and monetary integration that will have taken 35 years (from 1957 when the Treaty of Rome was first signed until the end of 1992, the target date for the completion of the single European market), the plans of the SCCM appear ambitious.

Cf. European Economic Community; Latin American Integration Association.

See also customs union; common external tariff; direct investment; harmonization; export-oriented industrialization; Southern Cone.

South Pacific Bureau for Economic Cooperation (SPEC) is a regional international organization, established in 1971, to assist the economic development of the smaller developing countries of the region on the basis of "economic partnership" with Australia and New Zealand.

The SPEC has negotiated the reduction (and for some goods, the entire removal) of tariffs between members, and it aims to coordinate and harmonize all trade, customs, transportation, and communications services between them.

The organization has its headquarters in Suva, Fiji, and it comprises the following members: Australia, Cook Islands, Fiji, Nauru, New Zealand, Tonga, and Western Samoa.

See also Pacific Forum.

South Pacific Commission (SPC) is a regional international organization, formed in 1947 by six countries with dependent territories in the region: Australia, France, the Netherlands, New Zealand, the United Kingdom, and the United States. The organization has its headquarters in Nouméa, New Caledonia, an "overseas territory" of France.

The purpose of the SPC was to act as a loose forum for liaison between the members on regional matters of mutual economic concern.

With the rise of major international development organizations, such as the United Nations Economic and Social Commission for Asia and the Pacific (UN/ESCAP), which has its entire focus on the region, and the strengthening of European integration (within the framework of the European Economic Community (EEC)), the *raison d'être* for the SPC has diminished.

Cf. Southeast Asia Treaty Organization.

See also United Nations Economic and Social Commission for Asia and the Pacific.

South Pacific Forum (SPF) is a regional organization formed in 1971 to promote the exchange of information on common regional problems through discussion among the Heads of State of the member countries.

The organization's headquarters are in Suva, Fiji. The SPF originated the idea for the establishment of the South Pacific Bureau for Economic Cooperation (SPEC).

The original seven SPF members (which recommended the formation of the SPEC) are Australia, Cook Islands, Fiji, Nauru, New Zealand, Tonga, and Western Samoa.

After gaining their political independence, the following countries joined the original seven: Kiribati, Niue, Papua New Guinea (PNG), Solomon Islands, and Tuvalu.

See also South Pacific Bureau for Economic Cooperation.

sovereign entity, from the French *sous la reine* meaning "under the queen," is, in international law, a country, duly recognized by custom or (formally) accorded recognition by the United Nations.

> **Example:** Tradition has it that the Holy See (Vatican City) is a sovereign entity, although its territorial jurisdiction has been whittled back to one square mile in Rome.
>
> On the other hand, the Palestine Liberation Organization (PLO), while recognized *(de jure)* by the Arab League as the exclusive legal government of Palestine, has no physical land upon which to stake its claim and assert its jurisdiction. Thus, the United Nations system continues to recognize Israel as the sovereign entity having exclusive legitimacy (over what the PLO claims is "occupied Palestine") in matters of domestic policy, external trade, and political relations.

See also international law.

sovereign immunity *See* Appendix VI (sovereign (sovereignty)).

Special Drawing Right (SDR, plural **SDRs)**, also known as *paper gold*, created by the International Monetary Fund (IMF) in 1969 as an international reserve asset supplemental to gold, is the unit of account of the IMF.

See also International Monetary Fund (2. Special Drawing Right (SDR)).

special economic zones (SEZs) are the Soviet equivalent of foreign trade zones (FTZs).

> The U.S.S.R. is in the process of establishing SEZs in the Maritime Territory adjoining Nakhodka and Vladivostok. Unlike established FTZs, the Soviet SEZs are proposed as being "zones of joint ventures," which would retain all the other characteristics of export-oriented industrial enclaves.

See also foreign trade zones.

Special Import Measures Act (SIMA) refers to Canadian enabling legislation, passed by the Federal Parliament in 1984, empowering the Canadian Import Tribunal—equivalent to the U.S. International Trade Commission—and the Department of National Revenue—under whose authority Canadian Customs and Excise falls—to (1) investigate and report its findings in the areas of export subsidization, countervailing duties, dumping, antidumping duties, and safeguards; and (2) to advise the government on appropriate action in light of its findings, in accordance with Canadian obligations under the General Agreement on Tariffs and Trade and under the Canada-U.S. Free Trade Agreement of 1989.

Cf. U.S. International Trade Commission.

See also Canadian Import Tribunal.

Specialized Credit, a special lending facility of the Export Development Corporation (EDC) to provide loans to Canadian companies involved in exporting, is available where a Canadian company requires a loan to purchase Canadian goods either (1) for permanent lease to another company outside Canada or (2) for permanent use by the Canadian company itself outside Canada.

This credit facility is the only EDC program in which it can extend credit to a Canadian firm, since the EDC is mandated to cooperate (*vis-à-vis* compete) with private Canadian lending institutions, and the extension of Special Credit is contingent on the existence of a valid and legally binding contract for permanent use or lease of goods outside Canada.

See also Export Development Corporation.

specific duty is a tax or tariff placed on imported goods and based on a stipulated levy per number, per weight, or per unit of volume of the goods.

> **Example:** The specific duty on imported shirts is $15 per hundredweight and is $16 per million cubic meters on exports of natural gas.

Cf. ad valorem duty; antidumping duty; compound duty; countervailing duty; end-use tariff; optimum tariff; prohibitive tariff.

See also duty.

Special Transaction Guarantees (STGs) refers to a program of the Export Development Corporation (EDC) whereby the EDC provides banks and other lenders of export financing (to foreign buyers of Canadian goods and services) with an unconditional coverage on nonrecourse supplier financing.

To qualify for these guarantees, the goods and services exported must be insured by the exporter with the EDC.

See also Export Development Corporation; export financing.

Specific Transaction Insurance (STI) is an insurance program of the Export Development Corporation (EDC), which protects Canadian exporters. STI provides "cover" for individual export transactions (from the time the goods are ordered or shipped until payment is received) against nonpayment of a credit from an export sale due to commercial risks and political risks.

See also Export Development Corporation; commercial risks; political risks.

sporadic dumping is the tactic of occasionally selling exported goods in foreign markets at a lower price than domestically.

The aim (of the alleged "dumper") is to dispose of a "temporary surplus"— the claim is that the excess was "unforeseen."

Had the excess production been "foreseeable," then a negative inference might have been drawn and the act branded as willful—dumping *per se* would be a reasonable conclusion.

See also dumping; predatory dumping; persistent dumping; antidumping duty.

Stabex •NW•, the abbreviation of the French *stabilisation des exports* meaning "stabilization of exports," is a program established under Lomé II (i.e., the Second Lomé Convention) between the European Economic Community (EEC) and African, Caribbean, and Pacific (ACP) nations.

The arrangements involve making funds available from the European Development Fund (EDF) for "stabilization of export earnings" of ACP states when the world price of their nonmineral exports fluctuates significantly, thus depriving them of anticipated hard currency.

Cf. *Sysmin •NW•*.

See also Lomé Convention.

stabilizing speculation *See* Appendix II.

standardize (standardizing) is a global marketing concept that involves a process of simplifying the procurement and production process, whereby the factors of production are secured from the cheapest, most accessible, and most reliable suppliers worldwide.

See also global marketing.

standards are (1) technical specifications as defined by the Agreement on Technical Barriers to Trade (Standards Code), which set out product attributes (such as levels of quality and purity); and (2) common sets of technical approaches (and benchmarks) to be used in the development, testing, certification, and production of goods.

> **Example:** One of the best cases of near-universally accepted standards are the hazardous-product symbols that graphically show that the contents (of containers) are acidic, caustic/corrosive, flammable, noxious, or explosive.

The United States and Canada have harmonized their standards in fields such as food and drugs and consumer product safety. Agencies such as the U.S. Food and Drug Administration (FDA) and the Consumer Product Safety Commission (CPSC) are the "lead agencies" in negotiations in the public sector (as is the U.S. American National Standards Institute (ANSI) in the private sector) aimed at harmonizing standards internationally. Competition between the European Economic Community and the United States around the question of "whose standards should be adopted," is proving to be a major nontariff barrier and is making it difficult for the U.S. government to assist U.S. industry to plan an industrial strategy.

Cf. European Organization for Testing and Certification.

See also harmonization; Standards Code.

Standards Code, officially the Agreement on Technical Barriers to Trade, is an international agreement resulting from the Tokyo Round of Multilateral Trade Negotiations.

The Code, signed by 39 countries as of the end of 1988, came into force on January 1, 1980. It was designed (1) with the specific intent to ensure that national administrative practices related to standards per se do not act as trade barriers and (2) for the purpose of regulating the manufacturing of industrial goods to accepted internationally established benchmarks.

> **Example:** The Standards Code was a genuine breakthrough in global trade talks since it pioneered a major normalization in the field of nontariff barriers. This is an area in which countries traditionally have enjoyed entrepreneurial autonomy. For example, in the past, to devise new definitions of purity (for domestic agricultural products) was to extend and deepen a nontariff barrier, winning valuable (domestic) political support.

The ongoing work of the General Agreement on Tariffs and Trade (GATT) Standards Committee, under the authority of the Standards Code, is aimed at eliminating duplication and promoting acceptance of unified standards of such international organizations as the International Standardization Organization (ISO), the International Electromechanical Commission (IEC) (which develops and promotes industry standards), and the FAO/WHO *Codex Alimentarius* Commission (which develops and promotes industry food standards).

Cf. European Organization for Testing and Certification.
See also International Standardization Organization; Tokyo Round.

standby arrangements are agreements negotiated between a borrower country and the International Monetary Fund (IMF) whereby the IMF extends "advance permission" to the country that, in the event of urgent need, agreed-upon amounts of reserve currencies will be made available "on demand."
See also International Monetary Fund; liquidity.

state trading nation (STN), also known as *state-trading country*, is a sovereign entity that relies on government-owned enterprise (e.g., a Crown Corporation) for wealth creation and for foreign trade.
A pure STN is a country with a command economy, as opposed to an open economy.

The Canadian mixed economy is, like the United Kingdom, a fundamentally open economy in which government has taken an active ownership and/or management role in some specific sector, usually because of market failure. Thus, because of a small domestic market located on an enormous land mass, the Canadian Crown Corporation (e.g., in broadcasting—Canadian Broadcasting Corporation, in railways—Canadian National Railways, and in mail services—Canada Post) has provided essential services due to lack of private investment.

In recent years, the global movement toward privatization has spurred the Canadian government to actively pursue the privatization of a significant number of its Crown Corporations.

Cf. open economy; mixed economy; Crown Corporation.
See also command economy; privatization.

statism (statist approach) is a political strategy involving, in varying degrees, the participation of government in the economy both as a "player" and as a "regulator" and, most critically, the acceptance by the population of such participation as "normal."

At the extreme, complete government direction of the economy characterizes a command economy. In political-economies like Canada, government involvement in the economy includes its market participation via Crown Corporations, thus converting and otherwise open economy into a mixed economy.

Cf. state trading nation.

steamship conference, also known as the *conference*, is a physical distribution/logistics (PD/L) international cartel that comprises independent owners/operators of marine transport vessels that come together and meet regularly to establish and maintain freight rates over important, high-traffic sea lanes (e.g., the North Atlantic Corridor).

Nonconference vessels (e.g., boats owned by companies and individuals that are not members of the price-fixing cartel) are called (pejoratively) "tramp steamers."

Sterling area *See* currency area.

straight bill of lading is a variation of *uniform straight bill of lading*.
See bill of lading.

strategic clusters (SCs) •NW• refer to the groupings of internationally competitive firms within geographic proximity to their major customers and to their supply networks.

According to Professors Alan Rugman and Joseph D'Cruz of the Faculty of Management, University of Toronto, SCs are an extension of the "diamonds of international competitiveness" (DIC) concept of Harvard University's Professor Michael Porter. The SC concept was developed to show how Canada in particular (but by inference, any industrialized country in general) can use the DIC concept to shape the groupings of its most internationally competitive industries.

The four principal determinants of a Porter "diamond" are:

1. a firm's strategy and the vigor of industry competition;
2. a firm's related and supporting industries;
3. the factor conditions in a firm's country; and
4. the demand conditions for a firm's goods and services.

Rugman and D'Cruz's strategic clusters are characterized by the following attributes:

1. a resource base, both physical and human;
2. supporting industries and infrastructure (e.g., the "hub-and-spoke" concept);
3. customers; and
4. leading firms in the industry that have established themselves in the cluster from which to compete globally.

The strategic clusters in Canada are denoted as follows:

1. Western Canadian forest-products cluster,
2. Alberta energy cluster,
3. Prairie farming cluster,
4. Eastern Canadian forest-products cluster,
5. Base-metal mining cluster,
6. Southwest Ontario automotive cluster,
7. Southern Ontario advanced manufacturing cluster,
8. Toronto financial services cluster,
9. Montreal aerospace/advanced transportation cluster,
10. Atlantic fisheries cluster.

It has been suggested that only under the Canada-U.S. Free Trade Agreement of 1989 (FTA) can Canada's 10 strategic clusters improve their international competitiveness and strengthen Canada's sovereignty (i.e., political independence from the United States). It is argued that the FTA actually helps maintain this sovereignty since the United States is FTA-bound to afford Canada "national treatment," thus ensuring its market access to the United States and thereby creating an incentive for Canadian firms within their SCs to improve their competitiveness.

This argument is persuasive, but it only convinces if one agrees that the United States has abandoned the "manifest destiny" idea (i.e., the geopolitical concept that the United States is fated to dominate the North American continent). If one sees "manifest destiny" as "on the move" however, then the whole argument changes. Rather than being taken as a friendly umbrella under which Canadian strategic clusters can develop competitively and contribute to Canadian sovereignty, one perceives the FTA as an analog of any other economically integrating program that the United States has pursued (e.g., the Caribbean Basin Initiative).

When the Europeans signed the Treaty of Rome in 1957, they ensured that it (subsequently strengthened by numerous amendments) contained a "social policy" that underpinned the European Economic Community (EEC). For example, when European workers are laid off and when companies close or relocate, the firms and the governments cooperate ahead of time, and throughout the entire process, to ensure that workers are adequately compensated and retrained. No such "social policy" was built into the FTA.

Further, in the EEC, all European strategic clusters are being integrated through the time-consuming process of explicit "harmonization." In North America, because the Canadian and American economies are already highly integrated, the "national treatment" provision under the FTA is an adequate tool with which to forge an eventual North American economic-monetary union (EMU), equivalent to the planned-for European EMU. From this viewpoint, while it will occur later, it may prove easier for the United States to achieve a full EMU with Canada than for the Europeans to reach it among themselves. In addition, it should be significantly easier for the United States to achieve its "manifest destiny" where a whole network of costly social programs do not have to be harmonized (with Canada) either because they do not exist or because (even if they did) there was no FTA-bound agreement to do so.

To those who accept the "manifest destiny" of the United States, this conclusion is not distressing. It is simply an acceptance of the logic of the globalization and an understanding that the ongoing process of homogenization of world culture is the likely end result.

Cf. cultural imperialism; dependent development.
See also globalization; free trade.

structural adjustment *See* adjustment.

structural change is a condition that occurs when there are significant shifts in the ownership and/or use of economic factors, such as the ownership of technology and the land tenure system.

Structural change can also result from shifts in the population base in a country due to factors such as war, famine, or migration. Changes can be either positive or negative, depending on the viewpoint (or the economic interest) of the observer.

> **Example:** If dependent development is the unacceptable course set (by the rich nations) for improving living conditions and productivity in Asia, Africa, and Latin America today, then the New International Economic Order (NIEO) can only be achieved by effecting structural change, not in the developed countries alone, but in the macroeconomic relations among the developed countries and the developing ones.

Positive Structural Changes: Changes in the structure of the economy are said to have taken place when a country, formerly a supplier of raw commodities, gets (via lease, joint venture, or independent development) the technology to process goods to add value to them and, thus, opens new markets for the distribution of those goods.

Negative Structural Changes: For instance, unskilled nonurban labor (paid in kind) is now attracted to cities to be trained for value-added manufacturing (paid in money). Urban migration disintegrates traditional *(Gemeinschaft)* rural life, and it ruins agricultural production. Food deficits result unless farm technology is used to increase agricultural productivity.

The need for improved (i.e., mechanised) farming tools is fulfilled if monetary authorities extend credit to farmers for capital-goods purchases. Where it is not fulfilled, powerful groups (e.g., *latifundistas*) usually struggle to monopolize most arable land and use it for cultivation of export cash crops.

These negative events result in a subsistence-crop shortfall and, consequently, the need to import staple foods with scarce foreign exchange. If the prices of the cash crops exported do not keep pace with the prices of the staple foods imported, the country, previously a poor developing country, now becomes an impoverished developing country, with unending external debts and no internal capacity to increase productivity to end the debt and establish a monetary equilibrium.

See also New International Economic Order; dependent development.

structural impediments initiative (SII) •NW• refers to bilateral negotiations between the governments of Japan and the United States, initiated by the latter in September 1989 with the explicit purpose of asking the Japanese government to make (relatively drastic) changes in six areas of its economy with the aim (ultimately) of redressing the negative U.S. balance of trade with Japan.

These six areas are:

1. domestic pricing, including predatory pricing specifically used among cooperating Japanese companies to block entry to the market, or attempts to expand distribution within it, by U.S. firms;
2. "rationalizing" the (notoriously complex) Japanese retail distribution system to permit greater market access by the United States;
3. gradually reducing Japan's savings rate, thus reducing the U.S.-dollar glut in Japan, which flows into the United States, keeping the value of the dollar, *vis-à-vis* other hard currencies, high;
4. reducing the power of the *keiretsu*, which are able (1) to effectively block industry penetration by the United States, as well as (2) to thwart U.S. attempts to procure Japanese government contracts;
5. discriminatory regulations regarding the purchase and use of land by U.S. firms;
6. exclusionary business practices, including nontariff measures, to block U.S. market entry.

At the end of four days (April 2–6, 1990) of top-level talks in Washington, D.C., Japan agreed to deregulate its distribution system and to gradually relax restrictions on the establishment of large stores. This will permit foreign retailers to open outlets in Japan. Japan also agreed to act against the *keiretsu* in areas of bid-rigging and government procurement.

See also keiretsu •NW•.

subcontract production is a component of a type of countertrade transaction called direct offsets in which an exporter agrees to permit a part of the total export contract to be produced "offshore."

The subcontract is usually a straight commercial arrangement, excluding licensed production.

See also offset deals.

subsidiary *See* foreign subsidiary.

Subsidies (and Countervailing Measures) Code is a code of conduct negotiated during the Tokyo Round (1973–1979) of Multilateral Trade Negotiations (MTNs) under the auspices of the General Agreement on Tariffs and Trade (GATT).

While not having defined "subsidies" per se, the Code established ways and means (i.e., protocols) whereby country X would inform country Y of its intention to levy a countervailing duty and also inform it of its plans to hold hearings into the matter.

Compliance with this protocol would be based upon the perception that country Y was acting contrary to the GATT principles by unfairly providing export subsidies and that the alleged offender (country Y) would be invited to respond at the hearings into the matter.

See also code of conduct; Tokyo Round.

subsidy *See* export subsidies.

Super 301 is the colloquial name for Section 301 of the U.S. Omnibus Trade Act of 1988, which is officially called Subtitle C–Response to Unfair International Trade Practices, Chapter I–Enforcement of United States Rights under Trade Agreements and Response to Certain Foreign Trade Practices, Sec. 301. Actions by United States Trade Representative.

The all-encompassing nature of Section 301, which enlarges the authority of the U.S. Trade Representative (USTR), can be described as follows:

(a) MANDATORY ACTION. Under Section 304 (a) (1) of the Act, time-limited investigations of unfair trading by foreign countries, under trade agreements to which the U.S. is a signatory—if there is a determination that—
(A) the rights of the United States under any trade agreement are being denied; or
(B) an act, policy, or practice of a foreign country—
(i) violates, or is inconsistent with, the provisions of, or otherwise denies benefits to the United States under, any trade agreement, or
(ii) is unjustifiable and burdens or restricts United States commerce";
the USTR "shall take action authorized in subsection (c) . . . to enforce such rights or to obtain the elimination of such act, policy, or practice."
(b) DISCRETIONARY ACTION.—If the Trade Representative determines . . . that
(1) an act, policy, or practice of a foreign country is unreasonable or dis-
. criminatory and burdens or restricts United States commerce, and
(2) action by the United States is appropriate, the Trade Representative shall take all appropriate and feasible action . . . within the power of the President that the President may direct the Trade Representative to take under this subsection, to obtain the elimination of that act, policy, or practice.
(c) SCOPE OF AUTHORITY.—
(1) For the purposes of carrying out the provisions of subsection (a) or (b), the Trade representative is authorized to—
(A) suspend, withdraw, or prevent the application of benefits of trade-agreement concessions to carry out a trade agreement with a foreign country referred to in such subsection;
(B) impose duties or other import restrictions on the goods of . . . such foreign country for such time as the Trade Representative determines appropriate; or
(C) enter into binding agreements with such foreign country that commits such foreign country to
(i) eliminate, or phase out, the act, policy or practice that is the subject of the action to be taken under subsection (a) or (b),
(ii) eliminate any burden or restriction on United States commerce resulting from such act, policy or practice, or
(iii) provide the United States with compensatory trade benefits . . ."

Subsection (d) of Super 301 defines the acts, policies, and practices that are unreasonable. They comprise—but are not limited to—such things as denial of market opportunities to U.S. traders, denial of opportunities for U.S. companies to invest in foreign countries, nonprovision of adequate protection for U.S. intellectual property, export targeting by foreign countries, and unfair export subsidizing by foreign countries.

Perhaps the part of Super 301 that is perceived as most discretionary (and arbitrarily self-serving) by foreign traders with the United States, is the following:

Section (d)(3)(A): "An act, policy, or practice is unreasonable if the act, policy, or practice, while not necessarily in violation of, or inconsistent with, the international legal rights of the United States is *otherwise unfair and inequitable*." (Italics added.)

Nothing in the Act defines what is meant by "otherwise unfair and inequitable." A negative inference is drawn by foreign traders: the sweeping scope of Super 301 gives the USTR (and the U.S. president, under whose direction the USTR acts) sufficient authority to define what is meant by "otherwise unfair and inequitable"; and such determinations may be rendered on the basis of political favors granted by, and allegiance shown to, the United States in matters dealing with U.S. geopolitical needs.

See also U.S. Trade Representative.

Supplier Credit Protocol (SCP) is an agreement between the Export Development Corporation (EDC) and a foreign financial institution whereby the foreign financial institution guarantees promissory notes issued by a foreign buyer as payment to a Canadian supplier.

The notes are then purchased by the EDC (at a discount), thus providing the Canadian supplier with capital to finance the export transaction.

Cf. Buyer Credit Protocol.
See also forfaiting; Export Development Corporation.

supplier credits refer to the finances made available to an exporter by the process that involves the purchase (by a financial institution) of promissory notes that are issued in deferred payment to an exporter by a foreign buyer.

Since the exporter is the original beneficiary of the notes, credit is extended to it by way of purchasing the notes at a discount before their maturity date by the institution that runs the risk of collecting on them when they fall due.

In common practice, supplier credits often refer to any form of term financial lending facilities made available to exporters.

See also Supplier Credit Protocol; Export Development Corporation.

supply-side economics *See* monetarism.

supranational institutions are organizations, bodies, or agencies that plan and implement programs that are not limited by the national jurisdiction of any state or group of states.
See also supranational objectives.

supranational objectives, from the Latin *supra* meaning "above," are the aims of international organizations (INTORGS) or associations (of states) whose mandates and actions are not delimited by domestic jurisdiction.

Implicitly, INTORGS owe allegiance to the international organization per se, and not to any individual country or any regional political organization.
See also Appendix V.

surcharge, from the French *sur* meaning "over" and *charge* meaning "burden"; also called a *surtax*, from the French *surtaxe* meaning "over" plus "tax"; is an additional tax, duty, or tariff added to an imported good or an addition to an existing tax (frequently used by a government as an emergency safeguard measure).

Cf. duty.

See also safeguards.

Surety Bond Insurance (SBI) is an insurance program of the Export Development Corporation (EDC), which insures a Canadian surety company against the risks associated with its provision of a performance bond to a foreign buyer on behalf of a Canadian exporter.

These risks include a call on the surety bond by the foreign buyer due to nonperformance by the Canadian company.

See also Export Development Corporation.

surplus (in the balance of payments) is the excess of credits over debits in the current account and capital account (or autonomous transactions), which is equal to the net debit balance in the official reserve account (or accommodating transactions).

Cf. deficit (in the balance of payments).

See also balance of payments.

sustainable development refers to the economic provision for the needs of the present generation without compromising the capability for the provision for the needs of future generations.

The concept is based on the fact that (1) the world ecosphere is finite; (2) economic growth in one industry, country, or region is always a "zero-sum game" (i.e., the competition is always at the expense at some other industry, country, or region); and therefore (3) intelligent economic growth must be in balance with the world ecosystem, otherwise extinction is inevitable as a result of the uncontrolled exploitation, decay, and irretrievable loss of the ecosystem itself.

Cf. developed country; developing country.

See also Valdez Principles.

swap arrangements *See* central bank swaps.

switch deals (switch trade), a type of countertrade transaction, refers to an agreement between exporter and importer that covers the practice of exchanging goods and funds that may be "trapped" under bilateral contractual constraints.

For example, when an importer is committed to a purchase but runs short of U.S. dollars, it may agree to "switch" the goods to a different country importer. If this intermediary has the U.S. dollars, the payment obligation is "switched" to it. Frequently, a countertrade importer may have agreed to counterpurchase goods for which it has little use, but to which it assented in order to conclude the deal.

Thus, third parties are in a favorable position to purchase such goods at a discount, especially when the original importer is pressed by its creditors to generate hard-currency liquidity. In such a case, the party to whom the obligation to pay has been transferred may be "switched" several times.

Cf. barter; buy-back; compensation trade; cooperation contracts; counterpurchase; offset deals.

See also countertrade.

Sysmin •NW•, the abbreviation of the French *système minéreaux des supports* meaning "system of mineral supports," is a program established under Lomé II that is similar to *Stabex* but that is designed to protect mineral producers in African, Caribbean, and Pacific (ACP) countries against unforeseen threats to their existing operations.

Sysmin, unlike *Stabex* does not compensate ACP countries for losses of export-earned mining revenue. The purpose of *Sysmin* is to help ACP states that are heavily dependent on mining to overcome temporary and unforeseen circumstances that compromise the industry's earning power.

> **Example:** Zaire is a major strategic producer and exporter of metals to the European Economic Community (EEC). Some years ago, it suffered an inability to export sufficient quantities to lead, zinc, copper, and tin to keep its mines in Shaba Province open. Lack of proper upkeep of the mining machinery, due to insufficient training of local personnel, suddenly gave way to a technological collapse of the industry. Under *Sysmin*, financial contributions were made to help Zaire rehabilitate obsolete capital equipment, maintain workable machinery, and close down (i.e., "rationalize") marginal mining operations, thus enabling the mining industry to regain its viability.

Cf. *Stabex* •NW•.
See also Lomé Convention.

t

tare (tare weight) is (1) the allowance made for the weight of a shipping container, a shipping box, or a transport carrier, without the cargo; or (2) the actual weight of an empty shipping container, an empty shipping box, or an empty carrier.

> The concept is useful in transport such as RO-RO: the tare (of the empty containers) plus the trailers on which the containers are "rolled on," must be calculated if the weight limits of the RO-RO vessel are not to be exceeded.

tariff, from the Arabic *ta'rifa* meaning "notify," is (1) a tax, also known as a *customs tariff*, levied by a government on goods imported into a country; (2) a schedule, list, or record (in some documentary form or in a computer data base) of a carrier's charges for transport services.

> Cf. duty.

Tariff Act of 1930 *See* Smoot-Hawley Tariff Act of 1930.

tariff barrier, from the laissez-faire (*vis-à-vis* the protectionist) viewpoint, is any tariff, regardless of its legitimacy, perceived as an impediment, which bars, limits, and hinders the free flow of goods and services.

> Cf. tariff wall.
> *See also* nontariff barriers.

tariff escalation refers to

1. an adversarial process of (usually) bilateral political conflict, when a duty levied on an import is "countervailed" by the exporting country, whereby it levies a duty against goods exported from its customer; this action is followed by successive rounds of tax reprisals by each of the players.

   If the conflict is unresolved, the cycle of increasing punitive duties expands beyond the original goods to other sectors, and the ultimate result is the halting of trade and a concurrent deterioration of political relations between the antagonists.

2. the gradient of duties set out in a tariff schedule, which, according to custom, imposes increasingly higher taxes on goods with increasingly higher valued-added levels.

    For example, duties on raw agricultural commodities would be nil or "low," those on semiprocessed items would be "moderate," and duties on fully manufactured and assembled items would be "high." From the viewpoint of developing countries, this graded system is discriminatory against them, and thus their demand for a New International Economic Order (NIEO).

    Cf. retaliation.
    See also tariff schedule; structural change; United Nations Conference on Trade and Development; New International Economic Order.

tariff factories, also called *branch plant operations*, are direct investments by international and global marketers in manufacturing, assembling, and processing operations in a foreign country with the specific objective of "jumping the tariff wall" (i.e., avoiding import tariffs).

tariff schedule is the comprehensive catalog comprising (1) all goods imported by a country; (2) their classification into categories (e.g., unprocessed, semiprocessed, knocked-down); and (3) the tariffs applicable.

tariff suspension is the withdrawal of a tariff, or other concessions, by a country that has a reasonable basis for claiming injurious action by a foreign exporter to the allegedly injured country.

    The legitimation for tariff suspension is a section in an international agreement called an escape clause.
    See also escape clause.

tariff wall, from the laissez-faire viewpoint, is the protective tax barrier with which a protectionist country surrounds itself (1) to shield domestic industry from global competition, (2) to generate government revenues by taxing imports, and (3) to create an incentive for direct investment by foreign exporters to "jump the tariff wall."

    See also economic nationalism; infant industry argument; protectionism; laissez-faire.

tariffy (tariffication) is the process of transforming nontariff barriers (NTBs)/nontariff measures (NTMs) (e.g., subsidies, performance bonds) into quantifiable tariffs for the purpose of (1) revealing the hidden protection afforded to domestic producers, (2) quantifying the protection, and (3) reducing and eliminating it on an equitable multilateral basis.

    The U.S. attempt to dismantle the European Economic Community (EEC) Common Agricultural Policy (CAP) has been characterized by America's traditional confrontational approach, and it has not been entirely successful. The breakdown (on December 7, 1990) of the then-current Uruguay Round of Multilateral Trade Negotiations (MTN) over the CAP resulted from the EEC's reluctance to slash subsidies by 75 percent, as requested by the United States, versus an EEC-proposed 30 percent. It might have been avoided entirely. The United States and the EEC might have approached the problem of opening each other's agricultural markets initially by agreeing (1) to tariffy the U.S. agricultural support and subsidy program and the CAP and (2) to mutually and reciprocally reduce tariffs between them, whether it be an across-the-board approach or an item-by-item approach.

See also tariff; nontariff barrier; subsidy; quota; Common Agricultural Policy; Uruguay Round; Multilateral Trade Negotiations; across-the-board tariff reductions; item-by-item tariff reductions.

tatemae •NW• from the Japanese meaning "official group stance," refers to the impersonal, "official," group-oriented behavior of Japanese when in decision-making groups.

In Japanese culture, *tatemae* is the only form of individual behavior socially acceptable within a group.

Cf. *honne* •NW•; *nemawashi* •NW•.

See also groupism •NW•.

tax haven is a country that has little or no taxation on foreign-source income, or capital gains, and for this reason is of interest to those who seek a place to shelter their funds.

See also offshore funds.

technical assistance refers to intellectual property (e.g., know-how, processes) made available to developing countries (usually free of charge or on concessional terms) either on a bilateral official development assistance (ODA) basis or via specialized bodies of the United Nations System, such as United Nations Industrial Development Organization (UNIDO).

Cf. technology transfer.

technical cooperation *See* technical assistance.

technology transfer

1. sometimes called *transfer of technology transactions*, is the making available of know-how (patents, industrial design, operational systems) from one trading partner to another.

   Technology transfer transactions can take two basic forms: commercial and noncommercial.

   • Commercially transferred technology is done via direct investment, including direct sale, the licensing of intellectual property, the contracting for consultancy services, and turnkey projects.

   • Noncommercially transferred technology takes the form of technical assistance funded by official government agencies (e.g., Canadian International Development Agency). It is otherwise called "official development assistance" (ODA) and can be provided either noncontractually (i.e., free of charge) or on concessional terms.

2. is a component of a type of countertrade transaction called "direct offsets" in which an exporter agrees either to make available technical assistance to the importer or to conduct research and development (R&D) in the host country as a condition of winning the export contract.

Example: A group of the Sahel nations agreed to Canadian exports of irrigation equipment provided that the companies funded local R&D in agronomy and hydrology aimed at reducing and ultimately eliminating their dependence on external agricultural inputs.

Cf. large scale industrial transfer; concessional financing.
See also official development assistance.

teleconferencing (teleconferencing network) is a communications technology, based on telephone-cable networks, applied to the business application of electronically convening an "audio meeting" of geographically separated individuals.

Until the introduction of the fiber optic cable, teleconferencing was the least expensive way of exchanging simultaneous audio signals between people widely separated geographically. For international communications, most teleconferencing uses commercial satellites and terrestrial (earth-based) satellite receiving stations.

Cf. videoconferencing.

term documentary credit *See* documentary credit.

term documentary draft is an instrument for the payment of exports.

When the importer presents the draft accompanied by documents to the bank that issued it, the instrument is "accepted" by the bank for payment and may be paid in full upon the maturity date of the draft. Such a draft is called a "banker's acceptance."

If the exporter is not prepared to wait for payment of this draft until its maturity date, she or he may receive payment for it earlier at a discount (i.e., the term draft may be discounted) by the bank, thus enabling the exporter to liquidate the receivable.

See also documentary draft; D/P draft; acceptance financing; banker's acceptance.

term draft, also called a *time draft*, is a bill of exchange, drawn against a letter of credit that orders payment of a specific amount within a specific time (e.g., 30, 60, 90, or 180 days) after its physical presentation to the payer.

Cf. sight draft.
See also documentary credit; documentary draft.

terms of sale are the legal conditions surrounding a commercial transaction (either export or import), which specify the obligations of both the buyer and the seller, including the payment conditions.

In the international and global marketing environments, some of these conditions are "uniform" (i.e., a worldwide concensus exists as to the meaning and use of the terms). In other cases, there exists a vocabulary of conditions of sale that do not enjoy a global concensus.

Cf. terms of trade.

See also Appendix III; Appendix IV; International Chamber of Commerce.

terms of trade, sometimes used synonymously, and incorrectly, with *terms of sale*, are the values derived from a transaction involving a quantity of export goods A from country A, which can be exchanged for an equivalent quantity of import goods B from country B.

> **Example:** The terms of trade for developing countries are considered to have deteriorated in recent years. For example, in 1965, it cost a typical Latin American country 50 tonnes of raw sugar to buy 1 Canadian tractor. In 1990, the same tractor cost 150 tonnes of the commodity. One of the reasons for this situation is the continuing surplus of commodities on the world market resulting in depressed prices for them. Consequently, commodity exporters are unable to generate sufficient hard-currency export earnings to afford high value-added capital-goods imports.
>
> Cf. terms of sale.

TEU (TEUs) is the abbreviation for **t**wenty-foot **e**quivalent **u**nit(s).

See container.

third-country dumping is the perception by the U.S. government that it is caused, or threatened to be caused, material injury by denying it "fair market access" to a foreign country when another country dumps competitive goods in that foreign country.

The concept derives from Section 1317 of the U.S. Omnibus Trade Act of 1988. Any country determined to be a "third-country dumper" can be dealt with accordingly under the Act by the United States Trade Representative (USTR).

> **Example:** When goods are sold into Canada by Taiwan at prices determined by the USTR (and the United States International Trade Commission) to be unfair to similar U.S. goods that might be marketed to Canada, Taiwan is determined to be guilty of third-country dumping. In this analysis, the United States is the "first country" and Canada, the target export country, is the "third country." Taiwan, determined to be guilty of the dumping, is cited as the "third-country dumper."
>
> *See also* dumping.

third-country national is a variation of *foreign expatriate*.

See expatriate.

Third Option is the international politico-economic policy of the Canadian government (in 1973) that sought to counterbalance perceived economic dependence on the United States by seeking "affiliate membership" for Canada in the European Economic Community (EEC).

The implementation of the strategy was unsuccessful, the consequences being that free trade with the United States became the only remaining option for Canada.

Third World (third world) is an ethnocentric reference to developing countries (LDCs).
    Cf. Fourth World.

Three Pillar Strategy, also called "Going Global," is the national trade approach of the Canadian government (toward the year 2000) that rests on orientations to the global triad of (1) North America, (2) the European Economic Community (EEC), and (3) a Japan-centered Asia-Pacific region.
    These orientations are as follows:

1. *North America:* Canada will increase its use of the Free Trade Agreement (FTA), will upgrade Canadian technology, and will expand Canadian research and development capabilities to compete with the European Economic Community (EEC) and Japan.

   The Canadian government has dubbed this the "USA Opportunities Strategy," and it comprises such programs as the New Exporters to Border States Program (NEBS) and New Exporters to the U.S. South Program (NEXUS).

2. *European Economic Community (EEC):* Foreseeing the ultimate unification of Europe (post-1992) as a Single Market and the real possibility of being "shut out" of entry to, or establishment in, that market, the following four initiatives are being implemented under the banner of a "Europe 1992 Strategy":
   i. *European Challenge Campaign*—a massive educational program directed at Canadian industry to explain the requirements and market opportunities of the (anticipated) Single Market of Europe in the post-1992 era;
   ii. *European Trade Policy Strategy*—Canada's use of the General Agreement of Tariffs and Trade (GATT) as the main vehicle for vigorous trade-liberalization efforts in Canada-EEC relations;
   iii. *European Trade and Investment Development Strategy*—major promotion of Canada-Europe two-way investment in "strategic corporate alliances" involving key industrial sectors, including the New Exporters Overseas program (NEXOS);
   iv. *Canada-Europe Science and Technology Strategy*—the enhancement of existing Canadian research-and-development (R&D) centers via Canada-Europe technology-transfer incentives, increased funding, and the establishment of new mechanisms for sharing in R&D between Canada and Europe.

3. *Japan-Centered Asia-Pacific Region:* in recognition of the ongoing importance of Japan (and its regional economic trade group), a "Pacific 2000 Strategy" has been initiated, comprising the following components:

i.   *Pacific Trade Strategy*—a program of "enhanced assistance" by the Canadian government to Canadian business to promote identification and penetration of Asian markets;

ii.   *Japan Science and Technology Fund*—a Canadian fund to capitalize basic research, applied technology, and technological innovation and to fund the commercialization of it through cooperation (and coordination) between Canadian and Japanese centers of research;

iii. *Pacific 2000 Language and Awareness Fund*—a fund designed to capitalize the establishment of educational centers (and expansion of current units within existing educational centers); to train teachers and develop curricula; to teach Canadians Asian languages; and to understand Asian cultures with the aim of improving and increasing long-term relationships among individuals, private institutions, and governments in Canada and Asia;

iv.   *Pacific 2000 Projects Fund*—a fund designed to promote major international events (e.g., Canada-Taiwan Trade Month): to form seminars on key regional issues; to fund visits to Canada by young Asian leaders of the Asian Region; to promote joint educational ventures with Asian educational institutions; to support research on priority policy areas; and to contribute to the funding of institutions such as the Pacific Economic Cooperation Group (PECG).

See also export support programs.

tied aid is a form of official development assistance (ODA) whereby the projects designed for a developing country by a developed country are linked to continued dependence by the former on the latter.

Example: Canadian ODA to India to provide a series of heavy-water (CANDU) nuclear reactors was tied to long-term Canadian exports of the U-235 fuel bundles needed to power the technology and of robotic technology required to safely handle the "spent fuel."

Cf. U.S. International Cooperation Development Agency ((c) Trade and Development Program).

tied loan is a nonrepayable credit granted by a sovereign state via a state agency that requires that the foreign borrower use the credit in the lender's country.

Example: The Canadian Federal Government uses its Canadian International Development Agency (CIDA) to extend tied loans to developing countries in Africa, Asia, and Latin America.

This directly benefits Canadian industry since the Canadian dollars never leave Canada but are simply moved from one side of the ledger to the other when the borrower government places its order for Canadian goods. It completely eliminates documentary collections and all the attendant commercial and political risks involved.

Cf. Official Development Assistance.

time draft is a nonstandard variation of *term draft*.
See documentary draft.

TOFC is the abbreviation for **trailer-on-flat-car**.
See container.

Tokyo Round, officially *The Tokyo Round of Multilateral Trade Negotiations*, the seventh round of trade negotiations (RTN) in the period 1973–1979, was held under the auspices of the General Agreement on Tariffs and Trade (GATT).

The major outcomes of the Tokyo Round were:

1. a concensus by all the Contracting Parties to across-the-board tariff reductions approaching 30 percent;
2. the agreement to adopt a globally standardized code of conduct for applying nontariff barriers; and
3. the negotiation of an acceptable code of conduct establishing procedural standards for proceedings involving countervailing duties and dispute settlement in the area of export subsidies, as well as seven other International Agreements.

According to some critics of the Tokyo Round, the GATT effectively died when the alleged benefits promised to the world as a result of the Tokyo Round failed to materialize. American protectionists cite the University of Michigan's 1986 review of the Tokyo Round, which claimed that the positive effects of the Round on U.S. trade, employment, and welfare should be measured in tenths (or even hundredths) of a percent!

While there is substantial evidence that can be used to disparage the Tokyo Round in particular, and the GATT in general (and even to proclaim that "the GATT is dead"), the truth is that U.S. expectations far exceeded the Tokyo Round's ability to deliver. The real cause of U.S. failure to benefit from the Tokyo Round is due to its own competitive failure in global competition. The current lead by Japan of the worldwide semiconductor industry and the steady decline of the U.S. share of the international aircraft industry are simply two well-known examples that support the facts.

The following cross references direct attention toward the specific Agreements, Arrangements, and Codes that resulted from the Tokyo Round.

See also Agreement on Antidumping Practices; Agreement on Customs Valuation; Agreement on Government Procurement; Agreement on Import Licensing; Subsidies (and Countervailing Measures) Code (Agreement on the Interpretation and Application of Articles VI, XVI, and XXIII of the GATT); Standards Code (Agreement on Technical Barriers to Trade); Agreement on Trade in Civil Aircraft; Arrangement Regarding Bovine Meat; International Dairy Arrangement.

tontine, from the French meaning "part in an annuity," or shared by a subscriber to a loan; derived from the Neapolitan financier Lorenzo Tonti, who originated them in France in the seventeenth century; is an "informal financial association" networks of which (1) exist in some African countries that were former French colonies, (2) operate parallel to the formal banking sector, and (3) provide substantial financing for rural "microprojects," such as small- and medium-size local manufacturing, trading, and agricultural enterprises.

The name *tontine* is used in Côte d'Ivoire, Cameroon, Congo, and Sénégal. In Nigeria, it is called *esusu*; in Liberia, *susu*; in Zambia, *cilimba*; and in Zaire, *likilemba*.

They are especially useful where the formal bank sector fails to provide financing for the purchase of seed, tools, machinery, and agricultural chemicals. In the Cameroon, under its financial laws, bank loans are only available if borrowers are *tontine* members, thus guaranteeing the existence of the informal sector that invests its funds in urban banks and helps increase the rural money supply.

Toronto Terms are a number of debt-rescheduling options that grew out of the so-called "Toronto Summit" in June 1988 and are considered the most recent approach by the Paris Club to debt rescheduling.

Cf. Venice Terms.

See also debt rescheduling; Paris Club.

total quality (TQ) is the idea that international businesses can only continue to exist by satisfying the needs of their customers and, especially, by exceeding their customers' expectations of service and satisfaction.

The two components of TQ are (1) the product-quality element (the "production orientation") and (2) the service-quality element (the "marketing orientation"). Companies that are leaders in their industries are deemed to have achieved a "good fit" between the two components.

The TQ idea, or "movement" (as perceptive sociologists have called it), began in the United States in the early 1980s as a response to Japanese competitive pressure. There are several characteristics of the "movement":

1. *Scholarly Legitimation:* the basis for TQ was laid through the work of American Professor G. Edward Deming in statistical quality control and just-in-time (JIT) systems.
2. *Charismatic Leadership:* the "acts of the corporate apostles" such as Lee Iaccoca, who "saved" Chrysler, have given the movement its dynamic and emotional role models.
3. *Social Reinforcement:* industry awards, such as the Awards for Business Excellence (Canada), the Baldrige Award (Japan), and the Deming Award (United States), give concrete social meaning to the belief in the free market and in the consumer-driven nature of it.

Operationally speaking, international companies that adopt a "total quality strategy" actively implement programs such as "quality circles" and "quality improvement." In so doing, they thereby promote the idea that their employees at every corporate level are the crucial ingredient in the firm's success.

From a sociological perspective, total quality can be considered a "constructed religion" designed to combat alienation by giving meaning to life in the workplace. This is not a cynical view, but rather one based on cross-cultural study. Consider, for example, the particular rites of passage *(rites de passage)* in large Japanese companies (e.g., the "initiation rites" and the daily ritual of singing the company song or "corporate anthem"). With the acceleration of secularization in the world, one should not be too surprised that social processes so successfully used in traditional religious institutions in *Gemeinschaft* society (like hymn singing) have been adopted by leaders in economic institutions (company-song singing) in our *Gesellschaft* society.

Cf. groupism •NW•; *nemawashi* •NW•.

See also Gemeinschaft; Gesellschaft.

trade refers to international transactions involving goods and/or services for monetary profit between legal entities (individuals, enterprises, states) that have different legal personalities.

Trade that is not entirely monetized is called "countertrade," and it comprises a variety of types of transactions, some devoid of money (e.g., barter), while others involve a money component (e.g., counterpurchase).

Trade that is carried out primarily for humanistic or altruistic motives (*vis-à-vis* the profit motive) and where the exchange is overwhelmingly one-sided is called "aid," or, more formally, "official development assistance" (ODA).

See also official development assistance; countertrade.

trade acceptance, sometimes called an *accepted bill of exchange,* is the negotiable instrument created when a documentary draft, drawn by the exporter on the importer, is acknowledged by the importer to be the obligation to pay, in consideration for goods shipped or services performed.

See also documentary draft; bill of exchange.

Trade Act of 1974 is important U.S. trade legislation that authorized the U.S. president to enter the Tokyo Round of Multilateral Trade Negotiations (MTN) (1973–1979) and that established the Office of the U.S. Trade Representative (USTR) as a branch of the Executive Office of the President.

The Act was notable for extending the Generalized System of Preferences (GSP) to developing countries and for having established guidelines to be followed for the granting of most-favored-nation (MFN) status to member countries of the Council for Mutual Economic Assistance (CMEA).

Section 201 of the Act provided for safeguards (as permitted under the General Agreement on Tariffs and Trade (GATT) Article XIX), and Section 301 of the Act enabled the U.S. president to withdraw concessions from, or impose quantitative restrictions on, "unfair traders" (i.e., countries that unfairly subsidized exports or blocked U.S. exports behind discriminatory tariff and nontariff barriers.)

Finally, the Act expanded the definition of international trade to include trade in services.

In 1984, fully 5 years following the end of the Tokyo Round and 10 years after the U.S. Act, the Canadian parliament passed legislation (the Special Import Measures Act of 1984), similar to the U.S. Trade Act of 1974, that incorporated Canadian rights and obligations that flowed from the Tokyo Round.

Cf. Omnibus Trade Act of 1988.

See also Tokyo Round; multilateral trade negotiations; Generalized System of Preferences; most-favored nation; Council for Mutual Economic Assistance; fast-track; safeguards; quantitative restrictions; Special Import Measures Act of 1984; U.S. Trade Representative.

Trade Agreements Act of 1934 is U.S. legislation that authorized then U.S. president Roosevelt (via Executive Branch officials) to negotiate mutual reductions of tariffs with U.S. trading partners under the most-favored-nation (MFN) principle.

See also most-favored nation.

Trade Agreements Act of 1979 is U.S. legislation that implemented the agreements reached at the Tokyo Round of Multilateral Trade Negotiations (MTN).
See also Tokyo Round.

Trade and Tariff Act of 1984 is U.S. legislation in the form of an "omnibus trade act" granting then-U.S. president Reagan authority to enter into negotiations with other countries with the aim of establishing free trade areas.

> The Act also authorized the president (1) to grant trade preferences, (2) to enforce quantitative restrictions (QRs) on (the import of) steel, and (3) to negotiate free trade agreements.
> It was under the authority of this Act that the United States negotiated two free trade agreements, one with Israel and the other with Canada.

See also Canada-U.S. Free Trade Agreement of 1989; U.S.-Israel Free Trade Agreement; preferences; quantitative restrictions.

trade bloc (trading bloc) is a group of countries that have formally come together to create an international (or supranational) commercial unit for the purpose of (1) trade among the members (e.g., Benelux) and (2) trade between the unit and other commercial groups (e.g., trade between the Benelux and the Association of Southeast Asian Nations).
See also Appendix V.

trade-creating customs union (also called a *trade-creating economic union*) refers to the economically desirable outcome that occurs when a regional, economically integrated group of countries generates more "external imports" from low-cost nongroup members than higher-cost imports from group-member countries.

> It is inferred that a trade-creating customs union must work well, as a consequence of the integration of member economies, when fewer high-cost imports are exchanged among group members than imports of lower-cost substitutes from nonmember countries.

Cf. trade-diverting customs union.
See also trade creation; trade diversion.

trade creation is a process that occurs whereby commercial transactions are generated by the displacement of domestic production by lower-cost imports.

> It is not suggested that all inefficient domestic production cease and be replaced by more efficient, lower-cost imports. It is suggested that wherever domestic production is inefficient (usually behind protective tariff barriers), the basis for trade creation exists.

Cf. trade deflection; trade diversion.

trade deflection is the process that occurs in a free trade area, common market, or customs union, which operates imperfectly (i.e., where the common external tariffs are neither equally common nor equally applied), when imports flow into the countries that apply the lowest tariffs to avoid the higher tariffs of the other member countries.

Cf. trade creation; trade diversion.

trade diversion is the process that occurs in a free trade area, common market, or customs union when lower-cost imports from outside the area are replaced by higher-cost imports from another member country of the trade group.

Cf. trade creation; trade deflection.

trade-diverting customs union, also called a *trade-diverting economic union*, is the economically undesirable outcome that occurs when a regional, economically integrated group of countries generates more "internal imports" from high-cost group members than lower-cost imports from nongroup countries.

It is inferred that a trade-diverting customs union must work imperfectly if, despite the integration of member economies, more high-cost imports are exchanged among group members than imports of lower-cost substitutes from nonmember countries.

Cf. trade-creating customs union.

See also trade creation; trade diversion.

trade effect of a tariff is the decrease in the volume of trade in the goods affected as a result of a tariff.

, The decrease is measured internationally: the reduction of export volume of the nation whose production of the goods has been curtailed plus the import volume of the nation whose consumption of the goods has been curtailed.

Cf. production effect of a tariff; consumption effect of a tariff.

See also duty.

Trade Expansion Act of 1962 is the U.S. legislation passed as an outcome of the Dillon Round (1960–1962) of Multilateral Trade Negotiations (MTN) under the auspices of the General Agreement on Tariffs and Trade (GATT).

The salient points of the Act empowered then-U.S. president Kennedy (via Executive Branch officials) (1) to negotiate across-the-board tariff reductions of up to 50 percent of their level in 1962 and (2) to participate in the up-coming Kennedy Round (1963–1967) of multilateral tariff negotiations (MTN).

See also round of trade negotiations.

trade fair, also called a *trade show* or a *trade exhibition*, is the physical presentation of export goods and services at a competitive event in a foreign market, held to bring buyers and sellers together for the purpose of sales.

There are two categories of trade fairs: government-sponsored trade fairs and industry-sponsored trade fairs. In the former, companies are invited to participate in the events, which are held under the auspices of the government (i.e., in a government-identified pavilion). In this case, the costs of participation are usually shared on some cooperative (i.e., cost-sharing) basis.

For industry-sponsored shows, the company usually participates on a "solo basis" (i.e., with little or no government direct assistance).

trade liberalization, called *liberalization,* is the ongoing process whereby tariff and nontariff barriers are removed (and eliminated) via multilateral trade negotiations (MTN) among trading nations that are Contracting Parties to the General Agreement on Tariffs and Trade (GATT).

Cf. protectionism.

See also liberalization; multilateral trade negotiations.

trade measures *See* nontariff barriers.

trade mission is a government-sponsored visit to a foreign country by a delegation of private-sector individuals (invited by the domestic government) to achieve specific commercial goals (e.g., technology transfer, direct exporting, promotion of direct investment).

Trade Opportunities Program (TOP) is a computerized "fee-for-service" program offered by the Foreign Commercial Service unit of the International Trade Administration section of the U.S. Department of Commerce in Washington, D.C.

The TOP (1) matches input from U.S. exporters with interest by foreign buyers and (2) mails "trade-opportunity notices" to U.S. TOP subscribers when a "match" occurs.

The TOP computer system is more advanced than any of the export-oriented information systems maintained by the Canadian government's Department of Industry, Science and Technology.

Cf. export trade information.

See also U.S. International Trade Administration.

trade policy refers to international commercial objectives of a government as formulated, publicly announced, and implemented by authorized officials.

For example, Canadian trade policy was, in the 1970s and early 1980s, highly protectionist and inward oriented.

Current Canadian trade policy (i.e., since the opening of FTA talks in 1985 and their successful conclusion in 1988) is free-market oriented and free-market driven. It can be succinctly called the Three Pillar Strategy, energetically supporting the drive of the General Agreement on Tariffs and Trade (GATT) to keep open the world trading system whose major political-economies are North America, the European Economic Community (EEC), and the Pacific/Asian megamarket of Japan and the Asian newly industrialized countries (NICs).

See also Three Pillar Strategy; Canada-U.S. Free Trade Agreement of 1989.

trade-related aspects of intellectual property rights (TRIPs) refers to one of the major Canadian government concerns at the Uruguay Round of multilateral trade negotiations (MTN). Canada has put forward proposals for a TRIPs Agreement to:

1. increase the levels of protection of intellectual property rights;
2. remove discriminatory practices worldwide; and

3. ensure that Canada in particular, and all General Agreement on Tariffs and Trade (GATT) members in general, have reasonable access to global technology.

The Canadian position is that "enhanced intellectual property protection" (via the adoption by GATT of a comprehensive set of enforcement rules on intellectual property rights) would act as an incentive for inventors of intellectual property, and for owners and users of it, to innovate and compete in the development and promotion of science and technology.

See also intellectual property; Uruguay Round.

trade-related investment measures (TRIMs) are nontariff barriers (NTBs) that restrict or distort trade, such as domestic content rules and conditions attached to remitting foreign exchange.

The reduction or elimination of TRIMs is one of the areas addressed by the Negotiating Group on Trade-Related Investment Measures of the General Agreement on Tariffs and Trade (GATT) and by the Tokyo Round of Multilateral Trade Negotiations (MTN).

See also General Agreement on Tariffs and Trade; Uruguay Round.

trade sanctions *See* embargo.

trade terms is the vocabulary of definitions used by those involved in the process of buying and selling goods and services internationally in order to establish an acceptable basis for accepting and carrying out one's responsibilities and obligations in the global commercial environment.

Cf. Appendix IV.

See also Appendix III.

trade visitor, also called an *incoming trade visitor*, is a formal invitee of a government who is brought to a country as a guest for the purpose of commercial activity.

The expectation is that the visitor will directly purchase or invest in, or will influence the purchase of or investment in, goods from the host country.

The activities of the foreign visitor may comprise (1) attending export-oriented trade fairs, (2) meetings with potential exporters (and export facilitators such as bankers) in the private sector, (3) discussions with government officials regarding direct-investment opportunities and incentives, and (4) (possibly) discussions with union functionaries about the variable costs of direct labor.

trade war is a sustained campaign (usually bilateral, and between two sovereign entities) involving measures aimed at reducing (to the point of elimination) the comparative advantage of a commercial antagonist.

Tactics used by the commercial belligerents may comprise any (or all) of the following tactics: predatory dumping, countervailing duties, retaliation, reprisals, predatory pricing, and embargo.

trading company *See* trading house.

trading house, also known as a *trading company* in North America (and not to be confused with a *sogososha*, a general trading company in Japan), refers to a business that functions as a trading principal, and that specializes in the import and export of particular kinds of goods from specific countries or geographic regions.

Trading houses buy and sell on their own account and, thus, are not indirect export intermediaries.

> **Example:** If a Canadian mining company negotiates a deal with a "cash-poor country" that can pay only 50 percent in dollars and 50 percent in smoked hams, a trading house can be used to (1) liquidate the hams immediately and (2) arrange sale of the countertraded commodity either to itself or to any other of its global customers anywhere in the world.

In Canada and the United States, countertrade transactions are handled by trading-house specialists whose volume of such business is so large globally that there is no cost incentive for a trader to do such a transaction independently, unless the deal is extraordinarily large.

Spar Aero-Space, Canadian builders of earth-tracking stations for the Brazilian (state) telecommunications agency Intelbras, concluded a countertrade deal with Brazil: Spar established their own trading house, Spar Trading Company, through which they agreed to market Brazilian tropical products and to accept the proceeds as partial payment, the remaining 50 percent being in cash.

Cf. offset deals.
See also Canadian Council of Trading Houses.

traditional economy *See Gemeinschaft.*

tramp (tramp ship, tramp steamer), from the Middle English *trampe* meaning "dissolute woman," is (1) an ocean-going vessel that carries cargo between ports on routes that offer neither conference-liner service nor nonconference-liner service; (2) an ocean-going vessel that provides irregular ocean-cargo service and whose standards of service are perceived to be "substandard," *vis-à-vis* conference-liner service.

tramp steamer *See* tramp.
See also steamship conference.

transactionability •NW• is the ease with which a currency is accepted in the international market.

A currency with high transactionability is called a convertible currency.
See also convertible currency.

transferable currency is a Soviet variation of *convertible currency.*
See convertible currency.
See also reserve currency country.

transferable rouble (Transferable Rouble) *See* International Bank for Economic Cooperation; International Investment Bank.

transfer cost (transfer costing), under a licensing agreement, is (1) the variable costs to a licensor of shipping capital equipment to the foreign-based licensee; or, as a variation, (2) all the ongoing costs to the licensor of maintaining the agreement, including any one-time costs for shipping capital equipment to the foreign-based licensee.

transfer of technology *See* technology transfer.

transfer payments are transactions between parent companies and their subsidiaries (and their affiliates) involving remittances of royalties to the parent company for the use of technology, intellectual property (e.g., trademarks), and supplies and operating equipment.
See also licensing.

transfer price (transfer pricing) refers to (1) the intracompany cost for the exchange of goods and services in the global environment of intercompany trade; or (2) the intracompany process of charging differential costs for goods and services depending upon the tax status of each of the company's units.

The conclusion to be drawn is that multinational and global companies engage in trade intracorporately and charge each of the company units prices for goods and services appropriate to the tax status of the company. The aim is to shift income and profits from high-tax countries to low-tax countries. No negative inference is intended (or should be drawn) regarding the motives for this activity.

transitional measures are short-term actions by governments put in place for a limited period of time during which a trade agreement is implemented.

> **Example:** The Tokyo Round (1973–1979) provided the Contracting Parties to the Agreement a period of eight years to fully implement the agreed-upon tariff cuts. Some of the short-term provisions available up to 1987 (and used by both Canada and the United States) were limited and emergency safeguards, used to protect domestic industry from potential injury due to extremely low-cost imports.

> *See also* safeguards; injury.

translation is the rendering of intellectual property (e.g., promotional materials, instruction manuals) in a forward direction, from one language (the source language) into another language (the target language).
When the process of interpretation involves the rendering of source-language sounds that do not naturally occur in the target language, the operation is called transliteration.

To translate the Islamic hortatory expression "God (Allah) is great" from Arabic to English, the result would be the transliteration *"ah-lahú ach-báar."* The "ach-" sound is the best English spelling to render an Arabic guttural sound, which has no natural equivalent in English and, consequently, no equivalent English spelling.

Cf. backtranslation.

transnational corporations (TNCs) *See* multinational corporations.

transnational enterprises (TNEs) *See* multinational corporations.

transparent refers to a high degree of visibility and openness to scrutiny of business practices and trade measures.

From the viewpoint of an open international trading system under the General Agreement on Tariff and Trade (GATT), tariffs are acknowledged as being the most highly visible of all trade barriers. Next in line are quotas, which are more transparent than subsidies since it is relatively easy to identify (1) who the quota-holders are, and (2) how much quota each holds. In contrast, it is much less easy to determine who receives subsidies and the amount of subsidy paid. It has been an ongoing working principle of the current Uruguay Round of Multilateral Tariff Negotiations (MTN) to keep all trade restrictions as transparent as possible so that they can be identified and addressed by all members of the international trading community.

> **Example:** At the request of Japan's Ministry of Finance (MOF), the Japanese Institute of Certified Public Accountants worked out a package of measures on March 26, 1991, aimed at increasing and strengthening the degree of disclosure on business transactions within Japanese *keiretsu*. The measures are intended to increase transparency in such business dealings and are Japan's response to an American government request under the Structural Impediments Initiative talks in 1990.

> *See also* quota; *keiretsu* •NW•; Structural Impediments Initiative •NW•.

transportation is the major core component of physical distribution (PD), which comprises the carriage of goods between the buyer and the seller.
See also physical distribution.

transportation costs are charges for freight, loading, unloading, insurance coverage, and interest rates while goods are in transit between the seller and the buyer.

Depending on the terms of sale, the cost of freight may (or may not) include the cost of loading, unloading, insurance coverage, and interest while the goods are in transit. Which party bears the onus for paying these costs depends upon the terms of sale.
See also terms of sale.

transshipment (trans-shipment) refers to (1) a handling function in physical distribution/logistics (PD/L) whereby goods are transferred intermodally (e.g., TOFC, COFC) to take advantage of transport efficiencies to effect promised customer service; or (2) goods transferred from one ship to another en route to the customer; for example, when containers from Japan, Korea, Hong Kong, and Taiwan that are destined for the United States are shipped to Singapore, where they are all consolidated aboard a container ship, the goods are said to have been "transshipped" to the United States via Singapore.

Treaty on Intellectual Property in Respect of Integrated Circuits is an international agreement adopted in Washington, D.C., on May 26, 1989, at a diplomatic conference to which all member states of the Paris Union and the Berne Union and/or WIPO were invited.

As of December 31, 1989, the following six states had signed it: Egypt, Ghana, Guatamala, Liberia, Yugoslavia, and Zambia.

Under the auspices of the World Intellectual Property Organization (WIPO), the Treaty establishes a framework of 20 articles under which signatories agree to protect the integrated circuits of their own nationals and of all other nationals of signatory countries from unauthorized reproduction and/or use.

Thus, Article 6 (1) is the focus of the protection provisions: signatory states agree to establish minimum standards for the protection of acts deemed unlawful, ". . . namely, and in particular, reproduction of a protected layout-design and the importation, sale, or other distribution for commercial purposes of a protected layout-design or an integrated circuit in which such a layout-design is incorporated, where said acts are performed without the authorization of the holder of the right."

See also World Intellectual Property Organization.

Treaty on International Registration of Audiovisual Works is an international agreement adopted in Geneva, Switzerland, during the period from April 10 to April 20, 1989, by a concensus of 59 states and 11 intergovernmental agencies.

As of December 31, 1989, the following 15 states had signed the Treaty: Austria, Brazil, Burkina Faso, Canada, Chile, Egypt, France, Greece, Guinea, Hungary, India, The Philippines, Poland, Sénégal, and the United States.

Under the auspices of the World Intellectual Property Organization (WIPO), the Treaty establishes an International Register (located in Austria) for "audiovisual works," comprising films made for television and cinema.

The aim of the Treaty is (1) to facilitate the legal, international flow of audiovisual works; (2) to increase the legal security for rightful owners of such works; and (3) to make a substantive contribution to the international effort against the unauthorized distribution and use ("piracy") of these works.

Under the Treaty, each country that is a signatory to it agrees to recognize that any entry in the International Register (by citizens of countries that have ratified the treaty) is considered to be a true statement of fact regarding the ownership of the works registered. For example, registration of a particular film by Egyptians, citizens of one of the signatory countries, would be taken in law as prima facie evidence (unless proven otherwise) that those who made the registration were people making a legal claim for having made the particular film and, thus, for having a legal right to make contracts for its use by others.

See also World Intellectual Property Organization.

Trevi Group, an abbreviation from the French Terrorisme, Radicalisme, Extrémisme, Violence Internationale, meaning "international terrorism, radicalism, extremism, and violence," is an international security organization consisting of the 12 European Economic Community countries, established to exchange information related to control of international political terrorism.

Cf. International Maritime Bureau.

trickle-down effect •NW• is the notion that government should selectively spend in the public sector to yield increased levels of down-stream growth, Western-style social change, and "enhanced levels of personal political freedom."

The effect assumes that limited government involvement in the economy can have "wealth-generating effects," but only so long as government ultimately withdraws its support, permitting industry to flourish independent of government assistance.

The trickle-down effect is a "soft" form of neoprotectionism: it is another way of saying the infant industry argument is "a good way" to generate and distribute wealth. In fact, protective tariffs are simply that, with the "tariff effects" well understood.

Moreover, it is always interesting when developing political-economies generate a trickle-down liberalization effect, remove their protective tariffs, and eliminate their subsidies—since it is such a rare event!

Cf. trickle-up effect •NW•.
See also protectionism; infant industry argument.

trickle-up effect •NW• is the notion that private capital investment in "developmentally prepared" sectors of a country, done on a gradual basis, eventually yields significant economic growth and an equitable social distribution of it.

The process is claimed to be social change by evolution, and the outcome is expected to be increasingly consumer-driven market economies, where economic growth is expected to yield increasingly favorable attitudes toward direct investment (by developed countries).

The political content of conservative international economists (in proposing the curtailing of public expenditures for social programs) suggests that individual entrepreneurial zeal, *vis-à-vis* government programs, carefully guided by sound monetary policy will yield trickle-up "benefits" for the population as a whole. It is a moot point whether reality supports the theory.

Cf. trickle-down effect •NW•.
See also monetarism; production effect of a tariff.

trigger mechanism is a set of specific events that set off other acts.
See also trigger price, trigger-price mechanism.

trigger price is (1) the world price, agreed upon by international commodity groups (ICGs), at which supplies of specific commodities (e.g., cocoa, coffee) held in inventory by producer countries would be released onto the world market to satisfy demand, thereby preventing the world price from exceeding an agreed-upon "price ceiling" and causing market disruption in consumer countries; or (2) the price of the lowest non-U.S. producer of steel that, under the U.S. trigger-price mechanism, acted as an "ignitor" to set off certain government actions.
See also international commodity agreement; trigger-price mechanism.

trigger-price mechanism (TPM) refers to the U.S. antidumping system developed in 1978 to protect the American steel industry from imports of under-priced steel from Canada, the European Economic Community (EEC), and Japan.

This system was characterized by two types of protectionist actions. If steel imported into the United States was priced below the lowest-cost non-U.S. producer, (1) a special countervailing duty would be set off ("triggered") to make the price equal to that of the lowest-cost foreign producer, and (2) an antidumping investigation would be set off ("triggered") by the U.S. International Trade Commission (USITC).

Trilateral Commission is a private organization, with bureaus in New York, London, and Tokyo, that represents the common interest of fostering the expansion and development of international capitalism in three trading regions: (1) North America, (2) West Europe, and (3) a Japan-centered Asian trading region.

Members of the body are important individuals who, as consultants to the governments of market economies, have significant input into the development and implementation of market-driven international trade policies.

The Commission has great influence. Its members have, over the years, represented the élite of the world's (market-driven) international economists, public-policy advisors, and specialists in key academic, research, and social-policy areas (e.g., Henry Kissinger, Zbigniew Brezhinski, and Arthur Schlesinger).

> **Example:** The Commission strives to maintain the perception of an arm's-length relationship with all governments. In this regard, if people who formerly were official government advisers move from that role to a political one within government, they resign their membership in the body. On the other hand, once government advisors and politicians resign their quasi- or full-government involvement, they may resume their membership in the organization.

Cf. *habatsu* •NW•.

trilateral trade is commercial exchange between three nations.
Cf. bilateral trade; quadrilateral trade; multilateral trade.

trilateral trade agreement is a formal exchange accord between three nations.
Cf. bilateral trade agreement; quadrilateral trade agreement; multilateral trade agreement.

trunk rooming (trunk room) •NW• is the usage of small-lot warehouses in Japan, mainly by companies, for the storage of nonmerchandise goods (e.g., computer tapes).

Trunk rooms themselves are located closer to Tokyo than are freight villas.

Cf. freight villa •NW•.

trust receipt, used widely in the United States and the United Kingdom, is a documentary acknowledgment by the importer that (1) possession of goods has been transferred (to the importer), but (2) ownership of the goods remains with the importer's bank (i.e., the issuing bank that issues the letter of credit on behalf of the exporter).

Only when the importer meets its obligations (i.e., pays its bank, which, in turn, pays the advising bank) does title to the imported goods pass to the importer.

See also issuing bank; letter of credit; consignment.

turnkey project is a business proposal in which the seller-exporter (or goods and/ or services) plans, organizes and manages, finances, and implements all phases of a scheme and hands it over to the buyer-importer after training of local personnel.

> **Example:** Canada's strategy for marketing its Canadian-deuterium-uranium (Candu) heavy-water nuclear reactor is to market it as a turnkey project. India purchased its first "peaceful" Candu nuclear reactor on that basis.
>
> Over a period of five years, from the surveying of the site and the turning of the sod to the flipping of the switch by Canadian-trained nuclear engineers and technicians, Canadian consortia of engineering, construction, and management companies handled every phase of the scheme, including the provision of "soft loans" and the guaranteeing of performance through the Export Development Corporation.

See also technology transfer.

𝓤

underselling refers to offering import items for sale in the United States at prices below those of comparable domestic U.S. goods.

There is considerable debate both in international business and in administrative law as to what represents legitimate "price cutting" or "discounting" and what represents underselling. Underselling implies selling at less than fair value (i.e., dumping).

The interest of the United States International Trade Commission (USITC) in matters concerning underselling stems from the USITC's mandate to undertake antidumping investigations. When American industry petitioners ask the USITC to levy antidumping duties on imported goods, they argue that the imported goods are underselling domestic goods, and, since domestic American manufacturers are "injured" because of this, the underselling is prima facie evidence of dumping.

This cause-effect argument is persuasive; but there is an equally sound rebuttal: underselling may be an above-board "pricing penetration" tactic used by the foreign exporter.

Example: Japanese automobile manufacturers used underselling as their main tactic when they began their export drive to North America in the 1950s and 1960s. The Japanese analyzed the automobile market, and they determined that there was a potentially large and untapped segment for a "down-sized car" (i.e., the "compact" and the "subcompact"). They penetrated the market aggressively by selling these at low prices, and they price-competed them against domestic American competitors who entered the market later.

These widely known marketing facts were considered attempts to cause the domestic automobile industry "injury" (as defined under the General Agreement on Tariffs and Trade) only in the 1980s when Japanese imports began seriously eroding the U.S. domestic-company share of the traditional "mid-size" American car market. At this point, the USITC was not used by the U.S. government to investigate charges of dumping. Rather, political solutions were arrived at. The Japanese agreed (1) to build automobile manufacturing and assembly plants in the United States and (2) to restrict finished-unit imports via mutually agreed-upon quantity restrictions called "voluntary export restraints."

Cf. price suppression; dumping.
See also quantity restrictions.

uncovered interest arbitrage *See* Appendix II.

UNCTAD (United Nations Conference on Trade and Development) Data Base on Trade Measures is a computer-based inventory of worldwide trade-control measures (i.e., nontariff barriers (NTBs) or nontariff measures (NTMs), comprising data on product-specific trade measures in over 100 developed and developing countries.

UNCTAD's Data Base on Trade Measures (UNCTAD Manufactures Division) and UNCTAD's Trade Information System (UNCTAD Division for Economic Cooperation among Developing Countries) and being integrated into a single data base—the Trade Control Measures Information System (TCMIS)—following an administrative reorganization of the UNCTAD Secretariat in Geneva, Switzerland. The integrated data base will contain complete records of NTBs in over 100 countries (including 85 less developed countries), which account for over 90 percent of the developing world's trade.

UNCTAD will make the data base available to any of its members faced with "market-access problems" due to nontariff barriers.

The nontariff measures that UNCTAD includes in the data base comprise all the elements in a broad definition of official, nontariff trade intervention: quotas, prohibitions, import authorizations, nonautomatic licenses (NALs), conditional import authorizations (CIAs), voluntary export restraints (VERs), international commodity agreements (ICAs) and arrangements (e.g., the MultiFiber Arrangement), variable levies, state monopolies on imports, state control of price levels of imports, import deposits, customs fees, surcharges, antidumping and countervailing duty actions, retaliation and reprisals, import surveillance, and automatic licenses. Excluded from the data base are all tariff and duty measures, including seasonal tariffs and NTBs such as standards, regulations, and taxes.

Cf. export trade information.
See also nontariff barriers.

unfair trade is discriminatory commercial exchange activities comprising goods that are either unfairly subsidized or dumped, or are otherwise illegitimate (e.g., gray-market goods or counterfeit goods).

Transactions involving any of these goods are called unfair trading practices.
See also U.S. International Trade Commission.

unfair trader is a country designated by the Executive Branch of the U.S. government, usually by the United States International Trade Commission (USITC) or the United States Trade Representative (USTR), as engaging in "unfair trading practices."

Example: Under Section 301 of the Omnibus Trade Act of 1988, the U.S. Trade Representative named Japan, Brazil, and India as unfair traders in June 1989; and under the authority of the Act, a range of specific retaliatory measures can be invoked against each of them.

uniform order bill of lading *See* bill of lading.

uniform straight bill of lading *See* bill of lading.

Union of Banana Exporting Countries (UBEC), also known as the *Unión de Paises Exportadores de Banano (UPEB)*, is a regional international commodity organization, established in Panamá in 1974 and comprising the following producer-member countries: Colombia, Costa Rica, Dominican Republic, Guatemala, Honduras, Nicaragua, Panamá, and Venezuela.

The main functions of the UBEC are (1) to address itself to the problems of supply and demand for its commodity and (2) to coordinate the exchange of scientific and technical information concerning disease control, product quality, and research into the formulation of food products involving bananas as a key ingredient.

1. *Supply and Demand:* To tackle this crucial area, UBEC established the Multinational Bureau for Commercialization of Banana (COMUNBANA) in 1977, which comprises all the UBEC members and which was conceived of as the OPEC-like arm of UBEC.
2. *Coordination of Information:* In this important field, UBEC maintains close relations with important international organizations such as the United Nations Food and Agricultural Organization (FAO), the United Nations Development Program (UNDP), and the United Nations Conference on Trade and Development (UNCTAD).

One of the facts that must weaken UBEC is that Ecuador, a regional country that alone is responsible for production of over 25 percent of the world production of bananas, is not a member of the organization. Research indicates that Ecuador's nonmembership may have been strongly influenced by the historically strong interrelationship between (1) the country's successive military and civilian political juntas, (2) its *latifundista* ruling families, and (3) the monopoly position in the banana-exporting industry of economically powerful (and politically influential) U.S. and European multinational corporations.

Cf. Organization of Petroleum Exporting Countries; international cartel.

Union Internationale pour la Protection des Obtentions Végétale (UPOV), also known as the *International Union for the Protection of New Varieties of Plants (IUPNVP)*, is an international organization created under the authority of the United Nations Convention for the Protection of New Varieties of Plants.

UPOV cooperates with the World Intellectual Property Organization (WIPO) to legally recognize the property right of the breeder of a new variety of plant. With its headquarters in the WIPO building in Geneva, Switzerland, UPOV is strategically located to avail itself of WIPO's administrative systems to fulfill its mandate.

As of February 1, 1989, the following 18 countries had acceded to the United Nations convention and, thus, had joined UPOV: Australia, Belgium, Denmark, France, Germany, Hungary, Ireland, Israel, Italy, Japan, the Netherlands, New Zealand, South Africa, Spain, Sweden, Switzerland, the United Kingdom, and the United States.

On March 19, 1991, 10 of these states (excepting Australia, Hungary, Ireland, Israel, Japan, New Zealand, Sweden, and the United States) signed a "revised Act of the Convention" in Geneva. The document strengthens the original accord by making protection of all species of plants mandatory for UPOV members. This new provision (1) increases the incentive for national plant breeders who know that their country (as a UPOV member) must afford them property rights to the new varieties they develop, and (2) lessens the threat to plant breeders from "piracy" (i.e., theft) of their protected plant varieties and plagiaristic breeding activities.

See also World Intellectual Property Organization.

United Arab Republic (UAR), now defunct, was a political attempt, in 1958, to establish a large, integrated Arab economy via the merger of Egypt and Syria. The initiative was perceived negatively by other Arab countries, which imputed economic and military-expansionist aims to the UAR.
Cf. Arab Union.

United Nations Capital Development Fund (UNCDF) is an organization of the United Nations System, founded in 1966 and fully operational in 1974.
Unlike the United Nations International Fund for Agricultural Development (IFAD), the UNCDF is not a specialized agency of the United Nations System. Rather, it is a specially constituted Fund of 24 members that allocate the Fund's resources to the world's 30 least developed countries (LLDCs) on a "rapid-deployment emergency basis" *vis-à-vis* the program-like activities of the IFAD.
Cf. International Fund for Agricultural Development.
See also United Nations System.

United Nations Center for Human Settlements (HABITAT) is an international organization of the United Nations System whose activities involve (1) planning for improved urban development and (2) developing strategies to implement improved systems of urban infrastructure, including health and education services, transportation, water supply, and waste disposal.
HABITAT is of interest to global marketers from the viewpoint of equipment purchases made by the Contracts and Procurement Section (CPS) at HABITAT's Nairobi, Kenya, headquarters.

United Nations Children's Fund (UNICEF, Unicef) is an international organization of the United Nations System that is involved in programs aimed at benefiting mothers and children in the fields of primary health care, primary child education, child-care education, shelter, water supply, and sanitation.
UNICEF cooperates and collaborates with other U.N. agencies (e.g., the World Health Organization (WHO)), in the development and implementation of programs such as nutrition education and Under-Five Clinics for postnatal care.

From the global marketing viewpoint, UNICEF procures an enormous quantity of goods, including routine and emergency medical supplies, hospital equipment, and pharmaceuticals.

UNICEF's Supply Division Procurement Services (UNICEF/SDPS) has two offices. One is located at UNICEF's New York headquarters. The other is in Copenhagen, Denmark. The New York UNICEF/SDPS procures for governments and U.N. agencies on a reimbursable basis. The Copenhagen UNICEF/SDPS offers the same service and, in addition, is UNICEF's global purchasing office for goods on a nonreimbursable basis. The facility for this is called the United Nations Packing and Assembly Center (UNIPAC).

United Nations Commission on International Trade Law (UNCITRAL) is a permanent subsidiary body of the United Nations General Assembly, established in 1966, comprised of representatives of 36 countries and devoted to progressively harmonizing and unifying international trade law worldwide.

UNCITRAL's main responsibilities are:

1. to coordinate the work of all international bodies working in the field of international commercial law;
2. to prepare international conventions (i.e., treaties) dealing with aspects of the field for signing by countries;
3. to promote an understanding of international law and of the means of ensuring the interpretation and application of international conventions.

Under its auspices, UNCITRAL has successfully developed a number of conventions in specific priority areas: arbitration, international sale of goods, and international payments. In the area of international arbitration, for example, UNCITRAL put forward a uniform set of rules in 1976 that was codified as the Model Law on International Commercial Arbitration. The United States has not formally adopted it but operates under rules enacted under the United States Uniform Arbitration Act that is in use in over half of the states plus the District of Columbia.

See also United Nations Convention on the Limitation Period on the International Sale of Goods; United Nations Convention on the Carriage of Goods by Sea; United Nations Convention on Contracts for the International Sales of Goods; United Nations Convention on International Bills of Exchange and International Promissory Notes.

United Nations Conference on Trade and Development (UNCTAD) is a functioning unit of the United Nations System as a permanent organ of the U.N. General Assembly, with headquarters in Geneva, Switzerland, devoted to promoting international trade, to assisting the acceleration of international economic cooperation and development among the world's regional trading groups, and to increasing the coordination, integration, and unification of all world trading groups and organizations into one harmonious world system.

UNCTAD was initiated in 1964 by the U.N. General Assembly, and membership comprises over 160 countries, regional trading entities (e.g., EEC), and international organizations.

After UNCTAD's inaugural meeting in 1964 in Geneva, UNCTAD II took place in New Delhi in 1968, and it was the forum for the development of the

Generalized System of Preferences (GSP). UNCTAD III convened in Santiago, Chile, in 1972; UNCTAD IV in Nairobi, Kenya, in 1976; UNCTAD V in Manila, The Philippines, in 1979; UNCTAD VI in Belgrade, Yugoslavia, in 1983; UNCTAD VII in Geneva, Switzerland, in 1987; and UNCTAD VIII is scheduled to be held in Punta del Este, Uruguay, in September/October 1991.

UNCTAD's focus has been predominantly on the perceived inequities in the world trading system, and its work has been in the furtherance of equity in the terms of trade between the developed and the developing countries. Implicitly, this has meant that UNCTAD has worked as the sponsor of such concepts as the Generalized System of Preferences (GSP), and the Common Fund for Commodities (CFC).

See also Group of Seventy-Seven; Generalized System of Preferences; Common Fund for Commodities; International Trade Centre UNCTAD/GATT; UNCTAD Data Base on Trade Measures.

United Nations Convention on the Carriage of Goods by Sea is an international agreement devised by the United Nations Commission on International Trade Law (UNCITRAL), and adopted in 1978, that sets uniform rules for international buyers and sellers concerning their obligations and responsibilities regarding the international physical distribution and movement of goods by sea.

Cf. Appendix IV.

See also United Nations Commission on International Trade Law; United Nations Convention on Contracts for the International Sales of Goods.

United Nations Convention on Conditions for Registration of Ships is an international agreement signed in 1986 under the auspices of the United Nations Conference on Trade and Development (UNCTAD).

This accord establishes new (and higher) standards of responsibility and accountability in international shipping. It also defines and establishes linkages between ships and the flags they fly (i.e., their registration).

Cf. flag of convenience.

See also United Nations Conference on Trade and Development.

United Nations Convention on Contracts for the International Sale of Goods (UN/CISG) is an international agreement, adopted in 1980, that was devised by the United Nations Commission on International Trade Law (UNCITRAL) as a uniform set of rules to help international buyers and sellers agree on their rights and obligations when making contracts.

The Convention has been ratified by the following countries: Austria, China, Egypt, Finland, France, Italy, Hungary, Lesotho, Mexico, Sweden, Syria, the United States, Yugoslavia, and Zambia. Ratification proceedings are under way in other countries.

Ratification by the United States brought the Convention into force on January 1, 1988, between the United States and the other 13 countries that accepted it.

See also Appendix IV; harmonization; United Nations Commission on International Trade Law.

United Nations Convention on International Bills of Exchange and International Promissory Notes is an international agreement devised by the United Nations Commission on International Trade Law (UNCITRAL) in 1987 that is still in draft form.

This treaty would aim to harmonize and unify on a long-term basis all existing national laws and regional rules surrounding the types of international bills of exchange used. Initially, the aim is to create a set of rules for interpreting various national and regional standards. Ultimately, the Convention would seek to create a single definition (i.e., a single interpretation) for bills of exchange and a standard format for them.

This "draft convention" is circulating among the 36 members of UNCITRAL and between them and other United Nations specialized bodies. Eventually it will be brought before the United Nations General Assembly for signing. Once countries have accepted the Convention, they will be responsible for returning to their individual countries to have it ratified in their national parliaments.

It is hoped to have this Convention accepted prior to the end of 1992 when it is anticipated that the Single European Market will have been completed.

See also United Nations Commission on International Trade Law.

United Nations Convention on International Multimodal Transport of Goods is an international agreement signed in 1980 under the auspices of the United Nations Conference on Trade and Development (UNCTAD).

This accord establishes a single set of rules for determining liability when goods are transported multimodally (i.e., via more than one manner of transport).

Cf. Code of Conduct for Liner Conferences.
See also United Nations Conference on Trade and Development.

United Nations Convention on the Limitation Period on the International Sale of Goods is an international agreement devised by the United Nations Commission on International Trade Law (UNCITRAL), and adopted in 1974, that sets a time limit of four years during which the parties to an international contract may sue for nonpayment.

See also United Nations Commission on International Trade Law.

United Nations Convention on the Recognition and Enforcement of Foreign Arbitration Awards (1972) (UNCREFAA) is an international accord binding its signatories (over 75 countries) to uphold foreign arbitral awards.

The 1972 convention was passed by the United Nations General Assembly in New York City following the earlier signing of the U.N. Geneva Convention on Arbitration (1972).

The UNCREFAA elevates the enforcement of arbitration awards to the level of a multilateral agreement (i.e., a treaty). Countries that have signed and ratified this Convention in their national parliaments are obligated to uphold its provisions.

Example: A French company, resident in the United States, took a matter of alleged patent infringement by a U.S. firm to the French Arbitration Association for disposition. An arbitration panel was established, and the arbitrators made a substantial monetary award to the French company, finding in favor of it and issuing a "cease and desist order" to prevent further infringing actions.

The U.S. firm petitioned the United States Court of International Trade (CIT) for a judicial review of the judgment, claiming that the panel had no jurisdiction over an American company. The firm hoped to have the CIT "stay" (i.e., reverse) the judgment. The CIT agreed to hear the plaintiff's argument upon which its appeal would be based. After the hearing, the CIT found that since the U.S. firm had voluntarily submitted itself to a legal arbitration process and bound itself to the outcome of it, the appeal was without merit. The CIT upheld the foreign arbitral award and upon being petitioned by the French firm, the CIT issued a judgment in its favor enforcing the award. The U.S. company tried to appeal the judgment, but no Federal court would hear the appeal since the United States was treaty-bound under the UNCREFAA.

See also United Nations Geneva Protocol on Arbitration (1923); United Nations Geneva Convention on Arbitration (1972).

United Nations Convention on the Settlement of Investment Disputes between States and Nationals of Other States is an international agreement, signed in 1965, that authorized the World Bank to establish (under its auspices) the International Center for the Settlement of Investment Disputes (ICSID).

See also World Bank International Center for the Settlement of Investment Disputes.

United Nations Development Program (UNDP) is an international organization of the United Nations System that is the world's largest and most important channel for multilateral financial investment and technical cooperation and assistance.

Established in 1965 through the merger of the U.N. Expanded Program for Technical Assistance (UN/EPTA) (established in 1949) and the United Nations Special Fund (UNSF) (established in 1958), the UNDP became operational in 1966.

The goal of the UNDP is to actively promote and accelerate economic growth (and higher physical standards of living) throughout developing countries (LDCs), which are mainly in Asia, Africa, and Latin America.

To achieve this, the UNDP works with over 150 governments and 35 international organizations, which support more than 4,000 projects in agriculture, education, public health, transportation, industry, trade, public administration, energy, communications, and environmental fields. The ongoing value of these UNDP projects exceeds U.S. $10 billion.

Cf. United Nations (Secretariat) Purchase and Transportation Service.

See also United Nations System; United Nations Development Program Division for Administrative and Management Services; United Nations Development Program Inter-Agency Procurement Services Office.

United Nations Development Program Division for Administrative and Management Services (UNDP/DAMS) is a service department of the UNDP, with offices in New York, that procures administrative support equipment and supplies (e.g., office equipment) for UNDP headquarters in New York and UNDP field offices (of which there are more than 100).

Cf. United Nations Development Program Office of Project Execution.

See also United Nations Development Program; United Nations Development Program Inter-Agency Procurement Services Office.

United Nations Development Program Inter-Agency Procurement Services Office (UNDP/IAPSO) is a service department of the UNDP that acts as a business information center; it assists global marketers to supply goods and services to UNDP/OPE, UNDP/DAMS, and UN/PTS.

In this regard, UNDP/IAPSO's key activities are:

1. to disseminate U.N. procurement information (i) via descriptive and technical bulletins and (ii) by publication and distribution of *Business Development*, the only U.N. publication that carries procurement notices for all the executive agencies of the UNDP (i.e., the multilateral development banks (MDBs)) and for all the U.N. Regional Economic Commissions;
2. to act as a liaison between the U.N. agencies with the aim of expediting the information exchange (i) between global suppliers and U.N. customers and (ii) among U.N. customers themselves;
3. to distribute "company profiles" to all organizations in the U.N. System.

Cf. United Nations Development Program Office of Project Execution; United Nations Development Program Division for Administrative and Management Services; United Nations (Secretariat) Purchase and Transportation Service.

See also United Nations Development Program.

United Nations Development Program Office for Project Execution (UNDP/OPE) is a service department of the UNDP, with offices in New York, that procures capital equipment and services for

1. the UNDP;
2. U.N. Regional Economic Commissions; and
3. other U.N. agencies whose projects either do not fall directly within the jurisdiction or competence of that program agency or that are multi- or interdisciplinary and involve two or more U.N. agencies.

Cf. United Nations Development Program Division for Administrative and Management Services.

See also United Nations Development Program; United Nations Development Program Inter-Agency Procurement Services Office.

United Nations Economic Commission for Africa (UN/ECA) is a Regional Economic Commission in the United Nations System, responsible for promoting long-term economic growth and development in the region by

1. the identification of project areas,
2. the development of project strategies,
3. the acquisition of project resources,

4. the implementation of the projects per se,
5. the monitoring of project execution, and
6. the evaluation of project feedback.

UN/ECA has its headquarters in Addis Ababa, Ethiopia. For global marketers, some procurement is done via the Commission's General Services Section (GSS) in Addis Ababa, but major procurement of goods and services is handled either by the UN/PTS in New York or through the Internal Services Section (ISS) at the U.N. Office at Geneva (UNOG), Switzerland.

See also United Nations (Secretariat) Purchase and Transportation Service; United Nations Development Program.

United Nations Economic Commission for Europe (UN/ECE) is a Regional Economic Commission in the United Nations System, originally responsible for promoting long-term economic growth and development in the less developed regions of Southern Europe. With the establishment and growth of both the European Economic Community (EEC) and the European Free Trade Association (EFTA), the development-assistance mandate of the UN/ECE has lessened considerably.

Most of the work of the UN/ECE, since its establishment in 1947, has been "inter-agency" in nature. For example, UN/ECE, as an executing agency of the United Nations Development Program (UNDP), liaises with the EEC and the EFTA and maintains close ties with the United Nations Conference on Trade and Development (UNCTAD). The UN/ECE also had established links with the former Council for Mutual Economic Assistance (CMEA), thus working to further the goal of a complete economic integration of Europe on nonideological lines.

The UN/ECE has its headquarters in Geneva, Switzerland. For global marketers, procurement is done in Geneva by the U.N. Internal Services Section (ISS) and by the U.N. Purchase and Transportation Service (UN/PTS) in New York.

See also United Nations (Secretariat) Purchase and Transportation Service; United Nations Development Program.

United Nations Economic Commission for Latin America and the Caribbean (UN/ECLAC), also co-officially *Comisión Económica Para América Latina Y El Caribe (CEPAL)*, is a Regional Economic Commission in the United Nations System that is responsible for promoting long-term economic growth and development in the region by

1. the identification of project areas,
2. the development of project strategies,
3. the acquisition of project resources,
4. the implementation of the projects per se,
5. the monitoring of project execution, and
6. the evaluation of project feedback.

UN/ECLAC has its headquarters in Santiago, Chile, and its subregional headquarters for the Caribbean in Port of Spain, Trinidad, where a permanent subsidiary body of the UN/ECLAC, called the Caribbean Development and Cooperation Committee (CDCC), has its offices.

For global marketers, some regional procurement is done through the Commission's General Services Unit (GSU) in Santiago, but major procurement of goods and services is handled by the U.N. Purchase and Transportation Service (UN/PTS) in New York.

See also Caribbean Development and Cooperation Committee; United Nations (Secretariat) Purchase and Transportation Service; United Nations Development Program.

United Nations Economic Commission for the Middle East (UN/ECME) is an idea, yet to be formally proposed, that suggests the formation of a Regional Economic Commission in the United Nations System that would be responsible for promoting long-term economic growth and development in the Middle East region by

1. identifying project areas (i) for immediate attention as a result of the Gulf Crisis (and the ensuing war) and (ii) for attention on a long-term development basis,
2. developing project strategies for these areas,
3. acquiring the project resources,
4. implementing the projects per se,
5. monitoring the execution of the project, and
6. evaluating project feedback.

On an interim basis, the headquarters of the United Nations Economic and Social Commission for Western Asia (UN/ESCWA) in Baghdad, Iraq, might house the new UN/ECME. Depending on the outcome of a regional peace conference (to deal with the consequences of the Persian Gulf War of 1991), permanent UN/ECME headquarters should be located either in some universally acceptable on-shore venue (e.g., Cairo or Ankara) or in some equivalently acceptable regional off-shore site (e.g., Cyprus).

See also Middle East Development Bank; Gulf Crisis.

United Nations Economic and Social Commission for Asia and the Pacific (UN/ESCAP) is a Regional Economic Commission in the United Nations System responsible for promoting long-term economic growth and development in the region by

1. the identification of project areas,
2. the development of project strategies,
3. the acquisition of project resources,
4. the implementation of the projects per se,
5. the monitoring of project execution, and
6. the evaluation of project feedback.

UN/ESCAP has its headquarters in Bangkok, Thailand. For global marketers, some regional procurement is done through the U.N. Purchase and Transportation Service (UN/PTS) in New York.

See also United Nations (Secretariat) Purchase and Transportation Service; United Nations Development Program.

United Nations Economic and Social Commission for Western Asia (UN/ESCWA) is a Regional Economic Commission in the United Nations System responsible for promoting long-term economic growth and development in the region by

1. the identification of project areas,
2. the development of project strategies,
3. the acquisition of project resources,
4. the implementation of the projects per se,
5. the monitoring of project execution, and
6. the evaluation of project feedback.

UN/ESCWA has its headquarters in Baghdad, Iraq. For global marketers, some regional procurement is done through the Commission's Purchase and Transportation Unit (PTU) in Baghdad, but major procurement of goods and services is handled either by the U.N. Purchase and Transportation Service (UN/PTS) in New York or through the Internal Service Section (ISS) at the U.N. Office at Geneva (UNOG).

See also United Nations (Secretariat) Purchase and Transportation Service; United Nations Development Program.

United Nations Educational, Scientific and Cultural Organization (UNESCO) is an international organization of the United Nations System whose activities cover the following major areas:

1. development and planning of education, at the primary, secondary, and tertiary levels, including vocational facilities and institutions;
2. training of educators;
3. promotion of literacy (both primary and adult);
4. training of mass communications specialists; and
5. advancement of research in science and in all fields of applied knowledge.

UNESCO is of interest to global marketers from the viewpoint of its equipment purchases. These are made by each of the Education, Science, and Communications Program Sectors and by the Field Equipment and Subcontracting Division. All of these offices are at UNESCO headquarters in Paris, France.

See also United Nations System.

United Nations Environment Program (UNEP) is an international body within the United Nations System, established in 1977 to coordinate environmental activities within the U.N. System.

Unlike other autonomous organizations within the U.N. System, UNEP is dependent on the U.N. for funding; consequently, because major country contributors to the U.N. have not considered UNEP a priority agency, it has had limited opportunity and scope to undertake initiatives or to develop programs.

UNEP has been of little interest from a global marketing viewpoint as a direct result of its limited funding, its limited capacity for influence, and its extremely limited procurement of goods and services by UNEP headquarters in Nairobi, Kenya. This may change in the 1990s with worldwide environmental awareness.

See also United Nations System.

United Nations Fund for Population Activities (UNFPA) is an international organ of the United Nations System, which reports to the U.N. General Assembly.

UNFPA was established in 1972 and became operational almost immediately, following adoption of the World Population Plan of Action (WPPA) in 1974 at the World Population Conference in Bucharest.

The activities of UNFPA, broadly speaking, include everything necessary to assist developing countries to undertake and implement programs of population planning. This mandate necessarily includes activities in the field of information gathering and analysis; studies on the interrelationship of food supplies and land-carrying capacities to population pressure; support for and training of specialists in the fields of health, education, nutrition, and community development in order to devise, coordinate, and implement programs.

UNFPA works closely with the United Nations Development Program (UNDP) and other autonomous agencies (e.g., the Food and Agricultural Organization (FAO) and the World Health Organization (WHO)).

From the global marketing viewpoint, UNFPA has an enormous influence on all programs within the United Nations System, and, inferentially, it procures significant volumes of capital equipment for medical work, communications, and teaching, plus medical supplies, through UNFPA headquarters in New York.

See also United Nations System.

United Nations Geneva Convention on Arbitration (1972) is an international accord that builds on the 1923 Geneva Protocol on Arbitration by requiring nations that signed the 1923 protocol to enforce the rules of an arbitration award made under an international contract covered by it.

See also Geneva Protocol on Arbitration (1923); United Nations Convention on the Recognition and Enforcement of Foreign Arbitration Awards (1972).

United Nations Geneva Protocol on Arbitration (1923) is an international accord signed in 1923 that binds countries to recognize the validity of arbitration agreements made between contracting parties regardless of where the arbitration agreement is executed (i.e., no matter where the actual arbitration process takes place).

See also Geneva Convention on Arbitration (1972); United Nations Convention on the Recognition and Enforcement of Foreign Arbitration Awards (1972).

United Nations Industrial Development Organization (UNIDO), created by the United Nations General Assembly in 1966 as a "technical body" within the U.N. Secretariat to promote and accelerate industrialization in the less developed countries (LDCs), became a specialized agency of the United Nations System in 1986.

UNIDO's activities cover the following fields:

1. promoting and accelerating the industrialization of developing countries via project identification, development, implementation, monitoring, and evaluation;

2. supporting the exchange of technical information (e.g., technical assistance and licensing) between developed countries and developing countries using UNIDO's Industrial Development Fund (IDF);
3. assisting in the establishment of pilot plants and pilot processes, and translating them into large-scale production entities;
4. procurement for UNIDO technical cooperation projects (TCPs) and for TCPs involving other U.N. bodies (e.g., initiated by the Food and Agricultural Organization (FAO), a joint FAO-UNIDO TCP, to hull genetically engineered cereal grains using European Economic Community (EEC) technology and processes).

A major international UNIDO-sponsored project is the establishment, together with the government of Italy, of an International Center for Science and High Technology (ICSHT), at Trieste. The agreement to fund the project was signed in June 1988 with contributions to UNIDO's IDF. The purpose of the ICSHT is to provide ways and means whereby UNIDO can provide Third World scientists with training, research facilities, and an opportunity to work with so-called "world class" researchers.

Three international units are planned for the ICSHT: (1) chemical-sciences research, (2) materials-science and high-technology research, and (3) earth and environmental sciences and technology.

UNIDO also supports two other research institutes:

1. together with the Italian government, UNIDO sponsors the International Center for Genetic Engineering and Biotechnology (ICGEB) at Trieste. The Center provides Third World scientists from 41 member nations with opportunities to carry on research in the field of molecular biology;
2. together with the Indian government, UNIDO sponsors, in New Delhi, an ICGEB laboratory whose work focuses on plant biology (including replication and transcription of plant genes), immunology, and the molecular biology of malaria and hepatitis.

UNIDO cooperates with the Trieste-based International Center for Theoretical Physics (ICTP), established by the International Atomic Energy Agency (IAEA) in 1964 and now operated jointly with the United Nations Educational Scientific and Cultural Organization (UNESCO).

UNIDO is of interest of global marketers from the viewpoint of its procurement of goods and services and from the outcomes of UNIDO-sponsored research. With regards to the procurement, this is done by UNIDO's Purchase and Contract Service (PAC) on behalf of UNIDO itself (and its projects) and for UNIDO joint projects. The PAC office is located at UNIDO headquarters in Vienna, Austria.

With regards to research outcome, contact with UNIDO headquarters in Vienna provides industrial opportunities, available resources, and calendars of fairs, exhibitions, seminars and, conferences.

See also International Atomic Energy Agency.

United Nations Regional Economic Commissions are five large "implementing agencies" that operate regionally within the framework of the United Nations System and under the authority of the United Nations Economic and Social Council.

They are the U.N. Economic Commissions for (1) Europe, (2) Africa, and (3) Latin America and the Caribbean, and (4) the Economic and Social Commissions for Asia and the Pacific, and (5) for Western Asia. Each can be found in the alphabetical listings.

In addition to these five established bodies, a sixth is proposed: the United Nations Economic Commission for the Middle East (UN/ECME). It would be an enduring and structurally permanent way to address the physical and social reconstruction of the region necessitated by the Gulf Crisis.

See United Nations Economic Commission for Europe; United Nations Economic Commission for Africa; United Nations Economic and Social Commission for Western Asia; United Nations Economic Commission for Latin America and the Caribbean; United Nations Economic and Social Commission for Asia and the Pacific.

See also Appendix V (D).

United Nation (Secretariat) Purchase and Transportation Service (UN/PTS) is the key service department of the United Nations Secretariat in New 5York. UN/PTS procures for

1. U.N. headquarters, New York;
2. U.N. peace-keeping forces (e.g., for UNIFIL (United Nations Interim Force in Lebanon)); and
3. the regular program activities of the U.N.'s Regional Economic Commissions (i.e., the Economic Commissions for Africa (UN/ECA), Europe (UN/ECE), Latin America and the Caribbean (UN/ECLAC), and the Economic and Social Commissions for Asia and the Pacific (UN/ESCAP), and for Western Asia (UN/ESCWA)).

UN/PTS also has a Contracts and Procurement Branch (CPB) in New York that, through its Department of Technical Cooperation for Development (DTCD), procures high-tech capital equipment, instruments and supplies, and expert consulting services for surveys, assessments, and feasibility studies.

Also, the U.N. Secretariat maintains an office at Geneva, Switzerland (UNOG). UNOG's Internal Services Section (ISS) procures for

1. some of the U.N. Regional Economic Commissions (e.g., UN/ECA), and
2. specialized U.N. international organizations, such as the United Nations Conference on Trade and Development (UNCTAD).

See also United Nations System; United Nations Regional Economic Commissions; Appendix V (D); United Nations Conference on Trade and Development.

United Nations System is a network of international organizations that cover an enormous range of structures, functions, mandates, and jurisdictions.

The system consists of the following key relationships:

1. U.N. Secretariat (at U.N. headquarters in New York), which liaises with the management of all other U.N. organizations and autonomous agencies;

2. U.N. Economic and Social Council (ECOSOC), to which U.N. Regional Economic Commissions report, as well as a host of specialized agencies and other U.N. bodies;
3. U.N. General Assembly to which report a variety of U.N. "organs" that are dependent upon the U.N. for their budgets (e.g., U.N. Conference on Trade and Development (UNCTAD), U.N. Development Program (UNDP), U.N. Environmental Program (UNEP), U.N. Fund for Population Activities (UNFPA), UNICEF, and HABITAT);
4. multilateral development banks (MDBs), which, while autonomous of the system (except the International Bank for Reconstruction and Development (IBRD), which reports to the U.N. Economic and Social Council), are designated as Executing Agencies of the United Nations Development Program (UNDP) and, thus, work closely with all Implementing Agencies (i.e., the U.N. Regional Economic Commissions) of the U.N. System.

See also United Nations (Secretariat) Purchase and Transportation Service; Appendix V (D); multilateral development banks.

Universal Postal Union (UPU) is a specialized agency of the United Nations involved in the organization and improvement of international postal services.

Historically, international postal services have been labor intensive and have involved considerable quantities of physical supplies and equipment. This has changed as a result of the advent of microcomputer technology, the diffusion internationally of that technology, and the acceleration of electronic data exchange between important global training centers.

The UPU, based in Basel, Switzerland, and the International Telecommunications Union (ITU), based in Geneva, are both ideally situated to cooperate and collaborate in the amelioration of contemporary postal services. Ultimately, replacement of today's paper systems by computer-based ones that generate electronic mail will advance international marketing toward its ultimate goal of a globally unified (and harmonized) information exchange system.

See also International Telecommunications Union.

unstable (foreign) exchange rate market *See* Appendix II.

up-stream pricing •NW• refers to the process of establishing a market value for commodities from which other goods are derived or other by-products are produced.

International marketers who control up-stream pricing have less control over the price of the original commodity (from which the by-products are derived) than those who produce the by-products.

Example: Members of the Asian and Pacific Coconut Community (APCC), the region's major coconut producers, have less control over the price paid to them for that commodity than have those Anglo-American soap manufacturers who manufacture and market the soap derived from the oil of the raw coconuts.

Cf. down-stream pricing.
See also commodity.

Uruguay Round is the eighth event in the continuing series of multilateral trade negotiations (MTN) held under the auspices of the General Agreement on Tariffs and Trade (GATT).

Named after Punta del Este, Uruguay, site of the 1986 inaugural meeting, this latest round will conclude with an Agreement in 1991/92.

The main goals of the Uruguay Round are as follows:

1. a one-third overall cut in tariffs,
2. reduction/elimination of nontariff barriers (NTBs),
3. a phase-out of the MultiFiber Arrangement (MFA),
4. strengthening the GATT Codes,
5. a comprehensive agreement on intellectual property protection,
6. guidelines to restrict the spread of trade-related investment measures (TRIMs),
7. an agreement applying the GATT rules to services,
8. reduction of agricultural support mechanisms,
9. updated GATT rules on the use of safeguards and voluntary export restraints (VERs),
10. improvement of the GATT dispute-settlement mechanisms.

The current Uruguay Round of Multilateral Tariff Negotiations (MTN) broke off on December 7, 1990, in Brussels, Belgium. The reason for the suspension was an impasse between the United States and the European Economic Community (EEC) regarding an agreement to reduce tariffs on agricultural imports. The United States held to a 75-percent across-the-board tariff reduction whereas the EEC's proposal was for a 30-percent staged-reduction approach.

On February 26, 1991, a decision to restart the talks was made by GATT's Trade Negotiations Committee (TNC). This followed weeks of back-room negotiating and resulted in the EEC deciding to take a softer stand on dismantling its Common Agricultural Policy (CAP). This change of approach was precipitated in part because of the lack of worldwide credibility and confidence generated as a result of the half-hearted physical and financial support rendered by the EEC to the United States in its leadership of the Coalition forces during the Gulf Crisis.

See also Common Agricultural Policy; Gulf Crisis; Agreement on AntiDumping Practices; Agreement on Technical Barriers to Trade (Standards Code); trade-related aspects of intellectual property rights; export subsidies; dispute-settlement system; round of trade negotiations.

U.S. Advisory Committee on Trade Policy Negotiations (ACTPN) is a body established by the U.S. president under the authority of Part 2, Section 135 (b) of the Omnibus Trade Act of 1988, which is the principal forum for advice to the U.S. Trade Representative (USTR).

The ACTPN is chaired by the USTR and comprises no more than 45 individuals representing every aspect of the U.S. political-economy, including labor, industry, agriculture, small business, consumers, retailers, and non-Federal U.S. government agencies.

See also United States Trade Representative.

U.S. Agency for International Development (USAID) *See* U.S. International Development Cooperation Agency.

U.S. Agricultural Adjustment Act (of 1933) is the United States legislation that permits the use of quantity restrictions (QRs) to limit imports into the country.

Section 22 of the Act authorizes the president to impose import fees or QRs on goods imported "under such conditions and in such quantities as to interfere with or render ineffective certain domestic commodity programs of the United States Department of Agriculture (USDA)." The Act also authorizes the president to (1) suspend or terminate such QRs "whenever he finds and proclaims that circumstances requiring the proclamation or provision thereof no longer exist," and (2) to change the fees or QRs "whenever he finds and proclaims that changed circumstances require modification." Further, the Act empowers the president to modify or terminate a QR at any time in an "emergency situation."

Whenever the president acts to change a QR either routinely or on an "emergency basis," he must do so after having received an investigation and recommendation report from the United States International Trade Commission (USITC).

The USDA "domestic commodity programs," which the QRs are designed to protect, refer to a large number of price-support and production-adjustment programs (e.g., direct payments, acreage restriction payments) for important agricultural products such as cereal grains (e.g., wheat, oats, rye, barley, rice), oil grains (e.g., peanut, soybean, canola), and foods (e.g., broiler chickens, eggs).

Imports of peanuts into the United States are under a global quota. This was set at 1,709,000 pounds (shelled basis) on June 8, 1953, by the president under Section 22 of the Agricultural Adjustment Act of 1933. The argument for the quota was as follows: (1) importing cheap peanuts would undercut domestic acreage control programs of the USDA that were designed to limit the supply of the commodity; (2) restricting domestic supply necessarily will force up the price paid to American peanut producers, which is desirable since it creates a financial incentive to keep American peanut farmers producing and, thus, ensures that the United States is independent of foreign (and potentially unpredictable) sources of supply.

Since 1953, USDA price-support programs for peanuts have changed. Current USDA programs consist of a two-tier price-support system that is tied to a maximum-poundage quota: peanuts produced subject to the poundage quota are supported at the higher of the two prices, while "over-quota peanuts" (i.e., peanuts from farms not having a quota) are supported at the lower price. For peanut producers who fail to fill their quotas within any given year, there is a USDA "overmarketing allowance" of 10 percent for the following year. Further, the USDA program permits peanut farmers to place their yields "under nonrecourse loan" with the Commodity Credit Corporation (CCC): farmers are allowed to borrow against their harvested crops at designated support prices.

Example: On October 12, 1990, a request was sent from the U.S. Peanut Butter and Nut Processors Association (PBNPA) to the USITC for an "expedited hearing and investigation" under Section 22(d) of the Agricultural Adjustment Act of 1933. The PBNPA wanted the USITC to recommend to the president (1) that QRs limiting the importation of peanuts be entirely removed and (2) that an immediate authorization be granted for the import of 400 million pounds of peanuts (on a shelled basis).

On December 3, 1990, the USITC undertook Investigation N. 22-52, pursuant to the request of the PBNPA. On January 22, 1991, a public hearing was held, and on March 22, 1991, the USITC issued its report to the president: it recommended "an increase in the quota for the growing year 1990/91 to

300 million pounds (shelled basis)." It was deemed that that quota would not interfere with or render ineffective current USDA support programs for peanuts.

Cf. Common Agricultural Policy; Canada Account (Comparable U.S. government programs).

See also Commodity Credit Corporation; U.S. International Trade Commission; quantity restrictions.

U.S.-Canada Free Trade Agreement (FTA) is the legally equivalent variation of the *Canada-U.S. Free Trade Agreement (FTA) of 1989.*

U.S. Customs Service (USCC) is the bureau of the U.S. Department of the Treasury that is headed by the Commissioner of Customs who reports to an Assistant Secretary (Enforcement).

The Customs Service is concerned with the following activities:

1. assessment and collection of revenues from tariffs levied and of other fees and penalties due on goods imported into the United States;
2. enforcement of U.S. customs laws and all export control laws, including the processing of people and cargo at all 240 Ports of Entry into the United States;
3. interdiction of all classes of "prohibited goods" (e.g., narcotics) and "controlled goods" (e.g., guns) within the territorial jurisdiction of the United States, including illegal narcotic substances, pornography, firearms and ammunition, and counterfeit negotiable instruments.

U.S. Department of Commerce (USDOC) is the major institution of the Executive Branch of U.S. government that promotes the economic growth of the United States of America.

The Department advances U.S. interests in world trade, and it acts to prevent unfair trade practices by foreign competitors.

See also U.S. International Trade Administration.

U.S. Export Administration Act (of 1979) is the U.S. legislation that authorizes the imposition of export controls on goods and services being exported from the United States.

The law empowers (1) the president to order that controls be put in place and (2) the United States Department of Commerce, via the Bureau of Export Administration (BXA), to monitor compliance with those controls.

Cf. nontariff barriers.

See also Bureau of Export Administration; export controls.

U.S. dollar area *See* currency area.

U.S. Industry Sector Advisory Committee (USISAC) is a body that is part of the staff structure that advises the U.S. Trade Representative (USTR), much like the U.S. Advisory Committee on Trade Policy Negotiations (ACTPN), during bi- and multilateral trade negotiations (MTN).

Cf. U.S. Advisory Committee on Trade Policy Negotiations.

U.S. Inter-Agency Trade Organization (USITO), under the Omnibus Trade Act of 1988, Section 1621, which amended the Trade Expansion Act of 1962, is a top-level Executive advisory body established by then-U.S. president Reagan to advise the president and the U.S. Trade Representative (USTR) on matters regarding (1) international trade policy formation and (2) the coordinated implementation of international trade policy worldwide.

The USITO is chaired by the USTR, and it consists of the following Executive Branch officers: Secretary of Commerce, Secretary of State, Secretary of the Treasury, Secretary of Agriculture, and Secretary of Labor.

Cf. U.S. Advisory Committee on Trade Policy Negotiations; U.S. Trade Representative.

U.S. International Development Cooperation Agency (USIDCA) is an autonomous agency of the U.S. government, established in 1979, that operates under the authority of the U.S. Foreign Assistance Act of 1961.

The USIDCA is the focus for the creation of policies and for the coordinated implementation of actions in terms of U.S. economic and developmental relations with developing countries.

The Agency, headed by a Director, comprises the following operational structure:

1. *USIDCA Proper:* the Agency is itself responsible for U.S. budget-setting, policy, and participation within the United Nations System, and specifically within the United Nations Development Program (UNDP), the U.N. Children's Fund (UNICEF), and the World Food Program (WFP).

   The Agency also sets budget and policy for involvement by the United States in technical-assistance programs of the Organization of American States (OAS).

   The Agency works jointly with the Department of the Treasury in budgeting for U.S. involvement in the World Bank Group and in U.S. participation with the five multilateral development banks (MDBs) that are the Executing Agencies for the UNDP.

   The Agency also administers the Food for Peace Program (Public Law 480) jointly with the Department of Agriculture.

2. *Agency for International Development (AID):* this operating unit of the USIDCA system executes development programs under the leadership of its Administrator. The AID is thus the "official development agency" of the U.S. government, equivalent to the Canadian International Development Agency (CIDA) and to the Overseas Development Administration in the British Ministry of Overseas Development (MOD).

   Under the U.S. Foreign Assistance Act of 1961, AID administers both official development assistance (ODA) and "economic support funds" (bureauspeak for a "slush fund") used to maintain and advance U.S. economic, political, and military interests in developing countries.

   Jointly with the Departments of State and Agriculture, AID executes the Agricultural Trade Development and Assistance Act of 1954 whereby agricultural commodities may be donated or sold on concessional terms.

Responsibility for executing the Food for Peace Program (PL 480) rests jointly with AID and the Department of Agriculture, whereby agricultural products must be donated or sold on concessional terms.

3. *Trade and Development Program (TDP):* this unit of the USIDCA operates under the authority of the Foreign Assistance Act of 1961, whereby
   i.   the TDP coordinates state-to-state technical assistance on a fully reimbursable, market-rate basis; and
   ii. the TDP functions as the "lead agency" (the "point man") in helping U.S. corporations participate in developmental projects that have as one of the U.S.-designed outcomes, the export potential for participating U.S. firms.

4. *Overseas Private Investment Corporation (OPIC):* the Chair of this unit of the USIDCA system is the Director of the USIDCA proper. This linkage ensures the best Executive-level policy coordination between the "soft side" of U.S. development assistance (i.e., the not-for-profit AID) and the "hard side" (i.e., the support for marketing-for-profit activities of OPIC).

   The Corporation's activities fall into two categories: export financing and export insurance, with major emphasis on the insurance: OPIC is the only U.S. quasi-government organization that provides export cover for political risks.

   i.   *Export Financing:* like its Canadian counterpart, the Export Development Corporation (EDC), OPIC offers U.S. exporters a number and variety of export-credit facilities for short-, medium-, and long-term overseas commercial activities.

   Example: For example, OPIC's direct loans are offered, under the Direct Investment Funds program, to small- and medium-sized U.S. firms at competitive market rates for medium- to long-term periods of 7 to 12 years for expansion and modernization of overseas facilities.

   ii. *Export Insurance:* OPIC insures U.S. exporters and direct overseas investors against the following political risks:
   - expropriation (of U.S. assets where invested);
   - inconvertibility of local currency into transferable currency;
   - damage and loss (of physical assets, capital, inventories, and human life) resulting from war, revolution, insurrection, and civil strife; and
   - wrongful calls against documentary credits (i.e., letters of credit) posted by U.S. companies either as bids or performance guarantees, or as advance-payment guarantees (against future performance).

   Cf. Export Development Corporation.
   See also tied aid; Export Development Corporation (4. Other Insurances Services).

U.S. International Trade Administration (USITA) is an important operating unit of the U.S. Department of Commerce, established in 1980 and headed by an Under Secretary for International Trade.

   The USITA has four subunits as follows:

1. *International Economic Policy:* headed by an Assistant Secretary, this unit advises on development and implementation of U.S. economic policies on a bilateral, multilateral, and regional basis.

2. *Import Administration:* headed by an Assistant Secretary, this group develops and implements policies within the broad meaning of the Tariff Act of 1930, including antidumping and countervailing duty laws.

   Under these laws, investigations are undertaken into dumping, antidumping, and countervailing duty actions at the request of U.S. government Executive Branch officers, such as the U.S. Trade Representative (USTR).

   If the Import Administration group establishes that export subsidization and dumping exist, the determination of injury is made by the U.S. International Trade Commission (USITC). Under U.S. law, the USTR has the authority to act on USITC findings.

3. *Trade Development:* headed by an Assistant Secretary, this group develops policies aimed at improving and promoting U.S. export competitiveness, and it implements such programs on a sectoral basis.

4. *U.S. and Foreign Commercial Service:* headed by a Director General, this subunit provides information support for U.S. exporters via promotional programs comprising trade fairs, trade missions, seminars, workshops, and conferences.

On the information/service side, the Foreign Commercial Service offers a number of "publications" and services to assist both novice and experienced American businesses in international trade:

1. *Potential Markets and Sales Leads*
   - "Foreign Trade Statistics"
   - "Global Market Surveys"
   - "Foreign Economic Trends"
   - "Foreign Market Reports"
   - "Market Share Reports"

2. *Market Research*
   - "Overseas Business Reports (OBPs)"
   - "Business America"
   - Commercial exhibitions (i.e., trade shows)

3. *Potential Foreign Distributors*
   - New Product Information Service (NPIS)
   - Trade Opportunity Program (TOP)
   - Industry/Special Trade Lists
   - "Commerce Business Daily"
   - Export Mailing List Service (EMLS)
   - Agent/Distributor Service (ADS)
   - Foreign Traders Index (FTI)

4. *Risk Insurance*
   - Foreign Credit Insurance Association (FCIA)
   - Export-Import Bank (Eximbank)

Cf. export support programs.

See also export promotion; U.S. International Trade Commission; U.S. Trade Representative; Super 301.

U.S. International Trade Commission (USITC), created by the U.S. Trade Act of 1974, is an autonomous agency of the U.S. government whose purpose is the regulation and protection of U.S. trade in consonance with U.S. laws and international treaties to which the U.S. government is a signatory.

From the global-marketing viewpoint, the Commission is of greatest interest in terms of its powers (1) to entertain petitions from U.S. industry claiming injury from imports allegedly dumped into the U.S. market; (2) to initiate fact-finding studies and hearings to investigate industry-generated complaints; and (3) to measure the impact of U.S. government actions on U.S. industry (e.g., countervailing duties) or of foreign governments' actions (e.g., quantitative restrictions).

The Commission's activities can be summarized according to the following broad categories:

1. advice concerning trade negotiations;
2. advice on the Generalized System of Preferences;
3. investigations (upon petition) for import relief or domestic industries;
4. monitoring of East-West trade, and specifically U.S.-WME trade;
5. investigations relating to imported manufactured goods or agricultural commodities alleged to be subsidized, unfairly traded, or dumped;
6. compilation and publication of tariff schedules of the United States, international trade statistics, and tariff summaries (i.e., summaries of trade and tariff information).

Under the 1974 legislation (and within the framework of the General Agreement on Tariffs and Trade (GATT)), the Commission has the authority to levy tariffs/duties in response to findings of unfair trading practices and injury.

Example: On September 13, 1989, by a three-to-two vote, the USITC determined that fresh, chilled, or frozen pork ("subsidized imports") from Canada threatened the pork industry in the United States with material injury. The Commission ordered a countervailing duty of eight cents per kilogram (or 3.6 cents per pound) to be levied on the imports.

On August 24, 1990, a binational dispute-settlement panel (to which the Canadian government appealed the decision), remanded the Commission's original decision for reconsideration because of a statistical error that affected the outcome. On October 23, 1990, the USITC again voted three to two to uphold its original determination; but its countervailing duty was adjusted downwards to six cents per kilogram, or 2.7 cents per pound. Again the Canadian government (as complainant) requested that the binational dispute-settlement panel review the USITC's "remand determination."

On January 22, 1991, the panel again remanded the determination to the USITC. The panel held that the USITC had erred and had exceeded its jurisdiction and that there was no evidence to support the determination that pork imports from Canada caused material injury to the domestic U.S. pork industry. Subsequently, on February 12, 1991, the USITC reversed its original determination. The countervailing duty was revoked, collection of further duties were ordered stopped, and $17 million in duties already collected were ordered repaid to Canadian exporters.

The USITC slammed the panel's decision, claiming that it circumscribed the Commission's discretion, violated the principles of the FTA, and contained "egregious errors under U.S. law." However, recognizing the binding nature of the panel's decisions as contained in the FTA Treaty, the USITC accepted the panel's decision because "they are legally binding on us."

In the interim, however, the United States Trade Representative (USTR), representing the U.S. National Pork Producers' Council, 38 U.S. Senators, and 51 Members of the U.S. House of Representatives, indicated that on March 28, 1991, it would formally challenge the panel's ruling under the FTA permitting "extraordinary challenges." These are fully provided for in Article 1904 of the FTA.

The extraordinary challenge procedure provides that the United States and Canada each will now select a judge to represent its side, and the two judges will select a third, all of whom will comprise an Extraordinary Challenge Committee. This Committee can (1) find in the USTR's favor, (2) return the matter to the binational dispute-settlement panel for further adjudication, or (3) reject the USTR's challenge, thus ending the matter.

The Extraordinary Challenge Committee is restricted in its authority to rule; and it can only make a final determination where (1) gross misconduct or conflict of interest influenced the original panel; (2) the panel seriously departed from a fundamental rule of procedure (i.e., "due process"); or (3) the panel manifestly exceeded its powers, authority, or jurisdiction.

It has been suggested that the USTR's challenge was a result of political pressure. Since the Bush Administration continues to woo Congress to continue its trade negotiating mandate (e.g., with the General Agreement on Tariffs and Trade and with Mexico), it is loathe to antagonize Congress. Even if the USTR loses the challenge, the Administration at least wants to be perceived as having stood up strongly for U.S. trade interests embedded within a trade treaty.

Cf. Appendix VI (judicial review).

See also Canada-U.S. Free Trade Agreement of 1989; binational dispute-settlement panel; North American Free Trade Agreement; injury; dumping.

U.S.-Israel Free Trade Agreement, also known as the *U.S.-Israel Free Trade Area Implementation Act* (of 1985), is the treaty providing for "special treatment" for specified products imported from Israel into the United States; the special treatment varies from preferential rates of duty to no rate of duty on specified products.

This treaty was negotiated under the authority of the Trade and Tariff Act of 1984.

Cf. Canada-U.S. Free Trade Agreement of 1989.

See also free trade area.

U.S. Maritime Administration (USMA) is an operating unit of the U.S. Department of Transportation that was transferred to it under the authority of The Maritime Act of 1981.

Aside from its main responsibilities of organizing the U.S. merchant marine and directing emergency merchant-ship operations, the USMA offers a War Risk Insurance Program (WRIP), which covers private carriers against losses caused by hostile acts. The WRIP is only offered if private, war-risk insurance is otherwise unavailable.

See also U.S. International Development Cooperation Agency (4. Overseas Private Investment Corporation).

U.S. "Superfund" was a planned-for windfall of export revenues to be generated by U.S. legislation that imposed (1) a surtax of 8.2 cents per barrel on domestic petroleum, oil, and lubricants (POL) and (2) a surtax of 11.7 cents per barrel on imported POL.

The "Superfund" was intended to generate U.S. $8.5 billion in revenue to be applied to environmental concerns such as cleanups following oil spills within U.S. territorial jurisdiction and toxic-waste dumping sites.

> **Example:** The U.S. "Superfund" law was passed in October 1986, took effect on January 1, 1987, and is scheduled to expire on December 31, 1991.
>
> At the request of Canada, Mexico, and the European Economic Community (EEC), a General Agreement on Tariffs and Trade (GATT) Panel was established to determine whether the 3.5-cents-per-barrel element (applied on Canadian POL exports to the U.S.) was consistent with U.S. obligations under GATT. In June 1987, the GATT panel found that the 11.7-cents-per-barrel surtax was GATT-inconsistent (i.e., illegal) because it was 3.5 cents per barrel higher on imported oil than on U.S.-produced oil.
>
> Nevertheless, the United States failed to remove the surtax. On March 10, 1989, Canada announced it was seeking GATT authority to withdraw "substantially equivalent concessions" from the United States, estimated to be worth $10 million annually.
>
> Subsequently, on June 15, 1989, Canada released a preliminary list of 70 commodities from which it was considering the selection for the application of a 2.5-percent surcharge above existing tariff rates. Parallel with the GATT approval being sought for the move by Canada, the U.S. House of Representatives Ways and Means Committee was recommending budget legislation to eliminate the Canadian element of the POL surtax.

Heading the list of the 70 U.S. commodities targeted for the surcharge were alcoholic grape wines. Mainly exported from California, all of them had benefited from immediate tariff reduction under the Free Trade Agreement (FTA) on January 1, 1989. The result was a significant export surge of them to Canada. Thus, the Canadian move could be interpreted as being a strictly legal but distinctly unfriendly form of retaliation.

> **Example:** On December 12, 1989, the U.S. president signed into law a change in the U.S. import fee under the Superfund that hurt Canadian oil companies. Under the new U.S. law, the Superfund tax would be equalized at 9.7 cents per barrel of oil, whether domestic or imported.

Finally, in November 1989, 2 1/2 years from the time the GATT had ruled the Superfund tax was illegal, the U.S. Congress moved to withdraw the tax. The law itself that withdrew the tax was contained in a bill extending restraints on imported steel through April 1992.

Observers who have commented that the U.S. Congress is somewhat quick in its pro-U.S. protectionist actions but slow in complying with worldwide trade liberalization may have some evidence to support this view.

U.S. Trade Representative (USTR) is the Cabinet-level officer (with the rank of Ambassador) in the U.S. government who heads the Office of the U.S. Trade Representative. The USTR is directly responsible to the president for the development and coordination of U.S. international trade policy and trade negotiations.

The Office of the USTR was established by Presidential Executive Order in 1963 as the Office of the U.S. Special Representative for Trade Negotiations. The Trade Act of 1974 established the Office as a branch of the Executive Office of the President. An Executive Branch reorganization of the Office in 1980 charged the USTR with the responsibility of being the chief U.S. trade representative at negotiations of (1) the General Agreement on Tariffs and Trade (GATT), (2) the Organization for Economic Cooperation and Development (OECD), and (3) the United Nations Conference on Trade and Development (UNCTAD).

With the passage of the Omnibus Trade Act of 1988, the powers of the USTR were strengthened significantly under Section 301 of the Act (referred to as Super 301).

The Canadian Cabinet Officer, who is the counterpart of the USTR, is the Minister of International Trade in the Department of External Affairs and International Trade Canada (EAITC).

Cf. Department of External Affairs and International Trade Canada.
See also Omnibus Trade and Competitiveness Act of 1988; Super 301.

vacation allowance *See* benefit allowance.

Valdez Principles •NW• is a corporate code of environmental conduct, adopted on September 17, 1989, as the follow-up to the *Exxon Valdez* oil-spill disaster in Alaska.

The oil-spill disaster occurred on Friday, March 24, 1989, when the very large crude carrier (VLCC), the *Exxon Valdez*, ran aground after having taken on a full load of Alaskan North Slope crude oil at Valdez and spilled millions of barrels of it, contaminating the fishery and killing wildlife over hundreds of kilometers of Alaskan coastline of Prince William Sound.

The Valdez Principles are envisioned as being comparable to the Sullivan Principles introduced in 1977 by Rev. Leon Sullivan, a member of the General Motors Board of Directors, and governing corporate conduct with South Africa. Drafted by the Social Investment Forum, a Boston-based trade group, and funded by Working Assets Money Fund of San Francisco, the code aims at incorporating its Principles into U.S. law.

The Principles are sponsored by the U.S. Coalition for Environmentally Responsible Economies (CERES), which includes some of the largest and most powerful environmental groups in the United States: the Sierra Club, the National Audubon Society, and the Humane Society of America.

The following is a summary of the Valdez Principles as they would be presented to U.S. corporations for signature:

1. *Protection of the Biosphere:* eliminate pollutants that damage air, water, and the earth.
2. *Wise Use of Energy:* use energy-efficient products and processes.
3. *Sustainable Use of Natural Resources:* use renewable resources whenever possible, and conserve nonrenewable resources.

4. *Marketing of Safe Products and Services:* disclose the environmental impact of products, processes, and services.
5. *Damage Compensation:* restore damaged environments, and compensate for human injury.
6. *Disclosure:* reveal manufacturing hazards and accidents, and protect employees who report them.
7. *Environmental Directors and Managers:* appoint at least one Board member who will be an "environmental expert," and name a "senior executive for environmental affairs."
8. *Assessment and Annual Audit:* conduct an annual environmental audit of worldwide operations, and make the audit public.

Cf. sustainable development; United Nations Environment Program.

valuation is the calculation of the worth of imported goods by customs authorities for the purpose of determining the amount of duty payable by the importer in the importing country.

The calculation is done using the General Agreement on Tariffs and Trade (GATT) formula.

Cf. American selling price.

See also GATT Customs Valuation Code.

value-added tax (VAT), in French, *IVA*, from impôt de valeur additionnel; in Spanish, *IVA*, from impuesto de valor adicional, is a tax levied at each level in a marketing channel, whereby each channel member who adds value to the goods purchased for processing, packaging, and/or distribution pays a tax only on the amount by which that member increases the worth of the goods.

Further, each seller receives a credit from the government for any VAT paid; thus, the VAT is pushed forward through the production and distribution channel to the consumer, who absorbs the VAT as part of the selling price but who receives no credit from the government.

> **Example:** A steel sheet purchased for $10 by a fabricator and stamped into a car door that is sold to the car assembler for $50 has added $40 worth of value and, thus, pays the VAT on the $40. The buyer of the door, who primes the unit, paints it, and attaches it to the car chassis, adds $210 to the unit since the finished door costs $250. The car assembler pays the VAT only on the $210 of added value.

In the European Economic Community (EEC), the VAT varies by country. In the United Kingdom, it is 16 percent, whereas in Denmark, it is 22 percent. When the United Kingdom made its application to join the EEC, one of the pre-conditions for entry was its imposition of a VAT (which was set at 10 percent upon entry in 1973 and was subsequently raised to current levels).

In Canada, a national VAT was introduced on January 1, 1991. Called the Federal Goods and Services Tax (GST), it was originally scheduled to be introduced at 9 percent. This was reduced to 7 percent upon introduction. It replaced the Federal manufacturers' sales tax (FMST), which was a 13.5-percent tax levied across the board on the total resale value of a manufacturer's goods and not on value added by the manufacturer. The new GST is thus conceived to be more equitable than the old

FMST. Whether this is so or not is a moot point. It will, in fact, be more broadly based than the FMST since it will be levied on every channel member's value-added component and not simply at the manufacturers' level. Food, however, is "zero-rated."

variable levy, also called a *variable import levy*, is a duty developed by the European Economic Community (EEC), designed to ensure that the price of imported agricultural products is equal to (if not higher than) a predetermined "gate price" of domestically produced competing commodities.

The "variable levy formula" works in the following way: say the predetermined "gate price" for butter (for the first two weeks in September) to French farmers is the equivalent of $6.30 per kilogram. During those two weeks, Canadian butter was the lowest quoted on the world market at, say, $3.00 per kilogram, and U.S. butter was quoted at $3.50 per kilogram, both prices being CIF (cost, insurance, and freight, Le Havre).

Thus, if a French firm wished to import, the variable levy (payable by the importer) would be as follows:

Step 1:	Predetermined French gate price:	$6.30 per kilo
minus	Lowest offer on CIF basis:	–3.00 per kilo
equals	Variable levy (benchmark):	$3.30 per kilo
Step 2:	U.S. offer price:	$3.50 per kilo
minus	Variable levy (benchmark):	–3.30 per kilo
equals	Variable levy increment on U.S. butter:	$0.20 per kilo

Thus, the French firm would have to pay $3.30 tax for every kilo of Canadian butter imported during the two-week period and the $3.30 base tax + the $0.20 increment, or $3.50 tax per kilo, for every kilo of American butter imported.

The amount of the levy is adjusted regularly for changes in world market conditions (i.e., daily for grains, bimonthly (or fortnightly) for dairy products, and quarterly for pork products).

See also Common Agricultural Policy; common external tariff.

Venice Terms are, in the context of international debt rescheduling, agreements between debtor countries and the Paris Club to afford the former longer maturities than the "standard 10-year period" allowed to debt that has been rescheduled by countries not benefiting by the Toronto Terms.

> **Example:** Under Venice Terms, Guyana applied for (and got) a 21-year maturity on its foreign debt, while Poland and Côte d'Ivoire received 15-year maturities. These improved repayment terms imply the creation of an "intermediate" category between the "standard 10-year-period" terms and the Toronto Terms.

> Cf. Toronto Terms.
> *See also* international debt; debt rescheduling; Paris Club.

video-conferencing (video-conferencing network) refers to communications technology, based on fiber-optic networks, applied to the business application of electronically convening a meeting of geographically separated individuals.

> **Example:** Olympia & York of Toronto, the international real-estate developer, has opened Canada's first domestic video-conferencing studio as part of its plan to develop a (joint venture) video-conferencing network with U.S. Sprint Communications Company, a unit of United Communications Inc.
>
> The Toronto studio is the fifth in Sprint's network of "Conference Express" studios in New York, Los Angeles, Chicago, and San Francisco. Through Sprint's electronic control and switching center in Atlanta, Georgia, Toronto business people can now video-conference with more than 500 other sites in North America and 22 studios in Europe and Asia.

The capacity of optical fiber (laid along railway rights-of-way) to carry many video images simultaneously makes fiber video-conferencing cheaper than satellite-based networks controlled by telephone companies.

Cf. teleconferencing.

Vienna Agreement Establishing an International Classification of the Figurative Elements of Marks, known as the *Vienna Agreement*, is a multilateral treaty signed by states to afford them substantial protection of intellectual property. The treaty is administered by the World Intellectual Property Organization (WIPO).

See also World Intellectual Property Organization.

Vienna Convention on the Law of Treaties is an international agreement, signed in Vienna, Austria, in 1968 and 1969, that established the way treaties concluded between states are to be negotiated, adopted, and otherwise modified.

This accord came into force in 1980.

Cf. Vienna Convention on the Law of Treaties between States and International Organizations or between International Organizations.

See also Appendix VI (international agreement).

Vienna Convention on the Law of Treaties between States and International Organizations or between International Organizations is an international agreement that established the way treaties between states and international organizations or between two or more international organizations are to be negotiated, adopted, and otherwise modified.

This accord was signed in Vienna, Austria, in 1986, but it has not yet come into force.

Cf. Vienna Convention on the Law of Treaties.

See also Appendix VI (international agreement).

visa *See* Appendix VI.

voluntary export restraints (VERs) *See* voluntary restraint agreements.

voluntary restraint agreements (VRAs) refer to a global arrangement entered into by consumer and producer countries to restrict the export of specific commodities to specific member countries over specific time periods in order to obviate injury to producers of the commodity in the consumer country.

Frequently called "orderly marketing arrangements" (OMAs), VRAs are intended to avoid market disruption by the process of negotiating an agreement to "manage trade."

Cf. international commodity agreements.

See also MultiFiber Arrangement; export quotas; market disruption.

war risk insurance (WRI) is "cover" (i.e., protection) for loss or damage to goods and investments in transit to or resident in a foreign country, against any act of belligerency.

Prior to the availability of coverage against this political risk by the Overseas Private Investment Corporation (OPIC), WRI in the United States was available exclusively through the American Cargo War Risk Reinsurance Exchange, a consortium of private insurers.

Cf. U.S. Maritime Administration; U.S. International Development Cooperation Agency (4. Overseas Private Investment Corporation).

Warsaw Treaty Organization (WTO), also known as the *Warsaw Pact*, and originally, the *Eastern European Mutual Assistance Treaty*, was a mutual defense pact signed in 1945 by the following original communist "fraternal allies": Albania, Czechoslovakia, German Democratic Republic (East Germany), Hungary, Poland, Romania, and the U.S.S.R.

> **Example:** The Warsaw Treaty Organization dissolved its military structure on March 31, 1991. The demilitarization was formalized on February 25, 1991, in Budapest, Hungary, which coincided with the formal dissolution of the Council for Mutual Economic Assistance (CMEA). This breakup of the communist military pact followed many years of violence and repression.
>
> In 1957, the WTO mobilized and invaded Hungary to physically suppress a nationalist uprising by the people. Prime Minister Imre Nagy (who unilaterally withdrew Hungary from the WTO) was executed by the Soviet Union, and his government was replaced by one led by a Soviet appointee, Janos Kadar.
>
> In 1968, the Warsaw Pact again mobilized and invaded Czechoslovakia to replace Alexandr [*sic*] Dubcek's nationalist government. Dubcek was removed and placed in "internal exile"; and a new government was installed, headed by Gustav Husak, a Soviet nominee.

In February 1990, following the peaceful fall of the country's communist government, Dubcek was "rehabilitated" as the country's titular Prime Minister in the elected government of (former dissident poet, now President) Vaclav Havel.

The Cold War is perceived to have ended in Paris on November 19, 1990, with the signing by the Warsaw Pact and NATO of (1) a Declaration of Non-Aggression and (2) a Treaty on Conventional Forces in Europe. These two instruments incorporated the ideas that NATO and the Warsaw Pact agreed not to use force against each other, and to automatically reduce the inventories of conventional military forces in Europe. On November 22, 1990, the Paris Charter for a New Europe was also signed in Paris.

The future of trade relations between East European countries that were CMEA members is uncertain. The collapse of communist regimes in Poland, East Germany, Hungary, and Czechoslovakia in 1989 has led to the start of transformation of these command economies into market economies. This beginning has been paralleled by a halting *perestroika* in the Soviet Union. However, the Soviet-abetted military repression in Lithuania in February 1991 to crush the nationalist movement has placed in doubt the long-term Soviet commitment to noninterference in the political-economies of East Europe, despite all words to the contrary.

Cf. North Atlantic Treaty Organization; Southeast Asia Treaty Organization.

See also perestroika; Council for Mutual Economic Assistance; Conference on Security and Cooperation in Europe; Paris Charter for a New Europe; nonmarket economy; open economy; closed economy.

Webb-Pomerene Act of 1918 (Webb-Pomerene Association) is U.S. legislation that permits two or more firms that are in the same industry to form a commercial partnership (i.e., an export association) within the United States for the sole purpose of export marketing, while exempting it (and its members) from provisions of U.S. antitrust laws, so long as it (and its members) do not restrain trade within the United States.

West African Economic Community (WAEC), also known as *Communauté Économique de l'Afrique de l'Ouest (CEAO)*, is a regional international trade group (ITG) established in 1973 in Abidjan, Côte d'Ivoire, by Burkina Faso, Côte d'Ivoire, Mali, Mauritania, Niger, and Sénégal in order to form a customs union between its member states.

The WAEC is headquartered in Ouagadougou, Burkina Faso.

Somewhat akin to the *Organisation Commune Africaine et Mauricienne* (OCAM), the establishment of WAEC has an interesting origin:

1. *1959:* the West African Customs Union (WACU), also known as *Union Douanière de l'Afrique de l'Ouest (UDAO)*, was established by five francophone West African countries, (prior to their political independence from France), which were members of the French Community.
2. *1966:* the Customs Union of West African States (CUWEAS), also known as *Union Douanière des États de l'Afrique de l'Ouest (UDEAO)*, was established (by the present members of the WAEC, plus Benin) to replace the WACU because, under the "guidance" of France, the organization was perceived to be ignoring the needs of its landlocked members.

3. *1973:* the present West African Economic Community (WAEC) was founded to replace the CUWEAS, without Benin.
4. *1975:* as a result of the efforts of regional economic integration by the WAEC (and successor organizations), a larger, more flexible and comprehensive regional organization was established to coordinate the objective of regional economic integration: the Economic Community of West African States (ECOWAS).

The WAEC, despite being somewhat overshadowed by ECOWAS, has excellent cooperative relations with it and works toward genuine customs union objectives as follows:

1. the unhindered movement of citizens (of member states between member states) was established in 1978;
2. a harmonized regional cooperations tax was introduced in 1976, to apply to industrial capital enterprises in all member countries; and
3. the internal customs system in member countries was entirely dismantled by the end of 1990, as was the consequent erection of a common external tax (CXT) on different commodity classes.

Cf. *Organisation Commune Africaine et Mauricienne.*
See also Economic Community of West African States.

West African Monetary Union (WAMU) is an international organization that was established in 1955 among francophone members of the French Community prior to their political independence to unify their financial policies and instruments.

It is inferred that France had self-interested motives at play whilst it guided the formation of WAMU.

WAMU comprises the same countries that are members of the Central Bank of West African States (CBWAS), officially, *Banque Centrale des États de l'Afrique de l'Ouest (BCEAO)*, the financial institution that acts as the exclusive issuer of notes and coins for the members of WAMU.

There are continuing moves to have CBWAS expand its role and enter into an agreement with both the WAEC and ECOWAS, since neither of these important international trading groups has a central bank that coordinates the balance-of-payments settlement systems within the two communities.

See also Central Bank of West African States; West African Economic Community; Economic Community of West African States; Appendix V (B).

Western European Union (WEU) is an international political group (IPG) established in 1955 as a successor to the Brussels Treaty Organization (BTO) and as the genuine forerunner of the Council of Europe.

Within the framework of the BTO, all the WEU's military functions have been transferred to the North Atlantic Treaty Organization (NATO), created in 1949. In addition, the Council of Europe per se, has taken over much of the work of the WEU, although the latter maintains a number of permanent committees to study such important areas as defense. The WEU thus has

ongoing relations with the Council of Europe, through which it has access to all the institutions of the European Economic Community (EEC).
See also Council of Europe; European Economic Community.

without recourse •NW• is the explicit acknowledgement that a financial institution that buys any type of deferred debt foregoes any right to claim any portion of the instrument's value from any of the previous holders of it.

with particular average (WPA) *See* Appendix III.

World Bank (WB) is the "short-form name" used to identify the International Bank for Reconstruction and Development (IBRD), which is the official name of the organization.
Cf. World Bank Group.
See International Bank for Reconstruction and Development.

World Bank Group is, collectively, a group of four international organizations involved in financing long-term development.
The charter member of The Group is the International Bank for Reconstruction and Development (IBRD), founded in 1944 at the Bretton Woods Conference. It is called the World Bank, and, when this name is used, the IBRD alone is denoted and none of the other entities in the Group.
The second member of the Group is the International Finance Corporation (IFC), established in 1956.
The third member of the Group is the International Development Association (IDA), which was formed in 1960.
The fourth member of the Group is the Multilateral Investment Guarantee Agency (MIGA), established in 1987.
See also International Bank for Reconstruction and Development; multilateral development banks; International Finance Corporation; International Development Association; Multilateral Investment Guarantee Agency.

World Bank International Center for the Settlement of Investment Disputes (ICSID) is an autonomous institution established by the World Bank in Washington, D.C., under the authority of the 1965 United Nations Convention on the Settlement of Investment Disputes between States and Nationals of Other States.
The aim of the ICSID is to resolve international disputes (via conciliation, if possible, and arbitration, if necessary) involving capital investments especially where a sovereign state, or an agency thereof, is a party to the dispute.

> **Example:** The kind of dispute that might lend itself to settlement by the ICSID might be one where the Overseas Private Investment Corporation (OPIC) participated in providing a private U.S. company with "direct investment funds" for investment in a Middle Eastern country's infrastructure that had been damaged as a result of the 1991 Persian Gulf War. Assume the following: (1) that the capital investment was shared as follows: OPIC (40 percent), U.S. private-sector capital (45 percent), and Middle Eastern country private-sector

co-financing (15 percent); (2) that there was some legal dispute (e.g., repatriating profits to the United States); and (3) that the country stepped in to block the transfer of U.S. funds and to contest the terms of repatriation.

To referee the matter, the U.S. company might approach the ICSID to "work things out" within the following framework: strict legal impartiality, sensitivity to the political conditions in the foreign country, and the desire of all parties to maintain a good long-term relationship.

Such disputes are inherently complex because of the complexities of international law, especially in the area of international finance, where there is scarce consensus on the proper arbitration of disputes involving services, and where code law systems and common law systems conflict.

See also arbitration; United Nations Commission on International Trade Arbitration Law; Appendix VI (sovereignty).

World Competitiveness Report (WCR) is an annual publication of the World Economic Forum and the International Management Development Institute (WEF/MDI), an academic consortium established in Geneva, Switzerland, in 1981.

The WCR explains what international competitiveness means and how it is measured; and it ranks countries according to 10 "competitiveness measures." This information is used by governments and by leaders of corporations worldwide.

The following is an overview of the WCR's 10 "competitiveness measures":

1. *Natural-Endowment Utilization:* measures the quantity of a country's physical resources and the efficiency with which they are used.
2. *Dynamism of the Economy:* examines macroeconomic measures such as economic growth, size of the gross domestic product, total foreign exchange reserves, and the expectation of recession.
3. *Industrial Efficiency:* measures (and examines) labor costs, productivity, corporate profit, inflation, and taxes.
4. *Market Orientation:* examines national markets on the precept that the ability to compete is partly contingent on how intensively (or "fiercely," as commentators on Japan are wont to say) the business community competes at home.
5. *Financial Dynamism:* assesses the capital market and the country's "financial environment." This includes a review of the government debt, its monetary policy, and the cost of capital.
6. *Human Resources:* reviews a country's comparative advantage based on its people's skills, their motivation and flexibility to work, and on the demographics of the working population (e.g., age structure, days absent due to ill health).
7. *Impact of the State:* evaluates the government's contribution to a country's competitiveness.
8. *International Orientation:* measures the presence of home-country companies in foreign markets and of home-country "openness" to imports and to foreign direct investment.
9. *Future Orientation:* examines the percentage of the gross domestic product invested in a country's research and development (R&D) and in sci-

ence and technology, the number of patent registrations in its national patent office, and its record of successful commercialization of new products.

10. *Socio-Political Stability:* reviews such things as labor relations, income distribution, incidence and distribution of crime, criminal conviction and imprisonment, and judicial independence.

The WCRs are an ethnocentric outgrowth of an economic deterministic *Weltanschauung* ("world-view"), which overvalues economic development. In the "global competitiveness sweepstakes," the WCR has become the secular equivalent of the Holy Grail.

Cf. sustainable development.

World Health Organization (WHO) is an autonomous, specialized, international organization of the United Nations System, officially established in 1958 in New York to create one global institution that would unify the pursuit of improving the health of the population of the world.

Predecessor world health institutions included (1) the *Office Internationale de l'Hygiène Publique (OIHP)*, founded in Paris in 1903; and (2) the *Pan-American Sanitary Bureau*, founded in Washington, D.C., in 1902.

The WHO has its headquarters in Geneva, Switzerland, and it assists over 150 member·countries. The WHO is responsible for planning, developing, and implementing programs for the prevention and treatment of human disease. Priority is given to research on and in-field implementation of ways and means to prevent, eradicate, and treat pandemics such as malaria, cholera, yellow fever, poliomyelitis, trypanosomiasis, and schistosomiasis, and conditions such as *kwashiorkor* (protein malnutrition), *marasmus* (protein-calorie malnutrition), and gastroenteritis.

The WHO works closely with joint programs involving important institutions in the United Nations System. From the global marketing viewpoint, therefore, the WHO procures an enormous volume of capital equipment, supplies, and expert services mainly from the WHO headquarters in Geneva, but also from its six regional offices as follows:

1. Regional Office for Africa: Brazzaville, Congo
2. Regional Office for the Americas (i.e., the Pan American Health Organization (PAHO)): Washington, D.C.
3. Regional Office for the Eastern Mediterranean: Alexandria, Egypt
4. Regional Office for Europe: Copenhagen, Denmark
5. Regional Office for Southeast Asia: New Delhi, India
6. Regional Office for the Western Pacific: Manila, Philippines.

See also United Nations Development Program; Food and Agricultural Organization; United Nations Fund for Population Activities; United Nations Education, Scientific and Cultural Organization.

World Intellectual Property Organization (WIPO) is the specialized agency of the United Nations System that functions to promote and coordinate intergovernmental cooperation in the field of intellectual property.

WIPO was established by an international convention signed in Stockholm,

Sweden, in 1967; and it came into force in 1970. Membership, as of 1990, was 125 countries. Under its auspices, WIPO has coordinated activity under international agreements respecting intellectual property, such as the Patent Cooperation Treaty (1970), the Paris Convention (1883), and the Berne Convention (1886), and as the central body for such programs as the CAPRI Project.

The following references are a comprehensive listing of the WIPO-administered multilateral agreements on intellectual property protection that are significant from an international business viewpoint.

See also Berne Convention; Budapest Treaty on the International Recognition of the Deposit of Microorganisms for the Purposes of Patent Procedure; CAPRI Project; Geneva Convention for the Protection of Producers of Phonograms against Unauthorized Duplication of their Phonograms; Hague Agreement Concerning the International Deposit of Industrial Designs; Madrid Agreement Concerning the International Registration of Marks; Nice Agreement Concerning the International Classification of Goods and Services for the Purposes of the Registration of Marks; Paris Convention; Patent Cooperation Treaty; Rome Convention for the Protection of Performers, Producers of Phonograms, and Broadcasting Organizations; Treaty on Intellectual Property in Respect of Integrated Circuits; Treaty on International Registration of Audiovisual Works; *Union Internationale pour la Protection des Obtentions Végétales (UPOV)*; Vienna Agreement Establishing an International Classification of the Figurative Elements of Marks.

World Meteorological Organization (WMO) is an autonomous international organization of the United Nations System that was formally established in Paris, France, in 1951.

The progenitor institution, the International Meteorological Organization, was founded in Utrecht in 1878. In 1947, at the twelfth IMO Conference in Washington, D.C., the Convention establishing the current WMO was drawn up.

The WMO functions to promote work in meteorological, geophysical, and hydrological fields pertinent to (1) ongoing research; (2) standardization of observations and statistics; (3) applications in shipping, aviation, and agriculture; and (4) collaborating with United Nations programs to provide relevant, accurate, and timely information for action.

The WMO is at the center of important global events:

1. *World Weather Watch Program:* coordinates the distribution to meteorological authorities in all countries of information based on data collection involving a network of World Meteorological Centers, 25 regional Meteorological Centers, national weather stations, and a system of geosynchronous and polar-orbiting weather satellites.
2. *Research and Development Program:* promotes work into improving both short- and long-term weather forecasting.
3. *Program on Research in Tropical Meteorology:* focuses work specifically to gain greater understanding about the predictability, causes, and geo-

physical and hydrological affects of tropical cyclones, monsoons, and droughts.

4. *Hydrology and Water Resources Program:* promotes cooperation in evaluating the world's hydrological resources and in establishing hydrological services to serve national and regional planning projects.

5. *World Climate Program:* is a global educational effort geared toward disseminating information on the world's climates, stimulating educational investment in the field, and raising global consciousness about economic and social consequences of climate changes.

The WMO has excellent working relations with all bodies in the United Nations System upon whose programs meteorological, geophysical, and hydrological considerations impact.

From the global-marketing viewpoint, the WMO has considerable importance and influence within the United Nations System. While its direct procurement through its Geneva, Switzerland, headquarters is not substantial, its authority to influence other specialized U.N. agencies, national governments, and their executing/implementing agencies is quite substantial.

See also United Nations System.

world trade center (WTC) is a site, in a city, that brings together under one roof all the services associated with international trade (e.g., international financial institutions, insurance facilities, customs brokers, freight forwarders, legal services, promotional services, export packaging services, and physical distribution/logistical facilities).

As of May 1, 1991, there were 211 operating WTCs in 223 cities in 211 countries.

A WTC usually comprises office space for its members, meeting rooms and exhibition halls (for workshops, seminars, trade shows, and training), a full range of telecommunications and clerical services, language services (including translation), and library facilities. WTCs frequently have hotel, dining, and recreational facilities as well, made available to their members and official guests. WTCs usually offer their members admittance to a WTC "Club" that provides access to special functions and receptions. All WTC clubs offer reciprocal privileges to their members worldwide.

At the hub of the WTC network is the World Trade Centers Association, which was founded in New Orleans, Louisiana, U.S.A., in 1968, but which is currently headquartered in New York City, New York.

World Trade Data Reports (WTDRs) are data in published form provided to U.S. exporters by the Foreign Commercial Service unit of the International Trade Administration section of the U.S. Department of Commerce to assist in assessing the reliability of foreign intermediaries.

The essence of each WTDR is that it provides an international "credit check" of a particular potential foreign distributor. Each WTDR is provided on a "fee-for-service" basis.

See also U.S. International Trade Administration.

yen, from the Chinese *yuan* meaning "round," is the official currency of Japan, issued by the Bank of Japan, and bearing the currency symbol "¥."

yen area (yen bloc) *See* currency area.

yen diplomacy •NW• is the use of strategically important regional measures by Japan to forge a yen area, or yen bloc. This refers to the establishing of arrangements with those Pacific Rim newly industrialized countries (NICs) who have close, ongoing ties in technology, finance, and trade with Japan.

Consequently, Japan aims to establish a long-term dependency on the Japanese "core" by the Asian nations on the "periphery" of the region.

An outline of these Japanese arrangements is as follows:

1. *New Asian Industries Development Plan:* called the "New AID Plan," a program for commitment of funds (as an incentive for Japanese business) to relocate industries to lower-cost offshore NICs.

   The New AID Plan is implemented in three steps:

   i.   *Targeting* of NIC industrial sectors and *master planning* to transfer Japanese experience and technical assistance to the target via the Japan International Cooperation Agency (JICA).
   ii. *Project development* and *policy reform* of the NICs by Japan, whereby infrastructure is redesigned, institutions are reorganized, and programs are designed to attract and retain Japanese direct investment.
   iii. *Program implementation* using the following Japanese financial facilities to build the infrastructure, recruit and train the technicians, and operate the industrial and logistical offshore export industries:

- Japan Overseas Economic Cooperation Foundation (JOEF) for bilateral funding of infrastructure;
- Japan External Trade Organization (JETRO) and Japan Overseas Development Corporation (JODC) for technical cooperation in training of local people in management, marketing, finance, logistics, promotion, and transportation;
- Association for Overseas Technical Scholarship (AOTC) for providing funding and support for NIC trainees brought to Japan for advancement.

2. *ASEAN-Japan Development Fund (AJDF):* a multi-agency effort to directly stimulate the formation of industrial Japanese-ASEAN joint ventures in ASEAN target countries.

There are three components to the AJDF:

- a capital fund allocated for bilateral JVs;
- a subfund set aside for regional JVs comprising, for then, one ASEAN country; and
- the Japan-ASEAN Investment Corporation (JAIC) for purchasing equity and bonds in Japanese-ASEAN JVs.

It is highly likely that out of the mix of the behind-the-scenes yen diplomacy with the highly vocal and visible Pacific Economic Cooperation Group (PECG), an integrated yen area with a common currency (or at least with linkages to the yen as the "peggable currency") and permanent monetary institutions will develop in the process of economically integrating the Asian "periphery" around a Japanese "core."

Cf. Three Pillar Strategy.
See also technology transfer; dependency theory.

"Yes, Yes" •NW• is a decision-avoidance paradigm developed as a *gedanken* idea (i.e., a "thought experiment") based on the work of Karel van Wolferen, the esteemed writer on the sociology of power in Japan.

The concept of "Yes, Yes" rests on the borrowed Japanese idea that Western managers can avoid confrontational decision making by adopting the Japanese practice of guiding groups to predetermined goals (i.e., *nemawashi*). It assumes that techniques used in Japan, which foster the Japanese penchant for compliance with management-engineered group norms, are transferable to solving "*nemawashi*-type" (i.e., group-based) problems in the West. Building on this assumption, "Yes, Yes" advances two ideas: (1) that Western managers should not feel obliged to make top-down decisions; and (2) that they should even avoid the pretense of making them, lest company members conclude that management is trying to "do a top-down job on them" (i.e., making decisions without democratic participation).

Is "Yes, Yes" correct? Is *nemawashi*-type problem solving transferable to the West, and is "Yes, Yes" reasonable?

The "Yes, Yes" idea incorrectly infers (but with every good intention) that Japanese decision avoidance is implicitly democratic since it is embedded within what Westerners see as a democratic group-based decision-making arena. Thus, decision avoidance is declared to have utility since it is presumed to be culturally congruent with implicitly democratic Western society.

The idea that Japanese decision avoidance is somehow desirable to import into the West, and to emulate, results from an incorrect perception that Japanese culture and decision making are genuinely group-based and democratic. The Japanese are under no such illusions. Japanese managers, deeply paternalistic and authoritarian, attempt to disguise the ethos of Japanese tyranny under the cover of the group-oriented "talk-it-out" format.

Social psychological analysis of "Yes, Yes" suggests why Western managers might engage in such unwitting self-deception: many managers fear the loss of their social assets ("face") as a result of (1) making incorrect decisions, (2) having their decisions rejected by superiors, or (3) having them go unsupported by subordinates. Thus, it is not unreasonable to conclude that Western managers who continue to believe in "Yes, Yes" may likely be suffering from low self-esteem.

See also cultural borrowing; *nemawashi* •NW•.

yoroshiku tanomu •NW•, from the Japanese meaning "act as you think fit" or "do as is appropriate," is verbal direction given by Japanese managers to Japanese worker teams to behave appropriately in a work situation, using both initiative and teamwork concepts where the situation demands it.

One can infer *yoroshiku tanomu* from the Japanese concept of situational conformity, that "the situation gives the orders." Thus, the expression *yoroshiku tanomu* assumes compliance by individual members of a work team with broadly based Japanese high-context cultural expectations.

Cf. low-context culture.

See also high-context culture; *nemawashi* •NW•; situational conformity •NW•.

Z

zaibatsu, an archaic term for the traditional, Japanese, family-dominated, economic monopolies, were, from the 1930s and 1940s to the end of the U.S. occupation of Japan (1945–1952), the Japanese equivalent of (hypothetical) North American megavertical marketing systems (VMSs).

Zaibatsu were characterized by vast networks of tight, interlocked directorships that coordinated business strategies based primarily on allegiance owed by family members to each other and from one family to others.

At the end of World War II, during the "American Occupation" (1945–1952), the *zaibatsu* were officially dismantled by the U.S. military occupation authorities, (1) because of their role in war-making and (2) because their structure conflicted with U.S. conceptions of antimonopoly behavior. Ironically, they were replaced (over time) by even more powerful modernized equivalents after the departure of the U.S. occupation forces.

Cf. *keiretsu* •NW•.

zaikai •NW• is the Japanese term that refers to the broad group of business functionaries in Japan who represent one level of the society's "power elite."

The *zaikai* does not represent only the leaders of Japan's business corporations. Rather, the *zaikai* is a four-headed organism that embodies the totality of the structure of power in Japan. The four heads are as follows:

1. *Keidanren* (Federation of Industrial Organizations) comprises all leading associations comprising all important business corporations in Japan.
2. *Nikkeiren* (Japan Federation of Employers' Associations) is the unit that works with Japan's labor unions (e.g., The Japanese Trade Union Confederation *(Rengo)* and The Japan Federation of Electrical Machine Workers Unions *(Denki Roren))* to control them.

3. *Keizai Doyukai* (The Committee for Economic Development) is the "inner cabinet" of top *zaikai* members who develop strategic international business policy for Japan.

4. *The Japan Chamber of Commerce* represents the interests of small businesses, which are defined as enterprises staffed by less than 300 employees and capitalized at less than ¥100 million.

See also *Keidanren* •NW•; *keiretsu* •NW•.

Zoll, from the German *Zoll* meaning "customs," is the word for "customs" in German, usually signifying a "customs post" for the purpose of examining imported goods.

See also customs; duty.

zona franca *See* foreign trade zone.

Foreign Exchange Contracts Vocabulary

What follows is a set of important terms used in international business where contracts for foreign currencies are bought and sold. This set covers the foreign exchange instruments, the contracts, and the ways of buying foreign exchange.

currency-option contract refers to the alternative to buy (or not to buy) or to sell (or not to sell) a quantity of currency at an agreed-upon exchange rate over a fixed period of time.

Any loss to the option holder by exercising this buy/sell alternative is limited to the cost of the option.

dual currency bond is a financial instrument that is denominated in one currency but that pays interest in another currency at a fixed exchange rate.

> **Example:** A 10-year Eurobond was issued by ASEA, the Swiss firm in the Swiss-Swedish joint venture ASEA, Brown, Boveri (ABB). Based in Zurich, ABB denominated the offering in Swiss-francs (CHF) but paid interest at 10 percent in Canadian dollars (CAD). The rate of exchange was fixed at CAD $1 = CHF 2.

Eurobond is a financial instrument denominated in one of the transferable currencies of West Europe but issued by a corporation nonresident in West Europe.

> **Example:** A series of one thousand 10-year 14-percent cumulative-interest-bearing Eurobonds was issued by the Canadian Export Development Corporation (EDC). Denominated in units of Deutsche marks (DEM) 500,000 each and available for purchase only in West Europe, the coupons clipped (and ultimately, the Eurobonds themselves) could only be cashed by a Canadian commercial bank resident in London and acting as the transfer agent for the nonresident EDC.

Eurocommercial paper is a short-term (i.e., 30-, 60-, 90-, or 180-day) unsecured note issued or offered by a nonbank corporation in the Euromarkets.

Eurocurrency is any currency being traded (i.e., bought and sold) outside the jurisdiction that issued the currency.

The term originally meant exclusively *Eurodollars* (i.e., U.S. dollars being traded in West Europe), which arose as a result of the massive increase in the world price of oil in the post-1973 period and the subsequent investment inflow of U.S. dollars to Europe from the Organization of Petroleum Exporting Countries (OPEC).

These petroleum-derived U.S. dollar revenues have been called "petrodollars."

See also Eurodollars.

Eurocurrency deposit is an account in which a currency denominated in a transferable West European currency has been placed by a person or a company not resident in the country of the currency.

> **Example:** When American subsidiaries resident in Japan accept payment in pound sterling (GBP) and make transfer deposits of the British currency to Italian banks, a Eurocurrency deposit has taken place.

Eurodollar deposit is an account in which a currency denominated in U.S. dollars is owned by a person or a company not resident in the United States.

> **Example:** Kjell Knutson, a Norwegian expatriate working for a U.S. company in Kenya, had a contract stating that part of his salary in U.S. dollars would be deposited directly into a British bank account opened in his name. This is a case where Kjell owns the Eurodollar account but does not make Eurodollar deposits into it.

Eurodollars were originally U.S. dollars being traded in West Europe subsequent to 1973.

In contemporary times, with the increasing monetary and customs unification of the European Economic Community (EEC) and the globalization of trade, Eurodollars have come to refer to accounts in financial institutions anywhere outside the territorial sovereignty of the United States in which the currency is U.S. dollars.

Eurolira *See* Eurocurrency.

Euromarks *See* Eurocurrency.

Euronotes is a variation of *Eurocommercial paper*.

Eurosterling (Europounds) *See* Eurocurrency.

Euroyen *See* Eurocurrency.

foreign exchange markets refer to buyers and sellers located mainly in international financial centers who buy and sell currencies both on a "spot" and a "forward" basis.

    See also international financial centers (in main entries).

forward contract is an agreement for the purchase or sale of a foreign currency at some future date at the exchange rate fixed on the date of the agreement.

forward exchange markets refer to buyers and sellers located mainly in international financial centers who make contracts for (and thereby engage in transactions in) the purchase or sale of currencies at some future date.

    See also forward contract.

petrodollars (Petrodollars) are OPEC (Organization of Petroleum Exporting Countries) revenues from the marketing of oil (in the post-1973 period) denominated in U.S. dollars (USD) and invested in Western nations.

    See also Eurocurrency.

spot deal is a contract for the purchase or sale of a foreign currency whereby the delivery of the currency, bought or sold, must occur within two business days from the day the contract is made at an exchange rate fixed on the day the contract was made.

    See also Appendix II (spot rate).

Foreign Exchange Risk Vocabulary

What follows is a set of essential terms that surround the concept of "risk" that is involved in buying and selling foreign currencies in international business.

accounting exposure refers to the inherent risks of depreciation or appreciation that potentially affect an accounting statement, or any entries in an accounting statement, expressed in a foreign currency.

See also exchange exposure.

appreciation is the decrease in the cost of a foreign currency as reflected by the decrease in the domestic currency price of a foreign currency.

Cf. depreciation.

arbitrage is the purchase of currency or securities in one market and the sale of them in another market in order to take profitable advantage of either (1) the spread (i.e., the price differences) or (2) the interest-rate differentials between the two markets.

bank swap, also known as *currency swap, bank-swapped deposit, swapped deposit,* and *foreign-exchange swap transaction,* is the purchase of a foreign currency (which remains deposited in the bank) with the forward sale of the same foreign currency on deposit at a future date that coincides with the maturity date of the deposit.

See also forward spread.

bank-swapped deposit *See* bank swap.

cash position is the situation of a trader of foreign exchange that reflects the fact that she or he has cash on hand for immediate use.

central bank swaps, commonly called *swap arrangements*, are exchanges of currencies between the central banks of different countries (usually by banks

within some integrated economic union) to provide transferable currency (usually, but not exclusively, U.S. dollars) to member countries so as to enable them to protect their own rates of inter- and extra-community exchange.
See Appendix V (B) for listed banks.

clean float (clean floating) refers to the rise and fall in price of a currency due solely to market forces and uninfluenced by government intervention in the market for the purpose of "administering" the float.
Cf. dirty float.

conversion exposure is the risk inherent in converting one currency into another or one balance sheet (expressed in one foreign currency, e.g., Canadian dollars) into a consolidated balance sheet (expressed in U.S. dollars).

cover *See forward cover.*

covered differential is the "spread" between comparable short-term rates of two convertible currencies (e.g., Canadian and U.S. dollars) after concession has been granted for the forward premium, or discount, on the U.S. dollar in Canada.

covered interest arbitrage refers to the transfer of short-term liquid funds from a domestic base to a foreign account with the aim of earning higher returns.
The risk that a downward fluctuation in exchange will occur is "covered" (1) by the purchase of the foreign currency on a spot basis and (2) by a simultaneous offsetting forward sale of it.
Cf. uncovered interest arbitrage.

currency swap *See* bank swap.

depreciation is the increase in the cost of a foreign currency as reflected by the increase in the domestic currency price of a foreign currency.
Cf. appreciation.

destabilizing speculation is the action of making a profit in the following ways:

1. selling a foreign currency when the domestic exchange rate is low or is falling in the expectation that the exchange rate will fall even lower, or
2. purchasing a foreign currency when the domestic exchange rate is high or is rising in the expectation that the exchange rate will rise even higher.

Cf. stabilizing speculation.

devaluation is the deliberate lowering of the value of one nation's currency in terms of the currency of one or more nations.
This is reflected as an increase in the exchange rate by the country that deliberately lowers the exchange value of its currency.

Example: In January, one U.S. dollar bought 200 Japanese yen. In June, it bought only 100 yen, a 50 percent devaluation in six months.

The reason for a competitive devaluation is to increase the attractiveness of a country's exports.

> **Example:** The 50 percent devaluation of the U.S. dollar against the yen reduced the domestic U.S. demand for Japanese imports because of the price increase of them in terms of the U.S. dollar. The U.S. balance-of-payments deficit was expected to be helped over the short term because of this.

dirty float (dirty floating) refers to the practice of a government "administering" a country's exchange rate to achieve goals other than those normally associated with monetary policy (e.g., the smoothing out of short-term exchange-rate fluctuations).

> **Example:** The Canadian government seems worried over the fact that since the FTA was signed, the Canadian dollar has been steadily rising toward parity with the U.S. dollar. For years, Canadian authorities have used the Bank of Canada to intervene in the free market to ensure that the Canadian dollar was undervalued *vis-à-vis* the U.S. dollar, making Canadian exports attractive to U.S. buyers, improving the Canadian trade balance, but worsening the U.S. deficit. In effect, the Canadian government was dirty floating its currency.

See also managed floating exchange rate system (in main entries).

discount *See* forward discount.

discount margin, sometimes referred to as a *negative premium*, is the condition under which the forward value of a currency is less than the spot price; thus, the currency is "at a discount."
Cf. premium margin; par.

effective exchange rate is a weighted average of the exchange rates between the domestic currency of a country and the currency of that nation's most important trading partners, with each currency weighted by the relative importance of each partner's trade with the domestic nation.

efficiency of foreign exchange markets is a situation that occurs if the future spot rate for foreign exchange is accurately predicated by the forward rate.

exchange exposure is the inherent risk that occurs whenever an asset or a liability (i.e., a credit or a debit) is expressed in a foreign currency.
Expressing accounts in foreign currency exposes the values to depreciation or appreciation.

exchange rate is the price of a foreign currency as expressed in local currency.

exchange spread is the difference between the buying rate and the selling rate for a currency.

export instability refers to the short-run fluctuations in export earnings and prices.

exposure *See* exchange exposure.

exposure netting refers to an open position in two or more currencies that reflects the fact that the strengths and weaknesses of each currency are perceived to balance each other.
>   Cf. square position.
>   *See also* open position.

fixed exchange rate is the transaction rate for a currency (which establishes its value in terms of other national currencies) as set by intergovernment agreement and by government intervention (where necessary) in world currency exchange markets.

>   **Example:** The Soviet Union had an agreement with its fraternal members of the Council for Mutual Economic Assistance (CMEA) to exchange Soviet roubles at fixed exchange rates. The significance of this is that there was an official multiple price system for the Soviet currency that is, regardless of its level, entirely artificial in that it was not "market driven," but rather created by the political needs of the nonmarket governments of the CMEA.

>   Cf. floating exchange rates.
>   *See also* dirty float; International Bank for Economic Cooperation (in main entries).

floating exchange rate is the transaction rate for a currency (which establishes its value in terms of other national currencies) as set by supply and demand for the currency in world markets.
>   Cf. fixed exchange rate.
>   *See also* clean float.

fluctuating exchange rate *See* floating exchange rate.

foreign exchange is a nondomestic, foreign currency.

foreign exchange exposure *See* exchange exposure.

foreign exchange reserve *See* reserve currency country (in main entries).

foreign exchange risk is the "danger" of possible depreciation or appreciation to which a foreign currency is exposed whenever transactions are made in nondomestic currencies or when assets or liabilities are held on a corporation's books in a foreign currency.
>   Cf. exchange exposure.

foreign-exchange swap transaction *See* bank swap.

forward contract *See* Appendix I.

forward cover is an agreement to provide protection against exchange rate fluctuations between the contract date and the due date (i.e., the date when payment is due).

The protection provided is in the form of a forward contract.

See also Appendix I (forward contract).

forward discount is the annual percentage by which the forward rate (on the foreign exchange) is below its spot rate.

Cf. forward premium.

forward position is the situation of a trader of foreign exchange that reflects the net difference between outstanding commitments for forward purchase and the sale of a foreign currency at a specific time.

forward premium is the annual percentage by which the forward rate (on the foreign exchange) is above its spot rate.

Cf. forward discount.

forward rate is the exchange rate in foreign currency transactions that is in effect at that time in the future (in a forward contract) when the currency contracted for must be delivered.

forward spread is the premium or discount on the forward portion of a bank swap.

See also bank swap.

futures contract is (1) in foreign exchange transactions, a standardized form of contract involving an agreement to deliver (at a specified time in the future) a specified quantity of currency; (2) in noncurrency commodity transactions, an agreement whereby contracting parties agree to buy (take delivery of) or sell (deliver) specific amounts of goods at specific prices at some specified time in the future.

gilt-edged market is a term used in the United Kingdom to mean all marketable securities, excluding Treasury Bills.

hedge (hedging) refers to actions taken to reduce exchange exposure in a foreign currency to avoid foreign exchange risk.

See also forward cover.

interest arbitrage is the transfer of short-term (i.e., 30-, 60-, and 90-day) funds from the domestic market to the foreign market to earn relatively higher interest rates there.

interest parity refers to the situation that reflects the following position: the forward discount on a particular foreign currency equals the positive interest differential (in favor of the foreign money center that is trading the currency).

interest rate swap is a transaction that uses the exchanging of interest "payment streams" by the parties as a hedging tactic.

There are three strategies:

1. *Cross-Currency (Interest-Rate) Swaps:* the exchange of a fixed rate in one currency for a floating rate in another currency;
2. *Basis (Interest-Rate) Swaps:* the exchange of one floating-rate index to another floating-rate index in the same currency;
3. *Coupon (Interest-Rate) Swaps:* the exchange of one floating-rate index to a fixed-rate index in the same currency.

intervention currency is a convertible currency (e.g., U.S. dollar, Swiss franc) used by the monetary authorities (i.e., by the central bank acting with political approval) to act in foreign exchange markets to keep a country's exchange rate within a range of fluctuations.

See also managed floating exchange rate system (in main entries).

LIBOR (London interbank offer rate), a variation of London interbank offered/offering rate, is the interest rate set in London, which reflects the deposit rate tendered by commercial banks to each other for the short-term (often overnight) deposit of funds.

The LIBOR is used as the base rate for Eurocurrency loan rates. It is also employed as a guide by the Canadian Export Development Corporation (EDC) to ensure that EDC rates of interest on official export financing do not exceed the concensus rates established by the Paris Club.

long position, sometimes called "being long," refers to (1) a situation of a trader of foreign exchange that reflects an excess of purchases over sales of a particular foreign currency; (2) a situation in which a company's assets in a foreign currency exceed its liabilities in that particular currency.

Cf. short position.

margin is the difference between the "spot" price of a currency and its "forward" price.

See also premium (margin); discount (margin).

mint parity, under the gold standard, meant that each nation defined the gold content of its currency, and each was prepared to buy and/or sell gold at that price.

For example, the unit of account of the International Bank for Economic Cooperation (IBEC) is the Transferable Rouble (TR), which has 0.987412 grams of gold, the same gold content as the Soviet rouble. Therefore, the mint parity of the Soviet (or Transferable) rouble is 0.987412 grams of gold, and it had a transactional value of U.S. $1.01, the equivalent of the former gold-standard price of U.S. $35.00 per ounce. Again, in theory, the Soviet Union would have been prepared to buy or sell units of gold in multiples of 0.987412 at U.S. $1.01 had it accepted the mint parity rule.

open position is the state of any trader in foreign exchange who has not yet made or received a payment in a foreign currency at some future date: the trader (and the currency) are "open to risk" (i.e., exposed to the possibility of some fluctuation in the exchange rate between the time the original contract was made and the settlement date).

Cf. accounting exposure; exchange exposure.

par is the condition where there is no margin: the forward price of a currency is equal to its spot price. The currency is thus "at par."

Cf. discount margin; premium margin.

position is the situation of a trader of foreign exchange in terms of the total amount of foreign currency bought or sold at any given time.

premium margin is the condition under which the forward price of a currency is greater than its spot price.

The currency is thus "at a premium."

Cf. discount margin; par.

risk position is the situation of a trader of foreign exchange that reflects the net amounts of spot and forward locations of a foreign currency being traded.

short position, sometimes called "being short," refers to (1) a situation of a trader of foreign exchange that reflects an excess of sales over purchases of a particular foreign currency; (2) a situation in which a company's liabilities in a foreign currency (i.e., its obligations to settle an account) exceed its assets in that particular currency.

Cf. long position.

speculation is the act of purposely engaging in transactions in which there is a degree of foreign exchange risk with the aim of making a profit as a consequence of the risks surrounding the transactions.

Cf. destabilizing speculation.

See also stabilizing speculation.

spot against forward refers to the extent to which "spot" holdings of foreign currency match "forward" currency sales.

The position is determined by subtracting forward purchases from forward sales.

See also long position; short position.

spot rate refers to the exchange rate in spot deals of foreign currency that calls for the exchange (and receipt) of the currencies within two business days from the day the contract was made.

See also Appendix I (spot deal).

spread is the difference between what is asked for a foreign currency and what is bid for it.

This invariably refers to a spot deal.

Cf. forward spread.

square position is the situation of the trader of foreign currency that reflects the fact that sales of a particular currency and purchases of the same currency are in balance during any specified accounting period.

Cf. exposure netting.

stabilizing speculation is the action of making a profit in the following ways:

1. purchasing a foreign currency when the domestic exchange rate is low or is falling in the expectation that the exchange rate will rise; or
2. selling a foreign currency when the domestic exchange rate is high or is rising in the expectation that the exchange rate will fall.

Cf. destabilizing speculation.

swapped deposit *See* bank swap.

translation risk refers to the inherent exchange risk in converting values in one currency to another, even when there are no transactions involved.

This risk is additional to the inherent risks involved in expressing an accounting statement in a foreign currency.

Cf. accounting exposure.

uncovered interest arbitrage is the transfer of short-term liquid funds from a domestic base to a foreign account with the aim of earning higher returns.

The risk that a downward fluctuation in exchange will occur is not "covered."

Cf. covered interest arbitrage.

unstable (foreign) exchange rate market is the characterization of a market for country currencies that varies from "unsteady" to "volatile," due to political and/or commercial disturbances.

Nonuniform Terms of Trade: Non-Incoterms

The following terms of trade are used as nonstandard terms of sale in international commercial transactions. While they have attained a good level of acknowledgment and acceptability among those who use them, their usage is neither extensive internationally nor sufficiently intensive (even regionally) to merit legitimation by the International Chamber of Commerce (ICC) and, hence, acceptance by the global marketing community.

Cost, Insurance, Freight, and Commission (CIF & C) means the seller is obligated to pay (1) the cost of the goods, (2) the cost of insurance against loss, (3) the freight charges to get them to the named port of destination, and (4) any commissions for services rendered by facilitating intermediaries (e.g., freight forwarders, customs brokers).

Cost, Insurance, Freight, and Exchange (CIF & E) means the seller is obligated to pay (1) the cost of the goods, (2) the cost of insurance against loss, (3) the freight charges to get them to the named port of destination, and (4) the foreign exchange (i.e., any costs associated with the conversion of the buyer's currency into the seller's currency or into any other designated currency of payment).

Cost, Insurance, Freight, and Interest (CIF & I) means the seller is obligated to pay (1) the cost of the goods, (2) the cost of insurance against loss, (3) the freight charges to get them to the named port of destination, and (4) interest on the value of the contract for any time period during which the goods have not been put into the buyer's hands.

Delivered Duty Exempt . . . (named Foreign/Free Trade Zone) (DDE) means the seller is obligated to pay (1) the cost of the goods; (2) the cost of insurance against loss; (3) the freight charges to get them to the named port of destination; and (4) any duties, surcharges, or taxes levied on the goods by the importing country.

Free on Board, Duty Exempt

The "named destination" is a foreign/free trade zone (FTZ), and it is assumed that no duties are due since the goods are not destined for import into the country in which the FTZ is an enclave. However, DDE exempts the buyer from paying any duties on the goods should the destination be altered or should the government of the importing country modify its customs laws.

Ex Dock . . . (named place of loading) means the seller is obligated to (1) clear the goods through customs and (2) place the goods on a specified import dock at the disposal of the buyer.

Free In (FI) means the charterer of the shipping vessel is obligated to pay only the cost of loading the goods at the port of export.

Free In and Out (FIO) means the charterer of the shipping vessel is obligated to pay both the cost of loading (at the port of export) and of unloading (at the port of import).

free of capture and seizure (FC&S) refers to an insurance clause in the export insurance policy of many private carriers that provides that any loss of goods is not insured if the loss is due to certain specified political risks.

free of particular average (FPA) is an insurance clause in the export marine insurance policy of many private carriers that provides that partial loss of or damage to goods is not insured.
    Cf. with particular average.

free of particular average American conditions (FPAAC) is an insurance clause in the export marine insurance policy of many private American carriers that provides that partial loss of goods is not insured unless caused by the vessel being sunk, stranded, in collision, or on fire.

free of particular average English conditions (FPAEC) is an insurance clause in the export marine insurance policy of many U.K. carriers that provides that partial loss of goods is not insured unless caused by the vessel being sunk, stranded, in collision, or on fire.

Free on Board . . . (named inland carrier) means the seller is obliged (1) to place the goods aboard a named carrier at a specified inland port and (2) to obtain a clean bill of lading attesting to this performance.
    The buyer is obligated to pay for the transportation from the specified inland port to the ultimate import destination.

Free on Board, Duty Exempt (FOB, Duty Exempt) means the seller is obliged to pay (1) for the goods; (2) for their transport to a specific FTZ; (3) for their loading aboard a named vessel in the FTZ; and (4) all taxes, duties, and surcharges that may be levied by customs authorities.

Free on Board, *Freight Allowed* (FOB, Freight Allowed) means the seller has the same performance obligations as with *Free on Board . . . (named inland carrier)*.

The buyer, likewise, is obligated to pay for the transportation from the specified inland port to the ultimate import destination, and the invoice of the seller is reduced by the amount of transport costs paid by the buyer.

Free on Board, Freight Prepaid (FOB, Freight Prepaid) means the seller is obliged (1) to place the goods aboard a named carrier at a specified inland port, (2) to obtain a clean bill of lading attesting to this performance, and (3) to pay the freight charges of the inland carrier.

Free Out (FO) means the charterer of the shipping vessel is obligated to pay only the cost of unloading the goods at the port of import.

general average is a deliberate loss or damage to goods (cargo) in the face of an imminent peril.

The sacrifice (of the cargo) is made to save the vessel and/or other goods. The cost of the lost goods is shared (i.e., "averaged") by the owners of the saved goods.

> **Example:** If $1 million in cargo was jettisoned to save other cargo that belonged to 10 shippers, the principle of general average would dictate that the cost of the lost cargo be shared equally by the 10 shippers of saved cargo (i.e., $1 million ÷ 10 shippers = $100,000 each).

with particular average (WPA) is an insurance clause in the export marine insurance policy of many private carriers that provides that partial loss of, or damage to, goods is insured.

Cf. free of particular average.

Uniform Terms of Trade: Incoterms

The Incoterms that follow are **not** listed in alphabetical order. They are presented in increasing order of responsibility: from the minimum responsibility of the seller to the maximum responsibility of the seller.

Ex Works . . . (named site of shipment/export) (ExW) is the generic expression that is changed, where appropriate, when the site of shipment/export varies as follows:

Site of Shipment	Incoterm
a factory	**Ex Factory (ExF)**
a mill	**Ex Mill (ExM)**
a plantation	**Ex Plantation (ExP)**
a warehouse	**Ex Warehouse (ExWH)**
a mine	**Ex Mine (ExM)**

The seller is obligated to make the goods available at the "works"—the factory, the mill, the plantation, the warehouse, or the mine. Further, the goods must be loaded on the rail cars, the trucks, the boats, or other agreed-upon means of transport at the seller's expense.

The buyer has to bear the costs and all risks of transportation from the point of shipment to the destination.

This term represents the level of least obligation for the seller.

Free on Rail/Free on Truck . . . (named port of shipment/export) (FOR/FOT) means the seller is obligated to deliver the goods to the railroad and to load the designated railway cars at the named port of shipment.

The buyer is obligated to bear the cost, and the risks, of transportation of the goods from the point of shipment to the destination.

The word *truck* has its derivation from the French word *wagon*, which refers to a "railway car" (*wagon de chemin de fer*: literally, "truck of a way of iron").

Free alongside . . . (named port of shipment/export) (FAS) means the seller is obligated to place the goods alongside the vessel.

For example, the seller may make the goods available on a designated quay, or in specific lighters (towed barges), in close proximity to the ship into which the goods will be loaded.

The actual loading of the ship itself, either from the quay or the lighter, is the obligation of the buyer, who bears all the costs and risks involved.

Likewise, the buyer is responsible for all the costs and risks of transportation of the goods from the port where the goods are loaded to the destination.

Free on Board . . . (named port or airport of shipment/export) (FOB) means the seller is obligated to bear the cost of transporting the goods to the named port or airport and for loading the goods aboard a specified ship or airplane.

Thereafter, the buyer bears the responsibility, the cost, and the risks of transporting the goods to the destination.

The term *Free on Board (FOB)* is equivalent to the French term *franco à bord (FAB)*.

Free Carrier . . . (named port of shipment/export) (FRC) means the seller is responsible, as in FOB, for transporting the goods to the named port of shipment and for delivering them to the first carrier (in a multimodal channel).

That first carrier is responsible for loading the goods on the specified mode of transport (e.g., a ship).

Unless the commercial agreement between buyer and seller specifically named the seller as being responsible for loading the first carrier and for bearing the costs of loading it, then the buyer bears these costs and risks.

All responsibility, beyond the first carrier, for the transport and handling of the goods, and the attendant risk, lies with the buyer: the seller's responsibilities end when the goods are delivered to and a bill of lading is exchanged with the first carrier.

Cost and Freight . . . (named port of destination/import) (C & F) means the seller is obligated to pay (1) the cost of the goods and (2) the freight charges to get them to the named port of designation.

The buyer is responsible for the goods once the seller loads them aboard the ship, since the seller has no obligation to insure the goods.

Cost, Insurance, and Freight . . . (named port of destination/import) (CIF) means the seller is obligated to pay (1) the cost of the goods, (2) the cost of insurance against loss, and (3) the freight charges to get them to the named port of destination.

"Marine insurance" is the nomenclature used whenever "cover" is required against loss or damage when goods are shipped by sea. The extensive citing of the term in international marketing literature results from the trade eras (predating global marketing) when the seas were, commercially and geopolitically, the preeminent medium of communications.

In the contemporary global-marketing environment, CIF often pertains to trade involving shipment by modes of transport different from sea. For example, where air cargo or (North American) Great Lakes water transport are used, the nomenclature for the "cover" against loss is simply an "insurance policy" (documented with an "insurance certificate") stating the protection against commercial and/or political risks, without any special naming of either air insurance or inland-waters transport insurance, respectively.

Ex Ship . . . (named port of destination/import) (ExS) means the seller is obliged to make the goods available to the buyer at the named port of destination.

Thus, until the ship arrives at the designated port, the seller bears the responsibility and the full costs and risks of loading and unloading, of handling and shipping.

When the ship arrives, the buyer is responsible for unloading the vessel, for any applicable customs matters, and for all necessary inland transport.

Ex Quay . . . (site at named port of destination/import) (ExQ) means the seller is obligated only to make the goods available on a designated wharf, pier, or jetty at a named port of entry.

Once the seller has discharged the responsibility of unloading the ship, all obligations, costs, and risks pass to the buyer for handling, customs, and inland transport.

Unless the commercial contract between buyer and seller names the seller, it is the buyer's responsibility to pay any applicable customs duties.

Ex Quay, duty on buyer's account . . . (named port of destination/import) (ExQ) means the seller is obligated only to make the goods available on a designated wharf, pier, or jetty at a named port of entry, and the buyer is explicitly responsible for paying any applicable customs duties.

Once the seller has discharged the responsibility of unloading the ship, all obligations, costs, and risks pass to the buyer for handling and inland transport.

Ex Quay, duty paid . . . (named port of destination/import) (ExQ) means the seller is obligated to make the goods available on a designated wharf, pier, or jetty at a named port of entry and is implicitly responsible for paying any applicable customs duties.

Once the seller has discharged the responsibility of unloading the ship and clearing the goods for import, all obligations, costs, and risks pass to the buyer for handling and inland transport.

Delivered at Frontier . . . (named place of delivery) (DAF) means the seller is obligated to make the goods available at a named frontier point between two sovereign jurisdictions.

The seller is not obliged to clear the goods through customs or to deliver them beyond the named frontier point. It is the responsibility of the buyer to clear the goods through customs, pay any applicable duties, and transport them from the named frontier point to their destination.

Delivered, duty paid . . . (named destination) (DDP) means the seller is obliged to bear all the responsibilities, costs, and risks associated with making the goods available at a named (foreign) destination, i.e., all the physical distribution and logistical functions comprising, where appropriate, export packaging, marking, loading, unloading, consolidation, deconsolidation, transshipment, shipping, handling, insurance, clearing customs and paying applicable duties, inland transport and local cartage, are the obligation of the seller.

International Organizations

What follows are listings of the world's most important international organizations. Their importance stems from their interconnectedness within the worldwide network of international (and supranational) institutions. (See the separate alphabetical entry for each organization for information regarding each group.)

The international organizations (INTORGs) are categorized in the following functional areas:

    A. International Trade Groups (ITGs).
    B. International Commercial/Financial Groups (ICFGs).
    C. International Political Groups (IPGs).
    D. International Organizations of the United Nations System.
    E. International Commodity Groups (ICGs).

A. INTERNATIONAL TRADE GROUPS (ITGs)	ACRONYM

Andean Common Market
   Also known as *El Pacto Andino, El Grupo Andino,*
   The Cartagena Agreement, Andean Development Corporation.
	ANCOM

Arab Common Market	ACM
Arab Mahgreb Union Also known as the *Mahgreb Common Market (MCM).*	AMU
Association of Southeast Asian Nations	ASEAN
Belgium-Netherlands-Luxembourg Customs Union	Benelux
Canada-U.S. Free Trade Agreement of 1989	FTA
Caribbean Common Market Officially, *Caribbean Community and Common Market.*	CARICOM
Caribbean Free Trade Association	CARIFTA

Central American Common Market Officially, *Mercado Común Centro-americano (MCC)*.	CACM
Commonwealth	——
Council for Mutual Economic Assistance Also known as *COMECON*.	CMEA
Customs and Economic Union of Central Africa Also known as *Union Douanière et Économique* *de l'Afrique Centrale (UDEAC)*.	CEUCA

East African Economic Community (defunct)
    Also known as the *East African Community (EAC)*
    and *East African Customs Union (EACU)*.
	EAEC

Economic Community of West African States
    Also known as the *Economic Community of*
    West Africa (ECWA).
	ECOWAS

European Economic Community
    Also known as the *European Community (EC)*,
    the *Common Market*, and *The Community*.
	EEC

European Free Trade Association	EFTA
Latin American Free Trade Association (defunct)	LAFTA

Latin American Integration Association
    Officially, *Asociación Latinoamericana de*
    Integración (ALADI)
	LAIA

Mahgreb Common Market	MCM
North American Free Trade Agreement Zone	NAFTA/NAFTZ
Preferential Trade Area for Eastern and Southern African States	PTA
Southern Cone Common Market	SCCM

West African Economic Community
    Also known as *Communauté Économique*
    de l'Afrique de l'Ouest (CEAO).
	WAEC

B. INTERNATIONAL COMMERCIAL/FINANCIAL
   GROUPS (ICFGs)

	ACRONYM
African Development Bank*	AfDB
Amazonian Cooperation Treaty Also known as the *Amazon Pact*.	ACT

Arab Bank for Economic Development in Africa
    Also known as *Banque Arabe pour le Développement*
    Économique en Afrique (BADEA).
	ABEDA

*See note on page 391.

Arab Fund for Economic and Social Development	AFESD
Arab Monetary Fund	AMF
Asian and Pacific Council	APC
Asian Development Bank*	AsDB, ADB

Asian-Pacific Economic Cooperation Group
    Also known as *Pacific Economic Cooperation
    Group (PECG)*.
	APEC

Asian Productivity Organization	APO
Bank of Central African States Officially, *Banque des États de l'Afrique Centrale (BEAC)*.	BCAS
Bank for International Settlements	BIS
Cairns Group	————
Caribbean Development Bank*	CDB
Caribbean Group for Cooperation in Economic Development	CGCED

Central American Bank for Economic Integration
    Also known as *Banco Centro-americano de
    Integración Económica (BCIE)*.
	CABEI

Central Bank of West African States
    Officially, *Banque Centrale des États de l'Afrique
    de l'Oeust (BCEAO)*.
	CBWAS

Colombo Plan
    Officially, *The Colombo Plan for Cooperative Economic
    and Social Development in Asia and the Pacific*.
	————

Commonwealth	————
Council of Arab Economic Unity	CAEU
Customs Cooperation Council	CCC
Danube Commission	————
East Asian Economic Grouping	EAEG

Economic Community of Great Lakes Countries
    Officially, *Communauté Économique des Pays
    des Grands Lacs (CEPGL)*.
	ECGC

Entente Council Also known as *Conseil de l'Entente*.	————

European Bank for Reconstruction and Development
    Officially, *Banque Européenne de Reconstruction et
    Développement (BERD)*.
	EBRD

European Investment Bank	EIB

*See note on page 391.

General Agreement on Tariffs and Trade	GATT
Group of Five	G-5
Group of Seven	G-7
Group of Seventy-seven	G-77
Group of Ten	G-10
Group of Thirteen	G-13
Group of Twenty-five	G-25
Group of Twenty-four	G-24
Inter-American Development Bank*	IDB, IaDB
International Bank for Economic Cooperation	IBEC
International Bank for Reconstruction and Development* Also known as the *World Bank*.	IBRD
International Chamber of Commerce	ICC
International Development Association	IDA
International Finance Corporation	IFC
International Investment Bank	IIB
International Maritime Satellite Organization	INMARSAT
International Monetary Fund	IMF
International Standardization Organization	ISO
International Telecommunications Satellite Organization	INTELSAT
International Trade Center UNTAD/GATT	ITC
International Trade Organization (defunct)	ITO
Islamic Development Bank	ISDB
Japan Sea Basin	JSB
Lake Chad Basin Commission Also known as *Commission du Bassin du Lac Chad (CBLC)*.	LCBC
Latin American Economic System Officially, *Sistema Económico Latinoamericano (SELA)*.	LAES
Lomé Convention	——
Mahgreb Permanent Consultative Committee Also known as *Permanent Consultative Committee of the Mahgreb (PCCM)*.	MPCC
Middle East Development Bank	MEDB

*See note on page 391.

Niger Basin Authority Officially, *Authorité du Bassin du Niger (ABN)*.	NBA
Nordic Council	NC
North Pacific Cooperation Security Dialog	NPCSD
OPEC Fund for International Development	OPEC/FID
Organization of Arab Petroleum Exporting Countries	OAPEC

Organization for the Development of the Sénégal River
   Officially, *Organisation pour la Mise en Valeur
   du Fleuve Sénégal (OMVFS)*.
	ODSR

Organization for Economic Cooperation and Development	OECD

Pacific Economic Cooperation Group
   Also called *Asian-Pacific Economic Cooperation
   Group (APECG)*.
	PECG

Regional Cooperation for Development	RCD
River Plate Basin System Officially, *El Sistema de la Cuenca del Plata (SICDEP)*.	RPBS
South Pacific Bureau for Economic Cooperation	SPEC
South Pacific Commission	SPC
South Pacific Forum	SPF
Southern African Development Coordination Conference	SADCC
West African Monetary Union	WAMU

World Bank*
   Officially, *International Bank for Reconstruction and
   Development (IBRD)*.
	WB

World Bank Group	——

*Note: The five multilateral development banks (MDBs) that are Executing Agencies for development projects financed by the United Nations Development Program (UNDP).

C. INTERNATIONAL POLITICAL GROUPS (IPGs)	**ACRONYM**
Arab Cooperation Council	ACC
Arab League Also known as *The League of Arab States*.	——
Arab Union (defunct)	——
Australia-New Zealand-U.S. Security Treaty	ANZUS Pact
Baghdad Pact	——

Central Treaty Organization	CENTO
Coordinating Committee for Multilateral Export Controls	COCOM
Council of Europe	——
Gulf Cooperation Council	GCC
North Atlantic Treaty Organization	NATO

Organisation Commune Africaine et Mauricienne
    Also known as *African and Mauritian Common*
    Organization (AMCO).
	OCAM

Organization of African Unity	OAU
Organization of American States Formerly, *Pan-American Union (PAU).*	OAS

Organization of Central American States
    Officially, *Organización de Estados*
    Centro-americanos (OECA).
	OCAS

Organization of the Islamic Conference	OIC
Southeast Asia Treaty Organization	SEATO
United Arab Republic (defunct)	UAR
Warsaw Treaty Organization Also called the *Warsaw Pact.*	WTO
Western European Union	WEU

D. INTERNATIONAL ORGANIZATIONS OF THE UNITED NATIONS SYSTEM

INTERNATIONAL ORGANIZATIONS OF THE UNITED NATIONS SYSTEM	ACRONYM
Caribbean Development and Cooperation Committee	CDCC
Food and Agricultural Organization	FAO
International Atomic Energy Agency	IAEA
International Civil Aviation Organization	ICAO
International Court of Justice Also known as the *World Court.*	ICJ
International Fund for Agricultural Development	IFAD
International Labor Organization	ILO
International Maritime Organization	IMO
International Telecommunications Union	ITU
United Nations Capital Development Fund	UNCDF
United Nations Center for Human Settlements	HABITAT

United Nations Children's Fund	UNICEF
United Nations Commission on International Trade Law	UNCITRAL
United Nations Conference on Trade and Development	UNCTAD
United Nations Development Program	UNDP
United Nations Economic Commission for Africa	UN/ECA
United Nations Economic Commission for Europe	UN/ECE
United Nations Economic Commission for Latin America and the Caribbean Also known as *Comisión Económica para América Latina y el Caribe (CEPAL).*	UN/ECLAC
United Nations Economic Commission for the Middle East	UN/ECME
United Nations Economic and Social Commission for Asia and the Pacific	UN/ESCAP
United Nations Economic and Social Commission for Western Asia	UN/ESCWA
United Nations Educational, Scientific and Cultural Organization	UNESCO
United Nations Environment Program	UNEP
United Nations Fund for Population Activities	UNFPA
United Nations Industrial Development Organization	UNIDO
Universal Postal Union	UPU
World Health Organization	WHO
World Intellectual Property Organization	WIPO
World Meteorological Organization	WMO

E. INTERNATIONAL COMMODITY GROUPS (ICGs)　　ACRONYM

African Groundnut Council Also known as *Counseil Africain de l'Arachide (CAA).*	AGC
African Timber Organization Also known as *Organisation Africaine du Bois (OAB).*	ATO
Asian and Pacific Coconut Community	APCC
Association of Iron Ore Exporting Countries Also known as *Association des Pays Exportateurs de Minerai de Fer (APEMF).*	AIOEC
Association of Natural Rubber Producing Countries	ANRPC
Cocoa Producers' Alliance	COPAL

Inter-African Coffee Organization   IACO
   Also known as *Organisation Inter-africaine de
   Café (OICAFE)*.

Inter-governmental Council of Copper Exporting Countries   ICCEC
   Also known as *Conseil Inter-gouvernemental des Pays
   Exportateurs de Cuivre (CIPEC)*.

International Bauxite Association   IBA

International Cocoa Organization   ICCO

International Coffee Organization   ICO

International Cotton Advisory Committee   ICAC

International Lead and Zinc Study Group   ILZSG

International Rubber Organization   IRO

International Rubber Study Group   IRSG

International Sugar Organization   ISO

International Tin Council   ITC

International Vine and Wine Study Group   IVWSG
   Officially, *Office Internationale de la Vigne et
   du Vin (OIVV)*.

International Wheat Council   IWC

International Wool Study Group   IWSG

Northwest Atlantic Fisheries Organization   NAFO

Organization of Petroleum Exporting Countries   OPEC

Union of Banana Exporting Countries   UBEC
   Also known as *Unión de Países Exportadores
   de Banano (UPEB)*.

International Law Vocabulary

International law is the system of rules generated by (1) treaties (see *international agreement*); (2) international customs (see *customary law*, and see *common law systems* and *code law systems* in main entries); (3) general principles of law (see *natural law* and *sovereignty*); and (4) judicial decisions (see *International Court of Justice*), which guide the conduct of states in their relations with each other and with international (and supranational) organizations.

The scope of international law is universal, and thus it is often called "public international law." Where the scope is less than universal, but where its application is between states on a bilateral basis (e.g., Canada, United States) or on a multilateral basis (e.g., EEC, ANCOM, ASEAN), international law is termed "private international law."

The subject of international law, both as a practiced profession and as a research discipline, is necessarily encyclopedic and complex. However, for the international business person, it need not be either.

International business people should not have to deal with a plethora of practically irrelevant and theoretically esoteric concepts and terms. What follows, therefore, is the purposeful effort to consolidate the vast amount of data in this field into a "kernel" international law vocabulary that is focused on and usefully relevant to international (and global) business activities. All entries are listed alphabetically. Cross-referencing is infrasectional unless the term is followed by "in main entries" (such terms are to be found in the main alphabetical listing of entires).

Act of State Doctrine is a concept in international law that advances the idea that every sovereign state can legally do what it likes within its own territory and that other states will not sit in judgment over these "acts of state."

The traditional absolutist view of this doctrine (i.e., the "divine right of kings" notion) has been substantially modified in recent times. Illegal acts committed by a state may be subject to accountability under international law. For example, the famous Nuremburg Trials, where Nazi "war criminals" were tried after the end of World War II, is evidence of this changed view. On the other hand, as of this writing, President

Saddam Hussein of Iraq, whose military commanders are alleged to have committed "war crimes" against the Iraqi, the Kuwaiti, and the Kurdish civilian populations before and during the Persian Gulf War of 1991, has yet to be brought to account for these "acts of state."

See also sovereignty.

adjudication is the legal process for settling international disputes when parties to a dispute submit them to a recognized court.

Cf. arbitration.

See also International Court of Justice.

administrative agency is a government body responsible for and authorized to implement legislation.

The U.S. International Trade Commission (USITC) is the administrative agency in the United States responsible for investigating antidumping complaints brought to its notice by U.S. industry that claims material injury or threat of material injury by foreign goods imported and sold at less than fair value in the United States.

See also U.S. International Trade Commission; antidumping duty; injury; less than fair value (all in main entries).

administrative law is specific legislation that governs the actions of administrative agencies.

The concept of a "determination" (i.e., a judgment) has its basis in administrative law whereby a duly authorized panel, tribunal, or other agency of government, or an administrative law judge presiding over some administrative agency process (e.g., an international dispute-settlement panel) and acting according to "due process," can make legal decisions.

See also judicial review; determination.

administrative law judge (ALJ) is a jurist who presides over tribunals and hearings into civil matters in the United States.

> **Example:** Notice is hereby given that the USITC has determined not to review the presiding ALJ's initial determination in the investigation on the basis of a settlement agreement between the parties.

See also determination.

administrative protection order (APO) is a directive, issued by the U.S. International Trade Commission (USITC) in connection with investigations under Title VII of the Tariff Act of 1930, that requires the Commission (under Section 1332 of the Omnibus Trade Act of 1988) to release to the authorized representatives of interested parties in dumping and countervailing duty investigations the business proprietary information (BPI) collected by the USITC in the course of such investigations.

The USITC, using implemented procedures governing the release of BPI under an APO, only provides BPI to "authorized applicants" who agree to be bound by the terms and conditions of the APO.

The main function of APOs is to protect the BPI of those who are parties to USITC investigations from having their BPI disseminated to unauthorized persons who might be in a position to use the BPI to misuse confidential information commercially. Such dissemination may occur willfully, or it may occur inadvertently due to failure to "bracket" BPI (i.e., use written brackets to set off BPI), which leads to disclosure, or failure to supervise junior attorneys and inexperienced clerical people in the proper handling of BPI at the law firms, or failure to destroy documents containing BPI (upon the termination of an USITC investigation), subject to the right to retain the documents during a judicial review of a USITC determination.

USITC sanctions for APO violations serve the interests of preserving the confidence of submitters of BPI in the USITC as a credible and reliable protector of BPI, punishing breachers and deterring future violations by past offenders and by others in a position to potentially offend. Sanctions include (1) forfeiture of legal practice before the USITC for up to seven years; (2) referral to a U.S. Attorney for potential criminal prosecution; (3) referral to an appropriate professional organization for discipline by its ethics advisor or ethics committee; (4) disallowing the information presented by any offender on behalf of the party represented; and (5) denial of further access to BPI in a current or any future proceedings before the USITC.

See also U.S. International Trade Commission (in main entries).

agreement of two instruments *See* international agreement.

alien (alien corporation, alien party) is (1) a person who is not a national of the country in which she or he is a resident or a visitor; or (2) a legal commercial entity (i.e., a corporation) that is owned less than 50 percent by nationals of a country.

Under international law, states have authority over aliens within their territorial jurisdiction, and they generally afford them near-equivalent national treatment in matters of civil rights, but not in political rights.

ambassador *See* diplomat.

American Arbitration Association (AAA) is a nonprofit organization, headquartered in New York City, that promotes the use of the arbitration process between disputing parties within the United States.

The AAA is located at 140 West 51st Street, New York, NY 10020 (telephone (212) 484-4000).

See also arbitration.

antitrust laws are laws that have been enacted to prevent profit-seeking firms from acting in ways that restrain trade to the detriment of the consumer or the industrial customer.

In the United States, the Federal antitrust laws are the Clayton Act (of 1914) and the Sherman Antitrust Act (of 1890). The Clayton Act is applicable to foreign trade and especially to interstate commerce. It mainly deals with restrictive business practices such as price discrimination. The Sherman Antitrust Act deals with domestic and foreign business activity and is aimed at prohibiting mergers, monopolies, and takeovers that are assumed to restrain trade. It also prohibits price fixing, bid rigging, and collusive agreements.

In Canada, all prohibitions against restraint-of-trade practices are contained in a single Federal law originally called the Combines Investigation Act and currently amended as the Competition Act.

In the European Economic Community (EEC), Articles 85 and 86 of the Treaty of Rome set out the competition laws of the EEC.

See also monopoly (in main entries).

arbitration is the process whereby parties to a dispute agree to present their cases before, and have the matter adjudged by, an independent third party, which is not a law court.

Where the parties to the dispute agree to accept an arbitration process and not to contest the final award, the process is called binding arbitration under the principle of *res judicata* (from the Latin *res* meaning "the thing" and *judicata* meaning "has been judged") unless the tribunal exceeded its jurisdiction as set out in the *compromis*.

Many experienced international marketers recommend that commercial contracts that are either intrinsically complex (such as countertrade agreements) or that involve substantial lead times include an arbitration clause that binds all parties to arbitration in the event of a contract dispute (e.g., nonperformance, negligent performance, breach of contract).

Cf. adjudication.

See also Court of Arbitration; arbitration clause; *compromis*.

arbitration clause is a clause in a sales contract between the exporter and the importer that specifies the method under which disputes relevant to the contract in question will be settled.

Example: It is agreed between the contracting parties that any and all disagreements and disputes occurring out of or in connection with this agreement will be settled by arbitration in New York City in accordance with the rules of the American Arbitration Association, and judgment of any and all awards under this arbitration may be entered in any court having jurisdiction thereof.

See also International Chamber of Commerce (in main entries).

attaché, from the French meaning "attached," is a middle-ranking person, with diplomatic status, who is attached to a diplomatic mission and who is the on-site specialist in a particular field (e.g., agriculture, science, commerce, economics).

award is the judgment of an independent third-party arbiter, arbitration court, commission, panel, or tribunal.

The judgment is in the form of a compensation to one of the parties, which can be an individual or a company, as well as a state.

The award itself can be in two parts:

1. *Compromis* (from the French *compromis* meaning "compromise"; implicitly, an "unsatisfactory solution" *vis-à-vis* an "agreeable solution" (in English)): this is a preliminary or "interim" arbitral award, usually on matters of jurisdiction.

2. *Final Award:* this is the arbitral judgment "on the merits" (i.e., on the substantive matters of the case being decided).

binding arbitration *See* arbitration.

blocking laws are laws that prevent the disclosure of confidential documents (by financial institutions that have them) to anyone outside the domestic jurisdiction of a state.
   See also secrecy laws.

Calvo clause, named after the Argentine jurist Carlos Calvo, is a provision sometimes inserted in a contract between a public enterprise and an alien corporation, or consortium, whereby

1. local legal processes and local legal remedies will be sought in case of commercial disputes with the public enterprise, and
2. the alien corporation will not call on its national government to intervene in matters acknowledged as being within the exclusive jurisdiction of the country in which the alien corporation is resident.

International law is moot on the Calvo clause. It can be argued that under international law, the legal right of a state to exercise its sovereign authority in exclusively domestic matters is violated when states intervene on behalf of their national corporations.
   It can be countered that states retain the right to deal with their nationals and national corporations (under international law) and that no person or corporation can "sign away" the obligation of its state to act.

citizen (citizenship) refers to the legal relationship between a person and a state with regard to the rights the person has as a member of a state and the obligation sowed to the person by the state of which she or he is a member.
   Citizenship may be acquired from one's parents at birth or by place of birth. It may also be acquired by voluntarily swearing allegiance to a state.
   See also law of blood *(jus sanguinis)*; law of soil *(jus solis)*; naturalization.

code law system *See* code law system (in main entries).

comity, formally called the *principle of comity*, is a precept of international law that "mutual respect of laws" is afforded to and expected from every state.
   Despite this principle, legal systems may be so different (e.g., the common law system of the United States as opposed to the Islamic code law system of Saudi Arabia) that a "conflict of laws" may result. In such cases, the "jurisdictional rule of reason" will be used to seek a resolution. This rule balances the vital interests of one party with those of the other.

Example: When a ship under the U.S. flag saw unknown terrorists planning to demolish a Cuban state vessel, the American naval officers boarded the ship to halt the planned terrorist acts. The U.S. officers were subsequently arrested and charged with illegally entering prohibited territory (i.e., Cuba).

The U.S. court that heard the case came to a decision using the jurisdictional rule of reason.

First of all, while U.S. law prohibiting illegal entry of a named "foreign enemy country" applied to the U.S. seamen, their motives for doing so and their actions upon doing so clearly complied with U.S. laws and United Nations Conventions against international terrorism. Secondly, within the international legal context, it was found not unreasonable to consider the American sailors (being uniformed officers in a legal armed force) "international peace officers" who acted with "objective concern for peace" in the case at hand. Thus, the court found that the vital interests of the United States were better served by the actions of the officers than by prosecuting them for the crime of trespass on "enemy territory." The naval officers were acquitted of the charges.

Cf. sovereign.
See also conflict of laws; Act of State Doctrine.

common law system *See* common law system (in main entries).

compromis *See* award.

conciliation is peaceful settlement of a political or commercial dispute by means less formal than arbitration or court proceedings.

The process of conciliation involves third-party intermediaries (which can be individual or group conciliators or mediators) who are invited to intervene between the disputing parties.

Cf. arbitration.

conflict of laws is the concept whereby there is a clash between the municipal laws of different states.

Conflicts typically occur between states when they have fundamentally different legal systems (e.g., the code law system of Continental Europe *vis-à-vis* the common law system of the United Kingdom).

> **Example:** The European Court of Justice in Brussels operates to try to apply a uniform set of laws throughout the European Community in matters of contracts, torts, labor, health and safety, civil rights, marriage, and divorce.

consul (consulate, consular mission, consular duties) refers to individuals sent to foreign countries to represent and promote the commercial interests of their state.

In Canada, they are called Trade Commissioners.

Consuls do not have diplomatic status, but their rights and obligations are codified in the 1963 Vienna Convention on Consular Relations.

Consular duties include the provision of services related to citizenship and visas, commerce, shipping and navigation, and the direct promotion of travel to and trade with the country that the consulate represents.

Court of Arbitration, also known colloquially as an *arbitration panel, arbitration board,* or *arbitration tribunal,* is an independent formal body, established by disputing commercial parties, that "tries" a matter (i.e., listens to the evidence and argument) and adjudges it.

Countries that have disputes frequently agree to establish ad hoc (i.e., "as the need arises") Courts of Arbitration.

The following are some important permanent Courts of Arbitration:

- *London Court of Arbitration* arbitrates disputes under English law in the United Kingdom and in other territories over which it has jurisdiction (e.g., Hong Kong);
- *Inter-American Commercial Arbitration Commission* arbitrates disputes in the United States and 21 American republics;
- *Canadian-American Commercial Arbitration Commission* arbitrates disputes between Canadian and American companies.

Example: The maritime dispute between Canada and France, in which there is no agreement as to the official boundary off the south coasts of the Canadian Province of Newfoundland and the French islands of Saint Pierre and Miquelon, was arbitrated by an *ad hoc* Court of Arbitration. The Court was established by France and Canada. It consisted of three foreign judges: Eduardo Jimenez de Arechaga, a former president of the International Court of Justice; Professor Oscar Schacter, Professor of Law, Columbia University, New York; and Professor Gaetano Arangio-Ruiz, of the University of Rome, Italy.

See also arbitration.

customary law is (1) used synonymously with "common law" in the common law system; and (2) one of the sources of international law, being the established and accepted practices of states toward each other.

Example: It was the historically observed practice of states to grant to all classes of accredited foreign diplomats immunity from all civil and criminal liability in their host country. This established behavior is classified as international customary law, and it has now become codified in international treaty law in the 1961 Vienna Convention on Diplomatic Relations.

determination (initial determination, final determination) is an order, emanating from an administrative law judge (ALJ), that has the full force of law and that pertains to civil matters such as trade and commerce.

See also administrative law judge.

diplomat is a person who is sent by a state to represent it in carrying out official state-to-state relations.

Such an emissary becomes officially accredited to carry out diplomatic functions when she or he presents a *letter of credence* to the head of the host country and when it is accepted.

The highest level of diplomatic representation is the embassy, headed by an ambassador, the highest level of diplomatic representative.

Only in a Commonwealth member country is the mission to it of another Commonwealth member country, at the highest level of diplomatic representation, termed a

"High Commission." This is equivalent to an embassy; it is headed by a High Commissioner who is equivalent to an ambassador. All Commonwealth countries engage in this diplomatic practice with each other—that of having themselves represented by a High Commissioner in the country of the other.

Cf. consul.

diplomatic mission refers to the physical premises where diplomats work that are a legal extension of the soil of the country whose diplomats represent it.

Thus the mission (and its diplomats) is recognized as not being subject to domestic jurisdiction of the host country.

Cf. consul.

diplomatic status (diplomatic immunity) refers to the standing of a diplomat regarding privileges and immunities as codified in the 1961 Vienna Convention on Diplomatic Status.

Accordingly, all accredited diplomats (i.e., those granted official diplomatic status) are granted complete immunity from any and all criminal and civil charges and legal processes that normally apply to individuals who are nondiplomats within the domestic jurisdiction of the state and who thus have nondiplomatic status.

Cf. consul.

Doctrine of Sovereign Compliance, also called the *Sovereign Compulsion Doctrine*, is the international legal principle that those accused of behaving in ways that are contrary to their home-country laws have as their defense the argument that they acted as they did under compulsion by the foreign state.

> **Example:** American managers in Canada must trade with Cuba under compulsion by Canada's Foreign Extraterritorial Measures Act. These managers are potentially liable for prosecution in a U.S. Federal Court for having traded with Cuba; but they could likely present a legal defense under the Doctrine of Sovereign Compliance.

Cf. sovereignty.

domestic jurisdiction, a variation of *municipal jurisdiction*, refers to those areas within states where the internal law of states has exclusive authority over individuals and other legal entities.

Drago Doctrine is the idea, put forward by Luis Maria Drago, the Foreign Minister of Argentina in 1902 (in a diplomatic note to the U.S. State Department), that opposed intervention by any state and the use of force to recover debts owed by a defaulting state to foreign states or to foreign nationals.

In the contemporary world, not only is the use of force against debt-defaulting nations legally unacceptable, but also it would be ineffective: if the less developed nation has no capacity to repay its debts with foreign earnings from its exports, the use of force has no utility in achieving debt repayment.

For example, were the United States to install a naval blockade against Brazil should it default on its foreign debt (as happened with Britain, Germany, and Italy in their blockade of Venezuela in 1902), it is highly likely that this action would only exacerbate Brazil's problems, inflame anti-American sentiments, and worsen Brazil's capacity to export and generate the foreign earnings necessary to meet its obligations.

Thus, as Hugo Grotius, "father of international law," wrote in his famous work *De Jure Belli et Pacis* (1625), the use of violence to settle international disputes between nations is ultimately self-defeating.

---

effects doctrine is the legal principle upon which U.S. courts act to uphold the extraterritorial application of U.S. antitrust laws if the actions of firms outside the United States have a direct and substantial negative "effect" on commerce within the country.

The U.S. Foreign Trade Antitrust Improvements Act of 1982 codified the effects doctrine.

See also extraterritoriality.

embassy *See* diplomat.

expatriation is the act of a person that may cause the loss of the person's citizenship.

Citizenship can be lost (1) by *commission* (i.e., by carrying out an act against the citizenship law of one's country); (2) by *omission* (i.e., by failing to comply with specific obligations of citizenship law); or (3) by *request* of the individual.

> **Example:** In the United States, serving with the armed forces of a foreign country without permission or taking an oath of allegiance to another flag is grounds for losing one's U.S. citizenship. In Canada, it is not.

> **Example:** In Canada, should a person who is born outside Canada but who obtains citizenship via *jus sanguinis* remain outside the country for a continuous period of 10 years, that person can have his or her citizenship revoked.

extradition (extradition treaty) refers to the process whereby individuals who are either charged with violating specific crimes or who have been convicted or sentenced or incarcerated for committing specific crimes are returned to the state from whence they have fled by a state that has signed a treaty to return them.

> **Example:** The Canada-U.S. Extradition Treaty is rigorous about the specific crimes for which a "fugitive from criminal justice" in each jurisdiction can be returned to the other. The treaty specifically excludes political crimes.
> The treaty also includes the "principle of comity," and the international legal concept of "sovereignty of states." For example, assume a person who is charged with homicide in the United States and who flees to Canada to escape possible capital punishment re-offends (e.g., by shoplifting) in Canada and is caught. The Extradition Treaty respects Canadian law and accepts that the offender will serve even a short jail term for the offense in Canada first, before any U.S. request for extradition will be entertained by the Canadian Minister of Justice.
> While public sentiment in Canada rejects extradition to any state that still uses the death penalty, the Canada-U.S. Extradition Treaty does not address itself to any questioning of the legal punishment: if the criminal offense is one that is extradictable, then the treaty is respected. Except on

"compassionate grounds," the Canadian Minister of Justice cannot use any legal prerogative (as granted in the Treaty) to block extradition.

extraterritoriality (extra-territoriality) is the application of the national laws of one country beyond the frontiers of that country to citizens or corporations of that country.

> **Example:** When it comes to a decision on whether to obey the laws of the host country or those of the United States, the U.S. government holds its citizens accountable under law to obey U.S. laws.
> The Trading with the Enemy Act is a law applicable to U.S. corporations (and officers of them) wherever in the world they reside. Thus, an American marketer working for a U.S.-Hungarian joint venture in Budapest that was specifically set up to countertrade goods among CMEA countries might have found herself or himself in an impossible position when required to trade Romanian machine tools to Cuba for citrus oil concentrates, which in turn are to be marketed to U.S. food-processor branch plants in England, Ireland, and Canada. Cuba is a specific country named as an "enemy" of the American people.

Federal Register is a U.S. government publication, published on every business day, that lists all administrative regulations, all presidential proclamations and orders, and any other documents as the president or Congress may direct.

In the United States, the Federal Register Act (1) requires an administrative agency to publish its regulations in the Federal Register and (2) provides that the printing *per se* is sufficient notice of the content of the regulation.

In Canada, administrative agencies must publish their regulations in a government document called the *Canada Gazette*. To have the full force of law, the printing must be in English and French, the official languages of Canada.

See also administrative agency.

friendship, commerce, and navigation (FCN) treaty, a variation of *freedom of commerce and navigation treaty*, is an international agreement that specifies the rights and obligations of each state toward the other regarding (1) their commercial (trading) relationship and (2) the use of each country's communications infrastructure, including roads, inland waterways, and territorial sea and airspace.

The following cross-references are types of FCN treaty listed in the main entries.

See most-favored nation; national treatment; identical treatment; equitable treatment; preferential treatment; good neighborly treatment; open door treatment (all in main entries).

hearing is the public meeting that administrative agencies are required to call (to conform to "due process") where all interested parties are entitled to be present.

Some administrative agencies are empowered to render a determination before calling a hearing. (This contrasts with law courts, which are not legally permitted to do so.)

However, if the agency's judgment is questioned, then a hearing must be called by the agency to deal with the objection. Agencies are careful about rendering determinations without holding hearings since the "onus" (i.e., the "burden of proof") is reversed: the party that objects to the agency's decision must bear the burden and the cost of pursuing this action.

Cf. open meeting.
See also administrative agency.

High Commission (High Commissioner) *See* diplomat.

international agreement is an official "instrument" whereby states (and some international organizations) formalize some understanding between or among them.

All instruments of international accord are governed by the law of treaties, a part of customary international law. They are defined by the 1969 Vienna Convention on the Law of Treaties. Some are a "single instrument," a common document signed by all parties to the accord. Another type is an "agreement of two instruments," an accord involving more than one document, thus, there is no common document signed by the parties.

Treaties are the most formal of international single instruments. Next in legal formality come the following single instruments: convention, agreement, protocol, declaration, charter, covenant, pact, statute, final act, general act, and Concordat, the last one referring to an accord between a state and the Holy See (i.e., The Vatican).

There are single instruments of less stringency called agreed minute and memorandum of agreement; and there are even less formal agreements comprising two or more instruments called exchange of notes, exchange of texts, and exchange of letters.

From the international business viewpoint, one of the kinds of international agreements that is of most interest is the friendship, commerce, and navigation (FCN) treaty.

See also friendship, commerce, and navigation treaty; Vienna Convention on the Law of Treaties (in main entries).

International Court of Justice (ICJ), also known as the *World Court*, is a specialized body of the United Nations System that provides a means of peacefully settling international disputes. The roots of the ICJ are as follows:

1. *1899:* The Permanent Court of Arbitration was established as a consequence of The Hague Peace Conference (and Convention) of 1899 and 1907.
2. *1920:* The Permanent Court of International Justice was established by the League of Nations, following World War I.
3. *1945:* The United Nations Charter provided for the establishment of the International Court of Justice, which replaced the Permanent Court of International Justice.

The ICJ's jurisdiction includes all matters provided for in the United Nations Charter or in treaties, conventions, accords, pacts, or other agreements in force between/among two or more nations. Thus, litigants before the ICJ can only be (1) sovereign states that, as U.N. members, are ipso facto parties to the Statue of the Permanent Court of International Justice, which is the governing instrument of the ICJ; or (2) nonsovereign entities that are "parties to the Statute" (e.g., the Palestine Liberation organization (PLO)).

International Criminal Police Organization, known as *Interpol,* is the coordinating body for worldwide criminal police forces of more than 125 countries.

The aim of Interpol is to promote the widest possible assistance between criminal police authorities globally in the enforcement of laws relating to (1) international terrorism; (2) drug trafficking; and (3) other organized criminal activities, such as counterfeiting and smuggling. From its headquarters in Paris, France, Interpol coordinates international police activity through data bases linking National Central *Bureaux,* one of which is located in the headquarters of each national police force (e.g., the Federal Bureau of Investigation (FBI) in Washington, D.C.; the Royal Canadian Mounted Police (RCMP) in Ottawa, Ontario; and Scotland Yard in London, England).

See also International Maritime Bureau (in main entries).

International Law Commission is an autonomous body of the United Nations General Assembly, created in 1947, to develop and codify international law.

The ILC consists of 34 people who are chosen as persons "of recognized competence in international law" to meet annually in Geneva, Switzerland, for a 12-week session. At these sessions, these experts being forward their work and, in coordination with other experts, work toward the following objectives:

1. *Development of New International Law:* the ILC is charged with the duty of preparing "draft conventions" on subjects that have yet to be regulated by existing international law.
2. *Codification of Existing International Law:* the ILC has been successful in acting as "lead agency" for the drafting of
   - laws on international security, such as the International Convention on the Taking of Hostages (adopted by the General Assembly in 1974) and the Draft Declaration on the Enhancement of the Effectiveness of the Principle of Refraining from the Threat or Use of Force in International Relations (adopted by the General Assembly in 1977);
   - laws on international commerce, such as the Law of the Sea; and
   - laws on diplomatic status.

See also consul; diplomatic status; Law of the Sea; Vienna Convention on the Law of Treaties (in main entries); Vienna Convention on the Law of Treaties Between States and International Organizations or Between International Organizations (in main entries).

judicial review is the process whereby the decision of a "lower court," arbitration panel, civil tribunal, or other government administrative agency is brought before and adjudicated by a "higher court."

In international trade disputes, judicial review involves the U.S. Court of International Trade (CIT). Appeals are brought to it by unsuccessful litigants before the U.S. International Trade Commission (USITC). The CIT, however, will not hear appeals on matters over which it has no jurisdiction (i.e., "treaty-bound disputes" between the United States and foreign countries").

> **Example:** The CIT has no jurisdiction in the area of decisions emanating from certain binational dispute-settlement panels. Those established under the Canada-U.S. Free Trade Agreement of 1989 (FTA) are empowered to impose "binding decisions" on Canadian and American litigants. Thus, both countries are "bound" neither to American nor Canadian law but to international treaty law to which both countries have agreed.

The following are the only legal criteria that qualify a judicial review by a "higher court" to reverse the decision by a "lower court," panel, tribunal, or agency: (1) the lower authority erred in law; (2) the lower authority exceeded its jurisdiction; (3) the lower authority "misbehaved" (i.e., clearly abused or arbitrarily or capriciously exercised its discretion).

See also U.S. International Trade Commission; binational dispute-settlement mechanism (of the FTA); Court of International Trade (all in main entries).

jurisdiction is the areas over which legal authority can be legitimately exerted.

In both domestic and international law (with reference to international and global marketing), jurisdictional issues are addressed by international treaties and other international law instruments of accord.

> **Example:** The Chicago Convention on International Civil Aviation recognized domestic jurisdiction over airspace above a state. It created the International Civil Aviation Organization (ICAO) in 1944 to ensure that all states respected the sovereignty of the airspace.
>
> In real terms, this means that without the permission to transit the airspace of a nation, the act of doing so is, technically, an unfriendly act: an "invasion of airspace." It is not, however, an act of belligerency (i.e., an act of armed attack with the intent of making war). The difference is, potentially, a critical one should a company jet accidentally stray off course and enter the airspace of a country. Witness the tragedy of Korean Airlines Flight #007, the alleged "off-course" invasion of Soviet airspace, and the catastrophic consequences.

See also domestic jurisdiction.

jurisdictional clause is a clause in an international contract between the exporter and the importer that specifies the law under which the agreement is to operate.

The purpose of a jurisdictional clause is to anticipate (and hopefully avoid) potential disputes (leading to arbitration) by explicitly agreeing that the parties will be bound by the laws of an agreed-upon jurisdiction.

> **Example:** It is agreed between the Contracting Parties that this agreement is made in the City of Chicago, Cook County, State of Illinois, U.S.A., and that any question regarding this agreement will be subject to and governed by the laws of the State of Illinois, U.S.A., where applicable.

Cf. arbitration clause.

jurisdictional rule of reason is the legal principle, based on comity, that balances the vital interests of one country against those of a foreign country.
See also comity.

law of blood, from the Latin *jus sanguinis*, is the legal rule that, at birth, an individual acquires the citizenship of its parents.

One area of significance of this international law rule for global and international marketing is that individuals may have multiple citizenships, providing multiple opportunities, but possibly presenting multiple problems.

> **Example:** A person born in Liberia of a Canadian father and a Ghanaian mother acquires Canadian citizenship, via the Canadian patrilineal "law of blood" rule, plus Ghanaian citizenship, via the Ghanaian matrilineal "law of blood" rule.
>
> Companies should be aware of these facts should they desire to domesticate an overseas operation, since there may be unforeseen outcomes to appointing local managers with multiple citizenships. In the case cited above, naturalized Canadians born abroad must not be absent from Canada for a continuous period of 10 years or more, or they can lose their citizenship. In hiring foreign managers, international recruiters should be aware of the existence of such potential problems.

Law of the Sea refers to international rules that pertain to the rights of states in maritime affairs *vis-à-vis* rules of navigation. Formalized in 1982 (under the auspices of the International Law Commission) as the United Nations Convention on the Law of the Sea, the Law is a multilateral treaty to which all signatories have bound themselves.

The Law of the Sea has evolved over time and, through various international conferences, can be summed up as follows:

1. All states have the right to use the "high seas" (i.e., waters beyond a state's 200-mile coastal economic zone) without interference.
2. Domestic jurisdiction is inviolable within a state's 12-mile "territorial sea" limit.
3. Domestic jurisdiction over a state's "coastal rights" can be exercised over all economic activities occurring within a 200-mile coastal economic zone.
4. All vessels have the right to peaceful passage through "commercial straits" (e.g., Straits of Malacca) and through "international commercial waterways" (e.g., Suez Canal, St. Lawrence Seaway).

See also Northwest Atlantic Fisheries Organization (in main entries).

law of soil, from the Latin *jus soli*, is the legal rule that a person has the legal right to the citizenship of the country on whose soil she or he was born.

> The concept is relevant to international marketing: a number of nonmarket economies in East Europe claim the right to retain and exert jurisdiction over individuals originally born in their countries even after they have emigrated to another country of which they have legally acquired citizenship through naturalization.
>
> The Canadian government respects this domestic jurisdictional claim, and it advises its naturalized Canadian citizens to verify their status carefully prior to stepping on

the soil of the land of birth, since the Canadian government may not be able to protect them.

---

less than fair value (LTFV) is a determination by the U.S. International Trade Commission (USITC) that foreign goods have been imported into the United States and sold there at a "dumped price."

Based on this determination, the goods may be the object of antidumping actions under the U.S. Tariff Act of 1930, and the alleged "dumpers" may be dealt with under the U.S. Omnibus Trade Act of 1988.

See also dumping; antidumping duty; U.S. International Trade Commission; Tariff Act of 1930; U.S. Omnibus Trade Act of 1988 (all in main entries).

letter of credence *See* diplomat.

like product means any good that, from the viewpoint of its inherent characteristics, can be substituted for any other good that has inherently equivalent characteristics.

> **Example:** In its original determination, the U.S. International Trade Commission (USITC) determined that the like product in question was pork whether fresh, chilled, or frozen. Further, the USITC found that the domestic U.S. industry was composed of "packers" who produced pork in either fresh, frozen, or chilled form. One USITC Commissioner differed in determining that the domestic industry of like producers included swine farmers; but this was not the majority USITC view.

See also determination.

municipal jurisdiction *See* domestic jurisdiction.

national (nationality) *See* citizen (citizenship).

naturalization is the acquisition of citizenship by the process of swearing allegiance to a state (i.e., by avowing to obey and uphold the laws of a state).

In practice, the vow of allegiance is not officially accepted by the state until and unless a variety of other conditions, which vary from state to state, are met—for example, residence in the state, nonviolation of criminal laws, literacy in the state's official language, knowledge of the state's laws.

natural law, from the Latin *jus naturale*, is the concept that reason and reasonableness, coupled with fairness and equity, form the basis of all law, both domestic and international.

It is evident that international law, codified from customary practices, legislation, and instruments of international agreements, while founded on natural law precepts, has gradually been displaced by law founded on legislation and treaties that delimit the rights and obligations of states and their citizens.

Thus, "natural rights" have given way to "civil rights," which have been transmuted into formal "legal rights." These have been codified in such documents as: The Bill of Rights, the first 10 Amendments to the Constitution of the United States (ratified

December 15, 1791); The International Convention on the Elimination of All Forms of Racial Discrimination (1965); and, more recently, the Canadian Charter of Rights and Freedoms (1982), which forms an integral part of the Canadian Constitution, formally called The Constitution Act 1982.

open meeting is the legal requirement in the United States under the Federal government's Sunshine Act of 1976 that administrative agencies have their hearings and investigations "open to the public."

The "openness" requirement is in accord with the fundamental democratic principle that those affected by government decisions have an inherent right to have input into them.

> *See also* natural law.

passport is an identity and travel document that is the property of the state and that is issued to an individual providing prima facie evidence of the person's identity and citizenship for the purpose of (1) travel between states and (2) attesting to the bearer's legitimate right to protection by the state that issued it. A passport identifies the bearer and carries a photograph of him or her. Each has pages for "endorsements and limitations" (i.e., space where governments can specify limits on the bearer's travel). Passports also have pages for visas.

> **Example:** If a state is engaged in belligerency (i.e., war) with another state, or if it is a third-party object of another state's belligerency or the object of nonstate belligerency, the passport will (most likely) carry the direction: NOT VALID FOR TRAVEL IN "X." U.S.-passport holders are thus advised by the U.S. State Department against travel in various parts of the world. Specifically, the State Department has "voided" U.S. passports for travel in Lebanon as a consequence of nonstate terrorist action there against U.S. citizens.

Every passport has its own official number. In recent years, passports issued in Canada and the U.S. have been "machine readable": they carry digits or markings that are recognizable by computer, permitting border officials to "computer process" an individual quickly, using a data-base management system. This system will, presumably, assist in the detection of illegal passports and, presumably, the apprehension of holders (and perhaps issuers) of them.

Traditionally, passports carry a request to allow the bearer to travel "without let or hindrance" and to "afford the bearer such assistance and protection as may be necessary."

public record *See* record.

quasi-international law refers to rules for the relationship between states and legal entities that do not have international personality (e.g., private corporations).

> **Example:** Concession agreements granted to a global petroleum company to carry out exploratory drilling in seas claimed to be the territorial waters of the state granting the concessions may be classed under quasi-international

law. The concession-grating state, nevertheless, retains the exclusive residual right to exercise its jurisdiction over the company.

recommended determination (RD) is a directive issued by an administrative law judge (ALJ) that pertains to some course of action to be taken respecting the violation of some order of a civil tribunal (e.g., the U.S. International Trade Commission).

> **Example:** On September 29, 1990, the U.S. International Trade Commission (USITC) referred the enforcement proceeding to an ALJ to hold an evidentiary hearing and to issue (within six months) a recommended determination (RD) concerning the question of violation of the USITC's March 16, 1989, cease and desist order (CDO).
>
> The original CDO directed the Atmel Corporation to refrain from importing and selling particular erasable, programmable, read-only memory (EPROM) chips found to be infringing valid U.S. patents owned by Intel Corporation.
>
> The USITC allowed the parties to express their views concerning the RD, to file exceptions to it, and to propose alternative findings of fact and conclusions of law prior to USITC disposition on the matter. The USITC finally adopted the RD with respect to the ALJ's determination that Atmel was in violation of the USITC's CDO and that the imposition of a $2,600,000 civil penalty was appropriate.

Cf. determination.
See also administrative law judge.

record (a noun) is, when referring to official trade investigations, (1) the body of written "historical information" pertaining to the case or (2) the "contemporaneous documentation" of information presented before and accepted by the investigating authorities in question (e.g., U.S. International Trade Commission).

The record may comprise the following documents:

- legislative acts and legal orders;
- determinations and findings;
- briefs, memoranda, notes, and notices;
- transcripts, depositions, written submissions, and affidavits;
- surveys, questionnaires, and financial audits.

Where a record is open to the public, it is called a "public record," in contrast to a "nonpublic record," which is not available for public scrutiny, sometimes because it contains business proprietary information (BPI).

See also business proprietary information; U.S. International Trade Commission (both in main entries).

retortion is a lawful but unfriendly act of retaliation.
See also retaliation (in main entries).

Rules of Navigation, officially, *International Regulations for Preventing Collisions at Sea*, is a set of formalized rules, based on British nineteenth-century regulations, which came into legal force in Washington, D.C., in 1889 and which today are administered by the International Maritime Organization (IMO), one of the specialized organs of the United Nations System.

See also International Maritime Organization (in main entries).

sanction, a variation of *embargo,* is

1. in formal international law, action taken against a state under the collective security system of the U.N. Security Council/U.N. General Assembly System;

   Example: In 1966, the U.N. Security Council imposed economic sanctions against the illegal government of Southern Rhodesia, declaring it a threat to international peace and security and requesting all states to cease all trade with it.

2. action taken either by a state unilaterally, or by a group of states (apart from the United Nations System) against another state judged to have endangered peace and security.

   Example: By Executive Order, legal trade sanctions were imposed against Nicaragua in the 1980s by the U.S. government. This was done to counter Nicaragua's alleged military and political destabilization of neighboring Central American states (Honduras and Costa Rica) and to exert economic pressure on the people to change their government. The sanctions were lifted in March 1990, following the electoral defeat of the Nicaraguan (Sandinista) government.

   See also embargo; Gulf Crisis •NW• (both in main entries).

secrecy laws are laws of confidentiality that apply to home-country financial institutions and that prohibit the disclosure of the identity of customers and their records.

Swiss secrecy laws have been notorious in preventing international police authorities (e.g., Interpol) from learning the identity of drug traffickers.

In 1991 these laws, called "Form B laws," were radically modified by the Swiss government to permit not only identification of certain Swiss bank customers but also disclosure (i.e., inspecting, copying, and removal) of relevant documents to prosecutors in foreign jurisdictions to be used as evidence in the worldwide anti-drug trafficking effort.

See also blocking laws.

single instrument *See* international agreement.

sovereign (sovereignty) refers to (1) historically, the "divine right of kings" to behave in any manner they deemed fit toward anyone within their territory; and (2) in the modern world, the exclusive right of states to deal with individuals within their jurisdiction, whether that be on their territorial land, within their territorial sea, or within their territorial airspace.

   Example: An Air Canada plane is under Canada's jurisdiction as long as it is over Canada's territory or is in "international airspace." Once the plane enters the airspace of another state, the passengers, flight crew, and the aircraft itself are all subject to the sovereignty of that other state.

   See also Act of State Doctrine; comity.

sovereign immunity, under international law, is the practice that accords states themselves exemption from litigation in their own national courts or in the courts of other countries unless they submit voluntarily.

See also sovereign; Act of State Doctrine.

state is the legal personality of an entity that is a definable territory, occupied by people, and that has the (governing) capacity (i.e., the government institutions) to exert its authority within the defined territory.

Recognition of states, once afforded, is not retractable.

This differs from diplomatic recognition, the political recognition of governments, that is a voluntary political act and, thus, revocable.

Example: The merging of the former states of North Vietnam and South Vietnam into a single nation involved, first of all, the *de facto* recognition of the new government, (i.e., the acknowledgement that a new government was in actual control of the politically united territory). This was followed by *de jure* recognition (i.e., acceptance of the legitimacy of the new government to be in legal control of a state called Vietnam).

De jure recognition of a government does not imply approval of a government. According to the doctrine of "necessary representation," states must (as a practical matter) deal with each other on an impersonal, objective (i.e., legal) basis in matters of mutual interest, such as trade and security, despite the political differences that differentiate one state from another.

United Nations Convention on the Law of the Sea *See* Law of the Sea.

visa, from the Latin *visa* meaning "seen," is an endorsement by officials of a state to be entered, by way of official stamps and signatures made in a passport, that permission has been granted to the bearer of the passport to enter the state.

Two groups of visas exist: (1) global-application and exit visas and (2) treaty-qualified visas. The former group applies to people not entitled to special treatment by virtue of a treaty, while the second group pertains to people who are entitled to "treaty-qualified" treatment.

1. *Global Application and Exit Visas:* There are different types of visas in this category: (i) general visa, (ii) tourist visa, (iii) commercial visa, (iv) transit visa, (v) re-entry visa, and (vi) exit visa.
   i. *General Visa:* This permits admission into a state for any purpose; that is, tourism, transit, or commerce.

   Example: "Consulate of Mozambique in Durban. Visa good for Mozambique. Valid for one voyage only, and to remain for three days. To be used within 120 days from date of issue."

   ii. *Tourist Visa:* This permits admission into a state exclusively for the purpose of tourism; it may be endorsed accordingly, with specific dates for exit and entry. When a documentary tourist visa is issued separate from and not affixed to a passport, it is called a "tourist card."

iii. *Commercial Visa:* This permits admission for the purpose of carrying out business for a short-term period (e.g., a business trip, a trade show). When the commercial purpose is that of residing in the foreign country to work there, the commercial visa is called a "work permit."

iv. *Transit Visa:* This permits admission for the exclusive purpose of allowing the individual to obtain transportation to a destination outside of the admitting state.

Since there are no official diplomatic relations between the governments of Nigeria and South Africa, air travelers with South African passports who fly on Pan Am from Johannesburg to London via Lagos are not granted transit visas by the Nigerian government.

Thus, upon arrival in Lagos, all transit passengers, except South African passport holders, are permitted to deplane and refresh themselves in the Transit Lounge. South African passport holders are not permitted to deplane and touch Nigerian soil: they must remain on the plane within the jurisdiction of Pan Am, the U.S. carrier.

v. *Re-Entry Visa:* This permits temporary departure from a host country; it is usually applicable to international business people who are resident in a host country and who are working under a work permit. The re-entry visa is sometimes called a *temporary exit visa* since it specifies the length of time a holder of a work permit may be away from the host country and still re-enter it without difficulty.

Example: "This endorsement constitutes authority to re-enter Zambia under Temporary Employment Permit #4-6785-301CA within 120 days of the issue hereof."

Example: "Bureau of Immigration & Naturalization, Department of Justice, Republic of Liberia. Permit to Re-Enter the Republic of Liberia. Pursuant to provisions of Section 14b of the Immigration and Naturalization Act, this permit is issued to the bearer, an alien previously lawfully admitted to the Republic, to re-enter Liberia if otherwise admissible as (1) an employee, or (2) a student, or (3) a treaty merchant. Good for one year only. Note: upon the expiration of its validity, this permit must be surrendered to the Bureau of Immigration & Naturalization."

vi. *Exit Visa:* This permits permanent departure from a country; it is only applicable to those who have been granted a commercial visa.

Example: In many African, Asian, and Latin American countries, holders of commercial visas (i.e., work permits) are usually free to come and go both internationally and within the host country, provided they have the appropriate documentation (e.g., re-entry visas). Permission to depart the host country permanently (i.e., the granting of an exit visa) is often not simply a bureaucratic formality. In some countries, exit visas can only be obtained after satisfying the authorities (usually by way of documentary evidence) that one has paid all personal income taxes to the state and all personal-consumption utility bills (e.g., household electricity bills).

In addition to the above classificatory differences, a visa can be granted to an individual as an "individual visa" or to individuals who are part of a group as a "group visa." With the former, the person can enter and exit the state independent of anyone else, as long as she or he complies with the conditions of entry. With the latter, the individual must enter and exit the country with the group on specified dates.

Example: The U.S. team left Washington on Aeroflot flight #274 without one of their key people. Dr. Sergei Balikov (a Soviet scientist who fled the U.S.S.R. in 1957 and later naturalized as an American) was stranded in Los Angeles due to inclement weather. He was urged to fly to New York, catch TWA flight 732 to London, and rejoin the group in the Transit Lounge at Heathrow no later than 10 A.M. local time.

If this failed, Soviet officials would definitely not admit Balikov since he was covered by a group visa, and the entire group had to enter and exit the Soviet Union together on the same day and on the same flight. There would be no time for Soviet authorities to change Balikov's status, grant him a new individual visa, and remove him from the group visa.

In any event, even if this could actually be done, the officials were not likely to do it: it was improbable that the Soviets would permit a scientifically savvy and politically astute nuclear scientist the freedom to come and go autonomously.

2. *Treaty-Qualified Visas:* Under the Canada-U.S. Free Trade Agreement (FTA) of 1989, national treatment is afforded cross-country nationals seeking entry into the United States and Canada for temporary purposes. For select classes of Canadian and U.S. citizens, no prequalification is necessary in order to secure the necessary visas and, subsequently, the appropriate work and residency documents.

The four classes of "FTA-qualified" persons are: (i) business visitors, (ii) intracompany transfers, (iii) traders and investors, and (iv) professionals in certain fields, as defined and detailed in Chapter 15, Article 1501–1506, and Annex 1502.1 (including Schedules 1 and 2) of the FTA.

  i. *Business Visitors:* A B-1 status is issued to bona fide Canadian business people, employed by Canadian companies, entering the United States for temporary business purposes on behalf of that company and as defined and listed in Annex 1502.1 and Schedule 1 of the FTA. Canadian business visitors need only identify themselves at a U.S. Port of Entry to be admitted for doing business for up to a single continuous six-month period per visit. The U.S. Customs Service issues neither physical documentation nor any passport stamp to support the B-1 status.

  ii. *Intracompany Transfers:* An L-1 visa is issued for Canadian intracompany transferees, as defined and listed in Annex 1502.1 and Schedule 1 of the FTA, who have been working for their Canadian-based company for a minimum of 12 months (prior to the transfer). The transfer must be for a temporary period of time, and the U.S. employer must complete Form I-129L with the U.S. Immigration and Naturalization Service (INS) on behalf of the transferee. The U.S. employer must be either a Canadian subsidiary or an affiliate of a U.S. parent, or a Canadian-U.S. joint venture owned on a 50–50 basis.

If the U.S. company has been in operation for at least one year, a three-year work permit may be issued. If the U.S. firm has been in business for less than one year, the permit issued will be for one year. The documentary work permit is issued at the U.S. Port of Entry by a Customs Inspector.

iii. *Traders and Investors:* An E-1 visa is issued to bona fide "treaty traders," and an E-2 visa to bona fide "treaty investors" (as defined and listed in Annex 1502.1 and Schedule 1 of the FTA) carrying on financial trade principally between Canada and the United States. These visas are issued at a U.S. Consulate. The actual documentary work permits themselves are issued at a U.S. Port of Entry.

iv. *Professionals:* A TC-1 visa is issued at the U.S. Port of Entry to persons defined as "professionals" and listed in Annex 1502.1 and Schedule 2 of the FTA. The visa has no time limitation attached to it, but since the work status of the professional is attached to the employer, release of the employee from the "sponsoring employer" terminates the validity of the visa unless, in the interim, the professional has converted the temporary status of the TC-1 permit to Permanent U.S. Resident status (i.e., the "Green Card").

To nonprofessionals who are "distinguished workers," an H-1 visa is issued at the U.S. border. A "distinguished worker" is defined as someone who, lacking the formal, professional, and/or academic qualifications to qualify as a "professional," is, nevertheless, an "eminent person" in a specialization or field of work. A U.S. employer must complete Form I-129B with the U.S. Immigration and Naturalization Service (INS). The H-1 has a five-year time-limitation period.

Selected Information Sources

What follows is an attempt to provide a discriminating list of sources from which researchers can get additional specialized data on the full range of international business entries covered in this volume.

The sources are categorized as follows:

A. United Nations System
B. Canadian Government
C. United States Government

D. Quasi-Government Organizations
E. International Organizations

A. UNITED NATIONS SYSTEM

African Development Bank
01 B.P. 1 387
Abidjan 01
CÔTE D'IVOIRE
Telephone: 32 07 11/32 50 10
TELEX: 3717/3498/3263/3282
Cable: AFDEV ABIDJAN
Fax: (225) 44 45 96

Asian Development Bank
2330 Roxas Boulevard
PO Box 789
Manila
PHILIPPINES 2800
Telephone: (63) (2) 834-4444
Telex: RCA 23103 adb ph;
            ITT 40571 adb pm
Cable: ASIANBANK MANILA

Caribbean Development Bank
PO Box 408 Wildey
St. Michael, Barbados
WEST INDIES
Telephone: (809) 426-1152
Telex: WB 2287

Food and Agricultural Organization of the United Nations
Via delle Terme di Caracalla
00100 Rome
ITALY
Telephone: (39) (6) 5797-6489
Telex: 611127
Cable: FOODAGRI ROME
Fax: (39) (6) 541-3047

General Agreement on Tariffs and Trade
Centre William Rappard
154, rue de Lausanne
1211 Geneva 21
SWITZERLAND
Telephone: (41) (22) 739-5111
Telex: 28787
Cable: GATT GENEVA
Fax: (44) (22) 731-4206

Inter-American Development Bank
1300 New York Avenue NW
Washington DC 20577
Telephone: (202) 623-1000
Telex: 64141/248352
Cable: INTAMBANC
Fax: (202) 623-3096/789-2835

International Atomic Energy Agency
Vienna International Center
PO Box 100
A-1400 Vienna
AUSTRIA
Telephone: (43) (1) 23600
Telex: 12645
Cable: INATOM VIENNA
Fax: (43) (1) 23 45 64

International Civil Aviation Organization
1000 Sherbrooke Street West
Montréal H3A 2R2
CANADA
Telephone: (514) 285-8081
Telex: (05) 24513
Cable: ICAO MONTREAL
Fax: (514) 288-4772

International Development Association
1818 H Street NW
Washington DC 20433
Telephone: (202) 477-1234

International Finance Corporation
1818 H Street NW
Washington DC 20433
Telephone: (202) 477-1234

International Fund for Agricultural Development
Via del Serafico 107
00142 Rome
ITALY
Telephone: (39) (6) 54591
Telex: 620330
Cable: IFAD ROME
Fax: (39) (6) 504-3463

International Labor Organization
International Labor Office
4 Route des Morillons
1211 Geneva 22
SWITZERLAND
Telephone: (41) (22) 799-7603
Telex: 415647 ILO CH
Cable: INTERLAB GVA
Fax: (41) (22) 798-9489

International Maritime Organization
4 Albert Embankment
London SE1 7SR
ENGLAND
Telephone: (44) (01) 735-7611
Telex: 23588
Cable: INTERMAR-LONDON, SE1
Fax: (44) (1) 587-3210

International Telecommunication Union
1211 Geneva 20
SWITZERLAND
Telephone: (41) (22) 730-5459
Telex: 421000 UIT CH
Cable: BURNINTERNA GVA
Fax: (41) (22) 730-5432

International Trade Center UNCTAD/ GATT
54-56 rue de Montbrillant
CH-1202 Geneva 10
SWITZERLAND
Telephone: (41) (22) 730-0111
Telex: 289052 ITC-CH
Fax: (41) (22) 733-4439

Pan-American Health Organization
525 23rd Street NW
Washington DC 20037
Telephone: (202) 861-3426
Telex: 248338-pasb
Cable: OFSANPAN
Fax: (202) 223-5971

United Nations Center for Human Settlements (HABITAT)
PO Box 30030
Nairobi
KENYA
Telephone: (254) (2) 333930;
520600; 520320
Telex: 22996
Cable: UNHABITAT
Fax: (254) (2) 520724

United Nations Children's Fund (UNICEF)
United Nations Plaza
New York NY 10017
Telephone: (202) 415-8384
Telex: WUI 62346
Cable: UNICEF NY

UNICEF Supply Division Procurement Services
UNIPAC
UNICEF Procurement and Assembly Center
UNICEF Plads
Freeport
DK-2100 Copenhagen Ø
DENMARK
Telephone: (45) 31 26 24 21
Telex: 19813 UNCF DK
Fax: (45) 31 26 94 21

United Nations Conference on Trade and Development (UNCTAD)
Palais des Nations
1211 Geneva 10
SWITZERLAND
Telephone: (41) (22) 734-6011
Telex: 289696
Cable: UNCTAD GVA
Fax: (41) (22) 733-9879

United Nations Department of Technical Cooperation for Development
Contracts and Procurement Service
United Nations Headquarters
Room DC1-15
New York NY 10017
Telephone: (212) 963-8947/8949/8954
Telex: 42 23 11 UNVI
Cable: UNATIONS NY
Fax: (212) 963-8941

United Nations Development Program (UNDP)
220 East 42nd Street, 14th floor
New York NY 10017
Telephone: (212) 906-6127
Telex: 662293 ops undp
            645495 ops undp
            824608 ops undp
Cable: UNOPSNEWYORK
Fax: (212) 906-6501/6502

UNDP Division for Administrative and Management Services
One United Nations Plaza
New York NY 10017
Telephone: (212) 906-5500
Telex: 236286
Cable: UNDEVPRO NY
Fax: (212) 826-2057

UNDP Inter-Agency Procurement Services Office
Norre Voldgade 94
DK-1358 Copenhagen K
DENMARK
Telephone: (45) (1) 33 15 40 88
Telex: 27 36819 iaps-dk
Fax: (45) (1) 33 15 32 51
            (45) (1) 33 13 15 99

United Nations Economic Commission for Africa
Africa Hall
PO Box 3001
Addis Ababa
ETHIOPIA
Telephone: (251) (1) 51 72 00
Telex: 21029 UNECA ET
Cable: ECA, ADDIS ABABA
Fax: (212) 963-4957

United Nations Economic Commission for Europe
Palais des Nations
1211 Geneva 10
SWITZERLAND
Telephone: (41) (22) 346-0111
Telex: 289696

United Nations Economic Commission for Latin America and the Caribbean
Casilla 179-D
Dag Hammarskjöld Plaza
Santiago
CHILE
Telephone: (56) (2) 485 051/485 071
Telex: 340295 (TRANSRADIO)
            441054 (ITT)
            240077 (TELEX CHILE)
Cable: UNATIONS SANTIAGO
Fax: (56) (2) 480 252

United Nations Economic and Social Commission for Western Asia
PO Box 27
Hay Al-Furat Baghdad
IRAQ
Telephone: (964) (1) 556-4282
Fax: (964) (1) 556-9437

United Nations Economic and Social Commission for Asia and the Pacific
United Nations Building
Rajdamnern Avenue
Bangkok
THAILAND
Telephone: (66) (2) 282-9161/9200/
9381/9389
Telex: 82392 ESCAP TH;
82315 ESCAP TH
Fax: (66) (2) 282-9602

United Nations Educational, Scientific and Cultural Organization (UNESCO)
7 Place de Fontenoy
75700 Paris
FRANCE
Telephone: (33) (1) 45 68 15 18/45 68 15 20
Telex: 201539 UNESQIP F
Cable: UNESCO PARIS
Fax: (33) (1) 47 83 20 43

United Nations Environment Program
PO Box 30552
Nairobi
KENYA
Telephone: (254) (2) 33 37 30
Telex: 22068/22173
Cable: UNITERRA, Nairobi
Fax: (254) (2) 52 08 31

United Nations Fund for Population Activities
220 East 42nd Street 17th floor
New York NY 10017
Telephone: (212) 850-5716
Telex: 422031
Cable: UNDEVPRO NY
Fax: (212) 850-5734

United Nations Industrial Development Organization
PO Box 300
A-1400 Vienna
AUSTRIA
Telephone: (43) (1) 230 7840/230 8272
Telex: 13 12 18 PAC A
Cable: UNIDO VIENNA
Fax: (43) (1) 230 7840/230 8272

United Nations Office at Geneva
1211 Geneva 10
SWITZERLAND
Telephone: (41) (22) 734-6011; 731-0211
Telex: 289696 UNO CH
Cable: UNATIONS GVA
Fax: (41) (22) 734-4560

United Nations Purchase and Transportation Service
United Nations Secretariat
New York NY 10017
Telephone: (212) 963-6225
Telex: 232422
Cable: UNATIONS NY
Fax: (212) 754-4879

Universal Postal Union
Case Postale
3000 Berne 15
SWITZERLAND
Telephone: (41) (31) 43 22 11
Telex: 32842
Cable: UPU BERNE
Fax: (41) (31) 43 22 10

World Bank
1818 H Street NW
Washington DC 20433
Telephone: (202) 477-3331; (202) 676-0320
Telex: RCA 248423
WUI 64145
TRT 197688
Cable: INTBAFRAD

World Food Program
Via delle Terme di Caracalla
00100 Rome
ITALY
Telephone: (39) (6) 57 97 63 18
Telex: 626675 WFPI
Cable: WORLDFOOD ROME
Fax: (39) (6) 57 97 56 52

World Health Organization
Avenue Appia, 20
1211 Geneva 27
SWITZERLAND
Telephone: (44) (22) 791-2801
Telex: 41546
Cable: UNISANTE GVA
Fax: (41) (22) 791-0536

World Intellectual Property Organization
34 Chemin des Colombettes
1211 Geneva 20
SWITZERLAND
Telephone: (41) (22) 730-9111
Telex: 412 912 OMPI CH
Cable: OMPI, Geneva
Fax: (41) (22) 733-5428

World Meteorological Organization
PO Box 2300
CH-1211 Geneva 2
SWITZERLAND
Telephone: (41) (22) 730-8111
Telex: 23260
Cable: METEOMOND GVA
Fax: (41) (22) 734-2326

B. CANADIAN GOVERNMENT

Canadian International Trade Tribunal
The Deputy Minister
Revenue Canada
Sir Richard Scott Building
191 Laurier Avenue West
Ottawa Ontario K1A 0L5
Telephone: (613) 990-2452
Fax: (613) 998-4783
             (613) 990-2439

Canadian Chamber of Commerce
Montréal Office:
Carnet Canada
The Candian Chamber of Commerce
1080 Du Beaver Hall Côté RM 710
Montréal Québec H2Z 1S8
Telephone: (514) 866-4334

Toronto Office:
Carnet Canada
The Canadian Chamber of Commerce
First Canadian Place STE 3370
PO Box 63
Toronto Ontario M5X 1B1
Telephone: (416) 868-6415

Vancouver Office:
Carnet Canada
The Canadian Chamber of Commerce
c/o Vancouver Board of Trade
500-1177 West Hastings Street
Vancouver BC V6E 2K3
Telephone: (604) 681-2111

Canadian Copyright and Industrial
  Design Office
Forms Office:
Copyright and Industrial Design Branch
Directorate of Intellectual Property
Consumer and Corporate Affairs Canada
Ottawa Ontario K1A 0C9
Telephone: (819) 997-1725

Search Office:
Place du Portage
50 Victoria Street
Hull Québec K1A 0S5

Canadian Department of Finance
Tariffs Division
Place Bell Canada
160 Elgin Street
Ottawa Ontario K1A 0G5
Telephone: (613) 992-1573

Canadian International Development
  Agency
Place du Centre
200 Promenade du Portage
Hull Québec K1A 0G4
Telephone: (819) 997-7775

Canadian Patent Office
Canadian Trade Marks Office
Patent Office Library and Trade Marks
  Office
Search Room
Place du Portage
Phase I
50 Victoria Street
Hull Québec K1A 0S5
Telephone: (819) 997-1936

Department of Industry, Science and
  Technology, Service Industries Branch
235 Queen Street
Ottawa Ontario K1A 0H5
Telephone: (613) 954-1984
Telex: 053-4123
Fax: (613) 954-1894

External Affairs and International Trade
  Canada
Export Controls Division:
125 Sussex Drive
Ottawa Ontario K1A 0G2
Telephone: (613) 996-2387

Import Controls Division:
125 Sussex Drive
Ottawa Ontario K1A 0G2
Telephone: (613) 995-8356

Trading House and Countertrade Section
125 Sussex Drive
Ottawa Ontario K1A 0G2
Telephone: (613) 995-7576
Telex: 053-3745
Fax: (613) 954-9103

INFO EXPORT HOTLINE
Toll Free: 1-800-267-8376
Ottawa area: (613) 993-6435
Telex: 053-3745 (BTC)
Fax: (613) 992-5791

Revenue Canada, Customs and Excise
Sir Richard Scott Building
191 Laurier Avenue West
Ottawa Ontario K1A 0L5
Telephone: Customs (613) 993-0534
                 Excise (613) 990-9908

Supply and Services Canada
Place du Portage 8B3
Hull Québec K1A 0S5
Telephone: (819) 994-0071

C. UNITED STATES GOVERNMENT

**Department of Agriculture, International
Affairs, and Commodity Programs,
Commodity Credit Corporation**
Fourteenth Street and Independence Avenue
SW
Washington DC 20250
Telephone: (202) 447-2791

**Department of Commerce, Bureau of
Export Administration**
Fourteenth Street between Constitution
Avenue and E Street
Washington DC 20230
Telephone: (202) 377-2000

**Department of State, Bureau of
International Organization Affairs**
2201 C Street NW
Washington DC 20520
Telephone: (202) 647-6400

**Department of Commerce, International
Trade Administration**
Fourteenth Street between Constitution
Avenue and E Street
Washington DC 20230
Telephone: (202) 377-2000

**Department of Commerce, Patent and
Trademark Office**
2021 Jefferson Davis Highway
Arlington, VA 20231
Telephone: (703) 557-3158

**Department of State, Bureau of Consular
Affairs**
Visa Services
2401 E Street NW
Washington DC 20520-0113
Telephone: (202) 647-0501

Passport Services
1425 K Street NW RM G
Washington DC 20524
Telephone: (202) 523-1355

**Department of State, Bureau of
Economic and Business Affairs**
2201 C Street NW
Washington DC 20520
Telephone: (202) 647-6575

**Department of State, Bureau of Politico-
Military Affairs**
2201 C Street NW
Washington DC 20520
Telephone: (202) 647-5104

**Department of Transportation
Maritime Administration**
400 Seventh Street SW
Washington DC 20590
Telephone: (202) 366-4000

**Department of the Treasury
U.S. Customs Service**
1301 Constitution Avenue NW
Washington DC 20229
Telephone: (202) 566-8195

Government Printing Office
North Capitol and H Streets NW
Washington DC 20401
Telephone: (202) 275-2051

**Library of Congress
Copyright Office**
James Madison Memorial Bldg
101 Independence Avenue SE RM LM-401
Washington DC 20540
Hotline Telephone: (202) 707-9100

Office of the U.S. Trade Representative
600 Seventeenth Street NW
Washington DC 20506
Telephone: (202) 395-3230

D. QUASI-GOVERNMENT ORGANIZATIONS

Central Intelligence Agency (CIA)
Washington DC 20505
Telephone: (in Arlington, VA)
 (703) 482-1101

Export Development Corporation
151 O'Connor Street
PO Box 655
Ottawa Ontario K1P 5T9
Telephone: (613) 598-2992
Fax: (613) 237-2690
Cable: EXCREDCORP

**Export-Import Bank of the United States
 (Eximbank)**
811 Vermont Avenue NW
Washington DC 20571
Telephone: (202) 566-8990

Federal Maritime Commission
1100 L Street NW
Washington DC 20571
Telephone: (202) 523-5773

**Federal Trade Commission
Bureau of Competition**
Pennsylvania Avenue at Sixth Street NW
Washington DC 20580
Telephone: (202) 326-2180

International Chamber of Commerce
801 2nd Avenue, Suite 1204
New York, NY 10017
Telephone: (212) 354-4480

Overseas Private Investment Corporation
1615 M Street NW
Washington DC 20527
Telephone: (202) 457-7200

U.S. Information Agency
(also known as USIS overseas)
301 Fourth Street SW
Washington DC 20547
Telephone: (202) 485-7700

**U.S. International Development
 Cooperation Agency (USIDCA)**
320 Twenty-First Street NW
Washington DC 20523-0001
Telephone: (202) 647-1850

**USIDCA Agency for International
 Development**
320 Twenty-First Street NW
Washington DC 20523-0001
Telephone: (202) 647-1850

**USIDCA Trade and Development
 Program**
SA-16 Room 309
Washington DC 20523-1602
Telephone: (703) 875-4357

U.S. International Trade Commission
500 E Street SW
Washington DC 20436
Telephone: (202) 252-1000

E. INTERNATIONAL ORGANIZATIONS

**Abu Dhabi Fund for Arab Economic
 Development**
PO Box 814
Abu Dhabi
UNITED ARAB EMIRATES
Telephone: (971) (2) 725-800
Telex: 22287 FUND EM
Cable: FUND
Fax: (971) (2) 728-890

**Arab Bank for Economic Development in
 Africa**
PO Box 2640
Khartoum
SUDAN
Telephone: 73645/6/7, 74709, 70498
Telex: 22248, 22739 BADEA SD
Cable: BADEA - Khartoum

Arab Fund for Economic and Social Development
PO Box 21923
SAFAT 13080 Kuwait City
KUWAIT
Telephone: (965) 245-1580
Telex: INMARABI 22143KT
Cable: INMARABI KUWAIT

Association of Southeast Asian Nations
6 Jalan Taman Pejambon
PO Box 2072
Jakarta
INDONESIA
Telephone: (62) (21) 348838

Bank of Central African States
Banque des États de l'Afrique Centrale
PO Box 1917
Yaoundé
CAMEROON
Telephone: (237) 22 25 05
Telex: BANETAC 8343 KN

Banque Centrale des États de l'Afrique de l'Ouest
(Central Bank of West African States)
PO Box 3108
Dakar
SÉNÉGAL
Telephone: (221) 273 72
Telex: BECEAO 3154 SG

Bank for International Settlements
Centralbahnplatz 2
4002 Basel
SWITZERLAND

Benelux Economic Union
39 rue de la Régence
1000 Brussels
BELGIUM
Telephone: (32) (2) 513-8680
Telex: 61540 BENELU B

Commission of the European Communities
200 rue de la Loi
1049 - Brussels
BELGIUM
Telephone: (32) (2) 235-1111
Telex: COMEURBRU 21877

Council for Mutual Economic Assistance
Prospekt Kalinina 56
Moscow 121205
USSR
Telephone: 290 91 11
Telex: 7141

Economic Community of West African States
6 George V Road
Lagos
NIGERIA
Telephone: (234) (1) 26001

European Free Trade Association
9-11 rue de Varembé
1211 Geneva 20
SWITZERLAND
Telephone: (41) (22) 34 90 00
Telex: 22660 EFTA CH

International Bank for Economic Cooperation
Kuznetski Most 15
Moscow 103031
USSR

International Investment Bank
Presnensky Val 17
Moscow 123557
USSR
Telephone: 225 58 51

International Sugar Organization
24 Haymarket
London SW1Y 4SS
ENGLAND
Telephone: (44) (1) 930-4128
Telex: 916128

International Wheat Council
24 Haymarket
London SW1Y 4SS
ENGLAND
Telephone: (44) (1) 930-4128
Telex: 916128

Islamic Development Bank
PO Box 5925
Jeddah 21432
SAUDI ARABIA
Telephone: (966) (2) 636-1400
Telex: 601137, 601407 ISDB J
Cable: BANISLAMI-JEDDAH

Latin American Economic System
(Sistema Económico Latinoamericano)
PO Box 17035
Caracas 101
VENEZUELA
Telephone: (58) (2) 32 49 11-17

Latin American Integration Association
(Asociación Latinoamericana de Integración)
Cebollati 1461
PO Box 577
Montevideo
URUGUAY
Telephone: (598) (2) 40 11 21-28

League of Arab States
Avenue Khéreddine Pacha
Tunis
TUNISIA
Telephone: (216) (1) 890-100

Mahgred Permanent Consultative Committee
14 rue Yahia Ibn Omar
Mutuelleville Tunis
TUNISIA
Telephone: (216) (1) 28 73 11
             (216) (1) 28 70 57
Telex: 337

North Atlantic Treaty Organization (NATO)
1110 Brussels
BELGIUM
Telephone: (32) (2) 241-0040
Telex: 23867

Northeast Atlantic Fisheries Commission
Great Westminster House
Horseferry Road
London SW1P 2AE
ENGLAND
Telephone: (44) (1) 216-6126
Telex: 21271

Northwest Atlantic Fisheries Organization
PO Box 638
Dartmouth
Nova Scotia B2Y 3Y9
CANADA
Telephone: (902) 469-9105
Telex: 019-31475

Organization of American States (OAS)
Seventeenth Street and
   Constitution Avenue NW
Washington DC 20006
Telephone: (202) 458-3000

Organization of Arab Petroleum Exporting Countries (OAPEC)
PO Box 20501
Kuwait City
KUWAIT
Telephone: (965) 44 82 00
Telex: 2166

Organization of Central American States
Oficina Centroamericana Paseo Escalón
San Salvador
EL SALVADOR
Telephone: (503) 23 51 36

Organization for Economic Cooperation and Development
2 rue André-Pascal
75775 Paris CEDEX 16
FRANCE
Telephone: (33) (1) 4524-8200

Organization of the Islamic Conference
Kilo 6
Mecca Road
PO Box 178
Jeddah
SAUDI ARABIA
Telephone: (966) (2) 687-3880

Organization of Petroleum Exporting Countries (OPEC)
Obere Donaustrasse 93
1020 Vienna
AUSTRIA
Telephone: (43) (222) 26 55 11
Telex: 74474

OPEC Fund for International Development
PO Box 995 A-1011
Vienna
AUSTRIA
Telephone: (43) (222) 51564-0
Telex: 1-31734 FUND A
Cable: OPECFUND

**South Pacific Bureau for Economic
  Cooperation**
PO Box 856
Suva
FIJI
Telephone: (679) 31 26 00
Telex: SPECSUVA FJ 2229

South Pacific Commission
PO Box D-5
Nouméa
NEW CALEDONIA
Telephone: (687) 26 20 00

Union of Banana Exporting Countries
(Unión de Países Exportadores de Banano)
PO Box 4275
Panama City 5
PANAMÁ

West African Economic Community
*(Communauté Économique de l'Afrique de
  l'Ouest)*
PO Box 643
Ouagadougou
BURKINA FASO
Telephone: 32 233

Reference Guides of Key Terms

The intent of these Reference Guides is to assist the reader to make the best possible use of this dictionary. Every term in the dictionary is listed in at least one appropriate Reference Guide; where there is important cross-functionality, terms are listed in more than one Guide where applicable. (Please see the Introduction of this book for a thorough explanation of the structure of the Reference Guides.)

Thus, the Reference Guides were designed to be useful in several specific ways. First of all, they are eminently suited to experienced business people who are major traders internationally and who wish to expand their operations to the global arena. Secondly, the Guides can functionally assist sophisticated exporters who tradition-ally trade with one region (e.g., West Europe) and who are considering trading with another one (e.g., East Europe). Thirdly, for the novice trader, the Reference Guides will be a profitable and useful tool to immediately assist in getting started in a new geographic market.

Reference Guides of Key Terms

1. Global Reference Guide of Key Terms

2. North American Reference Guide of Key Terms

3. Latin American and Caribbean Reference Guide of Key Terms

4. West European Reference Guide of Key Terms

5. East European Reference Guide of Key Terms

6. Middle East Reference Guide of Key Terms

7. African Reference Guide of Key Terms

8. Asian Reference Guide of Key Terms

9. Foreign Language Reference Guide of Key Terms

10. International Law Reference Guide of Key Terms

Bibliography

Adams, James H. *In the Canadian Interest: Third World Development in the 1980s.* Ottawa: North-South Institute, 1980.

"ADB/ADF Institutional Support to the PTA." *The Economist*, October 14, 1989, 9.

Afanasiev, L. *Economía Política del Capitalismo.* Havana: Editorial de Ciencias Sociales, 1979.

Alden, Vernon R. "Who Says You Can't Crack Japanese Markets?" *Harvard Business Review* 65 (January–February 1987): 52–56.

Alletzhauser, Al. "The Ultimate Company Men." *The Globe and Mail—Report on Business*, March 1990, 71–78.

Amaïzo, Ekoué Y. "UNIDO's Support to the PTA Bank." *Industry Africa* (Vienna), no. 1 (June 1989): 17–18.

Anderson, Charles H. *Sociological Essays and Research.* Homewood, IL: The Dorsey Press, 1970.

"Arab Bank for Economic Development in Africa." *Encyclopaedia Britannica*, 1985 ed., 1:504.

"Arab Fund for Economic and Social Development." *Encyclopaedia Britannica*, 1985 ed., 1:504.

"Arab League." *Encyclopaedia Britannica*, 1985 ed., 1:505.

"Arab Monetary Fund." *Encyclopaedia Britannica*, 1985 ed., 1:505.

Aron, Raymond. *The Century of Total War.* Boston: Beacon Press, 1965.

Asian Development Bank. *Asian Development Outlook, 1989.* Manila: ADB, 1989.

———. *Guidelines for Procurement Under Asian Development Bank Loans.* Manila: ADB, 1985.

———. *Guidelines on the Use of Consultants by Asian Development Bank and Its Borrowers.* Manila: ADB, 1985.

———. *Key Indicators of Developing Member Countries of the ADB.* Manila: ADB, July 1989.

"Asian Governments Eye At Potential of Biotechnology." *APO News* (Tokyo) 19, no. 10 (October 1989): 3.

Balassa, B. *Toward Renewed Economic Growth in Latin America.* Washington, D.C.: Institute for International Economics, 1966.

———. "The Purchasing Power Parity Doctrine: A Reappraisal." In *International Finance*, ed. R.N. Cooper. Baltimore: Penguin Books, 1969.

Balassa, B., et al. *The Structure of Protection in Developing Countries.* Baltimore: Johns Hopkins University Press, 1971.

Baldwin, R.E. *Nontariff Distortions of International Trade.* Washington, D.C.: The Brookings Institution, 1970.

Ball, Donald A., and Wendell H. McCulloch, Jr. *International Business: Introduction and Essentials.* 2nd ed. Plano, TX: Business Publications, 1985.

"Banks and Banking." *Encyclopaedia Britannica*, 1983 ed., 14:600–612.

Barnes, James F., Marshall Carter, and Max J. Skidmore. *The World of Politics: A Concise Introduction.* 2nd ed. New York: St. Martin's Press, 1984.

Bello, Daniel C., and Nicholas C. Williamson. "The American Export Trading Company: Designing a New International Marketing Institution." *Journal of Marketing* 49 (Fall 1985): 60–69.

Belov, A.P. "Legal Aspects of Compensation Agreements with Firms of Western Countries." *Soviet Export* 5, no. 140 (1982): 15.

Bendix, Reinhard. *Max Weber: An Intellectual Portrait.* London: Methuen, 1962.

Benedict, Ruth. *The Chrysanthemum and the Sword.* Boston: Houghton Mifflin, 1946.

Bennett, Peter D., ed. *Dictionary of Marketing Terms.* Chicago: American Marketing Association, 1988.

Bergsten, C. Fred, Sir Kit McMahon, and Tommasso Padoa-Schioppa. *The International Monetary System: The Next 25 years.* Basle: Per Jacobsson Foundation, International Monetary Fund, 1988.

Berlew, F. Kingston. "The Joint Venture—A Way into Foreign Markets." *Harvard Business Review* 62 (July–August 1984): 48, 50, 54.

Bernstein, Peter W. "Coke Strikes Back." *Fortune,* June 1, 1981, 30–36.

Bhagwati, J.N. "On the Equivalence of Tariffs and Quotas." In *Trade Growth and the Balance of Payments: Essays in Honor of Gottfried Haberler,* ed. R.E. Baldwin et al. Chicago: Rand McNally, 1965.

———. *Anatomy and Consequences of Exchange Control Regimes.* Cambridge, MA: Ballinger, 1978.

———. *Dependence and Interdependence.* Cambridge, MA: M.I.T. Press, 1985.

———. *Protectionism.* Cambridge, MA: M.I.T. Press, 1988.

———, ed. *The New International Economic Order: The North-South Debate.* Cambridge, MA: M.I.T. Press, 1977.

Bhatt, Gita. "Europe 1992." *Finance and Development* (Washington, D.C.) 26, no. 2 (June 1989): 40–42.

Black, George. *Triumph of the People—The Sandinista Revolution in Latin America.* London: Zed Press, 1981.

Black, S.W. "The Interrelationship Between Exchange Rate Policy in Ten Industrial Countries." In *Exchange Rate Theory and Practice,* ed. J.F.O. Bilson and R.C. Marston. Chicago: University of Chicago Press, 1984.

Boonekamp, Clemens F.J. "Voluntary Export Restraints." *Finance and Development* (Washington, D.C.) 24, December 1987: 2–5.

Bowles, Samuel, and Gerbert Gintis. *Democracy & Capitalism: Property, Community, and the Contradictions of Modern Social Thought.* New York: Basic Books, 1986.

"Brazil's Coffee Industry—Brewing a Quota." *The Economist,* March 30, 1991, 63.

Briggs, Asa. "Technology and Economic Development." In *Technology and Economic Development,* ed. Robert McGowan and Ed Ottensmeyer. Boulder, CO: Westview Press, 1987.

Brown, Michael Barrat. *The Economics of Imperialism.* Middlesex, England: Penguin Books, 1978.

Bueno, Gerardo M. "A Mexican View." In *Bilateralism, Multilateralism and Canada in U.S. Trade Policy,* ed. William J. Diebold, Jr. The Council on Foreign Relations Series on International Trade, ed. C. Michael Aho. New York: Ballinger Publishing Company, 1988.

Bullock, Alan. *Hitler: A Study in Tyranny.* Middlesex, England: Penguin Books, 1967.

Bunich, Andrei. "Black Holes in the Economy." *Soviet News & Views* (Moscow) no. 7 (April 1989): 14.

Burbach, Roger, and Patricia Flynn. *Agribusiness in the Americas.* New York: North American Congress on Latin America (NACLA), 1980.

Butterfield, Herbert. *The Statecraft of Machiavelli.* New York: Macmillan Co., 1956.

Buzzell, Robert D. "Can You Standardize Multinational Marketing?" In *Multinational Marketing Management: Cases & Readings*. Robert D. Buzzell and John A. Quelch. Boston: Addison-Wesley, 1988.

Calvet, A.L. "A Synthesis of Foreign Direct Investment Theories and Theories of Elite Multinational Firms." *Journal of International Business Studies*, Spring/Summer 1981: 43–59.

Canadian Association for Latin American and Caribbean Studies. *Directory of Canadian Theses on Latin American and Caribbean Topics: 1927–1980*. Ottawa: CALACS/ACELA, 1982.

Canadian Commercial Corporation. "U.S. Army Orders Tanker Trailers." *News Release*, no. 12 (May 3, 1989).

Canadian Government, Customs and Excise, Revenue Canada. *Canada-U.S. Free Trade Agreement—Exporter's Certificate of Origin*. Ottawa: Department of National Revenue, November 1988.

Canadian Government, Department of External Affairs. "External Affairs Announces New Export Control Lists." *News Release*, no. 050 (March 6, 1989).

———. "Speech by the Right Honourable (*sic*) Joe Clark, Secretary of State for External Affairs, to the Business Council of British Columbia." *Statement*, no. 89/14 (April 19, 1989).

Canadian Government, Department of External Affairs: Secretary of State for External Affairs. "Canada Signs Charter of the Organization of American States." *News Release*, no. 281 (November 13, 1989).

———. "Notes for Remarks by The Secretary of State for External Affairs, The Right Honourable (*sic*) Joe Clark, at the Meeting of the Council of the Organization of American States, Washington, D.C." *Statement*, no. 89/62 (November 13, 1989).

Canadian Government, Department of National Revenue. *Free Trade Agreement: An Explanation of the Regulations Respecting the Origin of Goods for Determining Entitlement to the United States Tariff*. Ottawa: Customs and Excise Canada, 1988.

Canadian Government, External Affairs and International Trade Canada (EAITC). "Carnets: The Way to Worry-Free Travel." *CanadExport* (Ottawa) 6, no. 9 (May 31, 1988): 1.

———. *Export Markets: The Trading House connection*. Hull, Quebec: Supply and Services Canada, 1988.

———. "Free Trade Bulletin." *CanadExport* (Ottawa) 7, no. 2 (January 31, 1989).

———. "Free Trade Bulletin." *CanadExport* (Ottawa) 7, no. 4 (February 28, 1989).

———. "Free Trade Bulletin." *CanadExport* (Ottawa) 7, no. 5 (March 15, 1989).

———. "Free Trade Bulletin." *CanadExport* (Ottawa) 7, no. 6 (March 31, 1989).

———. "Free Trade Bulletin." *CanadExport* (Ottawa) 7, no. 18 (December 1, 1989).

———. "International Trade Centers across the Country Offer Marketing Advice to Canadian Exporter." *CanadExport* (Ottawa) 7, no. 14 (September 15, 1989): 3–4.

———. *Meeting the Challenge of Global Competition: Canada's Year in Trade, 1988/89*. Hull, Quebec: Supply and Services Canada, 1989.

———. *1992 Implications of a Single European Market—Part 1: Effects on Europe*. Ottawa: EAITC, 1989.

Canadian Government, External Affairs Canada: *Countertrade Primer for Canadian Exporters*. Hull, Quebec: Supply and Services Canada, 1985.

———. *Free Trade Agreement Between Canada and the United States of America*. Ottawa: DEA/DMTN, 1989.

———. *International Financing Data: A Business Guide to Export Financing and Other Financial Assistance*. 6th ed. Hull, Quebec: Supply and Services Canada, 1988.

———. *Joint Ventures with the People's Republic of China: A Primer for Canadian Business*. Hull, Quebec: Supply and Services, Canada, 1988.

———. *So You Want to Export? A Resource*

Book for Canadian Exporters. Hull, Quebec: Supply and Services Canada, 1983.

———. *Tariff Schedule of the United States. Annex 401.2.* Ottawa: DEA/DMTN, 1987.

Canadian Government, Minister for International Trade. "Appointment of Ellen Beall to Head Canada Section of Binational Trade Dispute Secretariat Announced." *News Release*, no. 019 (February 1, 1989).

———. "Asia-Pacific Co-operation and Uruguay Round Progress Are Goals for Trade Ministers Meetings, November 5 to 23, 1989." *News Release*, no. 266 (October 31, 1989).

———. "Asia-Pacific Economic Co-operation (APEC) Meeting Termed a Success by International Trade Minister." *News Release*, no. 277 (November 7, 1989).

———. "Canada Acts under FTA Dispute Settlement." *News Release*, no. 0002 (January 4, 1989).

———. "Canada and North American Free Trade." *News Release*, no. 91/11 (February 18, 1991).

———. "Canada and the U.S. Announce FTA Auto Panel." *News Release*, no. 076 (April 6, 1989).

———. "Canada Requests Panel Review for Pork under Chapter 19 of the Canada-U.S. Free Trade Agreement." *News Release*, no. 194 (August 22, 1989).

———. "Canada to Seek Authority to Take Action against USA for Failure to Abide by GATT Panel Ruling." *News Release*, no. 064 (March 30, 1989).

———. "Crosbie Meets European Community Ambassadors in Ottawa." *News Release*, no. 265 (October 30, 1989).

———. *How to Secure and Enhance Canadian Access to Export Markets—Discussion Paper.* Ottawa: 1984.

———. "International Trade Advisory Committee (ITAC) Holds Quarterly Meeting in St. John's." *News Release*, no. 151 (June 22, 1989).

———. "Minister for International Trade, John C. Crosbie, Announces Composition of the New Sectoral Advisory Groups on International Trade (SAGITs)." *News Release*, no. 015 (January 27, 1989).

———. "Ministerial Meetings in Japan Yield Progress for Uruguay Round of Multilateral Trade Negotiations." *News Release*, no. 288 (November 17, 1989).

———. "Notes for an Address by The Minister for International Trade, John C. Crosbie, at the Annual Meeting of the World Economic Forum." *Statement*, no. 89/05 (January 28, 1989).

———. "Notes for an Address by The Minister for International Trade, John C. Crosbie, to The Atlantic Provinces' Economic Council." *Statement*, no. 89/49 (October 3, 1989).

———. "Notes for a Speech by The Minister for International Trade, John C. Crosbie, to the Federation of German Industries (BDI)." *Statement*, no. 89/53 (October 16, 1989).

———. "Notes for an Address by The Minister for International Trade, John C. Crosbie, to the Fisheries Council of Canada." *Statement*, no. 89/56 (October 25, 1989).

———. "Notes for a speech by The Minister for International Trade, John C. Crosbie, to the Canadian Chamber of Commerce, Tokyo, Japan." *Statement*, no. 89/63 (November 15, 1989).

———. "Panel Established under Chapter 19 under The Free Trade Agreement." *News Release*, no. 271 (November 3, 1989).

———. "Statement by The Minister for International Trade, John C. Crosbie, on Further Steps Against Foreign Overfishing." *Statement*, no. 89/50 (October 6, 1989).

———. "Support Levels Agreed to Under Canada-U.S. Free Trade Agreement." *News Release*, no. 130 (June 6, 1989).

———. "Trade Minister Crosbie Comments on Cairns Group Meeting in New Zealand." *News Release*, no. 060 (March 28, 1989).

———. "Trade Ministers Measure Potential for Progress in Multilateral Trade Negotiations." *News Release*, no. 203 (August 30, 1989).

———. "1989 Canada Export Award Program." *News Release*, no. 049 (March 6, 1989).

———. "1989 Canada Export Award Winners." *News Release*, no. 231 (October 2, 1989).

Canadian Government, Minister of Finance and Minister for International Trade. *Export Financing—Consultation Paper.* Ottawa: January 1985.

Canadian International Development Agency (CIDA). *Annual Report: 1982–1983.* Hull, Quebec: Supply and Services Canada, 1983.

———. *Annual Report: 1983–1984.* Hull, Quebec: Supply and Services Canada, 1984.

———. *Annual Report: 1984–1985.* Hull, Quebec: Supply and Services Canada, 1985.

———. *Annual Report: 1985–1986.* Hull, Quebec: Supply and Services Canada, 1986.

———. *Annual Report: 1986–1987.* Hull, Quebec: Supply and Services Canada, 1987.

———. *Annual Report: 1987–1988.* Hull, Quebec: Supply and Services Canada, 1988.

———. "The 20 Years of CIDA: from Maurice Strong to Margaret Catley-Carlson." *Development* (Hull, Quebec) Summer–Autumn 1988: 58–78.

Caribbean Development Bank. *Annual Report, 1985.* Wildey, Barbados, W.I.: Caribbean Development Bank, 1986.

———. *Annual Report, 1986.* Wildey, Barbados, W.I.: Caribbean Development Bank, 1987.

———. *Annual Report, 1987.* Wildey, Barbados, W.I.: Caribbean Development Bank, 1988.

———. *Annual Report, 1988.* Wildey, Barbados, W.I.: Caribbean Development Bank, 1989.

Cassirer, Ernst. *The Myth of the State.* New Haven, CT: Yale University Press, 1963.

Cateora, Philip R. *International Marketing.* 5th ed. The Irwin Series in Marketing. Homewood, IL: Irwin, 1983.

Cateora, Philip R., and Susan Keaveney. *Marketing, An International Perspective.* Homewood, IL: Irwin, 1987.

Cecchini, Paolo. *The European Challenge 1992: The Benefits of a Single Market.* Brussels: Commission of the European Communities, 1988.

Central African States' Development Bank. *Annual Report 1987/1988.* Brazzaville, Congo: BDEAC, 1989.

Chandavarkar, Anand G. *The International Monetary Fund: Its Financial Organization and Activities*, no. 42. Washington, D.C.: IMF, 1984.

Cline, W.R., et al. *Trade Negotiations in the Tokyo Round: A Quantitative Assessment.* Washington, D.C.: The Brookings Institution, 1978.

Comisión Económica Para América Latina y El Caribe (CEPAL). "Balance Preliminar de la Economía Latinoamericana, 1988." *Notas Sobre La Economía Y El Desarrolla* (Santiago de Chile), no. 470/471 (Diciembre de 1988).

———. "Balance Preliminar de la Economía Latinoamericana, 1989." *Notas Sobre La Economía Y El Desarrollo* (Santiago de Chile), no. 485/486 (Diciembre de 1989).

———. "ECLAC Y El Caribe." *Notas Sobre La Economía Y El Desarrollo*, (Santiago de Chile), no. 469 (Diciembre de 1988).

———. "PREALC/OIT: La Dueda Social en América Latina y El Caribe." *Notas Sobre La Economía Y El Desarrollo* (Santiago de Chile), no. 472/473 (Enero/Febrero de 1989).

———. "Structural Changes in Latin American Economic Policies and Their Relations with the Liner Shipping Industry." *Notas Sobre La Economía Y El Desarrollo* (Santiago de Chile), no. 477/478 (June 1989).

Commission of the European Communities. *Commission Regulation (EEC) No. 3272/88 of 24 October, 1988, Amending Regulation (EEC) No. 1496/80 on the Declaration of Particulars Relating to Customs Value and on Documents to be Furnished*. Official Journal of the European Communities (Brussels) no. L 291 (October 25, 1988): 49–50, plus Annex I and Annex II.

———. "Completing the Internal Market." *White Paper from the Commission to the European Council*. Brussels: 1985.

———. "Creation of a European Financial Area." *European Economy* (Brussels), no. 36 (1988).

———. "The Economics of 1992." *European Economy* (Brussels), no. 35 (1988).

———. "Report on Economic and Monetary Union in the European Community." *Report by the Committee for the Study of Economic and Monetary Union*. Brussels: 1989.

"Completion of Montréal Package: 'Good for Confidence in the Multilateral System,' Says Arthur Dunkel." *News of the Uruguay Round of Multilateral Trade Negotiations* (Geneva), no. 026 (April 12, 1989): 1–10.

Comte, Auguste. *System of Positive Philosophy*. London: Longman's Green, 1877.

"Consultations Continue in Geneva in Effort to Free Montréal Package." *News of the Uruguay Round of Multilateral Trade Negotiations* (Geneva), no. 024 (February 23, 1989): 1–3.

Cooper, R.N., et al., eds. *The International Monetary System Under Flexible Exchange Rates*. Cambridge, MA: Ballinger, 1982.

Copeland, Lennie. *Beyond Culture Shock*. Part 3 of *Going International*. 4 parts, ed. Rita Cummings. San Francisco: Copeland Griggs Productions, 1983.

———. *Bridging the Culture Gap*. Part 1 of *Going International*. 4 parts, ed. Rita Cummings. San Francisco: Copeland Griggs Productions, 1983.

———. *Managing the Overseas Assignment*. Part 2 of *Going International*. 4 parts, ed. Rita Cummings. San Francisco: Copeland Griggs Productions, 1983.

———. *Welcome Home, Stranger*. Part 4 of *Going International*. 4 parts, ed. Rita Cummings. San Francisco: Copeland Griggs Productions, 1983.

Corden, W.M. *The Theory of Protection*. London: Oxford University Press, 1971.

———. "The Normative Theory of International Trade." In *Handbook of International Economics*, vol. 1, ed. R.W. Jones and P.B. Kenen. New York: North-Holland, 1984.

CORE II™—Company Readiness to Export, Version 3.0: *User's Guide*, 1–19. East Lansing, MI: Dialog Systems Division, A.T. Kearney, Inc. September 1990.

"Council of Arab Economic Unity." *Encyclopaedia Britannica*, 1985 ed., 1:504.

Council of Canadian Trading Houses. *List of Members, 1986*. Ottawa: Council of Canadian Trading Houses, 1986.

Crane, David. *A Dictionary of Canadian Economics*. Edmonton, Alberta: Hurtig, 1980.

"The Culture of Islam." *Encyclopaedia Britannica*, 1985 ed., 22:31–43.

Czinkota, Michael A., and Ilkka A. Ronkainen. *International Marketing*. New York: The Dryden Press, 1988.

Dalton, George, ed. *Primitive, Archaic and Modern Economies Essays of Karl Polanyi*. New York: New American Library, 1972.

Daly, Donald J. "Canada's International Competitiveness." In *International Business in Canada: Strategies for Management*, ed. Alan M. Rugman. Scarborough, Ontario: Prentice-Hall, 1989.

Davis, M., and J.P. Krauter. *The Other Canadians*. Toronto: Methuen, 1971.

de Cecco, Marcello, and Alberto Giovannini, eds. *A European Central Bank?* London: Cambridge University Press, 1989.

Delegation of the Commission of the European Communities/Délégation de la Commission des Communautée Européennes. "Abolition of Border Controls: Schengen Group Moves into Top Gear." *European Community News/Communauté Européenne Nouvelles* no. (90) 05. (Brussels), (July 10, 1990).

A Developing World. Map. Hull, Québec: Canadian International Development Agency (CIDA), 1987.

de Wilde, Jim, and Don Simpson. "Export

Strategies for Innovative Canadian Firms: Finding Niches and Inventing Competitive Advantage." *Business Quarterly*, 53, no. 1 (Summer 1988): 72–76.

Dhawan, K.C., Hamid Etemad, and Richard W. Wright, eds. *International Business: A Canadian Perspective*. Don Mills, Ontario: Addison-Wesley, 1981.

Diebel, Linda. "Free Trade: The Mexican Connection." *The Toronto Star*, April 1, 1989, D1, D5.

———. "Border Industries Exploit Workers." *The Toronto Star*, April 1, 1989, D5.

Diebold Jr., William, ed. *Bilateralism, Multilateralism and Canada in U.S. Trade Policy*. The Council on Foreign Relations Series on International Trade. Ed. C. Michael Aho. New York: Ballinger Publishing Company, 1988.

"Dossier: Currency and Banking." *The Courier* (Brussels), no. 117 (September–October 1989): 50–91.

"Dossier: Regional Cooperation." *The Courier* (Brussels), no. 112 (November–December 1988): 47–85.

Dougherty, James E., and Robert L. Pfaltzgraff. *Contending Theories of International Relations: A Comprehensive Study*. 2nd ed. New York: Harper & Row, 1981.

Douglas, Susan, and Bernard DuBois. "Looking at the Cultural Environment for International Marketing Opportunities." *Columbia Journal of World Business*, 12 (Winter 1977): 102–109.

Drucker, Peter F. "Behind Japan's Success." *Harvard Business Review* 59 (January–February 1981): 83–90.

Dubois, Marguerite-Marie, ed. *Larousse Dictionnaire Moderne: Français-Anglais* (Larousse Modern Dictionary: English-French). Paris: Libraire Larousse, 1960.

Ellul, Jacques. *Propaganda—The Formation of Men's Attitudes*. New York: Alfred A. Knopf, Inc., Vintage Books Edition, 1973.

Enchin, Harvey. "How Canada Shapes Up." *The Globe and Mail—Report on Business*, April 25, 1991, B5.

Etzioni, A., and Eva Etzioni-Halevy, eds. *Social Change: Sources, Patterns and Consequences*. 2nd ed. New York: Basic Books, 1973.

"Europe." *The Europa Year Book 1986: A World Survey*. Vols. 1 and 2. London: Europa Publications, 1986.

European Investment Bank. *Annual Report, 1988*. Luxembourg: 1989.

———. "The EIB's Financial Product." *EIB-Information* (Luxembourg), no. 61 (October 1989).

———. "Lending for Industrial Development in the ACP States." *EIB-Information* (Luxembourg), no. 60 (July 1989).

———. "New Powerful Satellites for Telecommunications and Sea and Air Traffic." *EIB-Information* (Luxembourg), no. 58 (November 1988).

"European Bank Opens Its Doors." *The Globe and Mail—Report on Business*, April 6, 1991, B14.

Evans, Peter. *Dependent Development—The Alliance of Multinational, State, and Local Capital in Brazil*. Princeton, NJ: Princeton University Press, 1979.

Fagan, Drew. "Ottawa Pledges Better Airline Deal." *The Globe and Mail—Report on Business*, March 22, 1991, B1.

Farnsworth, Clyde H. "Canada-U.S. Panel Assailed in Congress on Pork Imports." *The New York Times—Business Day*, March 28, 1991, C1, C14.

Farrell, Shari. "Canadian Physical Distribution/ Logistics in the Automobile Industry." Undergraduate essay. Durham College of Applied Arts and Technology. Oshawa, Ontario: 1989.

Fautsch, E. "Businessmen Seize the Integration Initiative." *The IDB* (Washington, D.C.), December 1988: 6–7.

Feder, Barnaby J. "Who Will Subscribe to the Valdez Principles?" *The New York Times*, September 10, 1989, F6.

Feder, Ernest. *The Rape of the Peasantry—Latin America's Landholding System*. Garden City, NY: Doubleday & Company, 1967.

Federal Business Development Bank (FBDB).

Assistance to Business in Canada (ABC) 1984. 1984 ed. Montréal: FBDB, 1984.

Ferguson, Charles H. "Computers and the Coming of the U.S. Keiretsu." *Harvard Business Review* 68 (July–August 1990): 55–70.

"The Financial Challenge of 1992." *UBS International Finance* (Zurich) 1, no. 1 (Fall 1989): 1–8.

Fleming, M.J. "Domestic Financial Policies Under Fixed and Under Floating Exchange Rates." In *International Finance*, ed. R.N. Cooper. Baltimore: Penguin Books, 1969.

Food and Agricultural Organization of the United Nations. "Names of Countries." In *FAO Terminology Bulletin* (Rome) no. 20/rev. 8 (1986).

Forcese, D. *The Canadian Class Structure.* Oxford: Clarendon Press, 1942.

French, Carey. "Beware of Sharks Offering Cargo Deals." *The Globe and Mail—Report on Business*, March 26, 1991, B22.

Friberg, Eric G. "1992: Moves Europeans are Making." *Harvard Business Review* 67 (May–June 1989): 84–89.

Friedman, M. "The Case for Flexible Rates." In *Readings in International Economics.* ed. R.E. Caves and H.G. Johnson. Homewood, IL: Irwin, 1968.

"FTC Lays Down the Law to Monopolies." *The Japan Economic Journal*, February 2, 1991: 20.

Fucilla, Joseph G. *World-Wide Spanish Dictionary.* New York: CBS Publications, 1966.

Furtado, Celso. "The Development of Brazil." In *Technology and Economic Development*, ed. Robert McGowan and Ed Ottensmeyer. Boulder, CO: Westview Press, 1987.

Galeano, Eduardo. *Open Veins of Latin America.* Trans. Cedric Belfrage. London: Monthly Review Press, 1973.

General Agreement on Tariffs and Trade. *Chairman's Texts on Agriculture, Trade-Related Aspects of Intellectual Property Rights, Textiles and Clothing, and Safe-guards.* Geneva: Uruguay Round Trade Negotiations Committee, April 7, 1989.

———. *GATT International Trade 88–89.* Vol. I. Geneva: GATT, 1989.

———. *GATT International Trade 88–89.* Vol. II. Geneva: GATT, 1989.

———. *The General Agreement.* 8th ed. Geneva: GATT, 1985.

"German Party Approves Tax Surcharge." *The Globe and Mail—Report on Business*, February 25, 1991, B5.

Gerth, H.H., and C. Wright Mills, trans. and eds. *From Max Weber: Essays in Sociology.* New York: Oxford University Press, 1962.

Ghymn, Kyung-Il. "International Marketing Neglect Still Continues: An Examination of Teaching and Research." In *Proceedings of the American Marketing Association 1982 Summer Educators' Conference.* Chicago: AMA (1983): 161–164.

Giddy, Ian H. "The Demise of the Product-Cycle International Business Theory." *Columbia Journal of World Business*, Spring 1978, 90–97.

Gilibert, Pier-Luigi, and A. Steinherr. "The Impact of Financial Market Integration on the European Banking Industry." *Cahiers BEI/EIB Papers*, no. 8 (March 1989): 9–54.

Gilibert, Pier-Luigi, Bjørn Lygum, and Daniel Ottolenghi. "International Capital Markets in 1987." *Cahiers BEI/EIB Papers*, no. 6 (April 1988): 9–57.

Giurleo, Diego. "Foreign Exchange Explained." Part 1. *Canada Commerce*, Department of Industry, Trade and Commerce (Ottawa), February 1984: 12–14.

———. "Foreign Exchange Explained." Part 2. *Canada Commerce*, Department of Industry, Trade and Commerce (Ottawa), June 1984: 15–17.

González, Servando. *Fidel—Para Herejes y Otros Invertebrados.* Mérida, México: Producción Editorial Dante, S.A., 1986.

Gorbunov, Sergei. "Gradual Conversion of the Rouble." *Soviet News & Views* (Moscow), no. 2 (January 1989): 5.

Gottlieb, Richard S., et al. *"A Businessman's Guide to the Canada/United States Trade Agreement (FTA."* Toronto: Fraser & Beatty, Gottlieb, 1988.

Government of Canada. "Canada Announces Public Information Campaign to End EC Overfishing." *News Release*, no. 237 (October 6, 1989).

——. "Canada Proposes Intellectual Property Standards to Reduce Trade Problems." *News Release*, no. 260 (October 26, 1989).

——. "Canada Ratifies International Patent Cooperation Treaty." *News Release*, no. 233 (October 2, 1989).

——. "Government Targets Imports from U.S. for Action against U.S. 'SUPERFUND.'" *News Release*, no. 171 (July 19, 1989).

——. "Government to Consult on Initiatives Against U.S. 'SUPERFUND.'" *News Release*, no. 143 (June 15, 1989).

——. "Ministers Disappointed by U.S. Decision to Grant Extraordinary Challenge in Pork Countervail Case. *News Release*, no. 82 (March 28, 1991).

——. "New U.S. 'Mack Amendment' Will Be Blocked." *News Release*, no. 38 (February 19, 1991).

Government of the People's Republic of China. *CCPIT First National Congress*. Beijing: China Council for the Promotion of International Trade, 1986.

Grasmick, Joseph C. "How to Work in the U.S. under the Free Trade Agreement." *Business Quarterly* 54, no. 1 (Summer 1989): 63–65.

Gray, John. "German Officials Struggle with Details of Unification." *The Globe and Mail*, February 26, 1990, A8.

"Green Paper on the Development of European Standardization: Action for Faster Technological Integration in Europe." *Official Journal of the European Communities*, no. C (Brussels), January 28, 1991.

Greenspon, Edward. "Canadian and European Officials Pessimistic over Fishing Dispute." *The Globe and Mail*, September 12, 1989, B10.

——. "EC Offers Cash, Caution to East European Reformers." *The Globe and Mail*, December 10, 1989, A3.

Grubel, H.G., and H.G. Johnson. *Effective Tariff Protection*. Geneva: United Nations, 1971.

Hale, David D. "Global Finance and the Retreat to Managed Trade." *Harvard Business Review* 68 (January–February 1989): 150–162.

Hamel, Gary, and C.K. Prahalad. "Do You Really Have a Global Strategy?" In *Global Marketing Perspectives*, 95–107. Cincinnati: South-Western Publishing Company, 1989.

Harbron, John. "How Japan Executives Manage the New Zaibatsu." *Business Quarterly*, Summer 1980, 15–18.

Hart, Norman A., and John Stapleton. *Glossary of Marketing Terms*. 3rd ed. London: Heinemann Professional Publishing Ltd., 1987.

Hegel, G.W.F. *Philosophy of Right*. Oxford: Clarendon Press, 1942.

"Highlights of Productivity Programmes in 1988." *APO News* (Tokyo) 19, no. 2 (February 1989): 9–12.

Hird, H. Richard. *Working with Economics: A Canadian Framework*. 2nd ed. Toronto: Collier Macmillan, 1988.

Hobbes, Thomas. *Leviathan*. Ed. and intro. Michael Oakshott. Oxford: Basil Blackwell, 1942.

Hooper, W.H., and J.M. Stafford. "Re: Privatization." *Corporate Letter by the Petro-Canada Chairman and the President and Chief Operating Officer*, March 1991.

Hoselitz, Bert F., and Wilbert E. Moore, eds. *Industrialization and Society*. Paris: Mouton, 1963.

Hout, Thomas, et al. "How Global Companies Win Out." *Harvard Business Review* 60 (September–October 1982): 98–108.

"How to Win Friends and Influence Exports."

Canadian Business, February 1984, 97–98, 103–105.

Hoy, Harold J., and John J. Shaw. "The United States' Comparative Advantage and Its Relationship to the Product Life Cycle Theory and World Gross National Product Market Share." *Columbia Journal of World Business* 16, no. 1 (Spring 1981): 40–50.

Hughes, David R., and Evelyn Kallen. *The Anatomy of Racism: Canadian Dimensions.* Montréal: Harvest House, 1974.

Hume, David R. "A Treatise of Human Nature." In *The Essential David Hume.* Intro. Robert P. Wolff. New York: New American Library, 1969.

"Ideographic Word Processing Now Available for Customers in Asia." *TechKnowledge* 1, no. 11 (May 1985): 10.

"Idris Jazairy, President of IFAD: Combating Rural Poverty and Hunger." *The Courier* (Brussels), no. 115 (May–June 1989): 3–6.

"IFC—Promoting Private Sector Development." *Finance & Development* 25, no. 4 (December 1988): 22–42.

"India Presents Its Views on Intellectual Property and Investment Measures While Hong Kong and US Put Rules of Origin on the Negotiating Table." *News of the Uruguay Round of Multilateral Trade Negotiations* (Geneva), no. 031 (October 16, 1989): 1–15.

Inter-American Development Bank. *Annual Report, 1982.* Washington, D.C.: Inter-American Development Bank, 1983.

———. *Annual Report, 1983.* Washington, D.C.: Inter-American Development Bank, 1984.

———. *Annual Report, 1984.* Washington, D.C.: Inter-American Development Bank, 1985.

———. *Annual Report, 1985.* Washington, D.C.: Inter-American Development Bank, 1986.

———. *Annual Report, 1986.* Washington, D.C.: Inter-American Development Bank, 1987.

———. *Annual Report, 1987.* Washington, D.C.: Inter-American Development Bank, 1988.

———. *Annual Report, 1988.* Washington, D.C.: Inter-American Development Bank, 1989.

———. "Bridge across the Pacific." *The IDB* (Washington, D.C.), March 1991, 6–7.

———. "New Corporation Readies for Action." *The IDB* (Washington, D.C.), April/May 1989: 10–11.

———. "Yen Connection to Latin America—IDB Playing a Growing Role." *The IDB.* Washington, D.C.: December 1989: 8–9.

International Chamber of Commerce. *The Development of International Container Transport: Its Application in Developing Countries.* Paris: ICC, 1977.

"International Court of Justice." *World Book Encyclopaedia*, 1981 ed., 6:348.

"International Law." *Encyclopaedia Britannica*, 1985 ed., 21:724–731.

"International Law." *Worldmark Encyclopedia of the Nations*, 7th ed. New York: Worldmark Press Ltd. (John Wiley & Sons, Inc.), 1988.

International Monetary Fund. *Annual Report, 1986.* Washington, D.C.: IMF, 1989.

———. *Annual Report, 1987.* Washington, D.C.: IMF, 1989.

———. *Annual Report, 1988.* Washington, D.C.: IMF, 1989.

———. *Annual Report, 1989.* Washington, D.C.: IMF, 1989.

———. *Annual Report on Exchange Rate and Exchange Restrictions.* Washington, D.C.: IMF, 1986.

———. *Annual Report on Exchange Rate and Exchange Restrictions.* Washington, D.C.: IMF, 1987.

———. *Annual Report on Exchange Rate and Exchange Restrictions.* Washington, D.C.: IMF, 1988.

———. "Appointment of Chairman for Interim Committee." *Press Release*, no. 90/1 (January 3, 1990).

———. "Book Cites Benefits of Value-Added Tax, Examines Means of Implementation." *IMF Survey* (Washington, D.C.) 17, no. 21 (November 14, 1988): 357–359.

———. "A Brief Guide to Committees and Groups." *IMF Survey* (Washington, D.C.) 18, no. 8 (April 17, 1989): 117.

———. "Camdessus Urges Banks to Share in Debt Reduction and Provision of New Money to Debtor Countries." *IMF Survey* (Washington, D.C.) 18, no. 12 (June 12, 1989): 178–183.

———. "Delors Report Suggests Step-by-Step Process of European Integrations." *IMF Survey* (Washington, D.C.) 18, no. 14 (July 10, 1989): 209, 219–222.

———. "Economists Discuss Transition to Market-Oriented Economies." *IMF Survey* (Washington, D.C.) 20, no. 3 (February 4, 1991): 34–37.

———. "European Community Issues Directive to Liberalize All Capital Movements." *IMF Survey* (Washington, D.C.) 17, no. 17 (August 29, 1988): 283–294.

———. "European Monetary System: Faces Opportunities and Challenges in the Decade Ahead." *IMF Survey* (Washington, D.C.) 18, no. 23 (December 11, 1989): 375–377.

———. "Europe's Agricultural Policy is Costly, Distorts World Trade and Prices." *IMF Survey* (Washington, D.C.) 18, no. 4 (February 20, 1988): 49, 59–62.

———. *German Unification: Economic Issues.* Occasional Paper No. 75. Washington, D.C.: IMF, 1990.

———. "German Unification Requires Rapid Adjustment in the East." *IMF Survey* (Washington, D.C.) 20, no. 2 (January 21, 1991), 25–27.

———. "Group of 24 Communiqué: Officials Urge the Creation of a Committee on Reform of the International Monetary System." *IMF Survey—Annual Meetings* (Washington, D.C.) 18, no. 19 (October 16, 1989): 315–319.

———. *IMF Survey—Supplement on the Fund* (Washington, D.C.) 17 (September 1988).

———. *IMF Survey—Supplement on the Fund* (Washington, D.C.) 18 (August 1989).

———. *The Impact of the European Community's Internal Market on the EFTA.* Occasional Paper No. 74. Washington, D.C.: IMF, 1990.

———. "Industrial Nation Leaders Meet in Paris, Agree to Strengthen Cooperative Efforts." *IMF Survey* (Washington, D.C.) 18, no. 15 (July 24, 1989): 225, 233–236.

———. *International Financial Statistics* (Washington, D.C.) XXXIX (1986).

———. "Panelists at Fund Seminar Explore Implications of Protectionism." *IMF Survey* (Washington, D.C.) 18, no. 10 (May 15, 1989): 145, 157–159.

———. "Paris Club Implements Menu Approach for Low-Income Countries." *IMF Survey* (Washington, D.C.) 18, no. 7 (April 3, 1989): 103–104.

———. "Strengthen Policy Coordination, Says Former G-7 Deputy." *IMF Survey* (Washington, D.C.) 20, no. 8 (April 15, 1991): 120–122.

———. "Seminar on Latin America Focuses on Need for Policy Reform." *IMF Survey* (Washington, D.C.) 18, no. 21 (November 13, 1989): 337, 343–345.

———. "Singapore: A Profile." *IMF Survey* (Washington, D.C.) 18, no. 1 (January 9, 1989): 3–4.

———. *World Economic Outlook, 1989* (Washington, D.C.), October 1989.

———. "World Trade Value and Volume Continued to Expand Rapidly in 1988." *IMF Survey* (Washington, D.C.) 18, no. 20 (October 30, 1989): 321, 330–331.

International Rice Research Institute. "Prosperity Through Rice Stimulates Export Business." In *The IRRI Reporter* (Manila), no. 1/88 (March 1988).

International Sugar Organization. *Annual Report for the Year 1987.* London: ISO, 1987.

"International Trade." *Encyclopaedia Britannica,* 1983 ed., 21:824–854.

"Interpol." *Encyclopaedia Britannica,* 1985 ed., 6:355–356.

Iwata, Ryushi. *Japanese-Style Management: Its Foundations and Prospects.* Tokyo: Asian Productivity Organization, 1982.

Jackson, H. "The Jurisprudence of International Trade: The DISC Case in GATT." *American Journal of International Law* 72, no. 4 (October 1978): 747–781.

Jain, Subash C., and Lewis R. Tucker, Jr. *International Marketing: Managerial Perspectives.* Boston: CBI Publishing Company, 1979.

Japanese Government. *How to Succeed in Trade Shows and Exhibitions in Japan.* Tokyo: Japanese External Trade Relations Organization (JETRO), 1984.

Jatusripitak, Somkid, et al. "Strategic Global Marketing: Lessons from the Japanese." *Columbia Journal of World Business* 20, no. 1 (Spring 1985): 47–53.

Johnson, James C., and Donald F. Wood. *Contemporary Physical Distribution and Logistics.* 3rd ed. New York: Macmillan Co., 1986.

Kahler, Ruel. *International Marketing.* 5th ed. Cincinnati: South-Western Publishing Company, 1983.

Kandia, Peter. "ASEAN plus GATT equals EAEG." *Japan Economic Journal*, February 9, 1991, 10.

Kaplan, Morton A. *System and Process in International Politics.* New York: John Wiley & Sons, Inc., 1962.

Kashiwagi, Yusuke. *The Emergence of Global Finance.* Washington, D.C.: Per Jacobsson Foundation, International Monetary Fund, 1986.

Keegan, Warren J. *International Marketing Management.* Prentice-Hall International Series in Management. 2nd ed. Englewood Cliffs, NJ: Prentice-Hall, 1980.

"Keiretsu Disclosures Measures Mapped Out." *Nihon Keizai Shimbun*, March 27, 1991, 1.

Kelleway, Lucy. "Stereotyping Europe's Consumers." *The Financial Post*, February 6, 1990, 6.

Keynes, John Maynard. *The General Theory of Employment, Interest and Money.* London: Macmillan Company, 1936.

Khokhryakov, Gennady. "The Shadow Economy and The Administrative Command System." *Soviet News & Views* (Moscow), no. 3–4 (February 1989): 7.

Kirmani, Naheed. "The Uruguay Round: Revitalizing the Global Trading System." *Finance and Development* (Washington, D.C.) 26, no. 1 (March 1989): 6–8.

Kirpalani, V.H. *International Marketing.* New York: Random House, 1984.

Kurbarych, R.M. *Foreign Exchange Markets in the United States.* New York: The Federal Reserve Bank, 1983.

"Labor to Focus Demands on Shorter Work Hours." *The Japan Economic Journal*, February 9, 1991, 14.

Langer, Walter C. *The Mind Of Adolph Hitler: The Secret Wartime Reports.* New York: Basic Books, 1972.

Larkin, Margaret. "As Many as God Sends? Family Planning in Mexico." In *Sociological Essays and Research*, ed. Charles H. Anderson. Homewood, IL: The Dorsey Press, 1970.

"Latin American Integration—Getting Together." *The Economist*, March 30, 1991, 41–42.

Leamer, Edward. *Sources of International Comparative Advantage: Theory and Evidence.* Cambridge, MA: M.I.T. Press, 1985.

Leontief, Wassily F. "The Structure of Development." In *Technology and Economic Development*, ed. Robert McGowan and Ed Ottensmeyer. Boulder, CO: Westview Press, 1987. New York: Alfred A. Knopf, 1963.

Lerner, A.P. "The Symmetry between Import and Export Taxes." In *Readings in International Economics*, ed. R.E. Caves and H.G. Johnson. Homewood, IL: Irwin, 1968.

Levitt, Theodore. "The Globalization of Markets." *Harvard Business Review* 61 (May–June 1983): 92–102.

Lewington, Jennifer. "'Super-301' a Potent Tool for U.S. Trade Hawks." *The Globe and Mail*, May 8, 1989: B1.

Lewis, Paul. "Iraq Approval Starts Peace Schedule." *The New York Times*, April 7, 1991, 12.

Liddell, Henry R., and Robert Scott. *Greek—English Lexicon.* Oxford: Oxford University Press, 1935.

"Life, Death and Japan's Small Laundromats." *The Japan Economic Journal—Special U.S. Section*, March 9, 1991, A1.

Lipsey, Richard G., "The Theory of Customs Unions: A General Survey." In *Readings in International Economics*, ed. R.E. Caves and H.G. Johnson. Homewood, IL: Irwin, 1968.

Lipsey, Richard G., and Murray G. Smith. *Taking the Initiative: Canada's Trade Options in a Turbulent World*. Montréal: C.D. Howe Institute, 1985.

Lipsey, Richard G., and Robert York. "The Canada-U.S. Free Trade Agreement." In *International Business in Canada: Strategies for Management*, ed. Alan M. Rugman. Scarborough, Ontario: Prentice-Hall, 1989.

Lipschitz, Leslie, and Donogh McDonald (eds). *German Unification: Economic Issues*. Occasional Paper #75. Washington, D.C.: International Monetary Fund, 1990.

Little, J., et al. *Industries and Trade in Some Developing Countries*. London: Oxford University Press, 1970.

Litvak, Isaiah A. "Canadian Multinationals and Foreign Policy." In *International Business in Canada: Strategies for Management*, ed. Alan M. Rugman. Scarborough, Ontario: Prentice-Hall, 1989.

"The Lomé Trade Arrangements—What do they do for the ACPs?" *The Courier* (Brussels), no. 109 (May–June 1988): 5–10.

Lowenfeld, Andreas F. "What the GATT Says (Or Does Not Say)." In *Bilateralism, Multilateralism and Canada in U.S. Trade Policy*, ed. William J. Diebold, Jr. New York: Ballinger Publishing Company, 1988.

"Lumber Companies Trade Accusations in Tale of Softwood Smuggling." *The Globe and Mail*, May 23, 1989, B1, B6.

Lygum, Bjørn, Jacques Girard, Daniel Ottolenghi; Pier-Luigi Gilibert, and Alfred Steinherz. "International Capital Markets in 1988." *Cahiers BEI/EIB Papers*, no. 9 (March 1989): 9–84.

Machiavelli, Niccolo. *The Prince and the Discourses*. New York: Random House, 1940.

MacIntosh, Robert M. "Canadian Banking at the Crossroads." *Business Quarterly* 54, no. 3 (February 1990): 67–71.

Magee, John F. "1992: Moves Americans Must Make." *Harvard Business Review* 67 (May–June 1989): 78–84.

Mai, Ludwig H. *Men and Ideas in Economics: A Dictionary of World Economists Past and Present*. Totowa, NJ: Littlefield, Adams, 1975.

Main, Jeremy. "How to Go Global—And Why?" *Fortune*, August 28, 1989, 70–76.

"Major Proposals Tabled on Safeguards While First Sectoral Discussions Take Place in Services Group." *News of the Uruguay Round of Multilateral Trade Negotiations* (Geneva), no. 029 (July 7, 1989): 1–8.

"Many New Proposals Tabled as Year Ends—TNC Decides Dates for Brussels Ministerial Meeting." *News of the Uruguay Round of Multilateral Trade Negotiations* (Geneva), no. 033 (January 11, 1990): 1–21.

Marston, R.C. "Exchange Rate Unions as an Alternative to Flexible Rates: The Effects of Real and Monetary Disturbances." In *Exchange Rate Theory and Practice*, ed. John F. Bilson and Richard C. Marston. Chicago: University of Chicago Press, 1984.

Marx, Karl, and Fredrick Engels. *Manifesto of the Communist Party*. New York: International Publishers, 1932.

Mason, Edward S. "The Planning of Development." In *Technology and Economic Development*, ed. Robert McGowan and Ed Ottensmeyer. Boulder, CO: Westview Press, 1987.

McClelland, Charles A. *Theory and International Systems*. New York: Macmillan Co., 1966.

McClintock, Cynthia. *Peasant Cooperatives and Political Change in Peru*. Princeton, NJ: Princeton University Press, 1981.

McKechnie, Jean L., ed. *Webster's New Twentieth Century Dictionary of the En-*

glish Language. 2nd ed. New York: Simon & Schuster, 1979.

———. "A Dictionary of Foreign Words and Phrases." In the Supplement of Webster's New Twentieth Century Dictionary of the English Language. 2nd ed. New York: Simon & Schuster, 1979.

McMillan, Charles J. Bridge across the Pacific: Canada and Japan in the 1990's. Ottawa: Canada Japan Trade Council, 1988.

———. "How Japanese Use Technology for Competitive Success: Lessons for Canadian Management." Business Quarterly 54, no. 1 (Summer 1989): 34–38.

Meade, J. The Balance of Payments. London: Oxford University Press, 1951.

Meadows, Donella H., Dennis L. Meadows, Jorgen Randers, and William W. Behrens III. The Limits to Growth. New York: New American Library, 1972.

Meier, G. The International Economics of Development. New York: Harper & Row, 1968.

Meleka, Agia H. "The Changing Role of Multinational Corporations." Management International Review 25 (1985): 36–45.

Melly, Paul. "World Bank, IMF Policies Criticized by U.N. Agency." The Globe and Mail, September 6, 1989, B7.

Mentzer, John T., and Coskun Samili. "A Model for Marketing in Economic Development." Columbia Journal of World Business, Fall 1981, 91–101.

Merton, Robert K. Social Theory and Social Structure. New York: The Free Press, 1957.

"Mid-Term Review Agreements." News of the Uruguay Round of Multilateral Trade Negotiations (Geneva), no. 027 (April 24, 1989): 1–41.

Miliband, Ralph H. The State in the Capitalist Society. London: Quartet Books, 1973.

Mills, C. Wright. Power, Politics and People— The Collected Essays of C. Wright Mills. Ed. Louis Horowitz. New York: Ballantine Books, 1963.

———. The Sociological Imagination. New York: Oxford University Press, 1967.

———. Escucha Yanqui: La Revolución Cubana. Trans. Ramón Hernández Sol. Mexico City: Ediciónes Grijalbo, S.A., 1980.

Moha, Farida. "Rabat: The Maghreb . . . With Measured Tread . . ." Industry Africa (Vienna), no. 1 (June 1989): 5–7.

Moore, Wilbert E. Social Change. 2nd ed. Englewood Cliffs, NJ: Prentice-Hall, 1974.

Morgenthau, Hans, J. Politics Among Nations. 5th ed. New York: Alfred A. Knopf, 1978.

Morita, Akio, with Edwin M. Reingold and Mitsuko Shimomura. Made in Japan— Akio Morita and SONY. New York: NAL Penguin Inc., Signet Books, 1988.

Morse, Sir Jeremy. Do We Know Where We're Going? Seoul: Per Jacobsson Foundation, International Monetary Fund, 1985.

Moyer, Reed. International Marketing. The Irwin Series in Marketing. 5th ed. Homewood, IL: Irwin, 1983.

"Multinationals v. Globals." The Economist, May 5, 1984, 73.

Myint, H. "Infant Industry Arguments for Assistance to Industries in the Setting of Dynamic Trade Theory." In International Trade Theory in a Developing World, ed. R.F. Harrod and D.C. Hague. London: Macmillan & Co., 1963.

———. The Economics of Developing Countries. London: Hutchinson & Co., 1980.

"Negotiating Groups Restart Following the Mid-term Review." News of the Uruguay Round of Multilateral Trade Negotiations (Geneva), no. 028 (May 26, 1989): 1–4.

Neibuhr, Reinhold. Moral Man and Immoral Society. New York: Charles H. Scribner, 1947.

"The New Delors Commission." The Courier (Brussels), no. 114 (March–April 1989): 59–61.

The North-South Institute. In the Canadian Interest: Third World Development in the 1980s. Ottawa: The North-South Institute/ L'Institut Nord-Sud, 1980.

"Number of Rice Wholesalers to Be Halved in Four Years." The Nihon Keizai Shimbun, March 5, 1991, 1.

Ogley, Brian. *Exporting: Step by Step to Success*. London: Harper & Row, 1987.

Ohmae, Kenichi. *The Mind of the Strategist: The Art of Japanese Business*. New York: McGraw-Hill, 1982.

———. *Triad Power: The Coming Shape of Global Competition*. Glencoe, IL: Free Press, 1985.

———. *Beyond National Borders*. New York: Dow Jones-Irwin, 1987.

———. "The Global Logic of Strategic Alliances." *Harvard Business Review* 67 (March–April 1989): 143–154.

———. "Managing in a Borderless World." *Harvard Business Review* 67 (May–June 1989): 152–161.

Onkvisit, Sak, and John T. Shaw. "An Explanation of the International Product Life Cycle and Its Implications." *Columbia Journal of World Business* 18, no. 3 (February 1983): 73–79.

"Organization of Arab Petroleum Exporting Countries (OAPEC)." *Encyclopaedia Britannica*, 1985 ed., 1:505.

Organization for Economic Cooperation and Development. *1990 Catalogue of Publications Documents and Reference Works*. Development Center of the Organization for Economic Cooperation and Development (Paris, France), January 1990.

"Organization of the Islamic Conference." *Encyclopaedia Britannica*, 1985 ed., 6:411.

"Organization of Petroleum Exporting Countries (OPEC)." *Encyclopaedia Britannica*, 1985 ed., 6:345.

"Origin, Objectives and Characteristics of African State Trading Organizations (STOs)." *African Trade/Commerce Africain* (Addis Ababa) 13 (September 1988): 6–34.

Ostry, Sylvia. Interdependence: *Vulnerability and Opportunity*. Washington, D.C.: Per Jacobsson Foundation, International Monetary Fund, 1987.

Overgaard, Herman O.J., Maxime A. Crener, Bernard Z. Dasah, and Alfred L. Kahl, eds. *International Business: The Canadian Way*. Dubuque, IA: Kendall Hunt Publishing, 1983.

Oxfam-Ontario Committee. *Oxfam's Land, People, and Power: The Question of Third World Land Reform*. Toronto: OXFAM-Ontario, 1977.

"Pact on Coffee Prices Remains in Jeopardy." *The Globe and Mail*, February 23, 1989, B9.

Palanza, F. "Africa's Debt: An Analysis of the Crisis in the Eighties and of its Possible Remedies." *EIB Papers/Cahiers BEI*, no. 11 (November 1989): 7–51.

"Pan-American Union." *World Book Encyclopaedia*, 1981 ed., 15:96.

Pant, Pitambar. "The Development of India." In *Technology and Economic Development*, ed. Robert McGowan and Ed Ottensmeyer. Boulder, CO: Westview Press, 1987.

Park, Y.S., and J. Zwick. *International Banking in Theory and Practice*. Reading, MA: Addison-Wesley, 1985.

Pascale, R., and A. Athos. *The Art of Japanese Management*. New York: Simon & Schuster, 1981.

Pareto, Vilfredo. *The Mind and Society: A General Treatise on Sociology*. Trans. A. Bongiorno and A. Livingstone. New York: Dover, 1935.

Parkinson, C. Northcote. *Parkinson's Law or the Pursuit of Progress*. London: John Murray, 1962.

Parsons, Talcott. *Sociological Theory and Modern Society*. New York: The Free Press, 1967.

Parsons, Talcott, and Edward A. Shils, eds. *Toward a General Theory of Action*. New York: Harper & Row, 1962.

Paxton, John, ed. *The Statesman's Year-Book: Statistical and Historical Annual of the States of the World for the Year 1986–1987*. London: Macmillan Company, 1986.

Peter, Laurence J., and Raymond Hull. *The Peter Principle*. New York: Bantam Books, 1969.

Peterson, Peter G. *Economic Nationalism and International Interdependence: The Global Costs of National Choices*. Washington, D.C.: Per Jacobsson Foundation, International Monetary Fund, 1984.

Phatak, Arvind V. "International Dimensions of Management." *The Kent International Business Series*. Ed. David A. Ricks. Boston: Kent Publishing Company, 1983.

Plano, Jack C., and Roy Olton. *The International Relations Dictionary*. 3rd ed. Santa Barbara, CA: ABC-Clio, Inc., 1979.

"Poehl Calls Monetary Union a Disaster." *The Globe and Mail—Report on Business*, March 20, 1991, B7.

Polanyi, Karl. *The Great Transformation: The Political and Economic Origins of Our Time*. Boston: Beacon Press, 1967.

———. *Primitive, Archaic and Modern Economies*. Ed. George Dalton. Garden City, NY: Doubleday, 1968.

Polish Government. Foreign Investors Chamber of Industry and Commerce. *Polish Foreign Investment Law*. Warsaw: INTER-POLCOM, 1989.

"Pork Industry Stymied over Access to U.S." *The Globe and Mail—Report on Business*, March 29, 1991, B15.

Porter, John. *The Vertical Mosaic*. Toronto: Toronto University Press, 1965.

Porter, Michael G. *The Competitive Advantage of Nations*. New York: The Free Press (Macmillan Co.) 1990.

Powell, Dr. J.W. "Grass Roots Technology Transfer in Ghana." *The Courier* (Brussels), no. 109 (May–June 1988): 86–88.

Prebisch, R. *Towards a New Policy for Development*. New York: United Nations, 1964.

Presner, Lewis A. "Sociocultural Aspects of International Marketing Management: Probing 'The Japanese Problem.'" *Association of Marketing Educators (AME)* (Niagara Falls, NY), October 18, 1990.

Prestowitz, Clyde V., Alan Tonelson, and Robert W. Jerome. "The Last Gasp of GATTism." *Harvard Business Review* 69 (March–April 1991): 130–138.

"Promoting USSR Foreign Economic Relations." *Soviet Export* 1, no. 166 (1987): 16–17.

Quelch, John A., and Richard J. Hoff. "Customizing Global Marketing." In *Global Marketing Perspectives*, 17–31. Cincinnati: South-Western Publishing Company, 1989.

Rabbior, Gary. "'Black Monday': Why the Panic? Why the Plunge?" *Economic Bulletin* (Toronto), October 1987, 1–14.

———. *Export Canada: Opportunities and Challenges in the World Economy*. Toronto: Canadian Foundation for Economic Education (CFEE), 1989.

Ram, Sudha, and Sundaresan Ram. "Screening Financial Innovations: An Expert System Approach." *IEEE Expert*, August 1990, 20–28.

Reshitnyk, Michael J. "Canadian Trading Houses: A Growing Connection to Export Markets." *CanadExport* (Ottawa) 7, no. 16 (November 1, 1989): 9–11.

Ricks, David A. *Big Business Blunders: Mistakes in Multinational Marketing*. Homewood, IL: Dow Jones-Irwin, 1983.

Roberts, Jack. "Employment Equity a Trojan Horse." *The Globe and Mail—Commentary*, March 22, 1991, A17.

Rosenblatt, Julius, Thomas Mayer, Kaper Bartholdy, Dimitrios Demekas, Sanjeer Gupta, and Leslie Lipschitz. *The Common Agricultural Policy of the European Community—Principles and Consequences*, Occasional Paper #62. Washington, D.C.: International Monetary Fund, 1989.

Rosenthal, Gert. "III. The Crisis and the Current Situation: Significance and Implications." *Notas Sobre La Economía Y El Desarrollo* (Santiago de Chile), no. 470/471 (December 1988): 11–12.

Rugman, Alan M., and Joseph D'Cruz. *New Visions for Canadian Business: Strategies for Competing in the Global Economy*. Toronto: Kodak Canada, Inc., 1990.

———. *Fast Forward: Improving Canada's International Competitiveness*. Toronto: Kodak Canada, Inc., 1991.

Russell, Lord. *The Scourge of the Swastika: A Short History of Nazi War Crimes*. New York: Ballantine Books, 1954.

Sachs, Jim, and Marianne Kelly. "Many Exporters Missing the Boat." *The Free Trader* 2, no. 2 (February 1990): 2.

Saclier, Pierre. "The Lessons of the Franc Zone." *The Courier* (Brussels), no. 110 (July–August 1988): 85–88.

Safire, William. "A Foreign Affair." *The New York Times Magazine*, April 7, 1991, 14–16.

Salvatore, D., ed. *The New Protectionist Threat to World Welfare.* New York: North-Holland, 1987.

———. *Theory and Problems of International Economics.* 2nd ed. New York: McGraw-Hill, 1984.

———. *African Development Prospects: A Policy Modeling Approach.* New York: North-Holland, 1987.

Sarpkaya, S. *International Finance—In a Canadian Context.* Don Mills, Ontario: CCH Canadian Limited, 1983.

Schary, Philip B. *Logistics Decisions: Text & Cases.* Hinsdale, IL: The Dryden Press, 1984.

Schiavone, Giuseppe. *International Organizations: A Dictionary & Directory.* Chicago: St. James Press, 1983.

Sheth, Jagdish, and Abdolreza Eshghi, eds. *Global Marketing Perspectives.* Cincinnati: South-Western Publishing Company, 1989.

Silvert, K.H., ed. *Expectant Peoples—Nationalism and Development.* New York: Alfred A. Knopf, 1963.

Singh, Manmohan. "Revitalizing Development Cooperation Issues and Priorities." *Asian Development Review* 7, no. 1 (1989): 21–34.

Skeat, Walter W. *A Concise Etymological Dictionary of the English Language.* 7th ed. Oxford: Oxford University Press, 1965.

Solomon, R. *The International Monetary System.* New York: Harper & Row, 1982.

Sorokin, Pitrim A. *Social Change and Cultural Dynamics.* Boston: Porter Sargent, 1957.

Southerst, John. "Auto Mavericks." *Canadian Transportation and Distribution Management.* September 1989.

Spengler, Oswald. *The Decline of the West.* New York: Alfred A. Knopf, 1926.

Stolper, Wolfgang F. "The Development of Nigeria." In *Technology and Economic Development*, ed. Robert McGowan and Ed Ottensmeyer. Boulder, CO: Westview Press, 1987.

Stone, John. *Race, Ethnicity and Social Change.* Belmont, CA: Wadsworth, 1977.

"A Survey of America's Capital Markets." *The Economist*, June 11, 1988, 1–28.

"A Survey of the Arab East." *The Economist*, February 6, 1988, 1–30.

"A Survey of Canada." *The Economist*, October 8, 1988, 1–18.

"A Survey of the Caribbean." *The Economist*, August 6, 1988, 4–18.

"A Survey of Europe's Internal Market. *The Economist*, July 8, 1989, 1–48.

"A Survey of Europe's Internal Market." *The Economist*, July 9, 1988, 1–44.

"A Survey of International Banking." *The Economist*, March 25, 1989, 5–68.

"A Survey of International Banking." *The Economist*, March 26, 1988, 5–76.

"A Survey of Japanese Finance." *The Economist*, December 10, 1988, 1–34.

"A Survey of Japanese Technology." *The Economist*, December 2, 1989, 1–18.

"A Survey of South Korea." *The Economist*, May 21, 1988, 3–22.

"A Survey of the Soviet Economy." *The Economist*, April 8, 1988, 1–18.

"A Survey of the Third World." *The Economist*, September 23, 1989, 1–58.

"A Survey of the World Economy." *The Economist*, September 24, 1988, 5–72.

"A Survey of the Yen Block." *The Economist*, July 15, 1989, 1–20.

Svetlicic, Marjan. *Joint Ventures in Developing Countries: The Arab Experience.* Ljubljana, Yugoslavia: International Center for Public Enterprises in Developing Countries (ICPE), 1987.

Sweeny, T.A. "The Bi-National Dispute Settlement Mechanism in Anti-Dumping and Countervailing Duty Cases in the Context of the Canada-U.S. Trade Agreement." *Business Quarterly*, Spring 1988: 49–49.

Swierczek, Fredric William. "Privatization,

Policy and Market Issues: An Example from Thailand." *Public Enterprise* 8, no. 3 (1988): 211–218.

Sykes, J.B., ed. *Concise Oxford Dictionary of Current English.* 7th ed. Oxford: Oxford University Press, 1987.

"SYSMIN." *The Courier* (Brussels), no. 109 (May–June 1988): 14.

Szenberg, M., et al. *Welfare Effects of Trade Restrictions.* New York: Academic Press, 1977.

Tait, Alan A. *Value-Added Tax: International Practice and Problems.* Washington, D.C.: IMF, 1988.

Tajima, Mitsuo. "Japan's Cold Indifference Toward Old People." *The Wall Street Journal,* November 8, 1982, 23.

Taus, Andrew. "Open Skies Frighten Air Cargo Companies in Canada." *The Globe and Mail—Report on Business,* March 26, 1991, B22.

Tawney, R.H. *Religion and the Rise of Capitalism.* New York: Harcourt, Brace & World, 1926.

Tepperman, Lorne. *Social Mobility in Canada.* Toronto: McGraw-Hill Ryerson, 1975.

Terpstra, Vern. *The Cultural Environment of International Business.* Cincinnati: South-Western Publishing Company, 1978.

———. *International Marketing.* 2nd ed. New York: The Dryden Press, 1978.

———. *International Dimensions of Marketing.* The Kent International Business Series. Ed. David A. Ricks. Boston: Kent Publishing Company, 1982.

Terry, Edith. "LDP Back at Helm as Japan Sails into Sea of Economic Troubles." *The Globe and Mail—Report on Business,* February 23, 1990, B7.

———. "Electronics Empire Is Shifting Its Focus." *The Globe and Mail—Report on Business,* February 28, 1990, B1, B4.

Therberge, J. *Economics of Trade and Development.* New York: Oxford University Press, 1970.

"This Is Toyota/Esto es Toyota/Ceci est Toyota": *Corporate Information Book.*

Toyota City, Japan: Toyota Motor Company Ltd., 1979.

Thornton, Robert J. "Small FSCs. Why do they exist? What are they? Who wants them?" In *MS-DOS microcomputer disc file FSC-M.TXT.* Boston: Export FSC International, Ltd., June 1989.

"TNC Agrees on Final Ministerial Meeting in Brussels in Period 26 November–8 December, 1990." *News of the Uruguay Round of Multilateral Trade Negotiations* (Geneva), no. 030 (August 3, 1989): 1–18.

Tomberg, Igor, and Alexander Salitsky. "Special Economic Zones, What Are They?" *Soviet News & Views* (Ottawa), no. 6 (March, 1989), 4.

Tönnies, F. *Community and Society—Gemeinschaft und Gesellschaft.* Trans. and ed. Charles P. Loomis. East Lansing, MI: Michigan State University Press, 1957.

"The Top 50 Exporters." *The Financial Post 500,* Summer 1988, 116–118.

"Trade Liberalization May Kill US Sugar Industry." *The Reuter Sugar Newsletter* (November 6, 1989). In *International Sugar Organization Press Summary: November 30, 1989.* (London) December 11, 1989: 243.

"Trade Negotiations Committee to Meet from 2 April in Geneva." *News of the Uruguay Round of Multilateral Trade Negotiations* (Geneva), no. 025 (March 20, 1989): 1.

Tsunoda, R., W.T. de Bary, and D. Keene, eds. *Sources of Japanese Tradition.* Chicago: University of Chicago Press, 1958.

Tucker, Robert C. *Philosophy and Myth in Karl Marx.* Cambridge: Cambridge University Press, 1972.

Tyler, Patrick E. "Baghdad Formally Agrees to 'Unjust' U.N. Conditions for Permanent Cease-Fire." *The New York Times,* April 7, 1991, 1.

Union Bank of Switzerland. *Annual Report, 1983.* Zurich: UBS, 1984.

———. *Annual Report, 1984.* Zurich: UBS, 1985.

———. *Annual Report, 1985.* Zurich: UBS, 1986.

———. *Annual Report, 1986.* Zurich: UBS, 1987.

———. *Annual Report, 1987.* Zurich: UBS, 1988.

———. *Annual Report, 1988.* Zurich: UBS, 1989.

———. *The EC Internal Market: The Challenges and Opportunities for Switzerland* (Zurich), no. 109 (November 1989).

Union Internationale pour la Protection des Obtentions Végétales (UPOV). "Accession of Australia to the International Convention for the Protection of New Varieties of Plants." *Press Release* (Geneva) no. 4 (February 20, 1989).

———. "Diplomatic Conference for the Revision of the International Convention for the Protection of New Varieties of Plants." *Press Release* (Geneva) no. 8 (March 21, 1991).

United Nations. *African Trade Directory.* 1st ed. Addis Ababa: Federation of African Chambers of Commerce (FACC)/Economic Commission for Africa (ECA), 1987.

———. *General Business Guide: For Potential Suppliers of Goods and Services to the United Nations System.* 10th ed. Copenhagen: UNDP Inter-Agency Procurement Services Office (IAPSO), 1990.

———. *Handbook of Trade Control Measures of Developing Countries.* Geneva: United Nations Conference on Trade and Development (UNCTAD), 1987.

———. *The State of the World's Children.* New York: UNICEF, 1987.

———. *World Economic Survey.* New York: United Nations, 1986.

———. *World Economic Survey.* New York: United Nations, 1987.

———. *World Economic Survey.* New York: United Nations, 1988.

———. *World Health Statistics Annual, 1986.* Geneva: World Health Organization, 1986.

———. *World Population Prospects: Estimates and Projections as Assessed in 1984.* New York: UNICEF, 1986.

United Nations Conference on Trade and Development. "Automated System for Customs Data." *UNCTAD Bulletin* (Geneva), May–June 1990.

———. "Committee on Preferences Reaffirms Principles Underlying the Generalized System of Preferences." *UNCTAD Bulletin* (Geneva), no. 252 (May 1989): 2–3.

———. "The Common Fund for Commodities—Operation in Sight." *UNCTAD Bulletin* (Geneva), no. 245 (July 1988): 1–6.

———. "ECDC: First Regional Association of Trading Companies Established in Latin America." *UNCTAD Bulletin* (Geneva), no. 246 (August–September 1988): 15.

———. "From the President of Venezuela: The South's Contribution to International Cooperation." *UNCTAD Bulletin—Twenty-Fifth Anniversary Issue* (Geneva), (September–October 1989): 8–11.

———. "Insights into Two Modes of Transfer." In *Trade and Development Report, 1987,* Part 2, Chapter II (Geneva), 1988.

———. "The Least Developed Countries in the World Economy." *UNCTAD Bulletin* (Geneva), no. 251 (March–April 1989): 2.

———. "New International Agreement on Jute." *UNCTAD Bulletin* (Geneva), January–February 1990: 14–15.

———. "Operation of International Commodity Agreements." *UNCTAD Bulletin* (Geneva), no. 248 (November–December 1988): 8–9.

———. "Paris Club Rescheduling Practices: A Close Scrutiny." *UNCTAD Bulletin* (Geneva), no. 242 (April 1988): 1–4.

———. "The Review Conference on the United Nations Convention on a Code of Conduct for Liner Conferences." *UNCTAD Bulletin* (Geneva), no. 247 (October 1988): 5–9.

———. "Trade and Development Board to Carry Out Annual Review of Protectionism and Structural Adjustment." *UNCTAD Bulletin* (Geneva), no. 250 (February 1989): 3–10.

———. "UNCTAD and ECE Co-operate in Search for Solution to Proliferation of Container Characteristics." *UNCTAD*

Bulletin (Geneva), no. 254 (July–August 1989): 9–10.

———. "The UNCTAD Data Base on Trade Measures." *UNCTAD Bulletin* (Geneva), no. 244 (June 1988): 1–4.

———. "UNCTAD's Debt Management and Financial Analysis System in More Than 20 Countries." *UNCTAD Bulletin* (Geneva), no. 245 (July 1988): 7–9.

United Nations Economic Commission for Africa, Trade Section, Trade and Development Finance Division. *FLASH* (Addis Ababa), no. 43 (April 1989).

United Nations Industrial Development Organization. "High-Tech Science Center for Third World Under Way." *UNIDO Newsletter* (Vienna), no. 245. (September 1988): 1.

———. "More Money for Gen-Tech Center." *UNIDO Newsletter* (Vienna), no. 257 (September 1989): 2–3.

———. "Second International Rubber Conference at Tehran." *UNIDO Newsletter* (Vienna), no. 253 (May 1989): 2.

United States Government. *Public Law 100–418—August 23, 1988: An Act to Enhance the Competitiveness of American Industry, and for Other Purposes*. Congressional Record (Washington, D.C.), 134.

United States Government. *The United States Government Manual, 1989/90*. Washington, D.C.: Government Printing Office, 1989.

United States Government, Department of State. *GIST: Caribbean Basin Initiative (CBI)*. Washington, D.C.: Bureau of Public Affairs, 1987.

"United States Presents Draft Services Agreement—New Proposals Tabled on Agriculture and Trips." *News of the Uruguay Round of Multilateral Trade Negotiations* (Geneva), no. 032 (November 21, 1989): 1–14.

"United States Presents Draft Services Agreement." *Focus-GATT Newsletter* (Geneva), no. 67 (December 1989): 4–7.

University Microfilms International. *UMI Article Clearinghouse Catalog, 1988*. Ann Arbor, MI: University Microfilms International, 1988.

"U.N. Votes to Strip Iraq of Weapons." *The Globe and Mail*, April 4, 1991, A1, A10.

Urdang, Laurence, ed. *Dictionary of Advertising Terms*. Chicago: Crain Communications, 1983.

"Uruguay Round." *Focus-GATT Newsletter* (Geneva), no. 66 (November 1989): 3–8.

U.S. International Trade Commission. *The Effects of Greater Economic Integration Within The European Community On The United States*. Publication #2204. Washington, D.C.: July 1989.

———. *Fresh, Chilled or Frozen Pork from Canada—Views on Second Remand in Investigation No. 701-TA-298 (Final)*. Publication #2362. Washington, D.C.: February 1991.

———. *The Likely Impact on the United States of a Free Trade Agreement with Mexico*. Publication #2353. Washington, D.C.: February 1991.

———. "Possible Modifications to the International Harmonized System Nomenclature." *USITC—News Release* (Washington, D.C.), December 31, 1990.

———. *Profit Sharing: U.S. Imports under Harmonized Tariff Schedule Subheadings 9802.00.60 and 9802.00.80, 1986–1989*. Publication #2365. Washington, D.C.: March 1991.

———. "The United States Would Benefit Mostly from an FTA with Mexico, Says ITC." *USITC—News Release* (Washington, D.C.), February 22, 1991.

U.S. International Trade Commission, Office of Industries. "Agriculture: The United States Reviews Export Credit Guarantees to the Soviet Union." *Monthly Import/Business Review* (Washington, D.C.), March 1991: 4–5.

———. "Fresh, Chilled or Frozen Pork from Canada." *Monthly Import/Business Review* (Washington, D.C.), February 1991.

———. "Future Concerns for Caribbean Basin Textile and Apparel Suppliers." *Monthly Import/Business Review* (Washington, D.C.), February 1991, 6–7.

———. "Production Sharing: 'Agro-Maquilas'— U.S. Flower Growers And Food Processors Launch Operations In Mexico." *Monthly*

Import/Business Review (Washington, D.C.), March 1991, 32–33.

"U.S. Oil Tax Changes Boon for Canada." *The Globe and Mail*, December 13, 1989, B3.

Vincent, Jack E. *Handbook of International Relations*. New York: Barron's Educational Series, Inc., 1969.

Watanabe, Toshio. "Japan Sea Basin Needs Economic Cooperation; Soviet Far East Should Be Central to the New Zone." *Japan Economic Journal—Commentary*, March 30, 1991, 8.

Weekly, James K., and Raj Agarwal. *International Business: Operating in the Global Economy*. New York: The Dryden Press, 1987.

Weiner, Norbert. *The Human Use of Human Beings*. Garden City, NY: Doubleday, 1954.

Wheeler, Joseph C. "The Critical Role for Official Development Assistance in the 1990s." *Finance and Development* (Washington, D.C.) 26, no. 3 (September 1989): 38–40.

Whitney, Peter D. *The CBI: Important Incentives for Trade and Investment*. Current Policy No. 1065. Washington, D.C.: U.S. Department of State, Bureau of Public Affairs, 1988.

Wilcox, Clair. *A Charter for World Trade, 1949*. New York: The New York Times Publishing Company, 1972.

Williams, Andrew. "Harvesting the Oceans' Potential: ICOD." *Development* (Ottawa), Spring 1988: 24–27.

Williamson, J. *The Exchange Rate System*. Washington, D.C.: Institute for International Economics, 1985.

Winglee, Peter. "Agricultural Trade Policies of Industrial Countries." *Finance and Development* (Washington, D.C.) 26, no. 1 (March 1989): 9–11.

Witteveen, H. Johannes. *Developing a New International Monetary System: A Long-Term View*. Washington, D.C.: Per Jacobsson Foundation, International Monetary Fund, 1983.

Wolf, E. *Peasants*. Englewood Cliffs, NJ: Prentice-Hall, 1966.

Wonnacott, Paul. *The United States and Canada: The Quest for Free Trade*. Washington, D.C.: Institute for International Economics, 1987.

World Bank. *World Bank Development Report*. Washington, D.C.: World Bank, 1986.

———. *World Bank Development Report*. Washington, D.C.: World Bank, 1987.

———. *World Bank Development Report*. Washington, D.C.: World Bank, 1988.

"World Bank (IBRD)." *Worldmark Encyclopedia of the Nations*, 7th ed. New York: Worldmark Press Ltd. (John Wiley & Sons, Inc.), 1988.

World Intellectual Property Organization. "Accession by Czechoslovakia Brings to 49 the Number of Contracting States of the PCT." *Press Release PCT/54* (Geneva), March 22, 1991.

———. "Development of Trademark Classifications." *Report on the Activities of WIPO in the Year 1987* (Geneva), October 28, 1988: 105–106.

———. "Diplomatic Conference for the Conclusion of a Treaty on Intellectual Property in Respect of Integrated Circuits: Washington, May 8 to 26, 1989." *Newsletter* (Geneva), WIPO Publication no. 434(E)-27, October 1989.

———. "Diplomatic Conference for the Conclusion of a Treaty on the International Registration of Audiovisual Works." *Press Release* (Geneva) no. 83, April 20, 1989.

———. "Madrid Agreement Concerning the International Registration of Marks." In *Report on the Activities of WIPO in the Year 1987* (Geneva), October 28, 1988: 125–127.

———. "The Patent Cooperation Treaty (PCT) in 1988." *Press Release PCT/44* (Geneva), January 30, 1989.

———. "The Patent Cooperation Treaty (PCT) in 1990." *Press Release PCT/51* (Geneva), January 29, 1991.

———. "Ratification of the Patent Cooperation Treaty (PCT) by Canada Brings to 43 the Number of Contracting States to the PCT." *Press Release PCT/46* (Geneva), October 2, 1989.

———. *Report on the Activities of WIPO in the Year 1987* (Geneva), October 28, 1988.

———. "Treaties Providing for Simplified Possibilities for the International Protection of Inventions, Marks and Industrial Designs." *Report on the Activities of WIPO in the Year 1987* (Geneva), October 28, 1988, 108–109.

———. "Treaties Providing for the Substantive Protection of Intellectual Property." *Report on the Activities of WIPO in the Year 1987* (Geneva), October 28, 1988: 107–108.

———. "The United States of America Joins the Berne Convention for the Protection of Literary and Artistic Works." *Press Release 79* (Geneva), November 17, 1988.

———. "WIPO Worldwide Symposium on the Intellectual Property Aspects of Artificial Intelligence." *Press Release 87* (Geneva), March 18, 1991.

Wolferen, Karel van. *The Enigma of Japanese Power.* New York: Vintage Books, 1990.

"Worldwide Canadian Initiative." *The Economist*, April 13, 1991, 35.

Wortzel, Lawrence H., and Heidi Vernon Wortzel. "Export Marketing Strategies for NIC and LCD-Based Firms." *Columbia Journal of World Business* 16, no. 1 (Spring 1981): 51–60.

Wright, Richard W. "Networking—Japanese Style." *Business Quarterly* 54, no. 2 (Autumn 1989): 20–24.

———. "Japanese Investment in Canada." In *International Business in Canada: Strategies for Management*, ed. Alan M. Rugman. Scarborough, Ontario: Prentice-Hall, 1989.

Wright, Richard W., and Gunter A. Pauli. *The Second Wave: Japan's Global Assault on Financial Services.* New York: St. Martin's Press, 1988.

Yoshitomi, Masaru. "*Keiretsu*: An Insider's Guide to Japan's Conglomerates." *International Economic Insights* 6, no. 2 (1990): 10–14.

Yun, Yeo-Gyeong. "Promoting Small and Medium Industries: The Korean Experience." *Asian Development Review* 6, no. 2 (1988): 96–109.

Zaitsev, V.A. "Towards Integration: Following the Course of Scientific and Technological Progress." *Soviet Export* 6, no. 165 (1986): 6–9.